BASEBALL BURIAL SITES

Bob Bailey

ST. JOHANN PRESS
Haworth, NJ

ST. JOHANN PRESS

Published in the United States of America
by St. Johann Press
P.O. Box 241
Haworth, NJ 07641

Library of Congress Cataloging-in-Publication Data

Bailey, Bob, 1948–
    Baseball burial sites / Bob Bailey.
      p. cm.
   ISBN 1-878282-32-8 (alk. paper)
     1. Baseball players—United States—Death.
    2. Baseball players—Tombs—United States. I. Title.

   GV865.A1B32 2004
   796.357'02—dc22   2004050900

The paper used in this publication meets the minimum requirements of the
American National Standard for Information Sciences—Permanence of
Paper for Printed Library Materials, ANSI/NISO Z39/48-1992

Manufactured in the United States of America

Cover design by Gwendolyn Bailey
Book design and type composition by G&H SOHO.

TABLE OF CONTENTS

INTRODUCTION

In 1984 a friend invited me to attend a ceremony at Cave Hill Cemetery in Louisville, Kentucky. He had recently written an article about the career of Pete Browning, the nineteenth century baseball star of the Louisville Colonels. In the course of researching Browning's life he had visited Browning's gravesite at Cave Hill Cemetery. What he found was a simple granite stone with Pete's full name and the years of his birth and death. My friend was a little disappointed at the lack of recognition of Browning's baseball feats but was shocked to see that his first name was misspelled. For Pete Browning was born Louis Rogers Browning but the stone read "Lewis Rogers Browning."

This put him into action. He was determined to replace the stone with one that correctly spelled Browning's name and, he hoped, provided some recognition of his baseball career. Soon the Mayor, the Hillerich & Bradsby Corporation, and the Muldoon Monument Company were enlisted to donate materials, expertise, or money and a new monument was ordered.

The ceremony was held on a pleasant spring day with the Mayor, Pee Wee Reese, and members of the Hillerich family speaking or being introduced at the unveiling of the new grave marker. It was a handsome stone with Pete's name properly spelled and about 100 words describing his career in baseball.

As the event ended I was in the rear of the crowd by a pickup truck that had the old stone in the bed. I started chatting with the gentleman from the monument company that prepared and installed the new marker. When I asked what was going to happen to the old stone he told me nothing was planned but it probably would be crushed into gravel. When I got back to my office that morning I had the strange notion that the old stone was a valued piece of local Louisville history. I sent a letter to the monument company asking if I might save it for some undefined historical purpose. The manager called me the next day and said I was welcome to it if I could move the 400-pound stone out of their work yard. Somehow I did and for the next ten years Pete Browning's original gravestone resided in my garage. Something that did not thrill my wife, although some of the neighborhood children whispered that the Bailey's had a body buried in their garage.

But the tale does not end here. I wondered where in Louisville other baseball players were buried? And I set out to find out the answer to that question. First I went to the Baseball Encyclopedia to dig out the death dates of anyone who died in or around Louisville. Then to the library to find their obituary and then to the cemetery to find their final resting place. It wasn't long before my goal of finding everyone in the city became finding every ballplayer in the Metropolitan Area, then the state, and then neighboring states. Finally I said enough of half measures and began the hunt for the burial location of every deceased player who ever appeared in a box score.

The result of that project is this book. *Baseball Burial Sites* is a catalogue of what I have found over the past twenty plus years of tracking down the burial locations of ballplayers and others involved with professional baseball.

The largest numbers of the locations were found by researching newspaper obituaries. This involved finding libraries with holdings of papers and hand cranking through the microfilm for many hours. When I traveled I planned what libraries were on my route and what names were most likely to be found in their newspapers. So with my list of names and dates I would steal off for and hour or so of library time. But baseball people do not all live in major cities. So in addition to visiting libraries in Cincinnati, Philadelphia, San Francisco, and New York City I also found my self at the public library in Newark, Ohio, Hazleton, Pennsylvania, Johnson City, Tennessee, and Inverness, Florida.

Sometimes it was easy. Sometimes it wasn't. Many players die without any published obituary or with only the briefest mention of their passing. So I would find myself having exhausted the possibilities of all the libraries in an area and still having a substantial list of unfound names. Then I discovered the State Library system. In every state there is (for the most part) one library that has holdings of papers from the entire state, the daily papers of the mid-sized cities, the weeklies of rural America, and the back issues of papers that no longer exist. Some even have microfilm of death certificates. There were also uncounted letters, e-mails, and phone calls to cemeteries, funeral homes, and anyone else who might have a clue to where someone was.

Going through hundreds of reels of microfilm is solitary work. But as it turns out hunting for the burial location various types of famous and near famous people is not reserved for a rare few. As I was hunting for baseball burial sites I continued to run into others who were doing similar things. There are folks gathering burial data on Medal of Honor winners, politicians, musicians, and about any other category you can imagine. In the past several years there have been books published listing burial locations of Civil War generals, Hollywood celebrities, famous New Yorkers, and others.

The last source I want to mention is the relatively new tool of the Internet. Here you can read local newspapers from all over the country from your home, there are local history and genealogical sites with a wealth of information, and there are hundreds of cemetery transcriptions on-line. More and more cemeteries are putting their interments on their web sites and these are invaluable sources of data for the researcher. The Internet also allowed me to learn about Samoan burial customs, locate cemetery addresses, clarify situations where cemeteries merge or change their names, and dozens of other questions that arise in the course of research.

As with any endeavor like this you join this circle of kindred souls (or those who share your dementia). I have developed good friendships with many of these like-minded people. This is despite the fact that I have never met most of them. We communicate through e-mail, letters, and various web sites that several of them maintain. We exchange data sources, and suggestions. Occasionally it is a race to see who can find the final resting place of someone first. But for the most part we share finds with each other and go on hunts in our local areas to track down some specific piece of information someone needs.

I wish to acknowledge the many people who have contributed to this book. Deserving special notice are two faithful correspondents who have maintained a steady dialogue with me during this and, I'm sure, future research. They are David Lotz and Jim Springborn. Both of these gentlemen have hit the road and dug out data for me in places I could not travel. They have visited libraries and cemeteries and sent innumerable letters, e-mails, and good wishes over the years. I thank them most sincerely. Others who have provided help over the last twenty years are: Bruce Allardice, Tom Bailey, Pam Bailey, Jerry Beirne, Bill Carle, Rachel Cefalu, Dick Clark, Bill Deane, Russ Dodge, Cappy Gagnon, Rex Hamann, John Husman, Fred King, Ted Knorr, Steve Krah, Kit Krieger, Nancy Jo Leachman, Larry Lester, Richard Malatzky, Peter Mancuso, Mark Manuel, Rob Martindale, Sammy Miller, Peter Morris, Marty Myers, Rich Puff, John Russell, David Skinner, Bill Swank, Dick Thompson, Stew Thornley, and David Vincent. I am sure I am forgetting some people who have sent me material over the past two decades. I apologize for not remembering but thank you nonetheless. While they received mention above I must acknowledge my wife Pam, who tolerates quite a bit to allow me to indulge my interest in baseball research, and my children, Gwen, Rachel and Tom for those hours you waited while I was at some microfilm reader during our many trips.

The hunt for where baseball people made their final stop has taken me into more cemeteries than my family wishes to remember. As the family took trips throughout the country I would always add a cemetery or two to the itinerary. From Flat Rock Cemetery at a crossroads in rural Shelby County, Kentucky to the stately magnificence of Green-Wood Cemetery in Brooklyn to the solemn rows of simple markers at Chattanooga National Cemetery There is always a feeling of joy and sadness when you stand by the plot of one of these players. Even the least successful major league player is one of the elite players in the world just by making it to that level. Reading their names chiseled in granite or marble recalls their days as professional players. Then you look around and see wives, children, and parents in the family plot and remember that they had lives beyond the diamond. You remember that for most of them baseball was just a small part of their lives. They had careers and families, good times and bad, just like the rest of us.

This book is intended to be a guide to where people associated with baseball are buried. The basic format is alphabetical lists of components of the baseball world. These lists are Players and Managers, Negro Leaguers, Owners and Executives, Umpires and Writers and Broadcasters.

The individual lists are set up with the name of the individual, date of death and burial location. The players and managers list presents the player's names with their commonly used nickname followed by their given names. This pattern is repeated on subsequent lists.

The last list is a catalog by location. All the names from all lists are broken down by state, county, and cemetery. Want to find out who is buried at you local cemetery? This is the list to consult. Want to find a specific individual? Use the earlier lists. Within the state-by-state list all burials in a particular county are given regardless of municipality. There is also a notation with the county name as to what Metropolitan Area a county is located if want to venture a bit further afield.

There are several players who do not appear in any of the baseball reference books currently published. One reason for this is that there is ongoing research into birth and death data of many players. The Biographical Committee of the Society for American Baseball Research uncovers new facts about players every month. They identify lost or missing players, and sort out discrepancies in the biographical record. They find players who are incorrectly assigned the records of other players, dig out data about the 300 some odd players for whom the record of birth and death information is incomplete. I have tried to use the most up-to-date information as reported by this group in identifying the burial location of each player.

There are over 7,000 locations of players and several hundred additional locations of owners, umpires, writers, broadcasters, Negro Leaguers, and others who have made up the rich fiber of the history of the game; from the guy who appeared in only one game to every member of the

Baseball Hall of Fame; from all the Commissioners of Baseball to the guy who invented Cracker Jacks; from Bud Hillerich and Frank Bradsby of Louisville Slugger bat fame to Arch Ward who created the All Star Game. On all the lists except the players' list I have tried to include information to help identify why he is included.

The players' listing includes those who played in the National Association from 1871 to 1875. Any entry that includes the notation *"manager"* indicates a major league manager who never played in the majors. Occasional there are notes within the entries. These indicate if the individual was buried under a different name that he played. They also note where cemetery names have changed, or where a cemetery is known by multiple names.

Within these notes the term "cemetery removed" appears. This term is used when a cemetery closes and all the remains are removed, en mass, to a different cemetery. Commonly the new graves are unmarked with perhaps just a marker noting that a particular section of the new cemetery contains the remains removed from a cemetery no longer in existence. This was a common practice in New York City, Philadelphia, and San Francisco. New York City mandated an end to burials in Manhattan around the 1850s, so these changes had little effect on our subjects. Philadelphia, while still having many active cemeteries in the city limits, saw many cemeteries removed that had been abandoned or that sat on land needed for some other purpose. These removals occurred through the 1950s. San Francisco ordered the end to in ground burials early in the twentieth century and saw a huge exodus of cemeteries to neighboring San Mateo County, primarily to the town of Colma. Colma is now home to over a dozen cemeteries with more burials recorded that living population.

Notations of cremations use different forms in the lists. When you see an entry open with "Cremated at . . ." the location is where the cremation occurred, not necessarily where the ashes currently reside. When there is an entry that had the location followed by the word "cremated" it means the cremated remains are at the location mentioned.

This book contains over 80% of the locations of players for whom we have death data. There are still about 1,200 players to track down and hundreds of owners, umpires, Negro Leaguers, and others. I have made every effort to correctly identify the grave location of the individuals listed here. Unfortunately errors will occur in this type of list and for that I am responsible. Where localities have cemeteries with similar names I have tried to sort out all the information to get the right location. This was particularly difficult in Pittsburgh and Boston. Pittsburgh and Allegheny County have eight cemeteries containing the name "St. Mary's." Massachusetts has 17 cemeteries named for St. Patrick—13 of them in the Boston area.

There are over 3,600 cemeteries named in these lists. There are entries from every state in the union. Looking at the data from these lists shows the following cemeteries with the largest number of entries on the lists:

Cemetery	Total
Calvary Cemetery, St. Louis, MO	91
Holy Cross Cemetery, Colma, CA	48
Spring Grove Cemetery, Cincinnati, OH	47
Calvary Cemetery, Woodside, Queens, NY	38
Green-Wood Cemetery, Brooklyn, NY	37
Inglewood Park Cemetery, Inglewood, CA	36
Cave Hill Cemetery, Louisville, KY	35
Crown Hill Cemetery, Indianapolis, IN	29
Calvary Cemetery, Evanston, IL	28
Holy Cross Cemetery, Yeadon, PA	27

All but two of these cemeteries are located near an existing major league franchise. Colma is just outside San Francisco and Yeadon is a suburb of Philadelphia. But Crown Hill and Cave Hill, in Indianapolis and Louisville respectively, are a bit off the baseball path. But it was not always so. Both cities were members of various major leagues in the nineteenth century. Indianapolis was in and out of several leagues in the 1800s (and part of the Federal League in the 1910s), while Louisville was a mainstay of the American Association between stops as a charter member of the National League in 1876 and rejoining the NL in 1892.

Calvary Cemetery in St. Louis is by far the cemetery with largest number of baseball burials. They would also lead if we just counted players with 74 players buried there. If we counted only players the list would rearrange itself but fundamentally it would not change. Crown Hill Cemetery would fall off while Forest Lawn Memorial Park in Glendale, California would move into the ninth position.

You may know of baseball burial locations not listed here or know of errors or clarifications relevant to the listings. I would welcome hearing about them. I can even provide a list of missing players in any county in the country. You can send an e-mail with your information to *baseballburialsites@yahoo.com*.

PLAYERS AND MANAGERS

Name	DOD	Cemetery, City, State
Aaron, Tommie Lee	08/16/1984	Catholic Cemetery, Mobile, AL
Abadie, John	05/17/1905	St. Denis Cemetery, Havertown, PA
Abbaticchio, Ed (Edward James)	01/06/1957	St. Mary's Cemetery, Latrobe, PA
Abbey, Bert Wood	06/11/1962	Mountain View Cemetery, Essex Center, VT
Abbey, Charlie (Charles S.)	04/27/1926	Steele Cemetery, Falls City, NE
Abbott, Dan (Leander Franklin)	02/13/1930	Weston Cemetery, Weston, OH
Abbott, Fred (Harry Frederick)	06/11/1935	Valhalla Memorial Park, North Hollywood, CA
Abbott, Ody Cleon	04/13/1933	Monongahela Cemetery, Monongahela, PA
Aber, AL (Albert Julius)	05/20/1993	Cremated, Cleveland, OH. Ashes returned to family
Abernathy, Woody (Virgil Woodrow)	12/05/1994	Resthaven Memorial Park, Louisville, KY
Aberson, Cliff (Clifford Alexander)	06/23/1973	Suisun-Fairfield Cemetery, Fairfield, CA
Ables, Harry Terrell	02/08/1951	San Jose Burial Park, San Antonio, TX
Abrams, Cal (Calvin Ross)	02/25/1997	Star of David Memorial Gardens, North Lauderdale, FL
Abrams, George Allen	12/05/1986	Sylvan Abbey Memorial Park, Clearwater, FL
Abreu, Joseph Lawrence	03/17/1993	Evergreen-Washelli Cemetery, Seattle, WA. Cremated.
Abstein,Bill (William Henry)	04/08/1940	New Bethlehem Cemetery, St. Louis, MO
Ackley, Fritz (Florian Frederick)	05/22/2002	Greenwood Cemetery, Hayward, WI
Adair, Bill (Marion Danne) *manager*	06/17/2002	Pine Crest Cemetery, Mobile, AL
Adair, Jerry (Kenneth Jerry)	05/31/1987	Woodland Memorial Park, Sand Springs, OK
Adair, Jimmy (James Audrey)	12/09/1982	Sparkman Hillcrest Memorial Park, Dallas, TX
Adams, Babe (Charles Benjamin)	07/27/1968	Mount Moriah Cemetery, Mount Moriah, MO. Cremated at Fort Lincoln Cemetery, Brentwood, MD
Adams, Bert (John Bertram)	06/24/1940	Hollywood Forever Cemetery (formerly Hollywood Memorial Park), Hollywood, CA

Name	DOD	Cemetery, City, State
Adams, Bob (Robert Andrew)	03/06/1970	Cremated, Restlawn Memorial Park, Jacksonville, FL. Ashes given to family.
Adams, Bobby (Robert Henry)	02/13/1997	Cremated, Gig Harbor, WA
Adams, Buster (Elvin Clark)	09/01/1990	Eternal Hills Memorial Park, Oceanside, CA
Adams, Dan (Daniel Leslie)	10/06/1964	Resurrection Cemetery, Mackenzie, MO
Adams, Joe (Joseph Edward)	10/08/1952	Myers Cemetery, Herrick, IL
Adams, Karl Tutwiler	09/17/1967	Cypress Lawn Memorial Park, Everett, WA. Cremated.
Adams, Rick (Reuben Alexander)	03/10/1955	Providence Cemetery, Paris, TX
Adams, Sparky (Earl John)	02/24/1989	Reformed Cemetery, Tremont, PA
Adams, Sparky (Spencer Dewey)	11/24/1970	Kaysville and Layton Memorial Park, Kaysville, UT
Adcock, Joe (Joseph Wilbur)	05/03/1999	Holly Springs Cemetery, Martin, LA
Addy, Bob (Robert Edward)	04/09/1910	Mountain View Cemetery, Pocatello, ID
Aderholt, Morrie (Morris Woodrow)	03/18/1955	Appomattox Cemetery, Hopewell, VA
Adkins, Dick (Richard Earl)	09/12/1955	Electra Memorial Park, Electra, TX
Adkins, Grady Emmett	03/31/1966	Pine Crest Memorial Park, Alexander, AR
Adkinson, Henry Magee	05/01/1923	Oak Woods Cemetery, Chicago, IL
Agee, Tommie Lee	01/22/2001	Pine Crest Cemetery, Mobile, AL
Agganis, Harry	06/27/1955	Pine Grove Cemetery, Lynn, MA
Agler, Joe (Joseph Abram)	04/26/1971	Warstler Cemetery, Middlebranch, OH
Agnew, Sam (Samuel Lester)	07/19/1951	Chapel of the Chimes, Santa Rosa, CA. Cremated.
Aguirre, Hank (Henry John)	09/05/1994	San Gabriel Mission Cemetery, San Gabriel, CA
Aitchison, Raleigh Leonidas	09/26/1958	Columbus City Cemetery, Columbus, KS
Aiton, George Wilson	08/16/1976	Cremated, Van Nuys, CA
Ake, John Leckie	05/11/1887	Drowned in Mississippi River near LaCrosse, WI. Body never recovered
Akers, Bill (William G.)	04/13/1962	Chattanooga National Cemetery, Chattanooga, TN
Akers, Jerry (Albert Earl)	05/15/1979	Garden of Memories Cemetery, Tampa, FL
Albanese, Joe (Joseph Peter)	06/17/2000	St. George Cemetery, Neptune, NJ
Alberts, Fred (Frederick Joseph)	08/27/1917	Catholic Cemetery, Fort Wayne, IN
Alberts, Gus (Augustus Peter)	05/07/1912	Mount Olivet Cemetery, Wheat Ridge, CO
Albosta, Ed (Edward John)	01/07/2003	Mount Olivet Cemetery, Saginaw, MI. Cremated.
Albrecht, Ed (Edward Arthur)	12/29/1979	St. Joseph Cemetery, Dupo, IL
Albright, Jack (Harold John)	07/22/1991	Fort Rosecrans National Cemetery, LaJolla, CA. Cremated.
Alderson, Dale Leonard	02/12/1982	Alderson Family Cemetery, Belden, NE
Aldridge, Vic (Victor Eddington)	04/17/1973	New Trinity Cemetery, Trinity Springs, IN
Alexander, Bob (Robert Somerville)	04/07/1993	Cremated, Oceanside, CA. Ashes scattered at Point Loma, CA
Alexander, Dale (David Dale)	03/02/1979	Shiloh Cumberland Presbyterian Church Cemetery, Greeneville, TN
Alexander, Grover Cleveland	11/04/1950	Elwood Cemetery, St. Paul, NE
Alexander, Hugh	11/25/2000	Maple Grove Cemetery, Seminole, OK

Name	DOD	Cemetery, City, State
Alexander, Nin (William Henry)	12/22/1933	Mound Cemetery, Pana, IL
Alexander, Walt (Walter Ernest)	12/29/1978	Grove Hill Memorial Park, Dallas, TX
Allen, Bob (Robert Gilman)	05/14/1943	Roselawn Memorial Gardens Cemetery, Little Rock, AR
Allen, Bob (Robert)	12/18/1975	Bronswood Cemetery, Oak Brook, IL
Allen, Ethan Nathan	09/15/1993	Cremated, Brookings, OR. Ashes scattered.
Allen, Frank Erwin	02/06/1881	Dell Park Cemetery, Natick, MA
Allen, Hezekiah	09/21/1916	Willowbrook Cemetery, Norwalk, CT
Allen, Horace Tanner	07/05/1981	Oakdale Cemetery, Deland, FL
Allen, John Marshall	09/24/1967	Rose Hill Cemetery, Hagerstown, MD
Allen, Johnny (John Thomas)	05/29/1959	Forest Lawn Cemetery, Greensboro, NC
Allen, Myron Smith	03/08/1924	Rhinebeck Cemetery, Rhinebeck, NY
Allen, Nick (Artemus Ward)	10/16/1939	Ninnescah Cemetery, Udall, KS
Allen, Sled (Fletcher Manson)	10/16/1959	Lubbock City Cemetery, Lubbock, TX
Allison, Bob (William Robert)	04/09/1995	Cremated, Phoenix, AZ. Ashes returned to family
Allison, Doug (Douglas L.)	12/19/1916	Rock Creek Cemetery, Washington, DC
Allison, Mack Pendleton	03/13/1964	Mount Washington Cemetery, Independence, MO
Allison, Milo Henry	06/18/1957	Community Bible Church Cemetery, Lakewood, WI
Alperman, Whitey (Charles Augustus)	12/25/1942	Mount Royal Cemetery, Glenshaw, PA
Alston, Tom (Thomas Edison)	12/30/1993	New Goshen United Methodist Church Cemetery, Greensboro, NC
Alston, Walt (Walter Emmons)	10/01/1984	Darrtown Cemetery, Darrtown, OH
Alten, Ernie (Ernest Matthias)	09/09/1981	Yountville Cemetery, Yountville, CA
Altenburg, Jesse Howard	03/12/1973	North Star Cemetery, North Star, MI
Altizer, Dave (David Tilden)	05/14/1964	Crescent Heights Cemetery, Pleasant Hills, IL
Altrock, Nick (Nicholas)	01/20/1965	Vine Street Hill Cemetery, Cincinnati, OH
Ames, Red (Leon Kessling)	10/08/1936	Oakwood Cemetery, Warren, OH
Amole, Doc (Morris George)	03/07/1912	Fairview Cemetery, Coatesville, PA
Amoros, Sandy (Edmundo)	06/27/1992	Woodlawn Park Cemetery North, Miami, FL
Ancker, Walter	02/13/1954	George Washington Memorial Park, Paramus, NJ
Anderson, Alf (Alfred Walton)	06/23/1985	Crown Hill Cemetery, Albany, GA
Anderson, Andy Holm	07/18/1982	Evergreen-Washelli Cemetery, Seattle, WA
Anderson, Bill (William Edward)	03/13/1983	Forest Hill Cemetery, East Derry, NH
Anderson, Dave (David S.)	03/22/1897	Chester Rural Cemetery, Chester, PA
Anderson, Ferrell Jack	03/12/1978	Ozark Memorial Park Cemetery, Joplin, MO
Anderson, Fred (John Frederick)	11/08/1957	Salem Cemetery, Winston-Salem, NC
Anderson, George Jendrus	05/28/1962	All Souls Cemetery, Chardon, OH. Originally intered at Calvary Cemetery, Cleveland, OH. Moved in 1981.
Anderson, Goat (Edward John)	03/15/1923	Atlantic Cemetery, Atlantic, PA
Anderson, Hal (Harold)	05/01/1974	Calvary Cemetery, St. Louis, MO
Anderson, Harry Walter	06/11/1998	Wilimington & Brandywine Cemetery, Wilmington, DE

Name	DOD	Cemetery, City, State
Anderson, John Joseph	07/23/1949	Swedish Cemetery, Worcester, MA
Anderson, Red (Arnold Revola)	08/07/1972	Memorial Park Cemetery, Sioux City, IA
Anderson, Rick (Richard Lee)	06/23/1989	Cremated, Los Angeles, CA
Anderson, Varney Samuel	11/05/1941	Willwood Burial Park, Rockford, IL
Anderson, Walter Carl	01/06/1990	Fair Plains Cemetery, Grand Rapids, MI
Anderson, Wingo Charlie	12/19/1950	Crown Hill Cemetery, Dallas, TX
Andre, John Edward	11/25/1976	People's Cemetery, Chatham, MA
Andrews, Bill (William Walter)	01/20/1940	Memorial Park Cemetery, Indianapolis, IN
Andrews, Ed (George Edward)	08/12/1934	Woodlawn Cemetery, West Palm Beach, FL
Andrews, Elbert DeVore	11/25/1979	Edgewood Cemetery, Greenwood, SC
Andrews, Ivy Paul	11/24/1970	Shanghi Cemetery, Dora, AL
Andrews, Nate (Nathan Hardy)	04/26/1991	Rowland Cemetery, Rowland, NC
Andrus, Bill (William Morgan)	03/12/1982	Chattanooga National Cemetery, Chattanooga, TN
Andrus, Fred (Frederick Hotham)	11/10/1937	Woodlawn Cemetery, Detroit, MI (moved to Chicago June 14, 1938)
Andrus, Wiman (William Wiman)	06/17/1935	Miles City Cemetery, Miles City, MT
Angley, Tom (Thomas Samuel)	10/26/1952	Wichita Park Cemetery, Wichita, KS
Ankenman, Pat (Frederick Norman)	01/13/1989	Memorial Oaks Cemetery, Houston, TX
Annis, Bill (William Perley)	06/10/1923	Lindenwood Cemetery, Stoneham, MA
Anson, Cap (Adrian Constantine)	04/14/1922	Oak Woods Cemetery, Chicago, IL
Antonelli, John Lawrence	04/18/1990	Calvary Cemetery, Memphis, TN
Antonello, Bill (William James)	03/04/1993	Fort Snelling National Cemetery, Minneapolis, MN
Applegate, Fred (Frederick Romaine)	04/21/1968	Wildwood Cemetery, Williamsport, PA
Appleton, Ed (Edward Samuel)	01/27/1932	Arlington Cemetery, Arlington, TX
Appleton, Pete (Peter William)	01/18/1974	St. Gertrude's Cemetery, Colonia, NJ
Appling, Luke (Lucius Benjamin)	01/03/1991	Sawnee View Memorial Gardens, Cumming, GA
Aragon, Angel	01/24/1952	Gate of Heaven Cemetery, Hawthorne, NY
Aragon, Angel Valdes	04/04/1988	Serenity Gardens Memorial Park, Largo, FL
Archdeacon, Maurice John	09/05/1954	Memorial Park Cemetery, St. Louis, MO
Archer, Fred (Frederick Marvin)	10/31/1981	West Lawn Memorial Park, Landis, NC
Archer, Jimmy (James Patrick)	03/29/1958	Sacred Heart Cemetery, Boone, IA
Archie, George Albert	09/20/2001	Mount Olivet Cemetery, Nashville, TN
Ardner, Joe (Joseph A.)	09/15/1935	Woodland Cemetery, Cleveland, OH
Arellanes, Frank Julian	12/13/1918	Oak Hill Memorial Park, San Jose, CA
Arft, Hank (Henry Irven)	12/14/2002	St. John United Church of Christ Cemetery, Manchester, MO
Arlett, Buzz (Russell Loris)	05/16/1964	Lakewood Cemetery, Minneapolis, MN
Armbrust, Orville Martin	10/02/1967	Magnolia Cemetery, Mobile, AL
Armbruster, Charlie (Charles A.)	10/07/1964	Granite Hill Cemetery, Grants Pass, OR
Armbruster, Harry	12/10/1953	St. John's Cemetery, Cincinnati, OH
Armour, Bill (William Clark) manager	12/02/1922	Homestead Cemetery, Homestead, PA
Armstrong, George (Noble George)	07/24/1993	Cremated, Orange, NJ
Armstrong, Howard Elmer	03/08/1926	Woodlawn Cemetery, Wellsville, NY

Name	DOD	Cemetery, City, State
Arndt, Harry John	03/25/1921	Cedar Grove Cemetery, South Bend, IN
Arnold, Billy (Willis S.)	01/17/1899	Albany Rural Cemetery, Albany, NY
Arnovich, Morrie (Morris)	07/20/1959	Hebrew Cemetery, Superior, WI
Arntizen, Orie Edgar	01/28/1970	Cedar Memorial Park Cemetery, Cedar Rapids, IA
Arundel, Harry	03/25/1904	Woodland Cemetery, Cleveland, OH
Arundel, Tug (John Thomas)	09/05/1912	St. Joseph's Cemetery. Auburn, NY
Asbell, Jim (James Marion)	07/06/1967	Woodlawn Memorial Park, Colma, CA
Asbjornson, Robert Anthony (buried undername of Asby)	01/21/1970	Wildwood Cemetery, Williamsport, PA
Ash, Ken (Kenneth Lowther)	11/15/1979	Elk View Masonic Cemetery, Clarksburg, WV
Ashburn, Richie (Don Richard)	09/09/1997	Gladwyn Methodist Church Cemetery, Gladwyn, PA
Asmussen, Tom (Thomas William)	08/21/1963	Ridgewood Cemetery, Des Plaines, IL
Atkinson, Al (Albert Wright)	06/17/1952	Macedonia Cemetery, Stella, MO
Atkinson, Lefty (Hubert Burley)	02/12/1961	Mount Carmel Cemetery, Hillside, IL
Attreau, Dick (Richard Gilbert)	07/05/1964	Mount Olivet Cemetery, Chicago, IL
Atwood, Bill (William Franklin)	09/14/1993	Hillside Memorial Gardens, Snyder, TX
Atz, Jake (John Jacob)	05/22/1945	St. John's Cemetery, New Orleans, LA
Aubrey, Harry Herbert	09/18/1953	Loudon Park Cemetery, Baltimore, MD
Austin, Jimmy (James Philip)	03/06/1965	Melrose Abbey Memorial Park, Anaheim, CA
Autry, Chick (Martin Gordon)	01/26/1950	La Rosa Cemetery, Woodsboro, TX
Autry, Chick (William Askew)	01/16/1976	Chapel of the Chimes, Santa Rosa, CA. Cremated.
Averill, Earl (Howard Earl)	08/16/1983	G.A.R. Cemetery, Snohomish, WA
Avrea, Jim (James Epherium)	06/26/1987	Laurel Land Memorial Park, Dallas, TX
Ayers, Bill (William Oscar)	09/24/1980	Oak Hill Cemetery, Newnan, GA
Ayers, Doc (Yancy Wyatt)	05/26/1968	Grantham Cemetery, Draper, VA
Aylward, Dick (Richard John)	06/11/1983	Glen Abbey Memorial Park, Bonita, CA
Babb Charlie (Charles Amos)	03/19/1954	Cremated, Portland Memorial Cemetery, Portland, OR
Babe, Loren Rolland	02/14/1984	Calvary Cemetery, Omaha, NE
Babich, Johnny (John Charles)	01/19/2001	St. Joseph Cemetery, San Pablo, CA
Babington, Charlie (Charles Percy)	03/22/1957	Oakland Cemetery, Providence, RI
Backman, Les (Lester John)	11/08/1975	Spring Grove Cemetery, Cincinnati, OH
Bacon, Eddie (Edgar Suter)	10/02/1963	Peak's Mill Cemetery, Frankfort, KY
Baczewski, Fred (Frederic John)	11/14/1976	Holy Cross Cemetery, Culver City, CA
Bader, Art (Arthur Herman)	04/05/1957	Valhalla Cemetery, St. Louis, MO
Bader, Lore Verne	06/02/1973	Le Roy Cemetery, Le Roy, KS
Badgro, Red (Morris Hiram)	07/13/1998	Hillcrest Burial Park, Kent, WA
Baecht, Ed (Edward Joseph)	08/15/1957	Oak Grove Cemetery, Jerseyville, IL
Bagby, Jim (James Charles Jacob, Jr.)	09/02/1988	Westview Cemetery, Atlanta, GA
Bagby, Jim (James Charles Jacob, Sr.)	07/28/1954	Westview Cemetery, Atlanta, GA
Bagwell, Bill (William Mallory)	10/05/1976	Sibley Cemetery, Sibley, LA
Baichley, Grover Cleveland	06/28/1956	Golden Gate National Cemetery, San Bruno, CA

Name	DOD	Cemetery, City, State
Bailey, Bill (Harry Lewis)	10/27/1967	Acacia Memorial Park, Seattle, WA
Bailey, Fred (Frederick Middleton)	08/16/1972	Spring Hill Cemetery, Huntington, WV
Bailey, Harvey Francis	07/10/1922	Greenlawn Cemetery, Delta, OH
Bailey, King (Linwood C.)	11/19/1917	Riverside Cemetery, Macon, GA
Bailey, Sweetbreads (Abraham Lincoln)	09/27/1939	Elmhurst Cremetery, Joliet, IL
Bailey,Gene (Arthur Eugene)	11/14/1973	Hollywood Cemetery, Houston, TX
Bain, Loren (Herbert Loren)	11/24/1996	Cremated, Rice Lake, WI
Baird, Al (Albert Wells)	11/27/1976	Forest Park Cemetery, Shreveport, LA
Baird, Bob (Robert Allen)	04/11/1974	Lynnhurst Cemetery, Knoxville, TN
Baird, Doug (Howard Douglas)	06/13/1967	Valhalla Cemetery, St. Louis, MO
Bakely, Jersey (Edward Enoch)	12/17/1915	Greenmount Cemetery, Philadelphia, PA
Baker, Al (Albert Jones)	11/06/1982	Butler Family Cemetery, Kenedy, TX
Baker, Bock (Charles)	08/17/1940	New York City Cemetery (Potters Field), Bronx, NY
Baker, Charlie (Charles Arthur)	01/15/1937	Forest Vale Cemetery, Manchester, NH
Baker, Del (Delmer David)	09/11/1973	Sunset Memorial Park, San Antonio, TX
Baker, Ernie (Earnest Gould)	10/25/1945	Maple Grove Cemetery, Concord, MI
Baker, Frank (John Franklin)	06/28/1963	Spring Hill Cemetery, Easton, MD
Baker, Gene (Eugene Walter)	12/01/1999	Rock Island National Cemetery, Rock Island, IL
Baker, Howard Francis	01/16/1964	St. Michael's Cemetery, Stratford, CT
Baker, Jesse	07/29/1976	Pomona Cemetery, Pomona, CA
Baker, Jesse Ormond	09/26/1972	Mountain View Memorial Park, Tacoma, WA
Baker, Kirtley	04/15/1927	Greendale Cemetery, Lawrenceburg, IN
Baker, Neal Vernon	01/05/1982	Woodlawn Garden of Memories, Houston, TX
Baker, Norm (Norman Leslie)	02/20/1949	Wenonah Cemetery, Wenonah, NJ
Baker, Phil (Philip)	06/04/1940	Glenwood Cemetery, Washington, DC
Baker, Tom (Thomas Calvin)	01/03/1991	Greenwood Memorial Park, Fort Worth, TX
Baker, Tom (Thomas Henry)	03/09/1980	Laurel Grove Cemetery, Port Townsend, WA
Baker, Tracy Lee	03/14/1975	Westwood Hills Memorial Park, Placerville, CA
Balcena, Bobby (Robert Rudolph)	01/05/1990	Cremated, San Pedro, CA. Ashes scattered in Pacific Ocean.
Baldwin, Harry (Howard Edward)	01/23/1958	Oak Lawn Cemetery, Baltimore, MD
Baldwin, Kid (Clarence Geoghan)	07/10/1897	Longview Asylum Cemetery, Cincinnati, OH
Baldwin, Lady (Charles B.)	03/07/1937	Riverside Cemetery, Hastings, MI
Baldwin, Mark (Marcus Elmore)	11/10/1929	Allegheny Cemetery, Pittsburgh, PA
Baldwin, Ollie (Orson F.)	02/16/1942	Cremated, Los Angeles, CA
Baldwin, Ted (Henry Clay)	02/24/1964	Birmingham-LaFayette Cemetery, West Chester, PA
Balenti, Mike (Michael Richard)	08/04/1955	Altus Cemetery, Altus, OK
Ball, Art (Arthur)	12/26/1915	Mount Olivet Cemetery, Chicago, IL
Ball, Jim (James Chandler)	04/07/1963	Calvary Cemetery, Los Angeles, CA
Ball, Neal (Cornelius)	10/15/1957	Mountain Grove Cemetery, Bridgeport, CT
Ballenger, Pel (Pelham Ashby)	12/08/1948	Graceland Cemetery, Greenville, SC
Ballou, Win (Noble Winfield)	01/29/1963	Woodlawn Memorial Park, Colma, CA

Name	DOD	Cemetery, City, State
Bamberger, George Irvin	04/04/2004	Bay Pines National Cemetery, Bay Pines, FL
Bancroft, Dave (David James)	10/09/1972	Greenwood Cemetery, Superior, WI
Bancroft, Frank Carter *manager*	03/30/1921	Spring Grove Cemetery, Cincinnati, OH
Bankhead, Dan (Daniel Robert)	05/02/1976	Houston National Cemetery, Houston, TX
Banks, Bill (William)	09/08/1936	Odd Fellows Cemetery, Danville, PA
Banks, George Edward	03/01/1985	Pacolet Memorial Gardens, Pacolet, SC
Bankston, Everett (Wilborn Everett)	02/26/1970	Fredonia Congregational Christian Church Cemetery, Barnesville, GA
Banning, Jim (James M.)	10/14/1952	Calvary Cemetery, St. Paul, MN
Bannon, Jimmy (James Henry)	03/24/1948	St. Mary's Cemetery, Rochester, NH
Bannon, Tom (Thomas Edward)	01/26/1950	St. Joseph's Cemetery, Lynn, MA
Barbare, Walter Lawrence	10/28/1965	Graceland Cemetery, Greenville, SC
Barbeau, Jap (William Joseph)	09/10/1969	Holy Cross Cemetery, Milwaukee, WI
Barbee, Dave (David Monroe)	07/01/1968	Guilford Memorial Park, Greensboro, NC
Barber, Turner (Tyrus Turner)	10/20/1968	Oakwood Baptist Church Cemetery, Milan, TN
Barclay, Curt (Curtis Cordell)	03/25/1985	Cremated, Sunset Memorial Cemetery, Missoula, MT
Barclay, George Oliver	04/03/1909	Easton Cemetery, Easton, PA
Bare, Ray (Raymond Douglas)	03/29/1994	Miami Memorial Park, Miami, FL
Barfoot, Clyde Raymond	03/11/1971	Forest Lawn Memorial Park, Glendale, CA
Barger, Cy (Eros Bolivar)	09/23/1964	Columbia Cemetery, Columbia, KY
Barkley, Sam (Samuel E.)	04/20/1912	Peninsula Cemetery, Wheeling, WV
Barna, Babe (Herbert Paul)	05/18/1972	Mountain View Memorial Park, Charleston, WV
Barnabe, Charlie (Charles Edward)	08/16/1977	Rosemond Cemetery, Waco, TX
Barnes, Bob (Robert Avery)	12/08/1993	Lacon Cemetery, Lacon, IL
Barnes, Frank Samuel	09/27/1967	Forest Park (East) Cemetery, League City, TX
Barnes, Honey (John Francis)	06/18/1981	St. Mary's Cemetery, Fulton, NY
Barnes, Jesse Lawrence	09/09/1961	Westminster Memorial Park, Westminster, CA
Barnes, Junie Shoaf	12/31/1963	Barnes Family Cemetery, Churchland, NC
Barnes, Red (Emile Deering)	07/03/1959	Suggsville Cemetery, Suggsville, AL
Barnes, Ross (Roscoe Charles)	02/05/1915	Greenwood Cemetery, Rockford, IL
Barnes, Sam (Samuel Thomas)	02/19/1981	Fairmount Baptist Church Cemetery, Red Level, AL
Barnes, Virgil Jennings	07/24/1958	Holton Cemetery, Holton, KS
Barney, Rex Edward	08/12/1997	Lorraine Park Cemetery, Baltimore, MD
Barnhart, Clyde Lee	01/21/1980	Cedar Lawn Memorial Park, Hagerstown, MD
Barnhart, Ed (Edgar Vernon)	09/14/1984	Memorial Park Cemetery, Columbia, MO
Barnhart, Les (Leslie Earl)	10/07/1971	East Resthaven Park Cemetery, Phoenix, AZ
Barnie, Bill (William Harrison)	07/15/1900	Green-Wood Cemetery, Brooklyn, NY
Barr, Bob (Robert Alexander)	07/25/2002	Pine Grove Cemetery, Barrington, NH
Barr, Bob (Robert McClelland)	03/11/1930	Oak Hill Cemetery, Washington, DC
Barr, Scotty (Hyder Edward)	12/02/1934	Shannon Rose Hill Memorial Park, Fort Worth, TX

Name	DOD	Cemetery, City, State
Barrett, Bill (William Joseph)	01/26/1951	Cambridge Cemetery, Cambridge, MA
Barrett, Bob (Robert Schley)	01/18/1982	Westview Cemetery, Atlanta, GA
Barrett, Dick (Tracy Souter)	10/30/1966	Holyrood Cemetery, Seattle, WA
Barrett, Frank (Francis Joseph)	03/06/1998	Hillcrest Memorial Gardens, Leesburg, FL
Barrett, Jimmy (James Erigena)	10/24/1921	Mount Olivet Cemetery, Detroit, MI
Barrett, Johnny (John Joseph)	08/17/1974	Ridgewood Cemetery, North Andover, MA
Barrett, Marty (Martin F.)	01/29/1910	St. Jerome Cemetery, Holyoke, MA
Barrett, Red (Charles Henry)	07/28/1990	Evergreen Memorial Gardens, Wilson, NC
Barron, Frank John	09/18/1964	Odd Fellows Cemetery, St. Marys, WV
Barron, Red (David Irenus)	10/04/1982	Clarksville City Cemetery, Clarksville, GA
Barrow, Ed (Edward G.) *manager*	12/15/1953	Kensico Cemetery, Valhalla, NY
Barrows, Cuke (Roland)	02/10/1955	Eastern Cemetery, Portland, ME
Barry, Ed (Edward)	06/19/1920	Resurrection Catholic Cemetery, Madison, WI
Barry, Hardin	11/05/1969	Susanville Cemetery, Susanville, CA
Barry, Jack (John Joseph)	04/23/1961	Sacred Heart Cemetery, Meriden, CT
Barry, Shad (John C.)	11/27/1936	Calvary Cemetery, Los Angeles, CA
Barry, Tom (Thomas Arthur)	06/04/1946	Calvary Cemetery, St. Louis, MO
Bartell, Dick (Richard William)	08/04/1995	Cremated, Chapel of the Chimes Columbarium, Oakland, CA. Ashes given to family
Barthelson, Bob (Robert Edward)	04/14/2000	Beaverdale Memorial Park, New Haven, CT
Barthold, John Francis	11/04/1946	Holy Cross Cemetery, Yeadon, PA. Originally intered at St. Mary's Cemetery (Moore Street), Philadelphia. Cemtery removed in 1954.
Bartley, Bill (William Jackson)	05/17/1965	St. Joseph's New Cemetery, Cincinnati, OH
Bartling, Irv (Henry Irving)	06/12/1973	Grand Lawn Cemetery, Detroit, MI
Barton, Harry Lamb	01/25/1955	Cremated, West Laurel Hill Cemetery, Bala Cynwyd, PA. Ashes returned to family.
Barton, Vince (Vincent David)	09/13/1973	Cremated, Toronto, Ontario
Bartson, Charlie (Charles Franklin)	06/09/1936	Springdale Cemetery, Peoria, IL
Bashang, Al (Albert C.)	06/23/1967	Vine Street Hill Cemetery, Cincinnati, OH
Baskette, Jim (James Blaine)	07/30/1942	Cedar Grove Cemetery, Athens, TN
Bass, Doc (William Capers)	01/12/1970	Mount Zion Baptist Church Cemetery, Macon, GA
Bass, John Elias	09/25/1888	Riverside Cemetery, Denver, CO
Bassett, Charley (Charles Edwin)	05/28/1942	Moshassuck Cemetery, Central Falls, RI
Bassler, Johnny (John Landis)	06/29/1979	Woodlawn Cemetery, Santa Monica, CA
Bastian, Charlie (Charles J.)	01/18/1932	Holy Cross Cemetery, Yeadon, PA
Batch, Emil	08/23/1926	Evergreen Cemetery, Brooklyn, NY
Batchelder, Joe (Joseph Edward)	05/05/1989	Hamilton Cemetery, Hamilton, MA
Bates, Bud (Hubert Edgar)	04/29/1987	Cremated, Los Angeles, CA
Bates, Charlie (Charles William)	01/29/1980	Memorial Park Cemetery, Topeka, KS
Bates, John William	03/24/1919	Cremated, California Cremation, Oakland, CA.
Bates, Johnny (John William)	02/10/1949	Union Cemetery, Steubenville, OH
Bates, Ray (Raymond)	08/15/1970	Holy Hope Cemetery, Tucson, AZ

Name	DOD	Cemetery, City, State
Batsch, Bill (William McKinley)	12/31/1963	West Lawn Cemetery, Canton, OH
Battam, Larry (Lawrence)	01/27/1938	Holy Cross Cemetery, Brooklyn, NY
Battey, Earl Jesse	11/15/2003	Inglewood Park Cemetery, Inglewood, CA
Battin, Joe (Joseph V.)	12/10/1937	Glendale Cemetery, Akron, OH
Battle, Jim (James Milton)	09/30/1965	Glen Oaks Memorial Park, Chico, CA
Bauer, Albert	02/23/1944	Cremated, Columbus, OH.
Bauer, Lou (Louis Walter)	02/04/1979	Egg Harbor Cemetery, Egg Harbor, NJ
Bauers, Russ (Russell Lee)	01/21/1995	Trinity Lutheran Cemetery, Wabeno, WI
Baumann, Paddy (Charles John)	11/20/1969	Crown Hill Cemetery, Indianapolis, IN
Baumer, Jim (James Sloan)	07/08/1996	SS. Peter & Paul Cemetery, Springfield, PA
Baumgardner, George Washington	12/13/1970	Barboursville Cemetery, Barboursville, WV
Baumgartner, Harry E.	12/03/1930	City Cemetery, South Pittsburg, TN
Baumgartner, Stan (Stanwood Fulton)	10/04/1955	Holy Sepulchre Cemetery, Wyndmoor, PA
Bausewine, George W.	07/29/1947	Arlington Cemetery, Drexel Hill, PA
Baxes, Jim (Dimitrios Speros)	11/14/1996	Magnolia Memorial Park, Garden Grove, CA. Cremated
Baxter, Moose (John Morris)	08/07/1926	Greenwood Memorial Terrace Cemetery, Spokane, WA
Bay, Harry Elbert	03/20/1952	Parkview Cemetery, Peoria, IL
Bayless, Dick (Harry Owen)	12/16/1920	Forest Park Cemetery, Joplin, MO
Bayne, Bill (William Lear)	05/22/1981	Bellefontaine Cemetery, St. Louis, MO
Beadle, David A.	09/22/1925	Calvary Cemetery, Woodside, Queens, NY
Beall, Johnny (John Woolf)	06/13/1926	St. John's Cemetery, Beltsville, MD
Beall, Walter Esau	01/28/1959	Cedar Hill Cemetery, Suitland, MD
Beals, Tommy (Thomas L.)	10/02/1915	Cremated, Cypress Lawn Cemetery, Colma, CA.
Beam, Alex (Alexander Roger)	04/17/1938	Nogales City Cemetery, Nogales, AZ
Beam, Ernie (Ernest Joseph)	09/13/1918	Mansfield Cemetery, Mansfield, OH
Bean, Belv (Beveric Benton)	06/01/1988	White Point Cemetery, Comanche, TX
Bean, Joe (Joseph William)	02/15/1961	Westview Cemetery, Atlanta, GA
Beard, Ollie (Oliver Perry)	05/28/1929	Cremated, Cincinnati, OH.
Beard, Ralph William	02/10/2003	Cremated, West Palm Beach, FL
Bearden, Gene (Henry Eugene)	03/18/2004	Sunset Memorial Park, West Helena, AR
Bearnarth, Larry (Lawrence Donald)	12/31/1999	Memorial Park Cemetery, St. Petersburg, FL
Beatin, Ed (Ebenezer Ambrose)	05/09/1925	Oak Lawn Cemetery, Baltimore, MD
Beatty, Desmond (Aloysius Desmond)	10/06/1969	Pine Grove Cemetery, Falmouth, ME
Beaumont, Ginger (Clarence Howeth)	04/10/1956	Rochester Cemetery, Rochester, WI
Beazley, Johnny (John Andrew)	04/21/1990	Mount Olivet Cemetery, Nashville, TN
Becannon, Buck (James Melvin)	11/05/1923	Kensico Cemetery, Valhalla, NY
Bechler, Steve (Steven Scott)	02/17/2003	Cremated, Fort Lauderdale, FL. Ashes scattered at Camden Yards, Baltimore, MD
Beck, Boom-Boom (Walter William)	05/07/1987	Lutheran Cemetery, Decatur, IL
Beck, Clyde Eugene	07/15/1988	Cremated, Los Angeles, CA
Beck, Erve (Ervin Thomas)	12/23/1916	Mt. Carmel Cemetery (formerly St. Mary's Cemetery), Toledo, OH

Name	DOD	Cemetery, City, State
Beck, Fred (Frederick Thomas)	03/12/1962	Laurel Hill Cemetery, Havana, IL
Beck, George (Ernest George)	10/29/1973	Riverview Cemetery, South Bend, IN
Beck, Zinn Bertram	03/19/1981	Evergreen Cemetery, Sanford, FL
Beckendorf, Heinie (Henry Ward)	09/15/1949	Long Island National Cemetery, Farmingdale, NY
Becker, Beals (David Beals)	08/16/1943	Inglewood Park Cemetery, Inglewood, CA
Becker, Bob (Robert Charles)	10/11/1951	Assumption Cemetery, Syracuse, NY
Becker, Charlie (Charles S.)	07/30/1928	Arlington National Cemetery, Arlington, VA
Becker, Heinz Reinhard	11/11/1991	Restland Memorial Park, Dallas, TX
Becker, Joe (Joseph Edward)	01/11/1998	Mount Olive Cemetery of Lemay, St. Louis, MO
Becker, Marty (Martin Henry)	09/25/1957	Cremated, Cincinnati, OH.
Beckley, Jake (Jacob Peter)	06/25/1918	Riverside Cemetery, Hannibal, MO
Beckman, Jim (James Joseph)	12/05/1974	Gate of Heaven Cemetery, Montgomery, OH
Beckmann, William Aloysius	01/02/1990	Calvary Cemetery, St. Louis, MO
Bedford, Gene (William Eugene)	10/06/1977	Sunset Memorial Park, San Antonio, TX
Bedgood, Phil (Phillip Burlette)	11/08/1927	Baptist Church Cemetery, Harrison, GA
Bedient, Hugh Carpenter	07/21/1965	Levant Cemetery, Levant, NY
Bednar, Andy (Andrew Jackson)	11/26/1937	Nokomis Cemetery, Nokomis, IL
Beebe, Fred (Frederick Leonard)	10/30/1957	Parkholm Cemetery, LaGrange Park, IL
Beecher, Harry (Edward Harry)	09/12/1935	Mt. St. Benedict's Cemetery, Bloomfield, CT
Beecher, Roy (Leroy)	10/11/1952	South Swanton Cemetery, Swanton, OH
Beggs, Joe (Joseph Stanley)	07/19/1983	Cremated, Indianapolis, IN
Begley, Ed (Edward N.)	07/24/1919	New St. Joseph's Cemetery, Waterbury, CT
Begley, Jim (James Lawrence)	02/22/1957	Golden Gate National Cemetery, San Bruno, CA
Behan, Petie (Charles Frederick)	01/22/1957	St. Bernard's Cemetery, Bradford, PA
Behel, Steve (Stephen Arnold Douglas)	02/15/1945	Inglewood Park Cemetery, Inglewood, CA
Behrman, Hank (Henry Bernard)	01/20/1987	Calverton National Cemetery, Calverton, NY
Bejma, Ollie (Aloysius Frank)	01/03/1995	St. Joseph's Cemetery, South Bend, IN
Belanger, Mark Henry	10/06/1998	St. Joseph's Cemetery, Pittsfield, MA
Belardi, Wayne (Carroll Wayne)	10/21/1993	Cremated, Santa Cruz, CA. Ashes scattered in Pacific Ocean.
Bell, Beau (Roy Chester)	09/14/1977	Restever Memorial Park, Bryan, TX
Bell, Bill (William Samuel)	10/11/1962	Willow Dale Cemetery, Goldsboro, NC
Bell, Charlie (Charles C.)	02/07/1937	Baltimore Pike Cemetery, Cincinnati, OH
Bell, Frank Gustav	04/14/1891	Wesleyan Cemetery, Cincinnati, OH
Bell, Gus (David Russell)	05/07/1995	Gate of Heaven Cemetery, Montgomery, OH
Bell, Hi (Herman S.)	06/07/1949	Calvary Cemetery, Los Angeles, CA
Bell, Les (Lester Rowland)	12/26/1985	East Harrisburg Cemetery, Harrisburg, PA
Bell, Ralph Albert	10/18/1959	St. Peter's Catholic Church Cemetery, Keokuk, IA
Bell, Rudy (John)	07/28/1955	Sunset Memorial Park, Albuquerque, NM
Bellman, Jack (John Hutchins)	12/08/1931	Calvary Cemetery, Louisville, KY
Bemis, Harry Parker	05/23/1947	Elmhurst Park Cemetery, Avon, OH
Bender, Chief (Charles Albert)	05/22/1954	Hillside Cemetery (Ardsley Burial Park section), Roslyn, PA

Name	DOD	Cemetery, City, State
Benes, Joe (Joseph Anthony)	03/07/1975	St. Charles Cemetery, Farmingdale, NY
Benge, Ray (Raymond Adelphia)	06/27/1997	Concord Cemetery, Concord, TX
Bengough, Benny (Bernard Oliver)	12/22/1968	St. Dominic's Cemetery, Philadelphia, PA
Benn, Henry Omer	06/04/1967	Viola Cemetery, Viola, WI
Benners, Ike (Isaac B.)	04/18/1932	Fernwood Cemetery, Lansdowne, PA
Bennett, Bugs (Joseph Harley) (also played as Bugs Morris)	11/21/1957	White Rose Cemetery, Bartlesville, OK
Bennett, Charlie (Charles Wesley)	02/24/1927	Woodmere Cemetery, Detroit, MI
Bennett, Frank (Francis Allen)	03/18/1966	Gracelawn Memorial Park, New Castle, DE
Bennett, Fred (James Fred)	05/12/1957	Atkins City Cemetery, Atkins, AR
Bennett, Herschel Emmett	09/09/1964	Greenlawn Memorial Gardens, Springfield, MO
Bennett, Joe (Joseph Rosenblum)	07/11/1987	Cedar Park Cemetery, Paramus, NJ
Bentley, Jack (John Needles)	10/24/1969	Friends Cemetery, Sandy Spring, MD
Benton, Al (John Alton)	04/14/1968	Park Lawn Cemetery, City of Commerce, CA
Benton, Larry (Lawrence James)	04/03/1953	St. Joseph Cemetery, Cincinnati, OH
Benton, Rube (John Clebon)	12/12/1937	Baptist Church Cemetery, Salemburg, NC
Benton, Sid (Sidney Wright)	03/08/1977	Evergreen Cemetery, Fayetteville, AR
Benz, Joe (Joseph Louis)	04/22/1957	Holy Sepulchre Cemetery, Worth, IL
Berardino, John (Beradino)	05/19/1996	Holy Cross Cemetery, Culver City, CA
Berberet, Lou (Louis Joseph)	04/06/2004	All Souls Cemetery, Long Beach, CA
Berg, Moe (Morris)	05/29/1972	Cremated, Newark, NJ. Buried at unknown site in Israel
Bergamo, Augie (August Samuel)	08/19/1974	Forest Lawn Cemetery, Detroit, MI
Bergen, Bill (William Aloysius)	12/19/1943	St. John's Cemetery, Worcester, MA
Bergen, Boze (Louis William)	11/03/1992	Arlington National Cemetery, Arlington, VA
Bergen, Marty (Martin)	01/19/1900	St. Joseph's Cemetery, North Brookfield, MA
Berger, Clarence Edward	06/30/1959	Mount Olivet Cemetery, Frederick, MD
Berger, Heinie (Charles)	02/10/1954	Lake View Cemetery, Cleveland, OH
Berger, Joe (Joseph August)	03/06/1956	Memorial Park Cemetery, Rock Island, IL
Berger, Johnny (John Henne)	05/07/1979	Graceland Cemetery, Lake Charles, LA
Berger, Tun (John Henry)	06/10/1907	Oakland Cemetery, Pittsburgh, PA
Berger, Wally (Walter Anton)	11/30/1988	Inglewood Park Cemetery, Inglewood, CA
Bergh, John Baptist	04/17/1883	Holyhood Cemetery, Brookline, MA
Berghammer, Marty (Martin Andrew)	12/21/1957	St. Martin's Cemetery, Pittsburgh, PA
Bergman, Al (Alfred Henry)	06/20/1961	St. Charles Catholic Cemetery, Peru, IN
Berkelbach, Frank Pierce	06/10/1932	Arlington Cemetery, Pennsauken, NJ
Berkenstock, Nate (Nathan)	02/23/1900	Mount Peace Cemetery, Philadelphia, PA
Berly, Jack (John Chambers)	06/26/1977	Hollywood Cemetery, Houston, TX
Berman, Bob (Robert Leon)	08/02/1988	Gate of Heaven Cemetery, Hawthorne, NY
Bernard, Curt (Curtis Henry)	04/10/1955	Inglewood Park Cemetery, Inglewood, CA
Bernard, Joe (Joseph Carl)	09/22/1960	Calvary Cemetery, Springfield, IL
Bernhard, Bill (William Henry)	03/30/1949	Cremated, San Diego, CA.
Bernhardt, Walter Jacob	07/26/1958	Webster Rural Cemetery, Webster, NY
Bero, Johnny (John George)	05/11/1985	Holy Cross Cemetery, Culver City, CA
Berran, Dennis Martin	04/28/1943	New Calvary Cemetery, Mattapan, MA

17

Name	DOD	Cemetery, City, State
Berry, Charlie (Charles Francis)	09/06/1972	Belvidere Cemetery, Belvidere, NJ
Berry, Charlie (Charles Joseph)	02/16/1940	Mt. Olivet Cemetery, Newark, NJ
Berry, Claude Elzy	02/01/1974	Earlham Cemetery, Richmond, IN
Berry, Joe (Jonas Arthur)	09/27/1958	Huntsville Cemetery, Huntsville, AR
Berry, Joe (Joseph Howard)	03/13/1961	Westminster Cemetery, Bala Cynwyd, PA
Berry, Joe (Joseph Howard, Jr.)	04/29/1976	West Laurel Hill Cemetery, Bala Cynwyd, PA
Berry, Tom (Thomas Haney)	06/06/1915	Chester Rural Cemetery, Chester, PA
Berte, Harry Thomas	05/06/1952	Valhalla Memorial Park, North Hollywood, CA
Berthrong, Harry W.	04/24/1928	Woodbrook Cemetery, Woburn, MA
Bescher, Bob (Robert Henry)	11/29/1942	Kirkwood Cemetery, London, OH
Besse, Herman A.	08/13/1972	Calvary Cemetery, St. Louis, MO
Bessent, Don (Fred Donald)	07/07/1990	Oaklawn Cemetery, Jacksonville, FL
Bettencourt, Larry (Lawrence Joseph)	09/15/1978	Lake Lawn Cemetery, New Orleans, LA
Betts, Huck (Walter Martin)	06/13/1987	Millsboro Cemetery, Millsboro, DE
Betzel, Bruno (Christian Frederick Albert John Henry David)	02/07/1965	North Grove Cemetery, Celina, OH
Bevan, Hal (Harold Joseph)	10/05/1968	Greenwood Cemetery, New Orleans, LA
Bevens, Bill (Floyd Clifford)	10/26/1991	Restlawn Memory Gardens, Salem, OR
Bevil, Lou (Louis Eugene)	02/01/1973	Oakwood Cemetery, Dixon, IL
Beville, Charlie (Clarence Benjamin)	01/05/1937	Colusa Cemetery, Colusa, CA
Beville, Monte (Henry Monte)	01/24/1955	Oakwood Cemetery, Muskegon, MI
Bezdek, Hugo Frank *manager*	09/19/1952	Whitemarsh Memorial Park, Ambler, PA
Bickford, Vern (Vernon Edgell)	05/06/1960	Mount Zion Baptist Church Cemetery, New Canton, VA
Bickham, Dan (Daniel Denison)	03/03/1951	Woodland Cemetery, Dayton, OH
Biecher, Scrap Iron (Edward)	07/15/1939	St. Paul Churchyard Cemetery, Affton, MO
Bielaski, Oscar	11/08/1911	Arlington National Cemetery, Arlington, VA
Bieman, Charlie (Charles S.)	08/04/1879	Hoboken Cemetery, Hoboken, NJ
Biemiller, Harry Lee	05/25/1965	Glen Haven Memorial Park, Winter Park, FL
Bierbauer, Lou (Louis W.)	01/31/1926	Erie Cemetery, Erie, PA
Bigbee, Carson Lee	10/17/1964	Willamette National Cemetery, Portland, OR
Bigbee, Lyle Randolph	08/05/1942	Liberty Cemetery, Sweet Home, OR
Bigelow, Elliott Allardice	08/10/1933	Cycadia Cemetery, Tarpon Springs, FL
Biggs, Charlie (Charles Orval)	05/24/1954	Mount Lebanon Cemetery, French Lick, IN
Bigler, Pete (Ivan Edward)	04/01/1975	Harris Creek Cemetery, Bradford, OH
Bignell, George William	01/16/1925	St. Joseph's Cemetery, Taunton, MA
Bilbrey, Jim (James Melvin)	12/26/1985	New Belleville Ridge Cemetery, Dowling, OH
Bildilli, Emil	09/16/1946	Rose Lawn Cemetery, Terre Haute, IN
Bilko, Steve (Stephen Thomas)	03/07/1978	St. Joseph's Church Cemetery, Nanticoke, PA
Billiard, Harry Pree	06/03/1923	Wooster Cemetery, Wooster, OH
Billings, Haskell Clark	12/26/1983	Cremated, Greenbrae, CA
Billings, Josh (John Augustus)	12/30/1981	Body donated to UCLA Medical School, Los Angeles, CA
Biras, Steve (Stephen Alexander)	04/21/1965	Mount Carmel Cemetery, Belleville, IL
Birchall, Jud (Adoniram Judson)	12/22/1887	Milestown Baptist Church Cemetery, Philadelphia, PA

Name	DOD	Cemetery, City, State
Bird, Frank Zephrin	05/20/1958	Holy Rosary-St. Mary's Cemetery, Spencer, MA
Bird, George Raymond	11/09/1940	Stillman Valley Cemetery, Stillman Valley, IL
Bird, Red (James Edward)	03/23/1972	Oakdale Cemetery, Murfeesboro, AR
Birdsall, Dave (David Solomon)	12/30/1896	Mount Hope Cemetery, Mattapan, MA
Birkofer, Ralph Joseph	03/16/1971	St. Mary's Cemetery, Cincinnati, OH
Biscan, Frank Stephen	05/22/1959	Jefferson Barracks National Cemetery, St. Louis, MO
Bischoff, John George	12/28/1981	Sunset Hill Memorial Estates, Edwardsville, IL
Bishop, Bill (William Henry)	02/14/1956	Memorial Park Cemetery, St. Joseph, MO
Bishop, Bill (William Robinson)	12/15/1932	Homewood Cemetery, Pittsburgh, PA
Bishop, Charlie (Charles Tuller)	07/05/1993	White Rose Cemetery, Duluth, GA
Bishop, Frank H.	06/18/1929	Oak Woods Cemetery, Chicago, IL
Bishop, Jim (James Morton)	09/20/1973	Montgomery City Cemetery, Montgomery, MO
Bishop, Lloyd Clifton	06/18/1968	Clearwater Cemetery, Clearwater, KS
Bishop, Max Frederick	02/24/1962	Woodlawn Cemetery, Baltimore, MD
Bissonette, Del (Delphia Louis)	06/09/1972	Glenside Cemetery, Winthrop, ME
Bittmann, Red (Henry Peter)	11/08/1929	Vine Street Hill Cemetery, Cincinnati, OH
Bivin, Jim (James Nathaniel)	11/07/1982	Imperial Memorial Gardens, Pueblo, CO
Black, Bill (John William)	01/14/1968	East Cedar Hill Cemetery, Philadelphia, PA
Black, Bob (Robert Benjamin)	03/21/1933	Graceland Cemetery, Sioux City, IA
Black, Dave (David)	10/27/1936	Union Dale Cemetery, Pittsburgh, PA
Black, Don (Donald Paul)	04/21/1959	Good Shepherd Church Cemetery, McKenney, VA
Black, Joseph	05/17/2002	Cremated, Phoenix, AZ. Ashes given to family.
Blackburn, Earl Stuart	08/03/1966	Massillon Cemetery, Massillon, OH
Blackburn, Foster Edwin	03/09/1984	Irving Park Cemetery, Chicago. Cremated.
Blackburn, Jim (James Ray)	10/26/1969	Spring Grove Cemetery, Cincinnati, OH
Blackburn, Ron (Ronald Hamilton)	04/29/1998	Carolina Memorial Park, Kannapolis, NC
Blackburne, Lena (Russell Aubrey)	02/29/1968	Morgan Cemetery, Riverton, NJ
Blackerby, George Franklin	03/30/1987	Crestview Memorial Park, Wichita Falls, TX
Blackwell, Ewell	10/29/1996	Shepherd Memorial Park, Hendersonville, NC
Blackwell, Fred (Frederick William)	12/08/1975	Fairview Cemetery, Bowling Green, KY
Blades, Ray (Francis Raymond)	05/18/1979	IOOF Cemetery, McLeansboro, IL
Blaeholder, George Franklin	12/29/1947	Westminster Memorial Park, Westminster, CA
Blair, Footsie (Clarence Vick)	07/01/1982	Hillcrest Cemetery, Texarkana, TX
Blair, Walter Allen	08/20/1948	Lewisburg Cemetery, Lewisburg, PA
Blaisdell, Dick (Howard Carleton)	08/20/1886	Riverview Cemetery, Groveland, MA
Blake, Harry Cooper	10/14/1919	Greenlawn Cemetery, Portsmouth, OH
Blake, Sheriff (John Frederick)	10/31/1982	Sunset Memorial Park, Beckley, WV
Blakey, Linc (Lincoln Howard)	09/28/1976	Mountain View Cemetery, Oakland, CA
Blakiston, Bob (Robert J.)	12/25/1918	Holy Cross Cemetery, Colma, CA
Blanche, Al (Prosper Albert)	04/02/1997	Woodlawn Cemetery, Everett, MA

Name	DOD	Cemetery, City, State
Blanding, Fred (Frederick James)	07/16/1950	Franklin Cemetery, Birmingham, MI .
Blank, Coonie (Frank Ignatz)	12/08/1961	New St. Marcus Evangelical Cemetery, St. Louis, MO
Blankenship, Cliff (Clifford Douglas)	04/26/1956	Cremated, Oakland, CA
Blankenship, Homer	06/22/1974	Spring Hill Cemetery, Longview, TX
Blankenship, Ted (Theodore)	01/14/1945	Atoka Cemetery, Atoka, OK
Blanton, Cy (Darrell Elijah)	09/13/1945	Techumseh Cemetery, Techumseh, OK
Blatnik, Johnny (John Louis)	1/21/2004	Holly Memorial Gardens, Pleasant Grove, OH
Blauvelt, Henry Russell	12/28/1926	Cremated, Portland, OR
Blaylock, Marv (Marvin Edward)	10/23/1993	Pine Crest Memorial Park, Alexander, AR
Blefary, Curt (Curtis Leroy)	01/28/2001	Cremated, Pompano Beach, FL. Ashes scattered at site of Memorial Stadium, Baltimore, MD
Blemker, Ray (Raymond)	02/15/1994	Fairmount Cemetery, Huntingburg, IN
Blethen, Clarence Waldo	04/11/1973	Mount Olivet Cemetery, Frederick, MD
Bligh, Ned (Edwin Forrest)	04/18/1892	Holy Cross Cemetery, Brooklyn, NY
Bliss, Elmer Ward	03/18/1962	Oak Hill Cemetery, Bradford, PA
Bliss, Frank Eugene	01/08/1929	Oak Hill Cemetery, Janesville, WI
Bliss, Jack (John Joseph Albert)	10/23/1968	Cremated, Los Angeles, CA
Block, Bruno (James John)	08/06/1937	Saint Adalbert Cemetery, Milwaukee, WI
Blong, Joseph Myles	09/16/1892	Calvary Cemetery, St. Louis, MO
Blott, Jack (John Leonard)	06/11/1964	Cremated, Ann Arbor, MI
Blue, Burt (Bird Wayne)	09/02/1929	Woodlawn Cemetery, Detroit, MI
Blue, Lu (Luzerne Atwell)	07/28/1958	Arlington National Cemetery, Arlington, VA
Bluege, Ossie (Oswald Louis)	10/14/1985	Lakewood Cemetery, Minneapolis, MN
Bluege, Otto Adam	06/28/1977	Cremated, Chicago, IL
Bluejacket, Jim (James)	03/26/1947	St. Joseph Cemetery, West Peoria, IL
Bluhm, Red (Harvey Fred)	05/07/1952	Sunset Hills, Flint, MI
Blume, Clint (Clinton Willis)	06/12/1973	Ferncliff Cemetery, Hartsdale, NY
Boak, Chet (Chester Robert)	11/28/1983	SS. Philip & James Cemetery, New Castle, PA
Boardman, Charlie (Charles Louis)	08/10/1968	Cremated, Sacramento, CA
Bobb, Randy (Mark Randall)	06/13/1982	Cremated, Lake Tahoe, CA
Bodie, Ping (Frank Stephen)	12/17/1961	Holy Cross Cemetery, Colma, CA
Boeckel, Tony (Norman Doxie)	02/16/1924	Inglewood Park Cemetery, Inglewood, CA
Boehler, George Henry	06/23/1958	Greendale Cemetery, Lawrenceburg, IN
Boehling, Joe (John Joseph)	09/08/1941	Holy Cross Cemetery, Richmond, VA
Bogart, John Renzie	12/07/1986	Glenwood Cemetery, Geneva, NY
Boggs, Ray (Raymond Joseph)	11/27/1989	Orchard Mesa Municipal Cemetery, Orchard Mesa, CO
Bohen, Pat (Leo Ignatius)	04/08/1942	Tulocay Cemetery, Napa, CA
Bohn, Charlie (Charles)	08/01/1903	Woodland Cemetery, Cleveland, OH
Bohne, Sam (Samuel Arthur)	05/23/1977	Cremated, Palo Alto, CA
Boken, Bob (Robert Anthony)	10/08/1988	Bunker Brother's Memory Gardens Cemmetery, Las Vegas, NV
Bokina, Joe (Joseph)	10/25/1991	Lake Hills Memorial Gardens, Trenton, GA

Name	DOD	Cemetery, City, State
Boland, Bernie (Bernard Anthony)	09/12/1973	St. Hedwig Cemetery, Dearborn Heights, MI
Bold, Charlie (Charles Dickens)	07/29/1978	Central Cemetery, Carver, MA
Bolden, Bill (William Horace)	12/08/1966	Hillcrest Cemetery, Dandridge, TN
Bolen, Lefty (Stewart O'Neal)	08/30/1969	Pine Crest Cemetery, Jackson, AL
Boley, Joe (John Peter)	12/30/1962	St. Mary's Slovak Church Cemetery, Mahanoy City, PA
Bolling, Jack (John Edward)	04/13/1998	Kent-Forest Lawn Cemetery, Panama City, FL
Bolton, Cecil Glenford	08/25/1993	Greenville Cemetery, Greenville, MS
Bolton, Cliff (William Clifton)	04/21/1979	Holly Hill Memorial Park. Thomasville, NC
Bond, Tommy (Thomas Henry)	01/24/1941	Forest Hills Cemetery, Jamaica Plain, MA
Bond, Walt (Walter Franklin)	09/14/1967	Houston National Cemetery, Houston, TX
Bonds, Bobby Lee	08/23/2003	Skylawn Memorial Park, San Mateo, CA
Bone, George Drummond	05/26/1918	Oak Grove Cemetery, West Haven, CT
Bonetti, Julio Giacomo	06/17/1952	Holy Cross Cemetery, Colma, CA
Boney, Hank (Henry Tate)	06/12/2002	Wauchula Cemetery, Wauchula, FL
Bonham, Ernie (Ernest Edward)	09/15/1949	St. Mary's Catholic Cemetery, Sacramento, CA
Bonin, Luther (Ernest Luther)	01/03/1966	Bethel Cemetery, Sycamore, OH
Bonner, Frank J.	12/31/1905	Mount St. Mary's Cemetery, Kansas City, MO
Bonness, Bill (William John)	12/03/1977	Elmhurst Park Cemetery, Avon, OH
Bono, Gus (Adlai Wendell)	12/03/1948	Grand Lawn Cemetery, Detroit, MI
Bonura, Zeke (Henry John)	03/09/1987	Metairie Cemetery, Metairie, LA
Booe, Everitt Little	03/21/1969	Kenedy City Cemetery, Kenedy, TX
Bool, Al (Albert J.)	09/27/1981	Raymond Cemetery, Raymond, NE
Booles, Red (Seabron Jesse)	03/16/1955	Shiloh Cemetery, Bernice, LA
Boone, Danny (James Albert)	06/11/1968	Memory Hill Gardens Cemetery, Tuscaloosa, AL
Boone, George Morris	09/24/1910	Cave Hill Cemetery, Louisville, KY
Boone, Ike (Isaac Morgan)	08/01/1958	Tuscaloosa Memorial Park, Tuscaloosa, AL
Boone, Luke (Lute Joseph)	07/29/1982	Jefferson Memorial Park, Pleasant Hills, PA
Booth, Amos Smith	07/01/1921	Woodland Cemetery, Dayton, OH
Boozer, John Morgan	01/24/1986	Pilgrim Lutheran Church Cemetery, Lexington, SC
Borchers, George Bernard	10/24/1938	Sacramento City Cemetery, Sacramento, CA
Bordagaray, Frenchy (Stanley George)	04/13/2000	Pleasant Valley Cemetery, Coalinga, CA
Borden, Joe (Joseph Emley)	10/14/1929	Oaklands Cemetery, West Chester, PA
Borton, Babe (William Baker)	07/29/1954	Mountain View Cemetery, Oakland, CA
Boss, Harley (Elmer Harley)	05/15/1964	Woodlawn Memorial Park, Nashville, TN
Bosser, Mel (Melvin Edward)	03/26/1986	Crossville City Cemetery, Crossville, TN
Bostick,Henry Landers	09/16/1968	Fairmount Cemetery, Denver, CO
Bostock, Lyman Wesley	09/23/1978	Inglewood Park Cemetery, Inglewood, CA
Boswell, Andy (Andrew Cottrell)	02/03/1936	Holcombe-Riverview Cemetery, Lambertville, NJ
Bottomley, Jim (James Leroy)	12/11/1959	I.O.O.F. Cemetery, Sullivan, MO
Boucher, Al (Alexander Francis)	06/23/1974	Holy Cross Cemetery, Culver City, CA

Name	DOD	Cemetery, City, State
Boudreau, Lou (Louis)	08/10/2001	Pleasant Hill Cemetery, Frankfort, IL
Boultes, Jake (Jacob John)	12/24/1955	Resurrection Cemetery, Mackenzie, MO
Bowcock, Benny (Benjamin James)	06/16/1961	St. Mary's Cemetery, New Bedford, MA
Bowden, Tim (David Timon)	10/25/1949	Bethany Baptist Church Cemetery, Decatur, GA
Bowen, Chick (Emmons Joseph)	08/09/1948	St. Lawrence Cemetery, West Haven, CT
Bowen, Cy (Sutherland McCoy)	01/25/1925	Kingston Cemetery, Kingston, IN
Bowens, Sam (Samuel Edward)	03/28/2003	Greenlawn Memorial Gardens, Wilmington, NC
Bowerman, Frank Eugene	11/30/1948	Romeo Cemetery, Romeo, MI
Bowers, Billy (Grover Bill)	09/17/1996	Cogbill Cemetery, Wynne, AR
Bowes, Frank M.	01/21/1895	Calvary Cemetery, Woodside, Queens, NY
Bowler, Grant Tierney	06/25/1968	Mount Olivet Cemetery, Wheat Ridge, CO
Bowles, Charlie (Charles James)	12/23/2003	Cremated, Hickory, NC
Bowles, Emmett Jerome	09/03/1959	Mount Calvary Cemetery, Albuquerque, NM
Bowman, Abe (Alvah Edson)	10/11/1979	Memory Park Cemetery, Longview, TX
Bowman, Bob (Robert James)	09/04/1972	Woodlawn Memorial Park, Bluefield, WV
Bowman, Elmer (Elmari Wilhelm)	12/17/1985	Cremated, Los Angeles, CA
Bowman, Joe (Joseph Emil)	11/22/1990	Resurrection Cemetery, Lenexa, KS
Bowman, Roger Clinton	07/21/1997	Hagamans Mills Cemetery, Amsterdam, NY
Bowman, Sumner Sallade	01/11/1954	Oak Hill Cemetery, Millersburg, PA
Bowser, Red (James Harvey)	05/22/1943	Union Cemetery, Arnold, PA
Boyd, Bill (William J.)	10/01/1912	St. John's Cemetery, Middle Village, Queens, NY
Boyd, Frank Jay	12/16/1937	St. Joseph's Cemetery, Oil City, PA
Boyd, Jake (Jacob Henry)	08/12/1932	Evergreen Cemetery, Gettysburg, PA
Boyd, Ray (Raymond C.)	02/11/1920	Westfield Cemetery, Westfield, IN
Boyer, Ken (Kenton Lloyd)	09/07/1982	Friends Cemetery, Purcell, MO
Boyle, Buzz (Ralph Francis)	11/12/1978	St. Joseph's New Cemetery, Cincinnati, OH
Boyle, Eddie (Edward J.)	02/09/1941	St. Joseph's New Cemetery, Cincinnati, OH
Boyle, Henry J.	05/25/1932	Holy Cross Cemetery, Yeadon, PA
Boyle, Jack (John Anthony)	01/07/1913	St. Joseph's New Cemetery, Cincinnati, OH
Boyle, Jack (John Bellew)	04/03/1971	Hillside Cemetery, Ogema, WI
Boyle, Jim (James John)	12/24/1958	St. Joseph's New Cemetery, Cincinnati, OH
Brabender, Gene (Eugene Mathew)	12/27/1996	St. Barnabas Cemetery, Mazomanie, WI
Brack, Gibby (Gilbert Herman)	01/20/1960	Memoryland Memorial Park, Greenville, TX
Bracken, Jack (John James)	07/16/1954	Holy Sepulchre Cemetery, Southfield, MI
Brackenridge, John Givler	03/20/1953	Harrisburg Cemetery, Harrisburg, PA
Bradford, Larry	09/11/1998	Jackson City Cemetery, Jackson, GA
Bradford, Vic (Henry Victor)	06/10/1994	North Middletown Cemetery, North Middletown, KY
Bradley, Albert Joseph	02/05/1937	Calvary Cemetery, Altoona, PA
Bradley, Bill (William Joseph)	03/11/1954	Calvary Cemetery, Cleveland, OH
Bradley, Foghorn (George H.)	03/31/1900	Forest Hills Cemetery, Huntingdon Valley, PA. Originally intered at Philadelphia Cemetery. Cemetery removed in 1950.
Bradley, George Washington	10/02/1931	Northwood Cemetery, Philadelphia, PA

Name	DOD	Cemetery, City, State
Bradley, George Washington	10/19/1982	Lawrence County Memorial Gardens, Lawrenceburg, TN
Bradley, Herb (Herbert Theodore)	10/16/1959	Greenwood Cemetery, Clay Center, KS
Bradley, Hugh Frederick	01/26/1949	St. John's Cemetery, Worcester, MA
Bradley, Jack (John Thomas)	03/18/1969	Calvary Cemetery, Tulsa, OK
Bradshaw, Dallas Carl	12/11/1939	Herrin City Cemetery, Herrin, IL
Bradshaw, George Thomas	11/04/1994	Western Carolina State Veterans Cemetery, Black Mountain, NC
Brady, Bob (Robert Jay)	04/22/1996	East Cemetery, Manchester, CT
Brady, Cliff (Clifford Francis)	09/25/1974	Calvary Cemetery, St. Louis, MO
Brady, King (James Ward)	08/21/1947	Albany Rural Cemetery, Albany, NY
Brady, Neal (Cornelius Joseph)	06/19/1947	St. Mary's Cemetery, Fort Mitchell, KY
Brady, Steve (Stephen A.)	11/01/1917	Mt. St. Benedict's Cemetery, Bloomfield, CT
Brain, Dave (David Leonard)	05/25/1959	Cremated. Ashes scattered at Rose Hills Memorial Park, Whittier, CA
Brainard, Asa (Asahel)	12/29/1888	Green-Wood Cemetery, Brooklyn, NY
Brainerd, Fred (Frederick F.)	04/17/1959	Woodbine Cemetery, Artesia, NM
Braithwood, Al (Alfred)	11/24/1960	Aurora Cemetery, Aurora, WV
Brame, Erv (Ervin Beckham)	11/22/1949	Powell Cemetery, LaFayette, KY
Bramhall, Art (Arthur Washington)	09/04/1985	Resurrection Catholic Cemetery, Madison, WI
Branch, Norm (Norman Downs)	11/21/1971	Montgomery Cemetery, Montgomery, TX
Brandom, Chick (Chester Milton)	10/07/1958	Fairhaven Memorial Park, Santa Ana, CA
Brandt, Bill (William George)	05/16/1968	Concordia Cemetery, Fort Wayne, IN
Brandt, Ed (Edward Arthur)	11/01/1944	Fairmount Memorial Park, Spokane, WA
Brannan, Otis Owen	06/06/1967	Spring Hill Cemetery, Greenbrier, AR
Brannock, Mike (Michael J.)	10/07/1881	Calvary Cemetery, Evanston, IL
Branom, Dud (Edgar Dudley)	02/04/1980	Memorial Park Cemetery, Enid, OK
Bransfield, Kitty (William Edward)	05/01/1947	St. John's Cemetery, Worcester, MA
Brashear, Kitty (Norman C.)	12/22/1934	Cremated, Los Angeles, CA
Brashear, Roy Parks	04/20/1951	Cremated, Los Angeles, CA
Bratcher, Joe (Joseph Warwick)	10/13/1977	Mount Olivet Cemetery, Fort Worth, TX
Bratschi, Fred (Frederick Oscar)	01/10/1962	Rose Hill Memorial Park, Massillon, OH
Braxton, Garland (Edgar Garland)	02/26/1966	Woodlawn Memorial Gardens, Norfolk, VA
Bray, Buster (Clarence Wilbur)	09/04/1982	Locust Hill Cemetery, Evansville, IN
Brazill, Frank Leo	11/03/1976	Cremated, Oakland, CA
Brazle, Al (Alpha Eugene)	10/24/1973	Fairview Cemetery, Yellow Jacket, CO
Brecheen, Harry David	01/17/2004	Rosedale Cemetery, Ada, OK
Breckinridge, Bill (William Robertson)	08/23/1958	Memorial Park Cemetery, Tulsa, OK
Breitenstein, Alonzo	06/19/1932	Forest Hill Cemetery, Utica, NY
Breitenstein, Ted (Theodore P.)	05/03/1935	St. Peter's Cemetery, St. Louis, MO
Bremer, Herb (Herbert Frederick)	11/28/1979	Parkhill Cemetery, Columbus, GA
Brenegan, Sam (Olaf Selmar)	04/20/1956	Pine Cliff Cemetery, Galesville, WI
Brennan, Ad (Addison Foster)	01/07/1962	Forest Hill Cemetery, Kansas City, MO
Brennan, Don (James Donald)	04/26/1953	St. Mary's Cemetery, Augusta, ME
Brennan, Jim (Jack)	10/18/1904	Holy Cross Cemetery, Yeadon, PA
Brenner, Bert (Delbert Henry)	04/11/1971	Lakewood Cemetery, Minneapolis, MN

Name	DOD	Cemetery, City, State
Brenton, Lynn Davis	10/14/1968	Cremated, Los Angeles, CA
Brenzel, Bill (William Richard)	06/12/1979	Mountain View Cemetery, Oakland, CA
Bresnahan, Roger Philip	12/04/1944	Calvary Cemetery, Toledo, OH
Bressler, Rube (Raymond Bloom)	11/07/1966	Mt. Moriah Cemetery, Cincinnati, OH
Breton, Jimmy (John Frederick)	05/30/1973	Tabor Cemetery, Beloit, WI
Brett, Herb (Herbert James)	11/25/1974	Highland Burial Park, Danville, VA
Breuer, Marv (Marvin Howard)	01/17/1991	Rolla Cemetery, Rolla, MO
Brewer, Jack (John Herndon)	11/30/2003	Riverside National Cemetery, Riverside, CA
Brewer, Jim (James Thomas)	11/16/1987	Floral Haven Memorial Gardens, Broken Arrow, OK
Brickell, Fred (George Frederick)	04/08/1961	Old Mission Cemetery, Wichita, KS
Brickley, George Vincent	02/23/1947	Holy Cross Cemetery, Malden, MA
Brickner, Ralph Harold	05/09/1994	St. Aloysius Gonzaga Catholic Cemetery, Cincinnati, OH
Brideweser, Jim (James Ehrenfeld)	08/25/1989	Cremated, El Toro, CA. Ashes scattered in Pacific Ocean
Bridges, Marshall	09/03/1990	Garden Memorial Park, Jackson, MS
Bridges, Tommy (Thomas Jefferson Davis)	04/19/1968	Ridgewood Cemetery, Carthage, TN
Bridwell, Al (Albert Henry)	01/23/1969	Greenlawn Cemetery, Portsmouth, OH
Brief, Bunny (Anthony Vincent)	02/10/1963	Oakwood Cemetery, Traverse City, MI
Briggs, Buttons (Herbert Theodore)	02/18/1911	Calvary Cemetery, Cleveland, OH
Briggs, Grant	05/31/1928	North Side Catholic Cemetery, Pittsburgh, PA
Brill, Frank (Francis Hasbrouck)	11/19/1944	Flushing Cemetery, Flushing, NY
Brillheart, Jim (James Benson)	09/02/1972	Dublin Cemetery, Dublin, VA
Brinker, Bill (William Hutchinson)	02/05/1965	Cremated, Los Angeles, CA
Briody, Fatty (Charles F.)	06/22/1903	Oakwood Cemetery, Troy, NY
Britt, Jim (James Edward)	02/28/1923	Holy Cross Cemetery, Colma, CA
Brittain, Gus (August Schuster)	02/16/1974	Oakdale Cemetery, Wilmington, NC
Brittin, Jack (John Albert)	01/05/1994	Brittin Cemetery, Sherman, IL
Britton, Gil (Stephen Gilbert)	06/20/1983	Memorial Lawn Cemetery, Parsons, KS
Broaca, Johnny (John Joseph)	05/16/1985	St. Mary's Immaculate Conception Cemetery, Lawrence, MA
Brock, John Roy	10/27/1951	Lakewood Park Cemetery, St. Louis, MO
Brockett, Lew (Lewis Albert)	09/19/1960	Odd Fellows Cemetery, Norris City, IL
Broderick, Matt (Matthew Thomas)	02/26/1940	St. Ann's Cemetery, Freeland, PA
Brodie, Steve (Walter Scott)	10/30/1935	Woodlawn Cemetery, Baltimore, MD
Bronkie, Herman Charles	05/27/1968	West Cemetery, Somers, CT
Brooks, Bobby (Robert)	10/11/1994	Inglewood Park Cemetery, Inglewood, CA
Brooks, Harry (Henry Frank)	12/05/1945	North Cedar Hill Cemetery, Philadelphia, PA
Broskie, Sig (Sigmund Theodore)	05/17/1975	Forest Hill Cemetery, Canton, OH
Broughton, Cal (Cecil Calvert)	03/15/1939	Maple Hill Cemetery, Evansville, WI
Brouthers, Art (Arthur H.)	09/28/1959	Magnolia Cemetery, Charleston, SC
Brouthers, Dan (Dennis Joseph)	08/02/1932	St. Mary's Cemetery, Wappinger Falls, NY
Brovia, Joe (Joseph John)	08/15/1994	Holy Cross Cemetery, Santa Cruz, CA
Brower, Frank Willard	11/20/1960	Sudlersville Cemetery, Sudlersville, MD
Brown, Bill (William Verna)	05/13/1965	Resthaven Memorial Park, Lubbock, TX

Name	DOD	Cemetery, City, State
Brown, Boardwalk (Carroll William)	02/08/1977	Laurel Memorial Park Cemetery, Egg Harbor, NJ
Brown, Bob (Robert Murray)	08/03/1990	St. Joseph's Cemetery, West Roxbury, MA
Brown, Buster (Charles Edward)	02/09/1914	Onawa Cemetery, Onawa, IA
Brown, Charles E.	04/03/1938	Swan Creek Cemetery, Monclova, OH
Brown, Charles Roy	06/10/1968	Spring Hill Cemetery, Spring Hill, KS
Brown, Clint (Clinton Harold)	12/31/1955	Lakewood Park Cemetery, Rocky River, OH
Brown, Delos Hight	12/21/1964	Roselawn Cemetery, Pueblo, CO
Brown, Dick (Richard Ernest)	04/12/1970	Bellevue Cedar Hill Memory Gardens, Daytona Beach, FL
Brown, Drummond Nicol	01/27/1927	Line Creek Cemetery, Parkville, MO
Brown, Eddie (Edward William)	09/10/1956	Golden Gate National Cemetery, San Bruno, CA
Brown, Elmer Young	01/23/1955	Greenwood Cemetery, Greenwood, IN
Brown, Fred Herbert	02/03/1955	Ossipee Cemetery. Ossipee, NH
Brown, Freeman *manager*	12/27/1916	Hope Cemetery, Worcester, MA
Brown, Ike (Isaac)	05/17/2001	New Park Cemetery, Memphis, TN
Brown, Jake (Jerald Ray)	12/18/1981	Paradise North Cemetery, Houston, TX
Brown, Jim (James W.H.)	04/06/1908	Highland Cemetery, Lock Haven, PA
Brown, Joe (Joseph Henry)	03/07/1950	Forest Lawn Memorial Park, Glendale, CA
Brown, Jumbo (Walter George)	10/02/1966	Pinelawn Memorial Park & Cemetery, Farmingdale, NY
Brown, Lew (Lewis J.)	01/15/1889	Forest Hills Cemetery, Boston, MA
Brown, Lindsay (John Lindsay)	01/01/1967	Gooch Cemetery, Mason, TX
Brown, Lloyd Andrew	01/14/1974	Cremated, Miami, FL
Brown, Mace Stanley	03/24/2002	Westminster Gardens, Greensboro, NC
Brown, Myrl Lincoln	02/23/1981	Paxtang Cemetery, Harrisburg, PA
Brown, Norm (Norman Ladelle)	05/31/1995	Sunset Hill Memorial Park, Bennettsville, SC
Brown, Oliver Edward	09/23/1932	Green-Wood Cemetery, Brooklyn, NY
Brown, Ray (Paul Percival)	05/29/1955	Forest Lawn Memorial Park, Glendale, CA
Brown, Sam (Samuel Wakefield)	11/08/1931	Scottdale Cemetery, Scottdale, PA
Brown, Stub (Richard P.)	03/10/1948	Greenmount Cemetery, Baltimore, MD
Brown, Three Finger (Mordecai Peter Centennial)	02/14/1948	Rose Lawn Cemetery, Terre Haute, IN
Brown, Tom (Thomas Tarlton)	10/25/1927	Fort Lincoln Cemetery, Brentwood, MD
Brown, Walter Irving	02/03/1991	Bemus Point Cemetery, Bemus Point, NY
Brown, Willard (Willard M.)	12/20/1897	Holy Cross Cemetery, Colma, CA. Originally intered at Mount Calvary Cemetery, San Francisco. Cemetery removed.
Brown, Willard Jessie	08/08/1996	Houston National Cemetery, Houston, TX
Browne, Earl James	01/12/1993	Pine Crest Memorial Park, Alexander, AR
Browne, George Edward	12/09/1920	St. Peter's Cemetery, Poughkeepsie, NY
Browne, Pidge (Prentice Almont)	06/03/1997	Resthaven Memorial Gardens, Houston, TX
Browning, Frank	05/19/1948	Mission Burial Park North, San Antonio, TX
Browning, Pete (Louis Rogers)	09/10/1905	Cave Hill Cemetery, Louisville, KY
Brubaker, Bill (Wilber Lee)	04/02/1978	Cremated, Laguna Hills, CA
Bruce, Lou (Louis R.)	02/09/1968	Lake View Cemetery, Richfield Springs, NY

Name	DOD	Cemetery, City, State
Brucker, Earle Francis, Sr.	05/08/1981	Greenwood Memorial Park, San Diego, CA
Bruckmiller, Andy (Andrew)	01/12/1970	Elizabeth Cemetery, Elizabeth, PA
Bruggy, Frank Leo	04/05/1959	St. Gertrude's Cemetery, Colonia, NJ
Bruner, Jack Raymond	06/24/2003	Lincoln Memorial Park, Lincoln, NE
Bruner, Roy (Walter Roy)	11/30/1986	Resthaven Memorial Park, Louisville, KY
Brush, Bob (Robert)	04/02/1944	Cremated, San Bernardino, CA
Bruton, Billy (William Haron)	12/05/1995	Gracelawn Memorial Park, New Castle, DE
Bruyette, Ed (Edward T.)	08/05/1940	Cremated, Peshastin, WA
Bryant, George F.	06/12/1907	Mount Hope Cemetery, Mattapan, MA
Brynan, Charlie (Charles Ruley)	05/10/1925	Fernwood Cemetery, Lansdowne, PA
Bucha, Johnny (John George)	04/28/1996	Cedar Hill Memorial Park, Allentown, PA
Buchanan, Jim (James Forrest)	06/15/1949	Ridge Cemetery, Randolph, NE
Buckeye, Garland Maiers	11/14/1975	Ottawa Hills Memorial Park, Toledo, OH
Buckingham, Ed (Edward Taylor)	07/30/1942	Lawncroft Cemetery, Fairfield, CT
Buckles, Jess (Jesse Robert)	08/02/1975	Good Shepherd Cemetery, Huntington Beach, CA
Buckley, Dick (Richard D.)	12/12/1929	North Side Catholic Cemetery, Pittsburgh, PA
Buckley, John Edward	03/03/1942	Immaculate Conception Cemetery, Marlborough, MA
Buelow, Charlie (Charles John)	05/04/1951	Linwood Cemetery, Dubuque, IA
Buelow, Fritz (Frederick William Alexander)	12/27/1933	Woodlawn Cemetery, Detroit, MI
Bues, Art (Arthur Frederick)	11/07/1954	Pinelawn Memorial Park, Milwaukee, WI
Buffington, Charlie (Charles G.)	09/23/1907	Oak Grove Cemetery, Fall River, MA
Buhl, Bob (Robert Ray)	02/16/2001	Cremated, Orlando, FL. Ashes given to family in Titusville, FL
Buker, Harry (Henry L.)	08/10/1899	Rosehill Cemetery, Chicago, IL
Bullard, George Donald	12/23/2002	Puritan Lawn Memorial Park, Peabody, MA
Bullas, Sim (Simeon Edward)	01/14/1908	Woodland Cemetery, Cleveland, OH
Bullock, Red (Malton Joseph)	06/27/1988	Griffin Cemetery, Moss Point, MS
Bunce, Josh (Joshua)	04/28/1912	Green-Wood Cemetery, Brooklyn, NY
Burbrink, Nelson Edward	04/12/2001	The Garden Sanctuary Cemetery, Seminole, FL
Burch, Al (Albert William)	10/05/1926	St. John's Cemetery, Middle Village, Queens, NY
Burch, Ernie (Ernest A.)	10/12/1892	Summit View Cemetery, Guthrie, OK
Burchell, Fred (Frederick Duff)	11/20/1951	St. Patrick's Cemetery, Jordan, NY
Burdick, Bill (William Byron)	10/23/1949	St. Thomas Cemetery, Coeur D'Alene, ID
Burdock, Jack (John Joseph)	11/27/1931	Holy Cross Cemetery, Brooklyn, NY
Burgess, Smoky (Forrest Harrill)	09/15/1991	Sunset Memorial Park, Forest City, NC
Burgo, Bill (William Ross)	10/19/1988	Morgan City Cemetery, Morgan City, LA
Burk, Sandy (Charles Sanford)	10/11/1934	Cypress Hills National Cemetery, Brooklyn, NY
Burkam, Chris (Chauncey DePew)	05/09/1964	Mount Ever-Rest Cemetery, Kalamazoo, MI
Burkart, Elmer Robert	02/06/1995	Dulaney Valley Memorial Gardens, Timonium, MD
Burke, Billy (William Ignatius)	02/09/1967	St. John's Cemetery, Lancaster, MA

Name	DOD	Cemetery, City, State
Burke, Bobby (Robert James)	02/08/1971	St. Patrick's Cemetery, Joliet, IL
Burke, Dan (Daniel L.)	03/20/1933	St. Patrick's Cemetery, Rockland, MA
Burke, Eddie (Edward D.)	11/26/1907	St. Agnes Cemetery, Utica, NY
Burke, Frank Aloysius	09/17/1946	Holy Cross Cemetery, Culver City, CA
Burke, Glenn Lawrence	05/30/1995	Mountain View Cemetery, Oakland, CA
Burke, Jimmy (James Timothy)	03/26/1942	Calvary Cemetery, St. Louis, MO
Burke, Joe (Joseph A.)	11/03/1940	St. Joseph Cemetery, Cincinnati, OH
Burke, John Patrick	08/04/1950	St. Joseph's Church Cemetery, Keyport, NJ
Burke, Les (Leslie Kingston)	05/06/1975	Swampscott Cemetery, Swampscott, MA
Burke, Mike (Michael E.)	06/09/1889	St. Agnes Cemetery, Albany, NY
Burke, Pat (Patrick Edward)	07/07/1965	Resurrection Cemetery, Mackenzie, MO
Burkett, Jesse Cail	05/27/1953	St. John's Cemetery, Worcester, MA
Burnett, Hercules H.	10/04/1936	Eastern Cemetery, Louisville, KY
Burnett, Johnny (John Henderson)	08/12/1959	Garden of Memories Cemetery, Tampa, FL
Burnette, Wally (Wallace Harper)	02/12/2003	Highland Burial Park, Danville, VA
Burnham, George *manager*	11/18/1902	Oakwood Cemetery, Saline, MI
Burns, C.B. (Charles Birmingham)	06/06/1968	Angel Hill Cemetery, Havre de Grace, MD
Burns, Denny (Dennis)	05/21/1969	Rest Haven Cemetery, Sperry, OK
Burns, Dick (Richard Simon)	11/16/1937	Calvary Cemetery, Holyoke, MA
Burns, Eddie (Edward James)	05/30/1942	San Carlos Catholic Cemetery, Monterey, CA
Burns, George Joseph	08/15/1966	Our Lady of Mount Carmel Cemetery, Gloversville, NY
Burns, Jack (John Irving)	04/18/1975	Evergreen Cemetery, Brighton, MA
Burns, Jack (John Joseph)	06/24/1957	Jordan Cemetery, Waterford, CT
Burns, Joe (Joseph Francis)	07/12/1987	Highland Cemetery, Ipswich, MA
Burns, Joe (Joseph Francis)	01/07/1986	St. Mary's Cemetery, Trenton, NJ
Burns, Joe (Joseph James)	06/24/1974	St. Denis Cemetery, Havertown, PA
Burns, Oyster (Thomas P.)	11/11/1928	Holy Cross Cemetery, North Arlington, NJ
Burns, Sleepy Bill (William Thomas)	06/06/1953	Holy Cross Cemetery, San Diego, CA
Burns, Tioga George (George Henry)	01/07/1978	Calvary Catholic Cemetery, Seattle, WA
Burns, Tom (Thomas Everett)	03/19/1902	St. Michael's Cemetery, Springfield, MA
Burrell, Buster (Frank Andrew)	05/08/1962	Fairmount Cemetery, Weymouth, MA
Burris, Al (Alva Burton)	03/25/1938	Hollywood Cemetery, Harrington, DE
Burris, Paul Robert	10/03/1999	Williams Memorial Presbyterian Church Cemetery, Charlotte, NC
Burroughs, Henry S.	03/31/1878	Mount Pleasant Cemetery, Newark, NJ
Burrows, John	04/27/1987	Cremated, Coal Run, OH
Burrus, Dick (Maurice Lennon)	02/02/1972	New Hollywood Cemetery, Elizabeth City, NC
Burtsch, Moe (Edward Frank)	05/02/2004	St. Joseph's Old Cemetery, Cincinnati, OH
Burwell, Bill (William Edwin)	06/11/1973	Belleview Memorial Park, Daytona Beach, FL
Busby, Jim (James Franklin)	07/08/1996	Millen Cemetery, Millen, GA
Busch, Ed (Edgar John)	01/17/1987	O'Fallon City Cemetery, O'Fallon, IL
Bush, Bullet Joe (Leslie Ambrose)	11/01/1974	Cremated, Hollywood Memorial Gardens, Hollywood, FL. Ashes scattered

Name	DOD	Cemetery, City, State
Bush, Donie (Owen Joseph)	03/28/1972	Holy Cross Cemetery, Indianapolis, IN
Bush, Guy Terrell	07/02/1985	Shannon Cemetery, Shannon, MS
Bushelman, Jack (John Francis)	10/26/1955	Holston View Cemetery, Weber City, VA
Bushey, Frank (Francis Clyde)	03/18/1972	Mount Calvary Cemetery, St. Mary's, KS
Bushong, Doc (Albert John)	08/19/1908	Holy Cross Cemetery, Brooklyn, NY
Buskey, Joe (Joseph Henry)	04/11/1949	SS. Peter & Paul Cemetery, Cumberland, MD
Buskey, Tom (Thomas William)	06/07/1998	Blue Ridge Memorial Gardens, Harrisburg, PA
Butcher, Hank (Henry Joseph)	12/28/1979	St. Mary's Cemetery, Evergreen Park, IL
Butcher, Max (Albert Maxwell)	09/15/1957	Forest Lawn Cemetery, Pecks Mill, WV
Butland, Bill (Wilburn Rue)	09/19/1997	Roselawn Memorial Park, Terre Haute, IN
Butler, Art (Arthur Edward)	10/07/1984	Notre Dame Cemetery, Fall River, MA
Butler, Charlie (Charles Thomas)	05/10/1964	Frederica Cemetery, Saint Simon's Island, GA
Butler, Dick (Richard H.)	07/16/1917	Holy Cross Cemetery, Brooklyn, NY
Butler, Frank Dean	07/18/1945	Evergreen Cemetery, Jacksonville, FL
Butler, Ike (Isaac Burr)	03/17/1948	Cremated, Oakland, CA
Butler, John Albert	02/02/1950	Mount Calvary Cemetery, Roslindale, MA
Butler, Johnny (John Stephen)	04/29/1967	Angelus-Rosedale Cemetery, Los Angeles, CA
Butler, Kid (Frank Edward)	04/09/1921	Mount Calvary Cemetery, Roslindale, MA
Butler, Kid (Willis Everett)	02/22/1964	Golden Gate National Cemetery, San Bruno, CA
Butler, Ormond Hook *manager*	09/12/1915	Loudon Park Cemetery, Baltimore, MD
Buttery, Frank	12/16/1902	Old Silvermine Community Cemetery, New Canaan, CT
Buxton, Ralph Stanley	01/06/1988	Cremated, San Leandro
Byers, Bill (James William)	09/08/1948	Loudon Park Cemetery, Baltimore, MD
Byers, Burley	05/30/1933	Portland Cemetery, Louisville, KY
Byrd, Harry Gladwin	05/14/1985	Darlington Memory Gardens, Darlington, SC
Byrne, Bobby (Robert Matthew)	12/31/1964	Calvary Cemetery, St. Louis, MO
Byrne, Jerry (Gerald Wilford)	08/11/1955	Oakwood Cemetery, Grand Ledge, MI
Byrnes, Jim (James Joseph)	07/31/1941	Holy Cross Cemetery, Colma, CA
Byrnes, Milt (Milton John)	02/01/1979	Our Redeemer Cemetery, Affton, MO
Cadore, Leon Joseph	03/16/1958	Pinecrest Memorial Park, Sandpoint, ID
Cady, Hick (Forrest Leroy)	03/03/1946	Cremated, Cedar Rapids, IA
Cafego, Tom (Thomas)	10/29/1961	Cadillac Memorial Gardens West, Westland, MI
Caffyn, Ben (Benjamin Thomas)	11/22/1942	Springdale Cemetery, Peoria, IL
Cahill, John Patrick Parnell	10/31/1901	St. Mary's Cemetery, Oakland, CA
Cain, Bob (Robert Max)	04/08/1997	Cremated, Cleveland, OH. Ashes returned to family
Cain, Sugar (Merritt Patrick)	04/03/1975	Cremated, Atlanta, GA
Caithamer, George Theodore	06/01/1954	Bohemian National Cemetery, Chicago, IL
Calderone, Ivan	12/27/2003	Cementerio Municipal de Loiza, Loiza, Cuba
Caldwell, Bruce	02/15/1959	Swan Point Cemetery, Providence, RI
Caldwell, Charlie (Charles William)	11/01/1957	Cremated, Ewing Crematory, Ewing, NJ
Caldwell, Earl Welton	09/15/1981	Palm Valley Memorial Gardens, Pharr, TX
Caldwell, Ralph Grant	08/05/1969	Cemetery of the First Presbyterian Church, Ewing, NJ

Name	DOD	Cemetery, City, State
Caldwell, Ray (Raymond Benjamin)	08/17/1967	Randolph Cemetery, Randolph, NY
Calhoun, Bill (William Davitte)	01/28/1955	Rose Hill Cemetery, Rockmart, GA
Calhoun, Jack (John Charles)	02/27/1947	Cremated, Cincinnati, OH. Ashes given to family in Pittsburgh, PA
Callaghan, Marty (Martin Francis)	06/23/1975	Highland Cemetery, Norwood, MA
Callahan, Ed (Edward Joseph)	02/05/1947	Mount Benedict Cemetery, West Roxbury, MA
Callahan, Joe (Joseph Thomas)	05/24/1949	New Calvary Cemetery, Mattapan, MA
Callahan, Leo David	05/02/1982	Calvary Cemetery, Oil City, PA
Callahan, Nixey (James Joseph)	10/04/1934	St. Bernard's Church Cemetery, Fitchburg, MA
Callahan, Ray (Raymond James)	01/23/1973	Masonic Memorial Park, Olympia, WA
Callahan, Red (James Timothy)	03/09/1968	Mount Olivet Cemetery, Pittsburgh, PA
Callahan, Will (William T.)	12/20/1917	Holy Sepulchre Cemetery, Rochester, NY
Callaway, Frank Burnett	08/21/1987	Highland Memorial Park, Knoxville, TN
Camelli, Hank (Henry Richard)	07/14/1996	Woodlawn Cemetery, Wellesley, MA
Cameron, Jack (John Stanley)	07/12/1963	Forest Lawn Cemetery West, Charlotte, NC
Camilli, Dolph (Adolph Louis)	10/21/1997	Cypress Lawn Memorial Park, Colma, CA
Camnitz, Harry (Henry Richardson)	01/06/1951	Cave Hill Cemetery, Louisville, KY
Camnitz, Howie (Samuel Howard)	03/02/1960	Cave Hill Cemetery, Louisville, KY
Camp, Kid (Winfield Scott)	03/02/1895	Forest Lawn Memorial Park, Omaha, NE
Camp, Lew (Robert Plantagenet Llewellan)	10/01/1948	Forest Lawn Memorial Park, Omaha, NE
Campanella, Roy	06/26/1993	Cremated, Forest Lawn Memorial Park, Hollywood Hills, Los Angeles, CA. Ashes given to family
Campanis, Al (Alexander Sebastian)	06/21/1998	Loma Vista Memorial Park, Fullerton, CA
Campau, Count (Charles Columbus)	04/03/1938	Metairie Cemetery, Metairie, LA
Campbell, Archie (Archibald Stewart)	12/22/1989	Sierra Memorial Gardens, Reno, NV. Cremated.
Campbell, Billy (William James)	10/06/1957	Spring Grove Cemetery, Cincinnati, OH
Campbell, Bruce Douglas	06/17/1995	Cremated, Fort Myers, FL
Campbell, Gilly (William Gilthorpe)	02/21/1973	San Fernando Mission Cemetery, Mission Hills, CA
Campbell, Hugh F.	03/01/1881	Cemetery of the Holy Sepulchre, East Orange, NJ
Campbell, Hutch (Marc Thaddeus)	02/13/1946	New Bethlehem Cemetery, New Bethlehem, PA
Campbell, John Millard	04/24/1995	Bellevue Cedar Hill Memory Gardens, Daytona Beach, FL. Cremated.
Campbell, Michael	01/12/1926	Mt. Olivet Cemetery, Newark, NJ
Campbell, Vin (Arthur Vincent)	11/16/1969	Greenmount Cemetery, Baltimore, MD
Campfield, Sal (William Holton)	05/16/1952	Saegertown Cemetery, Saegertown, PA
Canavan, Hugh Edward	09/04/1967	St. John's Cemetery, Worcester, MA
Canavan, Jim (James Edward)	05/27/1949	St. Mary's Cemetery, New Bedford, MA
Candini, Milo Cain	03/17/1998	Park View Cemetery, Manteca, CA
Cantillon, Joe (Joseph D.) *manager*	01/31/1930	Mount Olivet Cemetery, Janesville, WI

Name	DOD	Cemetery, City, State
Cantwell, Ben (Benjamin Caldwell)	12/04/1962	North Lawn Cemetery, Salem, MO
Cantwell, Mike (Michael Joseph)	01/05/1953	Arlington National Cemetery, Arlington, VA
Cantwell, Thomas (Thomas Aloysius)	04/01/1968	Mount Olivet Cemetery, Washington, DC
Cantz, Bart (Bartholomew L.)	02/12/1943	Most Holy Redeemer Cemetery, Philadelphia, PA
Capron, Ralph Earl	09/19/1980	Forest Lawn Memorial Park, Hollywood Hills, Los Angeles, CA
Caraway, Pat (Cecil Bradford Patrick)	06/09/1974	Gordon Cemetery, Gordon, TX
Carbine, John C.	09/11/1915	Calvary Cemetery, Evanston, IL
Carden, John Bruton	02/08/1949	Mexia City Cemetery, Mexia, TX
Cardoni, Ben (Armand Joseph)	04/02/1969	St. John's Cemetery, Jessup, PA
Carey, Max George	05/30/1976	Woodlawn Park Cemetery North, Miami, FL
Carey, Rody (Roger J.)	02/08/1895	Calvary Cemetery, Woodside, Queens, NY
Carey, Scoops (George C.)	12/17/1916	Spring Grove Cemetery, East Liverpool, OH
Carey, Tom (Thomas Francis Aloysius)	02/21/1970	Holy Sepulchre Cemetery, Rochester, NY
Cargo, Bobby (Robert J.)	04/27/1904	St. Mary's Cemetery (Penn Ave.), Pittsburgh, PA
Carisch, Fred (Frederick Behlmer)	04/19/1977	Cremated, Los Angeles, CA
Carl, Fred (Frederick E.)	05/04/1919	Western Cemetery, Baltimore, MD. Cremated.
Carl, Lew (Lewis Adolph)	05/19/1885	Fairmount Cemetery, Newark, NJ
Carleton, Jim (James Leslie)	04/25/1910	Elmwood Cemetery, Detroit, MI
Carleton, Tex (James Otto)	01/11/1977	Oakwood Cemetery, Comanche, TX
Carlisle, Walter G.	05/27/1945	Inglewood Park Cemetery, Inglewood, CA
Carlsen, Don (Donald Herbert)	09/22/2002	Cremated, Denver, CO
Carlson, Hal (Harold Gust)	05/28/1930	Arlington Memorial Park, Rockford, IL
Carlson, Leon Alton	09/15/1961	Sunset Hill Cemetery, Lakewood, NY
Carlstrom, Swede (Albin Oscar)	04/23/1935	Evergreen Cemetery, Hillside, NJ
Carlyle, Cleo (Hiram Cleo)	11/12/1967	Forest Lawn Memorial Park, Glendale, CA
Carlyle, Roy Edward	11/22/1956	Norcross Cemetery, Norcross, GA
Carman, George Wartman	06/16/1929	Woodward Hill Cemetery, Lancaster, PA
Carmichael, Chet (Chester Keller)	08/22/1960	Honeoye Falls Cemetery, Honeoye Falls, NY
Carney, Bill (William John)	07/31/1938	Grand-View Park Cemetery, Hopkins, MN
Carney, John Joseph	10/19/1925	Pine Grove Cemetery, Manchester, NH
Carney, Pat (Patrick Joseph)	01/09/1953	St. John's Cemetery, Worcester, MA
Carpenter, Hick (Warren William)	04/18/1937	Mount Hope Cemetery, San Diego, CA
Carpenter, Lew (Lewis Emmett)	04/25/1979	Dawson Cemetery, Kennesaw, GA
Carpenter, Paul Calvin	03/14/1968	Wilson Cemetery, Newark, OH
Carr, Charlie (Charles Carbitt)	11/25/1932	Crown Hill Cemetery, Indianapolis, IN
Carr, Lew (Lewis Smith)	06/15/1954	Indian Mound Cemetery, Moravia, NY
Carreon, Camilo	09/02/1987	Hermosa Cemetery, Colton, CA
Carrick, Bill (William Martin)	03/07/1932	Oakwood Cemetery, Adrian, MI
Carrigan, Bill (William Francis)	07/08/1969	Riverside Cemetery, Lewiston, ME
Carroll, Cliff (Samuel Clifford)	06/12/1923	Lincoln Memorial Park (formerly Mount Scott Park Cemetery), Portland, OR

Name	DOD	Cemetery, City, State
Carroll, Dick (Richard Thomas)	11/22/1945	Calvary Cemetery, Cleveland, OH
Carroll, Dixie (Dorsey Lee)	10/13/1984	Evergreen Cemetery, Jacksonville, FL
Carroll, Doc (Ralph Arthur)	06/27/1983	St. John's Cemetery, Worcester, MA
Carroll, Ed (Edgar Fleischer)	10/13/1984	Gardens of Faith Memorial Gardens, Baltimore, MD
Carroll, Fred (Frederick Herbert)	11/07/1904	Odd Fellows Columbarium, San Francisco, CA
Carroll, Ownie (Owen Thomas)	06/08/1975	Gate of Heaven Cemetery, East Hanover, NJ
Carroll, Pat (Patrick)	02/14/1916	Holy Cross Cemetery, Yeadon, PA
Carroll, Scrappy (John E.)	11/14/1942	Mt. Olivet Cemetery, Tonawanda, NY
Carson, Al (Albert James)	11/26/1962	Cypress View Cemetery, San Diego, CA
Carson, Kit (Walter Lloyd)	06/21/1983	Forest Lawn Memorial Park, Cypress, CA
Carter, Arnold Lee	04/12/1989	Evergreen Cemetery, Louisville, KY
Carter, Blackie (Otis Leonard)	09/10/1976	Woodlawn Memorial Park, Greenville, SC
Carter, Howie (John Howard)	07/24/1991	Gate of Heaven Cemetery, Hawthorne, NY
Carter, Nick (Conrad Powell)	11/23/1961	Wye Mills Cemetery, Wye Mills, MD
Carter, Paul Warren	09/11/1984	Lake Park Cemetery, Lake Park, GA
Cartwright, Alexander Joy	07/13/1892	Oahu Cemetery, Honolulu, HI
Cartwright, Ed (Edward Charles)	09/03/1933	Oak Hill Cemetery, Youngstown, OH
Caruthers, Bob (Robert Lee)	08/05/1911	Graceland Cemetery, Chicago, IL
Case, Charlie (Charles Emmett)	04/16/1964	Spring Grove Cemetery, Cincinnati, OH
Case, George Washington	01/23/1989	Cemetery of the First Presbyterian Church, Ewing, NJ
Casey, Dan (Daniel Maurice)	02/08/1943	Fort Lincoln Cemetery, Brentwood, MD
Casey, Dennis Patrick	01/19/1909	Calvary-St. Patrick Cemetery, Johnson City, NY
Casey, Doc (James Patrick)	12/31/1936	Mount Olivet Cemetery, Detroit, MI
Casey, Hugh Thomas	07/03/1951	Mt. Paran Cemetery, Atlanta, GA
Casey, Joe (Joseph Felix)	06/02/1966	St. Patrick's Cemetery, Stoneham, MA
Cash, Norm (Norman Dalton)	10/12/1986	Pine Lake Cemetery, West Bloomfield, MI
Cashion, Jay Carl	11/17/1935	Greenwood Cemetery, Superior, WI
Caskin, Ed (Edward James)	10/09/1924	St. Mary's Cemetery, Danvers, MA
Cassady, Harry Delbert	04/19/1969	Cremated, Fresno, CA
Cassian, Ed (Edward T.)	09/10/1918	St. John's Cemetery, Middletown, CT
Cassidy, Joe (Joseph Phillip)	03/25/1906	Immaculate Heart of Mary Cemetery, Linwood, PA
Cassidy, John P.	07/03/1891	Flatbush Cemetery, Brooklyn, NY
Cassidy, Pete (Peter Francis)	07/09/1929	Cathedral Cemetery, Wilmington, DE
Caster, George Jasper	12/18/1955	Forest Lawn Memorial Park-Long Beach, Long Beach, CA
Castino, Vince (Vincent Charles)	03/06/1967	St. Mary's Catholic Cemetery, Sacramento, CA
Castle, John Francis	04/13/1929	St. Denis Cemetery, Havertown, PA
Castleman, Slick (Clydell)	03/02/1998	Woodlawn Memorial Park, Nashville, TN
Castleton, Roy (Royal Eugene)	06/24/1967	Salt Lake City Cemetery, Salt Lake City, UT
Castner, Paul Henry	03/03/1986	Calvary Cemetery, St. Paul, MN
Castro, Louis Manuel	09/24/1941	Mount St. Mary's Cemetery, Flushing, Queens, NY
Cates, Eli Eldo	05/29/1964	East Maplewood Cemetery, Anderson, IN

Name	DOD	Cemetery, City, State
Cather, Ted (Theodore Physick)	04/09/1945	Charlestown Cemetery, Charlestown, MD
Cathey, Hardin Abner	07/27/1997	Middle Tennessee Veterans Cemetery, Nashville, TN
Caton, Howdy (James Howard)	01/08/1948	Greenwood Cemetery, Zanesville, OH
Cattanach, John Leckie	11/10/1926	Oak Grove Cemetery, Pawtucket, RI
Catterson, Tom (Thomas Henry)	02/05/1920	Calvary Cemetery, South Portland, ME
Caufield, Jake (John Joseph)	12/16/1986	Holy Cross Cemetery, Colma, CA
Causey, Red (Cecil Algerton)	11/11/1960	Oak Hill Cemetery, Lake Placid, FL
Cavanaugh, John J.	01/14/1961	Cathedral Cemetery, Scranton, PA
Caveney, Ike (James Christopher)	07/06/1949	Holy Cross Cemetery, Colma, CA
Cavet, Pug (Tillar H.)	08/04/1966	Odd Fellows Cemetery, San Luis Obispo, CA
Caylor, O.P. (Oliver Perry) *manager*	01/31/1930	Woodland Cemetery, Dayton, OH
Cecil, Rex Rolston	10/30/1966	Westminster Memorial Park, Westminster, CA
Cermak, Ed (Edward Hugo)	11/22/1911	Woodland Cemetery, Cleveland, OH
Chadbourne, Chet (Chester James)	06/21/1943	Cremated, Los Angeles, CA
Chagnon, Leon Wilbur	07/30/1953	Mount Prospect Cemetery, Amesbury, MA
Chalmers, George W.	08/05/1960	Lutheran All Faiths Cemetery, Middle Village, Queens, NY
Chamberlain, Bill (William Vincent)	02/06/1994	Milton Cemetery, Milton, MA
Chamberlain, Icebox (Elton P.)	09/22/1929	Holy Cross Cemetery, Baltimore, MD
Chamberlain, Joe (Joseph Jeremiah)	01/28/1983	Holy Cross Cemetery, Colma, CA
Chambers, Bill (William Christopher)	03/27/1962	Covington Memorial Gardens, Fort Wayne, IN
Chambers, John (Johnnie Monroe)	05/11/1977	Oaklawn Cemetery, Jacksonville, FL
Chambers, Rome (Richard Jerome)	08/30/1902	Chambers Cemetery, Weaverville, NC
Chance, Frank Leroy	09/15/1924	Angelus-Rosedale Cemetery, Los Angeles, CA
Chandler, Spud (Spurgeon Ferdinand)	01/09/1990	Woodlawn Memory Gardens, St. Petersburg, FL
Chaney, Esty Clyon	02/05/1952	Hadley Cemetery, Hadley, PA
Channell, Les (Lester Clark)	05/07/1954	Fairmount Cemetery, Denver, CO
Chaplin, Ed (Bert Edgar)	08/15/1978	Oaklawn Park Cemetery, Sanford, FL
Chaplin, Tiny (James Bailey)	03/25/1939	Woodlawn Park Cemetery North, Miami, FL
Chapman, Ben (William Benjamin)	07/07/1993	Elmwood Cemetery, Birmingham, AL
Chapman, Ed (Edwin Volney)	05/03/2000	Lambert Cemetery, Lambert, MS
Chapman, Fred (Frederick Joseph)	12/14/1957	Evergreen Cemetery, Union City, PA
Chapman, Fred (William Fred)	03/27/1997	Carolina Memorial Park, Kannapolis, NC
Chapman, Glenn Justice	11/05/1988	Lutheran Cemetery, Pershing, IN
Chapman, Harry E.	10/21/1918	McPherson Cemetery, McPherson, KS
Chapman, Jack (John Curtis)	06/10/1916	Green-Wood Cemetery, Brooklyn, NY
Chapman, John Joseph	11/03/1953	St. Joseph's Cemetery, Fountain Springs, PA
Chapman, Ray (Raymond Johnson)	08/17/1920	Lake View Cemetery, Cleveland, OH
Chappell, Larry (LaVerne Ashford)	11/08/1918	Oak Grove Cemetery, Jerseyville, IL
Chartak, Mike (Michael George)	07/25/1967	Mt. Calvary Cemetery, Cedar Rapids, IA
Chase, Hal (Harold Homer)	05/18/1947	Oak Hill Memorial Park, San Jose, CA

Name	DOD	Cemetery, City, State
Chase, Ken (Kendall Fay)	01/16/1985	Plains Cemetery, Oneonta, NY
Chatham, Buster (Charles L.)	12/15/1975	Oakwood Cemetery, Waco, TX
Chatterton, Jim (James M.)	12/15/1944	Forest Dale Cemetery, Malden, MA
Chech, Charlie (Charles William)	01/31/1938	Calvary Cemetery, Los Angeles, CA
Cheek, Harry G.	06/25/1956	George Washington Memorial Park, Paramus, NJ
Cheeves, Virgil Earl	05/05/1979	Laurel Land Memorial Park, Dallas, TX
Chelini, Italo Vincent	08/25/1972	Holy Cross Cemetery, Colma, CA
Cheney, Larry (Laurence Russell)	01/06/1969	Shady Rest Cemetery, Holly Hill, FL
Cheney, Tom (Thomas Edgar)	11/01/2001	Morgan Cemetery, Morgan, GA
Chervinko, Paul	06/03/1976	Calvary Cemetery, Witt, IL
Chesbro, Jack (John Dwight)	11/06/1931	Howland Cemetery, Conway, MA
Chesnes, Bob (Robert Vincent)	05/23/1979	Evergreen Cemetery, Everett, WA
Chetkovich, Mitch (Mitchell)	08/24/1971	St. Patrick's Cemetery, Grass Valley, CA
Child, Harry Stephen Patrick	11/08/1972	Mount Comfort Memorial Park, Alexandria, VA
Childs, Cupid (Clarence Algernon)	11/08/1912	Loudon Park Cemetery, Baltimore, MD
Childs, Pete (Peter Pierre)	02/15/1922	West Laurel Hill Cemetery, Bala Cynwyd, PA
Childs, Sam (Samuel Beresford)	05/21/1938	Fairmount Cemetery, Denver, CO
Chiozza, Dino Joseph	04/23/1972	Calvary Cemetery, Memphis, TN
Chiozza, Lou (Louis Peo)	02/28/1971	Calvary Cemetery, Memphis, TN
Chipman, Bob (Robert Howard)	11/08/1973	Cemetery of Holy Rood, Westbury, NY
Chipple, Walt (Walter John)	06/08/1988	Elmlawn Cemetery, Tonawanda, NY
Chiti, Harry	01/31/2002	Rolling Hills Cemetery, Winter Haven, FL
Chouneau, Chief (William)	09/17/1946	LaPrairie Cemetery, Cloquet, MN
Christenbury, Lloyd Reid	12/13/1944	Forest Hill Cemetery, Birmingham, AL
Christensen, Cuckoo (Walter Neils)	12/20/1984	Cremated, Menlo Park, CA
Christian, Bob (Robert Charles)	02/20/1974	Alpine Cemetery, Alpine, CA
Christman, Mark (Marquette Joseph)	10/09/1976	Resurrection Cemetery, Mackenzie, MO
Christopher, Loyd Eugene	09/05/1991	Cremated, Richmond, VA
Christopher, Russ (Russell Ormand)	12/05/1954	Sunset View Cemetery, El Cerrito, CA. Cremated.
Church, Hi (Hiram Lincoln)	02/23/1926	West Evergreen Cemetery, Jacksonville, FL
Churry, John	02/08/1970	Maplewood Cemetery, New Lexington, OH
Ciaffone, Larry (Lawrence Thomas)	12/14/1991	Green-Wood Cemetery, Brooklyn, NY
Cicero, Joe (Joseph Francis)	03/30/1983	Curlew Hills Memory Gardens, Palm Harbor, FL
Cicotte, Al (Alva Warren)	11/29/1982	Holy Sepulchre Cemetery, Southfield, MI
Cicotte, Eddie (Edward Victor)	05/05/1969	Parkview Memorial Cemetery, Livonia, MI
Cieslak, Ted (Thaddeus Walter)	05/09/1993	Mount Olivet Cemetery, Milwaukee, WI
Cihocki, Ed (Edward Joseph)	11/09/1987	All Saints Cemetery, Newark, DE
Ciola, Lou (Louis Alexander)	10/18/1981	Calvary Cemetery, Austin, MN
Cissell, Bill (Chalmer William)	03/15/1949	Mount Hope Cemetery, Perryville, MO
Clabaygh, Moose (John William)	07/11/1984	Cremated, Tucson, AZ
Claire, Danny (David Matthew)	01/07/1956	Ludington Cemetery, Ludington, MI
Clancy, Al (Albert Harrison)	10/17/1951	Fairview Cemetery, Santa Fe, NM
Clancy, Bill (William Edward)	02/10/1948	Mount Olivet Cemetery, Whitesboro, NY

Name	DOD	Cemetery, City, State
Clancy, Bud (John William)	09/26/1968	St. Paul's Cemetery, Odell, IL
Clanton, Uke (Eucal)	02/24/1960	Memorial Park Cemetery, Ada, OK
Clapp, Aaron Bronson	01/13/1914	Tioga Point Cemetery, Athens, PA
Clapp, John Edgar	12/18/1904	Lakeview Cemetery, Ithaca, NY
Clare, Denny (Dennis J.)	11/26/1928	Holy Cross Cemetery, Brooklyn, NY
Clark, Bob (Robert H.)	08/21/1919	St. Mary's Cemetery, Fort Mitchell, KY
Clark, Bob (Robert William)	05/18/1944	Carlsbad Cemetery, Carlsbad, NM
Clark, Cap (John Carroll)	02/16/1957	Lafayette Memorial Park, Fayetteville, NC
Clark, Dad (Alfred Robert)	07/26/1956	Ogden City Cemetery, Ogden, UT
Clark, Danny (Daniel Curren)	05/23/1937	Rose Hill-Magnolia Cemetery, Meridian, MS
Clark, Earl (Bailey Earl)	01/16/1938	Cedar Hill Cemetery, Suitland, MD
Clark, George Myron	11/14/1940	Graceland Cemetery, Sioux City, IA
Clark, Jim (James)	10/24/1990	Cremated, Santa Monica, CA. Ashes scattered in Pacific Ocean
Clark, Jim (James Francis)	03/20/1969	Forest Lawn Memorial Park, Beaumont, TX
Clark, Mike (Michael John)	01/25/1996	New St. Mary's Cemetery, Bellmawr, NJ
Clark, Pep (Harry)	06/08/1965	Valhalla Memorial Park, Milwaukee, WI
Clark, Roy Elliott	11/01/1925	Mountain Grove Cemetery, Bridgeport, CT
Clark, Spider (Owen F.)	02/08/1892	Calvary Cemetery, Woodside, Queens, NY
Clark, Watty (William Watson)	03/04/1972	Dunedin Cemetery, Dunedin, FL
Clark, Win (William Winfield)	04/15/1959	Cremated, Los Angeles, CA
Clarke, Alan Thomas	03/11/1975	St. Mark's Cemetery, Germantown, MD
Clarke, Artie (Arthur Franklin)	11/14/1949	Walnut Hills Cemetery, Brookline, MA
Clarke, Boileryard (William Jones)	07/29/1959	Druid Ridge Cemetery, Pikesville, MD
Clarke, Dad (William H.)	06/03/1911	Calvary Cemetery, Lorain, OH
Clarke, Fred Clifford	08/14/1960	St. Mary's Cemetery, Winfield, KS
Clarke, Harry Corson	03/03/1923	Cremated, Los Angeles, CA
Clarke, Henry Tefft	03/28/1950	Forest Lawn Memorial Park, Omaha, NE
Clarke, Josh (Joshua Baldwin)	07/02/1962	Ivy Lawn Memorial Park, Ventura, CA
Clarke, Nig (Jay Justin)	06/15/1949	Woodmere Cemetery, Detroit, MI. Cremated.
Clarke, Rufus Rivers	02/08/1983	Elmwood Cemetery, Columbia, SC
Clarke, Stu (William Stuart)	08/26/1985	Holy Sepulchre Cemetery, Hayward, CA
Clarke, Tommy (Thomas Aloysius)	08/14/1945	St. John's Cemetery, Middle Village, Queens, NY
Clarkson, Bill (William Henry)	08/27/1971	Montlawn Memorial Park, Raleigh, NC
Clarkson, Buzz (James Buster)	01/18/1989	Brush Creek Cemetery, Irwin, PA
Clarkson, Dad (Arthur Hamilton)	02/05/1911	Cambridge Cemetery, Cambridge, MA
Clarkson, John Gibson	02/04/1909	Cambridge Cemetery, Cambridge, MA
Clarkson, Walter Hamilton	10/10/1946	Cambridge Cemetery, Cambridge, MA
Claset, Gowell Sylvester	03/08/1981	Cremated, National Cremation Society, St. Petersburg, FL
Clausen, Fritz (Frederick William)	02/11/1960	Forest Hill Cemetery-Midtown, Memphis, TN
Clauss, Al (Albert Stanley)	09/13/1952	St. Lawrence Cemetery, West Haven, CT
Clay, Bill (Frederick C.)	10/12/1917	Prospect Hill Cemetery, York, PA
Clay, Dain Elmer	08/28/1994	Glen Abbey Memorial Park, Bonita, CA
Clemens, Bob (Robert Baxter)	04/05/1964	Ridge Park Cemetery, Marshall, MO

Name	DOD	Cemetery, City, State
Clemens, Clem (Clement Lambert)	11/02/1967	St. Mary's Cemetery, Evergreen Park, IL
Clemensen, Bill (William Melville)	02/18/1994	Masonic Lawn Cemetery, Sacramento, CA
Clemente, Roberto	12/31/1972	Caribbean Sea off San Juan, PR. Remains not recovered
Clements, Jack (John J.)	05/23/1941	Arlington Cemetery, Drexel Hill, PA
Clemons, Verne James	05/05/1959	Bay Pines National Cemetery, Bay Pines, FL
Cleveland, Elmer Ellsworth	10/08/1913	Grandview Cemetery, Johnstown, PA
Clift, Harlond Benton	04/27/1992	Cremated, Yakima, WA. Ashes given to family
Clifton, Flea (Herman Earl)	12/22/1997	Bridgetown Cemetery, Cincinnati, OH
Cline, Monk (John P.)	09/23/1916	Cave Hill Cemetery, Louisville, KY
Clingman, Billy (William Frederick)	05/14/1958	Cave Hill Cemetery, Louisville, KY
Clinton, Lu (Luciean Louis)	12/06/1997	Lake View Cemetery, Wichita, KS
Clough, Ed (Edgar George)	01/30/1944	Wiconisco Cemetery, Wiconisco, PA
Clymer, Bill (William Johnston)	12/26/1936	North Cedar Hill Cemetery, Philadelphia, PA
Clymer, Otis Edgar	02/27/1926	Willow River Cemetery, Hudson, WI
Coakley, Andy (Andrew James)	09/27/1963	Kensico Cemetery, Valhalla, NY
Cobb, George Woodworth	08/19/1926	Evergreen Memorial Park, Riverside, CA
Cobb, Herb (Herbert Edward)	01/08/1980	Pinetops Baptist Church Cemetery, Pinetops, NC
Cobb, Ty (Tyrus Raymond)	07/17/1961	Rosehill Cemetery, Royston, GA
Coble, Dave (David Lamar)	10/15/1971	Lakeland Memorial Park, Monroe, NC
Cochran, A.J. (Alvah Jackson)	05/23/1947	College Park Memorial Cemetery, College Park, GA
Cochran, George Leslie	05/21/1960	Cremated, Los Angeles, CA
Cochrane, Mickey (Gordon Stanley)	06/28/1962	Cremated, Chicago, IL. Ashes scattered over Lake Michigan
Cocreham, Gene (Eugene)	12/27/1945	Luling City Cemetery, Luling, TX
Coffey, Jack (John Francis)	02/14/1966	Calvary Cemetery, Woodside, Queens, NY
Coffman, Dick (Samuel Richard)	03/24/1972	Athens City Cemetery, Athens, AL
Coffman, Slick (George David)	05/08/2003	Gatlin Cemetery, Ardmore, AL
Cogan, Dick (Richard Henry)	05/02/1948	Holy Sepulchre Cemetery, Totawa, NJ
Cohen, Alta Albert	03/11/2003	B'nai Abraham Memorial Park, Union, NJ
Cohen, Andy (Andrew Howard)	10/29/1988	B'nai Zion Cemetery, El Paso, TX
Cohen, Syd (Sydney Harry)	04/09/1988	B'nai Zion Cemetery, El Paso, TX
Coker, Jimmie Goodwin	10/29/1991	Throckmorton Cemetery, Throckmorton, TX
Colcolugh, Tom (Thomas Bernard)	12/10/1919	St. Lawrence Cemetery, Charleston, SC
Cole, Bert (Albert George)	05/30/1975	Cypress Lawn Memorial Park, Colma, CA
Cole, Ed (Edward William)	07/28/1999	Nashville National Cemetery, Madison, TN
Cole, King (Leonard Leslie)	01/06/1916	Woodlawn Cemetery, Toledo, IA
Cole, Willis Russell	10/11/1965	Milton Junction Cemetery, Milton, WI
Coleman, Bob (Robert Hunter)	07/16/1959	St. Joseph Cemetery, Evansville, IN
Coleman, Curt (Curtis Hancock)	07/01/1980	St. Paul Cemetery, St. Paul, OR
Coleman, Ed (Parke Edward)	08/05/1964	Zion Memorial Park, Canby, OR
Coleman, Gordy (Gordon Calvin)	03/12/1994	Arlington Memorial Gardens, Cincinnati, OH
Coleman, Joe (Joseph Patrick)	04/09/1997	Fort Myers Memorial Gardens, Fort Myers, FL

Name	DOD	Cemetery, City, State
Coleman, John W.	01/27/1915	St. Mark's Cemetery, Bristol, PA
Coleman, Percy (Pierce Devon)	02/16/1948	Los Angeles National Cemetery, Los Angeles, CA
Coles, Chuck (Charles Edward)	01/25/1996	Greene County Memorial Park, Waynesburg, PA
Colgan, Ed (William H.)	08/08/1895	Old Highland Cemetery, Great Falls, MT
Collamore, Allan Edward	08/08/1980	Oak Hill Cemetery, Battle Creek, MI
Collard, Hap (Earl Clinton)	07/09/1968	Casa Bonita Mausoleum, Stockton, CA
Collier, Orlin Edward	09/09/1944	Linwood Cemetery, Paragould, AR
Colliflower, Harry (James Harry)	08/12/1961	Mount Olivet Cemetery, Washington, DC
Collins, Bill (William J.)	06/08/1893	Mount Olivet Cemetery, Maspeth, Queens, NY
Collins, Bill (William Shirley)	06/26/1961	Bellevue Memorial Gardens, Ontario, CA
Collins, Chub (Charles Augustine)	05/20/1914	St. Augustine Cemetery, Dundas, Ontario, Canada
Collins, Eddie (Edward Trowbridge, Jr.)	11/02/2000	Union Hill Cemetery, Kennett Square, PA
Collins, Eddie (Edward Trowbridge, Sr.)	03/25/1951	Linwood Cemetery, Weston, MA
Collins, Hub (Hubert B.)	05/21/1892	Cave Hill Cemetery, Louisville, KY
Collins, Jimmy (James Joseph)	03/06/1943	Holy Cross Cemetery, Lackawanna, NY
Collins, Joe (Joseph Edward)	08/30/1989	Fairview Cemetery, Westfield, NJ
Collins, Orth Stein	12/13/1949	Evergreen Cemetery, Fort Lauderdale, FL
Collins, Pat (Tharon Patrick)	05/20/1960	Memorial Park Cemetery, Kansas City, KS
Collins, Phil (Philip Eugene)	08/14/1948	Holy Cross Cemetery, Calumet City, IL
Collins, Ray (Raymond Williston)	01/09/1970	Colchester Village Cemetery, Colchester, VT
Collins, Rip (Harry Warren)	05/27/1968	College Station Cemetery, College Station, TX
Collins, Rip (Robert Joseph)	04/19/1969	Jefferson Memorial Park, Pleasant Hills, PA
Collins, Ripper (James Anthony)	04/15/1970	Village Cemetery, Mexico, NY
Collins, Shano (John Francis)	09/10/1955	St. Mary's Cemetery, Needham, MA
Collins, Wilson (Cyril Wilson)	02/28/1941	Maplewood Cemetery, Tullahoma, TN
Collins, Zip (John Edgar)	12/19/1983	Cemetery of Holy Rood, Westbury, NY
Combs, Earle Bryan	07/21/1976	Richmond Cemetery, Richmond, KY
Combs, Merl (Merrill Russell)	07/07/1981	Riverside National Cemetery, Riverside, CA. Cremated
Comellas, Jorge (Pous)	09/13/2001	Woodlawn Park Cemetery North, Miami, FL
Comiskey, Charlie (Charles Albert)	10/26/1931	Calvary Cemetery, Evanston, IL
Comorosky, Adam Anthony	03/02/1951	St. Ignatius Cemetery, Kingston, PA
Compton, Jack (Harry Leroy)	07/04/1974	Hitler-Ludwig Cemetery, Circleville, OH
Compton, Pete (Anna Sebastian)	02/03/1978	Cremated, Kansas City, MO
Comstock, Ralph Remick	09/13/1966	Toledo Memorial Park, Sylvania, OH
Cone, Bob (Robert Earl)	05/24/1955	Galveston Memorial Park, Hitchcock, TX
Cone, Fred (Joseph Frederick)	04/13/1909	Graceland Cemetery, Chicago, IL
Congalton, Bunk (William Millar)	08/19/1937	Crown Hill Cemetery, Twinsburg, OH
Conger, Dick (Richard)	02/16/1970	Live Oak Memorial Park, Monrovia, CA
Conigliaro, Tony (Anthony Richard)	02/24/1990	Holy Cross Cemetery, Malden, MA
Conkwright, Red (Allen Howard)	07/30/1991	All Souls Cemetery, Long Beach, CA

Name	DOD	Cemetery, City, State
Conlan, Jocko (John Bertrand)	04/16/1989	Green Acres Memorial Gardens, Scottsdale, AZ
Conley, Ed (Edward J.)	10/16/1894	Mount Calvary Cemetery, Cumberland, RI
Conley, Snipe (James Patrick)	01/07/1978	Wheatland Cemetery, Dallas, TX
Conlon, Jocko (Arthur Joseph)	08/05/1987	Massachusetts National Cemetery, Bourne, MA
Conn, Bert (Albert Thomas)	11/02/1944	Oakland Cemetery, Philadelphia, PA
Connally, John M.	03/02/1896	Calvary Cemetery, Woodside, Queens, NY
Connally, Sarge (George Walter)	01/27/1978	Harris Creek Cemetery, McGregor, TX
Connaster, Bruce (Broadus Milburn)	01/27/1971	Highland Lawn Cemetery, Terre Haute, IN
Connaughton, Frank Henry	12/01/1942	St. Joseph's Cemetery, West Roxbury, MA
Connell, Gene (Eugene Joseph)	08/31/1937	St. Gabriel's Cemetery, Hazleton, PA
Connell, Joe (Joseph Bernard)	09/21/1977	Fairview Cemetery, Whitehall, PA
Connell, Terry (Terence G.)	03/25/1924	Holy Sepulchre Cemetery, Wyndmoor, PA
Connelly, Bill (William Wirt)	11/27/1980	Crestview Memorial Park, LaCrosse, VA
Connelly, Tom (Thomas Martin)	02/18/1941	Calvary Cemetery, Evanston, IL
Connolly, Bud (Mervin Thomas)	06/12/1964	St. Mary's Cemetery, Oakland, CA
Connolly, Ed (Edward Joseph, Jr.)	07/01/1998	Lakeview Cemetery, New Canaan, CT
Connolly, Ed (Edward Joseph, Sr.)	11/12/1963	St. Joseph's Cemetery, Pittsfield, MA
Connolly, Joe (Joseph Francis)	09/01/1943	St. Charles Cemetery, Blackstone, MA
Connolly, Joe (Joseph H.)	03/30/1960	Golden Gate National Cemetery, San Bruno, CA
Connolly, Tom (Thomas Francis)	05/14/1966	St. Joseph's Cemetery, West Roxbury, MA
Connor, Jim (James Matthew)	09/03/1950	Mount St. Mary's Cemetery, Pawtucket, RI
Connor, Joe (Joseph C.)	01/13/1891	Mount Olivet Cemetery, Wheat Ridge, CO. Originally interred at Mt. Calvary Cemetery, Denver, CO. Cemetery removed to Mount Olivet
Connor, Joe (Joseph Francis)	11/08/1957	Old St. Joseph's Cemetery, Waterbury, CT
Connor, John	11/14/1905	St. Patrick's Cemetery, Hudson, NH
Connor, Ned (Edward)	01/28/1898	Holy Cross Cemetery, Yeadon, PA
Connor, Roger	01/04/1931	Old St. Joseph's Cemetery, Waterbury, CT
Connors, Chuck (Kevin Joseph Aloysius)	11/10/1992	San Fernando Mission Cemetery, Mission Hills, CA
Conover, Ted (Theodore)	07/27/1910	Lexington Cemetery, Lexington, KY
Conroy, Ben (Bernard Patrick)	11/25/1937	Cathedral Cemetery, Philadelphia, PA
Conroy, Bill (William Frederick)	01/23/1970	Holy Sepulchre Cemetery, Worth, IL
Conroy, Bill (William Gordon)	11/13/1997	Mount Vernon Memorial Park, Fair Oaks, CA
Conroy, Wid (William Edward)	12/06/1959	Mount Carmel Cemetery, Moorestown, NJ
Constable, Jim (Jimmy Lee)	09/04/2002	Cremated, Johnson City, TN
Conway, Bill (William F.)	12/18/1943	St. Paul's Cemetery, Arlington, MA
Conway, Charlie (Charles Connell)	09/12/1968	Lake Park Cemetery, Youngstown, OH
Conway, Dick (Richard Butler)	09/09/1926	St. Mary's Immaculate Conception Cemetery, Lawrence, MA
Conway, Jack Clements	06/11/1993	Rosemond Cemetery, Waco, TX
Conway, Owen Sylvester	03/12/1942	Philadelphia National Cemetery, Philadelphia, PA

Name	DOD	Cemetery, City, State
Conway, Pat (Jerome Patrick)	04/16/1980	St. Jerome Cemetery, Holyoke, MA
Conway, Pete (Peter J.)	01/13/1903	St. Charles Cemetery, Drexel Hill, PA
Conway, Rip (Richard Daniel)	12/02/1972	St. Mary's Cemetery, White Bear Lake, MN
Conyers, Herb (Herbert Leroy)	09/16/1964	Knollwood Cemetery, Mayfield Heights, OH
Conzelman, Joe (Joseph Harrison)	04/17/1979	Elmwood Cemetery, Birmingham, AL
Coogan, Dale Roger	03/08/1989	Pacific View Memorial Park, Newport Beach, CA
Coogan, Dan (Daniel George)	10/28/1942	Holy Cross Cemetery, Yeadon, PA
Cook, Doc (Luther Almus)	06/30/1973	Lawrence County Memorial Gardens, Lawrenceburg, TN
Cook, Earl Davis	11/21/1996	Melville Cemetery, Stouffville, Ontario, Canada
Cook, Paul	05/25/1905	Holy Sepulchre Cemetery, Rochester, NY
Cook, Rollin Edward	08/11/1975	Woodlawn Cemetery, Toledo, OH
Cooke, Dusty (Allen Lindsey)	11/21/1987	Westview Memorial Gardens, Lillington, NC
Cooke, Fred (Frederick B.)	01/22/1923	Woodlawn Cemetery, Toledo, OH
Cooley, Duff Gordon	08/09/1937	Grove Hill Memorial Park, Dallas, TX
Coombs, Bobby (Raymond Franklin)	10/21/1991	Riverside Cemetery, Ogunquit, ME
Coombs, Cecil Lysander	11/25/1975	Mount Olivet Cemetery, Fort Worth, TX
Coombs, Jack (John Wesley)	04/15/1957	St. Joseph's Cemetery, Palestine, TX
Coon, William K.	08/30/1915	I.O.O.F. Cemetery, Burlington, NJ
Cooney, Bill (William Ambrose)	11/06/1928	New Calvary Cemetery, Mattapan, MA
Cooney, Bob (Robert Daniel)	05/04/1976	St. Mary's Cemetery, South Glens Falls, NY
Cooney, Jimmy (James Joseph)	07/01/1903	St. Ann's Cemetery, Cranston, RI
Cooney, Johnny (John Walter)	07/08/1986	Manasota Memorial Park, Bradenton, FL
Cooney, Scoops (James Edward)	08/07/1991	St. Ann's Cemetery, Cranston, RI
Cooper, Cal (Calvin Asa)	07/04/1994	Pinelawn Memorial Gardens, Clinton, SC
Cooper, Claude William	01/21/1974	Plainview Cemetery & Memorial Park, Plainview, TX
Cooper, Guy Evans	08/02/1951	Woodlawn Cemetery, Santa Monica, CA
Cooper, Mort (Morton Cecil)	11/17/1958	Salem Baptist Church Cemetery, Independence, MO
Cooper, Pat (Orge Patterson)	03/15/1993	Sharon Memorial Park, Charlotte, NC
Cooper, Wilbur (Arley Wilbur)	08/07/1973	Cremated, Encino, CA
Copeland, Mays	11/29/1982	Coachela Valley Cemetery, Coachella, CA
Coppola, Henry Peter	07/10/1990	St. Denis Cemetery, East Douglas, MA
Corbett, Joe (Joseph A.)	05/02/1945	Holy Cross Cemetery, Colma, CA
Corbitt, Claude Elliott	05/01/1978	Arlington Memorial Gardens, Cincinnati, OH
Corcoran, Art (Arthur Andrew)	07/27/1958	St. Joseph's Cemetery, West Roxbury, MA
Corcoran, John	12/28/1935	Jersey City Cemetery, Jersey City, NJ
Corcoran, Larry (Lawrence J.)	10/14/1891	Cemetery of the Holy Sepulchre, East Orange, NJ
Corcoran, Mickey (Michael Joseph)	12/09/1950	Holy Cross Cemetery, Lackawanna, NY
Corcoran, Tommy (Thomas William)	06/25/1960	Pachaug Cemetery, Pachaug, CT
Corey, Ed (Edward Norman)	09/17/1970	Sunset Ridge Memorial Park, Kenosha, WI

Name	DOD	Cemetery, City, State
Corey, Fred (Frederick Harrison)	11/27/1912	North Burial Grounds Cemetery (Potter's Field), Providence, RI
Corgan, Chuck (Charles Howard)	06/13/1928	Elmwood Cemetery, Wagoner, OK
Corhan, Roy George	11/24/1958	Holy Cross Cemetery, Colma, CA
Coridan, Phil (Philip F.)	07/01/1915	Holy Cross Cemetery, Indianapolis, IN
Corkhill, Pop (John Stewart)	04/03/1921	Bethel Memorial Park, Pennsauken, NJ
Corriden, John Michael, Jr.	06/04/2001	Washington Park East Cemetery, Indianapolis, IN
Corriden, Red (John Michael, Sr.)	09/28/1959	Mt. Hope Cemetery, Logansport, IN
Corridon, Frank Joseph	02/21/1941	St. Mary's Cemetery, Syracuse, NY
Cortazzo, Shine (John Francis)	03/04/1963	St. Joseph's Cemetery, East McKeesport, PA
Corwin, Al (Elmer Nathan)	10/23/2003	River Hills Memorial Park, Batavia, IL
Coscarart, Joe (Joseph Marvin)	04/05/1993	Dungeness Cemetery, Dungeness, WA
Coscarart, Pete (Peter John)	07/24/2002	Oak Hill Memorial Park, Escondido, CA
Costello, Dan (Daniel Francis)	03/26/1936	St. Mary's Catholic Cemetery, St. Mary's, PA
Cote, Henry Joseph	04/28/1940	St. Joseph's Cemetery, Troy, NY
Cote, Pete (Warren Peter)	10/17/1987	St. Paul's Cemetery, Arlington, MA
Cotter, Dan (Daniel Joseph)	09/04/1935	Mount Benedict Cemetery, West Roxbury, MA
Cotter, Dick (Richard Raphael)	04/04/1945	Holy Cross Cemetery, Brooklyn, NY
Cotter, Ed (Edward Christopher)	06/14/1959	Mt. St. Benedict's Cemetery, Bloomfield, CT
Cotter, Hooks (Harvey Louis)	08/06/1955	Forest Lawn Memorial Park, Glendale, CA
Cotter, Tom (Thomas Benedict)	11/22/1906	Calvary Cemetery, Waltham, MA
Cottrell, Ensign Stover	02/27/1947	Morningside Cemetery, Syracuse, NY
Couch, Johnny (John Daniel)	12/08/1975	Alta Mesa Memorial Park, Palo Alto, CA
Coughlin, Bill (William Paul)	05/07/1943	Cathedral Cemetery, Scranton, PA
Coughlin, Dennis	05/14/1913	Arlington National Cemetery, Arlington, VA
Coughlin, Ed (Edward E.)	12/25/1952	Mt. St. Benedict's Cemetery, Bloomfield, CT
Coughlin, Roscoe (William Edward)	03/20/1951	St. Patrick's Cemetery, Lowell, MA
Coulson, Bill (Robert Jackson)	09/11/1953	Beallsville Cemetery, Beallsville, PA
Coumbe, Fritz (Frederick Nicholas)	03/21/1978	Paradise Cemetery, Paradise, CA
Courtney, Clint (Clinton Dawson)	06/16/1975	Mount Zion Cemetery, Hall Summit, LA
Courtney, Henry Seymour	12/11/1954	Cremated, Lyme, CT
Cousineau, Dee (Edward Thomas)	07/14/1951	St. Patrick's Cemetery, Watertown, MA
Coveleski, Harry Frank	08/04/1950	St. Stanislaus Cemetery, Shamokin, PA
Coveleski, Stan (Stanley Anthony)	03/20/1984	St. Joseph Cemetery, South Bend, IN
Coveney, Jack (John Patrick)	03/28/1961	St. Patrick's Cemetery, Natick, MA
Covington, Chet (Chester Rogers)	06/11/1976	Vista Memorial Gardens, Hialeah, FL
Covington, Sam (Clarence Calvert)	01/04/1963	Oakwood Cemetery, Denison, TX
Covington, Tex (William Wilkes)	12/10/1931	Fairview Cemetery, Denison, TX
Cox, Bill (William Donald)	02/16/1988	Ashmore Cemetery, Ashmore, IL
Cox, Billy (William Richard)	03/30/1978	Newport Cemetery, Newport, PA
Cox, Dick (Elmer Joseph)	06/01/1966	Mountain View Cemetery, Altadena, CA
Cox, Ernie (Ernest Thompson)	04/29/1974	Forest Hill Cemetery, Birmingham, AL
Cox, Frank (Francis Bernard)	06/24/1928	St. Bernard's Cemetery, Rockville, CT
Cox, Larry Eugene	02/17/1990	Gethsemani Cemetery, Lima, OH
Cox, Red (Plateau Rex)	10/15/1984	Mountain View Cemetery, Vinton, VA

Name	DOD	Cemetery, City, State
Coyne, Toots (Martin Albert)	09/18/1939	Valhalla Cemetery, St. Louis, MO
Crabb, Jim (James Roy)	03/30/1940	Lewistown City Cemetery, Lewistown, MT
Crabtree, Estel Crayton	01/04/1967	Greenlawn Cemetery, Nelsonville, OH
Craddock, Walt (Walter Anderson)	07/06/1980	Blue Ridge Memorial Gardens, Prosperity, WV
Craft, Harry Francis	08/03/1995	Cremated, Conroe, TX. Ashes returned to family
Craft, Molly (Maurice Montague)	10/25/1978	Los Angeles National Cemetery, Los Angeles, CA. Cremated.
Craghead, Howard Oliver	07/15/1962	Fort Rosecrans National Cemetery, LaJolla, CA
Craig, George McCarthy	04/23/1911	Fernwood Cemetery, Lansdowne, PA
Cramer, Bill (William Wendell)	09/11/1966	Greenlawn Memorial Park, Fort Wayne, IN
Cramer, Doc (Roger Maxwell)	09/09/1990	Greenwood Cemetery, Tuckerton, NJ
Crandall, Doc (James Otis)	08/17/1951	Inglewood Park Cemetery, Inglewood, CA
Crane, Cannonball (Edward Nicholas)	09/20/1896	Holyhood Cemetery, Brookline, MA
Crane, Fred (Frederick William Hotchkiss)	04/27/1925	Green-Wood Cemetery, Brooklyn, NY
Crane, Sam (Samuel Byren)	11/12/1955	Hillside Cemetery, Roslyn, PA
Crane, Sam (Samuel Newhall)	06/26/1925	Lutheran All Faiths Cemetery, Middle Village, Queens, NY
Cravath, Gavy (Clifford Carlton)	05/23/1963	Melrose Abbey Memorial Park, Anaheim, CA
Craver, Bill (William H.)	06/17/1901	Oakwood Cemetery, Troy, NY
Crawford, Forrest A.	03/29/1908	Oakwood Cemetery, Austin, TX
Crawford, Glenn Martin	01/02/1972	Greenwood Cemetery, North Branch, MI
Crawford, Sam (Samuel Earl)	06/15/1968	Inglewood Park Cemetery, Inglewood, CA
Creamer, George W.	06/27/1886	Greenwood Cemetery, Philadelphia, PA
Cree, Birdee (William Franklin)	11/08/1942	Pomfret Manor Cemetery, Sunbury, PA
Creeden, Connie (Cornelius Stephen)	11/30/1969	Good Shepherd Cemetery, Huntington Beach, CA
Creeden, Pat (Patrick Francis)	04/20/1992	Calvary Cemetery, Brockton, MA
Creegan, Marty (Mark) (buried under birth name: Marcus Kragen)	09/29/1920	Holy Cross Cemetery, Colma, CA
Creel, Jack Dalton	08/13/2002	Memorial Oaks Cemetery, Houston, TX
Creely, Gus (August L.)	04/22/1934	Calvary Cemetery, St. Louis, MO
Cregan, Pete (Peter James)	05/18/1945	Calvary Cemetery, Woodside, Queens, NY
Creger, Bernie (Bernard Odell)	11/30/1997	Fort Hill Memorial Park, Lynchburg, VA
Cremins, Bob (Robert Anthony)	03/27/2004	Holy Sepulchre Cemetery, New Rochelle, NY
Crespi, Creepy (Frank Angelo Joseph)	03/01/1990	Calvary Cemetery, St. Louis, MO
Cress, Walker James	04/21/1996	Greenoaks Memorial Park, Baton Rouge, LA
Crews, Tim (Stanley Timothy)	03/23/1993	Woodlawn Memorial Park, Winter Garden, FL
Criger, Lou (Louis)	05/14/1934	Evergreen Cemetery, Tucson, AZ
Crisham, Pat (Patrick J.)	06/12/1915	Assumption Cemetery, Syracuse, NY

Name	DOD	Cemetery, City, State
Crisp, Joe (Joseph Shelby)	02/05/1939	Forest Hill Cemetery, Kansas City, MO
Criss, Dode	09/08/1955	Sherman Cemetery, Sherman, MS
Crist, Ches (Chester Arthur)	01/07/1957	Greenlawn Cemetery, Milford, OH
Cristante, Leo (Dante Leo)	08/24/1977	Our Lady of Hope Cemetery, Wyandotte, MI
Critchley, Morrie (Morris Arthur)	03/06/1910	Calvary Cemetery, Pittsburgh, PA
Critz, Hughie (Hugh Melville)	01/10/1980	I.O.O.F. Cemetery, Greenwood, MS
Crocker, Claude Arthur	12/19/2002	Rosemont Cemetery, Clinton, SC
Croft, Art (Arthur F.)	03/16/1884	Calvary Cemetery, St. Louis, MO
Croft, Harry (Henry T.)	12/11/1933	Mount Carmel Cemetery, Hillside, IL
Crolius, Fred Joseph	08/25/1960	Cremated, Daytona Beach, FL
Crompton, Herb (Herbert Bryan)	08/05/1963	Memorial Park Cemetery, Rock Island, IL
Cronin, Bill (William Patrick)	10/26/1966	Newton Cemetery, Newton, MA
Cronin, Dan (Daniel T.)	11/30/1885	Mount Calvary Cemetery, Roslindale, MA
Cronin, Jack (John J.)	07/12/1929	Ocean View Cemetery (formerly Valhalla Burial Grounds), Oakwood, Staten Island, NY
Cronin, Jim (James John)	06/10/1983	St. Joseph Cemetery, San Pablo, CA
Cronin, Joe (Joseph Edward)	09/07/1984	St. Francis Xavier Cemetery, Centerville, MA
Crooke, Tom (Thomas Aloysius)	04/05/1929	Mount Olivet Cemetery, Washington, DC
Crooks, Jack (John Charles)	02/02/1918	Valhalla Cemetery, St. Louis, MO
Crosby, George Washington	01/09/1913	Cypress Lawn Memorial Park, Colma, CA
Crosetti, Frank Peter Joseph	02/11/2002	Holy Cross Cemetery, Colma, CA
Cross, Amos C.	07/16/1888	Riverside Cemetery, Cleveland, OH
Cross, Clarence	06/23/1931	Cremated, Seattle, WA
Cross, Frank Atwell	11/02/1932	Riverside Cemetery, Cleveland, OH
Cross, Jeff (Joffre James)	07/23/1997	Memorial Oaks Cemetery, Houston, TX
Cross, Lave (Lafayette Napoleon)	09/06/1927	Woodlawn Cemetery, Toledo, OH
Cross, Lew (George Lewis)	10/09/1930	Pine Grove Cemetery, Manchester, NH
Cross, Monte (Montford Montgomery)	06/21/1934	Arlington Cemetery, Drexel Hill, PA
Crossen, Frank Patrick	12/06/1965	St. Mary's Cemetery, Wilkes-Barre, PA
Crothers, Dug (Douglas)	03/29/1907	Bellefontaine Cemetery, St. Louis, MO
Crotty, Joe (Joseph P.)	06/22/1926	St. Mary's Cemetery, Minneapolis, MN
Crouch, Bill (Wilmer Elmer)	12/26/1980	Lakeview Cemetery, Howell, MI
Croucher, Frank Donald	05/21/1980	Forest Park (Lawndale) Cemetery, Houston, TX
Crouse, Buck (Clyde Ellsworth)	10/23/1983	Elm Ridge Cemetery, Muncie, IN
Crowder, General (Alvin Floyd)	04/03/1972	Forsyth Memorial Park Cemetery, Winston-Salem, NC
Crowell, Cap (Minot Joy)	09/30/1962	Swan Point Cemetery, Providence, RI
Crowley, Bill (William Michael)	07/14/1891	New St. Mary's Cemetery, Bellmawr, NJ
Crowley, Ed (Edgar Jewel)	04/14/1970	Westview Cemetery, Atlanta, GA
Crowley, John A.	09/23/1896	St. Mary's Immaculate Conception Cemetery, Lawrence, MA
Crowson, Woody (Thomas Woodrow)	08/14/1947	Springfield Friends Church Cemetery, High Point, NC
Cruise, Walton Edwin	01/09/1975	Evergreen Memorial Cemetery, Sylacauga, AL
Crum, Cal (Calvin N.)	07/07/1945	Memorial Park Cemetery, Tulsa, OK
Crump, Buddy (Arthur Elliott)	09/26/1976	Raleigh National Cemetery, Raleigh, NC

Name	DOD	Cemetery, City, State
Crumpler, Roy Maxton	10/06/1969	Crumpler Family Cemetery, Salemburg, NC
Crutcher, Dick (Richard Louis)	06/19/1952	Frankfort Cemetery, Frankfort, KY
Cruthers, Press (Charles Preston)	12/27/1976	Sunset Ridge Memorial Park, Kenosha, WI
Cuccinello, Tony (Anthony Francis)	09/21/1995	Garden of Memories Cemetery, Tampa, FL
Cuccurullo, Cookie (Arthur Joseph)	01/23/1983	Rosedale Cemetery, Orange, NJ
Cudworth, Jim (James Alaric)	12/21/1943	Clark Cemetery, Lakeville, MA
Cuellar, Charlie (Jesus Patracis)	10/11/1994	Centro Austriano Memorial Park, Tampa, FL
Cuff, John Patrick	12/05/1916	Holy Name Cemetery, Jersey City, NJ
Culberson, Leon (Delbert Leon)	09/17/1989	Oaknoll Memorial Gardens, Rome, GA
Cullen, John Joseph	02/11/1921	Russian River Cemetery, Ukiah, CA
Cullenbine, Roy Joseph	05/28/1991	Christian Memorial Cultural Cemetery, Rochester, MI
Culler, Dick (Richard Broadus)	06/16/1964	Floral Garden Park Cemetery, High Point, NC
Cullop, Nick (Henry Nicholas)	12/01/1978	Mifflin Cemetery, Gahanna, OH
Culloton, Bud (Bernard Aloysius)	11/09/1976	St. Mary's Cemetery, Kingston, NY
Culp, Ben (Benjamin Baldy)	10/23/2000	Magnolia Cemetery, Philadelphia, PA
Culp, Bill (William Edward)	09/03/1969	Plum Creek Cemetery, New Kensington, PA
Cummings, Candy (William Arthur)	05/16/1924	Aspen Grove Cemetery, Ware, MA
Cummings, Jack (John William)	10/05/1962	North Side Catholic Cemetery, Pittsburgh, PA
Cunningham, Bert (Ellsworth Elmer)	05/14/1952	Lawn Croft Cemetery, Linwood, PA
Cunningham, Bill (William Aloysius)	09/26/1953	Holy Cross Cemetery, Colma, CA
Cunningham, Bill (William John)	02/21/1946	St. John's Cemetery, Schenectady, NY
Cunningham, Bruce Lee	03/08/1984	Cremated, Hayward, CA
Cunningham, George Harold	03/10/1972	Chattanooga Memorial Park, Chattanooga, TN
Cunningham, Mike (Mody)	12/10/1969	Bethlehem Baptist Church Cemetery, Lancaster, SC
Cuppy, Nig (George Joseph)	07/27/1922	Rice Cemetery, Elkhart, IN
Curley, Doc (Walter James)	09/23/1920	St. Mary's of the Assumption Catholic Cemetery, Milford, MA
Curran, Sammy (Simon Francis)	05/19/1936	Holy Cross Cemetery, Malden, MA
Currie, Clarence Franklin	07/15/1941	Highland Memorial Cemetery, Appleton, WI
Curry, George James	10/05/1963	Lakeview Cemetery, Bridgeport, CT
Curry, Jim (James L.)	08/02/1938	Lakeview Memorial Park, Cinnaminson, NJ
Curry, Wes (Wesley)	05/19/1933	Arlington Cemetery, Drexel Hill, PA
Curtis, Cliff (Clifton Garfield)	04/23/1943	Oak Grove Cemetery, Delaware, OH
Curtis, Edwin Russell *manager*	08/06/1914	Grove Cemetery, Bath, NY
Curtis, Fred (Frederick Marion)	04/05/1939	Cremated, Sunset Memorial Park Cemetery, Minneapolis, MN
Curtis, Gene (Eugene Holmes)	01/01/1919	Brooke Cemetery, Wellsburg, WV
Curtis, Harry Albert	08/01/1951	Calvary Cemetery, Evanston, IL
Curtis, Vern (Vernon Eugene)	06/24/1992	Roselawn Cemetery, Bardwell, KY
Curtiss, Ervin Duane	02/14/1945	Hillside Cemetery, North Adams, MA
Curtright, Guy Paxton	08/23/1997	Garden of Memories Cemetery, Tampa, FL
Cushman, Charlie *manager*	06/29/1909	Calvary Cemetery, Milwaukee, WI

Name	DOD	Cemetery, City, State
Cushman, Ed (Edgar Leander)	09/26/1915	Erie Cemetery, Erie, PA
Cushman, Harv (Harvey Barnes)	12/27/1920	Mount Royal Cemetery, Glenshaw, PA
Cusick, Jack (John Peter)	11/17/1989	George Washington Memorial Park, Paramus, NJ
Cusick, Tony (Andrew Daniel)	08/06/1929	Mount Olivet Cemetery, Chicago, IL
Cuthbert, Ned (Edgar Edward)	02/06/1905	Bellefontaine Cemetery, St. Louis, MO
Cutshaw, George William	08/22/1973	Cremated, Pacific Beach Mortuary, San Diego, CA. Ashes scattered in Pacific Ocean
Cuyler, Kiki (Hazen Shirley)	02/11/1950	St. Ann's Cemetery, Harrisville, MI
Cvengros, Mike (Michael John)	08/02/1970	Calvary Cemetery, Hot Springs, AR
Cypert, Al (Alfred Boyd)	01/09/1973	National Memorial Park, Falls Church, VA
Dagenhard, John Douglas	07/16/2001	Magnolia Cemetery, Magnolia, OH
Daglia, Pete (Peter George)	03/11/1952	Tulocay Cemetery, Napa, CA
Dahl, Jay Steven	06/20/1965	Montecito Memorial Park, Colton, CA
Dahlen, Bill (William Frederick)	12/05/1950	Evergreen Cemetery, Brooklyn, NY
Dahlgren, Babe (Ellsworth Tenney)	09/04/1996	Forest Lawn Memorial Park, Glendale, CA
Dailey, Vince (Vincent Perry)	11/14/1919	Rural Cemetery, Hornell, NY
Daily, Con (Cornelius F.)	06/14/1928	Lutheran All Faiths Cemetery, Middle Village, Queens, NY
Daily, Ed (Edward M.)	10/21/1891	Mount Olivet Cemetery, Washington, DC
Daily, John	01/08/1898	Calvary Cemetery, Woodside, Queens, NY
Daisy, George R.	04/27/1931	Rosehill Cemetery, Cumberland, MD
Daley, Bill (William)	05/04/1922	Poughkeepsie Rural Cemetery, Poughkeepsie, NY
Daley, John Francis	08/31/1988	Mansfield Catholic Cemetery, Mansfield, OH
Daley, Tom (Thomas Francis)	12/02/1934	Calvary Cemetery, Los Angeles, CA
Dallessandro, Dom (Nicholas Dominic)	04/29/1988	St. Joseph Cemetery, Indianapolis, IN
Dalrymple, Abner Frank	01/25/1939	Elmwood Cemetery, Warren, IL
Dalrymple, Bill (William Dunn)	07/14/1967	Greenwood Memorial Park, San Diego, CA
Daly, Bert (Albert Joseph)	09/03/1952	Holy Name Cemetery, Jersey City, NJ
Daly, George Josephs	12/12/1957	Holy Cross Cemetery, Lackawanna, NY
Daly, Joe (Joseph John)	03/21/1943	Holy Sepulchre Cemetery, Wyndmoor, PA
Daly, Tom (Thomas Daniel)	11/07/1946	Oak Grove Cemetery, Medford, MA
Daly, Tom (Thomas Peter)	10/29/1938	Holy Cross Cemetery, Brooklyn, NY
Dam, Bill (Elbridge Rust)	06/22/1930	Mount Wollaston Cemetery, Quincy, MA
Dammann, Bill (William Henry)	12/06/1948	Eastern Shore Chapel Cemetery, Virginia Beach, VA
Damrau, Harry Robert	08/21/1957	St. Peter's Cemetery, Staten Island, NY
Daney, Lee (Arthur Lee)	03/11/1988	Green Acres Memorial Gardens, Scottsdale, AZ
Danforth, Dave (David Charles)	09/19/1970	Loudon Park Cemetery, Baltimore, MD
Daniels, Bert (Bernard Elmer)	06/06/1958	Immaculate Conception Cemetery, Montclair, NJ
Daniels, Charlie (Charles L.)	02/09/1938	Mount Hope Cemetery, Mattapan, MA
Daniels, Lawrence Long	01/07/1929	Calvary Cemetery, Waltham, MA
Daniels, Pete (Peter J.)	02/13/1928	Holy Cross Cemetery, Indianapolis, IN

Name	DOD	Cemetery, City, State
Danner, Buck (Henry Frederick)	09/21/1949	Brookdale Cemetery, Dedham, MA
Danning, Ike (Isaac)	03/30/1983	Hillside Memorial Park, Los Angeles, CA
Dantonio, Fats (John James)	05/28/1993	Lake Lawn Cemetery, New Orleans, LA
Danzig, Babe (Harold Paul)	07/14/1931	Cremated, San Francisco, CA
Darby, George William	02/25/1937	Dixon Cemetery, Dixon, CA
Daringer, Cliff (Clifford Clarence)	12/26/1971	East Lawn Memorial Park, Sacramento, CA
Daringer, Rolla Harrison	05/23/1974	Hayden Cemetery, Hayden, IN
Darling, Dell (Conrad)	11/20/1904	Trinity Cemetery, Erie, PA
Darnell, Bob (Robert Jack)	01/03/1995	West Prong Cemetery, Medina, TX
Darr, Mike (Michael Curtis)	02/15/2002	Pierce Brothers Crestlawn Memorial Park, Riverside, CA
Darragh, Jack (James S.)	08/12/1939	Beaver Cemetery, Beaver, PA
Darrow, George Oliver	03/24/1983	Sunland Memorial Park, Sun City, AZ
Dashiell, Wally (John Wallace)	05/20/1972	Bayview Memorial Park, Pensacola, FL
Daub, Dan (Daniel William)	03/25/1951	Hickory Flats Cemetery, Overpeck, OH
Daubert, Harry J.	01/08/1944	Forest Lawn Cemetery, Detroit, MI
Daubert, Jake (Jacob Ellsworth)	10/09/1924	Charles Baber Cemetery, Pottsville, PA
Daughters, Bob (Robert Francis)	08/22/1988	St. Patrick's Cemetery, Watertown, MA
Dauss, Hooks (George August)	07/27/1963	Sunset Memorial Park, Affton, MO
Davenport, Claude Edwin	06/13/1976	Robstown Memorial Park, Robstown, TX
Davenport, Dave (David W.)	10/16/1954	Arlington Memorial Cemetery, El Dorado, AR
Davenport, Lum (Joubert Lum)	04/21/1961	Sparkman Hillcrest Memorial Park, Dallas, TX
Davidson, Bill (William Simpson)	05/23/1954	Waverly Rose Hill Cemetery, Waverly, NE
Davidson, Claude Boucher	04/18/1956	Blue Hill Cemetery, Braintree, MA
Davidson, Homer Hurd	07/26/1948	Grand Lawn Cemetery, Detroit, MI
Davies, Chick (Lloyd Garrison)	09/05/1973	Cremated, Middletown, CT
Davies, George Washington	09/22/1906	Village Cemetery, Waterloo, WI
Davis, Bud (John Wilbur)	05/26/1967	Williamsburg Memorial Park, Williamsburg, VA
Davis, Curt (Curtis Benton)	10/13/1965	Oakdale Memorial Park, Glendora, CA
Davis, Daisy (John Henry Albert)	11/05/1902	Pine Grove Cemetery, Lynn, MA
Davis, Dixie (Frank Talmadge)	02/04/1944	Christian Church Cemetery, Virgilina, VA
Davis, George Allen	06/04/1961	Lancaster Rural Cemetery, Lancaster, NY
Davis, George Stacey	10/17/1940	Fernwood Cemetery, Lansdowne, PA
Davis, Harry H	08/11/1947	Westminster Cemetery, Bala Cynwyd, PA
Davis, Ike (Isaac Marion)	04/02/1984	Cremated, Tucson, AZ
Davis, Jim (James Bennett)	11/30/1995	Cremated, San Mateo, CA
Davis, John Humphrey	04/26/2002	Spring Hill Cemetery, Laurel, MS
Davis, Jumbo (James J.)	02/14/1921	Calvary Cemetery, St. Louis, MO
Davis, Kiddo (George Willis)	03/04/1983	Park Cemetery, Bridgeport, CT
Davis, Lefty (Alfonzo DeFord)	02/07/1919	Holy Cross Cemetery, Lackawanna, NY
Davis, Peaches (Roy Thomas)	04/28/1995	Duncan City Cemetery, Duncan, OK
Davis, Ron (Ronald Everette)	09/05/1992	Davis Family Cemetery, Jackson, NC
Davis, Slats (James Ira)	12/21/1942	Lutheran All Faiths Cemetery, Middle Village, Queens, NY
Davis, Spud (Virgil Lawrence)	08/14/1984	Elmwood Cemetery, Birmingham, AL
Davis, Tod (Thomas Oscar)	12/31/1978	Rose Hills Memorial Park, Whittier, CA
Davis, Woody (Woodrow Wilson)	07/18/1999	Odum City Cemetery, Odum, GA

Name	DOD	Cemetery, City, State
Dawson, Joe (Ralph Fenton)	01/04/1978	Lakeview Memorial Gardens, Longview, TX
Dawson, Rex (Rexford Paul)	10/20/1958	Crown Hill Cemetery, Indianapolis, IN
Day, Bill (William M.)	08/16/1923	Cathedral Cemetery, Wilmington, DE
Day, Pea Ridge (Clyde Henry)	03/21/1934	Pea Ridge Cemetery, Pea Ridge, AR
Deagle, Ren (Lorenzo Burroughs)	12/24/1936	Elmwood Cemetery, Kansas City, MO
Deal, Charlie (Charles Albert)	09/16/1979	Pasadena Mausoleum, Altadena, CA
Deal, Lindsay (Fred Lindsay)	04/18/1979	Pine Crest Memorial Park, Alexander, AR
Deal, Snake (John Wesley)	05/09/1944	Florin Cemetery, Mt. Joy, PA
Dealy, Pat (Patrick E.)	12/17/1924	Holy Cross Cemetery, Lackawanna, NY
Dean, Chubby (Alfred Lovell)	12/21/1970	St. Peter's Church Cemetery, Riverside, NJ
Dean, Dizzy (Jay Hanna)	07/17/1974	Bond Cemetery, Bond, MS
Dean, Dory (Charles Wilson)	05/04/1935	Woodlawn Memorial Park, Nashville, TN
Dean, Harry (James Harry)	06/01/1960	Rose Hill Cemetery, Rockmart, GA
Dean, Paul Dee	03/17/1981	Oakland Cemetery, Clarksville, AR
Dean, Wayland Ogden	04/10/1930	Spring Hill Cemetery, Huntington, WV
Deane, Harry (John Henry)	05/31/1925	Crown Hill Cemetery, Indianapolis, IN
Dear, Buddy (Paul Stanford)	08/29/1989	Sunset Cemetery, Christiansburg, VA
DeArmond, Charlie (Charles Hommer)	12/17/1933	Shandon Cemetery, Shandon, OH
Deasley, John	12/25/1910	Mt. Moriah Cemetery, Philadelphia, PA
Deasley, Pat (Thomas H.)	04/01/1943	Mt. Moriah Cemetery, Philadelphia, PA
DeBerry, Hank (John Herman)	09/10/1951	Savannah Cemetery, Savannah, TN
DeBerry, Joe (Joseph Gaddy)	10/09/1944	Mount Hope Cemetery, Southern Pines, NC
DeBus, Adam Joseph	05/13/1977	St. Boniface Cemetery, Chicago, IL
Decatur, Art (Arthur Rue)	04/25/1966	Oak Hill Cemetery, Talladega, AL
Decker, Frank	02/05/1940	Valhalla Cemetery, St. Louis, MO. Cremated.
Decker, George A.	06/07/1909	Woodland Memorial Park, Compton, CA
Decker, Joe (George Henry)	03/02/2003	Buena Vista Cemetery, Storm Lake, IA
Dede, Artie (Arthur Richard)	09/06/1971	Evergreen Cemetery, Brooklyn, NY
Dee, Shorty (Maurice Leo)	08/12/1971	St. Patrick's Cemetery, Lowell, MA
Deering, John Thomas	02/15/1943	St. Mary Cemetery, Beverly, MA
DeFate, Tony (Clyde Herbert)	09/03/1963	Presbyterian Cemetery, Lafayette, LA
DeGroff, Rube (Edward Arthur)	12/17/1955	St. James Churchyard Cemetery, Hyde Park, NY
Deininger, Pep (Otto Charles)	09/25/1950	Forest Hills Cemetery, Boston, MA
Deisel, Pat (Edward)	04/17/1948	Spring Grove Cemetery, Cincinnati, OH
Deitrick, Bill (William Alexander)	05/06/1946	Arlington National Cemetery, Arlington, VA
Dejan, Mike (Michael Dan)	02/02/1953	Los Angeles National Cemetery, Los Angeles, CA
DeKonning, Bill (William Callahan)	07/26/1979	Curlew Hills Memory Gardens, Palm Harbor, FL
Delahanty, Ed (Edward James)	07/02/1903	Calvary Cemetery, Cleveland, OH
Delahanty, Frank George	07/22/1966	Calvary Cemetery, Cleveland, OH
Delahanty, Jim (James Christopher)	10/17/1953	Calvary Cemetery, Cleveland, OH
Delahanty, Joe (Joseph Nicholas)	01/29/1936	Calvary Cemetery, Cleveland, OH
Delahanty, Tom (Thomas James)	01/10/1951	All Souls Cemetery, Sanford, FL
DeLancey, Bill (William Pinkney)	11/28/1946	St. Francis Catholic Cemetery, Phoenix, AZ

Name	DOD	Cemetery, City, State
Delaney, Art (Arthur Dewey)	05/02/1970	Cremated, Chapel of the Chimes, Hayward, CA
Delaney, Bill (William L.)	03/01/1942	St. John's Catholic Church Cemetery, Canton, OH
Delhi, Flame (Lee William)	05/09/1966	Mount Tamalpais Cemetery, San Rafael, CA
Delker, Eddie (Edward Alberts)	05/14/1997	I.O.O.F. Cemetery, Saint Clair (Schuylkill Co.), PA
Dell, Wheezer (William George)	08/24/1966	Inglewood Park Cemetery, Inglewood, CA
Delmas, Bert (Albert Charles)	12/04/1979	Pacific View Memorial Park, Newport Beach, CA
Demarais, Fred (Frederick)	03/06/1919	St. John's Cemetery, Darien, CT
Demaree, Al (Albert Wentworth)	04/30/1962	Harbor Rest-Mount Olive Cemetery, Costa Mesa, CA
Demaree, Frank (Joseph Franklin)	08/30/1958	Glenwood Cemetery, Long Beach, CA. Cremated.
DeMiller, Harry	10/19/1928	Fairhaven Memorial Park, Santa Ana, CA
Demmitt, Ray (Charles Raymond)	02/19/1956	Mount Pulaski Cemetery, Mount Pulaski, IL
DeMontreville, Gene (Eugene Napoleon)	02/18/1935	Glenwood Cemetery, Washington, DC
DeMott, Ben (Benyew Harrison)	07/05/1963	Evergreen Cemetery, Basking Ridge, NJ
Denning, Otto George	05/25/1992	St. Joseph Cemetery, River Grove,IL
Denny, Jerry (Jeremiah Dennis)	08/16/1927	Holy Cross Cemetery, Houston, TX
Dent, Eddie (Elliott Estill)	11/25/1974	Elmwood Cemetery, Birmingham, AL
Dente, Sam (Samuel Joseph)	04/21/2002	Holy Cross Cemetery, North Arlington, NJ
Denzer, Roger	09/18/1949	Mound Cemetery, Le Seuer, MN
DePangher, Mike (Michael Anthony)	07/07/1915	Holy Cross Cemetery, Colma, CA
Derby, Gene (Eugene A.)	09/13/1917	Pine Grove Cemetery, Waterbury, CT
Derrick, Claud Lester	07/15/1974	Clayton Cemetery, Clayton, GA
Derringer, Paul (Samuel Paul)	11/17/1987	Cremated, Sarasota, FL. Ashes given to family.
Des Jardien, Shorty (Paul Raymond)	03/07/1956	Glenwood Cemetery, Long Beach, CA. Cremated.
DeSa, Joe (Joseph)	12/20/1986	Hawaiian Memorial Park, Kaneohe, HI
Desautels, Gene (Eugene Abraham)	11/05/1994	New Calvary Catholic Cemetery, Flint, MI
DeShong, Jimmie (James Brooklyn)	10/16/1993	East Harrisburg Cemetery, Harrisburg, PA
Dessau, Rube (Frank Rolland)	05/06/1952	Locust Grove Cemetery, Ellwood City, PA
Detore, George Francis	02/07/1991	Calvary Cemetery, Utica, NY
Deutsch, Mel (Melvin Elliott)	11/18/2001	Caldwell Masonic Cemetery, Caldwell, TX
Devens, Charlie (Charles)	08/13/2003	Mount Auburn Cemetery, Cambridge, MA
Devine, Jim (Walter James)	01/11/1905	St. Agnes Cemetery, Syracuse, NY
Devine, Mickey (William Patrick)	10/01/1937	Our Lady of Angels Cemetery, Albany, NY
Deviney, Hal (Harold John)	01/04/1933	Brookdale Cemetery, Dedham, MA
DeViveiros, Bernie (Bernard John)	07/05/1994	Mountain View Cemetery, Oakland, CA
Devlin, Art (Arthur McArthur)	09/18/1948	Congressional Cemetery, Washington, DC
Devlin, Jim (James Alexander)	10/10/1883	New Cathedral Cemetery, Philadelphia, PA
Devlin, Jim (James H.)	12/14/1900	St. John's Cemetery, Troy, NY

Name	DOD	Cemetery, City, State
Devlin, Jim (James Raymond)	01/15/2004	New Rosemont Cemetery, Bloomsburg, PA
DeVogt, Rex Eugene	11/09/1935	Riverside Cemetery, Alma, MI
Devore, Josh (Joshua D.)	10/06/1954	New Marshfield Cemetery, New Marshfield, OH
DeVormer, Al (Albert E.)	08/29/1966	Fair Plains Cemetery, Grand Rapids, MI
Devoy, Walt (Walter Joseph)	12/17/1953	Calvary Cemetery, St. Louis, MO
Dewald, Charlie (Charles H.)	08/22/1904	Woodland Cemetery, Cleveland, OH
Dexter, Charlie (Charles Dana)	06/09/1934	Glendale Cemetery, Des Moines, IA
Dibut, Pedro	12/04/1979	Vista Memorial Gardens, Hialeah, FL
Dickerman, Leo Louis	04/30/1982	Atkins City Cemetery, Atkins, AR
Dickerson, Buttercup (Lewis Pessano)	07/23/1920	Loudon Park Cemetery, Baltimore, MD
Dickerson, George Clark	07/09/1938	Frankford Cemetery, Dallas, TX
Dickey, Bill (William Malcolm)	11/12/1993	Roselawn Memorial Gardens Cemetery, Little Rock, AR
Dickey, George Willard	07/16/1976	Roselawn Memorial Gardens Cemetery, Little Rock, AR
Dickman, Emerson (George Emerson)	04/27/1981	George Washington Memorial Park, Paramus, NJ
Dickshot, Johnny (John Oscar)	11/04/1997	Ascencion Cemetery, Libertyville, IL
Dickson, Murry Monroe	09/21/1989	Sunset Memory Gardens, Leavenworth, KS
Dickson, Walt (Walter R.)	12/09/1918	East Mound Cemetery, Greenville, TX
Diddlebock, Harry (Henry H.) *manager*	02/05/1900	West Laurel Hill Cemetery, Bala Cynwyd, PA
Diehl, Ernie (Ernest Guy)	11/06/1958	Spring Grove Cemetery, Cincinnati, OH
Diehl, George Krause	08/24/1986	Oak Hill Cemetery, Kingsport, TN
Dietz, Dutch (Lloyd Arthur)	10/29/1972	Forest Lawn Memorial Park, Beaumont, TX
Diggs, Reese Wilson	10/30/1978	Gwynns Island Cemetery, Gwynn, VA
Dignan, Steve (Stephen E.)	07/11/1881	Mount Calvary Cemetery, Roslindale, MA
Dillard, Pat (Robert Lee)	07/22/1907	Forest Hills Cemetery, Chattanooga, TN
Dillhoefer, Pickles (William Martin)	02/23/1922	Magnolia Cemetery, Mobile, AL
Dillinger, Harley Hugh	01/08/1959	Calvary Cemetery, Cleveland, OH
Dillon, Pop (Frank Edward)	09/12/1931	Forest Lawn Memorial Park, Glendale, CA
DiMaggio, Joe (Joseph Paul)	03/08/1999	Holy Cross Cemetery, Colma, CA
DiMaggio, Vince (Vincent Paul)	10/03/1986	Rose Memorial Park, Fort Bragg, CA
Dineen, Bill (William Henry)	01/13/1955	St. Agnes Cemetery, Utica, NY
Dinges, Vance George	10/04/1990	Cedarwood Cemetery, Edinburg, VA
Disch, George Charles	08/25/1950	Mountain View Cemetery, Rapid City, SD
Distel, Dutch (George Adam)	02/12/1967	St. Patrick's Cemetery, Madison, IN
Diven, Frank Robert	05/30/1914	Evergreen Cemetery, Brooklyn, NY
Divis, Moxie (Edward George)	12/19/1955	Holy Cross Cemetery, Cleveland, OH
Dixon, Leo Moses	04/11/1984	Holy Sepulchre Cemetery, Worth, IL
Doak, Bill (William Leopold)	11/26/1954	Cremated, Bradenton, FL.
Doane, Walt (Walter Rudolph)	10/19/1935	East Caln Friends Buring Grounds, Downingtown, PA
Dobb, John Kenneth	07/31/1991	Mona View Jewish Cemetery, Muskegon, MI
Dobbs, Johnny (John Gordon)	09/09/1934	Forest Hills Cemetery, Chattanooga, TN
Dobens, Ray (Raymond Joseph)	04/21/1980	Mount Calvary Cemetery, Manchester, NH

Name	DOD	Cemetery, City, State
Dobernic, Jess (Andrew Joseph)	07/16/1998	Cremated, St. Louis, MO.
Dobson, Joe (Joseph Gordon)	06/23/1994	Evergreen Cemetery, Jacksonville, FL
Doby, Larry (Lawrence Eugene)	06/18/2003	Cremated, Monclair, NJ
Dockins, George Woodrow	01/22/1997	Mount Hope Cemetery, Clyde, KS
Dodd, Ona Melvin	12/17/1956	Dodd Family Cemetery, Detroit, TX
Dodge, John Lewis	06/19/1916	Cave Hill Cemetery, Louisville, KY
Dodge, Sam (Samuel Edward)	04/05/1966	New Forest Cemetery, Utica, NY
Doe, Fred (Alfred George)	10/04/1938	Oak Grove Cemetery, Gloucester, MA
Dolan, Biddy (Leon Mark)	07/15/1950	Holy Cross Cemetery, Indianapolis, IN
Dolan, Cozy (Albert James)	12/10/1958	All Saints Cemetery, Des Plaines, IL
Dolan, Cozy (Patrick Henry)	03/29/1907	St. Paul's Cemetery, Arlington, MA
Dolan, Joe (Joseph)	03/24/1938	Holy Sepulchre Cemetery. Omaha, NE
Dolan, John	05/04/1948	Calvary Cemetery, Springfield, OH
Dolan, Tom (Thomas J.)	01/16/1913	Calvary Cemetery, St. Louis, MO
Dole, Lester Carrington	12/10/1918	St. Paul School Cemetery, Concord, NH
Doljack, Frank Joseph	01/23/1948	Calvary Cemetery, Cleveland, OH
Donahue, Jiggs (John Augustus)	07/19/1913	Calvary Cemetery, Springfield, OH
Donahue, Jim (James Augustus)	04/19/1935	South Lockport Cemetery, Lockport, IL
Donahue, John Frederick	10/03/1949	St. Joseph's Cemetery, West Roxbury, MA
Donahue, Pat (Patrick William)	01/31/1966	Woodland/St. Ambrose Cemetery, Des Moines, IA
Donahue, Red (Francis Rostell)	08/25/1913	New St. Joseph's Cemetery, Waterbury, CT
Donahue, She (Charles Michael)	08/28/1947	St. Paul's Cemetery, Oswego, NY
Donahue, Tim (Timothy Cornelius)	06/12/1902	St. Joseph's Cemetery, Taunton, MA
Donalds, Ed (Edward Alexander)	07/03/1950	Forest Lawn Cemetery, Columbus, OH
Dondero, Len (Leonard Peter)	01/01/1999	Holy Sepulchre Cemetery, Hayward, CA
Donlin, Mike (Michael Joseph)	09/24/1933	Glenwood Cemetery, Long Branch, CA. Cremated.
Donnelly, Blix (Sylvester Urban)	06/20/1976	St. Aloysius Catholic Cemetery, Olivia, MN
Donnelly, Ed (Edward Vincent)	12/25/1992	St. Michael's Catholic Cemetery, Weimar, TX
Donnelly, Ed (Edward)	11/28/1957	St. Raphael Cemetery, Poultney, VT
Donnelly, Franklin Marion	02/03/1953	Laurel Hill Cemetery, Havana, IL
Donnelly, Pete (Peter J.)	10/01/1890	St. Peter's Cemetery, Jersey City, NJ
Donohue, Pete (Peter Joseph)	02/23/1988	Greenwood Memorial Park, Fort Worth, TX
Donovan, Bill (Willard Earl)	09/25/1997	Chapel Hill Gardens West, Oakbrook Terrace, IL
Donovan, Dick (Richard Edward)	01/06/1997	Woodside Cemetery,Cohasset, MA
Donovan, Fred (Frederick Maurice)	03/07/1916	Oak Ridge Cemetery, Springfield, IL
Donovan, Jerry (Jeremiah Francis)	06/27/1938	St. Mary's Cemetery, Lock Haven, PA
Donovan, Mike (Michael Berchman)	02/03/1938	Calvary Cemetery, Woodside, Queens, NY
Donovan, Patsy (Patrick Joseph)	12/25/1953	St. Mary's Immaculate Conception Cemetery, Lawrence, MA
Donovan, Tom (Thomas Joseph)	03/25/1933	St. Patrick's Cemetery, Watervliet, NY
Donovan, Wild Bill (William Edward)	12/09/1923	Holy Cross Cemetery, Yeadon, PA
Dooin, Red (Charles Sebastian)	05/12/1952	Holy Sepulchre Cemetery, Rochester, NY

Name	DOD	Cemetery, City, State
Doolan, Mickey (Michael Joseph)	11/01/1951	Greenwood Cemetery, Orlando, FL
Doran, Bill (William James)	03/09/1978	Cremated, Santa Monica, CA
Doran, Tom (Thomas J.)	06/22/1910	St. Raymond's Cemetery, Bronx, NY
Dorgan, Jerry (Jeremiah F.)	06/10/1891	St. John's Cemetery, Middletown, CT
Dorgan, Mike (Michael Cornelius)	04/26/1909	St. Agnes Cemetery, Syracuse, NY
Dorish, Harry	12/31/2000	St. Mary's Annunciation Church Cemetery, Pringle, PA
Dorman, Charlie (Charles William)	11/15/1928	Woodlawn Memorial Park, Colma, CA
Dorman, Red (Charles Dwight)	12/07/1974	Westminster Memorial Park, Westminster, CA
Dorner, Gus (Augustus)	05/04/1956	Corpus Christi Cemetery, Chambersburg, PA
Dorr, Bert (Charles Albert)	06/16/1914	Glenwood Cemetery, Port Dickinson, NY
Dorsett, Cal (Calvin Leavelle)	10/22/1970	Fairlawn Cemetery, Elk City, OK
Dorsey, Jerry (Michael Jeremiah)	11/03/1938	St. Joseph's Cemetery, Auburn, NY
Doscher, Herm (John Henry, Sr.)	03/20/1934	Elmlawn Cemetery, Tonawanda, NY
Doscher, Jack (John Henry, Jr.)	05/27/1971	Mount Carmel Cemetery, Tenafly, NJ
Dotterer, Dutch (Henry John)	10/09/1999	Assumption Cemetery, Syracuse, NY
Doty, Babe (Elmer L.)	11/20/1929	Clay Cemetery, Genoa, OH
Dougherty, Charlie (Charles William)	02/18/1925	Forest Home Cemetery, Milwaukee, WI
Dougherty, Patsy (Patrick Henry)	04/30/1940	St. Mary's Cemetery, Bolivar, NY
Dougherty, Tom (Thomas James)	11/06/1953	Wisconsin Memorial Park, Brookfield, WI
Douglas, John Franklin	02/11/1984	Woodlawn Park Cemetery West, Hialeah, FL
Douglas, Larry (Lawrence Howard)	11/04/1949	Jellico Cemetery, Jellico, TN
Douglas, Phil (Phillip Brooks)	08/02/1952	Tracy City Cemetery, Tracy City, TN
Douglass, Astyanax Saunders	01/26/1975	Evergreen East Cemetery, El Paso, TX
Douthit, Taylor Lee	05/28/1986	Cremated, Fremont, CA
Dow, Clarence G.	03/11/1893	Woodlawn Cemetery, Everett, MA
Dowd, Kip (James Joseph)	12/20/1960	St. Jerome Cemetery, Holyoke, MA
Dowd, Snooks (Raymond Bernard)	04/04/1962	St. Michael's Cemetery, Springfield, MA
Dowd, Tommy (Thomas Jefferson)	07/02/1933	Calvary Cemetery, Holyoke, MA
Dowie, Joe (Joseph E.)	03/04/1917	St. Vincent de Paul Cemetery, New Orleans, LA
Dowling, Pete (Henry Peter)	06/30/1905	Odd Fellows Cemetery, LaGrande, OR
Downey, Red (Alexander Cummings)	07/10/1949	Woodlawn Cemetery, Detroit, MI
Downey, Tom (Thomas Edward)	08/03/1961	St. Michael's Cemetery, Stratford, CT
Downs, Red (Jerome Willis)	10/19/1939	Neola Township Cemetery, Neola, IA
Dowse, Tom (Thomas Joseph)	12/14/1946	Evergreen Memorial Park, Riverside, CA
Doyle, Carl (William Carl)	09/04/1951	Lynnhurst Cemetery, Knoxville, TN
Doyle, Connie (Cornelius J.)	07/29/1921	Evergreen Cemetery, El Paso, TX
Doyle, Jack (John Joseph)	12/31/1958	St. Jerome Cemetery, Holyoke, MA
Doyle, Jess (Jesse Herbert)	04/15/1961	Walnut Hill Cemetery, Belleville, IL
Doyle, Jim (James Francis)	02/01/1912	St. Agnes Cemetery, Syracuse, NY
Doyle, Joe (Judd Bruce)	11/21/1947	Evergreen Cemetery, Tannersville, NY
Doyle, John Aloysius	12/24/1915	St. Francis Cemetery, Pawtucket, RI
Doyle, Larry (Lawrence Joseph)	03/01/1974	St. Bernard's Cemetery, Saranac Lake, NY

Name	DOD	Cemetery, City, State
Drake, Delos Daniel	10/03/1965	St. Michael's Church Cemetery, Findlay, OH
Drake, Larry Francis	07/14/1985	Memorial Park Cemetery, Tyler, TX
Drake, Logan Gaffney	06/01/1940	Elmwood Cemetery, Columbia, SC
Drake, Lyman Daniel	02/06/1932	Maple Hill Cemetery, Plainfield, IN
Drake, Tom (Thomas Kendall)	07/02/1988	Marvin's Chapel Cemetery, Pinson, AL
Drescher, Bill (William Clayton)	05/15/1968	St. Peter's Cemetery, Haverstraw, NY
Dressen, Chuck (Charles Walter)	08/10/1966	Forest Lawn Memorial Park, Glendale, CA
Dressen, Lee August	06/30/1931	Prairie Home Cemetery, Diller, NE
Dresser, Bob (Robert Nicholson)	07/27/1924	Mount Wollaston Cemetery, Quincy, MA
Drews, Frank John	04/22/1972	St. Stanislaus Cemetery, Cheektowaga, NY
Drews, Karl August	08/15/1963	Hollywood Memorial Park, Hollywood, FL
Drill, Lew (Lewis L.)	07/04/1969	Sunset Memorial Park, Minneapolis, MN
Driscoll, Dennis F.	02/21/1901	Mount St. Mary's Cemetery, Pawtucket, RI
Driscoll, Denny (John F.)	07/11/1886	St. Patrick's Cemetery, Lowell, MA
Driscoll, Mike (Michael Columbus)	03/22/1953	Immaculate Conception Cemetery, Easton, MA
Driscoll, Paddy (John Leo)	06/28/1968	All Saints Cemetery, Des Plaines, IL
Drissel, Mike (Michael F.)	02/26/1913	SS. Peter & Paul Cemetery, St. Louis, MO
Drohan, Tom (Thomas F.)	09/17/1926	Pleasant View Cemetery, Kewanee, IL
Drott, Dick (Richard Fred)	08/16/1985	Queen of Heaven Cemetery, Hillside, IL
Drucke, Louis Frank	09/22/1955	Holy Cross Cemetery, Waco, TX
Druhot, Carl A.	02/11/1918	Lincoln Memorial Park (formerly Mount Scott Park Cemetery), Portland, OR
Drysdale, Don (Donald Scott)	07/03/1993	Cremated, Forest Lawn Memorial Park, Glendale, CA. Ashes given to family
Dubiel, Monk (Walter John)	10/23/1969	Rose Hill Memorial Park, Rocky Hill, CT
Dubuc, Jean Joseph Octave	08/28/1958	Fort Myers Memorial Gardens, Fort Myers, FL
Dudley, Clise (Elzie Clise)	01/12/1989	Lake City Memorial Park, Lake City, SC
Dudra, John Joseph	10/24/1965	Calvary Cemetery, Pana, IL
Duff, Pat (Patrick Henry)	09/11/1925	St. Ann's Cemetery, Cranston, RI
Duffee, Charlie (Charles Edward)	12/24/1894	Magnolia Cemetery, Mobile, AL
Duffy, Bernie (Bernard Allen)	02/09/1962	Elmwood Memorial Park, Abilene, TX
Duffy, Hugh	10/19/1954	Mount Calvary Cemetery, Roslindale, MA
Dugan, Bill (William H.)	07/24/1921	St. Mary's Cemetery, Kingston, NY
Dugan, Dan (Daniel Phillip)	06/25/1968	Resurrection Cemetery, Piscataway, NJ
Dugan, Jumping Joe (Joseph Anthony)	07/07/1982	St. Joseph's Cemetery, West Roxbury, MA
Dugas, Gus (Augustin Joseph)	04/14/1997	St. Mary's & St. Joseph's Cemetery, Norwich, CT
Dugdale, Dan (Daniel Edward)	03/09/1934	Calvary Catholic Cemetery, Seattle, WA
Dugey, Oscar Joseph	01/01/1966	Oakland Cemetery, Dallas, TX
Duggan, Jim (James Elmer)	12/05/1951	Holy Cross Cemetery, Indianapolis, IN
Duggleby, Bill (William James)	08/30/1944	Redfield Cemetery, Redfield, NY
Dumont, George Henry	10/13/1956	Lakewood Cemetery, Minneapolis, MN
Duncan, Jim (James William)	10/16/1901	Grove Hill Cemetery, Oil City, PA
Duncan, Pat (Louis Baird)	07/17/1960	Fairmount Cemetery, Jackson, OH
Duncan, Taylor McDowell	01/03/2004	Sunset Cemetery, Asheville, NC

Name	DOD	Cemetery, City, State
Duncan, Vern (Vernon Van Duke)	06/01/1954	Hillside Cemetery, Ormond Beach, FL
Dundon, Ed (Edward Joseph)	08/18/1893	Mount Calvary Cemetery, Columbus, OH
Dundon, Gus (Augustus Joseph)	09/01/1940	North Side Catholic Cemetery, Pittsburgh, PA
Dungan, Sam (Samuel Morrison)	03/16/1939	Fairhaven Memorial Park, Santa Ana, CA
Dunham, Llee (Leland Huffield)	05/11/1961	Atlanta Cemetery, Atlanta, IL
Dunham, Wiley (Henry Huston)	01/16/1934	Mound Cemetery, Piketon, OH
Dunkle, Davy (Edward Perks)	11/19/1941	Highland Cemetery, Lock Haven, PA
Dunlap, Bill (William James)	11/29/1980	Charles Evans Cemetery, Reading, PA
Dunlap, Fred (Frederick C.)	12/01/1902	Mount Peace Cemetery (Odd Fellows section), Philadelphia, PA
Dunleavy, Jack (John Francis)	04/11/1944	St. Mary's & St. Joseph's Cemetery, Norwalk, CT
Dunn, Jack (John Joseph)	10/22/1928	St. Mary's Cemetery, Baltimore, MD
Dunn, Joe (Joseph Edward)	03/19/1944	Calvary Cemetery, Springfield, OH
Dunn, Steve (Stephen B.)	05/05/1933	Woodland Cemetery, London, Ontario, Canada
Dupee, Frank Oliver	08/14/1956	Pine Grove Cemetery, Falmouth, ME
Durbin, Kid (Blaine Alphonsus)	09/11/1943	St. Peter's Catholic Cemetery, Kirkwood, MO
Durham, Bull (Louis Staub)	06/28/1960	Pleasant Valley Cemetery, Bentley, KS
Durham, Ed (Edward Fant)	04/27/1976	Hopewell Presbyterian Church Cemetery, Blackstock, SC
Durham, Jimmy (James Garfield)	05/07/1949	Douglass Cemetery, Douglass, KS
Durning, Dick (Richard Knott)	09/23/1948	Zachary Taylor National Cemetery, Louisville, KY
Durocher, Leo Ernest	10/07/1991	Forest Lawn Memorial Park, Hollywood Hills, Los Angeles, CA
Durrett, Red (Elmer Cable)	01/17/1992	Laurel Land Memorial Park, Dallas, TX
Durst, Cedric Montgomery	02/16/1971	El Camino Memorial Park, La Jolla, CA
Duryea, Jesse (James Newton)	08/19/1942	Riverview Cemetery, Algona, IA
Dusak, Erv (Ervin Frank)	11/06/1994	Woodlawn Cemetery, Forest Park, IL
Duzen, Bill (William George)	03/11/1944	White Chapel Memorial Park, Amherst, NY
Dwight, Al (Albert Ward)	02/20/1903	Cremated, San Francisco, CA
Dwyer, Double Joe (Joseph Michael)	10/21/1992	Gate of Heaven Cemetery, East Hanover, NJ
Dwyer, Frank (John Francis)	02/04/1943	St. Patrick's Cemetery, Geneva, NY
Dyer, Ben (Benjamin Franklin)	08/07/1959	Green Ridge Cemetery, Kenosha, WI
Dyer, Eddie (Edwin Hawley)	04/20/1964	Forest Park (Lawndale) Cemetery, Houston, TX
Dygert, Jimmy (James Henry)	02/08/1936	Greenwood Cemetery, New Orleans, LA
Dykes, Jimmy (James Joseph)	06/15/1976	St. Denis Cemetery, Havertown, PA
Dyler, John	08/15/1916	St. Louis Cemetery, Louisville, KY
Eagan, Bill (William)	02/13/1905	Mount Olivet Cemetery, Wheat Ridge, CO
Eagan, Truck (Charles Eugene)	03/19/1949	Greenlawn Memorial Park, Colma, CA
Eagle, Bill (William Lycurgus)	04/27/1951	Rockville Union Cemetery, Rockville, MD
Eakle, Charlie (Charles Emory)	06/15/1959	New Cathedral Cemetery, Baltimore, MD
Earle, Billy (William Moffat)	05/30/1946	Forest Lawn Memorial Park, Omaha, NE
Earley, Arnold Carl	09/29/1999	Sunset Hills Cemetery, Flint, MI

Name	DOD	Cemetery, City, State
Earley, Tom (Thomas Francis Aloysius)	04/05/1988	St. Mary's Cemetery, Nantucket, MA
Early, Jake (Jacob Willard)	05/31/1985	Brevard Memorial Park, Cocoa, FL
Earnshaw, George Livingston	12/01/1976	Memorial Gardens of Hot Springs, Hot Springs, AR
Eason, Mal (Malcolm Wayne)	04/16/1970	Black Oak Cemetery, Elgin, AZ
East, Carl (Carlton William)	01/15/1953	Mt. Pleasant Cemetery, Carrollton, GA
East, Hugh (Gordon Hugh)	11/02/1981	Valhalla Cemetery, Birmingham, AL
Easter, Luke (Luscious Luke)	03/29/1979	Highland Park Cemetery, Cleveland, OH
Easterday, Henry P.	03/30/1895	Fernwood Cemetery, Lansdowne, PA
Easterling, Paul	03/15/1993	Reidsville City Cemetery, Reidsville, GA
Easterly, Ted (Theodore Harrison)	07/06/1951	Lower Lake Cemetery, Lower Lake, CA
Easterwood, Roy Charles	08/24/1984	Pioneer Cemetery, Graham, TX
Easton, John David	07/28/2001	Cremated, Ewing Crematory, Ewing, NJ
Easton, John S.	11/28/1903	Tiltonsville-Indian Mound Cemetery, Tiltonsville, OH
Eaves, Vallie Ennis	04/19/1960	Woodland Cemetery, Cleveland, OK
Eayrs, Eddie (Edwin)	11/30/1969	Swan Point Cemetery, Providence, RI
Ebright, Hi (Hiram C.)	10/24/1916	Evergreen Cemetery, Milwaukee, WI
Eccles, Harry Josiah	06/02/1955	Riverside Cemetery, Kennedy, NY
Echols, Johnny (John Gresham)	11/13/1972	Greenwood Cemetery, Atlanta, GA
Eckert, Al (Albert George)	04/20/1974	Good Hope Cemetery, Milwaukee, WI
Eckert, Charlie (Charles William)	08/22/1986	Forest Hills Cemetery, Huntingdon Valley, PA
Eckhardt, Ox (Oscar George)	04/22/1951	Oakwood Cemetery, Austin, TX
Edelen, Ed (Edward Joseph)	02/01/1982	St. Ignatius Cemetery, Port Tobacco, MD
Eden, Charlie (Charles M.)	09/17/1920	Cremated, Cincinnati, OH
Edington, Stump (Jacob Frank)	11/11/1969	Prairie Chapel Cemetery, Lyons, IN
Edmondson, George Henderson	07/11/1973	Restland Cemetery, Waco, TX
Edmondson, Paul Michael	02/13/1970	Valley Oaks Memorial Park, Westlake Village, CA
Edmundson, Bob (Robert E.)	08/14/1931	Oak Hill Cemetery, Lawrence, KS
Edwards, Bruce (Charles Bruce)	04/25/1975	Masonic Lawn Cemetery, Sacramento, CA
Edwards, Foster Hamilton	01/04/1980	Cremated, Orleans, MA
Edwards, Hank (Henry Albert)	06/22/1988	Fairhaven Memorial Park, Santa Ana, CA
Edwards, Jim Joe (James Corbette)	01/19/1965	Pontotoc Cemetery, Pontotoc, MS
Edwards, Sherman Stanley	03/08/1992	Woodlawn Cemetery, El Dorado, AR
Egan, Ben (Arthur Augustus)	02/18/1968	St. Helen's Church Cemetery, Sherrill, NY
Egan, Dick (Richard Joseph)	07/07/1947	St. Helena Cemetery, St. Helena, CA
Egan, Rip (John Joseph)	12/22/1950	St. Ann's Cemetery, Cranston, RI
Egan, Wish (Aloysius Jerome)	04/13/1951	Woodmere Cemetery, Detroit, MI
Eggert, Moose (Elmer Albert)	04/09/1971	Mount Hope Cemetery, Rochester, NY
Eggler, Dave (David Daniel)	04/05/1902	Holy Cross Cemetery, Lackawanna, NY
Ehmke, Howard Jonathan	03/17/1959	Cremated, Philadelphia, PA. Ashes scattered at Valley Forge, PA
Ehret, Red (Philip Sydney)	07/28/1940	Baltimore Pike Cemetery, Cincinnati, OH
Ehrhardt, Rube (Welton Claude)	04/27/1980	Trinity Lutheran Cemetery, Crete, IL
Eibel, Hack (Henry Hack)	10/16/1945	Westview Cemetery, Atlanta, GA
Eichrodt, Fred (Frederick George)	07/14/1965	Memorial Park Cemetery, Indianapolis, IN

Name	DOD	Cemetery, City, State
Eisenhart, Hank (Jacob Henry)	12/20/1987	Mount Union Cemetery, Huntingdon, PA
Eisenstat, Harry	03/21/2003	Mount Olive Cemetery, Cleveland, OH
Eiteljorge, Ed (Edward Henry)	12/05/1942	Forest Hill Cemetery, Greencastle, IN
Elberfeld, Kid (Norman Arthur)	01/13/1944	Chattanooga Memorial Park, Chattanooga, TN
Elder, Heinie (Henry Knox)	11/13/1958	Los Angeles National Cemetery, Los Angeles, CA
Elko, Pete (Peter)	09/17/1993	SS. Peter & Paul Ukrainian Catholic Church Cemetery, Plymouth, PA
Ellam, Roy	10/28/1948	Riverside Cemetery, West Norristown, PA
Eller, Hod (Horace Owen)	07/18/1961	Crown Hill Cemetery, Indianapolis, IN
Ellerbe, Frank (Francis Rogers)	07/08/1988	Haselden Family Cemetery, Sellars, SC
Ellick, Joe (Joseph J.)	04/21/1923	Mount Calvary Cemetery, Kansas City, KS
Elliott, Allen Clifford	05/06/1979	Laurel Hill Memorial Gardens, Pagedale, MO
Elliott, Bob (Robert Irving)	05/04/1966	Greenwood Memorial Park, San Diego, CA
Elliott, Carter Ward	05/21/1959	Welwood Murray Cemetery, Palm Springs, CA
Elliott, Claud Judson	06/21/1923	Pardeeville Cemetery, Pardeeville, WI
Elliott, Gene (Eugene Birminghouse)	01/05/1976	Riverview Cemetery, Huntingdon, PA
Elliott, Glenn (Herbert Glenn)	07/27/1969	Odd Fellows Cemetery, Myrtle Creek, OR
Elliott, Hal (Harold William)	04/25/1963	National Memorial Cemetery of the Pacific, Honolulu, HI
Elliott, Jumbo (James Thomas)	01/07/1970	Rose Lawn Cemetery, Terre Haute, IN
Elliott, Rowdy (Harold Bell)	02/12/1934	San Francisco National Cemetery, San Francisco, CA
Ellis, Rube (George William)	03/13/1938	Rose Hills Memorial Park, Whittier, CA
Ellison, Babe (Herbert Spencer)	08/11/1955	Golden Gate National Cemetery, San Bruno, CA
Ellison, George Russell	01/20/1978	Cremated, San Francisco, CA
Elmore, Verdo Wilson	08/05/1969	Gordo Cemetery, Gordo, AL
Elston, Donald Ray	01/02/1995	Cremated, Chicago, IL
Ely, Bones (William Frederick)	01/10/1952	Cremated, Berkeley, CA
Embrey, Slim (Charles Akin)	10/10/1947	Mount Olivet Cemetery, Nashville, TN
Emerson, Chester Arthur	07/02/1971	Hope Cemetery, Kennebunk, ME
Emig, Charlie (Charles Henry)	10/02/1975	Memorial Park Cemetery, Oklahoma City, OK
Emmerich, Bob (Robert George)	11/22/1948	Lakeview Cemetery, Bridgeport, CT
Emslie, Bob (Robert Daniel)	04/26/1943	St. Thomas West Avenue Cemetery, St. Thomas, Ontario, Canada
Engel, Joe (Joseph William)	06/12/1969	Forest Hills Cemetery, Chattanooga, TN
Engle, Charlie August	10/12/1983	Sunset Memorial Park, San Antonio, TX
Engle, Clyde (Arthur Clyde)	12/26/1939	Woodland Cemetery, Dayton, OH
English, Charlie (Charles Dewie)	06/25/1999	Cremated, Pasadena, CA
English, Gil (Gilbert Raymond)	08/31/1996	Mount Vernon United Methodist Church Cemetery, Trinity, NC
English, Woody (Elwood George)	09/26/1997	Fredonia Cemetery, Fredonia, OH
Ennis, Del (Delmer)	02/08/1996	Hillside Cemetery, Roslyn, PA
Ennis, Russ (Russell Elwood)	01/21/1949	Calvary Cemetery, Superior, WI

Name	DOD	Cemetery, City, State
Enright, Jack (Jackson Percy)	08/17/1975	Forest Lawn Central Cemetery, Fort Lauderdale, FL
Ens, Jewel Winklemeyer	01/17/1950	Memorial Park Cemetery, St. Louis, MO
Ens, Mutz (Anton)	06/28/1950	Memorial Park Cemetery, St. Louis, MO
Enwright, Charlie (Charles Massey)	01/19/1917	St. Joseph's Cemetery, Sacramento, CA
Epps, Aubrey Lee	11/13/1984	Concord Cemetery, Ackerman, MS
Erautt, Joe (Joseph Michael)	10/06/1976	Willamette National Cemetery, Portland, OR
Erickson, Eric George Adolph	05/19/1965	Sunset Hill Cemetery, Lakewood, NY
Erickson, Hank (Henry Nels)	12/13/1964	Glen Oak Cemetery, Hillside, IL
Erickson, Paul Walford	04/05/2002	Shrine of Rest Mausoleum, Fond du Lac, WI
Erickson, Ralph Lief	06/27/2002	Valley of the Sun Cemetery, Chandler, AZ
Errickson, Dick (Richard Merriwell)	11/28/1999	Cremated, Vineland, NJ
Erwin, Tex (Ross Emil)	04/05/1953	Holy Sepulchre Cemetery, Rochester, NY
Esmond, Jimmy (James J.)	06/26/1948	St. Agnes Cemetery, Albany, NY
Esper, Duke (Charles H.)	08/31/1910	Northwood Cemetery, Philadelphia, PA
Essick, Bill (William Earl)	10/12/1951	Inglewood Park Cemetery, Inglewood, CA
Estalella, Bobby (Roberto)	01/06/1991	Vista Memorial Gardens, Hialeah, FL
Esterbrook, Dude (Thomas John)	04/30/1901	Green-Wood Cemetery, Brooklyn, NY
Etchison, Buck (Clarence Hampton)	01/24/1980	St. Louis Cemetery, Clarksville, MD
Etten, Nick (Nicholas Raymond Thomas)	10/18/1990	Queen of Heaven Cemetery, Hillside, IL
Eubank, John Franklin	11/03/1958	Riverside Cemetery, Bellevue, MI
Eubanks, Uel Melvin	11/21/1954	Laurel Land Memorial Park, Dallas, TX
Eunick, Ferd (Fernandes Bowen)	12/09/1959	New Cathedral Cemetery, Baltimore, MD
Eustace, Frank John	10/16/1932	Charles Baber Cemetery, Pottsville, PA (aka Mount Laurel Cemetery)
Evans, Al (Alfred Hubert)	04/06/1979	Kenly Cemetery, Kenly, NC
Evans, Art (William Arthur)	01/08/1952	Sterling Community Cemetery, Sterling, KS
Evans, Bill (William James)	12/21/1946	Pine Hill Cemetery, Burlington, NC
Evans, Bill (William Lawrence)	11/30/1983	Orchard Mesa Municipal Cemetery, Orchard Mesa, CO
Evans, Chick (Charles Franklin)	09/02/1916	Vale Cemetery, Schenectady, NY
Evans, Jack (Uriah L. P.)	01/16/1907	Baltimore Cemetery, Baltimore, MD
Evans, Red (Russell Edison)	06/14/1982	Kirby's Tucker Memorial Cemetery, Mountain Home, AR
Evans, Steve (Louis Richard)	12/28/1943	Calvary Cemetery, Cleveland, OH
Everitt, Bill (William Lee)	01/19/1938	Crown Hill Cemetery, Wheat Ridge, CO
Evers, Hoot (Walter Arthur)	01/25/1991	Memorial Oaks Cemetery, Houston, TX
Evers, Joe (Joseph Francis)	01/04/1949	St. Agnes Cemetery, Albany, NY
Evers, Johnny (John Joseph)	03/28/1947	St. Mary's Cemetery, Troy, NY
Evers, Tom (Thomas Francis)	03/23/1925	Oak Hill Cemetery, Washington, DC
Ewell, George W.	10/20/1910	Mt. Moriah Cemetery, Philadelphia, PA
Ewing, Bob (George Lemuel)	06/20/1947	Walnut Hill Cemetery, New Hampshire, OH
Ewing, Buck (William)	10/20/1906	Mount Washington Cemetery, Cincinnati, OH
Ewing, John	04/23/1895	Mount Washington Cemetery, Cincinnati, OH
Ewing, Reuben (born Cohen)	10/05/1970	Emanuel Synagogue Cemetery, Wethersfield, CT

Name	DOD	Cemetery, City, State
Ewoldt, Art (Arthur Lee)	12/08/1977	Glendale Cemetery, Des Moines, IA
Ezzell, Homer Estell	08/03/1976	Mission Burial Park North, San Antonio, TX
Faber, Red (Urban Clarence)	09/25/1976	Acacia Park Cemetery, River Forest, IL
Fabrique, Bunny (Albert LaVerne)	01/10/1960	Riverside Cemetery, Clinton, MI
Faeth, Tony (Anthony Joseph)	12/22/1982	Calvary Cemetery, St. Paul, MN
Fagan, Bill (William A.)	03/21/1930	St. Agnes Cemetery, Albany, NY
Fagan, Everett Joseph	02/16/1983	Cremated, Morristown, NJ
Fahey, Frank (Francis Raymond)	03/19/1954	St. Mary's Cemetery, Uxbridge, MA
Fahey, Howard Simpson	10/24/1971	Oak Grove Cemetery, Medford, MA
Fahrer, Pete (Clarence Willie)	06/10/1967	Big Prairie-Everitt Cemetery, White Cloud, MI
Fain, Ferris Roy	10/18/2001	Georgetown Pioneer Cemetery, Georgetown, CA
Fairbank, Jim (James Lee)	12/27/1955	New Forest Cemetery, Utica, NY
Faircloth, Rags (James Lamar)	10/05/1953	Evergreen Cemetery, Tucson, AZ
Falch, Anton C.	03/31/1936	Union Cemetery, Milwaukee, MI
Falk, Bibb August	06/08/1989	Austin Memorial Park, Austin, TX
Falk, Chet (Chester Emanuel)	01/07/1982	Austin Memorial Park, Austin, TX
Falkenberg, Cy (Frederick Peter)	04/15/1961	Holy Cross Cemetery, Colma, CA
Fallenstein, Ed (Edward Joseph) (buried under birth name: Fallenstin)	11/24/1971	Hollywood Memorial Park, Union, NJ
Fallon, George Decatur	10/25/1994	Palm Beach Memorial Park, Lantana, FL
Falsey, Pete (Peter James)	05/23/1976	St. Bernard's Cemetery, West Haven, CT
Fannin, Cliff (Clifford Bryson)	12/11/1966	Toledo Memorial Park, Sylvania, OH
Fanning, Jack (John Jacob)	06/10/1917	Fern Hill Cemetery, Aberdeen, WA
Fanwell, Harry Clayton	07/15/1965	Woodlawn Cemetery, Baltimore, MD
Farmer, Alex (Alexander Johnson)	02/05/1920	Woodlawn Cemetery, Bronx, NY
Farrar, Sid (Sidney Douglas)	05/07/1935	Ferncliff Cemetery, Hartsdale, NY. Cremated.
Farrell, Dick (Richard Joseph)	06/10/1977	Forest Park (Westheimer) Cemetery, Houston, TX
Farrell, Doc (Edward Stephen)	12/20/1966	Calvary-St. Patrick Cemetery, Johnson City, NY
Farrell, Duke (Charles Andrew)	02/15/1925	Immaculate Conception Cemetery, Marlborough, MA
Farrell, Jack (John A.)	02/09/1914	Cemetery of the Holy Sepulchre, East Orange, NJ
Farrell, Jack (John J.)	12/02/1918	Mount Olivet Cemetery, Chicago, IL
Farrell, Jack (John)	11/15/1916	Mt. St. Benedict's Cemetery, Bloomfield, CT
Farrell, Joe (Joseph F.)	04/17/1893	Holy Cross Cemetery, Brooklyn, NY
Farrell, John Sebastian	05/14/1921	Forest Hill Cemetery, Kansas City, MO
Farrell, Kerby (Major Kerby)	12/17/1975	Woodlawn Memorial Park, Nashville, TN
Farrow, Jack (John Jacob)	12/31/1914	Cemetery of the Holy Sepulchre, East Orange, NJ
Fass, Frederick Peter	07/05/1930	Mountain View Cemetery, Pueblo, CO
Faulkner, Jim (James Leroy)	06/01/1962	Pinecrest Cemetery, Lake Worth, FL
Fausett, Buck (Robert Shaw)	05/02/1994	Restlawn Memorial Park, Sulphur Springs, TX

Name	DOD	Cemetery, City, State
Faust, Victory (Charles Victor)	06/18/1915	Western Washington State Hospital Memorial Cemetery, Tacoma, WA
Fautsch, Joe (Joseph Roamon)	03/16/1971	St. Mary's Cemetery, Minneapolis, MN
Fauver, Clay (Clayton King)	03/03/1942	Westwood Cemetery, Oberlein, OH
Fear, Vern (Luvern Carl)	09/06/1976	Lakeland Memorial Gardens, Spirit Lake, IA
Fee, Jack (John)	03/03/1913	St. Rose of Lima Cemetery, Carbondale, PA
Felderman, Marv (Marvin Wilfred)	08/06/2000	Riverside National Cemetery, Riverside, CA
Feldman, Harry	03/16/1962	Roselawn Cemetery, Fort Smith, AR
Felix, Gus (August Guenther)	05/12/1960	Greenwood Cemetery, Montgomery, AL
Felsch, Happy (Oscar Emil)	08/17/1964	Wisconsin Memorial Park, Brookfield, WI
Fennelly, Frank (Francis John)	08/04/1920	St. Patrick's Cemetery, Fall River, MA
Fenner, Hod (Horace Alfred)	11/20/1954	Riverside Cemetery, Kalamazoo, MI
Ferens, Stan (Stanley)	10/07/1994	St. Clair Cemetery, Greensburg, PA. Cremated.
Ferguson, Alex (James Alexander)	04/26/1976	Conejo Mountain Memorial Park, Camarillo, CA
Ferguson, Bob (Robert Vavasour)	05/03/1894	Evergreen Cemetery, Brooklyn, NY
Ferguson, Charlie (Charles J.)	04/29/1888	Maplewood Cemetery, Charlottesville, VA
Ferguson, George Cecil	09/05/1943	Woodlawn Park Cemetery North, Miami, FL
Fernandes, Ed (Edward Paul)	11/27/1968	Holy Sepulchre Cemetery, Hayward, CA
Fernandez, Nanny (Froilan)	09/19/1996	Green Hills Memorial Park, Rancho Palos Verdes, CA
Ferrazzi, Bill (William Joseph)	08/10/1993	Forest Meadows Memorial Park Central, Gainesville, FL
Ferrell, Rick (Richard Benjamin)	07/27/1995	New Garden FriendsCemetery, Greensboro, NC
Ferrell, Wes (Wesley Cheek)	12/09/1976	New Garden FriendsCemetery, Greensboro, NC
Ferrick, Tom (Thomas Jerome)	10/15/1996	SS. Peter & Paul Cemetery, Springfield, PA
Ferry, Cy (Alfred Joseph)	09/27/1938	St. Joseph's Cemetery, Pittsfield, MA
Ferry, Jack (John Francis)	08/29/1954	St. Joseph's Cemetery, Pittsfield, MA
Fessenden, Wally (Wallace Clifton) manager	05/15/1935	Green-Wood Cemetery, Brooklyn, NY
Fette, Lou (Louis Henry William)	01/03/1981	Sunset Hills Cemetery, Warrensburg, MO
Fetzer, Willy (William McKinnon)	05/03/1959	Oakwood Cemetery, Concord, NC
Fewster, Chick (Wilson Lloyd)	04/16/1945	St. John's Cemetery, Baltimore, MD
Fieber, Clarence Thomas	08/20/1985	Cremated, Redwood City, CA
Field, Jim (James C.)	05/13/1953	Holy Cross Cemetery, Yeadon, PA
Field, Sam (Samuel Jay)	10/28/1904	Aulenbach Cemetery, Mt. Penn, PA
Fields, George W.	09/22/1933	Riverside Cemetery, Waterbury, CT
Fields, Jocko (John Joseph)	10/14/1950	Holy Name Cemetery, Jersey City, NJ
Fiene, Lou (Louis Henry)	12/22/1964	Calvary Cemetery, Evanston, IL
Figgemeier, Frank Y.	04/15/1915	Calvary Cemetery, St. Louis, MO
Files, Eddie (Charles Edward)	05/10/1954	Riverside Cemetery, Cornish, ME
Filipowicz, Steve (Stephen Charles)	02/21/1975	St. Casimar's Church Cemetery, Kulpmont, PA
Filley, Marc (Marcus Lucius)	01/20/1995	Oakwood Cemetery, Troy, NY
Fillingim, Dana	02/03/1961	Tuskegee Cemetery, Tuskegee, AL

Name	DOD	Cemetery, City, State
Fincher, Bill (William Allen)	05/07/1946	Greenwood Cemetery, Shreveport, LA
Finigan, Jim (James Leroy)	05/16/1981	St. Peter's Cemetery, Quincy, IL
Fink, Herman Adam	08/24/1980	Carolina Memorial Park, Kannapolis, NC
Finlayson, Pembroke	03/06/1912	Green-Wood Cemetery, Brooklyn, NY
Finley, Bill (William James)	10/06/1912	Calvary Cemetery, Woodside, Queens, NY
Finley, Bobby (Robert Edward)	01/02/1986	Grove Hill Memorial Park, Dallas, TX
Finn, Neal (Cornelius Francis)	07/07/1933	Calvary Cemetery, Woodside, Queens, NY
Finneran, Happy (Joseph Ignatius)	02/03/1942	Gate of Heaven Cemetery, East Hanover, NJ
Finney, Hal (Harold Wilson)	12/20/1991	Chapel Hill Cemetery, Lafayette, AL
Finney, Lou (Louis Klopsche)	04/22/1966	Chapel Hill Cemetery, Lafayette, AL
Firth, Ted (John E.)	06/23/1902	Tewksbury Hospital Cemetery, Tewksbury, MA
Fischer, Carl (Charles William)	12/10/1963	Mount Ridge Cemetery, Royalton Center, NY
Fishburn, Sam (Samuel E.)	04/11/1965	Cedar Hill Memorial Park, Allentown, PA
Fishel, Leo	05/19/1960	Babylon Cemetery, Babylon, NY
Fisher, Bob (Robert Taylor)	08/04/1963	Evergreen Cemetery, Jacksonville, FL
Fisher, Charles G.	02/18/1917	Eagle Cemetery (formerly Fort Egbert Cemetery), Eagle, AK
Fisher, Cherokee (William Charles)	09/26/1912	Mount Carmel Cemetery, Hillside, IL
Fisher, Clarence Henry	11/02/1965	Suncrest Cemetery, Point Pleasant, WV
Fisher, Don (Donald Raymond)	07/29/1973	Whitehaven Park, Mayfield Village, OH
Fisher, Ed (Edward Fredrick)	07/24/1951	Glenwood Cemetery, Wayne,MI
Fisher, Gus (August Harris)	04/08/1972	River View Cemetery, Portland, OR
Fisher, Newt (Newton)	02/28/1947	Holy Sepulchre Cemetery, Worth, IL
Fisher, Ray Lyle	11/03/1982	Washtenong Memorial Park, Ann Arbor, MI
Fisher, Red (John Gus)	01/31/1940	Walnut Ridge Cemetery, Jeffersonville, IN
Fisher, Showboat (George Aloys)	05/15/1994	St. Benedict's Catholic Cemetery, Avon, MN
Fisher, Tom (Thomas Chalmers)	09/03/1972	East Maplewood Cemetery, Anderson,IN
Fisher, Wilbur McCullough	10/24/1960	Spring Hill Cemetery, Huntington, WV
Fiske, Max (Maximilian Patrick)	05/25/1928	Holy Sepulchre Cemetery, Worth, IL
Fittery, Paul Clarence	01/28/1974	White Cemetery, White, GA
Fitzberger, Charlie (Charles Caspar)	01/25/1965	Oak Lawn Cemetery, Baltimore, MD
Fitzgerald, Dennis S.	10/16/1936	Mount St. Peter's Cemetery, Derby, CT
Fitzgerald, Howard Chumney	02/27/1959	Masonic Cemetery, Eagle Lake, TX
Fitzgerald, John H.	03/31/1921	New Calvary Cemetery, Mattapan, MA
Fitzgerald, Justin Howard	01/17/1945	St. John's Cemetery, San Mateo, CA
Fitzgerald, Matty (Matthew William)	09/22/1949	St. Agnes Cemetery, Albany, NY
Fitzgerald, Ray (Raymond Francis)	09/06/1977	St. Mary's Cemetery, Westfield, MA
Fitzke, Paul (Robert Paul)	06/30/1950	Morris Hill Cemetery, Boise, ID
Fitzpatrick, Ed (Edward Henry)	10/23/1965	Fairmount Cemetery, Phillipsburg, NJ
Fitzsimmons, Freddie (Frederick Landis)	11/18/1979	Montecito Memorial Park, Colton, CA
Fitzsimmons, Tom (Thomas William)	12/20/1971	St. Mary's Cemetery, Oakland, CA
Flack, Max John	07/31/1975	Walnut Hill Cemetery, Belleville, IL
Flager, Wally (Walter Leonard)	12/16/1990	Restlawn Memory Gardens, Salem, OR
Flagstead, Ira James	03/13/1940	Masonic Memorial Park, Olympia, WA
Flaherty, Martin John	06/10/1920	St. Ann's Cemetery, Cranston, RI

Name	DOD	Cemetery, City, State
Flaherty, Pat (Patrick Henry)	01/28/1946	Calvary Cemetery, Evanston, IL
Flair, Al (Albert Dell)	07/25/1988	Metairie Cemetery, Metairie, LA
Flanagan, Charlie (Charles James)	01/08/1930	San Francisco National Cemetery, San Francisco, CA
Flanagan, Ed (Edward J.)	11/10/1926	St. Patrick's Cemetery, Lowell, MA
Flanagan, Steamer (James Paul)	04/21/1947	St. Mary's Cemetery, Wilkes-Barre, PA
Flanigan, Ray (Raymond Arthur)	03/28/1993	Moreland Memorial Park, Parkville, MD
Flaskamper, Ray (Raymond Harold)	02/03/1978	Sunset Memorial Park, San Antonio, TX
Flater, Jack (John William)	03/20/1970	Pleasant Grove Cemetery, Finksburg, MD
Fleet, Frank H.	06/13/1900	Linden Hill Cemetery, Flushing, NY
Fleming, Les (Leslie Harvey)	03/05/1980	Forest Lawn Memorial Park, Beaumont, TX
Fleming, Tom (Thomas Vincent)	12/26/1957	Lakeview Cemetery, Upton, MA
Fletcher, Art (Arthur)	02/06/1950	Glenwood Cemetery, Collinsville, IL
Fletcher, Elbie (Elburt Preston)	03/09/1994	Milton Cemetery, Milton, MA
Fletcher, Frank (Oliver Frank)	10/07/1974	Royal Palm Cemetery, St. Petersburg, FL
Fletcher, George Horace Elliot	06/18/1879	Green-Wood Cemetery, Brooklyn, NY
Flick, Elmer Harrison	01/09/1971	Crown Hill Memorial Park, Twinsburg, OH
Flick, Lew (Lewis Miller)	12/07/1990	Oak Hill Cemetery, Kingsport, TN
Flinn, Don Raphael	03/09/1959	Hucksby Cemetery, Stephenville, TX
Flint, Silver (Frank Sylvester)	01/14/1892	Bethany Cemetery, St. Louis, MO
Flitcraft, Hilly (Hildreth Milton)	04/02/2003	Sacred Heart of Mary Catholic Cemetery, Boulder, CO
Flohr, Mort (Moritz Herman)	06/02/1994	Woodlawn Cemetery, Canisteo, NY
Flood, Curt (Curtis Charles)	01/20/1997	Inglewood Park Cemetery, Inglewood, CA
Flood, Tim (Timothy A.)	06/15/1929	Calvary Cemetery, St. Louis, MO
Florence, Paul Robert	05/28/1986	Orange Hill Cemetery, Williston, FL
Flores, Jesse Sandoval	12/17/1991	Queen of Heaven Cemetery, Rowland Heights, CA
Flowers, Dicky (Charles Richard)	10/05/1892	Laurel Hill Cemetery, Philadelphia, PA
Flowers, Jake (D'Arcy Raymond)	12/27/1962	Cambridge Cemetery, Cambridge, MD
Flowers, Wes (Charles Wesley)	12/31/1988	Cogbill Cemetery, Wynne, AR
Fluhrer, John Lister	07/17/1946	St. Joseph's Cemetery, Lockbourne, OH
Flynn, Carney (Cornelius Francis Xavier)	02/10/1947	St. Joseph's New Cemetery, Cincinnati, OH
Flynn, Edward J.	08/28/1929	Graceland Cemetery, Chicago, IL
Flynn, Jocko (John A.)	12/31/1907	St. Mary's Immaculate Conception Cemetery, Lawrence, MA
Flynn, Joe (Joseph Nicholas)	12/22/1933	St. Francis Cemetery, Pawtucket, RI
Flynn, John Anthony	03/23/1935	St. Francis Cemetery, Pawtucket, RI
Flynn, Mike (Michael J.)	06/16/1941	Forest Lawn Memorial Park, Glendale, CA
Flythe, Stuart McGuire	10/18/1963	Cedar Grove Cemetery, New Bern, NC
Fogarty, John J.	03/28/1918	Holy Cross Cemetery, Colma, CA
Fogel, Horace S. *manager*	11/15/1928	Mount Peace Cemetery, Philadelphia, PA
Fohl, Lee (Leo Alexander)	10/30/1965	Calvary Cemetery, Cleveland, OH
Foley, Curry (Charles Joseph)	10/20/1898	Mount Calvary Cemetery, Roslindale, MA
Foley, Ray (Raymond Kirwin)	03/22/1980	St. James Cemetery, Naugatuck, CT
Foley, Will (William Brown)	11/12/1916	Graceland Cemetery, Chicago, IL
Fondy, Dee Virgil	08/19/1999	Montecito Memorial Park, Colton, CA

Name	DOD	Cemetery, City, State
Fonseca, Lew (Lewis Albert)	11/26/1989	All Saints Cemetery, Des Plaines, IL
Force, Davy (David W.)	06/21/1918	Brookside Cemetery, Englewood, NJ
Ford, Gene (Eugene Matthew)	09/07/1970	Corpus Christi Cemetery, Fort Dodge, IA
Ford, Gene (Eugene Wyman)	08/23/1973	Sylvan Abbey Memorial Park, Clearwater, FL
Ford, Hod (Horace Hills)	01/29/1977	Wildwood Cemetery, Winchester, MA
Ford, Russ (Russell William)	01/24/1960	Leak Family Cemetery, Rockingham, NC
Ford, Tom (Thomas Walter)	05/27/1917	Forest Hills Cemetery, Chattanooga, TN
Ford, William B.	04/06/1994	Mount Vernon Cemetery, Mckeesport, PA
Foreman, Brownie (John Davis)	10/10/1926	Druid Ridge Cemetery, Pikesville, MD
Foreman, Frank (Francis Isaiah)	11/19/1957	St. Mary's Cemetery, Baltimore, MD
Foreman, Happy (August G.)	02/13/1953	Beth David Cemetery, Elmont, NY
Forman, Bill (William Orange)	10/02/1958	Lafayette Memorial Park, Brier Hill, PA
Forster, Tom (Thomas W.)	07/17/1946	Mount Hope Cemetery, Hastings-on-Hudson, NY
Forsyth, Ed (Edward James)	06/22/1956	Holy Name Cemetery, Jersey City, NJ
Fortune, Gary (Garrett Reese)	09/23/1955	Kenly Cemetery, Kenly, NC
Foss, George Dueward	11/10/1969	Limona Cemetery, Brandon, FL
Foster, Eddie (Edward Cunningham)	01/15/1937	Columbia Gardens Cemetery, Arlington, VA
Foster, Elmer Ellsworth	07/22/1946	Lakewood Cemetery, Minneapolis, MN
Foster, Pop (Clarence Francis)	04/16/1944	Princeton Cemetery, Princeton, NJ
Foster, Reddy (Oscar E.)	12/19/1908	Oakwood Cemetery, Richmond, VA
Foster, Rube (George)	03/01/1976	Milton Cemetery, Hot Springs, OK
Foster, Slim (Edward Lee)	03/01/1929	Oakwood Cemetery, Montgomery, AL
Fothergill, Bob (Robert Roy)	03/20/1938	Massillon Cemetery, Massillon, OH
Fournier, Jack (John Frank)	09/05/1973	Fern Hill Cemetery, Aberdeen, WA
Fouser, Bill (William C.)	03/01/1919	Lawnview Cemetery, Rockledge, PA. Originally intered at Monument Cemetery. Cemetery removed in 1956.
Foutz, Dave (David Luther)	03/05/1897	Loudon Park Cemetery, Baltimore, MD
Foutz, Frank Hayes	12/25/1961	Woodlawn Cemetery, Lima, OH
Fowler, Boob (Joseph Chester)	10/08/1988	Restland Memorial Park, Dallas, TX
Fowler, Dick (Richard John)	05/22/1972	Plains Cemetery, Oneonta, NY
Fowler, Jesse Peter	09/23/1973	Zion Hill Baptist Church Cemetery, Spartanburg, SC
Fox, Bill (William Henry)	05/07/1946	St. Mary's Cemetery, Minneapolis, MN
Fox, Charlie (Charles Francis)	02/16/2004	Holy Cross Cemetery, Colma, CA
Fox, Henry	06/06/1927	Forest Hill Cemetery, Scranton, PA
Fox, Howie (Howard Francis)	10/09/1955	Laurel Hill Cemetery, Springfield, OR
Fox, Jack (John Paul)	06/28/1963	Aulenbach Cemetery, Mt. Penn, PA
Fox, John Joseph	04/18/1893	Mount Benedict Cemetery, West Roxbury, MA
Fox, Nellie (Jacob Nelson)	12/01/1975	St. Thomas Cemetery, St. Thomas, PA
Fox, Pete (Ervin)	07/05/1966	Woodlawn Cemetery, Detroit, MI
Foxen, Bill (William Aloysius)	04/17/1937	Mount Carmel Cemetery, Tenafly, NJ
Foxx, Jimmie (James Emory)	07/21/1967	Flagler Memorial Park, Miami, FL
France, Ossie (Osman Beverly)	05/02/1947	Greensburg Cemetery, North Canton, OH
Francis, Earl Coleman	07/03/2002	Homewood Cemetery, Pittsburgh, PA

Name	DOD	Cemetery, City, State
Francis, Ray James	07/06/1934	Greenwood Cemetery, Atlanta, GA
Frank, Charlie (Charles)	05/24/1922	Forest Hill Cemetery-Midtown, Memphis, TN
Frank, Fred (Frederick)	03/27/1950	Catlettsburg Cemetery, Catlettsburg, KY
Frankhouse, Fred (Frederick Meloy)	08/17/1989	New Church Hill Cemetery, Port Royal, PA
Franklin, Jack Wilford	11/15/1991	Garden of Memories, Panama City, FL
Franklin, Moe (Murray Asher)	03/16/1978	Hillside Memorial Park, Los Angeles, CA
Fraser, Chick (Charles Carrolton)	05/08/1940	Jerome Cemetery, Jerome, ID
Frasier, Vic (Victor Patrick)	01/10/1977	Mount Bethel Cemetery, Gary, TX
Freed, Eddie (Edwin Charles)	11/15/2002	Grand View Memorial Park, Rock Hill, SC
Freed, Roger Vernon	01/09/1996	Oakdale Memorial Park, Glendora, CA
Freeman, Buck (Alexander Vernon)	02/21/1953	Fort Sam Houston National Cemetery, San Antonio, TX
Freeman, Buck (John Frank)	06/25/1949	Evergreen Cemetery, Kingston, PA
Freeman, Harvey Bayard	01/10/1970	Mount Olivet Cemetery, Kalamazoo, MI
Freeman, Jerry (Frank Ellsworth)	09/30/1952	Cremated, Los Angeles, CA
Freeman, John Edward	04/14/1958	St. Joseph's Cemetery, West Roxbury, MA
Freeman, Julie (Julius Benjamin)	06/10/1921	Bellefontaine Cemetery, St. Louis, MO
Freeze, Jake (Carl Alexander)	04/09/1983	Fairmount Cemetery, San Angelo, TX
Freiburger, Vern Donald	02/27/1990	Good Shepherd Cemetery, Huntington Beach, CA
Freigau, Howard Earl	07/18/1932	Woodland Cemetery, Dayton, OH
Freitas, Tony (Antonio)	03/14/1994	St. Mary's Catholic Cemetery, Sacramento, CA
French, Charlie (Charles Calvin)	03/30/1962	Washington Park East Cemetery, Indianapolis, IN
French, Larry (Lawrence Herbert)	02/09/1987	Visalia Cemetery, Visalia, CA
French, Ray (Raymond Edward)	04/03/1978	Holy Sepulchre Cemetery, Hayward, CA
Frey, Benny (Benjamin Rudolph)	11/01/1937	Woodland Cemetery, Jackson, MI
Friberg, Bernie (Bernard Albert)	12/08/1958	Pine Grove Cemetery, Lynn, MA
Fricano, Marion John	05/18/1976	Holy Spirit Church Cemetery, North Collins, NY
Friday, Skipper (Grier William)	08/25/1962	Oakwood Cemetery, Gastonia, NC
Fried, Cy (Arthur Edwin)	10/10/1970	Sunset Memorial Park, San Antonio, TX
Friedrich, Bob (Robert George)	04/15/1997	Shiloh Cemetery, Jasper, IN
Friel, Bill (William Edward)	12/24/1959	Resurrection Cemetery, Mackenzie, MO
Friel, Pat (Patrick Henry)	01/15/1924	St. Francis Cemetery, Pawtucket, RI
Friend, Danny (Daniel Sebastian)	06/01/1942	Greenlawn Cemetery, Chillicothe, OH
Friend, Frank (buried under birth name: Lawrence L. Freund)	11/05/1933	Walnut Ridge Cemetery, Jeffersonville, IN
Frierson, Buck (Robert Lawrence)	06/26/1996	Chicota Presbyterian Church Cemetery, Chicota, TX
Fries, Pete (Peter Martin)	07/30/1937	Oak Woods Cemetery, Chicago, IL
Frill, John Edmond	09/28/1918	Riverbend Cemetery, Westerly, RI
Frink, Fred (Frederick Ferdinand)	05/19/1995	Woodlawn Park Cemetery South, Miami, FL
Frisbee, Charlie (Charles Augustus)	11/07/1954	Alden Cemetery, Alden, IA
Frisch, Frankie (Frank Francis)	03/12/1973	Woodlawn Cemetery, Bronx, NY
Frisella, Danny (Daniel Vincent)	01/01/1977	Cremated. Ashes scattered in Oroville, CA
Frisk, Emil (John Emil)	01/27/1922	Lake View Cemetery, Seattle, WA
Fritz, Charlie (Charles Cornelius)	07/30/1943	Magnolia Cemetery, Mobile, AL

Name	DOD	Cemetery, City, State
Fritz, Harry Koch	11/04/1974	Green Lawn Cemetery, Columbus, OH
Froats, Bill (William John)	02/09/1998	Gate of Heaven Cemetery, Hawthorne, NY
Frock, Sam (Samuel William)	11/03/1925	Loudon Park Cemetery, Baltimore, MD
Froelich, Ben (William Palmer)	09/01/1916	36th Ward Cemetery (Banksville), Pittsburgh, PA
Fromme, Art (Arthur Henry)	08/24/1956	Rose Hills Memorial Park, Whittier, CA
Fry, Jay (Johnson)	04/07/1959	Spring Hill Cemetery, Huntington, WV
Frye, Charlie (Charles Andrew)	05/25/1945	Friendship Lutheran Church Cemetery, Taylorsville, NC
Fuchs, Charlie (Charles Thomas)	06/10/1969	George Washington Memorial Park, Paramus, NJ
Fuhr, Lefty (Oscar Lawrence)	03/27/1975	Laurel Land Memorial Park, Dallas, TX
Fuhrman, Ollie (Alfred George)	01/11/1969	Spirit Hill Cemetery, Jordan, MN
Fuller, Ed (Edward Aston White)	03/15/1935	Fort Lincoln Cemetery, Brentwood, MD
Fuller, Frank Edward	10/29/1965	Mount Olivet Cemetery, Detroit, MI
Fuller, Nig (Charles F.)	11/12/1947	Woodlawn Cemetery, Toledo, OH
Fullerton, Curt (Curtis Hooper)	01/09/1975	Winthrop Cemetery, Winthrop, MA
Fullis, Chick (Charles Philip)	03/28/1946	Odd Fellows Cemetery, Tamaqua, PA
Fulmer, Chick (Charles John)	02/15/1940	Fernwood Cemetery, Lansdowne, PA
Fulmer, Chris (Christopher)	11/09/1931	New St. Jerome's Cemetery, Tamaqua, PA
Fulmer, Washington Fayette	12/08/1907	Fernwood Cemetery, Lansdowne, PA
Fultz, Dave (David Lewis)	10/29/1959	Oakdale Cemetery, Deland, FL
Funk, Liz (Elias Calvin)	01/16/1968	Fairlawn Cemetery, Oklahoma City, OK
Furillo, Carl Anthony	01/21/1989	Forest Hills Memorial Park, Reiffton, PA
Fusselman, Les (Lester Leroy)	05/21/1970	Acadia Memorial Park, Mayfield Heights, OH
Gabler, Frank Harold	11/01/1967	Cremated, Long Beach, CA
Gables, Ken (Kenneth Harlin)	01/02/1960	Rose Hill Cemetery, Willard, MO
Gaddy, John Wilson	05/03/1966	Fairview Memorial Park, Albemarle, NC
Gaedel, Eddie (Edward Carl)	06/18/1961	St. Mary's Cemetery, Evergreen Park, IL
Gaffke, Fabian Sebastian	02/08/1992	St. Adalbert Cemetery, Milwaukee, WI
Gaffney, John *manager*	08/08/1913	Calvary Cemetery, Woodside, Queens, NY
Gagnier, Ed (Edward James)	09/13/1946	Mount Olivet Cemetery, Detroit, MI
Gagnon, Chick (Harold Dennis)	04/30/1970	St. John's Cemetery, Worcester, MA
Gainer, Del (Dellos Clinton)	01/29/1947	Maplewood Cemetery, Elkins, WV
Gaines, Nemo (Willard Roland)	01/26/1979	Arlington National Cemetery, Arlington, VA
Gaiser, Fred (Frederick Jacob)	10/09/1918	Riverview Cemetery, Trenton, NJ
Galan, Augie (August John)	12/28/1993	St. Joseph Cemetery, San Pablo, CA
Galatzer, Milt (Milton)	01/29/1976	Ridgelawn Cemetery, Chicago, IL
Galehouse, Denny (Dennis Ward)	12/12/1998	Doylestown Cemetery), Doylestown, OH. (aka Chestnut Hill Cemetery)
Gallagher, Ed (Edward Michael)	12/22/1981	Mosswood Cemetery, Cotuit, MA
Gallagher, Gil (Lawrence Kirby)	01/06/1957	Arlington National Cemetery, Arlington, VA
Gallagher, Joe (Joseph Emmett)	02/25/1998	Cushing Cemetery, Cushing, TX
Gallagher, John Carroll	03/30/1952	Forest Lawn Cemetery, Norfolk, VA
Gallagher, William Howard	03/11/1950	St. Patrick's Cemetery, Lowell, MA
Gallia, Bert (Melvin Allys)	03/19/1976	St. Joseph Cemetery, Devine, TX
Galligan, John T.	07/17/1901	Easton Cemetery, Easton, PA
Gallivan, Phil (Philip Joseph)	11/24/1969	Willow River Cemetery, Hudson, WI

Name	DOD	Cemetery, City, State
Galloway, Chick (Clarence Edward)	11/07/1969	Rosemont Cemetery, Clinton, SC
Galloway, Jim (James Cato)	05/03/1950	Odd Fellows Cemetery, Georgetown, TX
Galvin, Jim (James Joseph)	09/30/1969	Resthaven Garden of Memories, Decatur, GA
Galvin, John A.	04/20/1904	Holy Cross Cemetery, Brooklyn, NY
Galvin, Pud (James Francis)	03/07/1902	Calvary Cemetery, Pittsburgh, PA
Gamble, Lee Jesse	10/05/1994	Morningside Cemetery, DuBois, PA
Gammons, Daff (John Ashley)	03/24/1963	Oak Grove Cemetery, New Bedford, MA
Gandil, Chick (Arnold)	12/13/1970	St. Helena Cemetery, St. Helena, CA
Gandy, Bob (Robert Brinkley)	06/19/1945	Oaklawn Cemetery, Jacksonville, FL
Ganley, Bob (Robert Stephen)	10/09/1945	St. Patrick's Cemetery, Lowell, MA
Gannon, Bill (William G.)	04/26/1927	Greenwood Memorial Park, Fort Worth, TX
Gannon, Gussie (James Edward)	04/12/1966	Trinity Cemetery, Erie, PA
Gannon, Joe (Michael Joseph)	03/19/1931	Calvary Cemetery, St. Louis, MO
Gantenbein, Joe (Joseph Steven)	08/02/1993	Valley Memorial Park, Novato, CA
Ganzel, Charlie (Charles William)	04/07/1914	Mount Wollaston Cemetery, Quincy, MA
Ganzel, John Henry	01/14/1959	Cremated, Orlando, FL
Garbark, Bob (Robert Michael)	08/15/1990	St. Brigid's Cemetery, Geneva, PA
Garbark, Mike (Nathaniel Michael)	08/31/1994	Evergreen Cemetery, Charlotte, NC
Garcia, Mike (Edward Miguel)	01/13/1986	Visalia Cemetery, Visalia, CA
Gardiner, Art (Arthur Cecil)	10/21/1954	Long Island National Cemetery, Farmingdale, NY
Gardner, Alex (Alexander)	06/18/1926	Holten Cemetery, Danvers, MA
Gardner, Earle McClurkin	03/02/1943	Caledonia Cemetery, Sparta, IL
Gardner, Gid (Franklin Washington)	08/01/1914	Cambridge Cemetery, Cambridge, MA
Gardner, Glenn (Miles Glenn)	07/07/1964	Cremated, Rochester, NY
Gardner, Harry Ray	08/02/1961	Zion Memorial Park, Canby, OR
Gardner, Jim (James Anderson)	04/24/1905	Homewood Cemetery, Pittsburgh, PA
Gardner, Larry (William Lawrence)	03/11/1976	Cremated, Burlington. Ashes scattered at St. Paul's Episcopal Cathedral, Burlington, VT
Gardner, Ray (Raymond Vincent)	05/03/1968	St. John's Cemetery, Frederick, MD
Garibaldi, Art (Arthur Edward)	10/19/1967	Mount Vernon Memorial Park, Fair Oaks, CA
Garland, Lou (Louis Lyman)	08/30/1990	Cremated, Idalho Falls, ID
Garms, Debs C.	12/16/1984	Squaw Creek Cemetery, Glen Rose, TX
Garoni, Willie (William)	09/09/1914	Fairview Cemetery, Fairview, NJ
Garrett, Clarence Raymond	02/11/1977	Big Run Church Cemetery, Cameron, WV
Garriott, Cecil (Virgil Cecil)	02/20/1990	Riverside National Cemetery, Riverside, CA
Garrison, Cliff (Clifford William)	08/25/1994	Capay Cemetery, Esparto, CA
Garrison, Ford (Robert Ford)	06/06/2001	Memorial Park Cemetery, St. Petersburg, FL
Garrity, Hank (Francis Joseph)	09/01/1962	St. Joseph's Cemetery, West Roxbury, MA
Garry, Jim (James Thomas)	01/15/1917	Fairview Cemetery, Dalton, MA
Garvin, Ned (Virgil Lee)	06/16/1908	Mountain View Cemetery, Fresno, CA
Gaspar, Harry Lambert	05/14/1940	Holy Sepulchre Cemetery, Orange, CA
Gassaway, Charlie (Charles Cason)	01/15/1992	Woodlawn Park Cemetery South, Miami, FL
Gastall, Tommy (Thomas Everett)	09/20/1956	St. Patrick's Cemetery, Fall River, MA
Gastfield, Ed (Edward)	12/01/1899	Forest Home Cemetery, Forest Park, IL
Gaston, Alex (Alexander Nathaniel)	02/08/1976	Cremated, Santa Monica, CA
Gaston, Milt (Nathaniel Milton)	04/26/1996	Garden of Memories Cemetery, Tampa, FL
Gaston, Welcome Thornburg	12/13/1944	Northwood Cemetery, Cambridge, OH

Name	DOD	Cemetery, City, State
Gastright, Hank (Henry Carl)	10/09/1937	St. Joseph Cemetery, Newport, KY
Gatins, Frank Anthony	11/08/1911	St. John's Catholic Church Cemetery, Geistown, PA
Gaule, Mike (Michael John)	01/24/1918	New Cathedral Cemetery, Baltimore, MD
Gautreau, Doc (Walter Paul)	08/23/1970	Mount Auburn Cemetery, Cambridge, MA
Gautreaux, Sid (Sidney Allen)	04/19/1980	Garden of Memories Cemetery, Houma, LA
Gaw, Chippy (George Joseph)	05/26/1968	Calvary Cemetery, Waltham, MA
Gazella, Mike (Michael)	09/11/1978	Holy Cross Cemetery, Culver City, CA
Gear, Dale Dudley	09/23/1951	Mount Hope Cemetery, Topeka, KS
Gearin, Dinty (Dennis John)	03/11/1959	St. Francis Cemetery, Pawtucket, RI
Geary, Bob (Robert Norton)	01/03/1980	Arlington Memorial Gardens, Cincinnati, OH
Geary, Huck (Eugene Francis Joseph)	01/27/1981	Holy Cross Cemetery, Lackawanna, NY
Gedeon, Joe (Elmer Joseph)	05/19/1941	East Lawn Memorial Park, Sacramento, CA
Gedney, Count (Alfred W.)	03/26/1922	Green-Wood Cemetery, Brooklyn, NY
Gee, Johnny (John Alexander)	01/23/1988	Cremated, Cortland, NY
Geggus, Charlie (Charles Frederick)	01/16/1917	Holy Cross Cemetery, Colma, CA
Gehrig, Lou (Henry Louis)	06/02/1941	Kensico Cemetery, Valhalla, NY. Cremated.
Gehring, Henry	04/18/1912	Forest Lawn Memorial Park, St. Paul, MN
Gehringer, Charlie (Charles Leonard)	01/21/1993	Holy Sepulchre Cemetery, Southfield, MI
Gehrman, Paul Arthur	10/23/1986	Greenwood Cemetery, Bend, OR
Geier, Phil (Philip Louis)	09/25/1967	St. Joseph's Cemetery, Spokane, WA
Geiger, Gary Merle	04/24/1996	Pleasant Grove Memorial Park, Murphysboro, IL
Geiss, Bill (William J.)	09/18/1924	St. Boniface Cemetery, Chicago, IL
Geiss, Emil August	10/04/1911	St. Boniface Cemetery, Chicago, IL
Gelbert, Charley (Charles Magnus)	01/13/1967	Norland Cemetery, Chambersburg, PA
Genewich, Joe (Joseph Edward)	12/21/1985	Holy Sepulchre Cemetery, Bath, NY
Gennis, Frank (C. Frank)	09/30/1922	Cremated, St. Louis, MO
Gentile, Sam (Samuel Christopher)	05/04/1998	Woodlawn Cemetery, Everett, MA
Gentry, Rufe (James Ruffus)	07/03/1997	Gardens of Memory, Walkertown, NC
George, Bill (William M.)	08/23/1916	Mount Calvary Cemetery, Wheeling, WV
George, Lefty (Thomas Edward)	05/13/1955	Prospect Hill Cemetery, York, PA
Georgy, Oscar John	01/15/1999	Greenwood Cemetery, New Orleans, LA
Geraghty, Ben (Benjamin Raymond)	06/18/1963	Evergreen Cemetery, Jacksonville, FL
Gerber, Wally (Walter)	06/19/1951	Green Lawn Cemetery, Columbus, OH
Gerhardt, Joe (John Joseph)	03/11/1922	Prospect Hill Cemetery, Washington, DC
Gerhauser, Al (Albert)	05/28/1972	Mount Hope Cemetery, Webb City, MO
Gerken, George Herbert	10/23/1977	Forest Lawn Memorial Park, Covina Hills, Covina, CA
Gerkin, Steve (Stephen Paul)	11/08/1978	Cremated, St. Petersburg, FL
German, Les (Lester Stanley)	06/10/1934	Baker Cemetery, Aberdeen, MD
Gervais, Lefty (Lucien Edward)	10/19/1950	Calvary Cemetery, Los Angeles, CA
Gessler, Doc (Harry Homer)	12/24/1924	St. Bernard's Cemetery, Indiana, PA
Gessner, Charlie (Charles)	05/25/1922	Finn's Piont National Cemetery, Salem, NJ
Gettig, Charlie (Charles Henry)	04/11/1935	Trinity Cemetery, Baltimore, MD

Name	DOD	Cemetery, City, State
Gettinger, Tom (Lewis Thomas Leyton)	07/26/1943	St. Michael's Cemetery, Pensacola, FL
Gettman, Jake (Jacob John)	10/04/1956	Fairmount Cemetery, Denver, CO
Getzein, Charlie (Charles H.)	06/19/1932	Concordia Cemetery, Forest Park, IL
Geyer, Rube (Jacob Bowman)	10/12/1962	Oakwood Cemetery, Mora, MN
Geygan, Chappy (James Edward)	03/15/1966	St. Michael's Cemetery, Columbus, OH
Gharrity, Patsy (Edward Patrick)	10/10/1966	Calvary Cemetery, Beloit, WI
Giannini, Joe (Joseph Francis)	09/26/1942	Holy Cross Cemetery, Colma, CA
Giard, Joe (Joseph Oscar)	07/10/1956	Our Lady of Mount Carmel Cemetery, Ware, MA
Gibson, Bob (Robert Murray)	12/19/1949	Homewood Cemetery, Pittsburgh, PA
Gibson, Charles (Charles Ellsworth)	11/22/1954	Oakwood Cemetery, Sharon, PA
Gibson, Frank Gilbert	04/27/1961	Memory Gardens of Edna (formerly Edna Cemetery), Edna, TX
Gibson, Norwood Ringold	07/07/1959	Springdale Cemetery, Peoria, IL
Gibson, Sam (Samuel Braxton)	01/31/1983	Forest Lawn Cemetery, Greensboro, NC
Gibson, Whitey (Leighton P.)	10/12/1907	Lancaster Cemetery, Lancaster, PA
Giebel, Joe (Joseph Henry)	03/17/1981	Gate of Heaven Cemetery, Silver Spring, MD
Giel, Paul Robert	05/22/2002	Lakewood Cemetery, Minneapolis, MN
Gifford, James *manager*	12/19/1901	Green Lawn Cemetery, Columbus, OH
Gilbert, Alfred Gideon	12/17/1927	Angel Hill Cemetery, Havre de Grace, MD
Gilbert, Andy (Andrew)	08/29/1992	St. Vincent's Cemetery, Latrobe, PA
Gilbert, Billy (William Oliver)	08/08/1927	Gate of Heaven Cemetery, Hawthorne, NY
Gilbert, Charlie (Charles Mader)	08/13/1983	Lake Lawn Cemetery, New Orleans, LA
Gilbert, Harry H.	12/23/1909	Edgewood Cemetery, Pottstown, PA
Gilbert, Jack (John Robert)	07/07/1941	St. Mary's Cemetery, South Glens Falls, NY
Gilbert, John B.	11/12/1903	Pottstown Cemetery (West), Pottstown, PA
Gilbert, Larry (Lawrence William)	02/17/1965	Greenwood Cemetery, New Orleans, LA
Gilbert, Pete (Peter)	01/01/1912	St. Michael's Cemetery, Springfield, MA
Gilbert, Tookie (Harold Joseph)	06/23/1967	Lake Lawn Cemetery, New Orleans, LA
Gilbert, Wally (Walter John)	09/07/1958	Sunrise Memorial Park, Hermantown, MN
Gilgras, Joe (Joseph John)	09/06/1947	St. Peter's Roman Catholic Church Cemetery, Saratoga Springs, NY
Gilham, George Lewis	04/25/1937	Shamokin Cemetery, Shamokin, PA
Gilhooley, Frank Patrick	07/11/1959	Calvary Cemetery, Toledo, OH
Gilks, Bob (Robert James)	08/21/1944	Palmetto Cemetery, Brunswick, GA
Gill, Ed (Edward James)	10/10/1995	Mount Benedict Cemetery, West Roxbury, MA
Gill, George Lloyd	02/21/1999	Raymond Town Cemetery, Raymond, MS
Gill, Haddie (Harold Edward)	08/01/1932	Calvary Cemetery, Brockton, MA
Gill, Jim (James C.)	04/10/1923	Prospect Hill Cemetery, York, PA
Gill, Johnny (John Wesley)	12/26/1984	Calvary Cemetery, Nashville, TN
Gill, Warren Darst	11/26/1952	Cremated, Laguna Beach, CA
Gillen, Tom (Thomas J.)	01/26/1889	Cathedral Cemetery, Philadelphia, PA
Gillenwater, Carden Edison	05/10/2000	Cremated, Largo, FL
Gillespie, Bob (Robert William)	11/04/2001	Parklawn Memorial Garden, Winston-Salem, NC
Gillespie, Jim (James Wheatfield)	09/05/1921	Elmlawn Cemetery, Tonawanda, NY
Gillespie, John Patrick	02/15/1954	St. Vincent's Cemetery, Vallejo, CA

Name	DOD	Cemetery, City, State
Gillespie, Paul Allen	08/11/1970	Westview Cemetery, Atlanta, GA
Gillespie, Pete (Peter Patrick)	05/05/1910	St. Rose of Lima Cemetery, Carbondale, PA
Gilliam, Jim (James William)	10/08/1978	Inglewood Park Cemetery, Inglewood, CA
Gilligan, Barney (Andrew Bernard)	04/01/1934	Pine Grove Cemetery, Lynn, MA
Gilligan, Jack (John Patrick)	11/19/1980	St. Stanislaus Catholic Cemetery, Modesto, CA
Gillis, Grant	02/04/1981	Gosport Cemetery, Gosport, AL
Gillpatrick, George F.	12/15/1941	Freeman Cemetery, Freeman, MO
Gilman, Jim (James Joseph)	12/21/1912	St. Joseph's Cemetery, Cleveland, OH
Gilman, Pit (Pitkin Clark)	08/17/1950	Butternut Ridge Cemetery, North Eaton, OH
Gilmore, Frank T.	07/21/1929	Mt. St. Benedict's Cemetery, Bloomfield, CT
Gilmore, Grover (Ernest Grover)	11/25/1919	Oakridge Cemetery, Hillside, IL
Gilmore, Jim (James)	11/18/1928	Greenmount Cemetery, Baltimore, MD
Gilroy, John M.	08/04/1897	Mount Olivet Cemetery, Washington, DC
Ging, Billy (William Joseph)	09/14/1950	SS. Peter & Paul Cemetery, Elmira, NY
Ginn, Tinsley Rucker	08/30/1931	Rosehill Cemetery, Royston, GA
Girard, Charlie (Charles August)	08/06/1936	Cypress Hills Cemetery, Brooklyn, NY
Gladd, Jim (James Walter)	11/08/1977	Citizens Cemetery, Fort Gibson, OK
Glade, Fred (Frederick Monroe)	11/21/1934	Grand Island City Cemetery, Grand Island, NE
Gladmon, Buck (James Henry)	01/13/1890	Mount Olivet Cemetery, Washington, DC
Glaiser, John Burke	03/07/1959	Forest Park (Lawndale) Cemetery, Houston, TX
Glass, Tom (Thomas Joseph)	12/15/1981	Moriah United Methodist Church Cemetery, Gilmer, NC
Glasscock, Jack (John Wesley)	02/24/1947	Greenwood Cemetery, Wheeling, WV. Moved from Peninsula Cemetery in 1964.
Glavenich, Luke Frank	05/22/1935	Jackson Catholic Cemetery, Jackson, CA
Glaviano, Tommy (Thomas Giatano)	01/19/2004	Cremated, Sacramento. Ashes scattered over Sonoma, CA
Glaze, Ralph (Daniel Ralph)	10/31/1968	Cremated, Atascadero, CA
Gleason, Bill (William G.)	07/21/1932	Calvary Cemetery, St. Louis, MO
Gleason, Bill (William Patrick)	01/09/1957	St. Jerome Cemetery, Holyoke, MA
Gleason, Bill (William)	12/02/1893	St. Joseph's Cemetery, Cleveland, OH
Gleason, Harry Gilbert	10/21/1961	Locustwood Memorial Park, Cherry Hill, NJ
Gleason, Jack (John Day)	09/04/1944	Calvary Cemetery, St. Louis, MO
Gleason, Joe (Joseph Paul)	09/08/1990	St. Francis Cemetery, Phelps, NY
Gleason, Kid (William J.)	01/02/1933	Northwood Cemetery, Philadelphia, PA
Gleeson, Jimmy (James Joseph)	05/01/1996	Calvary Cemetery, Kansas City, MO
Gleich, Frank Elmer	03/27/1949	St. Joseph's Cemetery, Lockbourne, OH
Glendon, Martin J.	11/06/1950	St. Joseph Cemetery, River Grove, IL
Glenn, Bob (Burdette)	06/03/1977	Cremated, Richmond, CA
Glenn, Ed (Edward D.)	12/06/1911	St. Joseph Cemetery, Newport, KY
Glenn, Harry Melville	10/12/1918	Highland Lawn Cemetery, Terre Haute, IN
Glenn, Joe (Joseph Charles)	05/06/1985	St. Mary's Visitation Parish Cemetery, Dickson City, PA
Gliatto, Sal (Salvador Michael)	11/02/1995	Restland Memorial Park, Dallas, TX
Glockson, Norm (Norman Stanley)	08/05/1955	Mount Greenwood Cemetery, Chicago, IL
Glossop, Al (Alban)	07/02/1991	Valhalla Gardens of Memory, Belleville, IL

Name	DOD	Cemetery, City, State
Goar, Jot (Joshua Mercer)	04/04/1947	New Lisbon Cemetery, New Lisbon, IN
Gochnaur, John Peter	09/27/1929	Fairview Cemetery, Altoona, PA
Godar, John Michael	06/23/1949	All Saints Cemetery, Des Plaines, IL
Godwin, John Henry	05/05/1956	Spring Hill Cemetery, Wellsville, OH
Goebel, Ed (Edwin)	08/12/1959	Maple Grove Park Cemetery, Hackensack, NJ
Goeckel, Billy (William John)	11/01/1922	St. Nicholas Cemetery, Shavertown, PA
Golden, Mike (Michael Henry)	01/11/1929	St. Mary/St. James Cemetery, Rockford, IL
Golden, Roy Kramer	10/04/1961	Cremated, Cincinnati, OH
Goldman, Jonah John	08/17/1980	Westchester Hills Cemetery, Hastings-on-Hudson, NY
Goldsberry, Gordon Frederick	02/23/1996	Cremated, Lake Forest, CA
Goldsby, Walt (Walton Hugh)	01/11/1924	Oakland Cemetery, Dallas, TX
Goldsmith, Fred (Fredrick Ernest)	03/28/1939	Roseland Park Cemetery, Berkley, MI
Goldsmith, Hal (Harold Eugene)	10/20/1985	Southold Presbyterian Cemetery, Southold, NY
Goldstein, Izzy (Isidore)	09/24/1993	Eternal Light Memorial Gardens, Boynton Beach, FL
Goliat, Mike (Michael Mitchell)	01/13/2004	All Saints Cemetery, Northfield, OH
Golvin, Walt (Walter George)	06/11/1973	Holy Cross Cemetery, Culver City, CA
Gomez, Lefty (Vernon Louis)	02/17/1989	Mount Tamalpais Cemetery, San Rafael, CA
Gonzales, Joe Madrid	11/16/1996	Cremated, Torrance, CA. Ashes scattered in Pacific Ocean.
Gonzalez, Mike (Miguel Angel)	02/19/1977	Cemeterio de Cristobal Colon, Havana, Cuba
Gooch, Charlie (Charles Furman)	05/30/1982	Fort Lincoln Cemetery, Brentwood, MD
Gooch, Johnny (John Beverley)	03/15/1975	Mount Olivet Cemetery, Nashville, TN
Gooch, Lee Currin	05/18/1966	Wake Forest Cemetery, Wake Forest, NC
Good, Gene (Eugene J.)	08/06/1947	New Calvary Cemetery, Mattapan, MA
Good, Ralph Nelson	11/24/1965	Riverview Cemetery, Farmington, ME
Good, Wilbur David	12/30/1963	Brooksville Cemetery, Brooksville, FL
Goodall, Herb (Herbert Frank)	01/20/1938	Prospect Cemetery, Mansfield, PA
Goodell, John Henry William	09/21/1993	Laurel Land Memorial Park, Dallas, TX
Goodenough, Bill (William B.)	05/24/1905	Calvary Cemetery, St. Louis, MO
Goodfellow, Mike (Michael J.)	02/12/1920	Fairmount Cemetery, Newark, NJ
Goodman, Billy (William Dale)	10/01/1984	Mount Olivet United Methodist Church Cemetery, Concord, NC
Goodman, Ival Richard	11/25/1984	Oak Hill Cemetery, Cincinnati, OH
Goodman, Jake (Jacob)	03/09/1890	Charles Evans Cemetery, Reading, PA
Goodwin, Art (Arthur Ingram)	06/19/1943	Jefferson Cemetery, Jefferson, PA
Goodwin, Pep (Claire Vernon)	02/15/1972	Cremated, Oakland, CA
Gorbous, Glen Edward	06/12/1990	Mountain View Memorial Gardens Cemetery, Calgary, Alberta, Canada
Gordinier, Ray (Raymond Cornelius)	11/15/1960	Holy Sepulchre Cemetery, Rochester, NY
Gordon, Joe (Joseph Lowell)	04/14/1978	Cremated, Sacramento, CA
Gordon, Sid (Sidney)	06/17/1975	New Montefiore Cemetery, Pinelawn, NY
Gorman, Herb (Herbert Allen)	04/05/1953	Oak Hill Memorial Park, San Jose, CA
Gorman, Howie (Howard Paul)	04/29/1984	Queen of Heaven Cemetery, Venetia, PA
Gorman, Jack (John F.)	09/09/1889	Calvary Cemetery, St. Louis, MO

Name	DOD	Cemetery, City, State
Gorman, Tom (Thomas Aloysius)	12/26/1992	Cemetery of Holy Rood, Westbury, NY
Gorman, Tom (Thomas David)	08/11/1986	George Washington Memorial Park, Paramus, NJ
Gormley, Joe (Joseph)	07/02/1950	GAR Cemetery, Summit Hill, PA
Gornicki, Hank (Henry Frank)	02/16/1996	Royal Palm Memorial Gardens, West Palm Beach, FL
Gorsica, Johnny (John Joseph Perry)	12/16/1998	Sunset Memorial Park, Beckley, WV
Goslin, Goose (Leon Allen)	05/15/1971	Baptist Cemetery, Salem, NJ
Gossett, Dick (John Star)	10/06/1962	Rose Hill Memorial Park, Massillon, OH
Goulait, Ted (Theodore Lee)	07/15/1936	St. Mary's Cemetery, St. Clair, MI
Gould, Al (Albert Frank)	08/08/1982	Los Gatos Memorial Park, San Jose, CA. Cremated.
Gould, Charlie (Charles Harvey)	04/10/1917	Spring Grove Cemetery, Cincinnati, OH
Goulish, Nick (Nicholas Edward)	03/15/1984	Calvary Cemetery, Youngstown, OH
Gouzzie, Claude	09/21/1907	Charleroi Cemetery, Charleroi, PA
Gowdy, Hank (Henry Morgan)	08/01/1966	Union Cemetery, Columbus, OH
Grabowski, Al (Alons Francis)	10/29/1966	Sacred Heart Cemetery, Syracuse, NY
Grabowski, Johnny (John Patrick)	05/23/1946	Park View Cemetery, Schenectady, NY
Grabowski, Reggie (Reginald John)	04/02/1955	Sacred Heart Cemetery, Syracuse, NY
Grace, Earl (Robert Earl)	12/22/1980	Greenwood Memory Lawn Cemetery, Phoenix, AZ
Grace, Joe (Joseph LaVerne)	09/18/1969	Ava Evergreen Cemetery, Ava, IL
Grady, John J.	07/15/1893	St. Patrick's Cemetery, Lowell, MA
Grady, Mike (Michael William)	12/03/1943	St. Partick's Cemetery, Kennett Square, PA
Graf, Fred (Frederick Gottleib)	10/04/1979	Mizpah Congregation Julia Cemetery, Chattanooga, TN
Graff, John J.	04/02/1932	Congressional Cemetery, Washington, DC
Graham, Barney (Bernard W.)	10/30/1886	Catholic Cemetery, Mobile, AL
Graham, Bert	06/19/1971	Valley View Cemetery, Clarksdale, AZ
Graham, Charlie (Charles Henry)	08/29/1948	Holy Cross Cemetery, Colma, CA
Graham, Kyle	12/01/1973	Oak Grove Missionary Baptist Church Cemetery, Oak Grove, AL
Graham, Moonlight (Archibald Wright)	08/25/1965	Calvary Cemetery, Rochester, MN
Graham, Oscar M.	10/15/1931	Riverside Cemetery, Moline, IL
Graham, Peaches (George Frederick)	07/25/1939	Cremated, Long Beach, CA
Graham, Skinny (Arthur William)	07/10/1967	Woodlawn Cemetery, Everett, MA
Graham, Tiny (Dawson Francis)	12/29/1962	Calvary Cemetery, Nashville, TN
Grahame, Bill (William James)	02/15/1936	Maple Ridge Cemetery, Holt, MI
Graney, Jack (John Gladstone)	04/20/1978	Bowling Green Memorial Gardens, Bowling Green, MO
Grant, Eddie (Edward Leslie)	10/05/1918	Meuse-Argonne American Cemetery, Romagne, France
Grant, George Addison	03/25/1986	Oak Hill Cemetery, Prattville, AL
Grant, Jim (James Ronald)	11/30/1985	Mount Hope Cemetery, Mardrid, IA
Grant, Jimmy (James Charles)	07/08/1970	West Lawn Memorial Park, Racine, WI

Name	DOD	Cemetery, City, State
Grantham, George Farley	03/16/1954	Mountain View Cemetery, Kingman, AZ
Grasso, Mickey (Newton Michael)	10/15/1975	Cremated, Miami, FL
Graves, Joe (Joseph Ebenezer)	12/22/1980	Waterside Cemetery, Marblehead, MA
Graves, Sid (Samuel Sidney)	12/26/1983	Hope Cemetery, Kennebunk, ME
Gray, Charlie (Charles A.)	06/01/1900	Crown Hill Cemetery, Indianapolis, IN
Gray, Chummy (George Edward)	08/14/1913	Acorn Cemetery, Rockland, ME
Gray, Dolly (William Denton)	04/03/1956	Sutter Cemetery, Sutter, CA
Gray, Milt (Milton Marshall)	06/30/1969	Resthaven Memorial Park, Louisville, KY
Gray, Pete (Peter J.)	06/30/2002	St. Mary's Cemetery, Wilkes-Barre, PA
Gray, Reddy (James W.)	01/31/1938	Homewood Cemetery, Pittsburgh, PA
Gray, Sam (Samuel David)	04/16/1953	Van Alstyne Cemetery, Van Alstyne, TX
Gray, Stan (Stanley Oscar)	10/11/1964	Evergreen Cemetery, Ballinger, TX
Gray, William Tolan	12/08/1932	Ivy Hill Cemetery, Philadelphia, PA
Green, Danny (Edward)	11/09/1914	New Camden Cemetery, Camden, NJ
Green, Freddie (Fred Allen)	12/22/1996	Harbourton Cemetery, Harbourton Village, NJ
Green, Gene Leroy	05/23/1981	Resurrection Cemetery, Mackenzie, MO
Green, Harvey George	07/24/1970	McGowen Memorial Cemetery, Jeanerette, LA
Green, James F.	12/12/1912	Calvary Cemetery, Cleveland, OH
Green, Joe (Joseph Henry)	02/04/1972	Arlington Cemetery, Drexel Hill, PA
Greenberg, Hank (Henry Benjamin)	09/04/1986	Hillside Memorial Park, Los Angeles, CA
Greene, June (Julius Foust)	03/19/1974	Cremated, Los Angeles, CA
Greene, Nelson George	04/06/1983	Mt. Lebanon Cemetery, Lebanon, PA
Greene, Paddy (Patrick Joseph)	10/20/1934	St. Francis Cemetery, Pawtucket, RI
Greenfield, Kent	03/14/1978	Highland Cemetery, Guthrie, KY
Greenig, John A.	07/28/1913	North Cedar Hill Cemetery, Philadelphia, PA
Greenwood, Bill (William F.)	05/02/1902	Mt. Moriah Cemetery, Philadelphia, PA
Gregg, Dave (David Charles)	11/12/1965	Clarkston Vineland Cemetery, Clarkston, WA
Gregg, Hal (Harold Dana)	05/13/1991	Cremated, Bishop, CA
Gregg, Vean (Sylveanus Augustus)	07/29/1964	Cremated, Hoquiam, WA. Ashes given to family
Gregory, Frank Ernst	11/05/1955	Eastlawn Cemetery, Beloit, WI
Gregory, Howie (Howard Watterson)	05/30/1970	Memorial Park Cemetery, Tulsa, OK
Gregory, Paul Edwin	09/16/1999	Oakwood Cemetery, Tunica, MS
Gremminger, Ed (Lorenzo Edward)	05/26/1942	Forest Hill Cemetery, Canton, OH
Gremp, Buddy (Lewis Edward)	01/30/1995	Lakewood Memorial Park, Hughson, CA
Grevell, Bill (William J.)	06/21/1923	M.E. Church Cemetery, Williamstown, NJ
Grey, Reddy (Romer Carl)	11/08/1934	Mountain View Cemetery, Altadena, CA
Griesenbeck, Tim (Carlos Phillipe)	03/25/1953	San Fernando Archdiocesan Cemetery, San Antonio, TX
Griffin, James Linton	02/11/1950	Elmo Cemetery, Elmo, TX
Griffin, Marty (Martin John)	11/19/1951	All Souls Cemetery, Long Beach, CA
Griffin, Mike (Michael Joseph)	04/10/1908	St. Agnes Cemetery, Utica, NY
Griffin, Pat (Patrick Richard)	06/07/1927	Calvary Cemetery, Youngstown, OH
Griffin, Pug (Francis Arthur)	10/12/1951	Calvary Cemetery, Lincoln, NE
Griffin, Thomas William	04/17/1933	St. Mary's-St. James Cemetery, Rockford, IL
Griffith, Bert (Bartholomew Joseph)	05/05/1973	Big Pine Cemetery, Big Pine, CA

Name	DOD	Cemetery, City, State
Griffith, Clark Calvin	10/27/1955	Fort Lincoln Cemetery, Brentwood, MD
Griffith, Tommy (Thomas Herman)	04/13/1967	Cremated, Cincinnati, OH
Griggs, Art (Arthur Carle)	12/19/1938	Cremated, Los Angeles, CA
Grigsby, Denver Clarence	11/10/1973	South Heights Cemetery, Sapulpa, OK
Grim, Bob (Robert Anton)	10/23/1996	Maple Hill Cemetery, Kansas City, KS
Grim, John Helm	07/28/1961	Crown Hill Cemetery, Indianapolis, IN
Grimes, Burleigh Arland	12/06/1985	Clear Lake Cemetery, Clear Lake, WI
Grimes, Ed (Edward Adelbert)	10/05/1974	Rosehill Cemetery, Chicago, IL
Grimes, John Thomas	01/17/1964	Golden Gate National Cemetery, San Bruno, CA
Grimes, Oscar Ray, Jr.	05/19/1993	Sunset Memorial Park, North Olmstead, OH
Grimes, Ray (Oscar Ray, Sr.)	05/25/1953	East Lawn Cemetery, Minerva, OH
Grimes, Roy (Austin Roy)	09/13/1954	East Lawn Cemetery, Minerva, OH
Grimm, Charlie (Charles John)	11/15/1983	Cremated. Some ashes scattered at Wrigley Field, Chicago, IL remainder given to family.
Grimshaw, Myron Frederick	12/11/1936	Fort Plain Cemetery, Fort Plain, NY
Grimsley, Ross Albert, Sr.	02/06/1994	Woodhaven Cemetery, Millington, TN
Griner, Dan (Donald Dexter)	06/03/1950	Bethlehem Methodist Cemetery, Bishopville, SC
Grissom, Lee Theo	10/04/1998	Sunset Hill Cemetery, Corning, CA
Grob, Connie (Conrad George)	09/28/1997	St. Francis Xavier Cemetery, Cross Plains, WI
Groh, Heinie (Henry Knight)	08/22/1968	Spring Grove Cemetery, Cincinnati, OH
Groh, Lew (Lewis Carl)	10/20/1960	Mt. Hope Cemetery, Rochester, NY
Gromek, Steve (Stephen Joseph)	03/12/2002	Holy Sepulchre Cemetery, Southfield, MI
Groom, Bob (Robert)	02/19/1948	Walnut Hill Cemetery, Belleville, IL
Gross, Emil Michael	08/24/1921	Graceland Cemetery, Chicago, IL
Gross, Turkey (Ewell)	01/11/1936	Mesquite Cemetery, Mesquite, TX
Grossart, George Albert	04/18/1902	Greendale Cemetery, Meadville, PA
Groth', Ernie (Ernest John)	05/23/1950	Cremated, Milwaukee, WI
Grove, Lefty (Robert Moses)	05/22/1975	Frostburg Memorial Park, Frostburg, MD
Grove, Orval Leroy	04/20/1992	Calvary Catholic Cemetery, Citrus Heights, CA
Grover, Charlie (Charles Byrd)	05/24/1971	Floral Lawn Memorial Gardens, Battle Creek, MI
Grubb, Harvey Harrison	01/25/1970	Oakwood Cemetery, Corsicana, TX
Grubbs, Tom (Thomas Dillard)	01/28/1986	Machpelah Cemetery, Mount Sterling, KY. Cremated.
Grube, Frank (Franklin Thomas)	07/02/1945	Easton Cemetery, Easton, PA
Gruber, Henry John	09/26/1932	St. Bernard's Cemetery, West Haven, CT
Gryska, Sig (Sigmund Stanley)	08/27/1994	Resurrection Cemetery, Justice, IL
Gudat, Marv (Marvin John)	03/01/1954	Meyersville Catholic Cemetery, Meyersville, TX
Guerra, Mike	10/09/1992	Flagler Memorial Park, Miami, FL
Guese, Whitey (Theodore)	04/08/1951	Wheeler Cemetery, Wapakoneta, OH
Guiney, Ben (Benjamin Franklin)	12/05/1930	Mount Elliott Cemetery, Detroit, MI
Guintini, Ben (Benjamin John)	12/02/1998	San Joaquin Valley National Cemetery, Gustine, CA
Guise, Witt Orison	08/13/1968	Little Rock National Cemetery, Little Rock, AR

Name	DOD	Cemetery, City, State
Guisto, Lou (Louis Joseph)	10/15/1989	Tulocay Cemetery, Napa, CA
Gulley, Tom (Thomas Jefferson)	11/24/1966	Roselawn Memorial Gardens Cemetery, Little Rock, AR
Gullic, Tedd Jasper	01/28/2000	Howell County Memorial Park Cemetery, West Plains, MO
Gumbert, Ad (Addison Courtney)	04/23/1925	Homewood Cemetery, Pittsburgh, PA
Gumbert, Billy (William Skeen)	04/13/1946	Homewood Cemetery, Pittsburgh, PA
Gunkel, Red (Woodward William)	04/19/1954	Sheffield Cemetery, Sheffield, IL
Gunning, Hy (Hyland)	03/28/1975	Maine Veterans Memorial Cemetery, Augusta, ME
Gunning, Tom (Thomas Francis)	03/17/1931	North Burial Ground, Fall River, MA
Gunson, Joe (Joseph Brook)	11/15/1942	Northwood Cemetery, Philadelphia, PA
Gust, Ernie (Ernest Herman Frank)	10/26/1945	Elm Lawn Park Cemetery, Bay City, MI
Gustine, Frankie (Frank William)	04/01/1991	Resurrection Cemetery, Coraopolis, PA
Guth, Bucky (Charles J.)	07/05/1883	Graceland Cemetery, Chicago, IL
Gyselman, Dick (Richard Ronald)	09/20/1990	Acacia Memorial Park, Seattle, WA
Haas, Bert (Berthold John)	06/23/1999	Cremated, Tampa, FL
Haas, Bruno Philip	06/05/1952	Hope Cemetery, Worcester, MA
Haas, Mule (George William)	06/30/1974	Immaculate Conception Cemetery, Montclair, NJ
Habenicht, Bob (Robert Julius)	12/24/1980	Riverview Cemetery, Richmond, VA
Haberer, Emil Karl	10/19/1951	Spring Grove Cemetery, Cincinnati, OH
Hach, Irv (Irvin William)	08/13/1936	Cave Hill Cemetery, Louisville, KY
Hack, Stan (Stanley Camfield)	12/15/1979	Grand Detour Cemetery, Grand Detour, IL
Hacker, Warren Louis	05/22/2002	Oakridge Cemetery, New Athens, IL
Hackett, Charles M. *manager*	08/01/1898	Calvary Cemetery, Holyoke, MA
Hackett, Jim (James Joseph)	03/28/1961	St. Mary's Cemetery, Evergreen Park, IL
Hackett, Mert (Mortimer Martin)	02/22/1938	St. Paul's Cemetery, Arlington, MA
Hackett, Walter Henry	10/02/1920	St. Paul's Cemetery, Arlington, MA
Haddix, Harvey	01/08/1994	Asbury Cemetery, Springfield, OH
Haddock, George Silas	04/18/1926	Forest Hills Cemetery, Boston, MA
Hadley, Bump (Irving Darius)	02/15/1963	Swampscott Cemetery, Swampscott, MA
Haefner, Bill (William Bernard)	01/27/1982	Mount Peace Cemetery, Philadelphia, PA
Haefner, Mickey (Milton Arnold)	01/03/1995	Oakridge Cemetery, New Athens, IL
Hafey, Bud (Daniel Albert)	07/27/1986	St. Joseph Cemetery, San Pablo, CA
Hafey, Chick (Charles James)	07/02/1973	Holy Cross Catholic Cemetery, St. Helena, CA
Hafey, Tom (Thomas Francis)	10/02/1996	Sunset View Cemetery, El Cerrito, CA
Hafford, Leo Edgar	10/02/1911	Holy Cross Cemetery, Malden, MA
Hafner, Frank (Francis R.)	03/02/1957	Mount Olivet Cemetery, Hannibal, MO
Hagan, Art (Arthur Charles)	03/25/1936	St. Ann's Cemetery, Cranston, RI
Hagerman, Rip (Zerah Zequiel)	01/30/1930	Mount Calvary Cemetery, Albuquerque, NM
Hague, Joe (Joe Clarence)	11/05/1994	Sunset Memorial Park, San Antonio, TX
Hahn, Dick (Richard Frederick)	11/05/1992	Woodlawn Memorium, Orlando, FL
Hahn, Ed (William Edgar)	11/29/1941	Pine Hill Cemetery, Des Moines, IA
Hahn, Noodles (Frank George)	02/06/1960	Forest Lawn Memorial Park, Enka, NC
Haid, Hal (Harold Augustine)	08/13/1952	St. Vincent's Cemetery, Latrobe, PA
Haigh, Ed (Edward E.)	02/13/1953	Atlantic City Cemetery, Pleasantville, NJ
Haines, Hinkey (Henry Luther)	01/09/1979	Middletown Cemetery, Media, PA

Name	DOD	Cemetery, City, State
Haines, Jesse Joseph	08/05/1978	Bethel Cemetery, Phillipsburg, OH
Hairston, Sammy (Samuel Harding)	10/31/1997	Elmwood Cemetery, Birmingham, AL
Haislip, Jim (James Clifton)	01/22/1970	Grove Hill Memorial Park, Dallas, TX
Halas, George Stanley	10/31/1983	St. Adalbert's Cemetery, Niles, IL
Halbriter, Ed (Edward L.)	08/09/1936	Forest Lawn Memorial Park, Glendale, CA
Haldeman, John Avery	09/17/1899	Cave Hill Cemetery, Louisville, KY
Hale, Dad (Ray Luther)	02/01/1946	Oakwood Cemetery, Allegan, MI
Hale, Odell (Arvel Odell)	06/09/1980	Arlington Memorial Cemetery, El Dorado, AR
Hale, Sammy (Samuel Douglas)	09/06/1974	Wheeler Cemetery, Wheeler, TX
Hall, Bill (William Bernard)	08/15/1947	Grandview Memorial Park, Dunbar, WV
Hall, Bill (William Lemuel)	01/01/1986	New Bethel Cemetery, Meigs, GA
Hall, Bob (Robert Lewis)	03/12/1983	Cremated, St. Petersburg, FL. Ashes scattered.
Hall, Bob (Robert Prill)	12/01/1950	Forest Hills Cemetery, Boston, MA
Hall, Charlie (Charles Louis)	12/06/1943	Ivy Lawn Memorial Park, Ventura, CA
Hall, Charlie (Charles Walter)	06/24/1921	Toulon Municipal Cemetery, Toulon, IL
Hall, George William	06/11/1923	Evergreen Cemetery, Brooklyn, NY
Hall, Herb (Herbert Silas)	07/01/1970	Belmont Memorial Park, Fresno, CA
Hall, Johnny (John Sylvester)	01/17/1995	Sunny Lane Cemetery, Oklahoma City, OK
Hall, Marc (Marcus)	02/24/1915	Diamond Cemetery, Diamond, MO
Hall, Russ (Robert Russell)	07/01/1937	Inglewood Park Cemetery, Inglewood, CA
Halla, John Arthur	09/30/1947	Pacific Crest Cemetery, Redondo Beach, CA
Hallahan, Bill (William Anthony)	07/08/1981	Calvary-St. Patrick Cemetery, Johnson City, NY
Hallett, Jack Price	06/11/1982	United Church of Christ Cemetery, Holgate, OH
Halliday, Newt (Newton Schurz)	04/06/1918	St. Joseph Cemetery, River Grove, IL
Halligan, Jocko (William E.)	02/13/1945	Mount Olivet Cemetery, Tonawanda, NY
Hallinan, Ed (Edward S.)	08/24/1940	Holy Cross Cemetery, Colma, CA
Hallinan, Jimmy (James H.)	10/28/1879	Calvary Cemetery, Evanston, IL
Hallman, Bill (William Harry)	04/23/1950	Mount Peace Cemetery, Philadelphia, PA
Hallman, Bill (William Wilson)	09/11/1920	Holy Sepulchre Cemetery, Wyndmoor, PA
Halpin, Jim (James Nathaniel)	01/04/1893	Mount Calvary Cemetery, Roslindale, MA
Halt, Al (Alva William)	01/22/1973	Calvary Cemetery, Sandusky, OH
Ham, Ralph A.	02/13/1905	St. Peter's Cemetery, Troy, NY
Hamann, Doc (Elmer Joseph)	01/11/1973	Wisconsin Memorial Park, Brookfield, WI
Hamberg, Charlie (Charles H.)	05/18/1931	Evergreen Cemetery, Hillside, NJ
Hamby, Jim (James Sanford)	10/21/1991	Camp Butler National Cemetery, Springfield, IL
Hamill, John Alexander Charles	12/06/1911	North Burial Ground, Bristol, RI
Hamilton, Billy (William Robert)	12/16/1940	Eastwood Cemetery, South Lancaster, MA
Hamilton, Earl Andrew	11/17/1968	Melrose Abbey Memorial Park, Anaheim, CA
Hamilton, Steve (Steven Absher)	12/02/1997	Forest Lawn Memorial Gardens, Morehead, KY
Hamilton, Tom (Thomas Bail)	11/29/1973	Capitol Memorial Park, Austin, TX
Hamlin, Luke Daniel	02/18/1978	East Lawn Memory Gardens, Okemos, MI
Hammond, Jack (Walter Charles)	03/04/1942	Cremated, Kenosha, WI

Name	DOD	Cemetery, City, State
Hamner, Granny (Granville Wilbur)	09/12/1993	Cremated, Harleigh Cemetery Crematory, Camden, NJ. Ashes given to family
Hamner, Ralph Conant	05/22/2001	Walnut Hill Cemetery, Bradley, AR
Hamric, Bert (Odbert Herman)	08/04/1984	Springboro Cemetery, Springboro, OH
Hancock, Fred James	03/12/1986	Cremated, Clearwater, FL.
Handiboe, Jim (James Edward)	11/08/1942	St. Joseph's Cemetery, Lockbourne, OH
Handiboe, Mike (Aloysius James)	01/31/1953	Catholic Cemetery, Savannah, GA
Handley, Jeep (Lee Elmer)	04/08/1970	Resurrection Cemetery, Coraopolis, PA
Hanebrink, Harry Aloysius	09/09/1996	Jefferson Barracks National Cemetery, St. Louis, MO
Haney, Fred Girard	11/09/1977	Holy Cross Cemetery, Culver City, CA
Hanford, Charlie (Charles Joseph)	07/19/1963	St. Mary's Cemetery, Trenton, NJ
Hankins, Don (Donald Wayne)	05/16/1963	Forsyth Memorial Park Cemetery, Winston-Salem, NC
Hankinson, Frank Edward	04/05/1911	Green-Wood Cemetery, Brooklyn, NY
Hanley, Jim (James Patrick)	05/01/1961	St. Francis Cemetery, Pawtucket, RI
Hanlon, Ned (Edward Hugh)	04/14/1937	New Cathedral Cemetery, Baltimore, MD
Hanna, John	11/07/1930	Cedar Hill Cemetery, Philadelphia, PA
Hannah, Truck (James Harrison)	04/27/1982	Cremated, Fountain Valley, CA
Hannifan, Pat (Patrick James)	11/05/1908	St. Michael's Cemetery, Springfield, MA
Hannifin, Jack (John Joseph)	10/27/1945	St. Jerome Cemetery, Holyoke, MA
Hanning, Loy Vernon	06/24/1986	Anaconda City Cemetery, Anaconda, MO
Hansen, Doug (Douglas William)	09/16/1999	Orem City Cemetery, Orem, UT
Hansen, Roy Inglof	02/09/1977	Eastlawn Cemetery, Beloit, WI
Hansen, Snipe (Roy Emil Frederick)	09/11/1978	Rosehill Cemetery, Chicago, IL
Hansford, Frank Cicero	12/14/1952	Evergreen Cemetery, Fort Scott, KS
Hanski, Don (Donald Thomas)	09/02/1957	Fairmount Willow Hills Park, Worth, IL
Hanson, Harry Francis	10/05/1966	Bonaventure Cemetery, Savannah, GA
Hanson, Ollie (Earl Sylvester)	08/19/1951	Laurel Grove Cemetery, Totowa, NJ
Hanyzewski, Ed (Edward Michael)	10/08/1991	St. Joseph Cemetery, South Bend, IN
Happenny, Cliff (John Clifford)	12/29/1988	Our Lady Queen of Heaven Cemetery, North Lauderdale, FL
Harbridge, Bill (William Arthur)	03/17/1924	Fernwood Cemetery, Lansdowne, PA
Harder, Mel (Melvin Leroy)	10/20/2002	Cremated, Chardon, OH. Ashes scattered at Mel Harder Park, Chardon, OH
Hardesty, Scott Durbin	10/29/1944	Bellville Cemetery, Bellville, OH
Hardgrove, Pat (William Henry)	01/26/1973	White Chapel Cemetery, Wichita, KS
Hardie, Lou (Lewis W.)	03/05/1929	Cremated, Oakland, CA
Hardin, Bud (William Edgar)	07/28/1997	Fort Rosecrans National Cemetery, LaJolla, CA
Hardin, Jim (James Warren)	03/09/1991	Cremated, Key West, FL. Ashes scattered at sea.
Harding, Charlie (Charles Harold)	10/30/1971	Calvary Cemetery, Nashville, TN
Hardy, Alex (David Alexander)	04/22/1940	Memorial Park Cemetery, Scarborough, Ontario, Canada
Hardy, Harry	09/04/1943	Union Cemetery, Steubenville, OH
Hardy, Jack (John Doolittle)	10/20/1921	Lakewood Park Cemetery, Rocky River, OH
Hardy, Red (Francis Joseph)	08/15/2003	St. Francis Catholic Cemetery, Phoenix, AZ

Name	DOD	Cemetery, City, State
Hargrave, Bubbles (Eugene Franklin)	02/23/1969	Union Cemetery, Montgomery, OH
Hargrave, Pinky (William McKinley)	10/03/1942	Greenlawn Memorial Park, Fort Wayne, IN
Hargreaves, Charlie (Charles Russell)	05/09/1979	Holcombe-Riverview Cemetery, Lambertville, NJ
Harkins, John Joseph	11/20/1940	St. Peter's Cemetery, New Brunswick, NJ
Harkness, Specs (Frederick Harvey)	05/18/1952	Calvary Cemetery, Los Angeles, CA
Harley, Dick (Henry Risk)	05/16/1961	Ferncliff Cemetery, Springfield, OH
Harley, Dick (Richard Joseph)	04/03/1952	Cathedral Cemetery, Philadelphia, PA
Harmon, Bob (Robert Green)	11/27/1961	Riverview Burial Park, Monroe, LA
Harper, Bill (William Homer)	06/17/1951	Memorial Park Cemetery, Memphis, TN
Harper, George B.	12/11/1931	Stockton Rural Cemetery, Stockton, CA
Harper, George Washington	08/18/1978	New Hope Cemetery, Magnolia, AR
Harper, Harry Clayton	04/23/1963	Hainesville Cemetery, Layton, NJ
Harper, Jack (Charles William)	09/30/1950	Holy Cross Cemetery, Jamestown, NY
Harrell, Ray (Raymond James)	01/28/1984	Byers Cemetery, Byers, TX
Harrell, Slim (Oscar Martin)	04/30/1971	Grandview Cemetery, Grandview, TX
Harrington, Andy (Andrew Francis)	11/12/1938	Mount Calvary Cemetery, Roslindale, MA
Harrington, Andy (Andrew Matthew)	01/29/1979	Morris Hill Cemetery, Boise, ID
Harrington, Joe (Joseph C.)	09/13/1933	St. Patrick's Cemetery, Fall River, MA
Harris, Ben Franklin	04/01/1927	Mount Olivet Cemetery, Nashville, TN
Harris, Bill (William Milton)	08/21/1965	Sharon Memorial Park, Charlotte, NC
Harris, Bob (Robert Arthur)	08/09/1989	Fort McPherson National Cemetery, Maxwell, NE
Harris, Bucky (Stanley Raymond)	11/08/1977	St. Peter's Lutheran Church Cemetery, Hughestown, PA
Harris, Charlie (Charles Jenkins)	03/14/1963	Evergreen Cemetery, Gainesville, FL
Harris, Dave (David Stanley)	09/18/1973	Resthaven Garden of Memories, Decatur, GA
Harris, Frank Walter	11/26/1939	County Home Cemetery, Freeport, IL
Harris, Herb (Herbert Benjamin)	01/18/1991	Cremated, Crystal Lake, IL
Harris, Joe (Joseph White)	04/12/1966	Wyoming Cemetery, Melrose, MA
Harris, Joe (Joseph)	12/10/1959	Sunset Hill Memorial Gardens, Cranberry, PA
Harris, Lum (Chalmer Luman)	11/11/1996	Elmwood Cemetery, Birmingham, AL
Harris, Mickey (Maurice Charles)	04/15/1971	Holy Sepulchre Cemetery, Southfield, MI
Harris, Ned (Robert Ned)	12/18/1976	Hillcrest Memorial Park, West Palm Beach, FL
Harris, Spencer (Anthony Spencer)	07/03/1982	Lakewood Cemetery, Minneapolis, MN
Harriss, Slim (William Jennings Bryan)	09/19/1963	Bangs Cemetery, Bangs, TX
Harshaney, Sam (Samuel)	02/01/2001	Sunset Memorial Park, San Antonio, TX
Harstad, Oscar Theander	11/14/1985	Oaklawn Memorial Park, Corvallis, OR
Hart, Bill (William Franklin)	09/19/1936	Rest Haven Memorial Park, Cincinnati, OH
Hart, Bill (William Woodrow)	07/29/1968	Wiconisco Cemetery, Wiconisco, PA
Hart, Bob (Robert Lee)	05/14/1944	Riverside Cemetery, Hannibal, MO
Hart, Hub (James Henry)	10/10/1960	Greenlawn Memorial Park, Fort Wayne, IN

Name	DOD	Cemetery, City, State
Hart, James *manager*	07/18/1919	Girard Cemetery, Girard, PA. Cremated.
Hart, Tom (Thomas Henry)	09/17/1939	St. Bernard's Church Cemetery, Fitchburg, MA
Harter, Frank (Franklin Pierce)	04/14/1959	Kendree Chapel Cemetery, Keyesport, IL
Hartford, Bruce Daniel	05/25/1975	Cremated, Los Angeles, CA. Ashes scattered in Pacific Ocean
Hartje, Chris (Christian Henry)	06/26/1946	Golden Gate National Cemetery, San Bruno, CA
Hartley, Chick (Walter Scott)	07/18/1948	Cathedral Cemetery, Wilmington, DE
Hartley, Grover Allen	10/19/1964	Cremated, Daytona Beach, FL
Hartman, Charlie (Charles Otto)	10/22/1960	Inglewood Park Cemetery, Inglewood, CA
Hartnett, Gabby (Charles Leo)	12/20/1972	All Saints Cemetery, Des Plaines, IL
Hartranft, Ray (Raymond Joseph)	02/10/1955	Fernwood Cemetery, Royersford, PA
Hartsel, Topsy (Tully Frederick)	10/14/1944	Woodlawn Cemetery, Toledo, OH. Cremated.
Hartzell, Roy Allen	11/06/1961	Golden Cemetery, Golden, CO
Harvel, Luther Raymond	04/10/1986	Mount Olivet Cemetery, Kansas City, MO
Hasbrook, Ziggy (Robert Lyndon)	02/09/1976	Restland Memorial Park, Dallas, TX
Haslin, Mickey (Michael Joseph)	03/07/2002	St. Mary's Cemetery, Wilkes-Barre, PA
Hasney, Pete (Peter James)	05/24/1908	New Cathedral Cemetery, Philadelphia, PA
Hassett, Buddy (John Aloysius)	08/23/1997	Garden of Memories, Old Tappan, NJ
Hassler, Joe (Joseph Frederick)	09/04/1971	Duncan City Cemetery, Duncan, OK
Hasson, Gene (Charles Eugene)	07/30/2003	Cremated, San Dimas, CA
Hasson, Gene (Charles Eugene)	07/30/2003	Cremated, Pomona, CA
Hastings, Charlie (Charles Morton)	08/03/1934	Parkersburg Memorial Gardens (formerly Odd Fellows Cemetery), Parkersburg, WV
Hastings, Scott (Winfield Scott)	08/14/1907	Los Angeles National Cemetery, Los Angeles, CA
Hasty, Bob (Robert Keller)	05/28/1972	Marietta City Cemetery, Marietta, GA
Hatfield, Fred James	05/22/1998	Meadowwood Memorial Park, Tallahassee, FL
Hatfield, Gil (Gilbert)	05/26/1921	Fairview Cemetery, Fairview, NJ
Hatfield, John Van Buskirk	02/20/1909	Mount Olivet Cemetery, Maspeth, Queens, NY
Hatten, Joe (Joseph Hilarian)	12/16/1988	Ogburn Inwood Cemetery, Shingletown, CA
Haugstad, Phil (Philip Donald)	10/21/1998	Riverside Cemetery, Black River Falls, WI
Hauser, Joe (Joseph John)	07/11/1997	Calvary Cemetery, Sheboygan, WI
Hausmann, Clem (Clemens Raymond)	08/29/1972	Earthman Memory Gardens Cemetery, Baytown, TX
Hautz, Charlie (Charles A.)	01/24/1929	SS. Peter & Paul Cemetery, St. Louis, MO
Hawes, Bill (William Hildreth)	06/16/1940	Edson Cemetery, Lowell, MA
Hawk, Ed (Edward)	03/26/1936	Gibson Cemetery, Neosho, MO
Hawke, Bill (William Victor)	12/11/1902	Wilimington & Brandywine Cemetery, Wilmington, DE
Hawks, Chicken (Nelson Louis)	05/26/1973	Cypress Lawn Memorial Park, Colma, CA. Cremated.
Hawley, Marv (Marvin Hiram)	04/28/1904	Evergreen Cemetery, Painesvile, OH
Hawley, Pink (Emerson P.)	09/19/1938	Oakwood Cemetery, Beaver Dam, WI
Haworth, Howie (Homer Harold)	01/28/1953	Willamette National Cemetery, Portland, OR
Hayden, Jack (John Francis)	08/03/1942	St. Denis Cemetery, Havertown, PA

Name	DOD	Cemetery, City, State
Hayes, Frankie (Frank Witman)	06/22/1955	Fernwood Cemetery, Jamesburg, NJ
Hayes, Jackie (Minter Carney)	02/09/1983	Clanton Cemetery, Clanton, AL
Hayes, Jim (James Millard)	11/27/1993	Fairview Memorial Gardens, Stockbridge, GA
Haynes, Joe (Joseph Walton)	01/06/1967	Fort Lincoln Cemetery, Brentwood, MD
Hayworth, Ray (Raymond Hall)	09/25/2002	Guilford Memorial Park, Greensboro, NC
Hazle, Bob (Robert Sidney)	04/25/1992	Crescent Hill Memorial Gardens, Columbia, SC
Hazleton, Doc (Willard Carpenter)	03/10/1941	Lakeview Cemetery, Burlington, VT
Head, Ed (Edward Marvin)	01/31/1980	Sardis Cemetery, West Monroe, LA
Head, Ralph	10/08/1962	Hollywood Cemetery, Tallapoosa, GA
Healy, Egyptian (John J.)	03/16/1899	Calvary Cemetery, St. Louis, MO
Healy, Fran (Francis Xavier Paul)	02/12/1997	St. Jerome Cemetery, Holyoke, MA
Healy, Thomas Fitzgerald	01/10/1977	Calvary Cemetery, Cleveland, OH
Heard, Jay (Jehosie)	11/18/1999	New Grace Hill Cemetery, Birmingham, AL
Hearn, Bunny (Charles Bunn)	10/19/1959	Maplewood Cemetery, Wilson, NC
Hearn, Bunny (Elmer Lafayette)	03/31/1974	Gulf Pines Memorial Park, Englewood, FL
Hearn, Jim (James Tolbert)	06/10/1998	Cremated, Boca Grande, FL
Hearne, Ed (Edmund)	09/08/1952	Los Angeles National Cemetery, Los Angeles, CA
Hearne, Hughie (Hugh Joseph)	09/22/1932	St. Mary's Cemetery, Troy, NY
Heath, Jeff (John Geoffrey)	12/09/1975	Lake View Cemetery, Seattle, WA
Heath, Spencer Paul	01/25/1930	St. Boniface Cemetery, Chicago, IL
Heathcote, Cliff (Clifton Earl)	01/18/1939	Mt. Carmel Cemetery, Littlestown, PA
Hechinger, Mike (Michael Vincent)	08/13/1967	St. Boniface Cemetery, Chicago, IL
Hecker, Guy Jackson	12/03/1938	Wooster Cemetery, Wooster, OH
Hedgpeth, Harry Malcolm	07/30/1966	Westhampton Memorial Park, Richmond, VA
Heffner, Don (Donald Henry)	08/01/1989	Mountain View Cemetery, Altadena, CA. Cremated.
Hegan, Jim (James Edward)	06/17/1984	Swampscott Cemetery, Swampscott, MA
Heidrick, Emmet (Robert Emmet)	01/20/1916	Clarion Cemetery, Clarion, PA
Heifer, Frank (Franklin)	08/29/1893	Charles Evans Cemetery, Reading, PA
Heilbrunner, Louis Wilbur *manager*	12/21/1933	Lindenwood Cemetery, Fort Wayne, IN
Heilman, Chink (John George)	07/19/1940	Vine Street Hill Cemetery, Cincinnati, OH
Heilmann, Harry Edwin	07/09/1951	Holy Sepulchre Cemetery, Southfield, MI
Heimach, Fred (Frederick Amos)	06/01/1973	Fort Myers Memorial Gardens, Fort Myers, FL
Heine, Bud (William Henry)	09/02/1976	Cremated, Fort Lauderdale, FL. Ashes scattered at sea
Heinzman, Jack (John Peter)	11/10/1914	St. Louis Cemetery, Louisville, KY
Heise, Clarence Edward	05/30/1999	Highland Memorial Park, Apopka, FL
Heismann, Crese (Christian Ernest)	11/19/1951	Spring Grove Cemetery, Cincinnati, OH
Heitmann, Henry Anton	12/15/1958	Cypress Hills National Cemetery, Brooklyn, NY
Heitmuller, Heinie (William Frederick)	10/08/1912	Olivet Memorial Park, Colma, CA
Helf, Hank (Henry Hartz)	10/27/1984	Capital Memorial Park, Austin, TX
Helfrich, Ty (Emory Wilbur)	03/18/1955	Atlantic City Cemetery, Pleasantville, NJ
Hellman, Tony (Anthony Joseph)	03/29/1898	St. Mary's Cemetery, Cincinnati, OH

Name	DOD	Cemetery, City, State
Hemingway, Ed (Edson Marshall)	07/05/1969	Sheridan Cemetery, Sheridan, MI
Hemming, George Earl	06/03/1930	Oak Grove Cemetery, Springfield, MA
Hemp, Duck Y (William H.)	03/06/1923	Calvary Cemetery, St. Louis, MO
Hemphill, Frank Vernon	11/16/1950	Oak Forest Cemetery, Oak Forest, IL
Hemsley, Rollie (Ralston Burdett)	07/31/1972	George Washington Cemetery, Adelphi, MD
Henderson, Bernie (Bernard)	06/04/1966	St. Williams Cemetery, Douglassville, TX
Henderson, Bill (William Maxwell)	10/06/1966	Bayview Memorial Park, Pensacola, FL
Henderson, Hardie (James Harding)	02/06/1903	Fernwood Cemetery, Lansdowne, PA
Hendrick, Harvey	10/29/1941	Munford Cemetery, Covington, TN
Hendricks, Ed (Edward)	11/28/1930	Roseland Memorial Gardens, Jackson, MI
Hendricks, Jack (John Charles)	05/13/1943	Mount Carmel Cemetery, Hillside, IL
Hendrix, Claude Raymond	03/22/1944	Arlington Memorial Park, Allentown, PA
Hendryx, Tim (Timothy Green)	08/14/1957	Rose Hill Memorial Park, Corpus Christi, TN
Hengle, Moxie (Emery J.)	12/11/1924	Forest Home Cemetery, Forest Park, IL
Henion, Lafayette Marion	07/22/1955	Odd Fellows Cemetery, San Luis Obispo, CA
Henley, Weldon	11/16/1960	West View Cemetery, Palatka, FL
Henline, Butch (Walter John)	10/09/1957	Manasota Memorial Park, Bradenton, FL
Hennessey, George	01/15/1988	Our Lady of Lourdes Cemetery, Trenton, NJ
Hennessey, Les (Lester Baker)	11/20/1976	St. Joseph's Cemetery, Lynn, MA
Henning, Pete (Ernest Herman)	11/04/1939	Maplewood Cemetery, Crown Point, IN
Henrich, Fritz (Frank Wilde)	05/01/1959	Holy Sepulchre Cemetery, Wyndmoor, PA
Henriksen, Olaf	10/17/1962	St. Mary's Cemetery, Canton, MA
Henry, Dutch (Frank John)	08/23/1968	Calvary Cemetery, Cleveland, OH
Henry, George Washington	12/30/1934	Cremated, Lynn, MA
Henry, Jim (James Francis)	08/15/1976	Forest Hill Cemetery-Midtown Memphis, TN
Henry, John Michael	06/11/1939	Mt. St. Benedict's Cemetery, Bloomfield, CT
Henry, John Park	11/24/1941	Evergreen Cemetery, Bisbee, AZ
Henry, Snake (Frederick Marshall)	10/12/1987	Montlawn Memorial Park, Raleigh, NC
Henshaw, Roy Kniklebine	06/08/1993	Mount Hope Cemetery, Chicago, IL
Hensiek, Phil (Philip Frank)	02/21/1972	Calvary Cemetery, St. Louis, MO
Herbel, Ron (Ronald Samuel)	01/20/2000	Mountain View Memorial Park, Tacoma, WA
Herbert, Ernie Albert	01/13/1968	Mount Olivet Cemetery, Marceline, MO
Herman, Art (Arthur)	09/20/1955	Inglewood Park Cemetery, Inglewood, CA
Herman, Babe (Floyd Caves)	11/27/1987	Forest Lawn Memorial Park, Glendale, CA
Herman, Billy (William Jennings Bryan)	09/05/1992	Riverside Memorial Park, Tequesta, FL
Hernon, Tom (Thomas H.)	02/04/1902	St. Mary's Cemetery, New Bedford, MA
Herrell, Walt (Walter William)	01/23/1949	Cedar Hill Cemetery, Suitland, MD
Herring, Art (Arthur L.)	12/02/1995	Grant Memorial Park, Marion, IN
Herring, Bill (William Francis)	09/10/1962	Pine Grove Cemetery, South Sterling, PA
Herring, Herb (Herbert Lee)	04/22/1964	Holy Hope Cemetery, Tucson, AZ
Herrmann, Leroy George	07/03/1972	San Joaquin Catholic Cemetery, Stockton, CA
Herrmann, Marty (Martin John)	09/11/1956	St. Mary's Cemetery, Cincinnati, OH
Hershberger, Willard McKee	08/03/1940	Visalia Cemetery, Visalia, CA
Hershey, Frank	12/15/1949	Gorham Cemetery, Gorham, NY
Herzog, Buck (Charles Lincoln)	09/04/1953	Grace Methodist Church Cemetery, Denton, MD

Name	DOD	Cemetery, City, State
Hess, Otto C.	02/25/1926	Fairview Park Cemetery, North Olmstead, OH
Hess, Tom (Thomas)	12/15/1945	St. Agnes Cemetery, Albany, NY
Hesselbacher, George Edward	02/18/1980	Northwood Cemetery, Philadelphia, PA
Hesterfer, Larry (Lawrence)	09/22/1943	Mt. Olivet Cemetery, Bloomfield, NJ
Hetling, Gus (August Julius)	10/13/1962	Wichita Park Cemetery, Wichita, KS
Heubel, George A.	01/22/1896	Leverington Cemetery, Philadelphia, PA
Heusser, Ed (Edward Burlton)	03/01/1956	Bountiful City Cemetery, Bountiful, UT
Heving, Joe (Joseph William)	04/11/1970	St. Mary's Cemetery, Fort Mitchell, KY
Heving, Johnnie (John Aloysius)	12/24/1968	Rowan Memorial Park, Salisbury, NC
Hewett, Walter F. *manager*	10/07/1944	Glenwood Cemetery, Washington, DC
Heydon, Mike (Michael Edward)	10/13/1913	Holy Cross Cemetery, Indianapolis, IN
Hibbard, John Denison	11/17/1937	Cremated, Los Angeles, CA. Ashes scattered in Pacific Ocean
Hickey, Eddie (Edward A.)	03/25/1941	Calvary Cemetery, Tacoma, WA
Hickey, Jim (James Robert)	09/20/1997	St. Patrick's Cemetery, Rockland, MA
Hickey, John William	12/28/1941	Calvary Catholic Cemetery, Seattle, WA
Hickey, Mike (Michael Francis)	06/11/1918	Calvary Cemetery, Chicopee, MA
Hickman, Charlie (Charles Taylor)	04/19/1934	East Oak Grove Cemetery, Morgantown, WV
Hickman, Ernie (Ernest P.)	11/19/1891	St. Peter's Cemetery, St. Louis, MO
Hicks, Nat (Nathan Woodhull)	04/21/1907	St. Peter's Cemetery, Weehawken, NJ
Higbe, Kirby (Walter Kirby)	05/06/1985	Elmwood Cemetery, Columbia, SC
Higbee, Mahlon Jesse	04/07/1968	Evergreen Cemetery, Louisville, KY
Higdon, Bill (William Travis)	04/30/1986	Greenwood Cemetery, Montgomery, AL
Higginbotham, Irv (Irving Clinton)	06/12/1959	Acacia Memorial Park, Seattle, WA
Higgins, Bill (William Edward)	04/25/1919	Silverbrook Cemetery, Wilmington, DE
Higgins, Bob (Robert Stone)	05/25/1941	Greenwood Cemetery, Chattanooga, TN
Higgins, Pinky (Michael Franklin)	03/21/1969	Sparkman Hillcrest Memorial Park, Dallas, TX
High, Andy (Andrew Aird)	02/22/1981	Ava Evergreen Cemetery, Ava, IL
High, Bunny (Hugh Jenkin)	11/16/1962	Bellefontaine Cemetery, St. Louis, MO
High, Charlie (Charles Edwin)	09/11/1960	Portland Memorial Cemetery, Portland, OR
High, Ed (Edward Thomas)	02/20/1926	Western Cemetery, Baltimore, MD
Higham, Dick (Richard)	03/18/1905	Mount Hope Cemetery, Chicago, IL
Hiland, John William	04/10/1901	Greenwood Cemetery (Knights of Pythias section), Philadelphia, PA
Hilcher, Whitey (Walter Frank)	11/21/1962	Fort Snelling National Cemetery, Minneapolis, MN
Hildebrand, George Albert	05/30/1960	Valhalla Memorial Park, North Hollywood, CA
Hildebrand, Oral Clyde	09/08/1977	Forest Lawn Memorial Gardens, Greenwood, IN
Hildebrand, Palmer Marion	01/25/1960	Shauck Cemetery (formerly Johnsville Cemetery), Shauck, OH
Hill, Belden L.	10/22/1934	Oak Hill Cemetery, Cedar Rapids, IA
Hill, Carmen Proctor	01/01/1990	Crown Hill Cemetery, Indianapolis, IN
Hill, Herbert Lee	09/02/1970	Laurel Land Memorial Park, Dallas, TX
Hill, Hunter Benjamin	02/22/1959	Austin Memorial Park, Austin, TX
Hill, Jesse Terrill	08/31/1993	Corona Cemetery, Corona, CA
Hill, Oliver Clinton	09/20/1970	Douglasville City Cemetery, Douglasville, GA
Hill, Red (Clifford Joseph)	08/11/1938	Evergreen Cemetery, El Paso, TX

Name	DOD	Cemetery, City, State
Hill, Still Bill (William Cicero)	01/28/1938	Evergreen Cemetery, Southgate, KY
Hiller, Frank Walter	01/10/1987	Cremated, Malvern, PA.
Hiller, Hob (Harvey Max)	12/27/1956	Evergreen Cemetery, Jim Thorpe, PA
Hilley, Ed (Edward Garfield)	11/14/1956	Calvary Cemetery, Cleveland, OH
Hillibrand, Homer Hiller Henry	01/20/1974	Elsinore Valley Cemetery, Lake Elsinore, CA
Hillis, Mack (Malcolm David)	06/16/1961	Cambridge Cemetery, Cambridge, MA
Hilly Pat (William Edward)	07/25/1953	St. Wendelin Church Cemetery, Fostoria, OH
Himes, Jack (John Herb)	12/16/1949	St. John the Baptist Cemetery, Joliet, IL
Himsl, Vedie (Avitus Bernard) *manager*	03/15/2004	St. Joseph's Cemetery, River Grove, IL
Hinchman, Bill (William White)	02/20/1963	St. Joseph's Cemetery, Lockbourne, OH
Hinchman, Harry Sibley	01/19/1933	Toledo Memorial Park, Sylvania, OH
Hinkle, Gordie (Daniel Gordon)	03/19/1972	Woodlawn Garden of Memories, Houston, TX
Hinrichs, Dutch (William Louis)	04/18/1972	Kingsburg Cemetery, Kingsburg, CA
Hinson, Paul (James Paul)	09/23/1960	Green Hills Cemetery, Muskogee, OK
Hippauf, Herb (Herbert August)	07/17/1995	Santa Clara Mission Cemetery, Santa Clara, CA
Hitchcock, Jimmy (James Franklin)	06/23/1959	Greenwood Cemetery, Montgomery, AL
Hitt, Bruce Smith	11/10/1973	Willamette National Cemetery, Portland, OR
Hitt, Roy Wesley	02/08/1956	Pomona Cemetery, Pomona, CA
Hoag, Myrill Oliver	07/28/1971	High Springs Cemetery, High Springs, FL
Hoak, Don (Donald Albert)	10/09/1969	Fishing Creek Cemetery, Roulette, PA
Hobbs, Bill (William Lee)	01/05/1945	St. Stephen's Cemetery, Hamilton, OH
Hoblitzell, Dick (Richard Carleton)	11/14/1962	Valley Cemetery, Marietta, OH
Hoch, Harry Keller	10/26/1981	Townsend Cemetery, Townsend, DE
Hock, Ed (Edward Francis)	11/21/1963	St. Peter's Catholic Cemetery, Wheelersburg, OH
Hockett, Oris Leon	03/23/1969	Inglewood Park Cemetery, Inglewood, CA
Hodapp, Johnny (Urban John)	06/14/1980	Oak Hill Cemetery, Cincinnati, OH
Hodes, Charles	02/14/1875	Lutheran All Faiths Cemetery, Middle Village, Queens, NY
Hodges, Edward Burton	01/08/2001	Forest Grove Freewill Baptist Church Cemetery, Knoxville, TN
Hodges, Gil (Gilbert Raymond)	04/02/1972	Holy Cross Cemetery, Brooklyn, NY
Hodnett, Charlie (Charles)	04/25/1890	Calvary Cemetery, St. Louis, MO
Hoelskoetter, Art (Arthur H.)	08/03/1954	Calvary Cemetery, St. Louis, MO
Hoerner, Joe (Joseph Walter)	10/04/1996	Resurrection Cemetery, Mackenzie, MO
Hoerst, Frank Joseph	02/18/2000	Holy Sepulchre Cemetery, Wyndmoor, PA
Hoey, Jack (John Bernard)	11/14/1947	St. James Cemetery, Naugatuck, CT
Hoff, Red (Chester Cornelius)	09/17/1998	Dale Historical Cemetery, Ossining, NY
Hoffer, Bill (William Leopold)	07/21/1959	Linwood Cemetery, Cedar Rapids, IA
Hofferth, Stew (Stewart Edward)	03/07/1994	St. Paul Lutheran Church Cemetery, Kouts, IN
Hoffman, Danny (Daniel John)	03/14/1922	St. Michael's Cemetery, Stratford, CT
Hoffman, Dutch (Clarence Casper)	12/06/1962	Lake View Memorial Gardens, Belleville, IL
Hoffman, Izzy (Harry C.)	11/13/1942	North Cedar Hill Cemetery, Philadelphia, PA
Hoffman, Larry (Lawrence Charles)	12/29/1948	Bohemian National Cemetery, Chicago, IL
Hoffman, Tex (Edward Adolph)	05/19/1947	Carrollton Cemetery, New Orleans, LA

Name	DOD	Cemetery, City, State
Hoffmeister, Jesse H.	01/14/1933	Glendale Cemetery, Des Moines, IA
Hofman, Bobby (Robert George)	04/05/1994	Bethlehem Cemetery, Bellefontaine, MO
Hofman, Solly (Arthur Frederick)	03/10/1956	New Bethlehem Cemetery, St. Louis, MO
Hofmann, Fred	11/19/1964	Golden Gate National Cemetery, San Bruno, CA
Hogan, George A.	02/22/1922	Marion Cemetery, Marion, OH
Hogan, Kenny (Kenneth Timothy)	01/02/1980	Calvary Cemetery, Cleveland, OH
Hogan, Marty (Martin F.)	08/15/1923	Calvary Cemetery, Youngstown, OH
Hogan, Mortimer Edward	03/17/1923	Calvary Cemetery, Evanston, IL
Hogan, Shanty (James Francis)	04/07/1967	Oak Grove Cemetery, Medford, MA
Hogan, Willie (William Henry)	09/28/1974	Oak Hill Memorial Park, San Jose, CA
Hogg, Bert (Wilbert George)	11/05/1973	Forest Lawn Cemetery, Detroit, MI
Hogg, Bill (William Johnston)	12/08/1909	Lutheran All Faiths Cemetery, Middle Village, Queens, NY
Hogg, Brad (Carter Bradley)	04/02/1935	Tazewell Cemetery, Tazewell, GA
Hogriever, George C.	01/26/1961	Riverside Cemetery, Appleton, WI
Hohman, Bill (William Henry)	10/29/1968	Cedar Hill Cemetery, Brooklyn Park, MD
Hohnhorst, Ed (Edward Hicks)	03/28/1916	Highland Cemetery, Fort Mitchell, KY
Holbrook, Sammy (James Marbury)	04/10/1991	Memorial Park, Meridian, MS
Holden, Bill (William Paul)	09/14/1971	Pfeiffer Cemetery, Pensacola, FL
Holden, Socks (Joseph Francis)	05/10/1996	Queen of the Universe Cemetery, Branchdale, PA
Holdsworth, Jim (James)	03/22/1918	Woodlawn Cemetery, Bronx, NY
Holke, Walter Henry	10/12/1954	Rose Lawn Memorial Gardens, Crystal City, MO
Holland, Dutch (Robert Clyde)	06/16/1967	Oak Grove Cemetery, Maxton, NC
Holland, Mul (Howard Arthur)	02/16/1969	Mount Hebron Cemetery, Winchester, VA
Holland, Will (Willard A.)	07/19/1930	Montrose Cemetery, Upper Darby, PA
Holley, Ed (Edward Edgar)	10/26/1986	Mt. Carmel Cemetery, Paducah, KY
Holliday, Bug (James Wear)	02/15/1910	Spring Grove Cemetery, Cincinnati, OH
Holling, Carl	07/18/1962	Santa Rosa Memorial Park, Santa Rosa, CA
Hollingshead, Holly (John Samuel)	10/06/1926	Glenwood Cemetery, Washington, DC
Hollingsworth, Al (Albert Wayne)	04/28/1996	Wimberley Cemetery, Wimberley, TX
Hollingsworth, Bonnie (John Burnette)	01/04/1990	Greenwood Cemetery, Knoxville, TN
Hollison, John Henry	08/19/1969	Acacia Park Cemetery, River Forest, IL
Hollmig, Stan (Stanley Ernest)	12/04/1981	Oakridge Cemetery, Hondo, TX
Hollocher, Charlie (Charles Jacob)	08/14/1940	Oak Hill Cemetery, Kirkwood, MO
Holloman, Bobo (Alva Lee)	05/01/1987	Evergreen Memorial Park, Athens, GA
Holloway, Jim (James Madison)	04/15/1997	Grace Memorial Park, Plaquemine, LA. Cremated, Baton Rouge, LA.
Holloway, Ken (Kenneth Eugene)	09/25/1968	Laurel Hill Cemetery, Thomasville, GA
Holly, Ed (Edward William)	11/27/1973	Mound Cemetery, Williamsport, PA
Holm, Billy (William Frederick)	07/27/1977	Calvary Cemetery, Portage, IN
Holm', Wattie (Roscoe Albert)	05/19/1950	Barnes Township Cemetery, Linn Grove, IA
Holmes, Chick (Elwood Marter)	04/15/1954	Evergreen Cemetery, Lumberton, NJ
Holmes, Ducky (Howard Elbert)	09/18/1945	Woodland Cemetery, Dayton, OH

Name	DOD	Cemetery, City, State
Holmes, Ducky (James William)	08/06/1932	Hartman Cemetery, Truro, IA
Holmes, Jim (James Scott)	03/10/1960	Riverside Memorial Park, Jacksonville, FL
Holshouser, Herm (Herman Alexander)	07/26/1994	Oakwood Cemetery, Concord, NC
Holt, Red (James Emmett Madison)	02/02/1961	Elmwood Cemetery, Birmingham, AL
Honan, Matty (Martin Weldon)	08/20/1908	Calvary Cemetery, Evanston, IL
Hood, Abie (Albie Larrison)	10/14/1988	Riverside Memorial Park, Norfolk, VA
Hood, Wally (Wallace James, Sr.)	05/02/1965	Rose Hills Memorial Park, Whittier, CA
Hooker, Buck (William Edward)	07/02/1929	Riverview Cemetery, Richmond, VA
Hooks, Alex (Alexander Marcus)	06/19/1993	Oak Hill Cemetery, Edgewood, TX
Hooper, Bob (Robert Nelson)	03/17/1980	Immaculate Conception Cemetery, Montclair, NJ
Hooper, Harry Bartholomew	12/18/1974	Aptos Cemetery, Aptos, CA
Hooper, Mike (Michael H.)	12/02/1917	Baltimore Cemetery, Baltimore, MD
Hoover, Buster (William James)	04/16/1924	Cremated, Garden State Crematory (formerly NY & NJ Crematory), North Bergen, NJ
Hoover, Dick (Richard Lloyd)	04/12/1981	St. Joseph's Cemetery, Lockbourne, OH
Hoover, Joe (Robert Joseph)	09/02/1965	Banning-Cabazon Cemetery, Banning, CA
Hopkins, Buck (John Winton)	10/02/1929	Oakland Cemetery, Hampton, VA
Hopkins, Marty (Meredith Hilliard)	11/20/1963	Restland Memorial Park, Dallas, TX
Hopkins, Mike (Michael Joseph)	02/05/1952	Mount Calvary Cemetery, McKees Rocks, PA
Hopkins, Paul Henry	01/02/2004	Fountain Hill Cemetery, Deep River, CT
Hopp, Johnny (John Leonard)	06/01/2003	Parkview Cemetery, Hastings, NE
Hopper, Bill (William Booth)	01/14/1965	Brown's Chapel Cemetery, Jackson, TN
Hopper, Jim (James McDaniel)	01/23/1982	Evergreen Cemetery, Charlotte, NC
Horan, Shags (Joseph Patrick)	02/13/1969	Angeles Abbey Memorial Park, Compton, CA
Horne, Trader (Berlyn Dale)	02/03/1983	Cremated, Woodland Cemetery, Dayton, OH
Horner, Jack (William Frank)	07/14/1910	Cremated, New Orleans, LA
Hornsby, Rogers	01/05/1963	Hornsby Cemetery, Hornsby Bend, TX
Hornung, Joe (Michael Joseph)	10/30/1931	Holy Cross Cemetery, Brooklyn, NY
Horsey, Hanson	12/01/1949	Asbury Methodist Church Cemetery, Millington, MD
Horstmann, Oscar Theodore	05/11/1977	Cremated, Independence, MO.
Hoskins, Dave (David Taylor)	04/02/1970	River Rest Cemetery, Flint, MI
Hostetler, Chuck (Charles Cloyd)	02/18/1971	Blue Eye Cemetery, Blue Eye, MO
Hotaling, Pete (Peter James)	07/03/1928	Lake View Cemetery, Cleveland, OH
Houck, Byron Simon	06/17/1969	Angelus-Rosedale Cemetery, Los Angeles, CA. Cremated.
Houck, Sadie (Sargent Perry)	05/26/1919	Glenwood Cemetery, Washington, DC
House, Fred (Willard Edwin)	11/16/1923	Mount Washington Cemetery, Independence, MO
Householder, Charlie (Charles W.)	09/03/1913	Mt. Vernon Cemetery, Philadelphia, PA
Houser, Ben (Benjamin Franklin)	01/15/1952	New Gloucester Cemetery, New Gloucester, ME. Cremated in Augusta, ME.
Houser, Joe (Joseph William)	01/03/1953	Forest Hill Cemetery, Canton, OH
Houtz, Lefty (Fred Fritz)	02/15/1959	St. Joseph Cemetery, Wapakoneta, OH
Hovlik, Joe (Joseph)	11/03/1951	Mayflower Cemetery, Oxford Junction, IA

Name	DOD	Cemetery, City, State
Howard, David Austin	01/26/1956	Calvary Hill Cemetery, Dallas, TX
Howard, Del (George Elmer)	12/24/1956	Evergreen-Washelli Cemetery, Seattle, WA. Cremated.
Howard, Earl Nycum	04/04/1937	Everett Cemetery, Everett, PA
Howard, Elston Gene	12/14/1980	George Washington Memorial Park, Paramus, NJ
Howard, Ivan Chester	03/30/1967	Henly-Hornbrook Cemetery, Hornbrook, CA
Howard, Paul Joseph	08/29/1968	Winthrop Cemetery, Winthrop, MA
Howe, Les (Lester Curtis)	07/26/1976	Long Island National Cemetery, Farmingdale, NY
Howell, Dixie (Homer Elliott)	10/05/1990	Cave Hill Cemetery, Louisville, KY
Howell, Dixie (Millard)	03/18/1960	Oak Lawn Cemetery, Wilkes-Barre, PA
Howell, Harry (Henry Harry)	05/22/1956	Greenwood Memorial Terrace, Spokane, WA
Howell, Red (Murray Donald)	10/01/1950	Travelers Rest Cemetery, Travelers Rest, SC
Howell, Roland Boatner	03/31/1973	Roselawn Memorial Park, Baton Rouge, LA
Howerton, Bill (William Ray)	12/18/2001	St. Catherine's Cemetery, Moscow, PA
Howley, Dan (Daniel Philip)	03/10/1944	St. Francis Xavier Cemetery, Weymouth, MA
Howser, Dick (Richard Dalton)	06/17/1987	Tallahassee Memory Gardens, Tallahassee, FL
Hoy, Dummy (William Ellsworth)	12/15/1961	Cremated, Cincinnati Cremation Co. Cincinnti, OH. Ashes given to family
Hoyle, Tex (Roland Edison)	07/04/1994	St. Anthony's Cemetery, Forest City, PA
Hoyt, Waite Charles	08/25/1984	Spring Grove Cemetery, Cincinnati, OH
Hubbard, Al (Allen)	12/14/1930	Newton Cemetery, Newton, MA
Hubbell, Bill (Wilbert William)	08/03/1980	Crown Hill Cemetery, Wheat Ridge, CO
Hubbell, Carl Owen	11/21/1988	Meeker New Hope Cemetery, Meeker, OK
Hubbs, Ken (Kenneth Douglass)	02/15/1964	Montecito Memorial Park, Colton, CA
Huber, Clarence Bill	02/22/1965	Laredo Municipal Cemetery, Laredo, TX
Huber, Otto	04/09/1989	St. Nicholas Cemetery, Lodi, NJ
Hudgens, Jimmy (James Price)	08/26/1955	St. Matthews Cemetery, St. Louis, MO
Hudlin, Willis (George Willis)	08/05/2002	Hazlehurst City Cemetery, Hazlehurst, MS
Hudson, Johnny (John Wilson)	11/07/1970	Bryan City Cemetery, Bryan, TX
Hudson, Nat (Nathaniel P.)	03/14/1928	Rosehill Cemetery, Chicago, IL
Huenke, Mack (Albert Alfred)	09/20/1974	German-Protestant Cemetery, New Bremen, OH
Huff, George A. *manager*	10/01/1936	Roselawn Cemetery (aka New Mount Hope Cemetery), Champaign, IL
Hug, Ed (Edward Ambrose)	05/11/1953	St. Joseph's Cemetery, Cincinnati, OH
Huggins, Miller James	09/25/1929	Spring Grove Cemetery, Cincinnati, OH
Hughes, Bill (William Nesbert)	02/25/1963	Elmwood Cemetery, Birmingham, AL
Hughes, Bill (William R.)	08/25/1943	Fairhaven Memorial Park, Santa Ana, CA
Hughes, Ed (Edward J.)	10/14/1927	Mount Carmel Cemetery, Hillside, IL
Hughes, Jim (James Jay)	06/02/1924	St. Joseph's Cemetery, Sacramento, CA
Hughes, Jim (James Robert)	08/13/2001	Holy Sepulchre Cemetery, Worth, IL
Hughes, Joe (Joseph Thompson)	03/13/1951	Grove Cemetery, Beaver Falls, PA
Hughes, Mickey (Michael F.)	04/10/1931	Holy Name Cemetery, Jersey City, NJ
Hughes, Roy John	03/05/1995	Guardian Angel Cemetery, Cincinnati, OH
Hughes, Thomas Franklin	08/10/1989	Forest Lawn Memorial Park, Beaumont, TX
Hughes, Thomas James	02/08/1956	St. Joseph Cemetery, River Grove, IL

Name	DOD	Cemetery, City, State
Hughes, Tom (Thomas L.)	11/01/1961	Forest Lawn Memorial Park, Glendale, CA
Hughes, Tommy (Thomas Owen)	11/28/1990	Cremated, Maple Hill Crematory, Wilkes-Barre, PA
Hughes, Vern (Vernon Alexander)	09/26/1961	Sylvania Hills Memorial Park, Rochester, PA
Hughey, Jim (James Ulysses)	03/29/1945	Lester Cemetery, California, MI
Hughson, Tex (Cecil Carlton)	08/06/1993	San Marcos Cemetery, San Marcos, TX
Huhn, Emil Hugo	09/05/1925	Oakwood Cemetery, Adrian, MI
Hulen, Billy (William Franklin)	10/02/1947	Cypress Hill Memorial Park, Petaluma, CA
Hulihan, Harry Joseph	09/11/1980	Evergreen Cemetery, Rutland, VT
Hulswitt, Rudy (Rudolph Edward)	01/16/1950	Calvary Cemetery, Louisville, KY
Hulvey, Jim (James Hensel)	04/09/1982	Lebanon Church of the Bretheran Cemetery, Mount Sidney, VA
Hummel, John Edwin	05/18/1959	St. Jerome Cemetery, Holyoke, MA
Humphrey, Al (Albert)	05/13/1961	Chestnut Grove Cemetery, Ashtabula, OH
Humphrey, Bill (Byron William)	02/13/1992	Iberia Cemetery, Iberia, MO
Humphries, John Henry	11/29/1933	Cremated, Salinas, CA
Humphries, John William	06/24/1965	Metairie Cemetery, Metairie, LA
Hungling, Bernie (Bernard Herman)	03/30/1968	Calvary Cemetery, Dayton, OH
Hunnefield, Bill (William Fenton)	08/28/1976	Cremated, Nantucket, MA
Hunt, Ben (Benjamin Franklin)	09/27/1927	Greybull Cemetery, Greybull, WY
Hunt, Dick (Richard M.)	11/20/1895	Green-Wood Cemetery, Brooklyn, NY
Hunt, Joel (Oliver Joel)	07/24/1978	Greenwood Cemetery, Teague, TX
Hunt, Ken (Kenneth Lawrence)	06/08/1997	Holy Cross Cemetery, Fargo, ND
Hunter, Bill (William Ellsworth)	04/10/1934	Ridge Lawn Cemetery, Cheektowaga, NY
Hunter, Catfish (James Augustus)	09/09/1999	Cedarwood Cemetery, Hertford, NC
Hunter, Eddie (Edison Franklin)	03/14/1967	Gate of Heaven Cemetery, Montgomery, OH
Hunter, Fred (Frederick Creighton)	10/26/1963	Green Lawn Cemetery, Columbus, OH
Hunter, George Henry	01/11/1968	Rolling Green Memorial Park, Camp Hill, PA
Hunter, Lem (Robert Lemuel)	11/09/1956	Fairfield Cemetery, West Lafayette, OH
Huntzinger, Walter Henry	08/11/1981	Arlington Cemetery, Drexel Hill, PA
Hurd, Tom (Thomas Carr)	09/05/1982	Cremated, Waterloo, IA
Hurley, Jerry (Jeremiah Joseph)	09/17/1950	Holy Cross Cemetery, Malden, MA
Hurley, Jerry (Jeremiah)	12/27/1919	Calvary Cemetery, Woodside, Queens, NY
Hurst, Don (Frank O'Donnell)	12/06/1952	Cremated, Pacific Crest Crematory, Redondo Beach, CA
Husta, Carl Lawrence	11/06/1951	Egg Harbor Cemetery, Egg Harbor, NJ
Husted, Bill (William J.)	05/17/1941	Cedar Grove Cemetery, Glassboro, NJ
Husting, Bert (Berthold Juneau)	09/03/1948	Graceland Cemetery, Mayville, WI
Huston, Harry Emanuel Kress	10/13/1969	IOOF Cemetery, Blackwell, OK
Huston, Warren Llewellyn	08/30/1999	Cremated, Wareham, MA
Hutcheson, Joe (Joseph Johnson)	02/23/1993	Springtown Cemetery, Springtown, TX
Hutchings, Johnny (John Richard Joseph)	04/27/1963	Holy Cross Cemetery, Indianapolis, IN
Hutchinson, Ed (Edwin Forrest)	07/19/1934	Colfax Cemetery, Colfax, CA
Hutchinson, Fred (Frederick Charles)	11/12/1964	Mt. Olivet Pioneer Cemetery, Renton, WA
Hutchinson, Ira Kendall	08/21/1973	Chapel Hill Gardens South, Oak Lawn, IL
Hutchison, Bill (William Forrest)	03/19/1926	Yantic Cemetery, Norwich, CT

Name	DOD	Cemetery, City, State
Hutson, Roy Lee	05/20/1957	Cypress View Cemetery, San Diego, CA
Hyatt, Ham (Robert Hamilton)	09/11/1963	Holy Cross Cemetery, Spokane, WA
Hyndman, Jim (James Harvey)	01/16/1934	Alamosa Cemetery, Alamosa, CO
Hynes, Pat (Patrick J.)	03/12/1907	Calvary Cemetery, St. Louis, MO
Iburg, Ham (Herman Edward)	02/11/1945	Holy Cross Cemetery, Colma, CA
Imlay, Doc (Harry Miller)	10/07/1948	Christ Churchyard, Bordentown, NJ
Ingersoll, Bob (Robert Randolph)	01/13/1927	Crystal Lake Cemetery, Minneapolis, MN
Ingerton, Scotty (William John)	06/15/1956	St. Vincent's Cemetery, Akron, OH
Ingram, Mel (Melvin David)	10/28/1979	Hillcrest Memorial Park, Grants Pass, OR
Inks, Bert (Albert John)	10/03/1941	Oak Park Cemetery, Ligionier, IN
Iott, Happy (Frederick Bidds)	02/17/1941	Smyrna Cemetery, Smyrna, ME
Iott, Hooks (Clarence Eugene)	04/17/1980	Memorial Park Cemetery, St. Petersburg, FL
Ireland, Ha; (Harold)	07/16/1944	Cremated, Carmel, IN
Irwin, Art (Arthur Albert)	07/16/1921	Long Island Sound, NY. Remains never recovered
Irwin, Bill (William Franklin)	08/07/1933	Calvary Cemetery, Moscow, OH
Irwin, Charlie (Charles Edwin)	09/21/1925	Holy Sepulchre Cemetery, Worth, IL
Irwin, John	02/28/1934	Mount Hope Cemetery, Mattapan, MA
Irwin, Tommy (Thomas Andrew)	04/25/1996	Calvary Cemetery, Altoona, PA
Isbell, Frank (William Frank)	07/15/1941	Old Mission Cemetery, Wichita, KS
Jablonski, Ray (Raymond Leo)	11/25/1985	Resurrection Cemetery, Justice, IL
Jacklitsch, Fred (Frederick Lawrence)	07/18/1937	Green-Wood Cemetery, Brooklyn, NY
Jackson, Bill (William Riley)	09/24/1958	Springdale Cemetery, Peoria, IL
Jackson, Charlie (Charles Bernard)	11/23/1957	Fairview Cemetery, Scottsbluff, NE
Jackson, Charlie (Charles Herbert)	05/27/1968	Oak Grove Cemetery, Pilot, VA
Jackson, George Christopher	11/25/1972	Blum Cemetery, Blum, TX
Jackson, Jim (James Benner)	10/09/1955	Arlington Cemetery, Drexel Hill, PA
Jackson, Joe (Joseph Jefferson)	12/05/1951	Woodlawn Memorial Park, Greenville, SC
Jackson, John Lewis	10/22/1956	Westminster Cemetery, Bala Cynwyd, PA
Jackson, Larry (Lawrence Curtis)	08/28/1990	Cremated, Boise, ID
Jackson, Lou (Louis Clarence)	05/29/1969	Monroe City Cemetery, Monroe, LA
Jackson, Travis Calvin	07/27/1987	Waldo Cemetery, Waldo, AR
Jacobs, Art (Arthur Edward)	06/08/1967	Cremated, Inglewood, CA
Jacobs, Bucky (Newton Smith)	06/15/1990	Forest Lawn Cemetery, Richmond, VA
Jacobs, Elmer (William Elmer)	02/10/1958	Cedar Grove Cemetery, Salem, MO
Jacobs, Mike (Morris Elmore)	03/21/1949	Eastern Cemetery, Louisville, KY
Jacobs, Otto Albert	11/19/1955	Acacia Park Cemetery, River Forest, IL
Jacobs, Ray (Raymond Frederick)	04/05/1952	Holladay Cemetery, Holladay, UT
Jacobs, Tony (Anthony Robert)	12/21/1980	Spring Hill Cemetery, Nashville, TN
Jacobson, Baby Doll (William Chester)	01/16/1977	Dayton Corners Cemetery, Colona, IL
Jacobson, Beany (Albert L.)	01/31/1933	Fairlawn Cemetery, Decatur, IL
Jacobson, Merwin John William	01/13/1978	Govans Presbyterian Cemetery, Baltimore, MD
Jacobus, Larry (Stuart Louis)	08/19/1965	Spring Grove Cemetery, Cincinnati, OH
Jacoby, Harry M.	07/22/1900	North Cedar Hill Cemetery, Philadelphia, PA
Jaeger, Charlie (Charles Thomas)	09/27/1942	Ottawa Avenue Cemetery, Ottawa, IL
Jaeger, Joe (Joseph Peter)	12/13/1963	Hampton Cemetery, Hampton, IA

Name	DOD	Cemetery, City, State
Jahn, Art (Arthur Charles)	01/09/1948	Roselawn Memorial Gardens Cemetery, Little Rock, AR
Jakucki, Sig (Sigmund)	05/29/1979	Calvary Cemetery, Galveston, TX
Jamerson, Charlie (Charles Dewey)	08/04/1980	Cremated, Mocksville, NC
James, Bernie (Robert Byrne)	08/01/1994	Holy Cross Cemetery, San Antonio, TX
James, Bert (Berton Hulon)	01/02/1959	Greenwood Cemetery, Adairville, KY
James, Bill (William Henry)	05/25/1942	Los Angeles National Cemetery, Los Angeles, CA
James, Bill (William Lawrence)	03/10/1971	Memorial Park Cemetery, Oroville, CA
James, Lefty (William A.)	05/03/1933	Ridgewood Cemetery, Wellston, OH
Jamieson, Charlie (Charles Devine)	10/27/1969	Valleau Cemetery, Ridgewood, NJ
Janowicz, Vic (Victor Felix)	02/27/1996	St. Joseph's Cemetery, Lockbourne, OH
Jansen, Ray (Raymond William)	03/19/1934	Valhalla Cemetery, St. Louis, MO
Janvrin, Hal (Harold Chandler)	03/01/1962	Exeter Cemetery, Exeter, NH
Jarvis, Roy (Leroy Gilbert)	01/13/1990	Lofland Cemetery, Wyandotte, OK
Jasper, Hi (Henry W.)	05/22/1937	Memorial Park Cemetery, St. Louis, MO
Javery, Al (Alva William)	08/16/1977	St. Roch's Cemetery, Oxford, MA
Jeanes, Tex (Ernest Lee)	04/05/1973	Memory Park Cemetery, Longview, MA
Jeffcoat, George Edward	10/13/1978	Old Lexington Baptist Church Cemetery, Lexington, SC
Jeffries, Irv (Irvine Franklin)	06/08/1982	Evergreen Cemetery, Louisville, KY
Jelincich, Frank Anthony	06/27/1992	Oak Hill Memorial Park, San Jose, CA
Jenkins, Joe (Joseph Daniel)	06/21/1974	Belmont Memorial Park, Fresno, CA
Jenkins, John Robert	08/03/1968	Van Horn Cemetery, Tina, MO
Jenkins, Tom (Thomas Griffith)	05/03/1979	Pine Hill Cemetery, Quincy, MA
Jennings, Alamazoo (Alfred Gorden)	11/02/1894	Evergreen Cemetery, Southgate, KY
Jennings, Hughie (Hugh Ambrose)	02/01/1928	St. Catherine's Cemetery, Moscow, PA
Jensen, Jackie (Jack Eugene)	07/14/1982	Amherst Cemetery, Amherst, VA
Jessee, Dan (Daniel Edward)	04/30/1970	Cremated, Venice, FL.
Jethroe, Sam (Samuel)	06/16/2001	Erie Cemetery, Erie, PA
Jewett, Nat (Nathan W.)	02/23/1914	Kensico Cemetery, Valhalla, NY
Johns, Ollie (Oliver Tracy)	06/17/1961	Miltonville Cemetery, Miltonville, OH
Johns, Pete (William R.)	08/09/1964	Knollwood Cemetery, Mayfield Heights, OH
Johns, Tommy (Thomas Pearce)	04/13/1927	Greenmount Cemetery, Baltimore, MD
Johnson, Adam Rankin, Sr.	07/02/1972	Montoursville Cemetery, Mountoursville, PA
Johnson, Art (Arthur Gilbert)	06/07/1982	Cremated, Sarasota, FL
Johnson, Bill (William Lawrence)	11/05/1950	Los Angeles National Cemetery, Los Angeles, CA
Johnson, Bob (Robert Lee)	07/06/1982	Cremated. Mountain View Memorial Park, Tacoma, WA. Ashes returned to family
Johnson, Charlie (Charles Cleveland)	08/28/1940	Lawn Croft Cemetery, Linwood, PA
Johnson, Chet (Chester Lillis)	04/10/1983	Cremated, Seattle, WA
Johnson, Chief (George Howard)	06/12/1922	Agency Cemetery, Winnebago, NE
Johnson, Darrell Dean	05/03/2004	Rockville Cemetery, Fairfield, CA
Johnson, Deron Roger	04/23/1992	Dearborn Memorial Park, Poway, CA
Johnson, Ed (Edwin Cyril)	07/03/1975	St. Ann Cemetery, Morganfield, KY

Name	DOD	Cemetery, City, State
Johnson, Ellis Walter	01/14/1965	Hillside Cemetery, Minneapolis, MN
Johnson, Elmer Ellsworth	10/31/1966	Bunnell Cemetery, Frankfort, IN
Johnson, Ernie (Ernest Rudolph)	05/01/1952	Fairhaven Memorial Park, Santa Ana, CA
Johnson, Fred (Frederick Edward)	06/14/1973	Sunset Memorial Park, San Antonio, TX
Johnson, Hank (Henry Ward)	08/20/1982	Fogartyville Cemetery, Bradenton, FL
Johnson, Jing (Russell Conwell)	12/06/1950	Parker Ford Baptist Church Cemetery, Parker Ford., PA
Johnson, Johnny (John Clifford)	06/26/1991	Norway Township Cemetery, Norway, MI
Johnson, Lloyd William	10/08/1980	Cherokee Memorial Park, Lodi, CA
Johnson, Louis (John Louis)	01/28/1941	Floral Hills Memorial Gardens, Kansas City, MO
Johnson, Otis L.	11/09/1915	Floral Park Cemetery, Johnson City, NY
Johnson, Paul Oscar	02/14/1973	Laurel Hill Cemetery, Mission, TX
Johnson, Roy Cleveland	09/10/1973	Cremated, Tacoma, WA
Johnson, Roy J.	01/10/1986	Cremated, Scottsdale. Ashes scattered at Camelback Mountain, Phoenix, AZ
Johnson, Si (Silas Kenneth)	05/12/1994	Elerding Cemetery, Sheridan, IL
Johnson, Syl (Sylvester)	02/20/1985	Portland Memorial Cemetery, Portland, OR
Johnson, Walter Perry	12/10/1946	Rockville Union Cemetery, Rockville, MD
Johnson, Youngy (John Godfred)	08/28/1936	Holy Cross Cemetery, Colma, CA
Johnston, Dick (Richard Frederick)	04/04/1934	St. Mary's Cemetery, Kingston, NY
Johnston, Doc (Wheeler Roger)	02/17/1961	Brainerd Methodist Church Cemetery, Chattanooga, TN
Johnston, Fred (Wilfred Ivy)	07/14/1959	Oakwood Cemetery, Tyler, TX
Johnston, Jimmy (James Harle)	02/14/1967	Forest Hills Cemetery, Chattanooga, TN
Johnston, Johnny (John Thomas)	03/07/1940	Cremated, San Diego, CA.
Joiner, Roy Merrill	12/26/1989	Vina-Carter Cemetery, Vina, CA
Jok, Stan (Stanley Edward)	03/06/1972	St. Stanislaus Cemetery, Cheektowaga, NY
Jolley, Smead Powell	11/17/1991	Cremated, Oakland, CA. Ashes scattered in Pacific Ocean
Jolly, Dave (David)	05/27/1963	Stony Point Cemetery, Stony Point, NC
Jones, Alex (Alexander H.)	04/04/1941	Homestead Cemetery, Homestead, PA
Jones, Art (Arthur Lennox)	11/25/1980	Kershaw City Cemetery, Kershaw, SC
Jones, Bill (William Dennis)	10/10/1946	Millinocket Cemetery, Millinocket, ME
Jones, Binky (John Joseph)	05/13/1961	Resurrection Cemetery, Mackenzie, MO
Jones, Bob (Robert Walter)	08/30/1964	El Camino Memorial Park, La Jolla, CA
Jones, Broadway (Jesse Frank)	09/07/1977	Millsboro Cemetery, Millsboro, DE
Jones, Bumpus (Charles Leander)	06/25/1938	North Cemetery, Cedarville, OH
Jones, Charlie (Charles F.)	09/15/1922	St. Raymond's Cemetery, Bronx, NY
Jones, Cobe (Coburn Dyas)	06/03/1969	Mount Olivet Cemetery, Wheat Ridge, CO
Jones, Cowboy (Albert Edward)	02/09/1958	Golden Cemetery, Golden, CO
Jones, Dale Eldon	11/08/1980	Arlington National Cemetery, Arlington, VA
Jones, Davy (David Jefferson)	03/30/1972	Roseland Park Cemetery, Berkley, MI
Jones, Deacon (Carroll Elmer)	12/28/1952	LeRoy Cemetery, Oskaloosa, KS
Jones, Dick (Decatur Poindexter)	08/02/1994	Mount Zion Cemetery, Meadville, MS
Jones, Earl Leslie	01/24/1989	Belmont Memorial Park, Fresno, CA
Jones, Elijah Albert	04/29/1943	Oxford Cemetery, Oxford, MI

Name	DOD	Cemetery, City, State
Jones, Fielder Allison	03/13/1934	Portland Memorial Cemetery, Portland, OR
Jones, Frank M.	02/04/1936	Valley Cemetery, Marietta, OH
Jones, Gordon Bassett	04/25/1994	East Lawn Sierra Hills Cemetery, Sacramento, CA
Jones, Henry Monroe	05/31/1955	Oak Grove Cemetery, Manistee, MI
Jones, Howie (Howard)	07/15/1972	Irwin Union Cemetery, Irwin, PA
Jones, Jake (James Murrell)	12/13/2000	Epps Cemetery, Epps, LA
Jones, Jim (James Tilford)	05/06/1953	A.R. Dyche Memorial Cemetery, London, KY
Jones, John William	11/03/1956	Fairview Cemetery, Coatesville, PA
Jones, Johnny (John Paul)	06/05/1980	Greenwood Cemetery, Ruston, LA
Jones, Jumping Jack (Daniel Albion)	10/19/1936	East Lawn Cemetery, East Haven, CT
Jones, Ken (Kenneth Frederick)	05/15/1991	Cremated, Hartford, CT
Jones, Nippy (Vernal Leroy)	10/03/1995	South East Lawn Memorial Park, Elk Grove, CA
Jones, Oscar Lafayette	03/16/1953	Garden of Memories Memorial Park, Fort Worth, TX
Jones, Percy Lee	03/18/1979	Grove Hill Memorial Park, Dallas, TX
Jones, Red (Morris E.)	06/30/1974	Cremated, Lincoln, CA
Jones, Sad Sam (Samuel Pond)	07/06/1966	Oak Lawn Cemetery, Woodsfield, OH
Jones, Sam (Samuel)	11/05/1971	Woodlawn Cemetery, Fairmont, WV
Jones, Tex (William Roderick)	02/26/1938	Old Mission Cemetery, Wichita, KS
Jones, Willie Edward	10/18/1983	Hillside Memorial Cemetery, Laurinburg, NC
Jonnard, Bubber (Clarence James)	08/23/1977	Sparkman Hillcrest Memorial Park, Dallas, TX
Jonnard, Claude Alfred	08/27/1959	Mount Olivet Cemetery, Nashville, TN
Jordan, Buck (Baxter Byerly)	03/18/1993	Chestnut Hill Cemetery, Salisbury, NC
Jordan, Charlie (Charles T.)	06/01/1928	Hazleton Cemetery, Hazleton, PA
Jordan, Dutch (Adolf Otto)	12/23/1972	Jefferson Memorial Park, Pleasant Hills, PA
Jordan, Jimmy (James William)	12/04/1957	Forest Lawn Cemetery, Charlotte, NC
Jordan, Mike (Michael Henry)	09/25/1940	St. Mary's Immaculate Conception Cemetery, Lawrence, MA
Jordan, Milt (Milton Mignot)	05/13/1993	Cremated, Ithaca, NY
Jordan, Rip (Raymond Willis)	06/05/1960	Ceneter Conway Cemetery, Conway, NH
Jordan, Slats (Clarence Veasey)	12/07/1953	Loudon Park Cemetery, Baltimore, MD
Jorgens, Art (Arndt Ludwig)	03/01/1980	Memorial Park Cemetery, Skokie, IL
Jorgensen, Pinky (Carl)	05/02/1996	Cremated, Santa Cruz, CA.
Josephson, Duane Charles	01/30/1997	New Hampton City Cemetery, New Hampton, IA
Joss, Addie (Adrian)	04/14/1911	Woodlawn Cemetery, Toledo, OH
Jourdan, Ted (Theodore Charles)	09/23/1961	St. John's Cemetery, New Orleans, LA
Joy, Pop (Aloysius C.)	06/28/1937	Mount Olivet Cemetery, Washington, DC
Joyce, Bill (William Michael)	05/08/1941	Bellefontaine Cemetery, St. Louis, MO
Joyce, Bob (Robert Emmett)	12/10/1981	San Joaquin Catholic Cemetery, Stockton, CA
Joyce, George W.	11/09/1895	Oak Hill Cemetery, Washington, DC
Judd, Ralph Wesley	05/06/1957	Oregon Township Cemetery, Lapeer, MI
Jude, Frank	05/04/1961	Rose Lawn Memorial Gardens, Brownsville, TX
Judge, Joe (Joseph Ignatius)	03/11/1963	Gate of Heaven Cemetery, Silver Spring, MD

Name	DOD	Cemetery, City, State
Judnich, Walt (Walter Franklin)	07/10/1971	Grand View Memorial Park, Glendale, CA
Judy, Lyle Leroy	01/15/1991	San Lerenzo Cemetery, St. Augustine, FL
Juelich, Red (John Samuel)	12/25/1970	SS. Peter & Paul Cemetery, St. Louis, MO
Jumonville, George Benedict	12/12/1996	Magnolia Cemetery, Mobile, AL
Jungels, Ken (Kenneth Peter)	09/09/1975	Wisconsin Memorial Park, Brookfield, WI
Jurisich, Al (Alvin Joseph)	11/03/1981	Greenwood Cemetery, New Orleans, LA
Just, Joe (Joseph Erwin)	11/22/2003	St. Adalbert Cemetery, Milwaukee, WI
Justis, Walt (Walter Newton)	10/04/1941	Greendale Cemetery, Lawrenceburg, IN
Juul, Earl Herold	01/04/1942	Irving Park Cemetery, Chicago, IL
Juul, Herb (Herbert Victor)	11/14/1928	Mount Olivet Cemetery, Chicago, IL
Kading, Jack (John Frederick)	06/02/1964	St. Boniface Cemetery, Chicago, IL
Kafora, Jake (Frank Jacob)	03/23/1928	St. Adalbert's Cemetery, Niles, IL
Kahdot, Ike (Isaac Leonard)	03/31/1999	Altoona Cemetery, Altoona, KS
Kahl, Nick (Nicholas Alexander)	07/13/1959	Coulterville Cemetery, Coulterville, IL
Kahle, Bob (Robert Wayne)	12/16/1988	Holy Cross Cemetery, Culver City, CA
Kahler, George Runnells	02/07/1924	West Union Street Cemetery, Athens, OH
Kahn, Owen Earle	01/17/1981	Maury Cemetery, Richmond, VA
Kahoe, Mike (Michael Joseph)	05/14/1949	Holy Cross Cemetery, Akron, OH
Kaiser, Al (Alfred Edward)	04/11/1969	St. Joseph's Cemetery, Cincinnati, OH
Kaiserling, George	03/02/1918	Union Cemetery, Steubenville, OH
Kalahan, John Joseph	06/20/1952	Holy Cross Cemetery, Yeadon, PA
Kalbfus, Charlie (Charles Henry)	11/18/1941	Oak Hill Cemetery, Washington, DC
Kalfass, Bill (William Philip)	09/08/1968	Germonds Presbyterian Church Cemetery, New City, NY
Kalin, Frank Bruno	01/12/1975	St. Paul's Catholic Cemetery, Weirton, WV
Kallio, Rudy (Rudolph)	04/06/1979	Lone Fir Cemetery, Portland, OR
Kamm, Willie (William Edward)	12/21/1988	Cypress Lawn Memorial Park, Colma, CA. Cremated.
Kamp, Ike (Alphonse Francis)	02/25/1955	Mount Calvary Cemetery, Roslindale, MA
Kampouris, Alex (Alexis William)	05/29/1993	St. Mary's Catholic Cemetery, Sacramento, CA
Kane, Frank (Francis Thomas)	12/02/1962	Calvary Cemetery, Brockton, MA
Kane, Harry	09/15/1932	St. Mary's Cemetery, Portland, OR
Kane, Jerry (William Jeremiah)	06/16/1949	Mount Carmel Cemetery, Belleville, IL
Kane, Jim (James Joseph)	10/02/1947	Holy Sepulchre Cemetery, Omaha, NE
Kane, John Francis	01/28/1934	Riverview Cemetery, St. Anthony, ID
Kane, Tom (Thomas Joseph)	11/26/1973	St. Joseph Cemetery, River Grove, IL
Kantlehner, Erv (Erving Leslie)	02/03/1990	Capay Cemetery, Esparto, CA. Cremated.
Kappel, Heinie (Henry)	08/27/1905	Most Holy Redeemer Cemetery, Philadelphia, PA
Kappel, Joe (Joseph)	07/08/1929	Most Holy Redeemer Cemetery, Philadelphia, PA
Kardow, Paul Otto	04/27/1968	Mission Burial Park North, San Antonio, TX
Karger, Ed (Edwin)	09/09/1957	Delta Municipal Cemetery, Delta, CO
Karl, Andy (Anton Andrew)	04/08/1989	Mission San Luis Rey Cemetery, San Luis Rey, CA
Karlon, Bill (William John)	12/07/1964	St. Anne's Cemetery, Palmer, MA
Karns, Bill (William Arthur)	11/15/1941	Masonic Memorial Park, Olympia, WA
Karow, Marty (Martin Gregory)	04/27/1986	College Station Cemetery, College Station, TX

Name	DOD	Cemetery, City, State
Karpel, Herb (Herbert)	01/24/1995	Eden Memorial Park, Mission Hills, CA
Karr, Benn (Benjamin Joyce)	12/08/1968	Crittenden Memorial Park, Marion, AR
Karst, John Gottlieb	05/21/1976	Sunset Memorial Park, Feasterville, PA
Katt, Ray (Raymond Frederick)	10/19/1999	Guadalupe Valley Memorial Park, New Braunfels, TX
Katz, Bob (Robert Clyde)	12/14/1962	Resurrection Catholic Cemetery, St. Joseph, MI
Kauff, Benny (Benjamin Michael)	11/17/1961	Union Cemetery, Columbus, OH
Kauffman, Dick (Howard Richard)	04/16/1948	Lewisburg Cemetery, Lewisburg, PA
Kaufmann, Tony (Anthony Charles)	06/04/1982	Mount Emblem Cemetery, Elmhurst, IL
Kavanagh, Charlie (Charles Hugh)	09/06/1973	Calvary Cemetery, Reedsburg, WI
Kavanagh, Leo Daniel	08/10/1950	Mount Carmel Cemetery, Hillside, IL
Kavanagh, Marty (Martin Joseph)	07/28/1960	Mount Olivet Cemetery, Detroit, MI
Kazak, Eddie (Edward Terrance)	12/15/1999	Assumption Cemetery, Austin, TX
Keane, Johnny (John Joseph) *manager*	01/06/1967	Memorial Oaks Cemetery, Houston, TX
Kearns, Teddy (Edward Joseph)	12/21/1949	St. Mary's Cemetery, Trenton, NJ
Kearse, Eddie (Edward Paul)	07/15/1968	Holy Sepulchre Cemetery, Hayward, CA
Keas, Ed (Edward James)	01/12/1940	Mount Olivet Cemetery, Dubuque, IA
Keating, Bob (Robert M.)	01/19/1922	St. Michael's Cemetery, Springfield, MA
Keating, Chick (Walter Francis)	07/13/1959	Holy Sepulchre Cemetery, Wyndmoor, PA
Keating, Ray (Raymond Herbert)	12/28/1963	St. Mary's Catholic Cemetery, Sacramento, CA
Keck, Cactus (Frank Joseph)	02/06/1981	Bellerive Heritage Gardens, Creve Coeur, MO
Keefe, Bob (Robert Francis)	12/06/1964	St. John's Catholic Cemetery, Folsom, CA
Keefe, Dave (David Edwin)	02/04/1978	Our Lady of the Holy Rosary Cemetery, Richmond, VT
Keefe, George Washington	08/24/1935	Cedar Hill Cemetery, Suitland, MD
Keefe, John Thomas	08/10/1937	St. Bernard's Church Cemetery, Fitchburg, MA
Keefe, Tim (Timothy John)	04/23/1933	Cambridge Cemetery, Cambridge, MA
Keeler, Willie (William Henry)	01/01/1923	Calvary Cemetery, Woodside, Queens, NY
Keeley, Burt (Burton Elwood)	05/03/1952	Ely Cemetery, Ely, MN
Keen, Bill (William Brown)	07/16/1947	Ferncliff Cemetery, Springfield, OH
Keen, Vic (Howard Victor)	12/10/1976	First Baptist Cemetery, Pembroke, MD
Keenan, Jim (James William)	06/05/1980	Cremated, National Cremation Society, St. Petersburg, FL
Keenan, Jim (James William)	09/21/1926	Spring Grove Cemetery, Cincinnati, OH
Keener, Harry (Joshua Harry)	03/25/1912	Easton Heights Cemetery, Easton, PA
Keesey, Jim (James Ward)	09/05/1951	Lincoln Memorial Park, Portland, OR
Kehn, Chet (Chester Lawrence)	04/05/1984	Cremated, San Diego, CA.
Keifer, Katsy (Sherman Carl)	02/19/1927	Charleroi Cemetery, Charleroi, PA
Keister, Bill (William Hoffman)	08/19/1924	Loudon Park Cemetery, Baltimore, MD
Kelb, George Francis	10/20/1936	Forest Cemetery, Toledo, OH
Keliher, Mickey (Maurice Michael)	09/07/1930	Mount Olivet Cemetery, Washington, DC
Kelleher, Duke (Albert Aloysius)	09/28/1947	Pinelawn Memorial Park and Cemetery, Farmingdale, NY
Kelleher, Frankie (Francis Eugene)	04/13/1979	Cremated, Stockton, CA
Kelleher, Hal (Harold Joseph)	08/27/1989	St. Mary's Cemetery, Cape May, NJ

Name	DOD	Cemetery, City, State
Kelleher, John Patrick	08/21/1960	Walnut Hills Cemetery, Brookline, MA
Keller, Charlie (Charles Ernest)	05/23/1990	Christ Reformed Church Cemetery, Middletown, MD
Kellert, Frank William	11/19/1976	Rose Hill Cemetery, Oklahoma City, OK
Kellett, Red (Donald Stafford)	11/03/1970	Druid Ridge Cemetery, Pikesville, MD
Kelley, Dick (Richard Anthony)	12/11/1991	Cremated, Northridge, CA
Kelley, Harry Leroy	03/23/1958	Cogbill Cemetery, Wynne, AR
Kelley, Joe (Joseph James)	08/14/1943	New Cathedral Cemetery, Baltimore, MD
Kelley, Mike (Michael Joseph)	06/06/1955	Lakewood Cemetery, Minneapolis, MN
Kelliher, Frank (Francis Mortimer)	03/04/1956	Oak Grove Cemetery, Medford, MA
Kellner, Alex (Alexander Raymond)	05/03/1996	Cremated, Tucson, AZ
Kellogg, Al (Albert Clement)	07/21/1953	Lincoln Memorial Park, Portland, OR
Kellogg, Bill (William Dearstyne)	12/12/1971	New Cathedral Cemetery, Baltimore, MD
Kellum, Win (Winford Ansley)	08/10/1951	Highland View Cemetery, Big Rapids, MI
Kelly, Billy (William Joseph)	06/03/1940	Lakeside Cemetery, Port Huron, MI
Kelly, George Lange	10/13/1984	Holy Cross Cemetery, Colma, CA
Kelly, Herb (Herbert Barrett)	05/18/1973	Pine Crest Cemetery, Mobile, AL
Kelly, Joe (Joseph Henry)	08/16/1977	Mount Olivet Cemetery, St. Joseph, MO
Kelly, Joe (Joseph James)	11/24/1967	Rockville Cemetery, Rockville Center, NY
Kelly, John (John Francis)	04/13/1908	Holy Sepulchre Cemetery, Totawa, NJ
Kelly, John Benedict	03/19/1944	Baltimore Cemetery, Baltimore, MD
Kelly, Kick (John O.)	03/27/1926	Calvary Cemetery, Woodside, Queens, NY
Kelly, King (Michael Joseph)	11/08/1894	Mount Hope Cemetery, Mattapan, MA
Kelly, Red (Albert Michael)	02/04/1961	Oakside Cemetery, Zephyrhills, FL
Kelly, Ren (Reynolds Joseph)	08/24/1963	Oak Hill Memorial Park, San Jose, CA
Kelly, Speed (Robert Brown)	05/06/1949	Violette Cemetery, Goshen, IN
Kelly, Will (William Henry)	04/08/1990	St. Agnes Cemetery, Syracuse, NY
Kelsey, Billy (George William)	04/25/1968	Cremated, Springfield, OH
Keltner, Ken (Kenneth Frederick)	12/12/1991	Wisconsin Memorial Park, Brookfield, WI
Kelty, John James	04/13/1929	Holy Name Cemetery, Jersey City, NJ
Kemmler, Rudy (Rudolph)	06/20/1909	Concordia Cemetery, Forest Park, IL
Kemner, Dutch (Herman John)	01/16/1988	Calvary Cemetery, Quincy, IL
Kenna, Ed (Edward Benninghaus)	03/22/1912	Spring Hill Cemetery, Charleston, WV
Kenna, Eddie (Edward Aloysius)	08/21/1972	Cypress Lawn Memorial Park, Colma, CA. Cremated.
Kennedy, Bill (William Aulton)	04/09/1983	Evergreen-Washelli Cemetery, Seattle, WA
Kennedy, Bill (William Gorman)	08/20/1995	Mount Comfort Memorial Park, Alexandria, VA
Kennedy, Brickyard (William Park)	09/23/1915	Greenwood Cemetery, Bellaire, OH
Kennedy, Ed (Edward)	05/20/1905	Calvary Cemetery, Woodside, Queens, NY
Kennedy, Jim *manager*	04/20/1904	Calvary Cemetery, Woodside, Queens, NY
Kennedy, John Irvin	04/27/1998	Evergreen Cemetery, Jacksonville, FL
Kennedy, Monte (Montia Calvin)	03/01/1997	Dale Memorial Park, Chesterfield, VA
Kennedy, Ray (Raymond Lincoln)	01/18/1969	Glen Haven Memorial Park, Winter Park, FL
Kennedy, Ted (Theodore A.)	10/28/1907	Calvary Cemetery, St. Louis, MO
Kennedy, Vern (Lloyd Vernon)	01/28/1993	Mendon Cemetery, Mendon, MO
Kent, Maury (Maurice Allen)	04/19/1966	Cremated, Iowa City, IA
Kenworthy, Bill (William Jennings)	09/21/1950	Mountain View Cemetery, Oakland, CA

Name	DOD	Cemetery, City, State
Keriazakos, Gus (Constantine Nicholas)	05/04/1996	Cremated, Hilton Head, SC
Kerins, Jack (John Nelson)	09/08/1919	Cave Hill Cemetery, Louisville, KY
Kerksieck, Bill (Wayman William)	03/11/1970	Lone Tree Cemetery, Stuttgart, AR
Kerlin, Orie Milton	10/29/1974	Arlington Cemetery, Homer, LA
Kerns, Russ (Russell Eldon)	08/21/2000	Oakwood Cemetery, Fremont, OH
Kerr, Dickie (Richard Henry)	05/04/1963	Forest Park (Lawndale) Cemetery, Houston, TX
Kerr, Doc (John Jonas)	01/09/1937	Richmond Cemetery, Richmond, OH
Kerr, John Francis	10/19/1993	All Souls Cemetery, Long Beach, CA. Cremated.
Kerr, Mel (John Melville)	08/09/1980	Cremated, Vero Beach, FL
Kerwin, Dan (Daniel Patrick)	07/13/1960	Holy Cross Cemetery, Yeadon, PA
Kessler, Henry	01/09/1900	Venango County Poor Farm Cemetery, Sugar Creek Township, PA
Ketter, Phil (Philip)	04/09/1965	St. Paul's Churchyard Cemetery, St. Louis, MO
Keupper, Hank (Henry J.)	08/14/1960	Lake View Cemetery, Johnston City, IL
Kibbie, Hod (Horace Kent)	10/19/1975	Shannon Rose Hill Memorial Park, Fort Worth, TX
Kibble, Jack (John Westly)	12/13/1969	Custer Battlefield National Cemetery, Crow Agency, MT
Kiefer, Joe (Joseph William)	07/05/1975	Mount Olivet Cemetery, Whitesboro, NY
Kiely, Leo Patrick	01/18/1984	Holy Cross Cemetery, North Arlington, NJ
Kilduff, Pete (Peter John)	02/14/1930	St. Mary's Cemetery, Pittsburg, KS
Kile, Daryl Andrew	06/22/2002	Cremated, Chicago, IL. Ashes given to family
Kiley, John Frederick	12/18/1940	Highland Cemetery, Norwood, MA
Killefer, Bill (William)	07/03/1960	Prospect Hill Cemetery, Paw Paw, MI
Killefer, Red (Wade)	09/04/1958	Cremated, Los Angeles, CA.
Killian, Ed (Edwin Henry)	07/18/1928	Woodlawn Cemetery, Detroit, MI
Killilay, Jack (John William)	10/21/1968	Memorial Park Cemetery, Tulsa, OK
Kilroy, Matt (Matthew Aloysius)	03/02/1940	Holy Sepulchre Cemetery, Wyndmoor, PA
Kilroy, Mike (Michael Joseph)	10/02/1960	New Cathedral Cemetery, Philadelphia, PA
Kimball, Gene (Eugene Boynton)	08/02/1882	Mt. Hope Cemetery, Rochester, NY
Kimber, Sam (Samuel Jackson)	11/07/1925	Westminster Cemetery, Bala Cynwyd, PA
Kimble, Dick (Richard Lewis)	05/07/2001	Ottawa Hills Memorial Park, Toledo, OH
Kime, Hal (Harold Lee)	05/16/1939	Union Cemetery, Columbus, OH
Kimmick, Walt (Walter Lyons)	07/24/1989	William Penn Memorial Cemetery, Churchill, PA
Kimsey, Chad (Clyde Elias)	12/03/1942	Fairview Cemetery, Pryor, OK. (aka Pryor Cemetery)
Kinder, Ellis Raymond	10/16/1968	Highland Memorial Gardens, Jackson, TN
King, Lee	09/16/1967	Shinnstown Masonic Cemetery, Shinnstown, WV
King, Lee (Edward Lee)	09/07/1938	Mount Benedict Cemetery, West Roxbury, MA
King, Lynn Paul	05/11/1972	Villisca Cemetery, Villisca, IA
King, Mart (Marshall Ney)	10/19/1911	Oakwood Cemetery, Troy, NY
King, Sam (Samuel Warren)	08/11/1922	King Cemetery, Peabody, MA

Name	DOD	Cemetery, City, State
King, Silver (Charles Frederick)	05/21/1938	New St. Marcus Evangelical Cemetery, St. Louis, MO
King, Steve (Stephen F.)	07/08/1895	Oakwood Cemetery, Troy, NY
Kingdon, Wes (Westcott William)	04/19/1975	Cremated, San Juan Capistrano, CA
Kingman, Henry Lees	12/27/1982	Cremated, Oakland, CA
Kinlock, Billy (William Francis) (buried under birth name: Kinloch)	02/15/1931	Calvary Cemetery, Woodside, Queens, NY
Kinney, Walt (Walter William)	07/01/1971	Cremated, Escondido, CA
Kinsella, Bob (Robert Francis)	12/30/1951	Calvary Cemetery, Springfield, IL
Kinsella, Ed (Edward William)	01/17/1976	St. Mary's Cemetery, Bloomington, IL
Kinsler, William H.	08/11/1963	Mount Carmel Cemetery, Tenafly, NJ
Kinslow, Tom (Thomas F.)	02/22/1901	Congressional Cemetery, Washington, DC
Kinzie, Walt (Walter Harris)	11/05/1909	Graceland Cemetery, Chicago, IL
Kinzy, Slim (Harry)	06/22/2003	Oakland Cemetery, Dallas, TX
Kippert, Ed (Edward August)	06/03/1960	Evergreen Cemetery, Detroit, MI
Kirby, Clay (Clayton Laws)	10/11/1991	National Memorial Park, Falls Church, VA
Kirby, John F.	10/06/1931	Sunset Memorial Park, Affton, MO
Kirby, LaRue	06/10/1961	Eureka Cemetery, Eureka, MI
Kircher, Mike (Michael Andrew)	06/26/1972	Irondequoit Cemetery, Irondequoit, NY
Kirk, Tom (Thomas Daniel)	08/01/1974	Resurrection Cemetery, Cornwells Heights, PA
Kirke, Jay (Judson Fabian)	08/31/1968	Machpelah Cemetery, Pascagoula, MS
Kirkpatrick, Enos Claire	04/14/1964	Calvary Cemetery, Pittsburgh, PA
Kirsch, Harry Louis	12/25/1925	Mount Lebanon Cemetery, Mount Lebanon, PA
Kish, Ernie (Ernest Alexander)	12/21/1993	Lake View Cemetery, Cleveland, OH
Kisinger, Bill (William Francis)	04/20/1929	Evergreen Cemetery, Southgate, KY
Kisinger, Rube (Charles Samuel)	07/17/1941	Oakwood Cemetery, Adrian, MI
Kitson, Frank R.	04/14/1930	Hudson Corners Cemetery, Allegan, MI
Klaerner, Hugo Emil	01/03/1982	Der Stadt Friedhof, Fredericksburg, TX
Klee, Ollie Chester	02/09/1977	Dayton Memorial Park, Dayton, OH
Klein, Chuck (Charles Herbert)	03/28/1958	Holy Cross Cemetery, Indianapolis, IN
Klein, Lou (Louis Frank)	06/20/1976	St. Joseph Cemetery #3, New Orleans, LA
Kleine, Hal (Harold John)	12/10/1957	Resurrection Cemetery, Mackenzie, MO
Kleinhans, Ted (Theodore Otto)	07/24/1985	Serenity Gardens Memorial Park, Largo, FL
Kleinke, Nub (Norbert George)	03/16/1950	Mountain View Cemetery, Oakland, CA
Kleinow, Red (John Peter)	10/09/1929	Lutheran All Faiths Cemetery, Middle Village, Queens, NY
Klepfer, Ed (Edward Lloyd)	08/09/1950	Rose Hill Memorial Park, Tulsa, OK
Klieman, Eddie (Edward Frederick)	11/15/1979	Cremated, Homosassa, FL
Kline, Bob (Robert George)	03/16/1987	Green Lawn Cemetery, Columbus, OH
Kline, Ron (Ronald Lee)	06/22/2002	Browndale Cemtery, Renfrew, PA
Kling, Bill (William)	08/26/1934	Calvary Cemetery, Kansas City, MO
Kling, Johnny (John)	01/31/1947	Mount Moriah Cemetery, Kansas City, MO
Kling, Rudy (Rudolph A.)	03/14/1937	New St. Marcus Cemetery, St. Louis, MO
Klinger, Bob (Robert Harold)	08/19/1977	Allen Cemetery, Allenton, MO
Klinger, Joe (Joseph John)	07/31/1960	Pine Crest Memorial Park, Alexander, AR

Name	DOD	Cemetery, City, State
Klippstein, Johnny (John C.)	10/10/2003	St. Mary's Catholic Cemetery, Huntley, IL
Klobedanz, Fred (Frederick Augustus)	04/12/1940	Pine Grove Cemetery, Waterbury, CT
Klopp, Stan (Stanley Harold)	03/11/1980	Heidelberg Cemetery, Robesonia, PA
Kloza, Jack (John Clarence)	06/11/1962	Holy Cross Cemetery, Milwaukee, WI
Klugmann, Joe (Josie)	07/18/1951	Oakland Cemetery, Moberly, MO
Klumpp, Elmer Edward	10/18/1996	Pinelawn Memorial Park, Milwaukee, WI
Kluszewski, Ted (Theodore Bernard)	03/29/1988	Gate of Heaven Cemetery, Montgomery, OH
Kluttz, Clyde Franklin	05/12/1979	Rowan Memorial Park, Salisbury, NC
Knabe, Otto (Franz Otto)	05/17/1961	New Cathedral Cemetery, Philadelphia, PA
Knaupp, Cotton (Henry Antone)	07/06/1967	Mission Burial Park South, San Antonio, TX
Kneisch, Rudy (Rudolph Frank)	04/06/1965	Lorraine Park Cemetery, Baltimore, MD
Knell, Phil (Philip Louis)	06/05/1944	Cremated, Santa Monica, CA
Knepper, Charlie (Charles)	02/06/1946	Beech Grove Cemetery, Muncie, IN
Knerr, Lou (Wallace Luther)	03/27/1980	Fairview Cemetery, Denver, PA
Knetzer, Elmer Ellsworth	10/03/1975	St. Wendelin Cemetery, Pittsburgh, PA
Knickerbocker, Austin Jay	02/18/1997	Stanford Cemetery, Stanfordville, NY
Knickerbocker, Bill (William Hart)	09/08/1963	Golden Gate National Cemetery, San Bruno, CA
Knight, John Wesley	12/19/1965	Cremated, Chapel of the Chimes Oakland, CA
Knight, Lon (Alonzo P.)	04/23/1932	Laurel Hill Cemetery, Philadelphia, PA
Knisely, Pete (Peter Cole)	07/01/1948	Hewitt Cemetery, Rices Landing, PA
Knode, Mike (Kenneth Thomson)	12/20/1980	Violette Cemetery, Goshen, IN
Knode, Ray (Robert Troxell)	04/13/1982	Memorial Park Cemetery, Battle Creek, MI
Knoll, Punch (Charles Elmer)	02/08/1960	Locust Hill Cemetery, Evansville, IN
Knolls, Hub (Oscar Edward)	07/01/1946	Jewish Waldheim Cemetery, Forest Park, IL
Knothe, Fritz (Wilfred Edgar)	03/27/1963	Holy Cross Cemetery, North Arlington, NJ
Knott, Jack (John Henry)	10/13/1981	Greenleaf Cemetery, Brownwood, TX
Knouff, Ed (Edward)	09/14/1900	Holy Cross Cemetery, Yeadon, PA
Knowles, Jimmy (James)	02/11/1912	New York Bay Cemetery, Jersey City, NJ
Knowlson, Tom (Thomas Herbert)	04/11/1943	Woodlawn Park Cemetery North, Miami, FL
Knowlton, Bill (William Young)	02/25/1944	Fernwood Cemetery, Lansdowne, PA
Knox, Andy (Andrew Jackson)	09/14/1940	Lawnview Cemetery, Rockledge, PA
Knox, Cliff (Clifford Hiram)	09/24/1965	Forest Cemetery, Oskaloosa, IA
Kocher, Brad (Bradley Wilson)	01/13/1965	Laurel Cemetery, White Haven, PA
Koehler, Ben (Bernard James)	05/21/1961	Highland Cemetery, South Bend, IN
Koehler, Pip (Horace Levering)	12/08/1986	Calvary Cemetery, Tacoma, WA
Koenecke, Len (Lenard George)	09/17/1935	Mt. Repose Cemetery, Friendship, WI
Koenig, Mark Anthony	04/22/1993	Cremated, Willows, CA
Koenigsmark, Will (Willis Thomas)	07/01/1972	Waterloo City Cemetery, Waterloo, IL
Koestner, Elmer Joseph	10/27/1959	Calvary Cemetery, Piper City, IL
Kohler, Harry (Henry C.)	08/27/1934	Loudon Park Cemetery, Baltimore, MD
Kokos, Dick (Richard Jerome)	04/09/1986	St. Adalbert's Cemetery, Niles, IL
Kolloway, Don (Donald Martin)	06/30/1994	Cedar Park Cemetery, Claumet Park, IL
Kolp, Ray (Raymond Carl)	07/29/1967	St. Stephen's Cemetery, Fort Thomas, KY
Kolseth, Karl Dickey	05/03/1956	SS. Peter & Paul Cemetery, Cumberland, MD

Name	DOD	Cemetery, City, State
Kommers, Fred (Frederick Raymond)	06/14/1943	Cedar Park Cemetery, Calumet Park, IL
Konetchy, Ed (Edward Joseph)	05/27/1947	Greenwood Memorial Park, Fort Worth, TX
Konikowski, Alex (Alexander James)	09/28/1997	St. Augustine's Cemetery, Seymour, CT
Konnick, Mike (Michael Aloysius)	07/09/1971	St. Mary's Cemetery, Wilkes-Barre, PA
Konopka, Bruno Bruce	09/27/1996	Cremated, Denver, CO
Konstanty, Jim (Casimir James)	06/11/1976	Maple Grove Cemetery, Worcester, NY
Koob, Ernie (Ernest Gerald)	11/12/1941	Calvary Cemetery, St. Louis, MO
Koonce, Cal (Calvin Lee)	10/28/1993	Lafayette Memorial Park, Fayetteville, NC
Kopf, Larry (William Lorenz)	10/15/1986	Mt. Moriah Cemetery, Cincinnati, OH
Kopf, Wally (Walter Henry)	04/30/1979	Calvary Cemetery, Cincinnati, OH
Kopp, Merlin Henry	05/06/1960	St. Mary's Catholic Cemetery, Sacramento, CA
Kopshaw, George Karl	12/26/1934	St. Mary's Cemetery, East Orange, NJ
Kores, Art (Arthur Emil)	03/26/1974	Wisconsin Memorial Park, Brookfield, WI
Korwan, Jim (James)	07/24/1899	Green-Wood Cemetery, Brooklyn, NY
Koshorek, Clem (Clement John)	09/08/1991	White Chapel Memorial Cemetery, Troy, MI
Koslo, Dave (George Bernard)	12/01/1975	St. John's Catholic Church Cemetery, Menasha, WI
Kosman, Mike (Michael Thomas)	12/10/2002	St. Mary's Cemetery, Lafayette, IN
Koster, Fred (Frederick Charles)	04/24/1979	Cave Hill Cemetery, Louisville, KY
Koupal, Lou (Louis Laddie)	12/08/1961	Resurrection Cemetery, Montebello, CA
Kowalik, Fabian Lorenz	08/14/1954	Falls City Cemetery, Falls City, TX
Kracher, Joe (Joseph Peter)	12/24/1981	Lawnhaven Memorial Gardens, San Angelo, TX
Kraft, Clarence Otto	03/26/1958	Greenwood Memorial Park, Fort Worth, TX
Krakauskas, Joe (Joseph Victor Lawrence)	07/08/1960	Holy Sepulchre Cemetery, Burlington, Ontario, Canada
Kramer, Jack (John Henry)	05/18/1995	Greenwood Cemetery, New Orleans, LA
Krapp, Gene (Eugene Hamlet)	04/13/1923	Woodmere Cemetery, Detroit, MI
Kraus, Tex (John William)	01/02/1976	Fort Sam Houston National Cemetery, San Antonio, TX
Krause, Charlie (Charles)	03/30/1948	Woodmere Cemetery, Detroit, MI
Krause, Harry William	10/23/1940	Holy Cross Cemetery, Colma, CA
Krausse, Lew (Lewis Bernard, Sr.)	09/06/1988	Palms Memorial Park, Sarasota, FL
Kreeger, Frank	07/14/1899	Linwood Cemetery, Pana, IL
Kreevich, Mike (Michael Andreas)	04/25/1994	Union Miners Cemetery, Mount Olive, IL
Krehmeyer, Charlie (Charles L.)	02/10/1926	New St. Marcus Evangelical Cemetery, St. Louis, MO
Kreiger, Kurt Ferdinand	08/16/1970	Sunset Memorial Park, Affton
Kreitner, Mickey (Albert Joseph)	03/06/2003	Spring Hill Cemetery, Nashville, TN
Kreitz, Ralph Wesley	07/20/1941	Lincoln Memorial Park, Portland, OR
Kremer, Ray (Remy Peter)	02/08/1965	Sunset View Cemetery, El Cerrito, CA
Kress, Red (Ralph)	11/29/1962	Forest Lawn Memorial Park, Glendale, CA
Krichell, Paul Bernard	06/04/1957	Kensico Cemetery, Valhalla, NY
Krieg, Bill (William Frederick)	03/25/1930	Chillicothe City Cemetery, Chillicothe, IL
Krist, Howie (Howard Wilbur)	04/23/1989	Delevan Cemetery, Delevan, NY

Name	DOD	Cemetery, City, State
Kroh, Rube (Floyd Myron)	03/17/1944	Garden of Memories, Metairie, LA
Krol, Jack *manager*	05/30/1994	Parklawn Memorial Garden, Winston-Salem, NC
Kroner, John Harold	04/26/1968	Memorial Park Cemetery, St. Louis, MO
Krueger, Ernie (Ernest George)	04/22/1976	Oak Woods Cemetery, Chicago, IL
Krueger, Otto (Arthur William)	02/20/1961	Resurrection Cemetery, Mackenzie, MO
Krug, Henry Charles	01/14/1908	Cypress Lawn Memorial Park, Colma, CA
Krug, Marty (Martin John)	06/27/1966	Forest Lawn Memorial Park, Glendale, CA
Kruger, Abe (Abraham)	07/04/1962	SS. Peter & Paul Cemetery, Elmira, NY
Kruger, Art (Arthur T.)	11/28/1949	Holy Cross Cemetery, Culver City, CA
Kucab, Johnny (John Albert)	05/26/1977	St. John's Cemetery, Campbell, OH
Kuczynski, Bert (Bernard Carl)	01/19/1997	Schoenersville Cemetery, Schoenersville, PA
Kuehne, Bill (William J.)	10/27/1921	Union Cemetery, New Washington, OH
Kuenn, Harvey Edward	02/28/1988	Sunland Memorial Park, Sun City, AZ
Kuhel, Joe (Joseph Anthony)	02/26/1984	Forest Hill Cemetery, Kansas City, MO
Kuhn, Bub (Bernard Daniel)	11/20/1956	Evergreen Cemetery, Lansing, MI
Kuhn, Walt (Walter Charles)	06/14/1935	Belmont Memorial Park, Fresno, CA
Kuhns, Charlie (Charles Benton)	07/15/1922	Freeport Cemetery, Freeport, PA
Kunkel, Bill (William Gustave James)	05/04/1985	Cremated, Middletown, NJ. Ashes given to family
Kunz, Earl Dewey	04/14/1963	St. Mary's Catholic Cemetery, Sacramento, CA
Kurowski, Whitey (George John)	12/09/1999	Gethsemane Cemetery, Reading, PA
Kusel, Ed (Edward Daniel)	10/20/1948	Brooklyn Heights Cemetery, Brooklyn Heights, OH
Kush, Emil Benedict	11/26/1969	St. Joseph Cemetery, River Grove, IL
Kutina, Pete (Joseph Peter)	04/13/1945	Bohemian National Cemetery, Chicago, IL
Kyle, Andy (Andrew Ewing)	09/06/1971	Park Lawn Cemetery, Toronto, Ontario, Canada
Laabs, Chet (Chester Peter)	01/26/1983	St. Clement Cemetery, Center Line, MI
LaChance, Candy (George Joseph)	08/18/1932	Calvary Cemetery, Waterbury, CT
Lackey, William D.	05/15/1941	Union Cemetery, Columbus, OH
Lacy, Guy (Osceola Guy)	11/19/1953	Triplett Cemetery, Cleveland, TN
Ladd, Hi (Arthur Clifford)	05/07/1948	Knotty Oak Cemetery, Anthony, RI
Lade, Doyle Marion	05/18/2000	National Memorial Cemetery of Arizona, Phoenix, AZ
Lafferty, Flip (Frank Bernard)	02/08/1910	Wilimington & Brandywine Cemetery, Wilmington, DE
Lafitte, Ed (Edward Francis)	04/12/1971	Ivy Hill Cemetery, Philadelphia, PA
LaForest, Ty (Byron Joseph)	05/05/1947	Mount Pleasant Cemetery, Arlington, MA
Lagger, Ed (Edwin Joseph)	11/10/1981	Mount Olivet Cemetery, Joliet, IL
Lajeskie, Dick (Richard Edward)	08/15/1976	Maryrest Cemetery, Mahwah, NJ
Lajoie, Napoleon	02/07/1959	Bellevue Cedar Hill Memory Gardens, Daytona Beach, FL
Lake, Eddie (Edward Erving)	06/07/1995	Holy Sepulchre Cemetery, Hayward, CA
Lake, Fred (Frederick Lovett)	11/24/1931	Oak Grove Cemetery, Medford, MA
Lake, Joe (Joseph Henry)	06/30/1950	St. John's Cemetery, Middle Village, Queens, NY

Name	DOD	Cemetery, City, State
Lakeman, Al (Albert Wesley)	05/25/1976	Roselawn Memorial Gardens, Inman, SC
Lally, Dan (Daniel J.)	04/14/1936	Mount Olivet Cemetery, Milwaukee, WI
LaManna, Frank	09/01/1980	St. Mary's Cemetery, Syracuse, NY
Lamanske, Frank James	08/04/1971	Oak Hill Cemetery, Taylorville, IL
Lamar, Bill (William Harmong)	05/24/1970	Baltimore National Cemetery, Baltimore, MD
LaMaster, Wayne (Noble Wayne)	08/04/1989	Kraft-Graceland Memorial Park, New Albany, IN
Lambert, Clay (Clayton Patrick)	04/03/1981	Aultorest Memorial Park, Ogden, UT
Lambert, Gene (Eugene Marion)	02/10/2000	Memorial Park Cemetery, Memphis, TN
Lambeth, Otis Samuel	06/05/1976	Moran Cemetery, Moran, KS
Lamer, Pete (Pierre)	10/24/1931	Cypress Hills Cemetery, Brooklyn, NY
Lamlein, Fred (Frederick Arthur)	09/20/1970	Mount Hope Catholic Cemetery, Port Huron, MI
LaMotte, Bobby (Robert Eugene)	11/02/1970	Bonaventure Cemetery, Savannah, GA
Lampe, Henry Joseph	09/16/1936	Cedar Grove Cemetery, Dorchester, MA
Land, Doc (William Gilbert)	04/14/1986	Belmont Community Cemetery, Belmont, AL
Land, Grover Cleveland	07/22/1958	Greenwood Memory Lawn Cemetery, Phoenix, AZ
Landenberger, Ken (Kenneth Henry)	07/28/1960	Whitehaven Park, Mayfield Village, OH
Landrum, Don (Donald Leroy)	01/09/2003	Holy Cross Cemetery, Antioch, CA
Landrum, Jesse Glenn	06/27/1983	Forest Lawn Memorial Park, Beaumont, TX
Lane, Hunter (James Hunter)	09/12/1994	Elmwood Cemetery, Memphis, TN
Lane, Jery (Jerald Hal)	07/24/1988	Chattanooga National Cemetery, Chattanooga, TN
Lanford, Sam (Lewis Grover)	09/14/1970	Bethel Cemetery, Woodruff, SC
Lanfranconi, Walt (Walter Oswald)	08/18/1986	Hope Cemetery, Barre, VT
Lang, Marty (Martin John)	01/13/1968	Crown Hill Cemetery, Wheat Ridge, CO
Lange, Bill (William Alexander)	07/23/1950	Holy Cross Cemetery, Colma, CA
Lange, Erv (Erwin Henry)	04/24/1971	Oakridge Cemetery, Hillside, IL
Lange, Frank Herman	12/26/1945	Hillside Cemetery, Columbus, WI
Langford, Sam (Elton)	07/31/1993	Plainview Cemetery & Memorial Park, Plainview, TX
Langsford, Bob (Robert William)	01/10/1907	Cave Hill Cemetery, Louisville, KY
Lanning, Johnny (John Young)	11/08/1989	Tweed's Chapel Cemetery, Asheville, NC
Lanning, Les (Lester)	06/13/1962	Pine Hill Cemetery, Westfield, MA
Lanning, Tom (Thomas Newton)	11/04/1967	Georgia Memorial Park Cemetery, Marietta, GA
Lansing, Gene (Eugene Hewitt)	01/18/1945	Albany Rural Cemetery, Albany, NY
Lapan, Pete (Peter Nelson)	01/05/1953	Los Angeles National Cemetery, Los Angeles, CA
LaPointe, Ralph Robert	09/13/1967	St. Stephen's Cemetery, Winooski, VT
LaPorte, Frank Breyfogle	09/25/1939	Union Cemetery, Uhrichsville, OH
Lapp, Jack (John Walker)	02/06/1920	Mount Peace Cemetery, Philadelphia, PA
Larkin, Ed (Edward Francis)	03/28/1934	SS. Peter & Paul Cemetery, North Towanda, PA
Larkin, Henry E.	01/31/1942	St. Peter's Cemetery, Reading, PA
Larkin, Steve (Stephen Patrick)	05/02/1969	St. Mary's Cemetery, Cincinnati, OH

Name	DOD	Cemetery, City, State
Larmore, Bob (Robert McKahan)	01/15/1964	New St. Marcus Cemetery, St. Louis, MO
LaRocque, Sam (Simeon Henry Jean)	06/05/1933	Mount Olivet Cemetery, Detroit, MI
LaRoss, Spike (Harry Raymond)	03/22/1954	Oak Woods Cemetery, Chicago, IL
Lary, Al (Alfred Allen)	07/10/2001	Carroll's Creek Baptist Church Cemetery, Northport, AL
Lary, Lyn (Lynford Hobart)	01/09/1973	All Souls Cemetery, Long Beach, CA
Lasley, Bill (Willard Almond)	08/21/1990	Acacia Memorial Park, Seattle, WA
Latham, Arlie (Walter Arlington)	11/29/1952	Greenfield Cemetery, Uniondale, NY
Lathers, Chick (Charles Ten Eyck)	07/26/1971	Greenwood Cemetery, Petoskey, MI
Lathrop, Bill (William George)	11/20/1958	Oak Hill Cemetery, Janesville, WI
Latimer, Tacks (Clifford Wesley)	04/24/1936	Greenlawn Cemetery, Milford, OH
Lattimore, Bill (William Hershel)	10/30/1919	Evergreen Cemetery, Paris, TX
Lau, Charlie (Charles Richard)	03/18/1984	Moreland Memorial Park, Parkville, MD
Lauder, Billy (William)	05/20/1933	Norwalk Cemetery, Norwalk, CT
Lauterborn, Bill (William Bernard)	04/19/1965	Hillside Cemetery, Andover, NY
Lavagetto, Cookie (Harry Arthur)	08/10/1990	Holy Cross Catholic Cemetery, St. Helena, CA
Lavan, Doc (John Leonard)	05/29/1952	Arlington National Cemetery, Arlington, VA
Lavender, Jimmy (James Sanford)	01/12/1960	Felton Cemetery, Montezuma, GA
LaVigne, Art (Arthur David)	07/18/1950	Hope Cemetery, Worcester, MA
Lawlor, Mike (Michael H.)	08/03/1918	St. Mary's Cemetery, Troy, NY
Lawrence, Bill (William Henry)	06/15/1997	Cypress Lawn Memorial Park, Colma, CA
Lawrence, Brooks Ulysses	04/27/2000	Ferncliff Cemetery, Springfield, OH
Lawry, Otis Carroll	10/23/1965	Maplewood Cemetery, Fairfield, ME
Lawson, Al (Alfred Voyle)	04/09/1977	Dibble Cemetery, Stockport, IA
Lawson, Bob (Robert Baker)	10/28/1952	Chapel Hill Cemetery, Chapel Hill, NC
Layden, Gene (Eugene Francis)	12/12/1984	Queen of Heaven Cemetery, Venetia, PA
Layden, Pete (Peter John)	07/18/1982	Layden Family Cemetery, Edna, TX
Layne, Herman	08/27/1973	Kirkland Memorial Gardens, Point Pleasant, WV
Lazzeri, Tony (Anthony Michael)	08/06/1946	Sunset View Cemetery, El Cerrito, CA
Leach, Freddy (Frederick)	12/10/1981	Hagerman Cemetery, Hagerman, ID
Leach, Tommy (Thomas William)	09/29/1969	Forest Hill Cemetery, Haines City, FL
Leadley, Bob (Robert H.) *manager*	05/19/1936	Inglewood Park Cemetery, Inglewood, CA
Leahy, Dan (Daniel C.)	12/25/1915	Calvary Cemetery, Knoxville, TN
Leahy, Tom (Thomas Joseph)	06/11/1951	St. Lawrence Cemetery, West Haven, CT
Lear, Fred (Frederick Francis)	10/13/1955	St. Mary's Cemetery, Grassmere, Staten Island, NY
Lear, King (Charles Bernard)	10/31/1976	Cedar Hill Cemetery, Greencastle, PA
Leard, Bill (William Wallace)	01/15/1970	Cypress Lawn Memorial Park, Colma, CA. Cremated.
Leary, Frank (Francis Patrick)	10/04/1907	St. Patrick's Cemetery, Natick, MA
Leary, John Louis	08/18/1961	Calvary Cemetery, Waltham, MA
Leathers, Hal (Harold Langford)	04/12/1977	Lakewood Memorial Park, Hughson, CA
Leber, Emil Bohmiel	11/06/1924	Riverside Cemetery, Cleveland, OH
LeBourveau, Bevo (DeWitt Wiley)	12/09/1947	Cremated, Nevada City, CA
Ledbetter, Razor (Ralph Overton)	02/01/1969	Burke Memorial Park, Morganton, NC
Ledwith, Mike (Michael)	01/02/1929	St. Raymond's Cemetery, Bronx, NY

Name	DOD	Cemetery, City, State
Lee, Big Bill (William Crutcher)	06/15/1977	Protestant Cemetery, Plaquemine, LA
Lee, Billy (William Joseph)	01/06/1984	Calvary Cemetery, Drums, PA
Lee, Cliff (Clifford Walker)	04/25/1980	Crown Hill Cemetery, Wheat Ridge, CO. Cremated.
Lee, Dud (Ernest Dudley)	01/07/1971	Fairmount Cemetery, Denver, CO
Lee, Hal (Harold Burnham)	09/04/1989	Jackson County Memorial Park, Pascagoula, MS
Lee, Leonidas Pyrrhus	06/11/1912	Rosehill Cemetery, Chicago, IL
Lee, Roy Edwin	11/11/1985	Frieden's Evangelical Church Cemetery, Troy, IL
Lee, Tom (Thomas Frank)	03/04/1886	Catholic Cemetery, Milwaukee, WI
Lee, Watty (Wyatt Arnold)	03/06/1936	Mount Olivet Cemetery, Washington, DC
Leever, Sam (Samuel)	05/19/1953	Goshen Cemetery, Goshen, OH
LeFevre, Al (Alfred Modesto)	01/21/1982	Calvary Cemetery, Woodside, Queens, NY
Lefler, Wade Hampton	03/06/1981	Eastview Cemetery, Newton, NC
Legett, Lou (Louis Alfred)	03/06/1988	Masonic Cemetery, New Orleans, LA
Lehan, James Francis	07/18/1946	St. Patrick's Cemetery, Hartford, CT
Leheny, Regis Francis	11/02/1976	St. Paul's Cathedral Cemetery, Pittsburgh, PA
Lehner, Paul Eugene	12/27/1967	Highland Memorial Gardens, Bessemer, AL
Lehr, Clarence Emanuel	01/31/1948	Forest Hill Cemetery, Ann Arbor, MI
Lehr, Norm (Norman Carl Michael)	07/17/1968	Leicester Cemetery, Leicester, NY
Leiber, Hank (Henry Edward)	11/08/1993	East Lawn Palms Cemetery, Tucson, AZ
Leibold, Nemo (Harry Loran)	02/04/1977	Holy Sepulchre Cemetery, Southfield, MI
Leifer, Elmer Edwin	09/26/1948	Pine City Cemetery, Pine City, WA
Leighton, John Atkinson	10/31/1956	Pine Grove Cemetery, Lynn, MA
Leinhauser, Bill (William Charles)	04/14/1978	Holy Cross Cemetery, Yeadon, PA
Leip, Ed (Edgar Ellsworth)	11/24/1983	Princeton Memorial Park, Robbinsville, NJ
Leiper, John Henry Thomas	08/23/1960	Leiper Church Cemetery, Swarthmore, PA
Leith, Bill (William)	07/16/1940	Fishkill Rural Cemetery, Beacon, NY
Leitner, Doc (George Aloysius)	05/18/1937	Rockland Cemetery, Sparkill, NY
Leitner, Dummy (George Michael)	02/20/1960	Loudon Park Cemetery, Baltimore, MD
Leja, Frank John	05/03/1991	Greenlawn Cemetery, Nahant, MA
LeJeune, Larry (Sheldon Aldenbert)	04/21/1952	Our Lady-Mount Carmel Cemetery, Wyandotte, MI
Lelivelt, Bill (William John)	02/14/1968	St. Adalbert's Cemetery, Niles, IL
Lelivelt, Jack (John Frank)	01/20/1941	Grand View Memorial Park, Glendale, CA
Lembo, Steve (Stephen Neal)	12/04/1989	St. Charles Cemetery, Farmingdale, NY
Lemon, Bob (Robert Granville)	01/11/2000	Cremated, Forest Lawn Memorial Park-Long Beach, Long Beach, CA. Ashes given to family
Lennon, Billy (William H.)	08/19/1910	Holy Cross Cemetery, Yeadon, PA
Lennon, Ed (Edward Francis)	09/13/1947	Holy Cross Cemetery, Yeadon, PA
Lennox, Ed (James Edgar)	10/26/1939	Evergreen Cemetery, Camden, NJ
Leon, Isidoro	07/25/2002	Miami Memorial Park, Miami, FL
Leonard, Andy (Andrew Jackson)	08/21/1903	New Calvary Cemetery, Mattapan, MA
Leonard, Dutch (Emil John)	04/17/1983	Auburn Cemetery, Auburn, IL
Leonard, Dutch (Hubert Benjamin)	07/11/1952	Mountain View Cemetery, Fresno, CA
Leonard, Elmer Ellsworth	05/27/1981	Tulocay Cemetery, Napa, CA

Name	DOD	Cemetery, City, State
Leopold, Rudy (Rudolph Matas)	09/03/1965	Roselawn Memorial Park, Baton Rouge, LA
Leovich, John Joseph	02/03/2000	Willamette National Cemetery, Portland, OR
LePine, Pete (Louis Joseph)	12/03/1949	Precious Blood Cemetery, Woonsocket, RI
Lerchen, Dutch (Bertram Roe)	01/07/1962	Roseland Park Cemetery, Berkley, MI
Lerian, Walt (Walter Irvin)	10/22/1929	New Cathedral Cemetery, Baltimore, MD
LeRoy, Louis Paul	10/10/1944	St. Francis Solanus Catholic Church Cemetery, Gresham, WI
Leslie, Roy Reid	04/09/1972	Arledge Ridge Cemetery, Bonham, TX
Leslie, Sam (Samuel Andrew)	01/21/1979	Jackson County Memorial Park, Pascagoula, MS
Letchas, Charlie	03/14/1995	Laurel Hill Cemetery, Thomasville, GA
Levan, Jesse Roy	11/30/1998	Charles Evans Cemetery, Reading, PA
Leverenz, Walt (Walter Fred)	03/19/1973	Atascadero Cemetery, Atascadero, CA
Leverett, Dixie (Gorham Vance)	02/20/1957	Riverview Abbey Mausoleum, Portland, OR
Leverette, Hod (Horace Wilbur)	04/10/1958	Parkview Cemetery, Peoria, IL
Levey, Jim (James Julius)	03/14/1970	Restland Memorial Park, Dallas, TX
Levis, Charlie (Charles H.)	10/16/1926	Calvary Cemetery, St. Louis, MO
Levsen, Dutch (Emil Henry)	03/12/1972	Wyoming Cemetery, Wyoming, IA
Lewis, Buddy (William Henry)	10/24/1977	Memorial Park Cemetery, Memphis, TN
Lewis, Burt (William Burton)	03/24/1950	Sweeney Cemetery, North Tonawanda, NY
Lewis, Duffy (George Edward)	06/17/1979	Holy Cross Cemetery, Londonderry, NH
Lewis, Fred (Frederick Miller)	06/05/1945	Forest Hill Cemetery, Utica, NY
Lewis, Jack (John David)	02/25/1956	Mt. Calvary Cemetery, Steubenville, OH
Lewis, Phil (Philip)	08/08/1959	Dorchester Cemetery, Dorchester, GA
Lewis, Ted (Edward Morgan)	05/24/1936	Durham Community Cemetery, Durham, NH
Libby, Steve (Stephen Augustus)	03/31/1935	Evergreen Cemetery, New Haven, CT
Liddle, Don (Donald Eugene)	06/05/2000	Highland Memorial Gardens, Mt. Carmel, IL
Lieber, Dutch (Charles Edwin)	12/31/1961	Los Angeles National Cemetery, Los Angeles, CA
Liebhardt, Glenn Ignatius	03/14/1992	Forsyth Memorial Park Cemetery, Winston-Salem, NC
Liebhardt, Glenn John	07/13/1956	Calvary Cemetery, Cleveland, OH
Liese, Fred (Frederick Richard)	06/30/1967	Cremated, Los Angeles, CA
Lillard, Gene (Robert Eugene)	04/12/1991	Goleta Cemetery, Goleta, CA
Lillie, Jim (James J.)	11/09/1890	Mount St. Mary's Cemetery, Kansas City, MO
Lilly, Bryce Lewis	10/17/2002	Tahoma National Cemetery, Kent, WA
Lincoln, Ezra Perry	05/07/1951	Raynham Cemetery, Raynham, MA
Lind, Carl (Henry Carl)	08/02/1946	St. John's Cemetery, New Orleans, LA
Lindaman, Vive (Vivan Alexander)	02/13/1927	Calvary Cemetery, Charles City, IA
Linde, Lymie (Lyman Gilbert)	10/26/1995	Leipsic Cemetery, Beaver Dam, WI
Lindell, Johnny (John Harlan)	08/27/1985	Cremated, Newport Beach, CA
Lindemann, Bob (John Frederick Mann)	12/19/1951	Mound Cemetery, Williamsport, PA
Lindemann, Ernie (Ernest)	12/27/1951	Lutheran All Faiths Cemetery, Middle Village, Queens, NY
Lindquist, Carl Emil	09/03/2001	Newton Cemetery, Emporium, PA
Lindsay, Bill (William Gibbons)	07/14/1963	New Garden Friends Cemetery, Greensboro, NC

Name	DOD	Cemetery, City, State
Lindsay, Chris (Christian Haller)	01/25/1941	Old Monaca Cemetery, Monaca, PA. (aka Union Cemetery)
Lindsey, Jim (James Kendrick)	10/25/1963	Greensburg Cemetery, Greensburg, LA
Lindstrom, Fred (Frederick Charles)	10/04/1981	All Saints Cemetery, Des Plaines, IL
Link, Fred (Frederick Theodore)	05/22/1939	Rosewood Memorial Park, Humble, TX
Linton, Bob (Claud Clarence)	04/03/1980	Magnolia Memorial Park, Magnolia, AR
Lipon, Johnny (John Joseph)	08/17/1998	Memorial Oaks Cemetery, Houston, TX
Lipp, Tom (Thomas Charles)	05/30/1932	New Freedom Cemetery, New Freedom, PA
Lipscomb, Nig (Gerard)	02/27/1978	Sharon Memorial Park, Charlotte, NC
Lisenbee, Hod (Horace Milton)	11/14/1987	Liberty Presbyterian Church Cemetery, Clarksville, TN
Liska, Ad (Adolph James)	11/30/1998	Mount Calvary Cemetery, Portland, OR
Little, Jack (William Arthur)	07/27/1961	Oakwood Cemetery, Waco, TX
Littlefield, Dick (Richard Bernard)	11/20/1997	Grand Lawn Cemetery, Detroit, MI
Lively, Jack (Henry Everett)	12/05/1967	Hebron Church of Christ Cemetery, Joppa, AL
Livengood, Wes (Wesley Amos)	09/02/1996	Salem Cemetery, Winston-Salem, NC
Livingston, Mickey (Thompson Orville)	04/03/1983	Newberry Memorial Gardens, Newberry, SC
Livingston, Paddy (Patrick Joseph)	09/19/1977	Calvary Cemetery, Cleveland, OH
Lizotte, Abe (Abel)	12/04/1926	St. Mary's Cemetery, Wilkes-Barre, PA
Llewellyn, Clem (Clement Manly)	11/26/1969	Oakwood Cemetery, Concord, NC
Loane, Bob (Robert Kenneth)	12/11/2002	El Carmelo Cemetery, Pacific Grove, CA. Cremated.
Lobert, Frank John	05/29/1932	St. George's Cemetery, Pittsburgh, PA
Lobert, Hans (John Bernard)	09/14/1968	Philadelphia Memorial Park, Frazer, PA
Lochhead, Harry (Robert Henry)	08/22/1909	Stockton Rural Cemetery, Stockton, CA
Locke, Marshall Pinkney Wilder	03/06/1940	Ashland Cemetery, Ashland, OH
Lockwood, Milo Hathaway	10/09/1897	Lake View Cemetery, Cleveland, OH
Loftus, Dick (Richard Joseph)	01/21/1972	Sleepy Hollow Cemetery, Concord, MA
Loftus, Frank (Francis Patrick)	10/27/1980	Mount Hope Cemetery, Belchertown, MA
Loftus, Tom (Thomas Joseph)	04/16/1910	Mount Olivet Cemetery, Dubuque, IA
Logan, Bob (Robert Dean)	05/20/1978	Oaklawn Memorial Gardens, Indianapolis, IN
Lohr, Howard Sylvester	01/09/1977	Arlington Cemetery, Drexel Hill, PA
Lollar, Sherm (John Sherman)	09/24/1977	Rivermonte Memorial Gardens, Springfield, MO
Lombardi, Ernie (Ernesto Natali)	09/26/1977	Mountain View Cemetery, Oakland, CA
Lombardi, Vic (Victor Alvin)	12/03/1997	Cemetery Tulare, Tulare, CA
Lonergan, Walter E.	01/23/1958	Mount Calvary Cemetery, Roslindale, MA
Long, Dale (Richard Dale)	01/27/1991	Cheshire Cemetery, Cheshire, MA
Long, Dan (Daniel W.)	04/30/1929	St. Mary's Cemetery, Oakland, CA
Long, Herman C.	09/17/1909	Concordia Cemetery, Forest Park, IL
Long, Jim (James M.)	12/12/1932	Resthaven Memorial Park, Louisville, KY
Long, Jimmie (James Albert)	09/14/1970	Corpus Christi Cemetery, Fort Dodge, IA
Long, Lep (Lester)	10/21/1958	Oak Hill Memorial Cemetery, Birmingham, AL
Long, Tom (Thomas Francis)	09/16/1973	St. Louis Cemetery, Louisville, KY
Loos, Pete (Ivan)	02/23/1956	Mount Peace Cemetery, Philadelphia, PA

Name	DOD	Cemetery, City, State
Lopat, Eddie (Edmund Walter)	06/15/1992	St. Mary's Cemetery, Greenwich, CT
Lopez, Jose Ramon	09/04/1982	Woodlawn Park Cemetery North, Miami, FL
Lord, Bris (Bristol Robotham)	11/13/1964	Lawn Croft Cemetery, Linwood, PA
Lord, Harry Donald	08/09/1948	Riverside Cemetery, Kezar Falls, ME
Lorenzen, Lefty (Adolph Andreas)	03/05/1963	Fairmont Cemetery, Davenport, IA
Loudell, Art (Arthur)	02/19/1961	Mount Moriah Cemetery, Kansas City, MO
Louden, Baldy (William P.)	12/08/1935	Philos Cemetery, Westernport, MD
Loudenslager, Charlie (Charles Edward)	10/31/1933	Loudon Park Cemetery, Baltimore, MD
Loughran, William H.	08/07/1917	Calvary Cemetery, Woodside, Queens, NY
Love, Slim (Edward Haughton)	11/30/1942	Calvary Cemetery, Memphis, TN
Lovelace, Tom (Thomas Rivers)	07/12/1979	Cremated, Restland Memorial Park, Dallas, TX. Ashes returned to family.
Lovett, John	12/05/1937	Green Lawn Cemetery, Nelsonville, OH
Lovett, Len (Leonard Walker)	11/18/1922	Head of Christiana Presbyterian Church Cemetery, Newark, DE
Lovett, Tom (Thomas Joseph)	03/19/1928	St. Ann's Cemetery, Cranston, RI
Lovitto, Joe (Joseph)	05/19/2001	Moore Memorial Gardens, Arlington, TX
Low, Fletcher	06/06/1973	Dartmouth Cemetery, Hanover, NH
Lowdermilk, Grover Cleveland	03/31/1968	Peaceful Valley Cemetery, Odin, IL
Lowdermilk, Lou (Louis Bailey)	12/27/1975	Summit Prarie Cemetery, Salem, IL
Lowe, Bobby (Robert Lincoln)	12/08/1951	Evergreen Cemetery, Detroit, MI
Lowe, George Wesley	09/03/1981	Seaside Cemetery, Marmora, NJ
Lowrey, Peanuts (Harry Lee)	07/02/1986	Holy Cross Cemetery, Culver City, CA
Luby, Hal (Hugh Max)	05/04/1986	Rest-Haven Memorial Park, Eugene, OR
Lucadello, Johnny (John)	10/30/2001	Fort Sam Houston National Cemetery, San Antonio, TX
Lucas, Fred (Frederick Warrington)	03/11/1987	Dorchester Memorial Park, Cambridge, MD
Lucas, Johnny (John Charles)	10/31/1970	Buck Road Cemetery, Glen Carbon, IL
Lucas, Red (Charles Frederick)	07/09/1986	Spring Hill Cemetery, Nashville, TN
Luce, Frank Edward	02/03/1942	Forest Home Cemetery, Milwaukee, WI
Lucey, Joe (Joseph Earl)	07/30/1980	Calvary Cemetery, Holyoke, MA
Lucid, Con (Cornelius Cecil)	06/25/1931	Holy Cross Cemetery, Houston, TX
Luderus, Fred (Frederick William)	01/05/1961	Pinelawn Memorial Park, Milwaukee, WI
Ludolph, Willie (William Francis)	04/08/1952	Holy Sepulchre Cemetery, Hayward, CA
Ludwig, Bill (William Lawrence)	09/05/1947	Calvary Cemetery, Louisville, KY
Luebbe, Roy John	08/21/1985	Forest Lawn Memorial Park, Omaha, NE
Luebke, Dick (Richard Raymond)	12/04/1974	Cremated, San Diego, CA
Luff, Henry T.	10/11/1916	Laurel Hill Cemetery, Philadelphia, PA
Luhrsen, Bill (William Ferdinand)	08/15/1973	Edgewood Memorial Park, North Little Rock, AR
Lukon, Eddie (Edward Paul)	11/07/1996	Our Lady of Lourdes Cemetery, Burgettstown, PA
Lumley, Harry Garfield	05/22/1938	Floral Park Cemetery, Johnson City, NY
Lundbom, Jack (John Frederick)	10/31/1949	Oak Grove Cemetery, Manistee, MI
Lundgren, Carl Leonard	08/21/1934	Marengo City Cemetery, Marengo, IL
Lundgren, Del (Ebin Delmer)	10/19/1984	Elmwood Cemetery, Lindsborg, KS
Lunte, Harry August	07/27/1965	St. John's Cemetery, St. Louis, MO

Name	DOD	Cemetery, City, State
Luque, Adolfo	07/03/1957	Cemeterio de Cristobal Colon, Havana, Cuba
Lush, Ernie (Ernest Benjamin)	02/26/1937	St. Michael's Cemetery, Stratford, CT
Lush, Johnny (John Charles)	11/18/1946	Calvary Cemetery, Los Angeles, CA
Luskey, Charlie (Charles Melton)	12/20/1962	Fort Lincoln Cemetery, Brentwood, MD
Lutenberg, Luke (Charles William)	12/24/1938	Greenmount Cemetery, Quincy, IL
Luttrell, Lyle Kenneth	07/11/1984	Chattanooga National Cemetery, Chattanooga, TN
Lutz, Red (Louis William)	02/22/1984	St. Stephen's Cemetery, Southgate, KY
Lutzke, Rube (Walter John)	03/06/1938	Valhalla Memorial Park, Milwaukee, WI
Lwaing, Garland Frederick	09/27/1996	Sharon Memorial Park, Charlotte, NC
Lyle, Jim (James Charles)	10/10/1977	Mount Carmel Cemetery, Williamsport, PA
Lynch, Adrian Ryan	03/16/1934	Glendale Cemetery, Des Moines, IA
Lynch, Danny (Matthew Daniel)	06/30/1978	Restland Memorial Park, Dallas, TX
Lynch, Henry W.	11/23/1925	St. John's Cemetery, Worcester, MA
Lynch, Jack (John H.)	04/20/1923	Gate of Heaven Cemetery, Hawthorne, NY
Lynch, Mike (Michael Joseph)	04/02/1927	St. Francis Cemetery, Pawtucket, RI
Lynch, Mike (Michael Joseph)	04/01/1947	Terrace Heights Memorial Park, Yakima, WA
Lynch, Tom (Thomas James)	03/28/1955	St. Agnes Cemetery, Cohoes, NY
Lynch, Walt (Walter Edward)	12/21/1976	Oakwood Cemetery, East Aurora, NY
Lynn, Byrd	02/05/1940	Cremated, Napa, CA
Lynn, Jerry (Jerome Edward)	09/25/1972	St. Catherine's Cemetery, Moscow, PA
Lynn, Red (Japhet Monroe)	10/27/1977	Oak Knoll Cemetery, Bellville, TX
Lyon, Russ (Russell Mayo)	12/24/1975	Forest Lawn Memorial Gardens, Abbeville, SC
Lyons, Al (Albert Harold)	12/20/1965	Inglewood Park Cemetery, Inglewood, CA
Lyons, Denny (Dennis Patrick Aloysius)	01/03/1929	St. Joseph's New Cemetery, Cincinnati, OH
Lyons, George Tony	08/12/1981	Newton Burial Park, Nevada, MO
Lyons, Harry Pratt	06/29/1912	West Laurel Hill Cemetery, Baba Cynwyd, PA
Lyons, Pat (Patrick Jerry)	01/20/1914	Calvary Cemetery, Springfield, OH
Lyons, Ted (Theodore Amar)	07/25/1986	Big Woods Cemetery, Vinton, LA
Lyons, Terry (Terence Hilbert)	09/09/1959	Dayton Memorial Park, Dayton, OH
Lyons, Toby (Thomas Arthur)	08/27/1920	Holy Cross Cemetery, Malden, MA
Lyston, Bill (William Edward)	08/04/1944	Holy Redeemer Cemetery, Baltimore, MD
Lyston, John Michael	10/29/1909	New Cathedral Cemetery, Baltimore, MD
Lytle, Dad (Edward Benson)	12/21/1950	Forest Lawn Memorial Park-Long Beach, Long Beach, CA
Maas, Duke (Duane Frederick)	12/07/1976	Utica Cemetery, Utica, MI
MacArthur, Mac (Malcolm M.)	10/18/1932	Elmwood Cemetery, Detroit, MI
MacDonald, Bill (William Paul)	05/04/1991	Memory Garden of Contra Costa, Concord, CA
MacDonald, Harvey Forsyth	10/04/1965	Glenwood Memorial Gardens, Broomall, PA.
Mace Harry F.	04/26/1930	Glenwood Cemetery, Washington, DC
MacFayden, Danny (Daniel Knowles)	08/26/1972	Old North Cemetery, North Truro, MA
MacGamwell, Ed (Edward M.)	05/26/1924	St. Agnes Cemetery, Albany, NY
Mack, Bill (William Francis)	09/30/1971	SS. Peter & Paul Cemetery, Elmira, NY
Mack, Earle Thaddeus	02/04/1967	Forest Hill Cemetery, Morganton, NC
Mack, Frank George	07/02/1971	Mount Emblem Cemetery, Elmhurst, IL

Name	DOD	Cemetery, City, State
Mack, Ray (Raymond James)	05/07/1969	Oakwood Cemetery, Bucyrus, OH
Mack, Reddy (Joseph)	12/30/1916	St. Joseph Cemetery, Newport, KY
Mackiewicz, Felix Thaddeus	12/20/1993	Calvary Cemetery, St. Louis, MO
Mackinson, Johnny (John Joseph)	10/17/1989	Riverside National Cemetery, Riverside, CA
Macko, Steve (Steven Joseph)	11/15/1981	Moore Memorial Gardens, Arlington, TX
Macon, Max Cullen	08/05/1989	Resthaven Memorial Park, Louisville, KY
Macullar, Jimmy (James F.)	04/08/1924	Baltimore Cemetery, Baltimore, MD
Madden, Bunny (Thomas Francis)	01/20/1954	St. Joseph's Cemetery, West Roxbury, MA
Madden, kid (Michael Joseph)	03/16/1896	Calvary Cemetery, South Portland, ME
Madden, Len (Leonard Joseph)	09/09/1949	Calvary Cemetery, Toledo, OH
Madden, Tommy (Thomas Joseph)	07/26/1930	Holy Sepulchre Cemetery, Wyndmoor, PA
Maddern, Clarence James	08/09/1986	Evergreen Cemetery, Bisbee, AZ
Maddox, Nick (Nicholas)	11/27/1954	St. Augustine's Cemetery, Pittsburgh, PA
Madigan, Tony (William J.)	12/04/1954	Mount Olivet Cemetery, Washington, DC
Madison, Art (Arthur M.)	01/27/1933	South View Cemetery, North Adams, MA
Madison, Dave (David Pledger)	12/08/1985	Brooksville Cemetery, Brooksville, MS
Madrid, Sal (Salvator)	02/24/1977	Lindenwood Cemetery, Fort Wayne, IN
Magee, Lee (Leo Christopher)	03/14/1966	St. Joseph's Cemetery, Lockbourne, OH
Magee, Sherwood Robert	03/13/1929	Arlington Cemetery, Drexel Hill, PA
Maggert, Harl Vestin	01/07/1963	Sunset View Cemetery, El Cerrito, CA. Cremated.
Maggert, Harl Warren	07/10/1986	Calvary Catholic Cemetery, Citrus Heights, CA
Maglie, Sal (Salvatore Anthony)	12/28/1992	St. Joseph's Italian Cemetery, Niagara Falls, NY
Magner, Stubby (Edmund Burke)	09/06/1956	Dayton National Cemetery, Dayton, OH
Magnuson, Jim (James Robert)	05/30/1991	Forest Home Cemetery, Milwaukee, WI
Magoon, George Henry	12/06/1943	Cold Spring Cemetery, East Rochester, NH
Maguire, Freddie (Frederick Edward)	11/03/1961	St. John's Cemetery, Worcester, MA
Mahady, Jim (James Bernard)	08/09/1936	St. Mary's Cemetery, Cortland, NY
Mahaffey, Lou (Louis Wood)	10/26/1949	Inglewood Park Cemetery, Inglewood, CA
Mahaffey, Roy (Lee Roy)	07/23/1969	Forest Lawn Memorial Park, Anderson, SC
Mahar, Frank Edward	12/05/1961	Forestdale Cemetery, Malden, MA
Maharg, Billy (William Joseph)	11/20/1953	Holy Sepulchre Cemetery, Wyndmoor, PA
Mahon, Al (Alfred Gwinn)	12/26/1977	Evergreen Cemetery, New Haven, CT
Mahoney, Bob (Robert Paul)	08/27/2000	Lincoln Memorial Park Columbarium, Lincoln, NE. Cremated.
Mahoney, Chris (Christopher John)	07/15/1954	Visalia Cemetery, Visalia, CA
Mahoney, Dan (Daniel J.)	01/31/1904	St. Michael's Cemetery, Springfield, MA
Mahoney, Danny (Daniel Joseph)	09/28/1960	St. Bernard's Cemetery, Waterville, NY
Mahoney, Mike (George W.)	01/03/1940	Mount Calvary Cemetery, Roslindale, MA
Maier, Bob (Robert Phillip)	08/04/1993	Resurrection Cemetery, Piscataway, NJ
Mails, Duster (John Walter)	07/05/1974	Mount Olivet Catholic Cemetery, San Rafael, CA
Main, Alex (Miles Grant)	12/29/1965	Crestwood Memorial Cemetery, Grand Blanc, MI
Main, Woody (Forrest Harry)	06/27/1992	North Kern Cemetery, Delano, CA
Mains, Jim (James Royal)	03/17/1969	South High Street Cemetery, Bridgton, ME

Name	DOD	Cemetery, City, State
Mains, Willard Eben	05/23/1923	South High Street Cemetery, Bridgton, ME
Maisel, Charlie (Charles Louis)	08/25/1953	Lorraine Park Cemetery, Baltimore, MD
Maisel, Fritz (Frederick Charles)	04/22/1967	Lorraine Park Cemetery, Baltimore, MD
Maisel, George John	11/20/1968	Baltimore National Cemetery, Baltimore, MD
Majeski, Hank (Henry)	08/09/1991	Cremated, Staten Island, NY
Malarkey, Bill (William John)	12/12/1956	Mountain View Cemetery, Kingman, AZ
Malarkey, John S.	10/29/1949	St. Mary's Cemetery, Marion, OH
Malay, Charlie (Charles Francis)	09/18/1949	Holy Cross Cemetery, Brooklyn, NY
Malay, Joe (Joseph Charles)	03/19/1989	St. Michael's Cemetery, Stratford, CT
Malis, Cy (Cyrus Sol)	01/12/1971	Valhalla Memorial Park, North Hollywood, CA
Mallon, Les (Leslie Clyde)	04/17/1991	Acton Cemetery, Acton, TX
Mallonee, Ben (Howard Bennett)	02/19/1978	Druid Ridge Cemetery, Pikesville, MD
Mallonee, Jule (Julius Norris)	10/26/1934	Elmwood Cemetery, Charlotte, NC
Malloy, Alex (Archibald Alexander)	03/01/1961	Ferris Park Cemetery, Ferris, TX
Malloy, Herm (Herman)	05/09/1942	St. Joseph's Cemetery, Massillon, OH
Malmberg, Harry William	10/29/1976	Holy Cross Cemetery, Antioch, CA
Malone, Fergy (Fergus G.)	01/01/1905	New Cathedral Cemetery, Philadelphia, PA
Malone, Lew (Lewis Aloysius)	02/17/1972	St. Patrick's Cemetery, Southold, NY
Maloney, Billy (William Alphonse)	09/02/1960	Breckinridge City Cemetery, Breckinridge, TX
Maloney, Charlie (Charles Michael)	01/17/1967	St. Paul's Cemetery, Arlington, MA
Maloney, Pat (Patrick William)	06/27/1979	St. Joseph's Cemetery, Ashton, RI
Maloy, Paul Augustus	03/18/1976	St. Mary's Cemetery, Tiffin, OH
Maltzberger, Gordon Ralph	12/11/1974	Hermosa Cemetery, Colton, CA
Mamaux, Al (Albert Leon)	12/31/1962	Forest Lawn Memorial Park-Hollywood Hills, Los Angeles, CA
Mancuso, Gus (August Rodney)	10/26/1984	Forest Park (Lawndale) Cemetery, Houston, TX
Manda, Carl Alan	03/09/1983	Woodbine Cemetery, Artesia, NM
Maney, S. Vincent	03/13/1952	St. Joseph's Cemetery, Batavia, NY
Mangum, Leo Allan	07/09/1974	Cremated, Fort Wayne, IN
Mangus, George Graham	08/10/1933	St. Thomas the Apostle Cemetery, Red Creek, NY
Manion, Clyde Jennings	09/04/1967	Holy Sepulchre Cemetery, Southfield, MI
Manlove, Charlie (Charles Henry Weeks)	02/12/1952	Oakridge Cemetery, Altoona, PA
Mann, Fred J.	04/16/1916	Oak Grove Cemetery, Springfield, MA
Mann, Garth (Ben Garth)	09/11/1980	Laurel Land Memorial Park, Dallas, TX
Mann, Johnny (John Leo)	03/31/1977	Calvary Cemetery, Terre Haute, IN
Mann, Les (Leslie)	01/14/1962	Cremated, Pasadena, CA
Manning, Ernie (Ernest Devon)	04/28/1973	Greenwood Cemetery, Florala, AL
Manning, Jack (John E.)	08/15/1929	New Calvary Cemetery, Mattapan, MA
Manning, Jim (James H.)	10/22/1929	North Burial Ground, Fall River, MA
Manning, Rube (Walter S.)	04/23/1930	Wildwood Cemetery, Williamsport, PA
Manning, Tim (Timothy Edward)	06/11/1934	Calvary Cemetery, Evanston, IL
Manno, Don (Donald D.)	03/11/1995	Wildwood Cemetery, Williamsport, PA
Mansell, John	02/20/1925	St. Joseph's Cemetery, Auburn, NY
Mansell, Mike (Michael R.)	12/04/1902	St. Joseph's Cemetery, Auburn, NY
Mansell, Tom (Thomas E.)	10/06/1934	St. Joseph's Cemetery, Auburn, NY

Name	DOD	Cemetery, City, State
Manske, Lou (Louis Hugo)	04/27/1963	Arlington Park Cemetery, Milwaukee, WI
Mantle, Mickey Charles	08/13/1995	Sparkman Hillcrest Memorial Park, Dallas, TX
Manuel, Moxie (Mark Garfield)	04/26/1924	Kennett Cemetery, Kennett, MO
Manush, Frank Benjamin	01/05/1965	Good Shepherd Cemetery, Huntington Beach, CA
Manush, Heinie (Henry Emmett)	05/12/1971	Sarasota Memorial Park, Sarasota, FL
Mapel, Rolla Hamilton	04/06/1966	Fort Rosecrans National Cemetery, LaJolla, CA
Mapes, Cliff (Clifford Franklin)	12/05/1996	Graham Memorial Cemetery, Pryor, OK
Maple, Howard Albert	11/09/1970	Belcrest Memorial Park, Salem, OR
Mappes, George Richard	02/20/1934	Calvary Cemetery, St. Louis, MO
Maranville, Rabbit (Walter James Vincent)	01/05/1954	St. Michael's Cemetery, Springfield, MA
Marberry, Firpo (Frederick)	06/30/1976	Birdston Valley Cemetery, Streetman, TX
Marbet, Walt (Walter William)	09/24/1956	Swiss Cemetery, Hohenwald, TN
Marchildon, Phil (Philip Joseph)	01/10/1997	Cremated, Toronto, Ontario, Canada
Marcum, Johnny (John Alfred)	09/10/1984	Eminence Cemetery, Eminence, KY
Marion, Dan (Donald G.)	01/18/1933	Mount Olivet Cemetery, Milwaukee, WI
Marion, Red (John Wyeth)	03/13/1975	Cedar Lawn Memorial Park, Fremont, CA
Maris, Roger Eugene	12/14/1985	Holy Cross Cemetery, Fargo, ND
Markland, Gene (Cleneth Eugene)	06/15/1999	Fountainhead Memorial Park, Palm Bay, FL
Markle, Cliff (Clifford Monroe)	05/24/1974	Resurrection Cemetery, Montebello, CA
Marlowe, Dick (Richard Burton)	12/30/1968	Toledo Memorial Park, Sylvania, OH
Marne, Harry Sylvester	01/07/2002	SS. Peter & Paul Cemetery, Springfield, PA
Marquard, Rube (Richard William)	06/01/1980	Hebrew Cemetery, Baltimore, MD
Marquardt, Ollie (Albert Ludwig)	02/07/1968	Toledo Memorial Park, Sylvania, OH
Marquis, Jim (James Milburn)	08/05/1992	Cremated, Jackson, CA
Marr, Lefty (Charles W.)	01/11/1912	Fairview Cemetery, New Britain, CT
Marriott, William Earl	08/11/1969	Mountain View Cemetery, Oakland, CA
Marrow, Buck (Charles Kennon)	11/21/1982	Peninsula Memorial Park, Newport News, VA
Mars, Ed (Edward M.)	12/09/1941	Oak Woods Cemetery, Chicago, IL
Marsans, Armando	09/03/1960	Cemeterio de Cristobal Colon, Havana, Cuba
Marshall, Bill (William Henry)	05/05/1977	St. Mary's Catholic Cemetery, Sacramento, CA
Marshall, Doc (William Riddle)	12/11/1959	Woodlawn Cemetery, Clinton, IL
Marshall, Joe (Joseph Hanley)	09/11/1931	Angelus-Rosedale Cemetery, Los Angeles, CA
Marshall, Max (Milo May)	09/16/1993	Belcrest Memorial Park, Salem, OR
Marshall, Rube (Roy DeVerne)	06/11/1980	Evergreen Burial Park, New Philadelphia, OH
Marshall, Willard Warren	11/05/2000	Fairview Cemetery, Fairview
Martel, Doc (Leon Alphonse)	10/11/1947	Arlington National Cemetery, Arlington, VA
Martin, Barney (Barnes Robertson)	10/30/1997	Greenlawn Memorial Park, Columbia, SC
Martin, Billy (Alfred Manuel)	12/25/1989	Gate of Heaven Cemetery, Hawthorne, NY
Martin, Billy (William Lloyd)	09/14/1949	Cedar Hill Cemetery, Suitland, MD
Martin, Doc (Harold Winthrop)	04/14/1935	Milton Cemetery, Milton, MA
Martin, Frank	09/30/1924	Calvary Cemetery, Evanston, IL
Martin, Jack (John Christopher)	07/04/1980	Laurelton Cemetery, Laurelton, NJ
Martin, Joe (Joseph Samuel)	05/25/1964	Calvary Cemetery, Altoona, PA

Name	DOD	Cemetery, City, State
Martin, Pepper (Johnny Leonard Roosevelt)	03/05/1965	Memorial Park Cemetery, Oklahoma City, OK
Martin, Phonney (Alphonse Case)	05/24/1933	Cypress Hills National Cemetery, Brooklyn, NY
Martin, Speed (Elwood Good)	06/14/1983	Cremated, Lemon Grove, CA
Martina, Oyster Joe (John Joseph)	03/22/1962	Greenwood Cemetery, New Orleans, LA
Martinez, Tony (Gabriel Antonio)	08/24/1991	Vista Memorial Gardens, Hialeah, FL
Martini, Wedo (Guido Joe)	10/28/1970	SS. Peter & Paul Cemetery, Springfield, PA
Marty, Joe (Joseph Anton)	10/04/1984	St. Mary's Catholic Cemetery, Sacramento, CA
Masi, Phil (Philip Samuel)	03/29/1990	All Saints Cemetery, Des Plaines, IL
Maskrey, Harry H.	08/17/1930	Mercer Citizen's Cemetery, Mercer, PA
Maskrey, Leech (Samuel Leech)	04/01/1922	Mercer Citizen's Cemetery, Mercer, PA
Mason, Charlie (Charles E.)	10/21/1936	Hillside Cemetery, Roslyn, PA
Mason, Del (Adelbert William)	12/31/1962	Palm Cemetery, Winter Park, FL
Massey, Bill (William Herbert)	10/17/1971	Forest Park Cemetery, Shreveport, LA
Massey, Roy Hardee	06/23/1954	Westview Cemetery, Atlanta, GA
Masterson, Paul Nicholas	11/27/1997	Evergreen Cemetery, Evergreen Park, IL
Mathews, Bobby (Robert T.)	04/17/1898	New Cathedral Cemetery, Baltimore, MD
Mathews, Eddie (Edwin Lee)	02/18/2001	Santa Barbara Cemetery, Santa Barbara, CA
Mathewson, Christy (Christopher)	10/07/1925	Lewisburg Cemetery, Lewisburg, PA
Mathewson, Henry	07/01/1917	Evergreen-Woodlawn Cemetery, Factoryville, PA
Mathison, Jimmy (James Michael Ignatius)	07/04/1911	New Cathedral Cemetery, Baltimore, MD
Mattern, Al (Alonzo Albert)	11/06/1958	Pine Hill Cemetery, West Rush, NY
Matteson, C.V. (Clifford Virgil)	12/18/1931	Mound Hill Cemetery, Seville, OH
Matteson, Henry Edson	09/01/1943	Evergreen Cemetery, Portland, NY
Matthews, Bill (William Calvin)	01/23/1946	Calvary Cemetery, Mt. Carbon, PA
Matthews, Joe (John Joseph)	02/08/1968	Rose Hill Cemetery, Hagerstown, MD
Matthews, Wid Curry	10/05/1965	Roseland Park Cemetery, Hattiesburg, MS
Matthewson, Dale Wesley	02/20/1984	Union Memory Gardens, Blairsville, GA
Mattick, Wally (Walter Joseph)	11/05/1968	Calvary Cemetery, St. Louis, MO
Mattimore, Mike (Michael Joseph)	04/28/1931	Holy Cross Cemetery, Butte, MT
Mattingly, Earl (Laurence Earl)	09/08/1993	Cedar Hill Cemetery, Suitland, MD
Mattox, Cloy Mitchell	08/03/1985	Roselawn Burial Park, Martinsville, WA
Matuzak, Harry George	11/16/1978	Belforest Catholic Cemetery, Daphne, AL
Mauck, Al (Alfred Maris)	04/27/1921	Warnock Cemetery, Princeton, IN
Maul, Al (Albert Joseph)	05/03/1958	Most Holy Redeemer Cemetery, Philadelphia, PA
Mauldin, Mark (Marshall Reese)	09/02/1990	Forest Lawn Memorial Gardens, College Park, GA
Maun, Ernie (Ernest Gerald)	01/01/1987	Falfurrias Burial Park, Falfurrias, TX
Mauney, Dick (Richard)	02/06/1970	Fairview Memorial Park, Albemarle, NC
Maupin, Harry Carr	08/25/1952	Oakwood Cemetery, Parsons, KS
Mauro, Carmen Louis	12/19/2003	Calvary Catholic Cemetery, Citrus Heights, CA
Maxwell, Bert (James Albert)	12/10/1961	Rest Haven Cemetery, Brady, TX
May, Buckshot (William Herbert)	03/15/1984	Greenlawn Memorial Park, Bakersfield, CA
May, Jackie (Frank Spruiell)	06/03/1970	Montlawn Memorial Park, Raleigh, NC

Name	DOD	Cemetery, City, State
May, Jerry Lee	06/30/1996	Union Cemetery, Parnassus, VA
May, Pinky (Merrill Glend)	09/04/2000	Cedar Hill Cemetery, Corydon, IN
Mayer, Erskine John	03/10/1957	Forest Lawn Memorial Park, Glendale, CA
Mayer, Sam (Samuel Frankel)	07/01/1962	Decatur City Cemetery, Decatur, GA
Maynard, Buster (James Walter)	09/07/1977	Union Chapel Church Cemetery, Henderson, NC
Maynard, Chick (Leroy Evans)	01/31/1957	Millinocket Cemetery, Millinocket, ME
Mays, Al (Albert C.)	05/17/1905	Parkersburg Memorial Gardens (formerly Odd Fellows Cemetery), Parkersburg, WV
Mays, Carl William	04/04/1971	River View Cemetery, Portland, OR
Mazzera, Mel (Melvin Leonard)	12/17/1997	San Joaquin Catholic Cemetery, Stockton, CA
McAdams, Jack (George D.)	05/21/1937	Bryant Cemetery, Benton, AR
McAfee, Bill (William Fort)	07/08/1958	Crown Hill Cemetery, Albany, GA
McAleer, Jimmy (James Robert)	04/29/1931	Oak Hill Cemetery, Youngstown, OH
McAleese, Jack (John James)	11/14/1950	St. Mary's Cemetery, Sharon, PA
McAllester, Bill (William Lusk)	03/03/1970	Forest Hills Cemetery, Chattanooga, TN
McAllister, Sport (Lewis William)	07/17/1962	Mount Olivet Cemetery, Detroit, MI
McArthur, Dixie (Oland Alexander)	05/31/1986	Friendship Cemetery, Columbus, MS
McAtee, Bub (Michael James)	10/18/1876	St. John's Cemetery, Troy, NY
McAuley, Ike (James Earl)	04/06/1928	Maple Grove Cemetery, Wichita, KS
McAuliffe, Gene (Eugene Leo)	04/29/1953	St. Mary's Cemetery, Randolph, MA
McAvoy, Wickey (James Eugene)	07/06/1973	Holy Sepulchre Cemetery, Rochester, NY
McBee, Pryor Edward	04/19/1963	Roseville Cemetery, Roseville, CA
McBride, Algie (Algernon Griggs)	01/10/1956	Greenlawn Cemetery, Portsmouth, OH
McBride, George Florian	07/02/1973	Holy Cross Cemetery, Milwaukee, WI
McBride, Pete (Peter William)	07/03/1944	Maple Street Cemetery, Adams, MA
McBride, Tom (Thomas Ray)	12/26/2001	Cedarlawn Memorial Park, Sherman, TX
McCabe, Dick (Richard James)	04/11/1950	Mount Calvary Cemetery, Cheektowaga, NY
McCabe, Swat (James Arthur)	12/09/1944	New St. Joseph's Cemetery, Bristol, CT
McCabe, Tim (Timothy J.)	04/12/1977	Arcadia Valley Memorial Park, Ironton, MO
McCaffery, Harry Charles	04/29/1928	Calvary Cemetery, St. Louis, MO
McCaffery, Sparrow (Charles P.)	04/29/1894	New Cathedral Cemetery, Philadelphia, PA
McCage, Bill (William Francis)	09/02/1966	Mount Carmel Cemetery, Hillside, IL
McCahan, Bill (William Glenn)	07/03/1986	Greenwood Memorial Park, Fort Worth, TX
McCall, Dutch (Robert Leonard)	01/07/1996	Little Rock National Cemetery, Little Rock, AR
McCallister, Jack (John) *manager*	10/18/1946	Green Lawn Cemetery, Columbus, OH
McCann, Emmett (Robert Emmett)	04/15/1937	Cathedral Cemetery, Philadelphia, PA
McCann, Gene (Henry Eugene)	04/26/1943	St. John's Cemetery, Middle Village, Queens, NY
McCarren, Bill (William Joseph)	09/11/1983	Cremated, Denver, CO
McCarthy, Alex (Alexander George)	03/12/1978	Parsons Cemetery, Salisbury, MD
McCarthy, Bill (William John)	02/04/1928	Holyhood Cemetery, Brookline, MA
McCarthy, Bill (William Thomas)	05/29/1939	St. Bernard's Cemetery, Concord, MA
McCarthy, Jerry (Jerome Francis)	10/03/1965	Cemetery of Holy Rood, Westbury, NY
McCarthy, Joe (Joseph Vincent) *manager*	01/13/1978	Mt. Olivet Cemetery, Tonawanda, NY
McCarthy, Johnny (John Joseph)	09/13/1973	Ascension Cemetery, Libertyville, IL

Name	DOD	Cemetery, City, State
McCarthy, Tom (Thomas Patrick)	03/28/1933	Catholic Cemetery, Fort Wayne, IN
McCarthy, Tommy (Thomas Francis Michael)	08/05/1922	Mount Calvary Cemetery, Roslindale, MA
McCarton, Frank (Francis J.)	06/17/1907	Calvary Cemetery, Woodside, Queens, NY
McCarty, Lew (George Lewis)	06/09/1930	Hillside Cemetery, Catawissa, PA
McCauley, Al (Allen A.)	08/24/1917	Crown Hill Cemetery, Indianapolis, IN
McCauley, Bill (William H.)	01/27/1926	Congressional Cemetery, Washington, DC
McCauley, Jim (James Adelbert)	09/14/1930	Woodlawn Cemetery, Canadaigua, NY
McCauley, Pat (Patrick F.)	01/17/1917	Old Saint William's Cemetery, Ware, MA
McClanahan, Pete (Robert Hugh)	10/28/1987	Oakwood Cemetery, Coldspring, TX
McClellan, Bill (William Henry)	07/03/1929	Rosehill Cemetery, Chicago, IL
McClellan, Harvey McDowell	11/06/1925	Battle Grove Cemetery, Cynthiana, KY
McCleskey, Jeff (Jefferson Lamar)	05/11/1971	Oak Grove Cemetery, Americus, GA
McCloskey, Jim (James Ellwood)	08/18/1971	Holy Name Cemetery, Jersey City, NJ
McCloskey, John (James John)	06/05/1919	St. Mary's Cemetery, Wilkes-Barre, PA
McCloskey, John *manager*	11/17/1940	Calvary Cemetery, Louisville, KY
McClure, Hal (Harold Murray)	03/01/1919	Lewisburg Cemetery, Lewisburg, PA
McClure, Larry (Lawrence Ledwith)	08/31/1949	Woodmere Memorial Park, Huntington, WV
McCluskey, Harry Robert	06/07/1962	Forest Cemetery, Toledo, OH
McColl, Alex (Alexander Boyd)	02/06/1991	Mount Pleasant Cemetery, Geneva, OH
McConnaughey, Ralph James	06/04/1966	Cadillac Memorial Gardens West, Westland, MI
McConnell, Amby (Ambrose Moses)	05/20/1942	St. Peter's Cemetery, Utica, NY
McConnell, George Neely	05/10/1964	Forest Hills Cemetery, Chattanooga, TN
McConnell, Sam (Samuel Faulkner)	06/27/1981	Valley Forge Gardens, King of Prussia, PA
McCormick, Barry (William J.)	01/28/1956	St. Joseph's New Cemetery, Cincinnati, OH
McCormick, Frank Andrew	11/21/1982	Cemetery of Holy Rood, Westbury, NY
McCormick, Jim (James Ambrose)	02/01/1948	St. Mary's Cemetery, Biddeford, ME
McCormick, Jim (James)	03/10/1918	Laurel Grove Cemetery, Totowa, NJ
McCormick, Mike (Michael J.)	11/18/1953	Holy Name Cemetery, Jersey City, NJ
McCormick, Moose (Harry Elwood)	07/09/1962	Lewisburg Cemetery, Lewsiburg, PA
McCorry, Bill (William Charles)	03/22/1973	Westover Memorial Park, Augusta, GA
McCosky, William Barney	09/06/1996	Holy Sepulchre Cemetery, Southfield, MI
McCoy, Art (Arthur Gray)	03/22/1904	Odd Fellows Cemetery, Danville, PA
McCrea, Frank (Francis William)	02/25/1981	Locust Hill Cemetery, Dover, NJ
McCredie, Walt (Walter Henry)	07/29/1934	Cremated, Portland, OR
McCreery, Ed (Esley Porterfield)	10/19/1960	Holy Sepulchre Cemetery, Hayward, CA
McCreery, Tom (Thomas Livingston)	07/03/1941	Beaver Cemetery, Beaver, PA
McCue, Frank Aloysius	07/05/1953	St. Mary's Cemetery, Evergreen Park, IL
McCullough, Clyde Edward	09/18/1982	Rosewood Memorial Park, Virginia Beach, VA
McCullough, Paul Willard	11/07/1970	Oak Park Cemetery, New Castle, PA
McCullough, Phil (Pinson Lamar)	01/16/2003	Resthaven Cemetery, Alpharetta, GA
McCurdy, Harry Henry	07/21/1972	Cremated, Houston, TX
McDaniel, Von (Max Von)	08/20/1995	Dodson Cemetery, Dodson, TX
McDermott, Mike (Michael H.)	05/07/1947	St. Patrick's Cemetery, Fall River, MA

Name	DOD	Cemetery, City, State
McDermott, Mike (Michael Joseph)	06/30/1943	Calvary Cemetery, St. Louis, MO
McDermott, Sandy (Thomas Nathaniel)	11/23/1922	Mount Calvary Cemetery, Zanesville, OH
McDonald, Ed (Edward C.)	03/11/1946	St. Agnes Cemetery, Albany, NY
McDonald, Hank (Henry Monroe)	10/17/1982	Inglewood Park Cemetery, Inglewood, CA
McDonald, Jack (Daniel)	11/23/1880	Calvary Cemetery, Woodside, Queens, NY
McDonald, Jim (James Augustus)	09/14/1914	Holy Cross Cemetery, Colma, CA
McDonald, Joe (Malcolm Joseph)	05/30/1963	Cedarcrest Cemetery, Baytown, TX
McDonald, John Joseph	04/09/1950	Mt. Carmel Cemetery, Dunmore, PA
McDonald, Tex (Charles C.)	03/31/1943	I.O.O.F. Cemetery, Farmersville, TX
McDonough, Ed (Edward Sebastian)	09/02/1926	Bluff City Cemetery, Elgin, IL
McDougal, James H.	04/28/1935	Aledo Cemetery, Aledo, IL
McDougal, Sandy (John Auchanbolt)	10/02/1910	Forest Lawn Cemetery, Buffalo, NY
McElwee, Lee (Leland Stanford)	02/08/1957	Lowell Cemetery, Lowell, MA
McElyea, Frank	04/19/1987	Sunset Memorial Gardens, Evansville, IN
McEvoy, Lou (Louis Anthony)	12/17/1953	St. Patrick's Cemetery, Williamsburg, KS
McFadden, Guy G.	03/10/1911	Topeka Cemetery, Topeka, KS
McFarlan, Alex (Alexander Shepard)	03/02/1939	Floydsburg Cemetery, Crestwood, KY
McFarlan, Dan (Anderson Daniel)	09/24/1924	Flat Rock Cemetery, Shelby County, KY
McFarland, Chappie (Charles Amos)	12/14/1924	Glenwood Cemetery, Houston, TX
McFarland, Chris (Christopher)	05/24/1918	Oak Grove Cemetery, Fall River, MA
McFarland, Ed (Edward William)	11/28/1959	Lake View Cemetery, Cleveland, OH
McFarland, Herm (Hermas Walter)	09/21/1935	Riverview Cemetery, Richmond, VA
McFarland, Howie (Howard Alexander)	04/07/1993	Ringling Memorial Cemetery, Ringling, OK
McFarland, Monte (Lamont Amos)	11/15/1913	White Hall Cemetery, White Hall, IL
McFetridge, Jack (John Reed)	01/10/1917	Laurel Hill Cemetery, Philadelphia, PA
McGaffigan, Patsy (Mark Andrew)	12/22/1940	Carlyle Cemetery, Carlyle, IL
McGann, Dan (Dennis Lawrence)	12/13/1910	Grove Hill Cemetery, Shelbyville, KY
McGarr, Chippy (James B.)	06/06/1904	St. John's Cemetery, Worcester, MA
McGarvey, Dan (Daniel Francis)	03/07/1947	Holy Cross Cemetery, Yeadon, PA
McGeachey, Jack (John Charles)	04/05/1930	Woodlawn Cemetery, Clinton, MA
McGee, Bill (William Henry)	02/11/1987	St. Norbett's Catholic Cemetery, Hardin, IL
McGee, Frank (Francis D.)	01/30/1934	St. Joseph's Cemetery, Lockbourne, OH
McGee, Pat (Patrick)	06/20/1889	Calvary Cemetery, Woodside, Queens, NY
McGeehan, Connie (Cornelius Bernard)	07/04/1907	St. Ann's Cemetery, Freeland, PA
McGeehan, Dan (Daniel DeSales)	07/12/1955	Calvary Cemetery, Drums, PA
McGehee, Pat (Patrick Henry)	12/30/1946	Maplelawn Park Cemetery, Paducah, KY
McGhee, Bill (William Mac)	03/10/1984	Bayview Memorial Park, Pensacola, FL
McGhee, Ed (Warren Edward)	02/13/1986	Calvary Cemetery, Memphis, TN
McGill, Bill (William Jacob)	08/07/1959	Alva Municipal Cemetery, Alva, OK
McGill, Willie (William Vaness)	08/29/1944	Crown Hill Cemetery, Indianapolis, IN
McGillen, John Joseph	08/11/1987	SS. Peter & Paul Cemetery, Springfield, PA
McGilvray, Bill (William Alexander)	05/23/1952	Fairmount Cemetery, Denver, CO
McGinley, Jim (James William)	09/20/1961	Riverview Cemetery, Groveland, MA

Name	DOD	Cemetery, City, State
McGinnis, Gus (Albert)	04/20/1904	Southern Cemetery, Barnesville, OH
McGinnis, Jumbo (George Washington)	05/18/1934	Calvary Cemetery, St. Louis, MO
McGinnity, Joe (Joseph Jerome)	11/14/1929	Oak Hill Cemetery, McAllister, OK
McGlone, John T.	11/22/1927	Holy Cross Cemetery, Brooklyn, NY
McGlothin, Jim (James Milton)	12/23/1975	Burlington Cemetery, Burlington, KY
McGlynn, Stoney (Ulysses Simpson Grant)	08/26/1941	Evergreen Cemetery, Manitowoc, WI
McGovern, Art (Arthur John)	11/14/1915	Pine Grove Cemetery, Lynn, MA
McGowan, Beauty (Frank Bernard)	05/06/1982	St. Lawrence Cemetery, West Haven, CT
McGowan, Mickey (Tullis Earl)	03/08/2003	Greenlawn Cemetery, Waycross, GA
McGraner, Howard	10/22/1952	West Union Street Cemetery, Athens, OH
McGraw, Bob (Robert Emmett)	06/02/1978	Roselawn Cemetery, Pueblo, CO
McGraw, John (buried under birth name: Raymond Heir)	04/27/1967	Inglewood Park Cemetery, Inglewood, CA
McGraw, John Joseph	02/25/1934	New Cathedral Cemetery, Baltimore, MD
McGrew, Slim (Walter Howard)	08/21/1967	Rosewood Memorial Park, Humble, TX
McGrillis, Mark A.	05/16/1935	Cathedral Cemetery, Philadelphia, PA
McGuckin, Joe (Joseph W.)	12/31/1903	Holy Sepulchre Cemetery, Totawa, NJ
McGuinness, John James	12/19/1916	Calvary-St. Patrick Cemetery, Johnson City, NY
McGuire, Deacon (James Thomas)	10/31/1936	Riverside Cemetery, Albion, MI
McGuire, Tom (Thomas Patrick)	12/07/1959	Holy Sepulchre Cemetery, Worth, IL
McGunnigle, Bill (William Henry)	03/09/1899	St. Patrick's Cemetery, Brockton, MA
McHale, Bob (Robert Emmet)	06/09/1952	St. Mary's Catholic Cemetery, Sacramento, CA
McHale, Jim (James Bernard)	06/17/1959	San Gabriel Mission Cemetery, San Gabriel, CA
McHale, Marty (Martin Joseph)	05/07/1979	Cemetery of Holy Rood, Westbury, NY
McHenry, Austin Bush	11/27/1922	Moore's Chapel Cemetery, Blue Creek, OH
McIlveen, Irish (Henry Cooke)	10/18/1960	Ridge Hill Memorial Park, Amherst, OH
McInnis, Stuffy (John Phalen)	02/16/1960	Rosedale Cemetery, Manchester-by-the-Sea, MA
McIntire, Harry (John Reid)	01/09/1949	Woodland Cemetery, Dayton, OH
McIntyre, Frank W.	07/08/1887	Mount Elliott Cemetery, Detroit, MI
McIvor, Otto (Edward Otto)	05/04/1954	Greenwood Cemetery, Dallas, TX
McJames, Doc (James McCutchen) (buried under birth name: James McC. James	09/23/1901	Old St. David Episcopal Churchyard, Cheraw, SC
McKain, Archie Richard	05/21/1985	Highland Cemetery, Minneapolis, KS
McKain, Hal (Harold Leroy)	01/24/1970	Cedar Lawn Cemetery, Council Bluffs, IA
McKay, Reeve Stewart	01/18/1946	Restland Memorial Park, Dallas, TX
McKean, Ed (Edwin John)	08/16/1919	Calvary Cemetery, Cleveland, OH
McKechnie, Bill (William Boyd)	10/29/1965	Manasota Memorial Park, Bradenton, FL
McKee, Red (Raymond Ellis)	08/05/1972	Forest Lawn Cemetery, Saginaw, MI
McKeever, Jim (James)	08/19/1897	Holy Cross Cemetery, Malden, MA
McKeithan, Tim (Emmett James)	08/20/1969	Concord Baptist Church Cemetery, Bostic, NC
McKelvey, John Wellington	05/31/1944	Mt. Hope Cemetery, Rochester, NY

Name	DOD	Cemetery, City, State
McKelvey, Russ (Russell Errett)	10/19/1915	Forest Lawn Memorial Park, Omaha, NE
McKenna, Kit (James William)	03/31/1941	Holy Cross Cemetery, Lynchburg, VA
McKenry, Limb (Frank Gordon)	11/01/1956	Mountain View Cemetery, Oakland, CA
McKeon, Larry (Lawrence J.)	07/18/1915	St. Mary's Cemetery, Port Jervis, NY
McKinney, Bob (Robert Francis)	08/19/1946	Church of the Annunciation Cemetery, Hanover, PA
McKinnon, Alex (Alexander J.)	07/24/1887	Lowell Cemetery, Lowell, MA
McKnight, Jim (James Arthur)	02/24/1994	Blackwell Cemetery, Bee Branch, AR
McLane, Ed (Edward Cameron)	08/21/1975	New Cathedral Cemetery, Baltimore, MD
McLarney, Art (Arthur James)	12/20/1984	Laurel Grove Cemetery, Port Townsend, WA
McLarry, Polly (Howard Zell)	11/04/1971	Leonard Cemetery, Leonard, TX
McLaughlin, Barney (Bernard)	02/13/1921	St. Patrick's Cemetery, Lowell, MA
McLaughlin, Frank (Francis Edward)	04/05/1917	St. Patrick's Cemetery, Lowell, MA
McLaughlin, Jim (James Robert)	12/18/1968	Oakwood Cemetery, Mount Vernon, IL
McLaughlin, Jim (James Thomas)	11/16/1895	Riverside Cemetery, Cleveland, OH
McLaughlin, Jud (Justin Theodore)	09/27/1964	Belmont Cemetery, Belmont, MA
McLaughlin, Kid (James Anson)	11/13/1934	St. Bonaventure University Cemetery, St. Bonaventure, NY
McLaughlin, Pat (Patrick Elmer)	11/01/1999	Resthaven Memorial Gardens, Houston, TX
McLaughlin, Tom (Thomas)	07/21/1921	St. Michael's Cemetery, Louisville, KY
McLaughlin, Warren A.	10/22/1923	Hillside Cemetery, Metuchen, NJ
McLaurin, Ralph Edgar	02/11/1943	McColl Cemetery, McColl, SC
McLean, Larry (John Bannerman)	03/24/1921	Cedar Grove Cemetery, Dorchester, MA
McLean, Mac (Albert Eldon)	09/29/1990	Guilford Memorial Park, Greensboro, NC
McLeland, Wayne Gaffney	05/09/2004	Forest Park (Lawndale) Cemetery, Houston, TX
McLeod, Jim (Soule James)	08/03/1981	Roselawn Memorial Gardens Cemetery, Little Rock, AR
McMahon, Doc (Henry John)	12/11/1929	Calvary Cemetery, Woburn, MA
McMahon, Don (Donald John)	07/22/1987	Good Shepherd Cemetery, Huntington Beach, CA
McMahon, Jack (John Henry)	12/30/1894	St. Michael's Cemetery, Stratford, CT
McMahon, Sadie (John Joseph)	02/20/1954	St. Joseph's-on-the-Brandywine Church Cemetery, Greenville, DE
McMakin, John Weaver	09/25/1956	Wood Memorial Park, Greer, SC
McManus, George *manager*	10/02/1918	Woodlawn Cemetery, Bronx, NY
McManus, Joe (Joab Logan)	12/23/1955	Sunset Memorial Park, Beckley, WV
McManus, Marty (Martin Joseph)	02/18/1966	Calvary Cemetery, St. Louis, MO
McMillan, Norm (Norman Alexis)	09/28/1969	Magnolia Cemetery, Latta, SC
McMillan, Reddy (George A.)	04/18/1920	West Park Cemetery, Cleveland, OH
McMillan, Roy David	11/02/1997	Willow Wild Cemetery, Bonham, TX
McMillan, Tommy (Thomas Law)	07/15/1966	Woodlawn Memorial Park, Winter Garden, FL
McMullen, Hugh Raphael	05/23/1986	Rose Hills Memorial Park, Whittier, CA
McMullin, Fred Drury	11/21/1952	Inglewood Park Cemetery, Inglewood, CA
McMullin, John F.	04/11/1881	Cathedral Cemetery, Philadelphia, PA
McNabb, Edgar J.	02/28/1894	Mound View Cemetery, Mt. Vernon, OH
McNair, Eric (Donald Eric)	03/11/1949	Rose Hill-Magnolia Cemetery, Meridian, MS

Name	DOD	Cemetery, City, State
McNally, Dave (David Arthur)	12/01/2002	Yellowstone Valley Memorial Park, Billings, MT
McNally, Mike (Michael Joseph)	05/29/1965	St. Joseph's Cemetery, Scranton, PA
McNamara, Dinny (John Raymond)	12/20/1963	St. Bernard's Cemetery, Concord, MA
McNamara, George Francis	06/12/1990	Holy Sepulchre Cemetery, Worth, IL
McNamara, Tim (Timothy Augustine)	11/05/1994	St. Charles Cemetery, Blackstone, MA
McNamara, Tom (Thomas Henry)	05/05/1974	Annunciation Cemetery, Danvers, MA
McNaughton, Gordon Joseph	08/06/1942	Calvary Cemetery, Evanston, IL
McNeal, Harry (John Harley)	01/11/1945	Fern Dale Cemetery, Johnstown, NY
McNeely, Earl (George Earl)	07/16/1971	Mount Vernon Memorial Park, Fair Oaks, CA
McNeil, Norm (Norman Francis)	04/11/1942	United German & French Cemetery, Cheektowaga, NY
McNichol, Ed (Edwin Briggs)	11/01/1952	Woodland Cemetery, Salineville, OH
McNulty, Pat (Patrick Howard)	05/04/1963	Good Shepherd Cemetery, Huntington Beach, CA
McPhee, Bid (John Alexander)	01/03/1943	Cypress View Cemetery, San Diego, CA. Cremated.
McPherson, John Jacob	09/30/1941	Easton Heights Cemetery, Easton, PA
McQuaid, Herb (Herbert George)	04/04/1966	Chapel of the Chimes, Oakland, CA
McQuaid, Mart (Mortimer Martin)	03/05/1928	Calvary Cemetery, Evanston, IL
McQuery, Mox (William Thomas)	06/12/1900	Linden Grove Cemetery, Covington, KY
McQuillan, Hugh (Alvin Hugh)	08/26/1947	Calvary Cemetery, Woodside, Queens, NY
McQuinn, George Hartley	12/24/1978	Cremated, Alexandria, VA
McRae, Norm (Norman)	07/25/2003	Restland Memorial Park, Dallas, TX
McShannic, Pete (Peter Robert)	11/30/1946	Toledo Memorial Park, Sylvania, OH
McSorley, Trick (John Bernard)	02/09/1936	Calvary Cemetery, St. Louis, MO
McSweeney, Paul A.	08/12/1951	Calvary Cemetery, St. Louis, MO
McTamany, Jim (James Edward)	04/16/1916	St. Francis DeSales Cemetery, Chester Heights, PA
McTigue, Bill (William Patrick)	05/08/1920	Calvary Cemetery, Nashville, TN
McVey, Cal (Calvin Alexander)	08/20/1926	Cremated, San Francisco, CA
McWeeney, Doug (Douglas Lawrence)	01/01/1953	All Saints Cemetery, Des Plaines, IL
McWilliams, Bill (William Henry)	01/21/1997	Garland Memorial Park, Garland, TX. Cremated.
Meador, Johnny (John Davis)	04/11/1970	Forsyth Memorial Park Cemetery, Winston-Salem, NC
Meadows, Lee (Henry Lee)	01/29/1963	Resthaven Garden of Memories, Decatur, GA
Meadows, Rufus Rivers	05/10/1970	Resthaven Gardens of Memory, Wichita, KS
Meakim, George Clinton	02/17/1923	Mount Olivet Cemetery, Maspeth, Queens, NY
Meara, Charlie (Charles Edward)	02/08/1962	Long Island National Cemetery, Farmingdale, NY
Medwick, Joe (Joseph Michael)	03/21/1975	Saint Lucas Cemetery, St. Louis, MO
Mee, Tommy (Thomas William)	05/16/1981	Holy Sepulchre Cemetery, Worth, IL
Meegan, Pete (Peter James)	03/15/1905	Holy Cross Cemetery, Colma, CA
Meehan, Bill (William Thomas)	10/08/1982	Douglas Park Cemetery, Douglas, WY

Name	DOD	Cemetery, City, State
Meek, Dad (Frank J.)	12/22/1922	New Picker's Cemetery, Lemay, MO
Meeker, Roy (Charles Roy)	03/25/1929	Memorial Park Cemetery, Kansas City, KS
Meekin, Jouett (George Jouett)	12/14/1944	Fairview Cemetery, New Albany, IN
Meier, Dutch (Arthur Ernst)	03/23/1948	Graceland Cemetery, Chicago, IL
Meine, Heinie (Henry William)	03/18/1968	St. Trinity Lutheran Cemetery, St. Louis, MO
Meinert, Walt (Walter Henry)	11/09/1958	Fairlawn Cemetery, Decatur, IL
Meinke, Bob (Robert Bernard)	12/29/1952	Acacia Park Cemetery, River Forest, IL
Meinke, Frank Louis	11/08/1931	Montrose Cemetery, Chicago, IL
Meister, John F.	01/28/1923	Union Cemetery, Allentown, PA
Meister, Karl Daniel	08/15/1967	East Lawn Memorial Park, Marietta, OH
Meixell, Moxie (Merton Merrill)	08/17/1982	Cremated, Los Angeles, CA
Melillo, Oscar Donald	11/14/1963	Holy Sepulchre Cemetery, Worth, IL
Mellana, Joe (Joseph Peter)	11/01/1969	Mount Tamalpais Cemetery, San Rafael, CA
Mellor, Bill (William Harpin)	11/05/1940	Acotes Cemetery, Chepachet, RI
Meloan, Paul B.	02/11/1950	Cremated, Taft, CA
Melter, Steve (Stephen Blasius)	01/28/1962	Mount Calvary Cemetery, Cherokee, IA
Melton, Cliff (Clifford George)	07/28/1986	Holy Redeemer Cemetery, Baltimore, MD
Melton, Rube (Reuben Franklin)	09/11/1971	Woodlawn Memorial Park, Greenville, SC
Menefee, Jock (John)	03/11/1953	Cochran Cemetery, Dawson, PA
Menosky, Mike (Michael William)	04/11/1983	Holy Sepulchre Cemetery, Southfield, MI
Mensor, Ed (Edward)	04/20/1970	Buena Vista Cemetery, Independence, OR
Menze, Ted (Theodore Charles)	12/23/1969	St. Peter's Cemetery, St. Louis, MO
Meola, Mike (Emile Michael)	09/01/1976	Calvary Cemetery, Paterson, NJ
Mercer, Jack (Harry Vernon)	06/25/1945	Ferncliff Cemetery, Springfield, OH
Mercer, John Locke	12/22/1982	Greenwood Cemetery, Shreveport, LA
Mercer, Win (George Barclay)	01/12/1903	Spring Grove Cemetery, East Liverpool, OH
Merena, Spike (John Joseph)	03/09/1977	St. Michael's Cemetery, Stratford, CT
Merkle, Fred (Carl Frederick Rudolf)	03/02/1956	Bellevue Cedar Hill Memory Gardens, Daytona Beach, FL
Merrill, Ed (Edward Mason)	01/29/1946	Oakridge Cemetery, Hillside, IL
Merriman, Lloyd Archer	01/20/2004	Cremated, Clovis, CA
Merritt, Bill (William Henry)	11/17/1937	St. Patrick's Cemetery, Lowell, MA
Merritt, George Washington	02/21/1938	Memorial Park Cemetery, Memphis, TN
Merritt, Herm (Herman G.)	05/26/1927	Mount Washington Cemetery, Independence, MO
Merritt, John Howard	11/03/1955	Glenwood Cemetery, Tupelo, MS
Mertes, Sam (Samuel Blair)	03/11/1945	Woodlawn Memorial Park, Colma, CA
Mesner, Steve (Stephen Mathias)	04/06/1981	Greenwood Memorial Park, San Diego, CA
Messenger, Andy (Andrew Warren)	11/04/1971	Roselawn Cemetery, Perry, MI
Messenger, Bobby (Charles Walter)	07/10/1951	Richmond Cemetery, Richmond, ME
Messitt, Tom (Thomas John)	09/22/1934	Calvary Cemetery, Evanston, IL
Metcalf, Al (Alfred Tristram)	09/02/1914	Cypress Hills Cemetery, Brooklyn, NY
Metha, Scat (Frank Joseph)	03/02/1975	Rose Hills Memorial Park, Whittier, CA
Metheny, Bud (Arthur Beauregard)	01/02/2003	Colonial Grove Memorial Park, Virginia Beach, VA
Metivier, Dewey (George Dewey)	03/02/1947	St. Paul's Cemetery, Arlington, MA
Metkovich, Catfish (George Michael)	05/17/1995	El Toro Memorial Park, Lake Forest, CA

Name	DOD	Cemetery, City, State
Metz, Lenny (Leonard Raymond)	02/24/1953	Mountain View Cemetery, Boulder, CO
Metzler, Alex (Alexander)	11/30/1973	Mountain View Cemetery, Fresno, CA
Meusel, Bob (Robert William)	11/28/1977	Rose Hills Memorial Park, Whittier, CA
Meusel, Irish (Emil Frederick)	03/01/1963	Inglewood Park Cemetery, Inglewood, CA
Meyer, Benny (Bernhard)	02/06/1974	Hematite Methodist Cemetery, Hematite, MO
Meyer, Bill (William Adam)	03/31/1957	Lynnhurst Cemetery, Knoxville, TN
Meyer, George Francis	01/03/1992	Memory Gardens Cemetery, Arlington Heights, IL
Meyer, Jack (John Robert)	03/06/1967	Lakeview Memorial Park, Cinnaminson, NJ
Meyer, Leo	09/02/1968	Silverbrook Cemetery, Wilmington, DE
Meyer, Russ (Russell Charles)	11/16/1997	Peru City Cemetery, Peru, IL
Meyerle, Levi Samuel	11/04/1921	Oaklands Cemetery, West Chester, PA
Meyers, Chief (John Tortes)	07/25/1971	Green Acres Memorial Park, Bloomington, CA
Meyers, Henry L.	06/28/1898	Cathedral Cemetery, Harrisburg, PA
Meyers, Lou (Lewis Henry)	11/30/1920	Spring Grove Cemetery, Cincinnati, OH
Michaels, Cass (Casimir Eugene)	11/12/1982	Mount Olivet Cemetery, Detroit, MI
Michaels, John Joseph	11/18/1996	St. Michael's Cemetery, Stratford, CT
Michaels, Ralph Joseph	08/05/1988	St. Mary Church Cemetery (Sharpsburg), Pittsburgh, PA
Michaelson, John August	04/16/1968	Marenisco Cemetery, Marenisco, MI
Middleton, Jim (James Blaine)	01/12/1974	Argos Maple Grove Cemetery, Argos, IN
Middleton, John Wayne	11/03/1986	Llano Cemetery, Amarillo, TX
Midkiff, Dick (Richard James)	10/30/1956	Gonzales Memorial Park, Gonzales, TX
Midkiff, Ezra Millington	03/20/1957	Woodmere Memorial Park, Huntington, WV
Mihalic, John Michael	04/24/1987	Woodlawn Memorial Park, Nashville, TN
Milan, Clyde (Jesse Clyde)	03/03/1953	Clarksville Cemetery, Clarksville, TX
Milan, Horace Robert	06/29/1955	Fairview Cemetery, Clarksville, TX
Miles, Dee (Wilson Daniel)	11/02/1976	Elmwood Cemetery, Birmingham, Al
Miley, Mike (Michael Wilfred)	01/06/1977	Garden of Memories, Metairie, LA
Miljus, Johnny (John Kenneth)	02/11/1976	Cremated, Kalispell, MT
Millard, Frank E.	07/04/1892	Bellefontaine Cemetery, St. Louis, MO (Moved to unknown location on 03/23/1898)
Miller, Bert (Herbert A.)	06/14/1937	Flint Cemetery, Flint, MI
Miller, Bill (William Alexander)	09/09/1957	Knollwood Cemetery, Mayfield Heights, OH
Miller, Bill (William Francis)	02/26/1982	Holy Family Cemetery, Hannibal, MO
Miller, Bill (William Paul)	07/01/2003	Indiantown Gap National Cemetery, Annville, PA
Miller, Bing (Edmund John)	05/07/1966	Calvary Cemetery, West Conshohocken, PA
Miller, Bob (Robert Lane)	08/06/1993	Dearborn Memorial Park, Poway, CA
Miller, Bob (Robert W.)	05/23/1931	Fairmount Cemetery, Newark, NJ
Miller, Charlie (Charles Elmer)	04/23/1972	Sunset Hills Cemetery, Warrensburg, MO
Miller, Charlie (Charles Hess)	01/13/1951	Millersville Mennonite Cemetery, Millersville, PA
Miller, Chuck (Charles Marion)	06/16/1961	Forest Park (Lawndale) Cemetery, Houston, TX
Miller, Cyclone (Joseph H.)	10/13/1916	Comstock Cemetery, Montville, CT

Name	DOD	Cemetery, City, State
Miller, Doc (Roy Oscar)	07/31/1938	Cremated, Garden State Crematory (formerly NY & NJ Crematory), North Bergen, NJ
Miller, Doggie (George Frederick)	04/06/1909	Lutheran All Faiths Cemetery, Middle Village, Queens, NY
Miller, Dots (John Barney)	09/05/1923	Holy Cross Cemetery, North Arlington, NJ
Miller, Dusty (Charles Bradley)	09/03/1945	Forest Hill Cemetery-Midtown, Memphis, TN
Miller, Dusty (Dakin Evans)	04/19/1950	Stockton Rural Cemetery, Stockton, CA
Miller, Ed (Edwin Collins)	04/17/1980	Mt. Annville Cemetery, Annville, PA
Miller, Eddie (Edward Robert)	07/31/1997	Union Dale Cemetery, Pittsburgh, PA
Miller, Elmer	11/28/1944	Eastlawn Cemetery, Beloit, WI
Miller, Elmer Joseph	01/08/1987	Cremated, Riverside, CA
Miller, Frank Lee	02/19/1974	Rowe Cemetery, Allegan, MI
Miller, Fred (Frederick Holman)	05/02/1953	Maple Grove Cemetery, Brookville, IN
Miller, George C.	07/24/1929	Spring Grove Cemetery, Cincinnati, OH
Miller, Hack (Laurence H.)	09/16/1971	St. Mary's Cemetery, Oakland, CA
Miller, Hughie (Hugh Stanley)	12/24/1945	Jefferson Barracks National Cemetery, St. Louis, MO
Miller, Jake (Jacob George)	08/24/1974	Oak Lawn Cemetery, Baltimore, MD
Miller, Jake (Walter)	08/20/1975	Cremated, Venice, FL
Miller, Joe (Joseph A.)	04/23/1928	Mount Calvary Cemetery, Wheeling, WV
Miller, Ken (Kenneth Albert)	04/03/1991	Our Redeemer Cemetery, Affton, MO
Miller, Kohly (Frank A.)	03/29/1951	Gethsemane Cemetery, Reading, PA
Miller, Otto (Otis Louis)	07/26/1959	Walnut Hill Cemetery, Belleville, IL
Miller, Ralph Darwin	05/08/1973	Spring Grove Cemetery, Cincinnati, OH
Miller, Ralph Henry	02/18/1967	Sunset Memorial Park, Minneapolis, MN
Miller, Ralph Joseph	03/18/1939	Catholic Cemetery, Fort Wayne, IN
Miller, Ray (Raymond Peter)	04/07/1927	St. Mary's Roman Catholic Cemetery (Troy Hill), Pittsburgh, PA
Miller, Red (Leo Alphonso)	10/20/1973	Glen Haven Memorial Park, Winter Park, FL
Miller, Roger Wesley	04/26/1993	Indian Creek Baptist Church Cemetery, Mill Run, PA
Miller, Ronnie (Roland Arthur)	01/06/1998	Valhalla Cemetery, St. Louis, MO
Miller, Roscoe Clyde	04/18/1913	Cedar Hill Cemetery, Corydon, IN
Miller, Rudy (Rudel Charles)	01/22/1994	Mountain Home Cemetery, Kalamazoo, MI
Miller, Russ (Russell Lewis)	04/30/1962	Glen Rest Memorial Estate, Reynoldsburg, OH
Miller, Tom (Thomas P.)	05/29/1876	Evergreen Memorial Park, Bensalem, PA. Originally intered at Lafayette Cemetery, Philadelphia. Cemetery removed
Miller, Walt (Walter W.)	03/01/1956	Riverside Cemetery, Gas City, IN
Miller, Ward Taylor	09/04/1958	Oakwood Cemetery, Dixon, IL
Miller, Warren Lemuel	08/12/1956	Holy Sepulchre Cemetery, Wyndmoor, PA
Millies, Wally (Walter Louis)	02/28/1995	Chapel Hill Gardens South, Oak Lawn, IL
Milligan, Billy (William Joseph)	10/14/1928	St. Matthews Cemetery, Buffalo, NY
Milligan, Jocko (John)	08/29/1923	Mt. Moriah Cemetery, Philadelphia, PA
Milligan, John Alexander	05/15/1972	Fort Pierce Cemetery, Fort Pierce, FL

Name	DOD	Cemetery, City, State
Mills, Art (Arthur Grant)	07/23/1975	Forest Hill Cemetery, Utica, NY
Mills, Buster (Colonel Buster)	12/01/1991	Oakwood Cemetery, Waco, TX
Mills, Charlie (Charles F.)	04/09/1874	Cypress Hills Cemetery, Brooklyn, NY
Mills, Everett	06/22/1908	Fairmount Cemetery, Newark, NJ
Mills, Frank LeMoyne	08/31/1983	Forest Lawn Memorial Park, Youngstown, OH
Mills, Jack (Abbott Paige)	06/03/1973	Cremated, Washington, DC
Mills, Lefty (Howard Robinson)	09/23/1982	Green Hills Memorial Park, Rancho Palos Verdes, CA
Mills, Rupert Frank	07/20/1929	St. Mary's Cemetery, East Orange, NJ
Milne, Pete (William James)	04/11/1999	Mobile Memorial Gardens, Mobile, AL
Milner, John David	01/04/2000	College Park Cemetery, College Park, GA
Milstead, George Earl	08/09/1977	Godley Cemetery, Godley, TX
Minahan, Cotton (Edmund Joseph)	05/20/1958	Holy Cross Cemetery, North Arlington, NJ
Mincher, Edward M.	12/08/1918	Green-Wood Cemetery, Brooklyn, NY
Miner, Ray (Raymond Theodore)	09/15/1963	St. Mary's Cemetery, South Glens Falls, NY
Minnehan, Dan (Daniel Joseph)	08/08/1929	St. Joseph's Cemetery, Troy, NY
Miranda, Willie (Guillermo)	09/07/1996	Gardens of Faith Memorial Gardens, Baltimore, MD
Misse, John Beverly	03/18/1970	Highland Cemetery, Highland, KS
Mitchell, Bobby (Robert McKasha)	05/01/1933	Oak Hill Cemetery, Cincinnati, OH
Mitchell, Clarence Elmer	11/06/1963	Aurora Cemetery, Aurora, NE
Mitchell, Dale (Loren Dale)	01/05/1987	Cloud Chief Cemetery, Cloud Chief, OK
Mitchell, Fred (Frederick Francis)	10/13/1970	Brookside Cemetery, Stow, MA
Mitchell, Johnny (John Franklin)	11/04/1965	Mount Olivet Cemetery, Detroit, MI
Mitchell, Mike (Michael Francis)	07/16/1961	St. Francis Catholic Cemetery, Phoenix, AZ
Mitchell, Monroe Barr	09/04/1976	McLane Riverview Memorial Gardens, Valdosta, GA
Mitchell, Roy (Albert Roy)	09/08/1959	North Belton Cemetery, Belton, TX
Mitchell, Willie (William)	11/23/1973	Rose Hill Cemetery, Sardis, MS
Mitterling, Ralph	01/22/1956	Fairview Cemetery, Freeburg, PA
Mize, Johnny (John Robert)	06/02/1993	Yonah View Memorial Gardens, Demorest, GA
Mizell, Vinegar Bend (Wilmer David)	02/21/1999	Faith Missionary Alliance Church Cemetery, Winston-Salem, NC
Mizeur, Bill (William Francis)	08/27/1976	Calvary Cemetery, Decatur, IL
Modak, Mike (Michael)	12/12/1995	Tod Homestead Cemetery, Youngstown, OH
Moeller, Danny (Daniel Edward)	04/14/1951	Forest Hill Cemetery-Midtown, Memphis, TN
Moffett, Joe (Joseph William)	02/24/1935	Cremated, San Bernardino, CA
Moffett, Sam (Samuel R.)	05/05/1907	Greenwood Cemetery, Wheeling, WV
Mogridge, George Anthony	03/04/1962	Holy Sepulchre Cemetery, Rochester, NY
Mohardt, John Henry	11/14/1961	Fort Rosecrans National Cemetery, LaJolla, CA
Mohart, George Benjamin	10/02/1970	Glenwood Cemetery, Silver Creek, NY
Mokan, Johnny (John Leo)	02/10/1985	St. Augustine Cemetery, Lancaster, NY

Name	DOD	Cemetery, City, State
Molesworth, Carlton	07/25/1961	Mount Olivet Cemetery, Frederick, MD
Mollenkamp, Fred (Frederick Henry)	11/01/1948	St. Mary's Cemetery, Cincinnati, OH
Mollwitz, Fritz (Frederick August)	10/03/1967	Wisconsin Memorial Park, Brookfield, WI
Moncewicz, Fred (Frederick Alfred)	04/23/1969	Calvary Cemetery, Brockton, MA
Monroe, Ed (Edward Oliver)	04/29/1969	Calvary Cemetery, Louisville, KY
Montague, Ed (Edward Francis)	06/17/1988	Holy Cross Cemetery, Colma, CA
Moolic, George Henry	02/19/1915	St. Mary's Immaculate Conception Cemetery, Lawrence, MA
Moon, Leo	08/25/1970	Greenwood Cemetery, New Orleans, LA
Mooney, Jim Irving	04/27/1979	Evergreen Cemetery, Erwin, TN
Moore, Al (Albert J.)	11/29/1974	Plain Lawn Cemetery, Hicksville, NY
Moore, Anse (Anselm Winn)	10/29/1993	Union Baptist Church Cemetery, Puckett, MS
Moore, Bill (William Christopher)	01/24/1984	St. Mary's Cemetery, Corning, NY
Moore, Bill (William Henry)	05/24/1972	Calvary Cemetery, Kansas City, MO
Moore, Charley (Charles Wesley)	07/29/1970	Skyline Memorial Gardens, Portland, OR
Moore, Cy (William Austin)	03/28/1972	Stevens Family Cemetery, Sandy Cross, GA
Moore, Dee (D. C.)	07/02/1997	Riverview Cemetery, Williston, ND
Moore, Donnie Ray	07/18/1989	Peaceful Gardens Memorial Park, Woodrow, TX
Moore, Earl Alonzo	11/28/1961	Glen Rest Memorial Estate, Reynoldsburg, OH
Moore, Euel Walton	02/12/1989	Tishomingo Cemetery, Tishomingo, OK
Moore, Ferdie (Ferdinand DePaige)	05/06/1947	Laurel Memorial Park Cemetery, Egg Harbor, NJ
Moore, Gene (Eugene, Jr.)	03/12/1978	Lake Park Cemetery, Laurel, MS
Moore, Gene (Eugene, Sr.)	08/31/1938	Edgewood Cemetery, Lancaster, TX
Moore, Jim (James Stanford)	05/19/1973	Fairmount Cemetery, Denver, CO
Moore, Jimmy (James William)	03/07/1986	Memorial Park Cemetery, Memphis, TN
Moore, Johnny (John Francis)	04/04/1991	Manasota Memorial Park, Bradenton, FL
Moore, Jo-Jo (Joseph Gregg)	04/01/2001	Gause Cemetery, Gause, TX
Moore, Piggy (Frank J.)	05/20/1964	Greenlawn Cemetery, Portsmouth, OH
Moore, Randy (Randolph Edward)	06/12/1992	Omaha Cemetery, Omaha, TX
Moore, Ray (Raymond Leroy)	03/02/1995	Cedar Hill Cemetery, Suitland, MD
Moore, Scrappy (William Allen)	10/13/1964	Roselawn Memorial Gardens Cemetery, Little Rock, AR
Moore, Terry Bluford	03/29/1995	Holy Cross Lutheran Cemetery, Collinsville, IL
Moore, Whitey (Lloyd Albert)	12/10/1987	Union Cemetery, Uhrichsville, OH
Moore, Wilcy (William Wilcy)	03/29/1963	Fairmount Cemetery, Hollis, OK
Moorhead, Robert (Charles Robert)	12/03/1986	Parklawns Memorial Gardens, Chambersburg, PA
Moose, Bob (Robert Ralph)	10/09/1976	Twin Valley Memorial Park, Delmont, PA
Mooty, Jake T.	04/20/1970	Mount Olivet Cemetery, Fort Worth, TX
Moran, Bill (William L.)	04/08/1916	St. Patrick's Cemetery. Joliet, IL
Moran, Charles Vincent	04/11/1934	Mount Olivet Cemetery, Washington, DC
Moran, Charley (Charles Barthell)	06/14/1949	Horse Cave Cemetery, Horse Cave, KY
Moran, Harry Edwin	11/28/1962	Highlawn Memorial Park, Oak Hill, WV

Name	DOD	Cemetery, City, State
Moran, Herbie (John Herbert)	09/21/1954	Lake View Cemetery, Brockport, NY
Moran, Hiker (Albert Thomas)	01/07/1998	Greenridge Cemetery, Saratoga Springs, NY
Moran, Pat (Patrick Joseph)	03/07/1924	Saint Bernard's Cemetery, Fitchburg, MA
Moran, Roy Ellis	07/18/1966	Westview Cemetery, Atlanta, GA
Moran, Sam (Samuel)	08/27/1897	Holy Sepulchre Cemetery, Rochester, NY
More, Forrest Theodore	08/17/1968	Hillcrest Cemetery, North Vernon, IN
Morehart, Ray (Raymond Anderson)	01/13/1989	Restland Memorial Park, Dallas, TX
Moren, Lew (Lewis Howard)	11/02/1966	Homewood Cemetery, Pittsburgh, PA
Moreno, Julio	01/02/1987	Woodlawn Park Cemetery, Miami, FL
Morey, Dave (David Beale)	01/04/1986	Oak Grove Cemetery, Vineyard Haven, MA
Morgan, Bill (William)	09/07/1908	Lutheran All Faiths Cemetery, Middle Village, Queens, NY
Morgan, Chet (Chester Collins)	09/20/1991	Grand View Memorial Park, Pasadena, TX
Morgan, Cy (Cyril Arlon)	09/11/1946	East Harwich Cemetery, East Harwich, MA
Morgan, Cy (Harry Richard)	06/28/1962	Riverview Cemetery, Martins Ferry, OH
Morgan, Daniel	01/31/1910	Calvary Cemetery, St. Louis, MO
Morgan, Ed (Edward Carre)	04/09/1980	Garden of Memories, Metairie, LA
Morgan, Eddie (Edwin Willis)	06/27/1982	Hillcrest Memorial Park, Bedford Heights, OH
Morgan, Ray (Raymond Caryll)	02/15/1940	Cecilton Cemetery (now Zion Cemetery), Cecilton, MD
Morgan, Red (James Edward)	03/25/1981	Ferncliff Cemetery, Hartsdale, NY
Morgan, Tom Stephen	01/13/1987	Green Hills Memorial Park, Rancho Palos Verdes, CA
Morgan, Vern (Vernon Thomas)	11/08/1975	Emporia Cemetery, Emporia, VA
Moriarty, Bill (William Joseph)	12/25/1916	Mount Olivet Cemetery, Chicago, IL
Moriarty, Ed (Edward Jerome)	09/29/1991	Calvary Cemetery, Holyoke, MA
Moriarty, George Joseph	04/08/1964	St. Mary's Cemetery, Evergreen Park, IL
Morley, Bill (William M.)	05/14/1985	Lubbock City Cemetery, Lubbock, TX
Morrell, Bill (Willard Blackmer)	08/05/1975	Elmwood Cemetery, Birmingham, AL
Morrill, John Francis	04/02/1932	Holyhood Cemetery, Brookline, MA
Morris, Doyt Theodore	07/04/1984	Stanley Cemetery, Stanley, NC
Morris, Ed (Edward)	04/12/1937	Union Dale Cemetery, Pittsburgh, PA
Morris, Ed (Walter Edward)	03/03/1932	Oak Grove Cemetery, Flomaton, AL
Morris, Walter (John Walter)	08/02/1961	Restland Memorial Park, Dallas, TX
Morrisette, Bill (William Lee)	03/25/1966	Rosewood Memorial Park, Virginia Beach, VA
Morrison, Guy (Walter Guy)	08/14/1934	Sunset Memorial Park, Charleston, WV
Morrison, Hank (Stephen Henry)	09/30/1927	St. John's Cemetery, Attleboro, MA
Morrison, Johnny (John Dewey)	03/20/1966	Rose Hill Cemetery, Owensboro, KY
Morrison, Mike (Michael)	06/16/1955	Trinity Cemetery, Erie, PA
Morrison, Phil (Philip Melvin)	01/18/1955	Rose Hill Cemetery, Owensboro, KY
Morrison, Tom (Thomas J.)	03/27/1902	Calvary Cemetery, St. Louis, MO
Morrissey, Deacon (Michael Joseph)	02/22/1939	New Cathedral Cemetery, Baltimore, MD
Morrissey, Jack (John Albert)	10/30/1936	Mount Hope Cemetery, Lansing, MI
Morrissey, John J.	04/29/1884	Mount Olivet Cemetery, Janesville, WI
Morrissey, Jo-Jo (Joseph Anselm)	05/02/1950	St. John's Cemetery, Worcester, MA

Name	DOD	Cemetery, City, State
Morrissey, Tom (Thomas J.)	09/23/1941	Mount Olivet Cemetery, Janesville, WI ·
Morse, Bud (Newell Obediah)	04/06/1987	Cremated, Mountain View Cemetrery, Reno, NV.
Morse, Hap (Peter Raymond)	06/19/1974	Forest Lawn Memorial Park, St. Paul, MN
Morton, Carl Wendle	04/12/1983	Memorial Park Cemetery, Tulsa, OK
Morton, Charlie (Charles Hazen)	12/09/1921	Glendale Cemetery, Akron, OH
Morton, Guy, Sr.	10/18/1934	Vernon Cemetery, Vernon, AL
Moryn, Walt (Walter Joseph)	07/21/1996	Assumption Cemetery, Glenwood, IL
Moseley, Earl Victor	07/01/1963	Alliance City Cemetery, Alliance, OH
Moser, Walter Frederick	12/10/1946	West Laurel Hill Cemetery, Bala Cynwyd, PA
Moses, Wally (Wallace)	10/10/1990	Pine Crest Cemetery, Vidalia, GA
Moskiman, Doc (William Bankhead)	01/11/1953	Holy Sepulchre Cemetery, Hayward, CA
Mosolf, Jim (James Frederick)	12/28/1979	Woodbine Cemetery, Puyallup, WA
Moss, Charlie (Charles Crosby)	10/09/1991	Rose Hill-Magnolia Cemetery, Meridian, MS
Moss, Howie (Howard Glenn)	05/07/1989	Dulaney Valley Memorial Gardens, Timonium, MD
Moss, Mal (Charles Malcolm)	02/06/1983	Beaufort National Cemetery, Beaufort, SC
Moss, Ray (Raymond Earl)	08/09/1998	Hamilton Memorial Gardens, Chattanooga, TN
Mossor, Earl Dalton	12/29/1988	Mount Moriah Cemetery, Withamsville, OH
Mostil, Johnny (John Anthony)	12/10/1970	Ridgelawn-Mount Mercy Cemetery, Gary, IN
Motz, Frank H.	03/18/1944	Rose Hill Cemetery, Fairlawn, OH
Moulder, Glen Hubert	11/27/1994	Body donated to medical research. Atlanta, GA
Moulton, Allie (Albert Theodore)	07/10/1968	Pine Grove Cemetery, Warner, NH
Mountain, Frank Henry	11/19/1939	Most Holy Redeemer Cemetery, Schenectady, NY
Mountjoy, Billy (William Henry)	05/19/1894	Mount Pleasant Cemetery, London, Ontario, Canada
Mowrey, Mike (Harry Harlan)	03/20/1947	Lincoln Cemetery, Chambersburg, PA
Mowry, Joe (Joseph Aloysius)	02/09/1994	Resurrection Cemetery, Mackenzie, MO
Moyer, Charlie (Charles Edward)	11/18/1962	Cremated, Jacksonville, FL
Moynahan, Mike (Michael)	04/09/1899	Mount Olivet Cemetery, Chicago, IL
Mueller, Bill (William Lawrence)	10/24/2001	Memorial Park Cemetery, Skokie, IL
Mueller, Heinie (Clarence Francis)	01/23/1975	Park Lawn Cemetery, St. Louis, MO
Mueller, Heinie (Emmett Jerome)	10/03/1986	Woodlawn Cemetery, Winter Garden, FL
Mueller, Ray Coleman	06/29/1994	Harrisburg Cemetery, Harrisburg, PA
Mueller, Walter John	08/16/1971	Mount Lebanon Cemetery, St. Ann, MO
Muich, Joe (Ignatius Andrew)	07/02/1993	SS. Peter & Paul Cemetery, St. Louis, MO
Muir, Joe (Joseph Allen)	06/25/1980	Oriole Cemetery, Oriole, MD
Mulcahy, Hugh Noyes	10/19/2001	Beaver Cemetery, Beaver, PA
Mullane, Tony (Anthony John)	04/25/1944	Holy Sepulchre Cemetery, Worth, IL
Mulleavy, Greg (Gregory Thomas)	02/01/1980	Queen of Heaven Cemetery, Rowland Heights, CA
Mullen, Billy (William John)	05/04/1971	Jefferson Barracks National Cemetery, St. Louis, MO
Mullen, Charlie (Charles George)	06/06/1963	Evergreen-Washelli Cemetery, Seattle, WA
Mullen, Freddie (Frederick William)	10/20/1976	Cremated, Davis, CA
Mulligan, Dick (Richard Charles)	12/15/1992	Resurrection Cemetery, Victoria, TX

Name	DOD	Cemetery, City, State
Mulligan, Eddie (Edward Joseph)	03/15/1982	Holy Cross Cemetery, Colma, CA
Mulligan, Joe (Joseph Ignatius)	06/05/1986	St. Joseph's Cemetery, West Roxbury, MA
Mullin, George Joseph	01/07/1944	Falls Cemetery, Wabash, IN
Mullin, Henry J.	11/08/1937	St. Mary's Cemetery, Salem, MA
Mullin, Pat (Patrick Joseph)	08/14/1999	Lafayette Memorial Park, Brier Hill, PA
Mulrenan, Dominic Joseph	07/27/1964	Wyoming Cemetery, Melrose, MA
Mulroney, Frank (Francis Joseph)	11/11/1985	Fern Hill Cemetery, Aberdeen, WA
Mulvey, Joe (Joseph H.)	08/21/1928	Magnolia Cemetery, Philadelphia, PA
Munce, John Lewis	03/15/1917	Holy Cross Cemetery, Yeadon, PA
Munch, Jake (Jacob Ferdinand)	06/08/1966	Arlington Cemetery, Drexel Hill, PA
Muncrief, Bob (Robert Cleveland)	02/06/1996	Cedarlawn Memorial Park, Sherman, TX
Mundy, Bill (William Edward)	09/23/1958	Spring Hill Cemetery, Wellsville, OH
Munger, George David	07/23/1996	Forest Park (Lawndale) Cemetery, Houston, TX
Mungo, Van Lingle	02/12/1985	First Baptist Church Cemetery, Pageland, SC
Munn, Horatio Brinsmade	02/17/1910	Mount Pleasant Cemetery, Newark, NJ
Munns, Les (Leslie Ernest)	02/28/1997	Oakdale Cemetery, Crookston, MN
Munson, Joe (Joseph Martin Napoleon) (buried under birth name: Carlson)	02/24/1991	Arlington Cemetery, Drexel Hill, PA
Munson, Red (Clarence Hanford)	02/19/1957	Spring Grove Cemetery, Cincinnati, OH
Munson, Thurman Lee	08/02/1979	Sunset Hills Burial Park, Canton, OH
Munyan, John Baird	02/18/1945	Riverhurst Cemetery, Endicott, NY
Murchison, Tim (Thomas Malcolm)	10/20/1962	Fairview Cemetery, Liberty, NC
Murdoch, Wilbur Edwin	10/29/1941	Valhalla Memorial Park, North Hollywood, CA
Murname, Tim (Timothy Hayes)	02/07/1917	Old Dorchester Burial Ground, Dorchester, MA
Murphy, Buzz (Robert Sylvester)	05/11/1938	Mount Olivet Cemetery, Wheat Ridge, CO
Murphy, Con (Cornelius B.)	08/01/1914	St. John's Cemetery, Worcester, MA
Murphy, Connie (Cornelius David)	12/14/1945	St. Mary's Cemetery, New Bedford, MA
Murphy, Danny (Daniel Joseph)	12/14/1915	Holy Cross Cemetery, Brooklyn, NY
Murphy, Dave (David Francis)	04/08/1940	Maple Street Cemetery, Adams, MA
Murphy, Dummy (Herbert Courtland)	08/10/1962	Laurel Hill Cemetery, Thomasville, GA
Murphy, Ed (Edward J.)	01/29/1935	St. Joseph's Cemetery. Auburn, NY
Murphy, Ed (Edward Joseph)	12/10/1991	St. John the Baptist Cemetery, Joliet, IL
Murphy, Eddie (John Edward)	02/21/1969	Queen of Peace Cemetery, Hawley, PA
Murphy, Frank (Francis Patrick)	11/04/1912	Sleepy Hollow Cemetery, Tarrytown, NY
Murphy, Howard	10/05/1926	Mount Olivet Cemetery, Fort Worth, TX
Murphy, Joe (Joseph Akin)	03/28/1951	Calvary Cemetery, St. Louis, MO
Murphy, John Patrick	04/20/1949	St. Mary's Immaculate Conception Cemetery, Lawrence, MA
Murphy, Johnny (John Joseph)	01/14/1970	Woodlawn Cemetery, Bronx, NY
Murphy, Mike (Michael Jerome)	10/26/1952	Calvary-St. Patrick Cemetery, Johnson City, NY
Murphy, Morgan Edward	10/03/1938	St. Francis Cemetery, Pawtucket, RI
Murphy, Pat (Patrick J.)	05/16/1927	St. John's Cemetery, Worcester, MA
Murphy, Patrick Lawrence	10/06/1911	Crown Hill Cemetery, Indianapolis, IN
Murphy, Tony (Francis J.)	12/15/1915	Calvary Cemetery, Woodside, Queens, NY

Name	DOD	Cemetery, City, State
Murphy, Walter Joseph	03/23/1976	Memorial Oaks Cemetery, Houston, TX
Murphy, Yale (William Henry)	02/14/1906	St. John's Cemetery, Lancaster, MA
Murray, Amby (Ambrose Joseph)	02/06/1997	Cremated, Port Solerno, FL
Murray, Bill (William Allenwood)	09/14/1943	Mt. St. Benedict's Cemetery, Bloomfield, CT
Murray, Bobby (Robert Hayes)	01/04/1979	Edgewood Cemetery, Nashua, NH
Murray, Ed (Edward Francis)	11/08/1970	Mount Olivet Cemetery, Cheyenne, WY
Murray, George King	10/18/1955	Oakwood Cemetery, Brownsville, TN
Murray, Jim (James Francis)	07/15/1973	St. Catherine's Cemetery, Moscow, PA
Murray, Jim (James Oscar)	04/25/1945	Episcopal Cemetery, Galveston, TX
Murray, Miah (Jeremiah J.)	01/11/1922	Holyhood Cemetery, Brookline, MA
Murray, Pat (Patrick Joseph)	11/05/1983	St. John the Evangelist Cemetery, Spencerport, NY
Murray, Ray (Raymond Lee)	04/09/2003	Shannon Rose Hill Memorial Park, Fort Worth, TX
Murray, Red (John Joseph)	12/04/1958	SS. Peter & Paul Cemetery, Elmira, NY
Murray, Tony (Anthony Joseph)	03/19/1974	All Saints Cemetery, Des Plaines, IL
Murtaugh, Danny (Daniel Edward)	12/02/1976	SS. Peter & Paul Cemetery, Springfield, PA
Musser, Paul	07/07/1973	Fairview Cemetery, Millheim, PA
Mustaikis, Alex (Alexander Dominick)	01/17/1970	Cathedral Cemetery, Scranton, PA
Mutrie, Jim (James J.) *manager*	01/24/1938	Moravian Cemetery, New Dorp, Staten Island, NY
Myatt, Glenn Calvin	08/09/1969	Forest Park (Lawndale) Cemetery, Houston, TX
Myer, Buddy (Charles Solomon)	10/31/1974	Greenoaks Memorial Park, Baton Rouge, LA
Myers, Al (James Albert)	12/24/1927	Highland Lawn Cemetery, Terre Haute, IN
Myers, Billy (William Harrison)	04/10/1995	Rolling Green Memorial Park, Camp Hill, PA
Myers, Elmer Glenn	07/29/1976	Sunnyside Cemetery, York Springs, PA
Myers, George D.	12/14/1926	Holy Cross Cemetery, Lackawanna, NY
Myers, Hap (Ralph Edward)	06/30/1967	Golden Gate National Cemetery, San Bruno, CA
Myers, Henry C.	04/18/1895	Mt. Vernon Cemetery, Philadelphia, PA
Myers, Hy (Henry Harrison)	05/01/1965	Grove Hill Cemetery, Hanoverton, OH
Myers, Joe (Joseph William)	02/11/1956	Cathedral Cemetery, Wilmington, DE
Myers, Lynn (Lynnwood Lincoln)	01/19/2000	Rolling Green Memorial Park, Camp Hill, PA
Nabors, Jack (Herman John)	10/29/1923	Montevallo Cemetery, Montevallo, AL
Nagel, Bill (William Taylor)	10/08/1981	Beverly National Cemetery, Beverly, NJ
Nagelsen, Lou (Louis Marcellus)	10/21/1965	Catholic Cemetery, Fort Wayne, IN
Nagle, Judge (Walter Harold)	05/26/1971	Santa Rosa Memorial Park, Santa Rosa, CA. Cremated.
Nagle, Tom (Thomas Edward)	03/09/1946	Calvary Cemetery, Milwaukee, WI
Naleway, Frank	01/28/1949	Resurrection Cemetery, Justice, IL
Nance, Doc (William G.)	05/28/1958	Shannon Rose Hill Memorial Park, Fort Worth, TX
Napier, Buddy (Skelton Leroy)	03/29/1968	Hutchins Cemetery, Hutchins, TX
Napoleon, Danny (Daniel)	04/26/2003	Greenwood Cemetery, Trenton, NJ
Narleski, Bill (William Edward)	07/20/1964	Beverly National Cemetery, Beverly, NJ

Name	DOD	Cemetery, City, State
Narron, Sam (Samuel Woody)	12/31/1996	Antioch Baptist Church Cemetery, Middlesex, NC
Nash, Ken (Kenneth Leland)	02/16/1977	Highland Cemetery, Weymouth, MA
Nava, Sandy (Vincent Irwin)	06/15/1906	Trinity Cemetery, Baltimore, MD
Naylor, Rollie (Roleine Cecil)	06/18/1966	IOOF Cemetery, Denton, TX
Neal, Charlie (Charles Leonard)	11/18/1996	Grace Hill Cemetery, Longview, TX
Neale, Greasy (Alfred Earle)	11/02/1973	Parkersburg Memorial Gardens (formerly Odd Fellows Cemetery), Parkersburg, WV
Neale, Joe (Joseph Hunt)	12/30/1913	Mount Peace Cemetery, Akron, OH
Nealon, Jim (James Joseph)	04/02/1910	Holy Cross Cemetery, Colma, CA
Needham, Tom (Thomas Joseph)	12/14/1926	Mt. Calvary Cemetery, Steubenville, OH
Neher, Jim (James Gilmore)	11/11/1951	Forest Lawn Cemetery, Buffalo, NY
Nehf, Art (Arthur Neukom)	12/18/1960	Greenwood Memory Lawn Cemetery, Phoenix, AZ. Cremated
Neighbors, Cy (Flemon Cecil)	05/20/1964	Mountain View Memorial Park, Tacoma, WA
Neill, Tommy (Thomas White)	09/22/1980	Resthaven Memorial Gardens, Houston, TX
Neis, Bernie (Bernard Edmund)	11/29/1972	Oak Ridge Cemetery, Inverness, FL
Neitzke, Ernie (Ernest Frederick)	04/27/1977	Union Hill Cemetery, Bowling Green, OH
Nelson, Bill (William F.)	06/23/1941	St. Joseph's Cemetery, Terre Haute, IN
Nelson, Candy (John W.)	09/04/1910	Cypress Hills Cemetery, Brooklyn, NY
Nelson, Emmett (George Emmett)	08/25/1967	Zion Lutheran Church Cemetery, Garrettsville, SD
Nelson, Luke (Luther Martin)	11/14/1985	St. John's Cemetery, Viola, IL
Nelson, Lynn Bernard	02/15/1955	Mount St. Mary's Cemetery, Kansas City, MO
Nelson, Red (Albert Francis)	10/26/1956	Woodlawn Memorial Gardens, St. Petersburg, FL
Nelson, Tommy (Thomas Cousineau)	09/24/1973	Cremated, San Diego, CA
Netzel, Milo (Miles A.)	03/18/1938	Los Angeles National Cemetery, Los Angeles, CA
Neu, Otto Adam	09/19/1932	Ferncliff Cemetery, Springfield, OH
Neubauer, Hal (Harold Charles)	09/09/1949	Cremated, Oak Grove Cemetery, Fall River, MA
Neuer, Tex (John S.)	01/14/1966	West Side Cemetery, Shamokin Dam, PA
Neun, Johnny (John Henry)	03/28/1990	Immanuel Lutheran Cemetery, Baltimore, MD
Nevel, Ernie Wyre	07/10/1988	Ozarks Memorial Park, Branson, MO
Nevers, Ernie (Ernest Alonzo)	05/03/1976	Cremated, San Rafael, CA
Newell, John A.	01/28/1919	Cathedral Cemetery, Wilmington, DE
Newhouser, Hal (Harold)	11/10/1998	Oakland Hills Memorial Gardens, Novi, MI
Newkirk, Floyd Elmo	04/15/1976	Jefferson Barracks National Cemetery, St. Louis, MO
Newkirk, Joel Ivan	01/22/1966	Wolf Creek Cemetery, Eldorado, IL
Newlin, Maury (Maurice Milton)	08/14/1978	Brookside Memorial Park, Houston, TX
Newman, Charlie (Charles)	11/23/1947	Cremated, San Diego., CA
Newman, Fred (Frederick William)	06/24/1987	Walnut Hills Cemetery, Brookline, MA
Newnan, Patrick Henry	06/20/1938	St. Mary's Cemetery, San Antonio, TX
Newsom, Bobo (Louis Norman)	12/07/1962	Magnolia Cemetery, Hartsville, SC
Newsome, Skeeter (Lamar Ashby)	08/31/1989	Parkhill Cemetery, Columbus, GA

Name	DOD	Cemetery, City, State
Newton, Doc (Eustace James)	05/14/1931	Crown Hill Cemetery, Indianapolis, IN
Nicholl, Sam (Samuel Anderson)	04/19/1937	Mt. Calvary Cemetery, Wheeling, WV
Nicholls, Simon Burdette	03/12/1911	Holy Cross Cemetery, Yeadon, PA
Nichols, Art (Arthur Francis) (buried under birth name: Meikle)	08/09/1945	St. Joseph Cemetery, Willimantic, CT
Nichols, Chet (Chester Raymond, Jr.)	03/27/1995	Union Cemetery, North Smithfield, RI
Nichols, Chet (Chester Raymond, Sr.)	07/11/1982	Union Cemetery, North Smithfield, RI
Nichols, Dolan Levon	11/20/1989	Oak Hill Cemetery, Water Valley, MS
Nichols, Kid (Charles Augustus)	04/11/1953	Mount Moriah Cemetery, Kansas City, MO
Nichols, Roy	04/03/2002	Cremated, Hot Springs, AR.
Nichols, Tricky (Frederick C.)	08/22/1897	St. Michael's Cemetery, Stratford, CT
Nicholson, Frank Collins	11/10/1972	Jersey Shore Cemetery, Jersey Shore, PA
Nicholson, Ovid Edward	03/24/1968	Crown Hill Cemetery, Salem, IN
Nicholson, Parson (Thomas Clark)	02/28/1917	Greenwood Cemetery, Bellaire, OH
Nicholson, Swish (William Beck)	03/08/1996	Old St. Paul's Episcopal Church Cemetery, Chestertown, MD
Nicol, Hugh N.	06/27/1921	Grand View Cemetery, West Lafayette, IN
Niebergall, Charlie (Charles Arthur)	08/29/1982	Meadowland Memorial Gardens, New Port Richey, FL
Niehaus, Al (Albert Bernard)	10/14/1931	St. Joseph's Old Cemetery, Cincinnati, OH
Niehaus, Dick (Richard J.)	03/12/1957	Woodbury Cemetery, Woodbury, GA
Niehoff, Bert (John Albert)	12/08/1974	Inglewood Park Cemetery, Inglewood, CA
Nieman, Bob (Robert Charles)	03/10/1985	Fairhaven Memorial Park, Santa Ana, CA
Nieman, Butch (Elmer Leroy)	11/02/1993	Topeka Cemetery, Topeka, KS
Niemes, Jack (Jacob Leland)	03/04/1966	Oak Hill Cemetery, Cincinnati, OH
Niemiec, Al (Alfred Joseph)	10/29/1995	Sunset Hills Memorial Park, Bellevue, WA
Niggeling, Johnny (John Arnold)	09/16/1963	St. Mary's Catholic Cemetery, Remsen, IA
Niland, Tom (Thomas James)	04/30/1950	St. Mary's Cemetery, Lynn, MA
Niles, Bill (William E.)	07/03/1936	Ferncliff Cemetery, Springfield, OH
Niles, Harry (Herbert Clyde)	04/18/1953	Oak Lawn Cemetery, Sturgis, MI
Nill, Rabbit (George Charles)	05/24/1962	Catholic Cemetery, Fort Wayne, IN
Nitcholas, Otho James	09/11/1986	Altoga Cemetery, McKinney, TX
Nixon, Al (Albert Richard)	11/09/1960	Myrtle Grove Cemetery, Opelousas, LA
Nixon, Willard Lee	12/10/2000	East View Cemetery, Rome, GA
Noble, Ray (Rafael Miguel)	05/09/1998	Cypress Hills Cemetery, Brooklyn, NY
Noftsker, George Washington	05/08/1931	Spring Hill Cemetery, Shippensburg, PA
Nolan, The Only (Edward Sylvester)	05/18/1913	Holy Sepulchre Cemetery, Totawa, NJ
Noonan, Pete (Peter John)	02/11/1965	St. Peter's Catholic Cemetery, Great Barrington, MA
Nops, Jerry (Jeremiah H.)	03/26/1937	St. Paul's Catholic Cemetery, Norwalk, OH
Nordyke, Lou (Louis Ellis)	09/27/1945	Cremated, Los Angeles, CA
Norman, Bill (Henry Willis Patrick)	04/21/1962	Calvary Cemetery, St. Louis, MO
North, Lou (Louis Alexander)	05/15/1974	Pine Grove Cemetery, Ansonia, CT
Northen, Hub (Hubbard Elwin)	10/01/1947	Pine Crest Cemetery, Atlanta, TX
Northey, Ron (Ronald James)	04/16/1971	Fairfield Memorial Park, Stamford, CT

Name	DOD	Cemetery, City, State
Northrop, Jake (George Howard)	11/16/1945	Monroeton Cemetery, Monroeton, PA
Norton, Frank Prescott	08/02/1920	Setauket Cemetery, Port Jefferson, NY
Nourse, Chet (Chester Linwood)	04/20/1958	Oak Hill Cemetery, Newburyport, MA
Novikoff, Lou (Louis Alexander)	09/30/1970	Russian Molokan Cemetery, City of Commerce, CA
Novotney, Rube (Ralph Joseph)	07/16/1987	Holy Cross Cemetery, Culver City, CA
Noyes, Wynn (Winfield Charles)	04/08/1969	Cashmere City Cemetery, Cashmere, WA
Nunamaker, Les (Leslie Grant)	11/14/1938	Aurora Cemetery, Aurora, NE
Nusz, Emory Moberly	08/03/1898	Mount Olivet Cemetery, Frederick, MD
Nutter, Dizzy (Everett Clarence)	07/25/1958	Rose Hill Cemetery, Roseville, OH
Nyce, Charlie (Charles Reiff)	05/09/1908	Westminster Cemetery, Bala Cynwyd, PA
Oakes, Rebel (Ennis Telfair)	03/01/1948	Rocky Springs Cemetery, Lisbon, LA
Oana, Prince (Henry Kawaihoa)	06/19/1976	Oakwood Cemtetery, Austin, TX
Oberbeck, Henry A.	08/26/1921	Bellefontaine Cemetery, St. Louis, MO
Oberlander, Doc (Hartman Louis)	11/14/1922	Rockvale Cemetery, Pryor, MT
Oberlin, Frank Rufus	01/06/1952	Hamilton Cemetery, Hamilton, IN
O'Brien, Billy (William Smith)	05/26/1911	Mount St. Mary's Cemetery, Kansas City, MO
O'Brien, Buck (Thomas Joseph)	07/25/1959	New Calvary Cemetery, Mattapan, MA
O'Brien, Darby (John F.)	03/11/1892	St. Patrick's Cemetery, Watervliet, NY
O'Brien, Dink (Frank Aloysius)	11/04/1971	Willamette National Cemetery, Portland, OR
O'Brien, George Joseph	03/24/1966	Calvary Cemetery, West Conshohocken, PA
O'Brien, Jack (John Joseph)	06/10/1933	St. Agnes Cemetery, Albany, NY
O'Brien, John E.	12/31/1914	St. Patrick's Cemetery, Fall River, MA
O'Brien, John J.	05/13/1913	Mount Hope Cemetery, Lewiston, ME
O'Brien, Pete (Peter J.)	01/31/1917	St. Mary's Cemetery, Cortland, NY
O'Brien, Pete (Peter James)	06/30/1937	All Saints Cemetery, Des Plaines, IL
O'Brien, Ray (Raymond Joseph)	03/31/1942	Calvary Cemetery, St. Louis, MO
O'Brien, Tom (Thomas H.)	04/21/1921	St. John's Cemetery, Worcester, MA
O'Brien, Tom (Thomas J.)	02/03/1901	St. Mary's Roman Catholic Cemetery (Troy Hill), Pittsburgh, PA
O'Brien, Tommy (Thomas Edward)	11/05/1978	Edgemont Cemetery, Anniston, AL
Ockey, Walter Andrew (buried under birth name: Okpyeh)	12/04/1971	St. Peter's Cemetery, Staten Island, NY
O'Connell, Danny (Daniel Francis)	10/02/1969	Immaculate Conception Cemetery, Montclair, NJ
O'Connell, Jimmy (James Joseph)	11/11/1976	Greenlawn Memorial Park, Bakersfield, CA
O'Connell, John Charles	10/17/1992	Forest Hill Cemetery, Canton, OH
O'Connell, John Joseph	05/14/1908	St. Mary's Immaculate Conception Cemetery, Lawrence, MA
O'Connell, Pat (Patrick H.)	01/24/1943	Mount Hope Cemetery, Lewiston, ME
O'Connor, Andy (Andrew James)	09/26/1980	St. Joseph's Cemetery, West Roxbury, MA
O'Connor, Dan (Daniel Cornelius)	03/03/1942	Marymount Cemetery, Guelph, Ontario, Canada
O'Connor, Frank Henry	12/26/1913	Catholic Cemetery, Brattleboro, VT
O'Connor, Jack (John Joseph)	11/14/1937	Calvary Cemetery, St. Louis, MO
O'Connor, Johnny (John Charles)	05/30/1982	Leavenworth National Cemetery, Leavenworth, KS
O'Connor, Paddy (Patrick Francis)	08/17/1950	St. Michael's Cemetery, Springfield, MA

Name	DOD	Cemetery, City, State
O'Day, Hank (Henry Francis)	07/02/1935	Calvary Cemetery, Evanston, IL
O'Dea, Ken (James Kenneth)	12/17/1985	St. Agnes Cemetery, Avon, NY
O'Dea, Paul	12/11/1978	Myrtle Hill Cemetery, Valley City, OH
Odenwald, Ted (Theodore Joseph)	10/23/1965	St. Mark's Cemetery, Shakopee, MN
Odom, Heinie (Herman Boyd)	08/31/1970	Cedar Hill Cemetery, Rusk, TX
O'Donnell, Harry Herman	01/31/1958	St. Domonic's Cemetery, Philadelphia, PA
O'Doul, Lefty (Francis Joseph)	12/07/1969	Cypress Lawn Memorial Park, Colma, CA
Odwell, Feed (Frederick William)	08/19/1948	Paige Cemetery, Downsville, NY
Oeschger, Joe (Joseph Carl)	07/28/1986	St. Mary's Cemetery, Ferndale, CA
O'Farrell, Bob (Robert Arthur)	02/20/1988	Northshore Gardens of Memories, North Chicago, IL
Ogden, Curly (Warren Harvey)	08/06/1964	Lawn Croft Cemetery, Linwood, PA
Ogden, Jack (John Mahlon)	11/09/1977	Oxford Cemetery, Oxford, PA
Oglesby, Jim (James Dorn)	09/01/1955	Memorial Park Cemetery, Tulsa, OK
Ogrodowski, Bruce (Ambrose Francis)	03/05/1956	Cypress Lawn Memorial Park, Colma, CA
Ogrodowski, Joe (Joseph Anthony)	06/24/1959	Woodlawn Cemetery, Elmira, NY
O'Hagen, Hal (Harry P.)	01/14/1913	Cemetery of the Holy Sepulchre, East Orange, NJ
O'Hara, Bill (William Alexander)	06/13/1931	Mount Pleasant Cemetery, Toronto, Ontario, Canada
O'Hara, Kid (James Francis)	12/01/1954	Calvary Cemetery, Massillon, OH
O'Hara, Tom (Thomas F.)	06/08/1954	Mount Olivet Cemetery, Wheat Ridge, CO
Ohl, Joe (Joseph Earl)	12/18/1951	Upper Springfield Cemetery, Jobstown, NJ
Okrie, Frank Anthony	10/16/1959	Mount Olivet Cemetery, Detroit, MI
Oldfield, Dave (David)	08/28/1939	Oakland Cemetery, Philadelphia, PA
Oldham, Red (John Cyrus)	01/28/1961	Cremated, Newport Beach, CA
Oldring, Rube (Reuben Henry)	09/09/1961	Cohansey Bapist Church Cemetery, Roadstown, NJ
O'Leary, Charley (Charles Timothy)	01/06/1941	Mount Olivet Cemetery, Chicago, IL
O'Leary, Dan (Daniel)	06/24/1922	Mount Carmel Cemetery, Hillside, IL
Olin, Frank (Franklin Walter)	05/20/1951	Oak Grove Cemetery, St. Louis, MO
Olin, Steve (Steven Robert)	03/22/1993	Cremated Skyline Memorial Gardens, Portland, OR. Ashes scattered in Tualatin Mountains, near Portland,
Oliver, Tom (Thomas Noble)	02/26/1988	Greenwood Cemetery, Montgomery, AL
Olmstead, Fred (Frederic William)	10/22/1936	Elmwood Cemetery, Wagoner, OK
Olmsted, Hank (Henry Theodore)	01/06/1969	Manasota Memorial Park, Bradenton, FL
Olsen, Barney (Bernard Charles)	03/30/1977	Holy Cross Cemetery, Malden, MA
Olsen, Ole (Arthur Ole)	09/12/1980	Union Cemetery, Rowayton, CT
Olsen, Vern Jarl	07/13/1989	Arlington Cemetery, Elmhurst, IL
Olson, Ivy (Ivan Massie)	09/01/1965	Cremated, Los Angeles, CA
Olson, Marv (Marvin Clement)	02/05/1998	Gayville Cemetery, Gayville, SD
Olson, Ted (Theodore Otto)	12/09/1980	Church of St. John the Evangelist Cemetery, Hingham, MA
O'Mara, Ollie (Oliver Edward)	10/24/1989	All Saints Cemetery, Pleasant Prairie, WI
O'Meara, Tom (Thomas Edward)	02/16/1902	Catholic Cemetery, Fort Wayne, IN

Name	DOD	Cemetery, City, State
O'Neal, Skinny (Oran Herbert)	06/02/1981	Evergreen Cemetery, Republic, MO
O'Neil, Ed (Edward J.)	09/30/1892	St. Mary's Cemetery, Fall River, MA
O'Neil, Mickey (George Michael)	04/08/1964	Calvary Cemetery, St. Louis, MO
O'Neill, Denny (Dennis)	11/15/1912	St. Jerome Cemetery, Holyoke, MA
O'Neill, Emmett (Robert Emmett)	10/11/1993	Cremated, Sierra Crematroy, Reno, NV.
O'Neill, Harry Mink	03/06/1945	Arlington Cemetery, Drexel Hill, PA
O'Neill, Jack (John Joseph)	06/25/1935	St. Joseph's Cemetery, Minooka, PA
O'Neill, Jim (James Leo)	09/05/1976	St. Joseph's Cemetery, Minooka, PA
O'Neill, Mike (Michael Joyce)	08/12/1959	St. Joseph's Cemetery, Minooka, PA
O'Neill, Peaches (Philip Bernard)	08/02/1955	East Maplewood Cemetery, Anderson, IN
O'Neill, Steve (Stephen Francis)	01/26/1962	St. Joseph's Cemetery, Minooka, PA
Onis, Ralph (Manuel Dominguez)	01/04/1995	Centro Austriano Memorial Park, Tampa, FL
Onslow, Eddie (Edward Joseph)	05/08/1981	Grandview Cemetery, Scio, OH
Onslow, Jack (John James)	12/22/1960	Grandview Cemetery, Scio, OH
Ordenana, Tony (Antonio)	09/29/1988	Dade Memorial Park-South, Miami, FL
Orengo, Joe (Joseph Charles)	07/24/1988	Italian Cemetery, Colma, CA
O'Riley, Don (Donald Lee)	05/02/1997	Floral Hills Memorial Gardens, Kansas City, MO
Orme, George William	03/16/1962	Floral Park Cemetery, Indianapolis, IN
Orndorff, Jess (Jesse Walworth Thayer)	09/28/1960	Cremated, Cardiff-by-the-Sea, CA
O'Rourke, Blackie (James Francis)	05/14/1986	Graceland Memorial Park, Kenilworth, NJ
O'Rourke, Jim (James Henry)	01/08/1919	St. Michael's Cemetery, Stratford, CT
O'Rourke, Joe (Joseph Leo, Jr.)	06/27/1990	Holy Sepulchre Cemetery, Wyndmoor, PA
O'Rourke, John W.	06/23/1911	St. Michael's Cemtery, Stratford, CT
O'Rourke, Patsy (Joseph Leo, Sr.)	04/18/1956	Holy Sepulchre Cemetery, Wyndmoor, PA
O'Rourke, Queenie (James Stephen)	12/22/1955	Oak Lawn Cemetery, Baltimore, MD
O'Rourke, Tim (Timothy Patrick)	04/20/1938	Calvary Catholic Cemetery, Seattle, WA
O'Rourke, Tom (Thomas Joseph)	07/19/1929	Calvary Cemetery, Woodside, Queens, NY
Orr, Billy (William John)	03/10/1967	Holy Cross Cemetery, Colma, CA
Orr, Dave (David L.)	06/02/1915	Woodlawn Cemetery, Bronx, NY
Orrell, Joe (Forrest Gordon)	01/12/1993	La Vista Memorial Park, National City, CA
Orsatti, Ernie (Ernest Ralph)	09/04/1968	San Fernando Mission Cemetery, Mission Hills, CA
Orth, Al (Albert Lewis)	10/08/1948	Spring Hill Cemetery, Lynchburg, VA
Ortiz, Roberto Gonzalo	09/15/1971	Flagler Memorial Park, Miami, FL
Orwoll, Ossie (Oswald Christian)	05/08/1967	Decorah Lutheran Cemetery, Decorah, IA
Osborn, Bob (John Bode)	04/19/1960	Oakwood Cemetery, Paris, AR
Osborn, Fred (Wilferd Pearl)	09/02/1954	Oak Hill Cemetery, Upper Sandusky, OH
Osborne, Tiny (Earnest Preston)	01/05/1969	Riverview Memorial Park, Smyrna, GA
Osborne, Wayne Harold	03/13/1987	Cremated, Vancouver, WA
Ostdiek, Harry (Henry Girard)	05/06/1956	St. Mary's Cemetery, Minneapolis, MN
Osteen, Champ (James Champlin)	12/14/1962	Rose Hill Cemetery, Piedmont, SC
Ostendorf, Fred (Frederick K.)	03/02/1965	Woodlawn Cemetery, Baltimore, MD
Ostergard, Red (Roy Lund)	01/13/1977	San Jacinto Valley Cemetery, San Jacinto, CA
Osterhout, Charlie (Charles H.)	05/21/1933	St. Mary's Cemetery, Syracuse, NY

Name	DOD	Cemetery, City, State
Ostermueller, Fritz (Frederick Raymond)	12/17/1957	Calvary Cemetery, Quincy, IL
Ostrowski, Joe (Joseph Paul)	01/03/2003	St. Joseph's Polish Catholic Cemetery, West Wyoming, PA
Ostrowski, Johnny (John Thaddeus)	11/13/1992	Resurrection Cemetery, Justice, IL
Otero, Reggie (Regino Jose)	10/21/1988	Vista Memorial Gardens, Hialeah, FL
Otey, Bill (William Tilford)	04/23/1931	Brunsteter Cemetery, Austintown, OH
Otis, Bill (Paul Franklin)	12/15/1990	Forest Hill Cemetery, Duluth, MN
Otis, Harry George	01/29/1976	George Washington Memorial Park, Paramus, NJ
O'Toole, Marty (Martin James)	02/18/1949	Fern Hill Cemetery, Aberdeen, WA
Ott, Mel (Melvin Thomas)	11/21/1958	Metairie Cemetery, Metairie, LA
Otten, John G.	10/17/1905	Forest Home Cemetery (formerly Waldheim Cemetery), Forest Park, IL.
Otterson, Billy (William John)	09/21/1940	Union Dale Cemetery, Pittsburgh, PA
Oulliber, Johnny (John Andrew)	12/26/1980	Metairie Cemetery, Metairie, LA
Outen, Chink (William Austin)	09/11/1961	Mount Holly Cemetery, Mount Holly, NC
Overall, Orval	07/14/1947	Cremated, Fresno, CA.
Ovitz, Ernie (Ernest Gayhart)	09/11/1980	Laona Cemetery, Laona, WI
Owen, Frank Malcolm	11/24/1942	Grand Lawn Cemetery, Detroit, MI
Owen, Marv (Marvin James)	06/22/1991	Santa Clara Mission Cemetery, Santa Clara, CA
Owens, Frank Walter	07/02/1958	Cremated, Lakewood Cemetery, Minneapolis, MN. Ashes scattered
Owens, Jack (Furman Lee)	11/14/1958	Westview Cemetery, Easley, SC
Owens, Paul manager	12/26/2003	Woddbury Memorial Park, West Deptford, NJ
Owens, Red (Thomas Llewellyn)	08/20/1952	Prospect Hill Cemetery, Steelton, PA
Oyler, Andy (Andrew Paul)	10/24/1970	Rolling Green Memorial Park, Camp Hill, PA
Oyler, Ray (Raymond Francis)	01/26/1981	Sunset Hills Memorial Park, Bellevue, WA
Ozmer, Doc (Horace Robert)	12/28/1970	Crest Lawn Memorial Park, Atlanta, GA
Pabor, Charlie (Charles Henry)	04/23/1913	Mapledale Cemetery, New Haven, CT
Pabst, Ed (Edward D. A.)	06/19/1940	St. Peter's Cemetery, St. Louis, MO
Packard, Gene (Eugene Milo)	05/19/1959	Evergreen Memorial Park, Riverside, CA
Padden, Dick (Richard Joseph)	10/31/1922	St. Mary's Cemetery, Martins Ferry, OH
Padden, Tom (Thomas Francis)	06/11/1973	St. Joseph Cemetery, Bedford, NH
Paddock, Del (Delmer Harold)	02/06/1952	Ditson Cemetery, Girard, IL (aka Stephenson Cemetery)
Padgett, Ernie (Ernest Kitchen)	04/15/1957	Northwood Cemetery, Philadelphia, PA
Page, Joe (Joseph Francis)	04/21/1980	Greenwood Cemetery, New Kensington, PA
Page, Phil (Philippe Rausac)	07/27/1958	Hillcrest Park Cemetery, Springfield, MA
Page, Sam (Samuel Walter)	05/29/2002	First Presbyterian Church Cemetery, Woodruff, SC
Page, Vance Linwood	07/14/1951	Cedar Grove Cemetery, Elm City, NC
Paige, Pat (George Lynn)	06/08/1939	Rice Cemetery, Elkhart, IN
Paige, Satchel (Leroy Robert)	06/08/1982	Forest Hill Cemetery, Kansas City, MO
Paine, Phil (Phillips Steere)	02/19/1978	Hummelstown Cemetery, Hummelstown, PA
Palica, Erv (Ervin Martin)	05/29/1982	Holy Cross Cemetery, Culver City, CA

Name	DOD	Cemetery, City, State
Palmer, Eddie (Edwin Henry)	01/09/1983	Marlow Cemetery, Marlow, OK
Palmero, Emilio Antonio	07/15/1970	Ottawa Hills Memorial Park, Toledo, OH
Palmisano, Joe (Joseph)	11/05/1971	Gate of Heaven Catholic Cemetery, Albuquerque, NM
Papai, Al (Alfred Thomas)	09/07/1995	Brush Creek Cemetery, Divernon, IL
Pape, Larry (Laurence Albert)	07/21/1918	Spring Grove Cemetery, Cincinnati, OH
Pappalau, John Joseph	05/12/1944	Albany Rural Cemetery, Albany, NY
Parent, Fred (Frederick Alfred)	11/02/1972	St. Ignatius Cemetery, Sanford, ME
Parisse, Tony (Louis Peter)	06/02/1956	Holy Sepulchre Cemetery, Wyndmoor, PA
Park, Jim (James)	12/17/1970	Lexington Cemetery, Lexington, KY
Parker, Dixie (Douglas Wooley)	05/15/1972	Green Pond Cemetery, Green Pond, AL
Parker, Doc (Harley Park)	03/03/1941	All Saints Cemetery, Des Plaines, IL
Parker, Jay	06/08/1935	Maple Hill Cemetery, Hartford, MI
Parker, Pat (Clarence Perkins)	03/21/1967	Mountainview Cemetery, Claremont, NH
Parker, Roy William	05/17/1954	Masonic Cemetery, St. James, MO
Parker, Salty (Francis James)	07/27/1992	Forest Park (Westheimer) Cemetery, Houston, TX
Parkinson, Frank Joseph	07/04/1960	Beverly National Cemetery, Beverly, NJ
Parks, Art (Artie William)	12/06/1989	Oakwood Cemetery, Paris, AR
Parks, Bill (William Robert)	10/10/1911	Easton Cemetery, Easton, PA
Parmelee, Roy (Leroy Earl)	08/31/1981	Toledo Memorial Park, Sylvania, OH
Parnham, Rube (James Arthur)	11/25/1963	Mount Vernon Cemetery, Mount Vernon, PA
Parrott, Jiggs (Walter Edward)	04/14/1898	Lone Fir Cemetery, Portland, OR
Parrott, Tom (Thomas William)	01/01/1932	Lone Fir Cemetery, Portland, OR
Parson, Jiggs (William Edwin)	05/19/1967	Cremated, Los Angeles, CA
Parsons, Charlie (Charles James)	03/24/1936	Cherry Flats Cemetery, Cherry Flats, PA
Parsons, Dixie (Edward Dixon)	10/31/1991	Leesburg Cemetery, Pittsburg, TX
Partenheimer, Stan (Stanwood Wendell)	01/28/1989	Evergreen Memorial Garden, Wilson, NC
Partenheimer, Steve (Harold Philip)	06/16/1971	Green River Cemetery, Greenfield, MA
Partridge, Jay (James Bugg)	01/14/1974	Woodlawn Memorial Park, Nashville, TN
Paschal, Ben (Benjamin Edwin)	11/10/1974	Sharon Memorial Park, Charlotte, NC
Pasek, Johnny (John Paul)	03/13/1976	Holy Trinity Roman Catholic Cemetery, Lewiston, NY
Paskert, Dode (George Henry)	02/12/1959	St. Mary's Cemetery, Cleveland, OH
Pasquella, Mike (Michael John)	04/05/1965	St. Michael's Cemetery, Stratford, CT
Passeau, Claude William	08/30/2003	Magnolia Cemetery, Lucedale, MS
Pastorius, Jim (James W.)	05/10/1941	Southside Cemetery, Pittsburgh, PA
Pate, Joe (Joseph William)	12/26/1948	Oakwood Cemetery, Fort Worth, TX
Patrick, Bob (Robert Lee)	10/06/1999	Fort Smith National Cemetery, Fort Smith, AR
Pattee, Harry Ernest	07/17/1971	Prince's Hill Burial Ground, Barrington, RI
Patterson, Clare (Lorenzo Clare)	03/28/1913	Riverview Cemetery, Arkansas City, KS
Patterson, Ham (Hamilton)	11/25/1945	Walnut Hill Cemetery, Belleville, IL
Patterson, Hank (Henry Joseph)	09/30/1970	San Fernando Mission Cemetery, Mission Hills, CA
Patterson, Pat (William Jennings Bryan)	10/01/1977	Resurrection Cemetery, Mackenzie, MO
Patterson, Roy Lewis	04/14/1953	St. Croix Falls Cemetery, St. Croix Falls, WI

Name	DOD	Cemetery, City, State
Pattison, Jimmy (James Wells)	02/22/1991	Cremated, Melbourne, FL
Patton, Bill (George William)	03/15/1986	George Washington Memorial Park, Plymouth Meeting, PA
Patton, Harry Claude	06/09/1930	Masonic Cemetery, Trenton, MO
Paulette, Gene (Eugene Edward)	02/08/1966	Calvary Cemetery, Little Rock, AR
Paulsen, Gil (Guilford Paul Hans)	04/02/1994	Brighton Cemetery, Marne, IA
Pauxtis, Si (Simon Francis)	03/13/1961	SS. Peter & Paul Cemetery, Springfield, PA
Pawelek, Ted (Theodore John)	02/12/1964	Holy Cross Cemetery, Calumet City, IL
Payne, Fred (Frederick Thomas)	01/16/1954	Village Cemetery, Mexico, NY
Payne, George Washington	01/24/1959	Westminster Memorial Park, Westminster, CA
Paynter, George Washington	10/01/1950	Spring Grove Cemetery, Cincinnati, OH
Peacock, Johnny (John Gaston)	10/17/1981	Fremont Cemetery, Fremont, NC
Peak, Elias	12/17/1916	Fernwood Cemetery, Lansdowne, PA
Pearce, Dicky (Richard J.)	09/18/1908	Long Neck Cemetery, Onset, MA
Pearce, Ducky (William C.)	05/22/1933	Crown Hill Cemetery, Indianapolis, IN
Pearce, Frank (Franklin Johnson)	11/13/1926	Cave Hill Cemetery, Louisville, KY
Pearce, Frank (Franklin Thomas)	09/03/1950	Eastwood Cemetery, Eastwood, KY
Pearce, Harry James	01/08/1942	Holy Sepulchre Cemetery, Wyndmoor, PA
Pears, Frank H.	11/29/1923	Calvary Cemetery, St. Louis, MO
Pearson, Alex (Alexander Franklin)	10/30/1966	Irvin Cemetery, Rochester, PA
Pearson, Ike (Isaac Overton)	03/17/1985	Memphis National Cemetery, Memphis, TN
Pearson, Monte (Montgomery Marcellus)	01/27/1978	Cremated, Fresno, CA.
Peasley, Marv (Marvin Warren)	12/27/1948	Golden Gate National Cemetery, San Bruno, CA
Pechiney, George Adolphe	07/14/1943	Spring Grove Cemetery, Cincinnati, OH
Pechous, Charlie (Charles Edward)	09/13/1980	All Saints Cemetery, Pleasant Prairie, WI
Peck, Hal (Harold Arthur)	04/13/1995	Cremated, Milwaukee, WI
Peckinpaugh, Roger Thorpe	11/17/1977	Acadia Memorial Park, Mayfield Heights, OH
Peden, Les (Leslie Earl)	02/11/2000	Greenlawn Cemetery, Jacksonville, FL
Pedroes, Chick (Charles P.)	08/06/1927	Montrose Cemetery, Chicago, IL
Peek, Steve (Stephen George)	09/20/1991	Crown Hill Memorial Park, Kirkland, NY
Peerson, Jack Chiles	10/23/1966	Beal Memorial Cemetery, Fort Walton Beach, FL
Peery, Red (George Allan)	05/06/1985	Payson City Cemetery, Payson, UT
Peitz, Heinie (Henry Clement)	10/23/1943	St. Mary's Cemetery, Cincinnati, OH
Peitz, Joe (Joseph)	12/04/1919	Calvary Cemetery, St. Louis, MO
Pelouze, Louis Henri	01/09/1939	Kensico Cemetery, Valhalla, NY
Pelty, Barney	05/24/1939	Masonic Cemetery, Farmington, MO
Peltz, John	02/27/1906	Valence Street Cemetery, New Orleans, LA
Pence, Elmer Clair	09/17/1968	Olivet Memorial Park, Colma, CA. Cremated.
Pence, Russ (Russell William)	08/11/1971	Marine City Cemetery, Marine, IL
Pendleton, Jim (James Edward)	03/20/1996	Houston National Cemetery, Houston, TX
Penner, Ken (Kenneth William)	05/28/1959	Cremated, Sacramento, CA
Pennington, Kewpie (George Louis)	05/03/1953	Restland Memorial Park, East Hanover, NJ
Pennock, Herb (Herbert Jefferis)	01/30/1948	Union Hill Cemetery, Kennett Square, PA
Peoples, Jimmy (James Elsworth)	08/29/1920	Woodmere Cemetery, Detroit, MI

Name	DOD	Cemetery, City, State
Pepper, Bob (Robert Ernest)	04/08/1968	Ford City Cemetery, Ford City, PA
Pepper, Ray (Raymond Watson)	03/24/1996	Athens City Cemetery, Athens, AL
Peppers, Bill (William Harrison)	11/05/1903	Webb City Cemetery, Webb City, MO
Perdue, Hub (Herbert Rodney)	10/31/1968	Bethpage Cemetery, Bethpage, TN
Perkins, Charlie (Charles Sullivan)	05/25/1988	Cremated, Salem, OR. Ashes scattered in Willamette Valley
Perkins, Cy (Ralph Foster)	10/02/1963	Oak Grove Cemetery, Gloucester, MA
Perkovich, John Joseph	09/16/2000	Little Rock National Cemtery, Little Rock, AR
Pernoll, Hub (Henry Hubbard)	02/18/1944	Hillcrest Memorial Park, Grants Pass, OR
Perrin, Bill (William Joseph)	06/30/1974	St. John's Cemetery (Hope Mausoleum), New Orleans, LA
Perrin, John Stephenson	06/24/1969	Lakeview Cemetery, Escanaba, MI
Perrine, John Grover	08/13/1948	Memorial Park Cemetery, Kansas City, MO
Perring, Nig (George Wilson)	08/20/1960	Eastlawn Cemetery, Beloit, WI
Perritt, Pol (William Dayton)	10/15/1947	Arcadia Cemetery, Arcadia, LA
Perry, Boyd Glenn	06/29/1990	Spring Friends Cemetery, Snow Camp, NC
Perry, Clay (Clayton Shields)	01/16/1954	Nora Cemetery, Rice Lake, WI
Perry, Scott (Herbert Scott)	10/27/1959	Mount St. Mary's Cemetery, Kansas City, MO
Perryman, Parson (Emmett Key)	09/12/1966	Crosby Lake Cemetery, Starke, FL
Pertica, Bill (William Andrew)	12/28/1967	Willamette National Cemetery, Portland, OR
Peterman, Bill (William David)	03/13/1999	Hillside Cemetery, Roslyn, PA
Peters, John Paul	01/04/1924	New St. Marcus Cemetery, St. Louis, MO. Originally intered in Old St. Marcus Cemetery. Cemetery removed to New St. Marcus Cemetery.
Peters, John William	02/21/1932	Memorial Park Cemetery, Kansas City, MO
Peters, Rube (Otto Casper)	02/07/1965	New York Bay Cemetery, Jersey City, NJ
Peters, Rusty (Russell Dixon)	02/21/2003	Cremated, Harrisonburg, VA. Ashes scattered on grounds of the Unity of Roanoke Valley Church, Roanoke, VA
Peterson, Bob (Robert Andrew)	11/27/1962	West Laurel Hill Cemetery, Bala Cynwyd, PA
Peterson, Cap (Charles Andrew)	05/16/1980	Mountain View Memorial Park, Tacoma, WA
Peterson, Jim (James Niels)	08/08/1975	Our Lady Queen of Peace Cemetery, West Palm Beach, FL
Peterson, Kent Franklin	04/27/1995	Orem City Cemetery, Orem, UT
Peterson, Sid (Sidney Herbert)	08/29/2001	Cremated, Wichita Falls, TX. Ashes given to family.
Petoskey, Ted (Frederick Lee)	11/30/1996	Greenlawn Memorial Park, Columbia, SC
Pettee, Pat (Patrick E.)	10/09/1934	St. Patrick's Cemetery, Natick, MA
Pettigrew, Ned (Jim Ned)	08/20/1952	Duncan City Cemetery, Duncan, OK
Pettit, Bob (Robert Henry)	11/01/1910	Oak Cliffe Cemetery, Derby, CT
Pettit, Leon Arthur	11/21/1974	Memorial Park Cemetery, Memphis, TN
Petty, Jesse Lee	10/23/1971	Fort Snelling National Cemetery, Minneapolis, MN
Pezold, Larry (Lorenz Johannes)	10/22/1957	Greenoaks Memorial Park, Baton Rouge, LA
Pezzullo, Pretzel (John)	05/16/1990	Holy Redeemer Cemetery, DeSoto, TX
Pfeffer, Big Jeff (Francis Xavier)	12/19/1954	St. Mary's Cemetery, Champaign, IL

Name	DOD	Cemetery, City, State
Pfeffer, Fred (Nathaniel Frederick)	04/10/1932	All Saints Cemetery, Des Plaines, IL
Pfeffer, Jeff (Edward Joseph)	08/15/1972	Rock Island National Cemetery, Rock Island, IL
Pfeiffer, Monte	09/27/1941	Acacia Cemetery, Jamaica, Queens, NY
Pfiester, Jack (John Albert)	09/03/1953	Union Cemetery, Montgomery, OH
Pfister, George Edward	08/14/1997	Bound Brook Cemetery, Bound Brook, NJ
Pfyl, Monte (Meinhard Charles)	10/18/1945	Park View Cemetery, Manteca, CA
Phebus, Bill (Raymond William)	10/11/1989	Wildwood Cemetery, Bartow, FL
Phelan, Art (Arthur Thomas)	12/27/1964	Cremated, Fort Worth, TX. Ashes given to family
Phelan, Dan (Daniel T.)	12/07/1945	St. Lawrence Cemetery, West Haven, CT
Phelan, Dick (James Dickson)	02/13/1931	St. Mary's Cemetery, San Antonio, TX
Phelps, Babe (Ernest Gordon)	12/10/1992	Nichols Bethel United Methodist Church Cemetery, Odenton, MD
Phelps, Ed (Edward Jaykill)	01/31/1942	East Greenbush Cemetery, East Greenbush, NY
Phelps, Nealy (Cornelius Carmen)	02/12/1885	Green-Wood Cemetery, Brooklyn, NY
Phelps, Ray (Raymond Clifford)	07/07/1971	Fort Pierce Cemetery-Riverview Memorial Park, Fort Pierce, FL
Phillippe, Deacon (Charles Louis)	03/30/1952	Allegheny County Memorial Park, Allison Park, PA
Phillips, Bill (William B.)	10/07/1900	Graceland Cemetery, Chicago, IL
Phillips, Bill (William Corcoran)	10/25/1941	Mount Auburn Cemetery, Fayette City, PA
Phillips, Bubba (John Melvin)	06/22/1993	Cedar Lawn Cemetery, Philadelphia, MS
Phillips, Buz (Albert Abernathy)	11/06/1964	Eastview Cemetery, Newton, NC
Phillips, Eddie (Edward David)	01/26/1968	Mt. Calvary Cemetery, Cheektowaga, NY
Phillips, Jack (John Stephen)	06/16/1958	Resurrection Cemetery, Mackenzie, MO
Phillips, Lefty (Harold Ross) *manager*	06/12/1972	Mount Sinai Memorial Park, Los Angeles, CA
Phillips, Marr B.	04/01/1928	Union Dale Cemetery, Pittsburgh, PA
Phillips, Red (Clarence Lemuel)	02/01/1988	Old Mission Cemetery, Wichita, KS
Phillips, Tom (Thomas Gerard)	04/12/1929	Philipsburg Cemetery, Philipsburg, PA
Phyle, Bill (William Joseph)	08/06/1953	Holy Cross Cemetery, Culver City, CA
Piatt, Wiley Harold	09/20/1946	Heck's Cemetery, Augusta, KY
Picciuto, Nick (Nicholas Thomas)	01/10/1997	Cremated, Winchester, VA
Picinich, Val (Valentine John)	12/05/1942	Dunbar Cemetery, Nobleboro, ME
Pick, Charlie (Charles Thomas)	06/26/1954	Holy Cross Cemetery, Lynchburg, VA
Pick, Eddie (Edgar Everett)	05/13/1967	Cremated, Santa Monica, CA
Pickering, Ollie (Oliver Daniel)	01/20/1952	Fairview Cemetery, Vincennes, IN
Pickering, Urbane Henry	05/13/1970	Lakewood Memorial Park, Hughson, CA
Pickett, Charlie (Charles Albert)	05/20/1969	Glen Haven Memorial Gardens, New Carlisle, OH
Pickett, Dave (David T.)	04/22/1950	Holyhood Cemetery, Brookline, MA
Pickett, John Thomas	07/04/1922	Calvary Cemetery, Evanston, IL
Pickrel, Clarence Douglas	11/04/1983	Gretna Burial Park, Gretna, VA
Pickup, Ty (Clarence William)	08/02/1974	St. Domonic's Cemetery, Philadelphia, PA
Piechota, Al (Aloysius Edward)	06/13/1996	St. Adalbert's Cemetery, Niles, IL
Pieh, Cy (Edwin)	09/12/1945	Enderlin Cemetery, Enderlin, ND

Name	DOD	Cemetery, City, State
Pierce, George Thomas	10/11/1935	Plainfield Cemetery, Plainfield, IL
Pierce, Ray (Raymond Lester)	05/04/1963	Topeka Cemetery, Topeka, KS
Piercy, Andy (Andrew J.)	12/27/1932	Woodlawn Memorial Park, Colma, CA
Piercy, Bill (William Benton)	08/28/1951	Cremated, Long Beach, CA
Pieretti, Marino Paul	01/30/1981	Holy Cross Cemetery, Colma, CA
Pierotti, Al (Albert Felix)	02/12/1964	Glenwood Cemetery, Everett, MA
Pierson, Dave (David P.)	11/11/1922	Fairmount Cemetery, Newark, NJ
Pierson, Dick (Edmund Dana)	07/20/1922	Fairmount Cemetery, Newark, NJ
Pierson, Will (William Morris)	02/20/1959	Holy Cross Cemetery, Yeadon, PA
Piet, Tony (Anthony Francis)	12/01/1981	Resurrection Cemetery, Justice, IL
Piez, Sandy (Charles William)	12/29/1930	Atlantic City Cemetery, Pleasantville, NJ
Pike, Jess Willard	03/28/1984	Glen Abbey Memorial Park, Bonita, CA
Pike, Lip (Lipman Emanuel)	10/10/1893	Salem Fields Cemetery, Brooklyn, NY
Piktuzis, George Richard	11/28/1993	Cremated, Long Beach, CA
Pillette, Herm (Herman Polycarp)	04/30/1960	St. Mary's Catholic Cemetery, Sacramento, CA
Pillion, Squiz (Cecil Randolph)	09/30/1962	Homewood Cemetery, Pittsburgh, PA
Pilney, Andy (Antone James)	09/15/1996	Lake Lawn Cemetery, New Orleans, LA
Pinckney, George Burton	11/10/1926	Springdale Cemetery, Peoria, IL
Pinelli, Babe (Ralph Arthur)	10/22/1984	Holy Cross Cemetery, Colma, CA
Pinson, Vada Edward	10/21/1995	Rolling Hills Memorial Park, Richmond, CA
Pinto, Lerton (William Lerton)	05/13/1983	Ivy Lawn Memorial Park, Ventura, CA
Pipgras, Ed (Edward John)	04/13/1964	Restland Memory Gardens, Slayton, MN
Pipgras, George William	10/19/1986	Cremated, Memorial Park Cemetery, St. Petersburg, FL.
Pipp, Wally (Walter Clement)	01/11/1965	Woodlawn Cemetery, Grand Rapids, MI
Pippen, Cotton (Henry Harold)	02/15/1981	Sierra View Memorial Park, Marysville, CA
Pitler, Jake (Jacob Albert)	02/03/1968	Riverside Cemetery, Endicott, NY
Pittenger, Pinky (Clarke Alonzo)	11/04/1977	Cremated, Fort Lauderdale, FL. Ashes scattered
Pittinger, Togie (Charles Reno)	01/14/1909	Greencastle Cemetery, Greencastle, PA
Pitula, Stan (Stanley)	08/15/1965	Hackensack Cemetery, Hackensack, NJ
Pitz, Herman	09/03/1924	Evergreen Cemetery, Brooklyn, NY
Planeta, Emil Joseph	02/02/1963	Rose Hill Memorial Park, Rocky Hill, CT
Plank, Eddie (Edward Stewart)	02/24/1926	Evergreen Cemetery, Gettysburg, PA
Plarski, Don (Donald Joseph)	12/29/1981	Cremated, St. Louis, MO
Plaskett, Elmo Alexander	11/02/1998	Frederiksted Cemetery, Frederiksted, Virgin Islands
Platt, Whitey (Mizell George)	07/27/1970	Hillcrest Memorial Park, West Palm Beach, FL
Platte, Al (Alfred Frederick Joseph)	08/29/1976	Holy Trinity Cemetery, Grand Rapids, MI
Plitt, Norman William	02/01/1954	Prospect Hill Cemetery, York, PA
Poat, Ray (Raymond Willis)	04/29/1990	Chapel Hill Gardens South, Oak Lawn, IL
Podbielan, Bud (Clarence Anthony)	10/26/1982	St. Mary's Cemetery, Syracuse, NY
Podgajny, Johnny (John Sigmund)	03/02/1971	St. Francis DeSales Cemetery, Chester Heights, PA
Poetz, Joe (Joseph Frank)	02/07/1942	Resurrection Cemetery, Mackenzie, MO
Pofahl, Jimmy (James Willard)	09/14/1984	Maple Lawn Cemetery, Faribault, MN

Name	DOD	Cemetery, City, State
Poholsky, Tom (Thomas George)	01/06/2001	Oak Hill Cemetery, Kirkwood, MO
Poindexter, Jennings (Chester Jennings)	03/03/1983	Mount Olivet Cemetery, Pauls Valley, OK
Poland, Hugh Reid	03/30/1984	Highland Cemetery, Guthrie, KY
Polchow, Lou (Louis William)	08/15/1912	German Lutheran Cemetery, Mankato, MN
Polhemus, Mark S.	11/12/1923	Nyack Rural Cemetery, West Nyack, NY
Polivka, Ken (Kenneth Lyle)	07/23/1988	SS. Peter & Paul Cemetery, Naperville, IL
Pollet, Howie (Howard Joseph)	08/08/1974	Memorial Oaks Cemetery, Houston, TX
Polli, Lou (Louis Americo)	12/19/2000	Hope Cemetery, Barre, VT
Polly, Nick (Nicholas)	01/17/1993	Elmwood Cemetery, River Grove, IL
Pond, Ralph Benjamin	09/08/1947	Cremated, Cleveland, OH
Ponder, Elmer (Charles Elmer)	04/20/1974	Fairview Memorial Park, Albuquerque, NM
Pool, Harlin Welty	02/15/1963	Golden Gate National Cemetery, San Bruno, CA
Poole, Ed (Edward T.)	03/11/1919	Bethlehem Cemetery, Malvern, OH
Poole, Jim (James Robert)	01/02/1975	Linney's Grove Baptist Church Cemetery, Hiddenite, NC
Poorman, Tom (Thomas Iverson)	02/18/1905	Highland Cemetery, Lock Haven, PA
Pope, Dave (David)	08/28/1999	Lake View Cemetery, Cleveland, OH
Popowski, Eddie (Edward Joseph) manager	12/04/2001	New Calvary Cemetery, Parlin, NJ
Popp, Bill (William Peter)	09/05/1909	Calvary Cemetery, St. Louis, MO
Popplein, George J.	03/31/1901	Greenmount Cemetery, Baltimore, MD
Porter, Darrell Ray	08/05/2002	Longview Memorial Gardens, Kansas City, MO
Porter, Dick (Richard Twilley)	09/24/1974	Asbury United Methodist Church Cemetery, Allen, MD
Porter, Henry (Walter Henry)	12/30/1906	Calvary Cemetery, Brockton, MA
Porter, Irv (Irving Marble)	02/20/1971	St. Joseph's Cemetery, Lynn, MA
Porter, Jim (Odie Oscar)	05/02/1903	Pleasant Ridge Cemetery, Borden, IN
Porter, Ned Swindell	06/30/1968	Magnolia Cemetery, Apalachicola, FL
Porterfield, Bob (Erwin Cooledge)	04/28/1980	Sharon Memorial Park, Charlotte, NC
Portocarrero, Arnie (Arnold Mario)	06/21/1986	Cremated, Kansas City, MO
Posedel, Bill (William John)	11/28/1989	Cremated, Livermore, CA. Ashes scattered in Pacific Ocean,
Poser, Bob (John Falk)	05/21/2002	Hillside Cemetery, Columbus, WI
Post, Lew (Lewis G.)	08/21/1944	All Saints Cemetery, Des Plaines, IL
Post, Sam (Samuel Gilbert)	03/31/1971	Oak Grove Cemetery, Portsmouth, VA
Post, Wally (Walter Charles)	01/06/1982	Saint Henry's Church Cemetery, Saint Henry, OH
Pott, Nellie (Nelson Adolph)	12/03/1963	Baltimore Pike Cemetery, Cincinnati, OH
Potter, Dykes (Maryland Dykes)	02/27/2002	Bellefonte Memorial Gardens, Flatwoods, KY
Potter, Nels (Nelson Thomas)	09/30/1990	Oakwood Cemetery, Mount Morris, IL
Potter, Squire (Robert)	01/27/1983	Bellefonte Memorial Gardens, Flatwoods, KY
Potts, Dan (Vivian)	08/17/1934	Bristol Cemetery, Bristol, PA
Pounds, Bill (Jeared Wells)	07/07/1936	Laurel Grove Cemetery, Totowa, NJ
Powell, Ab (Charles Abner)	08/07/1953	St. John's Cemetery, New Orleans, LA

Name	DOD	Cemetery, City, State
Powell, Bill (William Burris)	09/28/1967	Columbiana County Memorial Park, East Liverpool, OH
Powell, Grover David	05/21/1985	Camptown Cemetery, Camptown, PA
Powell, Jack (Reginald Bertrand)	03/12/1930	Memphis National Cemetery, Memphis, TN
Powell, Jake (Alvin Jacob)	11/04/1948	St. John's Cemetery, Forest Glen, MD
Powell, Jake (John Joseph)	10/17/1944	Mount Carmel Cemetery, Hillside, IL
Powell, Jim (James Edwin)	11/20/1929	Mount Moriah Cemetery, Butte, MT
Powell, Martin J.	02/05/1888	St. Bernard's Church Cemetery, Fitchburg, MA
Powell, Ray (Raymond Raeth)	10/16/1962	Mount Zion Cemetery, Bogard, MO
Power, Tom (Thomas E.)	02/25/1898	Holy Cross Cemetery, Colma, CA
Powers, Doc (Michael Riley)	04/26/1909	St. Louis Cemetery, Louisville, KY
Powers, Ike (John Lloyd)	12/22/1968	United Methodist Churchyard, Hancock, MD
Powers, J.C. (John Calvin)	09/25/2001	Forest Hill Cemetery, Birmingham, AL
Powers, Les (Leslie Edwin)	11/13/1978	Holy Cross Cemetery, Culver City, CA
Powers, Mike (Ellis Foree)	12/02/1983	Floydsburg Cemetery, Crestwood, KY
Powers, Pat (Patrick Thomas) manager	08/27/1925	St. John's Cemetery, Trenton, NJ
Powers, Phil (Philip B.)	12/22/1914	St. Raymond's Cemetery, Bronx, NY
Pramesa, Johnny (John Steven)	09/09/1996	Cremated, Simi Valley, CA.
Pratt, Al (Albert G.)	11/21/1937	Union Dale Cemetery, Pittsburgh, PA
Pratt, Frank (Francis Bruce)	03/08/1974	Pineland Memorial Park, Centreville, AL
Pratt, Tom (Thomas Jefferson)	09/28/1908	Laurel Hill Cemetery, Philadelphia, PA
Pratt,Del (Derrill Burnham)	09/30/1977	Cremated, Texas City, TX
Preibisch, Mel (Melvin Aloysius)	04/12/1980	Sealy Cemetery, Sealy
Prendergast, Jim (James Bartholomew)	08/23/1994	Mt. Olivet Cemetery, Tonawanda, NY
Prendergast, Mike (Michael Thomas)	11/18/1967	Calvary Cemetery, Omaha, NE
Pressnell, Tot (Forest Charles)	01/06/2001	Maple Grove Cemetery, Findlay, OH
Price, Jackie (John Thomas Reid)	10/02/1967	Golden Gate National Cemetery, San Bruno, CA
Price, Joe (Joseph Preston)	01/15/1961	Monte Vista Burial Park, Johnson City, TN
Prichard, Bob (Robert Alexander)	09/25/1991	Highland Memorial Cemetery, Stamford, TX
Priddy, Jerry (Gerald Edward)	03/03/1980	Holy Cross Cemetery, Culver City, CA
Priest, Johnny (John Gooding)	11/05/1979	Oakwood Cemetery, Falls Church, VA
Prim, Ray (Raymond Lee)	04/29/1995	Calvary Cemetery, Los Angeles, CA
Prince, Walter Farr	03/02/1938	St. Joseph's Cemetery, Bristol, NH
Proctor, Red (Noah Richard)	12/17/1954	Cedar Grove Cemetery, Williamsburg, VA
Proeser, George	10/13/1941	Spring Grove Cemetery, Cincinnati, OH
Propst, Jake (William Jacob)	02/24/1967	Friendship Cemetery, Columbus, MS
Prothro, Doc (James Thompson)	10/14/1971	Memorial Park Cemetery, Memphis, TN
Prough, Bill (Herschel Clinton)	12/29/1936	Hoverstock Cemetery, Zanesville, IN
Pruess, Earl Henry	08/28/1979	Irving Park Cemetery, Chicago, IL
Pruett, Hub (Hubert Shelby)	01/28/1982	Bellefontaine Cemetery, St. Louis, MO
Pruiett, Tex (Charles Leroy)	03/06/1953	Ivy Lawn Memorial Park, Ventura, CA. Cremated.
Puccinelli, George Lawrence	04/16/1956	Holy Cross Cemetery, Colma, CA

Name	DOD	Cemetery, City, State
Puckett, Troy Levi	04/13/1971	Fountain Park Cemetery, Winchester, IN
Puhl, John G.	08/24/1900	Holy Name Cemetery (formerly Hudson County Catholic Cemetery), Jersey City, NJ
Pumpelly, Spence (Spencer Armstrong)	12/05/1973	Evergreen Cemetery, Owego, NY
Purdy, Pid (Everett Virgil)	01/16/1951	Evergreen Home Cemetery, Beatrice, NE
Purnell, Jesse Rhoades	07/04/1966	Oakland Cemetery, Philadelphia, PA
Purner, Oscar E.	12/04/1915	Douglas Cemetery, Douglas, AZ
Purtell, Billy (William Patrick)	03/17/1962	Mansion Memorial Park, Ellenton, FL
Puttmann, Ambrose Nicholas	06/21/1936	St. Joseph's Old Cemetery, Cincinnati, OH
Pyle, Ewald (Herbert Ewald)	01/10/2004	Sunset Memorial Park, DuQuoin, IL
Pyle, Harlan Albert	01/13/1993	Liberty Cemetery, Liberty, NE
Pyle, Shadow (Harry Thomas)	12/26/1908	Charles Evans Cemetery, Reading, PA
Pytlak, Frankie (Frank Anthony)	05/08/1977	St. Stanislaus Cemetery, Cheektowaga, NY
Quarles, Bill (William H.)	03/25/1897	Blandford Cemetery, Petersburg, VA
Quellich, George William	08/21/1958	Cremated, Chapel of the Chimes Oakland, CA
Quest, Joe (Joseph L.)	11/14/1924	Mount Hope Cemetery, San Diego, CA
Quick, Eddie (Edward)	06/19/1913	Fairmount Cemetery, Denver, CO
Quick, Hal (James Harold)	03/09/1974	Leavenworth National Cemetery, Leavenworth, KS
Quillen, Lee (Leon Abner)	05/14/1965	Oakland Cemetery, St. Paul, MN
Quinlan, Finners (Thomas Finners)	02/17/1966	St. Catherine's Cemetery, Moscow, PA
Quinlan, Frank (Francis Patrick)	05/04/1904	Immaculate Conception Cemetery, Marlborough, MA
Quinn, Jack (John Picus)	04/17/1946	Charles Baber Cemetery, Pottsville, PA
Quinn, Joe (Joseph J.)	11/12/1940	Calvary Cemetery, St. Louis, MO
Quinn, John Edward	04/09/1956	St. Mary's Cemetery, Mansfield, MA
Quinn, Paddy (Patrick J.)	01/02/1909	Calvary Cemetery, Evanston, IL
Quinn, Tad (Clarence Carr)	08/07/1946	Hillside Cemetery, Torrington, CT
Quinn, Tom (Thomas Oscar)	07/24/1932	Braddock Catholic Cemetery, Braddock, PA
Quinn, Wimpy (Wellington Hunt)	09/01/1954	Woodlawn Cemetery, Santa Monica, CA
Quisenberry, Dan (Daniel Raymond)	09/30/1998	Mount Moriah Cemetery, Kansas City, MO
Rabbitt, Joe (Joseph Patrick)	12/05/1969	St. Mary's & St. Joseph's Cemetery, Norwalk, CT
Rachunok, Steve (Stephen Stepanovich)	05/11/2002	Body donated to UC-Irvine College of Medicine, Irvine, CA
Radbourne, George B.	01/01/1904	Evergreen Memorial Cemetery, Bloomington, IL
Radbourne, Hoss (Charles Gardner)	02/05/1897	Evergreen Memorial Cemetery, Bloomington, IL
Radcliff, Rip (Raymond Allen)	05/23/1962	Memorial Park Cemetery, Enid, OK
Radcliffe, John Y.	07/26/1911	Harleigh Cemetery, Camden, NJ
Radebaugh, Roy	01/17/1945	Linwood Cemetery, Cedar Rapids, IA
Rader, Don (Donald Russell)	06/26/1983	Cremated, Walla Walla, WA
Radford, Paul Revere	02/21/1945	Brookdale Cemetery, Dedham, MA
Raffensberger, Ken (Kenneth David)	11/10/2002	Mt. Rose Cemetery, York, PA

Name	DOD	Cemetery, City, State
Rafter, Jack (John Cornelius)	01/05/1943	St. John's Cemetery, Troy, NY
Raftery, Tom (Thomas Francis)	12/31/1954	Dorchester North Cemetery, Dorchester, MA
Ragan, Pat (Don Carlos Patrick)	09/04/1956	Forest Lawn Memorial Park, Glendale, CA
Raines, Larry (Lawrence Glenn Hope)	01/28/1978	Evergreen-Mount Hope Cemetery, Lansing, MI
Rainey, John Paul	11/11/1912	Birmingham Cemetery, Birmingham, MI
Raleigh, John Austin	08/24/1955	Oak Hill Memorial Park, Escondido, CA
Ralston, Doc (Samuel Beryl)	08/29/1950	Cremated, Lancaster, PA
Ramazzotti, Bob (Robert Louis)	02/15/2000	Calvary Cemetery, Altoona, PA
Rambert, Pep (Elmer Donald)	11/16/1974	Royal Palm Memorial Gardens, West Palm Beach, FL
Rambo, Pete (Warren Dawson)	06/19/1991	Eglington Cemetery, Clarksboro, NJ
Ramsdell, Willie (James Willard)	10/08/1969	Riverview Cemetery, Kiowa, KS
Ramsey, Toad (Thomas A.)	03/27/1906	Crown Hill Cemetery, Indianapolis, IN
Rand, Dick (Richard Hilton)	01/22/1996	Cremated, Riverside, CA. Ashes scattered at sea.
Randall, Newt (Newton J.)	05/03/1955	Park Hill Cemetery, Duluth, MN
Raney, Ribs (Frank Robert Donald)	07/07/2003	Resurrestion Cemetery, Clinton Township, MI
Rapp, Earl Wellington	02/13/1992	St. Joseph's Cemetery, Swedesboro, NJ
Rapp, Goldie (Joseph Aloysius)	07/01/1966	Fort Rosecrans National Cemetery, La Jolla, CA
Rariden, Bill (William Angel)	08/28/1942	Green Hill Cemetery, Bedford, IN
Raschi, Vic (Victor John Angelo)	10/14/1988	Cremated, Livingston County, NY. Ashes returned to family
Rasmussen, Hans (Henry Florian)	01/01/1949	All Saints Cemetery, Des Plaines, IL
Rath, Morrie (Morris Charles)	11/18/1945	Arlington Cemetery, Drexel Hill, PA
Raub, Tommy (Thomas Jefferson)	02/15/1949	Fairmount Cemetery, Phillipsburg, NJ
Rawlings, Johnny (John William)	10/16/1972	Cremated, Inglewood, CA
Ray Farmer (Robert Henry)	03/11/1963	New Electra Cemetery, Electra, TX
Ray, Irv (Irving Burton)	02/21/1948	Forest Hills Cemetery, Harrington, ME
Raymer, Fred (Frederick Charles)	06/11/1957	Cremated, Los Angeles, CA
Raymond, Bugs (Arthur Lawrence)	09/07/1912	Montrose Cemetery, Chicago, IL
Raymond, Lou (Louis Anthony)	05/02/1979	Holy Sepulchre Cemetery, Rochester, NY
Reach, Al (Alfred James)	01/14/1928	West Laurel Hill Cemetery, Bala Cynwyd, PA
Reach, Bob (Robert)	05/19/1922	Oak Grove Cemetery, Springfield, MA
Reagan, Rip (Arthur Edgar)	06/08/1953	Calvary Cemetery, St. Louis, MO
Reardon, Jim (Jeremiah J.)	04/22/1907	Calvary Cemetery, St. Louis, MO
Reardon, Phil (Philip Michael)	09/28/1920	Holy Cross Cemetery, Brooklyn, NY
Reccius, John	09/01/1930	Cave Hill Cemetery, Louisville, KY
Reccius, Phil (Philip)	02/15/1903	Cave Hill Cemetery, Louisville, KY
Redding, Phil (Philip Hayden)	03/31/1928	Terry Cemetery, Terry, MS
Reder, Johnny (John Anthony)	04/12/1990	St. Patrick's Cemetery, Fall River, MA
Redfern, Buck (George Howard)	09/08/1964	Riverside Cemetery, Asheville, NC
Redmond, Harry John	07/10/1960	Holy Cross Cemetery, Cleveland, OH
Redmond, Jack (John McKittrick)	07/27/1968	Mesa Municipal Cemetery, Mesa, AZ
Reed, Howie (Howard Dean)	12/07/1984	Robstown Memorial Park, Robstown, TX
Reed, Hugh	11/03/1883	Graceland Cemetery, Chicago, IL
Reed, Milt (Milton D.)	07/27/1938	Crest Lawn Memorial Park, Atlanta, GA

Name	DOD	Cemetery, City, State
Reed, Ted (Ralph Edwin)	02/16/1959	Beaver Cemetery, Beaver, PA
Reeder, Icicle (Julius Edward)	01/15/1913	Spring Grove Cemetery, Cincinnati, OH
Reeder, Nick (Nicholas)	09/26/1894	Cave Hill Cemetery, Louisville, KY
Rees, Stan (Stanley Milton)	08/30/1937	Battle Grove Cemetery, Cynthiana, KY
Reese, Jimmy (James Herman)	07/13/1994	Cremated, Westwood Memorial Park, Los Angeles, CA
Reese, Pee Wee (Harold Henry)	08/14/1999	Resthaven Memorial Park, Louisville, KY
Reese, Randy (Andrew Jackson)	01/10/1966	Glenwood Cemetery, Tupelo, MS
Reeves, Bobby (Robert Edwin)	06/04/1993	Chattanooga National Cemetery, Chattanooga, TN
Regan, Bill (William Wright)	06/11/1968	Calvary Cemetery, Pittsburgh, PA
Regan, Joe (Joseph Charles)	11/18/1948	St. Thomas Cemetery, Southington, CT
Regan, Mike (Michael John)	05/22/1961	St. Agnes Cemetery, Albany, NY
Rego, Tony (Antone)	01/06/1978	Calvary Cemetery, Tulsa, OK
Rehg, Wally (Walter Phillip)	04/05/1946	Grand View Memorial Park, Glendale, CA
Reiber, Frank Bernard	12/26/2002	Cremated, Bradenton, FL.
Reichle, Dick (Richard Wendell)	06/13/1967	Resurrection Cemetery, Mackenzie, MO
Reid, Earl Percy	05/11/1984	Holly Pond Cemetery, Holly Pond, AL
Reidy, Bill (William Joseph)	10/14/1915	St. John's Cemetery, Cleveland, OH
Reilley, Duke (Alexander Aloysius)	03/04/1968	Holy Cross Cemetery, Indianapolis, IN
Reilly, Arch (Archer Edwin)	11/29/1963	St. Joseph's Cemetery, Lockbourne, OH
Reilly, Barney (Bernard Eugene)	11/15/1934	Mount Olivet Cemetery, St. Joseph, MO
Reilly, Charlie (Charles Thomas)	12/16/1937	Calvary Cemetery, Los Angeles, CA
Reilly, Hal (Harold John)	12/24/1957	Holy Sepulchre Cemetery, Worth, IL
Reilly, Jiosh (William Henry)	06/12/1938	Holy Cross Cemetery, Colma, CA
Reilly, John Good	05/31/1937	Spring Grove Cemetery, Cincinnati, OH
Reilly, Tom (Thomas Henry)	10/18/1918	St. Joseph Cemetery #3, New Orleans, LA
Reinbach, Mike (Michael Wayne)	05/20/1989	El Camino Memorial Park, La Jolla, CA
Reinhart, Art (Arthur Conrad)	11/11/1946	Oakwood Cemetery, Ackley, IA
Reinholz, Art (Arthur August)	12/29/1980	Cadillac Memorial Gardens West, Westland, MI
Reipschlager, Charlie (Charles W.)	03/16/1910	Lutheran All Faiths Cemetery, Middle Village, Queens, NY
Reis, Bobby (Robert Joseph Thomas)	05/01/1973	Willow River Cemetery, Hudson, WI
Reis, Jack (Harrie Crane)	07/20/1939	Vine Street Hill Cemetery, Cincinnati, OH
Reis, Laurie (Lawrence P.)	01/24/1921	Mount Greenwood Cemetery, Chicago, IL
Reiser, Pete (Harold Patrick)	10/25/1981	Desert Memorial Park, Cathedral City, CA
Reisgl, Bugs (Jacob)	02/24/1957	St. Mary's Cemetery, Fort Johnson, NY
Reising, Charlie (Charles)	07/26/1915	Cave Hill Cemetery, Louisville, KY
Reisling, Doc (Frank Carl)	03/04/1955	Rose Hill Memorial Park, Tulsa, OK
Reiss, Al (Albert Allen)	05/13/1989	Rosedale Cemetery, Linden, NJ
Rementer, Butch (Willis J.)	09/23/1922	Holy Cross Cemetery, Yeadon, PA
Renfer, Erwin Arthur	10/26/1958	Bluff City Cemetery, Elgin, IL
Renfroe, Marshall Daniel	12/10/1970	Bayview Memorial Park, Pensacola, FL
Reninger, Jim (James David)	08/23/1993	Cremated, Fort Myers, FL
Rensa, Tony (George Anthony)	01/04/1987	St. Mary's Cemetery, Wilkes-Barre, PA

Name	DOD	Cemetery, City, State
Repulski, Rip (Eldon John)	02/10/1993	Trinity Lutheran Church Cemetery, Sauk Rapids, MN
Ressler, Larry (Lawrence P.)	06/12/1918	St. Peter's Cemetery, Reading, PA
Rettger, George Edward	06/05/1921	Calvary Cemetery, Lakewood, OH
Rettig, Otto (Adolph John)	06/16/1977	Cremated, Stuart, FL
Reulbach, Ed (Edward Marvin)	07/17/1961	Immaculate Conception Cemetery, Montclair, NJ
Reyes, Nap (Napoleon Aguilera)	09/15/1995	Vista Memorial Gardens, Hialeah, FL
Reynolds, Allie Pierce	12/26/1994	Memorial Park Cemetery, Oklahoma City, OK
Reynolds, Bill (William Dee)	06/05/1924	Carnegie Cemetery, Carnegie, OK
Reynolds, Carl Nettles	05/29/1978	Wharton City Cemetery, Wharton, TX
Reynolds, Charlie (Charles Lawrence)	07/03/1944	Fairmount Cemetery, Denver, CO
Reynolds, Ross Ernest	06/23/1970	Rosedale Cemetery, Ada, OK
Rhawn, Bobby (Robert John)	06/09/1984	Elan Memorial Park Cemetery, Bloomsburg, PA
Rheam, Cy (Kenneth Johnston)	10/23/1947	Allegheny Cemetery, Pittsburgh, PA
Rhem, Flint (Charles Flint)	07/30/1969	Wood Memorial Park, Greer, SC
Rhiel, Billy (William Joseph)	08/16/1946	Calvary Cemetery, Youngstown, OH
Rhines, Billy (William Pearl)	01/30/1922	Sarah Thayer Memorial Cemetery, Ridgway, PA
Rhoads, Bob (Barton Emory)	02/12/1967	Mountain View Memorial Park, Barstow, CA
Rhodes, Charlie (Charles Anderson)	10/26/1918	Caney Sunnyside Cemetery, Caney, KS
Rhodes, Gordon (John Gordon)	03/22/1960	Los Angeles National Cemetery, Los Angeles, CA
Rhyne, Hal (Harold J.)	01/07/1971	East Lawn Memorial Park, Sacramento, CA. Cremated
Rice, Bob (Robert Turnbull)	02/20/1986	Masonic Cemetery, Elizabethtown, PA
Rice, Del (Delbert W.)	01/26/1983	Cremated, Buena Park, CA
Rice, Harry Francis	01/01/1971	Riverview Abbey Mausoleum, Portland, OR
Rice, Len (Leonard Oliver)	06/13/1992	Buena Vista Cemetery, Murphys, CA
Rice, Sam (Edgar Charles)	10/13/1974	Woodside Cemetery, Brinklow, MD
Rich, Woody (Woodrow Earl)	04/18/1983	South Mountain Baptist Church Cemetery, Morganton, NC
Richards, Paul Rapier	05/04/1986	Hillcrest Burial Park, Waxahachie, TX
Richardson, Bill (William Henry)	11/06/1949	Greendale Cemetery, Osgood, IN
Richardson, Hardy (Abram Harding)	01/14/1931	Forest Hill Cemetery, Utica, NY
Richardson, Ken (Kenneth Franklin)	12/07/1987	Cremated, Woodland Hills, CA
Richardson, Nolen (Clifford Nolen)	09/25/1951	Oconee Hill Cemetery, Athens, GA
Richardson, Tom (Thomas Mitchell)	11/15/1939	Graceland Cemetery, Onawa, IA
Richbourg, Lance Clayton	09/10/1975	Live Oak Memorial Park, Crestview, FL
Richie, Lew (Elwood Lewis)	08/15/1936	Rose Hill Cemetery, Ambler, PA
Richmond, Beryl Justice	04/24/1980	Highland Cemetery, Cameron, WV
Richmond, Don (Donald Lester)	05/24/1981	SS. Peter & Paul Cemetery, Elmira, NY

Name	DOD	Cemetery, City, State
Richmond, Lee (J Lee)	10/01/1929	Cremated, Woodlawn Cemetery, Toledo, OH
Richmond, Ray (Raymond Sinclair)	10/21/1969	Fillmore Glendale Cemetery, Fillmore, IL
Richter, John M.	10/04/1927	St. Louis Cemetery, Louisville, KY
Richter, Reggie (Emil Henry)	08/02/1934	Oak Hill Cemetery, Chicago, IL
Rickert, Joe (Joseph Francis)	10/15/1943	St. Bernard Cemetery, Springfield, OH
Rickert, Marv (Marvin August)	06/03/1978	Cremated, Oakville, WA
Ricketts, Dick (Richard James)	03/06/1988	Pughtown Baptist Cemetery, Spring City, PA
Rickey, Branch (Wesley Branch)	12/09/1965	Rushtown Cemetery, Rushtown, OH
Rickley, Chris (Christian)	10/25/1911	Greenmount Cemetery, Philadelphia, PA
Rico, Art (Arthur Ramon)	01/03/1919	Holyhood Cemetery, Brookline, MA
Riddle, Elmer Ray	05/14/1984	Parkhill Cemetery, Columbus, GA
Riddle, John H.	05/05/1931	New Camden Cemetery, Camden, NJ
Riddle, Johnny (John Ludy)	12/15/1998	Oaklawn Memorial Gardens, Fishers, IN
Riddlemoser, Dorsey Lee	05/11/1954	Mount Olivet Cemetery, Frederick, MD
Ridgway, Jack (Jacob Augustus)	02/23/1928	Westminster Cemetery, Bala Cynwyd, PA
Riebe, Hank (Harvey Donald)	04/16/2001	All Souls Cemetery, Chardon, OH
Rieger, Elmer Jay	10/21/1959	Inglewood Park Cemetery, Inglewood, CA
Riggert, Joe (Joseph Aloysius)	12/10/1973	Calvary Cemetery, Kansas City, MO
Riggs, Lew (Lewis Sidney)	08/12/1975	Rock Creek United Methodist Church Cemetery, Snow Camp, NC
Rigney, Johnny (John Dungan)	10/21/1984	Queen of Heaven Cemetery, Hillside, IL
Rigney, Topper (Emory Elmo)	06/06/1972	Sunset Memorial Park, San Antonio, TX
Rikard, Culley	02/25/2000	Boggan Cemetery, Lewisburg, MS
Riley, Billy (William James)	11/09/1887	St. Joseph's New Cemetery, Cincinnati, OH
Riley, Jim (James Joseph)	03/25/1949	Holy Cross Cemetery, Lackawanna, NY
Riley, Jim (James Norman)	05/25/1969	Guadalupe Valley Memorial Park, New Braunfels, TX
Riley, Lee (Leon Francis)	09/13/1970	Most Holy Redeemer Cemetery, Schenectady, NY
Ring, Jimmy (James Joseph)	07/06/1965	St. John's Cemetery, Middle Village, Queens, NY
Ringo, Frank C.	04/12/1889	Elmwood Cemetery, Kansas City, MO
Rinker, Bob (Robert John)	12/19/2002	Sky-View Memorial Park, Hometown, PA
Ripken, Cal, Sr. *manager*	03/25/1999	Baker Cemetery, Aberdeen, MD
Ripley, Walt (Walter Franklin)	10/07/1990	Massachusetts National Cemetery, Bourne, MA
Ripple, Charlie (Charles Dawson)	05/06/1979	Whiteville Memorial Cemetery, Whiteville, NC
Ripple, Jimmy (James Albert)	07/16/1959	Eastview Cemetery, Delmont, PA
Risberg, Swede (Charles August)	10/13/1975	Mount Shasta Memorial Park, Mount Shasta, CA
Ritchey, Claude Cassius	11/08/1951	Emlenton Cemetery, Emlenton, PA
Ritter, Floyd Alexander	02/07/1943	West Klickitat Cemetery, White Salmon, WA
Ritter, Hank (William Herbert)	09/03/1964	Rose Hill Burial Park, Fairlawn, OH
Ritter, Lew (Lewis Elmer)	05/27/1952	Liverpool Cemetery, Liverpool, PA
Ritterson, Ed (Edward West)	07/28/1917	Reform Cemetery, Perkasie, PA
Riviere, Tink (Arthur Bernard)	09/27/1965	Immaculate Conception Catholic Cemetery, Liberty, TX

Name	DOD	Cemetery, City, State
Rixey, Eppa	02/28/1963	Greenlawn Cemetery, Milford, OH
Rizzo, Johnny (John Costa)	12/04/1977	Forest Park (Westheimer) Cemetery, Houston, TX
Roach, John F.	04/02/1934	St. Mary's Cemetery, Peoria, IL
Roach, Roxy (Wilbur Charles)	12/26/1947	Tawas City Cemetery, Tawas City, MI
Roach, Skel (Rudolph Charles)	03/09/1958	Concordia Cemetery, Forest Park, IL
Roat, Fred (Frederick R.)	09/24/1913	River View Cemetery, Oregon, IL
Robello, Tommy (Thomas Vardasco)	12/25/1994	Mount Olivet Cemetery, Fort Worth, TX
Roberge, Skippy (Joseph Albert Armand)	08/17/1941	St. Joseph's Cemetery, Chelmsford, MA
Roberts, Curt (Curtis Benjamin)	11/14/1969	Evergreen Cemetery, Oakland, CA
Roberts, Jim (James Newsom)	06/24/1984	Friendship Cemetery, Columbus, MS
Roberts, Skipper (Clarence Ashley)	12/24/1963	All Souls Cemetery, Long Beach, CA
Robertson, Charlie (Charles Culbertson)	08/23/1984	Palo Pinto Cemetery, Palo Pinto, TX
Robertson, Dave (Davis Aydelotte)	11/05/1970	Forest Lawn Cemetery, Norfolk, VA
Robertson, Dick (Preston)	10/02/1944	St. Joseph Cemetery #2, New Orleans, LA
Robertson, Jerry Lee	03/24/1996	Cremated, Burlington, KS
Robertson, Sherry (Sherrard Alexander)	10/23/1970	Lakewood Cemetery, Minneapolis, MN
Robinson, Aaron Andrew	03/09/1966	Zion Methodist Church Cemetery, Lancaster, SC
Robinson, Charlie (Charles Henry)	05/18/1913	Riverbend Cemetery, Westerly, RI
Robinson, Fred (Frederic Henry)	12/18/1933	Forestvale Cemetery, Hudson, MA
Robinson, Hank (John Henry)	07/03/1965	Edgewood Memorial Park, North Little Rock, AR
Robinson, Jack (John W.)	07/22/1921	Riverside Cemetery, Macon, GA
Robinson, Jackie (Jack Roosevelt)	10/24/1972	Cypress Hills Cemetery, Brooklyn, NY
Robinson, Kenny (Kenneth Neal)	02/28/1999	Oaklawn Cemetery, Jacksonville, FL
Robinson, Rabbit (William Clyde)	04/09/1915	Wellsburg Cemetery, Wellsburg, WV
Robinson, Wilbert	08/08/1934	New Cathedral Cemetery, Baltimore, MD
Robinson, Yank (William H.)	08/25/1894	Calvary Cemetery, St. Louis, MO
Robison, Matthew Stanley, Jr. *manager*	03/24/1911	Lake View Cemetery, Cleveland, OH
Robitaille, Chick (Joseph Anthony)	07/30/1947	St. Joseph's Cemetery, Waterford, NY
Rocap, Adam	03/26/1892	Mount Peace Cemetery, Philadelphia, PA
Rocco, Mickey (Michael Dominick)	06/01/1997	Roselawn Cemetery, Roseville, MN
Roche, Jack (John Joseph)	03/30/1983	Resthaven Park Cemetery, Glendale, AZ
Rochelli, Lou (Louis Joseph)	10/23/1992	Resurrection Cemetery, Victoria, TX
Rock, Les (Lester Henry)	09/09/1991	Cremated, Davis, CA
Rodgers, Bill (Wilbur Kincaid)	12/24/1978	Berclair Cemetery, Berclair, TX
Rodgers, Bill (William Sherman)	05/13/2002	Woodland Memorial Gardens, Harrisburg, PA
Rodin, Eric Chapman	01/04/1991	Prospect Hill Cemetery, Flemington, NJ
Roe Clay (James Clay)	04/03/1956	Cleveland Cemetery, Cleveland, MS
Roettger, Oscar Frederick Louis	07/04/1986	Bethlehem Cemetery, Bellefontaine, MO
Roettger, Wally (Walter Henry)	09/14/1951	Riverview Cemetery, Streator, IL
Roetz, Ed (Edward Bernard)	03/16/1965	Beverly National Cemetery, Beverly, NJ

Name	DOD	Cemetery, City, State
Rogell, Billy (William George)	08/09/2003	Holy Sepulchre Cemetery, Southfield, MI
Rogers, Emmett E.	10/24/1941	Calvary Catholic Cemetery, Fort Smith, AR
Rogers, Jay Lewis	07/01/1964	Temple Hill Cemetery, Geneseo, NY
Rogers, Jim (James F.)	01/21/1900	St. Michael's Cemetery, Stratford, CT
Rogers, Lee Otis	11/23/1995	Roselawn Memorial Gardens Cemetery, Little Rock, AR
Rogers, Packy (Stanley Frank)	05/15/1998	Woodlawn National Cemetery, Elmira, NY
Rogers, Tom (Thomas Andrew)	03/07/1936	Spring Hill Cemetery, Nashville, TN
Rogge, Clint (Francis Clinton)	01/06/1969	Memphis Cemetery, Memphis, MI
Rogovin, Saul Walter	01/23/1995	Beth David Cemetery, Elmont, NY
Rohe, George Anthony	06/10/1957	Walnut Hills Cemetery, Cincinnati, OH
Rohwer, Ray	01/24/1988	Dixon Cemetery, Dixon, CA
Rojek, Stan (Stanley Andrew)	07/09/1997	Mt. Olivet Cemetery, Tonawanda, NY
Rolfe, Red (Robert Abial)	07/08/1969	Woodlawn Cemetery, Penacook, NH
Rolling, Ray (Raymond Copeland)	08/25/1966	Lakewview Cemetery, Mahtomedi, MN
Rollings, Red (William Russell)	12/31/1964	Pine Crest Cemetery, Mobile, AL
Romano, Jim (James King)	09/12/1990	Calverton National Cemetery, Calverton, NY
Romberger, Dutch (Allen Isaiah)	05/26/1983	St. Michael's Lutheran Church Cemetery, Klingerstown, PA
Rommel, Eddie (Edwin Americus)	08/26/1970	New Cathedral Cemetery, Baltimore, MD
Rondeau, Henri Joseph	05/28/1943	Precious Blood Cemetery, Woonsocket, RI
Rooks, George Brinton McClellan	03/11/1935	Jewish Waldheim Cemetery, Forest Park, IL
Rooney, Frank	04/06/1977	Hurley City Cemetery, Hurley, WI
Root, Charlie (Charles Henry)	11/05/1970	Cremated, Garden of Memories Crematory, Salinas, CA. Ashes given to family
Rosar, Buddy (Warren Vincent)	03/13/1994	Mount Calvary Cemetery, Cheektowaga, NY
Rose, Chuck (Charles Alfred)	08/04/1961	Mount Olivet Cemetery, Marceline, MO
Roseboro, John Junior	08/16/2002	Forest Lawn Memorial Park-Hollywood Hills, Los Angeles, CA
Rosebraugh, Zeke (Eli Ethelbert)	07/16/1930	Washington Colony Cemetery, Fresno, CA
Roseman, Chief (James John)	07/04/1938	St. John's Cemetery, Middle Village, Queens, NY
Rosenberg, Harry	04/13/1997	Hills of Eternity Memorial Park, Colma, CA. Cremated.
Rosenberg, Lou (Louis)	09/08/1991	Eternal Home Cemetery, Colma, CA
Rosenfield, Max	03/10/1969	Graceland Memorial Park, Miami, FL
Rosenthal, Larry (Lawrence John)	03/04/1992	Resurrection Cemetery, St. Paul, MN
Rosenthal, Si (Simon)	04/07/1969	Beth El Cemetery, West Roxbury, MA
Roser, Bunny (John William Joseph)	05/06/1979	Rose Hill Memorial Park, Rocky Hill, CT
Roser, Steve (Emerson Corey)	02/08/2002	Cedar Lake Cemetery, New Hartford, NY
Ross, Buster (Chester Franklin)	04/24/1982	Maplewood Cemetery, Mayfield, KY
Ross, Chet (Chester James)	02/21/1989	Holy Cross Cemetery, Lackawanna, NY
Ross, Cliff (Clifford Davis)	04/13/1999	Whitemarsh Memorial Park, Ambler, PA
Ross, Don (Donald Raymond)	03/28/1996	Resurrection Cemetery, Montebello, CA
Ross, Ernie (Ernest Bertram)	03/28/1950	Necropolis Cemetery, Toronto, Ontario, Canada
Ross, George Sidney	04/22/1935	Holy Trinity Cemetery, North Amityville, NY

Name	DOD	Cemetery, City, State
Rosso, Francis James	01/26/1980	St. Thomas Cemetery, West Springfield, MA
Roth, Braggo (Robert Frank)	09/11/1936	St. Mary's Cemetery, Burlington, WI
Roth, Frank (Francis Charles)	03/27/1955	St. Charles Cemetery, Burlington, WI
Rothel, Bob (Robert Burton)	03/21/1984	York Chapel Cemetery, Bellevue, OH
Rothrock, Jack (John Houston)	02/02/1980	Montecito Memorial Park, Colton, CA
Roush, Edd J.	03/21/1988	Montgomery Cemetery, Oakland City, IN
Rowan, Jack (John Albert)	09/29/1966	Dayton Memorial Park, Dayton, OH
Rowe, Dave (David Elwood)	12/09/1930	Forest Lawn Memorial Park, Glendale, CA
Rowe, Harland Stimson	05/26/1969	Riverside Cemetery, Springvale, ME
Rowe, jack (John Charles)	04/26/1911	Bellefontaine Cemetery, St. Louis, MO
Rowe, Schoolboy (Lynwood Thomas)	01/08/1961	Arlington Memorial Cemetery, El Dorado, AR
Rowell, Bama (Carvel William)	08/16/1993	New Home Missionary Baptist Church Cemetery, Citronelle, AL
Rowland, Chuck (Charlie Leland)	01/21/1992	Greenmount Cemetery, Raleigh, NC
Rowland, Pants (Clarence Henry) *manager*	05/17/1969	Holy Sepulchre Cemetery, Worth, IL
Roxburgh, Jim (James A.)	02/21/1934	Holy Cross Cemetery, Colma, CA
Roy, Charlie (Charles Robert)	02/10/1950	Gibson Mission Cemetery, Blackfoot, ID
Roy, Emil Arthur	01/05/1997	Cremated, Crystal River, FL
Roy, Luther Franklin	07/24/1963	Rest Lawn Memorial Park, Grand Rapids, MI
Rubeling, Al (Albert William)	01/28/1988	Parkwood Cemetery, Baltimore, MD
Ruble, Art (William Arthur)	11/01/1983	Logan Chapel United Methodist Church Cemetery, Maryville, TN
Rucker, Johnny (John Joel)	08/07/1985	Rucker Family Cemetery, Crabapple, GA
Rucker, Nap (George)	12/19/1970	Presbyterian Cemetery, Roswell, GA
Rudderham, John Edmund	04/03/1942	St. Mary's Cemetery, Randolph, MA
Rudolph, Dick (Richard)	10/20/1949	Woodlawn Cemetery, Bronx, NY
Rudolph, Don (Frederick Donald)	09/12/1968	Forest Lawn Memorial Park-Hollywood Hills, Los Angeles, CA
Rudolph, Dutch (John Herman)	04/17/1967	Mount Airy Cemetery, Natrona Heights, PA
Rudolph, Ernie (Ernest William)	01/13/2003	Riverside Cemetery, Black River Falls, WI
Ruel, Muddy (Herold Dominic)	11/13/1963	Alta Mesa Memorial Park, Palo Alto, CA
Ruether, Dutch (Walter Henry)	05/16/1970	Cremated, Greenwood Memorial Cemetery, Phoenix, AZ. Ashes given to family.
Ruffing, Red (Charles Herbert)	02/17/1986	Hillcrest Cemetery, Bedford Heights, OH
Ruiz, Chico (Hiraldo)	02/09/1972	El Camino Memorial Park, La Jolla, CA
Rullo, Joe (Joseph Vincent)	10/28/1969	Holy Cross Cemetery, Yeadon, PA
Rumler, William George	05/26/1966	Blue Mound Cemetery, Milford, NE
Runnels, Pete (James Edward)	05/20/1991	Forest Park (East) Cemetery, League City, TX
Rush, Andy (Jesse Howard)	03/16/1969	Washington Colony Cemetery, Fresno, CA
Rusie, Amos Wilson	12/06/1942	Acacia Memorial Park, Seattle, WA
Russ, John	01/18/1912	St. Michael's Cemetery, Louisville, KY
Russell, Allen E.	10/20/1972	Loudon Park Cemetery, Baltimore, MD
Russell, Harvey Holmes	01/08/1980	Ivy Hill Cemetery, Upperville, VA
Russell, Jack Erwin	11/03/1990	Sylvan Abbey Memorial Park, Clearwater, FL
Russell, Jim (James William)	11/24/1987	Mount Auburn Cemetery, Fayette City, PA
Russell, John Albert	11/20/1930	Cypress Lawn Memorial Park, Colma, CA

Name	DOD	Cemetery, City, State
Russell, Lefty (Clarence Dickson)	01/22/1962	Dulaney Valley Memorial Gardens, Timonium, MD
Russell, Lloyd Opal	05/24/1968	Oakwood Cemetery, Waco, TX
Russell, Reb (Ewell Albert)	09/30/1973	St. Joseph's Cemetery, Indianapolis, IN
Russell, Rip (Glen David)	09/26/1976	Holy Cross Cemetery, Culver City, CA
Ruszkowski, Hank (Henry Alexander)	05/31/2000	Calvary Cemetery, Cleveland, OH
Ruth, Babe (George Herman)	08/16/1948	Gate of Heaven Cemetery, Hawthorne, NY
Rutherford, Jim (James Hollis)	09/18/1956	Lakewood Park Cemetery, Rocky River, OH
Ryan, Blondy (John Collins)	11/28/1959	St. Joseph's Cemetery, Lynn, MA
Ryan, Buddy (John Budd)	07/09/1956	St. Mary's Catholic Cemetery, Sacramento, CA
Ryan, Connie (Cornelius Joseph)	01/03/1996	Metairie Cemetery, Metairie, LA
Ryan, Cyclone (Daniel R.)	01/30/1917	Holy Cross Cemetery, Malden, MA
Ryan, Jack	10/16/1949	Evergreen Cemetery, Gulfport, MS
Ryan, Jack (John Bernard)	08/21/1952	St. James Cemetery, Haverhill, MA
Ryan, Jimmy (James Edward)	10/26/1923	Calvary Cemetery, Evanston, IL
Ryan, Johnny (John Joseph)	03/22/1902	New Cathedral Cemetery, Philadelphia, PA
Ryan, Rosy (Wilfred Patrick Dolan)	12/10/1980	St. John's Cemetery, Worcester, MA
Ryba, Mike (Dominic Joseph)	12/13/1971	Resurrection Cemetery, Springfield, MO
Ryder, Tom (Thomas)	07/18/1935	Mount Olivet Cemetery, Dubuque, IA
Sabo, Alex (Alexander)	01/03/2001	Lake Nelson Cemetery, Piscataway, NJ
Sacka, Frank	12/07/1994	Michigan Memorial Park, Flat Rock, MI
Sadowski, Ed (Edward Roman)	11/06/1993	Holy Sepulchre Cemetery, Orange, CA
Sadowski, Ted (Theodore)	07/18/1993	All Saints Church Cemetery, Pittsburgh, PA
Sage, Harry	05/27/1947	Calvary Cemetery, Rock Island, IL
Saier, Vic (Victor Sylvester)	05/14/1967	Mount Hope Cemetery, Lansing, MI
Sale, Freddy (Frederick Link)	05/27/1956	Cremated, Hermosa Beach, CA
Sales, Ed (Edward A.)	08/10/1912	Mount Calvary Cemetery, Harrisburg, PA
Salisbury, Harry (Henry H.)	03/29/1933	Mount Hope Cemetery, Chicago, IL
Salisbury, Solly (William Ansel)	01/17/1952	Odd Fellows Cemetery, The Dalles, OR
Salkeld, Bill (William Franklin)	04/22/1967	Forest Lawn Memorial Park-Hollywood Hills, Los Angeles, CA
Sallee, Slim (Harry Franklin)	03/22/1950	Confidence Cemetery, Georgetown, OH
Salmon, Roger Elliott	06/17/1974	Grove Cemetery, Belfast, ME
Saltzgaver, Jack (Otto Hamlin)	02/01/1978	Greenglade Cemetery, Farmington, IA
Salve, Gus (Augustus William)	03/29/1971	Thomas Cemetery, Swansea, MA
Salveson, Jack (John Theodore)	12/28/1974	Loma Vista Memorial Park, Fullerton, CA
Salvo, Manny (Manuel)	02/07/1997	St. Mary's Catholic Cemetery, Sacramento, CA
Samuels, Ike (Samuel Earl)	01/01/1942	Rosemont Park Cemetery, Chicago, IL
Samuels, Joe (Joseph Jonas)	10/28/1996	Cathedral Cemetery, Scranton, PA
Sand, Heinie (John Henry)	11/03/1958	Cremated, San Francisco, CA
Sandberg, Gus (Gustave E.)	02/03/1930	Cremated, Los Angeles, CA
Sanders, Ben (Alexander Bennett)	08/29/1930	Sudley United Methodist Cemetery, Catharpin, VA
Sanders, Ray (Raymond Floyd)	10/28/1983	Mount Hope Cemetery, St. Louis, MO
Sanders, Roy Garvin	01/17/1950	Calvary Cemetery, Kansas City, MO
Sanders, Roy Lee	07/08/1963	Louisville Memorial Gardens, Louisville, KY
Sanders, War (Warren Williams)	08/03/1962	Forest Hills Cemetery, Chattanooga, TN

Name	DOD	Cemetery, City, State
Sanicki, Ed (Edward Robert)	07/06/1998	Holy Cross Burial Park, Jamesburg, NJ
Santry, Edward	03/06/1899	Calvary Cemetery, Evanston, IL
Sargent, Joe (Joseph Alexander)	07/05/1950	Holy Sepulchre Cemetery, Rochester, NY
Sauer, Ed (Edward)	07/01/1988	Cremated, Thousand Oaks, CA
Sauer, Hank (Henry John)	08/24/2001	Holy Cross Cemetery, Colma, CA
Saunders, Rusty (Russell Collier)	11/24/1967	Greenwood Cemetery, Trenton, NJ
Sauter, Al (Albert C.)	07/15/1928	Westminster Cemetery, Bala Cynwyd, PA
Savage, Don (Donald Anthony)	12/25/1961	Mt. Olivet Cemetery, Bloomfield, NJ
Savage, Jimmie (James H.)	06/26/1940	St. Thomas Cemetery, Southington, CT
Savidge, Don (Donald Snyder)	03/22/1983	Body donated to UCLA Medical School, Los Angeles, CA
Savidge, Ralph Austin	07/22/1959	Pine Grove Cemetery, Berwick, PA
Sawatski, Carl Ernest	11/24/1991	Pine Crest Memorial Park, Alexander, AR
Sawyer, Carl Everett	01/17/1957	Forest Lawn Memorial Park, Glendale, CA
Sawyer, Eddie (Edwin Milby) manager	09/22/1997	Body donated to Pennsylvania Medical Society, Philadelphia, PA
Sawyer, Will (Willard Newton)	01/05/1936	Standing Rock Cemetery, Kent, OH
Sax, Oliver (Erik Oliver)	03/21/1982	Arlington Cemetery, Kearney, NJ
Say, Jimmy (James I.)	06/23/1894	Loudon Park Cemetery, Baltimore, MD
Say, Lou (Louis I.)	06/05/1930	Harford County Home Cemetery, Bel Air, MD
Sayles, Bill (William Nisbeth)	11/20/1996	Cremated, Lincoln City, OR
Saylor, Phil (Philip Andrew)	07/23/1937	Fairview Cemetery, West Alexandria, OH
Scala, Jerry (Gerard Michael)	12/14/1993	Lorraine Park Cemetery, Baltimore, MD
Scalzi, John Anthony	09/27/1962	St. John's Cemetery, Darien, CT
Scalzi, Skeeter (Frank John)	08/25/1984	Upland Cemetery, Yorkville, OH
Scanlan, Doc (William Dennis)	05/29/1949	St. Joseph's Cemetery, Stockbridge, MA
Scanlan, Frank Aloysius	04/09/1969	St. John's Cemetery, Middle Village, Queens, NY
Scanlan, Mort (Mortimer J.)	12/29/1928	Calvary Cemetery, Evanston, IL
Scanlon, Michael B. manager	01/18/1929	Mount Olivet Cemetery, Washington, DC
Scantlebury, Pat (Patricio Athelstan)	05/24/1991	Glendale Cemetery, Bloomfield, NJ
Scarborough, Ray (Rae Wilson)	07/01/1982	Martin-Price Cemetery, Mount Olive, NC
Scarritt, Russ (Stephen Russell Mallory)	12/04/1994	St. John's Cemetery, Pensacola, FL
Scarsella, Les (Leslie George)	12/16/1958	Oakmont Memorial Park, Lafayette, CA
Schacht, Al (Alexander)	07/14/1984	New North Cemetery, Woodbury, CT. Originally intered at Beth El Cemetery, Waterbury, CT.
Schacht, Sid (Sidney)	03/30/1991	Cedar Park Cemetery, Paramus, NJ
Schaefer, Germany (Herman A.)	05/16/1919	St. Boniface Cemetery, Chicago, IL
Schafer, Harry C.	02/28/1935	Fernwood Cemetery, Lansdowne, PA
Schalk, Ray (Raymond William)	05/19/1970	Evergreen Cemetery, Evergreen Park, IL
Schaller, Biff (Walter)	10/09/1939	Mountain View Cemetery, Oakland, CA
Schang, Bobby (Robert Martin)	08/29/1966	St. Mary's Catholic Cemetery, Sacramento, CA
Schang, Wally (Walter Henry)	03/06/1965	Dixon Cemetery, Dixon, MO
Schanz, Charley (Charles Murrell)	05/28/1992	East Lawn Memorial Park, Sacramento, CA
Schardt, Bill (Wilburt)	07/20/1964	Lutheran Cemetery, Cleveland, OH
Scharein, Art (Arthur Otto)	07/02/1969	Sunset Memorial Park, San Antonio, TX

Name	DOD	Cemetery, City, State
Scharein, George Albert	12/23/1981	Fairlawn Cemetery, Decatur, IL
Scharf, Nick (Edward T.)	03/12/1937	New Cathedral Cemetery, Baltimore, MD
Schauer, Rube (Alexander John)	04/15/1957	St. Mary's Cemetery, Minneapolis, MN
Scheer, Al (Allen G.)	05/06/1959	Mt. Hope Cemetery, Logansport, IN
Scheer, Heinie (Henry William)	03/21/1976	Congregation Sinai Memorial Park, Allingtown, CT
Scheeren, Fritz (Frederick)	06/17/1973	North Forest Cemetery, Marienville, PA
Scheetz, Owen Franklin	09/28/1994	Glen Rest Memorial Estate, Reynoldsburg, OH
Scheffing, Bob (Robert Boden)	10/26/1985	St. Francis Catholic Cemetery, Phoenix, AZ
Scheibeck, Frank S.	10/22/1956	Mount Elliott Cemetery, Detroit, MI
Scheible, John G.	08/09/1897	Oak Hill Cemetery, Youngstown, OH
Schell, Danny (Clyde Daniel)	05/11/1972	West Deerfield Cemetery, West Deerfield, MI
Schelle, Jim (Gerard Anthony)	05/04/1990	Massachusetts National Cemetery, Bourne, MA
Schellhase, Al (Albert Herman)	01/03/1919	Oak Hill Cemetery, Evansville, IN
Schemanske, Fred (Frederick George)	02/18/1960	Woodmere Cemetery, Detroit, MI
Schemer, Mike (Michael)	04/22/1983	Southern Memorial Park, Miami, FL
Schenck, Bill (William G.)	01/29/1934	Cypress Hills Cemetery, Brooklyn, NY
Scheneberg, John Bluford	09/26/1950	Highland Cemetery, Huntington, WV
Schenz, Hank (Henry Leonard)	05/12/1988	Green Mound Cemetery, New Richmond, OH
Schepner, Joe (Joseph Maurice)	07/25/1959	Pine Crest Cemetery, Mobile, AL
Schesler, Dutch (Charles)	11/19/1953	Harrisburg Cemetery, Harrisburg, PA
Schettler, Lou (Louis Martin)	05/01/1960	Forest Lawn Memorial Park, Youngstown, OH
Schiappacasse, Lou (Louis Joseph)	09/20/1910	St. Thomas Catholic Cemetery, Ann Arbor, MI
Schillings, Red (Elbert Isaiah)	01/07/1954	Memorial Park Cemetery, Oklahoma City, OK
Schindler, Bill (Williams Gibbons)	02/06/1979	Mount Hope Cemetery, Perryville, MO
Schirick, Dutch (Harry Ernest)	11/12/1968	Mount Marion Cemetery, Mount Marion, NY
Schlafly, Larry (Harry Linton)	06/27/1919	Grandview Cemetery, Strasburg, OH
Schlei, Admiral (George Henry)	01/24/1958	Ridgelawn Memorial Park, Huntington, WV
Schliebner, Dutch (Frederick Paul)	04/15/1975	Cremated. Remains scattered over Lake Acacia in Toledo Memorial Park, Sylvania, OH
Schlitzer, Biff (Victor Joseph)	01/04/1948	Forest Hill Cemetery, Utica, NY
Schmandt, Ray (Raymond Henry)	02/02/1969	Calvary Cemetery, St. Louis, MO
Schmees, George Edward	10/30/1998	Oak Hill Memorial Park, San Jose, CA
Schmeltz, Gus (Gustavius Heinrich) *manager*	10/13/1925	Green Lawn Cemetery, Columbus, OH
Schmidt, Boss (Charles)	11/14/1932	St. Mary's Catholic Church Cemetery, Altus, AR
Schmidt, Butch (Charles John)	09/04/1952	Druid Ridge Cemetery, Pikesville, MD
Schmidt, Henry Martin	04/23/1926	Spring Hill Cemetery, Nashville, TN
Schmidt, Walter Joseph	07/04/1973	St. Stanislaus Catholic Cemetery, Modesto, CA
Schmit, Crazy (Frederick M.)	10/05/1940	Forest Home Cemetery (formerly Waldheim Cemetery), Forest Park, IL.
Schmutz, Charlie (Charles Otto)	06/27/1962	Cremated, Seattle, WA
Schneiberg, Frank Frederick	05/18/1948	Wanderer's Rest Cemetery, Milwaukee, WI

Name	DOD	Cemetery, City, State
Schneider, Pete (Peter Joseph)	06/01/1957	Inglewood Park Cemetery, Inglewood, CA
Schnell, Karl Otto	05/31/1992	Alta Mesa Memorial Park, Palo Alto, CA. Cremated.
Schoeneck, Jumbo (Lewis W.)	01/20/1930	Mount Emblem Cemetery, Elmhurst, IL
Schomberg, Otto H.	05/03/1927	Graceland Cemetery, Milwaukee, WI. Originally intered at Fairview Mausoleum, Milwaukee. Mausoleum removed in 1997.
Schorr, Ed (Edward Walter)	09/12/1969	Holy Cross Cemetery, Mays Landing, NJ
Schott, Gene (Arthur Eugene)	11/16/1992	Garden of Memories Cemetery, Tampa, FL
Schreckengost, Ossee Freeman	07/09/1914	Kittanning Cemetery, Kittanning, PA
Schreiber, Barney (David Henry)	10/06/1964	Floral Hills Memory Gardens, Chillicothe, OH
Schreiber, Hank (Henry Walter)	02/23/1968	Holy Cross Cemetery, Indianapolis, IN
Schreiber, Paul Frederick	01/28/1982	Riverside Memorial Park, Jacksonville, FL
Schuble, Heinie (Henry George)	10/02/1990	Forest Park (Lawndale) Cemetery, Houston, TX
Schulmerich, Wes (Edward Wesley)	06/26/1985	Valley Memorial Park, Hillsboro, OR
Schulte, Fred William	05/20/1983	Calvary Cemetery, St. Louis, MO
Schulte, Ham (Herman Joseph)	12/21/1993	St. Peter's Catholic Cemetery, St. Charles, MO
Schulte, Johnny (John Clement)	06/28/1978	Calvary Cemetery, St. Louis, MO
Schulte, Len (Leonard Bernard)	05/06/1986	Glen Haven Memorial Park, Winter Park, FL
Schulte, Wildfire (John Herman Frank)	08/17/1975	Resurrection Cemetery, Mount Clemens, MI
Schultz, Bob (Robert Duffy)	03/31/1979	Nashville National Cemetery, Madison, TN
Schultz, Joe (Joseph Charles, Jr.)	01/10/1996	Calvary Cemetery, St. Louis, MO
Schultz, Joe (Joseph Charles, Sr.)	04/13/1941	Calvary Cemetery, St. Louis, MO
Schultz, Webb (Wilbert Carl)	07/26/1986	Spring Grove Cemetery, Delavan, WI
Schulz, Al (Albert Christopher)	12/13/1931	Toledo Memorial Park, Sylvania, OH
Schulz, Walt (Walter Frederick)	02/27/1928	Sunset Memorial Park, Affton, MO
Schulze, John H.	05/19/1941	Calvary Cemetery, St. Louis, MO
Schumacher, Hal (Harold Henry)	04/21/1993	St. Joseph's Cemetery, Dolgeville, NY
Schumann, Hack (Carl J.)	03/25/1946	Mt. Calvary Cemetery, Cheektowaga, NY
Schupp, Ferdie (Ferdinand Maurice)	12/16/1971	Calvary Cemetery, Los Angeles, CA
Schuster, Bill (William Charles)	06/28/1987	Live Oak Memorial Park, Monrovia, CA
Schwartz, Bill (William Charles)	08/29/1961	Woodlawn Memorial Park, Nashville, TN
Schwartz, Pop (William August)	12/22/1940	Evergreen Cemetery, Southgate, KY
Schweitzer, Al (Albert Casper)	01/27/1969	Cedar Hill Cemetery, Newark, OH
Schwenck, Rudy (Rudolph Christian)	11/27/1941	Cave Hill Cemetery, Louisville, KY
Schwenk, Hal (Harold Edward)	09/03/1955	Memorial Park Cemetery, Sedalia, MO
Schwert, Pi (Pius Louis)	03/11/1941	Forest Avenue Cemetery, Angola, NY
Scott, Ed (Phillip Edwin)	11/01/1933	Toledo Memorial Park, Sylvania, OH
Scott, Everett (Lewis Everett)	11/02/1960	Elm Grove Cemetery, Bluffton, IN
Scott, George Wilson	12/03/1962	Willamette National Cemetery, Portland, OR
Scott, Jack (John William)	11/30/1959	Fairview Cemetery, Warrenton, NC
Scott, Jim (James Walter)	05/12/1972	Woodlawn Memorial Gardens, St. Petersburg, FL

Name	DOD	Cemetery, City, State
Scott, Jim (James)	04/07/1957	Inglewood Park Cemetery, Inglewood, CA
Scott, Lefty (Marshall)	03/03/1964	Glenwood Cemetery, Groveton, TX
Scott, LeGrant Edward	11/12/1993	Elmwood Cemetery, Birmingham, AL
Scott, Milt (Milton Parker)	11/03/1938	Loudon Park Cemetery, Baltimore, MD
Scott, Pete (Floyd John)	05/03/1953	Golden Gate National Cemetery, San Bruno, CA
Seaton, Tom (Thomas Gordon)	04/10/1940	Evergreen Cemetery, El Paso, TX
Seats, Tom (Thomas Edward)	05/10/1992	Woodlawn Memorial Park, Colma, CA
Sebring, Jimmy (James D.)	12/22/1909	Wildwood Cemetery, Williamsport, PA
Sechrist, Doc (Theodore O'Hara)	04/02/1950	Somerset Cemetery, Somerset, KY
Secory, Frank Edward	04/07/1995	Cremated, Port Huron, MI
Seeds, Bob (Ira Robert)	10/28/1993	Shamrock Cemetery, Shamrock, TX
Seerey, Pat (James Patrick)	04/28/1986	Calvary Cemetery, St. Louis, MO
Seery, Emmett (John Emmett)	08/07/1930	All Saints Cemetery, Jensen Beach, FL
Seibold, Socks (Harry)	09/21/1965	Beverly National Cemetery, Beverly, NJ
Selbach, Kip (Albert Karl)	02/17/1956	Green Lawn Cemetery, Columbus, OH
Selee, Frank Gibson *manager*	07/05/1909	Wyoming Cemetery, Melrose, MA
Selkirk, George Alexander	01/19/1987	Siloam United Methodist Church Cemetery, Harrisonville, PA
Sell, Epp (Lester Elwood)	02/19/1961	Forest Hills Memorial Park, Reiffton, PA
Sellers, Rube (Oliver)	01/14/1952	Jefferson Memorial Park, Pleasant Hills, PA
Sellman, Frank (Charles Francis)	05/06/1907	Greenmount Cemetery, Baltimore, MD
Selph, Carey Isom	02/24/1976	Pleasant Hill Cemetery, Donaldson, AR
Seminick, Andrew Wasil	02/22/2004	Melbourne Cemetery, Melbourne, FL
Sensenderfer, Count (John Phillips Jenkins)	05/03/1903	West Laurel Hill Cemetery, Bala Cynwyd, PA
Sentell, Paul (Leopold Theodore)	04/27/1923	St. Joseph Cemetery #3, New Orleans, LA
Senteney, Steve (Stephen Leonard)	06/18/1989	Sylvan Cemetery, Citrus Heights, CA
Serad, Will (William I.)	11/01/1925	Chester Rural Cemetery, Chester, PA
Serena, Bill (William Robert)	04/17/1996	Cremated, Hayward, CA
Sessi, Walter Anthony	04/18/1998	Mobile Memorial Gardens, Mobile, AL
Settlemire, Merle (Edgar Merle)	06/12/1988	Mount Tabor Cemetery, Gutman, OH
Severeid, Hank (Henry Levai)	12/17/1968	Sunset Memorial Park, San Antonio, TX
Seward, Ed (Edward William)	07/30/1947	West Park Cemetery, Cleveland, OH
Sewell, Joe (Joseph Wheeler)	03/06/1990	Tuscaloosa Memorial Park, Tuscaloosa, AL
Sewell, Luke (James Luther)	05/14/1987	Rose Hill Burial Park, Fairlawn, OH
Sewell, Rip (Truett Banks)	09/03/1989	Oaklawn Cemetery, Plant City, FL
Sewell, Tommy (Thomas Wesley)	07/30/1956	Greenwood Cemetery, Montgomery, AL
Sexton, Frank Joseph	01/04/1938	St. Patrick's Cemetery, Brockton, MA
Sexton, Tom (Thomas William)	02/08/1934	Calvary Cemetery, Rock Island, IL
Seybold, Socks (Ralph Orlando)	12/22/1921	Brush Creek Cemetery, Irwin, PA
Seymour, James Bentley	09/20/1919	Albany Rural Cemetery, Albany, NY
Shafer, Jake (John W.)	11/21/1926	Highland Cemetery, Lock Haven, PA
Shafer, Orator (George W.)	01/21/1922	West Laurel Hill Cemetery, Bala Cynwyd, PA
Shafer, Tilly (Arthur Joseph)	01/10/1962	Holy Cross Cemetery, Culver City, CA
Shallix, Gus (August)	10/28/1937	St. Joseph's Old Cemetery, Cincinnati, OH
Shaner, Wally (Walter Dedaker)	11/13/1992	Paradise Memorial Gardens, Las Vegas, NV

Name	DOD	Cemetery, City, State
Shanks, Howie (Howard Samuel)	07/30/1941	Old Monaca Cemetery, Monaca, PA. (aka Union Cemetery)
Shanley, Doc (Harry Root)	12/13/1934	Royal Palm Cemetery, St. Petersburg, FL
Shanley, James H.	11/04/1904	Calvary Cemetery, Woodside, Queens, NY
Shannabrook, Warren H.	03/10/1964	Massillon Cemetery, Massillon, OH
Shanner, Bill (Wilfred William)	12/18/1986	Sunset Memorial Gardens, Evansville, IN
Shannon, Dan (Daniel Webster)	10/24/1913	St. Michael's Cemetery, Stratford, CT
Shannon, Frank (John Francis)	02/27/1934	Mount Hope Cemetery, Mattapan, MA
Shannon, Owen Dennis Ignatius	04/10/1918	Holy Sepulchre Cemetery, Omaha, NE
Shannon, Red (Maurice Joseph)	04/12/1970	Holy Cross Cemetery, North Arlington, NJ
Shannon, Spike (William Porter)	05/16/1940	St. Mary's Cemetery, Minneapolis, MN
Shantz, Billy (Wilmer Ebert)	12/13/1993	Cremated, Fort Lauderdale, FL
Sharman, Ralph Edward	05/24/1918	Spring Grove Cemetery, Cincinnati, OH
Sharpe, Bud (Bayard Heston)	05/31/1916	Greenmount Cemetery, West Chester, PA
Sharrott, George Oscar	01/06/1932	Silver Mount Cemetery, Staten Island, NY
Sharrott, Jack (John Henry)	12/31/1927	Forest Lawn Memorial Park, Glendale, CA. Cremated.
Sharsig, Bill (William A.) *manager*	02/01/1902	Mt. Vernon Cemetery, Philadelphia, PA
Shaute, Joe (Joseph Benjamin)	02/21/1970	St. Catherine's Cemetery, Moscow, PA
Shaw, Al (Albert Simpson)	12/30/1974	Greasy Point Cemetery, Rardin, IL
Shaw, Al (Alfred)	03/25/1958	Union Cemetery, Uhrichsville, OH
Shaw, Ben (Benjamin Nathaniel)	03/16/1959	Aurora Cemetery, Aurora, OH
Shaw, Dupee (Frederick Lander)	01/12/1938	Glenwood Cemetery, Everett, MA
Shaw, Hunky (Royal N.)	07/03/1969	Terrace Heights Memorial Park, Yakima, WA
Shaw, James Aloysius	01/27/1962	St. Mary's Cemetery, Alexandria, VA
Shawkey, Bob (James Robert)	12/31/1980	Oakwood-Morningside Cemetery, Syracuse, NY
Shay, Danny (Daniel C.)	12/01/1927	Mount St. Mary's Cemetery, Kansas City, MO
Shay, Marty (Arthur Joseph)	02/20/1951	Mount Calvary Cemetery, Roslindale, MA
Shea, Gerry (Gerald J.)	05/03/1964	Calvary Cemetery, St. Louis, MO
Shea, John Michael Joseph	11/30/1956	Holy Cross Cemetery, Malden, MA
Shea, Merv (Mervyn David John)	01/27/1953	St. Mary's Catholic Cemetery, Sacramento, CA
Shea, Nap (John Edward)	07/08/1968	St. Mary's Cemetery, Ware, MA
Shea, Red (Patrick Henry)	11/17/1981	St. Thomas the Apostle Cemetery, Palmer, MA
Shea, Spec (Francis Joseph)	07/19/2002	St. James Cemetery, Naugatuck, CT
Shealy, Al (Albert Berly)	03/07/1967	Grand View Memorial Park, Rock Hill, SC
Shean, Dave (David William)	05/22/1963	St. Paul's Cemetery, Arlington, MA
Shearer, Ray Solomon	02/21/1982	Salem Union Cemetery, Jacobus, PA
Shearon, John M.	02/01/1923	St. Bernard's Cemetery, Bradford, PA
Shears, George Penfield	11/12/1978	Sunrise Ranch Cemetery, Loveland, CO. Cremated.
Sheckard, Jimmy (Samuel James Tilden)	01/15/1947	Laurel Hill Memorial Gardens, Columbia, PA
Sheehan, Biff (Timothy James)	10/21/1923	St. Patrick's Cemetery, Hartford, CT
Sheehan, Jack (John Thomas)	05/29/1987	Royal Palm Memorial Gardens, West Palm Beach, FL

Name	DOD	Cemetery, City, State
Sheehan, Jim (James Thomas)	12/02/2003	All Saints Cemetery, North Haven, CT
Sheely, Bud (Hollis Kimball)	10/17/1985	Cremated, Sacramento, CA
Sheely, Earl Homer	09/16/1952	East Lawn Memorial Park, Sacramento, CA
Sheerin, Chuck (Charles Joseph)	09/27/1986	Cemetery of Holy Rood, Westbury, NY
Shellenback, Frank Victor	08/17/1969	Newton Cemetery, Newton, MA
Shelley, Hugh (Hubert Leneirre)	06/16/1978	Magnolia Cemetery, Beaumont, TX
Shelton, Skeeter (Andrew Kemper)	01/09/1954	Spring Hill Cemetery, Huntington, WV
Shemo, Steve (Stephen Michael)	04/13/1992	Wilson Primitive Baptist Church Cemetery, Walnut Cove, NC
Shepard, Jack Leroy	12/31/1994	Cremated, Palo Alto, CA
Shepardson, Ray (Raymond Francis)	11/08/1975	St. Mary's Church Cemetery, Little Falls, NY
Sherdel, Bill (William Henry)	11/14/1968	Annunciation Church Cemetery, McSherrystown, PA
Sherid, Roy (Royden Richard)	02/28/1982	Oak Grove Cemetery, Parker Ford, PA
Sheridan, Red (Eugene Anthony)	11/25/1975	Long Island National Cemetery, Farmingdale, NY
Sherling, Ed (Edward Creech)	11/16/1965	Meadowland Memorial Park, Enterprise, AL
Sherlock, Monk (John Clinton)	11/26/1985	Forest Lawn Cemetery, Buffalo, NY
Sherlock, Vince (Vincent Thomas)	05/11/1997	Mt. Olivet Cemetery, Tonawanda, NY
Sherman, Babe (Lester Daniel)	09/16/1955	White Chapel Memorial Cemetery, Troy, MI
Sherman, Joe (Joel Powers)	12/21/1987	Riverbend Cemetery, Westerly, RI
Sherry, Fred Peter	07/27/1975	St. John's Cemetery, Honesdale, PA
Shetrone, Barry Steven	07/18/2001	Glen Haven Memorial Gardens, Glen Burnie, MD
Shettsline, Bill (William Joseph) manager	02/22/1933	Chelten Hills Cemetery, Philadelphia, PA
Shetzline, John Henry	12/15/1892	Philadelphia Memorial Park, Frazer, PA. Originally intered at American Mechanics Cemetery, Philadelphia. Cemetery removed in 1951.
Shevlin, Jimmy (James Cornelius)	10/30/1974	Our Lady Queen of Heaven Cemetery, North Lauderdale, FL
Shields, Ben (Benjamin Cowen)	01/24/1982	Hopewell Presbyterian Church Cemetery, Huntersville, NC
Shields, Charlie (Charles Jessamine)	08/27/1953	Elmwood Cemetery, Memphis, TN
Shields, Pete (Francis Leroy)	02/11/1961	Greenwood Cemetery, Jackson, MS
Shilling, Jim (James Robert)	09/12/1986	Memorial Park Cemetery, Tulsa, OK
Shinault, Ginger (Enoch Erskine)	12/29/1930	Forest Hill Cemetery-Midtown, Memphis, TN
Shindle, Billy (William)	06/03/1936	Union Cemetery, Gloucester, NJ
Shinners, Ralph Peter	07/23/1962	Holy Cross Cemetery, Milwaukee, WI
Shipke, Bill (William Martin)	09/10/1940	Westlawn Cemetery, Omaha, NE
Shires, Art (Charles Arthur)	07/13/1967	Italy Cemetery, Italy, TX
Shirey, Duke (Clair Lee)	09/01/1962	Rose Hill Cemetery, Hagerstown, MD
Shirley, Mule (Ernest Raeford)	08/03/1955	Willow Dale Cemetery, Goldsboro, NC
Shirley, Tex (Alvis Newman)	11/07/1993	Red Oak Cemetery, Red Oak, TX
Shiver, Ivey Merwin	08/31/1972	Greenwich Cemetery, Savannah, GA

Name	DOD	Cemetery, City, State
Shoch, George Quintus	09/30/1937	East Cedar Hill Cemetery, Philadelphia, PA
Shocker, Urban James	09/09/1928	Calvary Cemetery, St. Louis, MO
Shoemaker, Charlie (Charles Landis)	05/31/1990	Aulenbach Cemetery, Mt. Penn, PA
Shoffner, Milt (Milburn James)	01/19/1978	Madison Memorial Cemetery, Madison, OH
Shofner, Strick (Frank Strickland)	10/10/1998	Crawford Cemetery, Crawford, TX
Shook, Ray (Raymond Curtis)	09/16/1970	Riverview Cemetery, South Bend, IN
Shore, Ernie (Ernest Grady)	09/24/1980	Forsyth Memorial Park Cemetery, Winston-Salem, NC
Shores, Bill (William David)	02/19/1984	Lexington Cemetery, Lexington, OK
Short, Chris (Christopher Joseph)	08/01/1991	Union Cemetery, Georgetown, DE
Shorten, Chick (Charles Henry)	10/23/1965	Abington Hills Cemetery, Clarks Summit, PA
Shoun, Clyde Mitchell	03/20/1968	Sunset Memorial Park, Mountain City, TN
Shoupe, John F.	02/13/1920	Linden Grove Cemetery, Covington, KY
Shovlin, John Joseph	02/16/1976	St. Ann's Cemetery, Freeland, PA
Show, Eric Vaughn	03/16/1994	Olivewood Cemetery, Riverside, CA
Shreve, Lev (Leven Lawrence)	10/18/1942	Cave Hill Cemetery, Louisville, KY
Shriver, Harry Graydon	01/21/1970	Wadestown M.E. Cemetery, Wadestown, WV
Shugart, Frank Harry	09/09/1944	Luthersburg Cemetery, Luthersburg, PA
Shuman, Harry	10/25/1996	Haym Salomon Memorial Park, Frazer, PA
Shupe, Vince (Vincent William)	04/05/1962	Christ Evangelical Lutheran Cemetery (formerly Mapleton Cemetery), Mapleton, OH
Sicking, Ed (Edward Joseph)	08/30/1978	St. Mary's Cemetery, Cincinnati, OH
Siebert, Dick (Richard Walther)	12/09/1978	Lakewood Cemetery, Minneapolis, MN
Siefke, Fred (Frederick Edwin)	04/18/1893	Green-Wood Cemetery, Brooklyn, NY
Siegle, Johnny (John Herbert)	02/12/1968	Oakdale Cemetery, Urbana, OH
Siemer, Oscar Sylvester	12/05/1959	Calvary Cemetery, St. Louis, MO
Siever, Ed (Edward Tilden)	02/05/1920	Woodlawn Cemetery, Detroit, MI
Siffell, Frank	10/26/1909	Greenmount Cemetery, Philadelphia, PA
Sigafoos, Frank (Francis Leonard)	04/12/1968	Cremated, Indianapolis, IN
Siglin, Paddy (Wesley Peter)	08/05/1956	Santa Clara Mission Cemetery, Santa Clara, CA
Sigman, Tripp (Wesley Triplett)	03/08/1971	Westover Memorial Park, Augusta, GA
Signer, Walter Donald Aloysius	07/23/1974	Gate of Heaven Cemetery, Hawthorne, NY
Sigsby, Seth DeWitt	09/15/1953	Vale Cemetery, Schnectady, NY
Silber, Eddie (Edward James)	10/26/1976	Sylvan Abbey Memorial Park, Clearwater, FL
Silch, Ed (Edward)	01/15/1895	Calvary Cemetery, St. Louis, MO
Silva, Danny (Daniel James)	04/04/1974	Mosswood Cemetery, Cotuit, MA
Silvestri, Ken (Kenneth Joseph)	03/31/1992	Mount Carmel Cemetery, Hillside, IL
Simmons, Al (Aloysius Harry)	05/26/1956	Saint Adalbert Cemetery, Milwaukee, WI
Simmons, Hack (George Washington)	04/26/1942	Evergreen Cemetery, Brooklyn, NY
Simmons, Joe (Joseph S.) (buried under birth name: Chabriel)	07/24/1901	New York Bay Cemetery, Jersey City, NJ
Simmons, Pat (Patrick Clement)	07/03/1968	St. Patrick's Cemetery, Watervliet, NY
Simon, Mike (Michael Edward)	06/10/1963	Loma Vista Memorial Park, Fullerton, CA
Simons, Mel (Melbern Ellis)	11/10/1974	Greenlea Cemetery, Fulton, KY
Simpson, Harry Leon	04/03/1979	Dalton Cemetery-West Hill, Dalton, GA

Name	DOD	Cemetery, City, State
Simpson, Steve (Steven Edward)	11/02/1989	Memorial Park Cemetery, Topeka, KS
Sims, Pete (Clarence)	12/02/1968	Forest Rose Cemetery, Lancaster, OH
Sincock, Bert (Herbert Sylvester)	08/01/1946	Lake View Cemetery, Calumet, MI
Siner, Hosea John	06/10/1948	Mt. Zion Cemetery, Sullivan, IN
Singleton, Elmer (Bert Elmer)	01/05/1996	Plain City Cemetery, Plain City, UT
Singleton, John Edward	10/23/1937	Vine Street Hill Cemetery, Cincinnati, OH
Sisiler, George Harold	03/26/1973	Old Meeting House Presbyterian Church Cemetery, Frontenac, MO. Remains moved to presant locaton from Oak Grove Cemetery, St. Louis in 1990. Cremated.
Sisler, Dick (Richard Allan)	11/20/1998	Woodlawn Memorial Park, Nashville, TN
Sitton, Carl Vetter	09/11/1931	Presbyterian Cemetery, Pendleton, SC
Sivess, Pete (Peter)	06/01/2003	St. Peter's Episcopal Church Cemetery, Spottswood, NJ
Sixsmith, Ed (Edward)	12/12/1926	North Cedar Hill Cemetery, Philadelphia, PA
Skaff, Frank (Francis Michael)	04/12/1988	Dulaney Valley Memorial Gardens, Timonium, MD
Skeels, Dave (David)	12/02/1926	St. Mary of the Rosary Cemetery, Chewelah, WA
Sketchley, Bud (Harry Clement)	12/19/1979	Forest Lawn Memorial Park, Glendale, CA
Skinner, Camp (Elisha Harrison)	08/04/1944	Douglasville City Cemetery, Douglasville, GA
Skopec, John S.	10/20/1912	Bohemian Natrional Cemetery, Chicago, IL
Sladen, Art (Arthur W.)	02/28/1914	Edson Cemetery, Lowell, MA
Slagle, Jimmy (James Franklin)	05/10/1956	Oakridge Abbey Cemetery, Chicago, IL
Slagle, Walt (Walter Jennings)	06/14/1974	Rose Hills Memorial Park, Whittier, CA
Slapnicka, Cy (Cyril Charles)	10/20/1979	Cedar Memorial Park Cemetery, Cedar Rapids, IA
Slappey, Jack (John Henry)	06/10/1957	Oakview Cemetery, Albany, GA
Slattery, Jack (John Terrence)	07/17/1949	St. Joseph's Cemetery, West Roxbury, MA
Slattery, Mike (Michael J.)	10/16/1904	Holyhood Cemetery, Brookline, MA
Slattery, Phil (Philip Ryan)	03/02/1968	Westminster Memorial Park, Westminster, CA
Slaughter, Barney (Byron Atkins)	05/17/1961	Glenwood Cemetery, Smyrna, DE
Slauter, Enos Bradsher	08/12/2002	Allensville United Methdist Church Cemetery, Roxboro, NC
Slayton, Steve (Foster Herbert)	12/20/1984	Hope Cemetery, Barre, VT
Sloan, Bruce Adams	09/24/1973	Chapel Hill Memorial Gardens, Oklahoma City, OK
Sloan, Tod (Yale Yeastman)	09/12/1956	Chestnut Hill Memorial Park, Cuyahoga Falls, OH
Sloat, Dwain Clifford	04/18/2003	Union Cemetery, St. Paul, MN
Small, Charlie (Charles Albert)	01/14/1953	Lower Gloucester Cemetery, New Gloucester, ME
Smallwood, Walt (Walter Clayton)	04/29/1967	New Cathedral Cemetery, Baltimore, MD
Smaza, Joe (Joseph Paul)	05/30/1979	St. Hedwig Cemetery, Dearborn Heights, MI
Smiley, Bill (William B.)	07/11/1884	St. Patrick's Catholic Church Cemetery, Baltimore, MD
Smith, Al (Alfred John)	04/28/1977	Cremated, Brownsville, TX

Name	DOD	Cemetery, City, State
Smith, Al (Alfred Kendricks)	08/11/1995	Cremated, San Diego, CA
Smith, Aleck (Alexander Benjamin)	07/09/1919	Woodlawn Cemetery, Bronx, NY
Smith, Art (Arthur Laird)	11/22/1995	Cremated, Norwalk, CT
Smith, Bill (William Garland)	03/30/1997	Resurrection Cemetery, Clinton, MD
Smith, Bob (Robert Ashley)	12/27/1965	Cremated, Grand View Memorial Park, Glendale, CA
Smith, Bob (Robert Eldridge)	07/19/1987	Westview Cemetery, Atlanta, GA
Smith, Carr (Emanuel Carr)	04/14/1989	Cremated, Fort Lauderdale, FL
Smith, Charley (Charles William)	11/29/1994	Cremated, Reno, NV
Smith, Charlie (Charles Edwin)	01/03/1929	St. Joseph's Cemetery, Cleveland, OH
Smith, Chick (John William)	10/11/1935	St. Stephen's Cemetery, Fort Thomas, KY
Smith, Clay Jamieson	03/05/2002	Cambridge Cemetery, Cambridge, KS
Smith, Dave (David Merwin)	04/01/1998	Whiteville Memorial Cemetery, Whiteville, NC
Smith, Doug (Douglass Weldon)	09/18/1973	Highland Cemetery, Millers Falls, MA
Smith, Earl Leonard	03/14/1943	Memorial Burial Park, Wheelersburg, OH
Smith, Earl Sutton	06/08/1963	Little Rock National Cemetery, Little Rock, AR
Smith, Eddie (Edgar)	01/02/1994	Brigadier General William C. Doyle Memorial Cemetery (formerly New Jersey Veterans Memorial Cemetery), Wrightstown, NJ
Smith, Edgar Eugene	11/03/1892	Swan Point Cemetery, Providence, RI
Smith, Elmer Ellsworth	11/05/1945	Union Dale Cemetery, Pittsburgh, PA
Smith, Elmer John	08/03/1984	Cremated. Louisville Crematory, Louisville, KY
Smith, Ernie (Ernest Henry)	04/06/1973	Long Island National Cemetery, Farmingdale, NY
Smith, Frank Elmer	11/03/1952	Minersville Cemetery, Pittsburgh, PA
Smith, Frank L.	10/11/1928	Woodlawn Cemetery, Canadaigua, NY
Smith, Fred (Frederick)	02/04/1964	Inglewood Park Cemetery, Inglewood, CA
Smith, Fred Vincent	05/28/1961	Calvary Cemetery, Cleveland, OH
Smith, Frederick William (buried under birth name: Schmidt)	05/28/1928	Valence Street Cemetery, New Orleans, LA
Smith, George Allen	01/07/1965	Greenwood Union Cemetery, Rye, NY
Smith, George Cornelius	06/15/1987	Lincoln Cemetery, Gulfport, FL
Smith, George Shelby	05/26/1981	Sunset Memorial Park, Chester, VA
Smith, Germany (George J.)	12/01/1927	Calvary Cemetery, Altoona, PA
Smith, Hal (Harold Laverne)	09/27/1992	Parkview Cemetery, Peoria, IL Cremated.
Smith, Happy (Henry Joseph)	02/26/1961	Oak Hill Memorial Park, San Jose, CA
Smith, Harry (Harrison Morton)	07/26/1964	Wykula Cemetery, Nebraska City, NE
Smith, Harry (James Harry)	04/01/1922	Oak Lawn Cemetery, Baltimore, MD
Smith, Harry Thomas	02/17/1933	Lawnside Cemetery, Woodstown, NJ
Smith, Harvey Fetterhoff	11/12/1962	Harrisburg Cemetery, Harrisburg, PA
Smith, Hienie (George Henry)	06/25/1939	Elmlawn Cemetery, Tonawanda, NY
Smith, Jack	05/02/1972	Forest Home Cemetery, Forest Park, IL
Smith, Jake (Jacob John)	11/07/1948	Grandview Cemetery, East McKeesport, PA
Smith, Jimmy (James Lawrence)	01/01/1974	Calvary Cemetery, Pittsburgh, PA
Smith, John J.	01/06/1899	Holy Cross Cemetery, Colma, CA
Smith, John Marshall	05/09/1982	Parklawn Cemetery, Rockville, MD
Smith, Jud (Grant Judson)	12/07/1947	Cremated, Los Angeles, CA

Name	DOD	Cemetery, City, State
Smith, Klondike (Armstrong Frederick)	11/15/1959	Bellevue Cemetery, Lawrence, MA
Smith, Leo (Lionel H.)	08/30/1935	Riverview Cemetery, Trenton, NJ
Smith, Mike (Elwood Hope)	05/31/1981	Riverside Memorial Park, Norfolk, VA
Smith, Milt (Milton)	04/11/1997	Greenwood Memorial Park, San Diego, CA
Smith, Paddy (Lawrence Patrick)	12/02/1990	Gate of Heaven Cemetery, Hawthorne, NY
Smith, Paul Stoner	07/03/1958	Mount Zion Cemetery, Mount Zion, IL
Smith, Phenomenal (John Francis)	04/03/1952	St. Joseph Cemetery, Bedford, NH
Smith, Red (James Carlisle)	10/11/1966	Westview Cemetery, Atlanta, GA
Smith, Red (Marvin Harold)	02/19/1961	Fort Rosecrans National Cemetery, La Jolla, CA
Smith, Red (Richard Paul)	05/08/1978	Calvary Cemetery, Toledo, OH
Smith, Rufus Frazier	08/21/1984	St. Paul United Methodist Church Cemetery, New Ellenton, SC
Smith, Skyrocket (Samuel J.)	04/26/1916	Calvary Cemetery, St. Louis, MO
Smith, Tom (Thomas Edward)	03/02/1929	Mount Calvary Cemetery, Roslindale, MA
Smith, Tony (Anthony)	02/27/1964	Galveston Memorial Park, Hitchcock, TX
Smith, Vinnie (Vincent Ambrose)	12/14/1979	Body donated to Medical College of Virginia, Richmond, VA
Smith, Wib (Wilbur Floyd)	11/18/1959	Lakewood Cemetery, Minneapolis, MN
Smoll, Lefty (Clyde Hetrick)	08/31/1985	Union Cemetery, Quakertown, PA
Smoot, Homer Vernon	03/25/1928	Galestown Cemetery, Galestown, MD
Smoyer, Henry Neitz	02/28/1958	Morningside Cemetery, DuBois, PA
Smykal, Frank John	08/11/1950	Bohemian Natrional Cemetery, Chicago, IL
Smyth, Harry (William Henry)	08/28/1980	Westover Memorial Park, Augusta, GA
Smyth, Red (James Daniel)	04/14/1958	Holy Cross Cemetery, Culver City, CA
Snell, Charlie (Charles Anthony)	04/04/1988	East Harrisburg Cemetery, Harrisburg, PA
Snell, Wally (Walter Henry)	07/23/1980	Swan Point Cemetery, Providence, RI. Cremated.
Snipes, Roxy (Wyatt Eure)	05/01/1941	Rose Hill Cemetery, Marion, SC
Snodgrass, Fred (Frederick Charles)	04/05/1974	Cremated, Ivy Lawn Park, Ventura, CA
Snow, Charlie (Charles M.)	08/27/1929	Green-Wood Cemetery, Brooklyn, NY
Snyder, Bernie (Bernard Austin)	04/15/1999	Holy Cross Cemetery, Yeadon, PA
Snyder, Bill (William Nicholas)	10/08/1934	Vicksburg Cemetery, Vicksburg, MI
Snyder, Charles	03/03/1901	Cathedral Cemetery, Philadelphia, PA
Snyder, Gene Walter	06/02/1996	Mount Zion Cemetery, Delta, PA
Snyder, George T.	08/02/1905	Mt. Moriah Cemetery, Philadelphia, PA
Snyder, Jack (John William)	12/13/1981	Jefferson Memorial Park, Pleasant Hills, PA
Snyder, Jim (James C. A.)	12/01/1922	Cypress Hills Cemetery, Brooklyn, NY
Snyder, Josh (Joshua M.)	04/21/1881	Cypress Hills Cemetery, Brooklyn, NY
Snyder, Pancho (Frank Elton)	01/05/1962	Fort Sam Houston National Cemetery, San Antonio, TX
Snyder, Pop (Charles N.)	10/29/1924	Glenwood Cemetery, Washington, DC
Snyder, Redleg (Emanuel Sebastian)	11/11/1933	St. Peter's Church Cemetery, Riverside, NJ
Sockalexis, Lou (Louis Francis)	12/24/1913	Indian Island Cemetery, Old Town, ME
Sodd, Bill (William)	05/14/1998	Mount Olivet Cemetery, Fort Worth, TX

Name	DOD	Cemetery, City, State
Solaita, Tony (Tolia)	02/10/1990	Immediately outside his home in Village of Nu'uuli, American Samoa
Solomon, Eddie	01/12/1986	King's Chapel Cemetery, Perry, GA
Solomon, Mose Hirsch	06/25/1966	Mt. Nebo Memorial Gardens, Miami, FL
Solters, Moose (Julius Joseph)	09/28/1975	Calvary Cemetery, Pittsburgh, PA
Somerlott, Jock (John Wesley)	04/21/1965	Metz Cemetery, Metz, IN
Sommer, Joe (Joseph John)	01/16/1938	Highland Cemetery, Fort Mitchell, KY
Sommers, Rudy (Rudolph)	03/18/1949	Calvary Cemetery, Louisville, KY
Somon, Syl (Sylvester Adam)	02/28/1973	Locust Hill Cemetery, Evansville, IN
Songer, Don (Donald C.)	10/03/1962	Mount Moriah Cemetery, Kansas City, MO
Sorrell, Vic (Victor Garland)	05/04/1972	Raleigh Memorial Park, Raleigh, NC
Southwick, Clyde Aubra	10/14/1961	Chapel Hill Memorial Park, Freeport, IL
Southworth, Billy (William Harrison)	11/15/1969	Green Lawn Cemetery, Columbus, OH
Sowders, Bill (William Jefferson)	02/02/1951	Crown Hill Cemetery, Indianapolis, IN
Sowders, John	07/29/1939	Crown Hill Cemetery, Indianapolis, IN
Sowders, Len (Leonard)	11/19/1888	Crown Hill Cemetery, Indianapolis, IN
Spade, Bob (Robert)	09/07/1924	Springfield Center Presbyterian Cemetery, Akron, OH
Spahn, Warren Edward	11/25/2003	Elmwood Cemetery, Hartshorne, OK
Spalding, Al (Albert Goodwill)	09/09/1915	Cremated, Greenwood Cemetery, San Diego, CA. Ashes scattered at Point Loma.
Spalding, Cick (Charles Harry)	02/03/1950	Northwood Cemetery, Philadelphia, PA
Sparks, Tully (Thomas Frank)	07/15/1937	Edgemont Cemetery, Anniston, AL
Sparma, Joe (Joseph Blasè)	05/14/1986	Resurrection Cemetery, Worthington, OH
Speaker, Tris (Tristram E.)	12/08/1958	Fairview Cemetery, Hubbard, TX
Speece, Byron Franklin	09/29/1974	Elgin Cemetery, Elgin, OR
Speer, Floyd Vernie	03/22/1969	Carolan Cemetery, Booneville, AR
Spence, Harry *manager*	05/17/1908	Elmwood Cemetery, River Grove, IL
Spence, Stan (Stanley Orville)	01/09/1983	Maplewood Cemetery, Kinston, NC
Spencer, Ben (Lloyd Benjamin)	09/01/1970	Westminster Cemetery, Westminster, MD
Spencer, Chet (Chester Arthur)	11/10/1938	Greenlawn Cemetery, Portsmouth, OH
Spencer, Glenn Edward	12/30/1958	Vestal Hills Memorial Park, Vestal, NY
Spencer, Hack (Fred Calvin)	02/05/1969	Sunset Memorial Park, Minneapolis, MN
Spencer, Jim (James Lloyd)	02/10/2002	Cremated, Westminster, MD. Ashes returned to family.
Spencer, Roy Hampton	02/08/1973	Gulf Pines Memorial Park, Englewood, FL
Spencer, Tubby (Edward Russell)	02/01/1945	Woodlawn Memorial Park, Colma, CA
Spencer, Vern (Vernon Murray)	06/03/1971	New Hudson Cemetery, New Hudson, MI
Speraw, Paul Bachman	02/22/1962	Linwood Cemetery, Cedar Rapids, IA
Sperber, Ed (Edwin George)	01/05/1976	Spring Grove Cemetery, Cincinnati, OH
Sperry, Stan (Stanley Kenneth)	09/27/1962	Maple Hill Cemetery, Evansville, WI
Spies, Harry (Henry)	07/07/1942	Inglewood Park Cemetery, Inglewood, CA
Spognardi, Andy (Andrea Ettore)	01/01/2000	Forest Hills Cemetery, Jamaica Plain, MA
Spohrer, Al (Alfred Ray)	07/17/1972	Trinity Cemetery, Holderness, NH
Spongberg, Carl Gustav	07/21/1938	Forest Lawn Memorial Park, Glendale, CA
Spooner, Karl Benjamin	04/10/1984	Crestlawn Cemetery, Vero Beach, FL
Spotts, Jim (James Russell)	06/15/1964	Mount Laurel Cemetery, Mount Laurel, NJ

Name	DOD	Cemetery, City, State
Spragins, Homer Franklin	12/10/2002	I.O.O.F. Cemetery, Greenwood, MS
Springer, Brad (Bradford Louis)	01/04/1970	Holy Sepulchre Cemetery, Southfield, MI
Sprinz, Mule (Joseph Conrad)	01/11/1994	Holy Cross Cemetery, Colma, CA
Sproull, Charlie (Charles William)	01/13/1980	Greenwood Cemetery, Rockford, IL
Spurgeon, Freddy (Fred)	11/05/1970	Grand Prairie Cemetery, Kalamazoo, MI
Spurney, Ed (Edward Frederick)	10/12/1932	Woodland Cemetery, Cleveland, OH
St. Claire, Ebba (Edward Joseph)	08/22/1982	Our Lady of Angels Cemetery, Whitehall, NY
St. Vrain, Jim (James Marcellin)	06/12/1937	Mountain View Cemetery, Butte, MT
Stack, Eddie (William Edward)	08/28/1958	Mount Carmel Cemetery, Hillside, IL
Stafford, Bill (William Charles)	09/19/2001	Cremated, Plymouth, MI. Ashes given to family
Stafford, Bob (Robert M.)	08/20/1916	Oak Ridge Cemetery, Greensboro, NC
Stafford, General (James Joseph)	09/18/1923	Calvary Cemetery, Dudley, MA
Stafford, John Henry	07/03/1940	Calvary Cemetery, Dudley, MA
Stahl, Chick (Charles Sylvester)	03/28/1907	Lindenwood Cemetery, Fort Wayne, IN
Stahl, Jake (Garland)	09/18/1922	Oak Woods Cemetery, Chicago, IL
Stainback, Tuck (George Tucker)	11/29/1992	Cremated, Camarillo, CA
Staley, Gale (George Gaylord)	04/19/1989	Oakmont Memorial Park, Lafayette, CA
Staley, Harry (Henry Eli)	01/12/1910	Oak Hill Cemetery, Battle Creek, MI
Stallcup, Virgil (Thomas Virgil)	05/02/1989	Greenville Memorial Gardens, Piedmont, SC
Staller, George Walborn	07/03/1992	Hershey Cemetery, Hershey, PA
Stallings, George Tweedy	05/13/1929	Riverside Cemetery, Macon, GA
Stanceu, Charley (Charles)	04/03/1969	Forest Hill Cemetery, Canton
Standaert, Jerry (Jerome John)	08/04/1964	St. Mary's Cemetery, Evergreen Park, IL
Standridge, Pete (Alfred Peter)	08/02/1963	Holy Cross Cemetery, Colma, CA
Stankard, Tom (Thomas Francis)	06/13/1958	Calvary Cemetery, Waltham, MA
Stanky, Eddie (Edward Raymond)	06/06/1999	Catholic Cemetery, Mobile, AL
Stanley, Buck (John Leonard)	08/13/1940	Forest Lawn Cemetery, Norfolk, VA
Stanley, Joe (Joseph Bernard)	09/13/1967	Mount Olivet Cemetery, Washington, DC
Stansbury, Jack (John James)	12/26/1970	Fairmount Cemetery, Phillipsburg, NJ
Stanton, Buck (George Washington)	01/01/1992	Stantonsburg Cemetery, Stantonsburg, NC
Stanton, Tom (Thomas Patrick)	01/17/1957	Calvary Cemetery, St. Louis, MO
Stargell, Willie (Wilver Dornel)	04/09/2001	Oleander Memorial Gardens, Wilmington, NC
Stark, Dolly (Monroe Randolph)	12/01/1924	Elmwood Cemetery, Memphis, TN
Starkel, Con (Conrad)	01/19/1933	New Tacoma Memorial Park, Tacoma, WA
Starnagle, George Henry	02/15/1946	Walnut Hill Cemetery, Belleville, IL
Starr, Bill (William)	08/12/1991	Cypress View Cemetery, San Diego, CA
Starr, Charlie (Charles Watkin)	10/18/1937	Cremated, Pasadena, CA
Starr, Ray (Raymond Francis)	02/09/1963	Carlyle Cemetery, Carlyle, IL
Start, Joe (Joseph)	03/27/1927	Riverside Cemetery, Pawtucket, RI
Statz, Jigger (Arnold John)	03/16/1988	Holy Cross Cemetery, Culver City, CA
Stauffer, Ed (Charles Edward)	07/02/1979	Cremated, St. Petersburg, FL
Stearns, Bill (William E.)	12/30/1898	Arlington National Cemetery, Arlington, VA
Stearns, Ecky (Daniel Eckford)	06/28/1944	Calvary Cemetery, Los Angeles, CA
Stecher, Charlie (William Theodore)	12/26/1926	Riverside Cemetery, Riverside, NJ
Steele, Bill (William Mitchell)	10/19/1949	Memorial Park Cemetery, St. Louis, MO
Steele, Bob (Robert Wesley)	01/27/1962	Burlington Cemetery, Burlington, WI

Name	DOD	Cemetery, City, State
Steele, Elmer Rae	03/09/1966	Poughkeepsie Rural Cemetery, Poughkeepsie, NY
Steelman, Farmer (Morris James)	09/16/1944	Arlington Cemetery, Pennsauken, NJ
Steen, Bill (William John)	03/13/1979	Cremated, Los Angeles, CA
Steengrafe, Milt (Milton Henry)	06/02/1977	Rose Hill Cemetery, Oklahoma City, OK
Steere, Gene (Frederick Eugene)	03/13/1942	Cremated, San Mateo, CA
Stein, Ed (Edward F.)	05/10/1928	Elmwood Cemetery, Detroit, MI
Stein, Irv (Irvin Michael)	01/07/1981	Dendinger Memorial Cemetery, Madisonville, LA
Stein, Justin Marion	05/01/1992	Calvary Cemetery, St. Louis, MO
Steinbacher, Hank (Henry John)	04/03/1977	St. Mary's Catholic Cemetery, Sacramento, CA
Steinbrenner, Gene (Eugene Gass)	04/25/1970	Union Dale Cemetery, Pittsburgh, PA
Steinecke, Bill (William Robert)	07/20/1986	San Lerenzo Cemetery, St. Augustine, FL
Steineder, Ray (Raymond)	08/25/1982	Siloam Cemetery, Vineland, NJ
Steiner, Red (James Harry)	11/16/2001	Cremated, Gardena, CA
Steinfeldt, Harry M.	08/17/1914	Spring Grove Cemetery, Cincinnati, OH. Originally interred at Evergreen Cemetery, Southgate, KY. Moved in 1921.
Stellbauer, Bill (William Jennings)	02/16/1974	Bremond Cemetery, Bremond, TX
Stellberger, Bill (William F.)	11/09/1936	Woodmere Cemetery, Detroit, MI
Stemmeyer, Bill (William)	05/03/1945	Lakewood Park Cemetery, Rocky River, OH
Stengel, Casey (Charles Dillon)	09/29/1975	Forest Lawn Memorial Park, Glendale, CA
Stenson, Dernell Renauld	11/05/2003	Restlawn Memory Gardens, LaGrange, GA
Stenzel, Jake (Jacob Charles) (buried under birth name: Stelzle)	01/06/1919	St. Mary's Cemetery, Cincinnati, OH
Stephens, Bryan Maris	11/21/1991	Pacific View Memorial Park, Newport Beach, CA
Stephens, Clarence Wright	02/28/1945	Spring Grove Cemetery, Cincinnati, OH
Stephens, Jim (James Walter)	01/02/1965	Oxford Cemetery, Oxford, AL
Stephens, Vern (Vernon Decatur)	11/04/1968	Forest Lawn Memorial Park-Long Beach, Long Beach, CA
Stephenson, Dummy (Reuben Crandol)	12/01/1924	South Dennis Cemetery, South Dennis, NJ
Stephenson, Riggs (Jackson Riggs)	11/15/1985	Tuscaloosa Memorial Park, Tuscaloosa, AL
Stephenson, Walter McQueen	07/04/1993	Forest Park Cemetery, Shreveport, LA
Sterrett, Dutch (Charles Hurlbut)	12/08/1965	Church Hill Cemetery, Reedsville, PA
Stevens, Jim (James Arthur)	09/25/1966	Druid Ridge Cemetery, Pikesville, MD
Stewart, Ace (Asa)	04/17/1912	Highland Lawn Cemetery, Terre Haute, IN
Stewart, Glen Weldon	02/11/1997	Forest Hill Cemetery-Midtown, Memphis, TN
Stewart, Lefty (Walter Cleveland)	09/26/1974	Green Acres Memory Gardens, Crossville, TN
Stewart, Mack (William Macklin)	03/21/1960	Macon Memorial Park, Macon, GA
Stewart, Mark	01/17/1932	Maplewood Cemetery, Paris, TN
Stewart, Neb (Walter Nesbitt)	06/08/1990	Kirkwood Cemetery, London, OH
Stewart, Stuffy (John Franklin)	12/30/1980	Oakland Cemetery, Lake City, FL
Stewart, Tuffy (Charles Eugene)	11/18/1934	Oakridge Cemetery, Hillside, IL
Stiely, Fred Warren	01/06/1981	St. Andrews Church Cemetery, Valley View, PA

Name	DOD	Cemetery, City, State
Stimmel, Archie (Archibald Ray)	08/18/1958	Mount Hope Cemetery, Woodsboro, MD
Stimson, Carl Remus	11/09/1936	Forest Lawn Memorial Park, Omaha, NE
Stine, Harry C.	06/05/1924	Oakwood Cemetery, Niagara Falls, NY
Stires, Gat (Garrett)	06/13/1933	Byron Cemetery, Byron, IL
Stirnweiss, Snuffy (George Henry)	09/15/1958	Mt. Olivet Cemetery, Red Bank, NJ
Stivetts, Jack (John Elmer)	04/18/1930	Brock Cemetery, Ashland, PA
Stock, Milt (Milton Joseph)	07/16/1977	Catholic Cemetery, Mobile, AL
Stockdale, Otis Hinkley	03/15/1933	St. Paul's Cemetery, Arcadia, MD
Stokes, Art (Arthur Milton)	06/03/1962	Jerusalem Corners Cemetery, Pleasantville, PA
Stone, Arnie (Edwin Arnold)	07/29/1948	Union Cemetery, Fort Edward, NY
Stone, Dick (Charles Richard)	02/18/1980	Rose Hill Cemetery, Oklahoma City, OK
Stone, Dwight Ely	06/03/1976	Valhalla Memorial Park, North Hollywood, CA
Stone, George Robert	01/03/1945	Coleridge City Cemetery, Coleridge, NE
Stone, John Thomas	11/30/1955	Odd Fellows-Masonic Cemetery, Lynchburg, TN
Stone, Rocky (John Vernon)	11/12/1986	Fresno Memorial Gardens, Fresno, CA
Stone, Tige (William Arthur)	01/01/1960	Riverside Memorial Park, Jacksonville, FL
Stoneham, John Andrew	01/01/2004	Cremated, Tulsa, OK
Stoner, Lil (Ulysses Simpson Grant)	06/26/1966	Memorial Park Cemetery, Enid, OK
Storie, Howie (Howard Edward)	07/27/1968	St. Joseph's Cemetery, Pittsfield, MA
Storke, Alan Marshall	03/18/1910	Fort Hill Cemetery, Auburn, NY
Storti, Lin (Lindo Ivan)	07/24/1982	Bellevue Memorial Gardens, Ontario, CA
Stouch, Tom (Thomas Carl)	10/07/1956	Riverview Burial Park, Lancaster, PA
Stout, Allyn McClelland	12/22/1974	Garden of Memories Cemetery, Sikeston, MO
Stovall, George Thomas	11/05/1951	Aspen Grove Cemetery, Burlington, IA
Stovey, Harry Duffield	09/20/1937	Oak Grove Cemetery, New Bedford, MA
Strahs, Dick (Richard Bernard)	05/26/1988	Palm Vally View Cemetery, Las Vegas, NV
Strand, Paul Edward	07/02/1974	Salt Lake City Cemetery, Salt Lake City, UT
Strands, Larry (John Lawrence)	01/19/1957	Chapel Hill Gardens, Oak Lawn, IL
Strang, Sammy (Samuel Nicklin)	03/13/1932	Chattanooga National Cemetery, Chattanooga, TN
Strange, Alan Cochrane	06/27/1994	Calvary Catholic Cemetery, Seattle, WA
Stratton, Asa Evans	08/14/1925	Riverside Cemetery, Grafton, MA
Stratton, Monty Franklin Pierce	09/29/1982	Memoryland Memorial Park, Greenville, TX
Stratton, Scott (Chilton Scott)	03/08/1939	Valley Cemetery, Taylorsville, KY
Straub, Joe (Joseph J.)	02/13/1929	Roselawn Cemetery, Pueblo, CO
Strauss, Joe (Joseph) (buried under birth name: Strasser)	06/24/1906	Spring Grove Cemetery, Cincinnati, OH
Street, Gabby (Charles Evard)	02/06/1951	Ozark Memorial Park Cemetery, Joplin, MO
Strelecki, Ed (Edward Harold)	01/09/1968	Gate of Heaven Cemetery, East Hanover, NJ
Stremmel, Phil (Philip)	12/26/1947	Cedar Park Cemetery, Calumet Park, IL
Strick, Charles E.	11/18/1933	Erie Cemetery, Erie, PA
Stricker, Cub (John A.)	11/19/1937	West Laurel Hill Cemetery, Bala Cynwyd, PA
Stricklett, Elmer Griffin	06/07/1964	Cremated, IOOF Crematory, Santa Cruz, CA.
Stripp, Joe (Joseph Valentine)	06/10/1989	Woodlawn Memorial Park, Winter Garden
Strobel, Allie (Albert Irving)	02/10/1955	Hollywood Memorial Gardens, Hollywood, FL

Name	DOD	Cemetery, City, State
Stromme, Floyd Marvin	02/07/1993	Sunset Memorial Park Cemetery, Coos Bay, OR
Stroner, Jim (James Melvin)	12/06/1975	St. Mary's Cemetery, Evergreen Park, IL
Stroud, Sailor (Ralph Vivian)	04/11/1970	East Lawn Memorial Park, Sacramento, CA
Strueve, Al (Albert Frederick)	01/28/1929	Greenfield Cemetery, Greenfield, OH
Strunk, Amos Aaron	07/22/1979	Greenmount Cemetery, Philadelphia, PA
Stryker, Dutch (Sterling Alpa)	11/05/1964	Mt. Olivet Cemetery, Red Bank, NJ
Stuart, Bill (William Alexander)	10/14/1928	Branch Cemetery, State College, PA
Stuart, Johnny (John Davis)	05/13/1970	Mountain View Memorial Park, Charleston, WV
Stuart, Luke (Luther Lane)	06/15/1947	Guilford College Cemetery, Greensboro, NC
Stuart, Marlin Henry	06/16/1994	Wood's Chapel Cemetery, Paragould, AR
Studley, Seem (Seymour L.)	07/09/1901	Soldiers' & Sailors' Home Cemetery, Grand Island, NE
Stultz, George Irvin	03/19/1955	Portland Cemetery, Louisville, KY
Stumpf, Bill (William Frederick)	02/14/1966	Loudon Park Cemetery, Baltimore, MD
Stumpf, George Frederick	03/06/1993	Garden of Memories, Metairie, LA
Sturdy, Guy	05/04/1965	Colonial Gardens Cemetery, Marshall, TX
Sturgis, Dean Donnell	06/04/1950	Oak Lawn Cemetery, Uniontown, PA
Stutz, George	12/29/1930	Hillside Cemetery, Roslyn, PA
Styles, Lena (William Graves)	03/14/1956	Gurley Cemetery, Gurley, AL
Stynes, Neil (Cornelius William)	03/26/1944	St. Paul's Cemetery, Arlington, MA
Suche, Charley (Charles Morris)	02/11/1984	Sunset Memorial Park, San Antonio, TX
Suck, Tony (Charles Anthony)	01/29/1895	Oak Woods Cemetery, Chicago, IL
Sudhoff, Willie (John William)	05/25/1917	Bethany Cemetery, St. Louis, MO
Sugden, Joe (Joseph)	06/28/1959	North Cedar Hill Cemetery, Philadelphia, PA
Suggs, George Franklin	04/04/1949	Maplewood Cemetery, Kinston, NC
Suhr, Gus (August Richard)	01/15/2004	Olivet Memorial Park, Colma, CA
Sukeforth, Clyde Leroy	09/03/2000	Brookland Cemetery, Waldoboro, ME
Sulik, Ernie (Ernest Richard)	05/31/1963	Holy Sepulchre Cemetery, Hayward, CA
Sullivan, Andrew B.	02/14/1920	St. Luke's Cemetery, Westborough
Sullivan, Bill (William)	11/13/1884	St. Jerome Cemetery, Holyoke, MA
Sullivan, Billy (William Joseph, Sr.)	01/28/1965	St. James Catholic Cemetery, McMinnville, OR
Sullivan, Denny (Dennis J.)	12/31/1925	New Calvary Cemetery, Mattapan, MA
Sullivan, Denny (Dennis William)	06/02/1956	Los Angeles National Cemetery, Los Angeles, CA
Sullivan, Harry Andrew	09/22/1919	St. Mary/St. James Cemetery, Rockford, IL
Sullivan, Haywood Cooper	02/12/2003	Dothan City Cemetery, Dothan, AL
Sullivan, Jackie (Carl Mancel)	10/15/1992	Ridgeview Memorial Park, Allen, TX
Sullivan, Jim (Daniel James)	11/29/1901	Holy Cross Cemetery, Malden, MA
Sullivan, Joe	04/08/1985	Cremated, Sequim, WA. Ashes scattered in Okanogan County
Sullivan, Joe (Joseph Daniel)	11/02/1897	Holy Cross Cemetery, Malden, MA
Sullivan, John Jeremiah	07/07/1958	St. Mary's Cemetery, Evergreen Park, IL
Sullivan, John Lawrence	04/01/1966	Harmony Cemetery, Milton, PA
Sullivan, Lefty (Paul Thomas)	11/01/1988	Paradise Memorial Gardens, Scottsdale, AZ
Sullivan, Marty (Martin C.)	01/06/1894	St. Patrick's Cemetery, Lowell, MA

Name	DOD	Cemetery, City, State
Sullivan, Mike (Michael Joseph)	06/14/1906	Mount Calvary Cemetery, Roslindale, MA
Sullivan, Sleeper (Thomas Jefferson)	10/13/1909	Calvary Cemetery, St. Louis, MO
Sullivan, Suter Grant	04/19/1925	St. Mary's Cemetery, Baltimore, MD
Sullivan, Ted (Timothy Paul)	07/05/1929	Calvary Cemetery, Milwaukee, WI
Sullivan, Tom (Thomas Augustin)	09/23/1962	Mount Hope Cemetery, Mattapan, MA
Sullivan, Tom (Thomas Brandon)	08/16/1944	Calvary Catholic Cemetery, Seattle, WA
Sullivan, Tom (Thomas)	04/12/1947	Oak Hill Cemetery, Cincinnati, OH
Sullivan, William F.	10/08/1905	St. Francis Cemetery, Pawtucket, RI
Summa, Homer Wayne	01/29/1966	Grand View Memorial Park, Glendale, CA
Summers, Ed (Oron Edgar)	05/12/1953	Ladoga Cemetery, Ladoga, IN
Summers, Kid (William)	10/16/1895	St. James Cemetery, Toronto, Ontario, Canada
Sumner, Carl Ringdahl	02/08/1999	Pine Hill Cemetery, Tewksbury, MA
Sunday, Art (Arthur)	10/02/1926	Odd Fellows Cemetery, Reno, NV
Sunday, Billy (William Ashley)	11/06/1935	Forest Home Cemetery (formerly Waldheim Cemetery), Forest Park, IL.
Sundra, Steve (Stephen Richard)	03/23/1952	Calvary Cemetery, Cleveland, OH
Sunkel, Tom (Thomas Jacob)	04/06/2002	St. Mary's Cemetery, Paris, IL
Surkont, Max (Matthew Constantine)	10/08/1986	Notre Dame Cemetery, Pawtucket, RI
Susce, George Cyril Methodius	02/25/1986	Sarasota Memorial Park, Sarasota, FL
Susko, Pete (Peter Jonathan)	05/22/1978	St. Nicholas Russian Orthodox Cemetery, Akron, OH
Sutcliffe, Butch (Charles Inigo)	03/02/1994	Oak Grove Cemetery, Fall River, MA
Suter, Rube (Harry Richard)	07/24/1971	Assaria Cemetery, Assaria, KS
Sutherland, Dizzy (Howard Alvin)	08/21/1979	Cheltenham Veterans Cemetery, Cheltenham, MD
Sutherland, Suds (Harvey Scott)	05/11/1972	Pioneer Cemetery, Portland, OR
Sutthoff, Jack (John Gerhard)	08/03/1942	St. Joseph's New Cemetery, Cincinnati, OH
Swacina, Harry Joseph	06/21/1944	Elmwood Cemetery, Birmingham, AL
Swan, Andy (Andrew J.)	08/27/1885	Bellevue Cemetery, Lawrence, MA
Swan, Ducky (Harry Gordon)	05/09/1946	Smithfield East End Cemetery, Pittsburgh, PA
Swander, Pinky (Edward Ottis)	10/24/1944	Greenlawn Cemetery, Portsmouth, OH
Swanson, Bill (William Andrew)	10/14/1954	Calvary Cemetery, Woodside, Queens, NY
Swanson, Evar (Ernest Evar)	07/17/1973	Oak Lawn Memorial Gardens, Galesburg, IL
Swanson, Karl Edward	04/03/2002	Riverside Cemetery, Moline, IL
Swarback, Bill (William) (buried under birth name: Schwappach)	05/17/1949	St. John's Cemetery, Darien, CT
Swartwood, Ed (Cyrus Edward)	05/15/1924	Union Dale Cemetery, Pittsburgh, PA
Swartz, Bud (Sherwin Merle)	06/24/1991	Hillside Memorial Park, Los Angeles, CA
Swartz, Dazzy (Vernon Monroe)	01/13/1980	Germantown Cemetery, Germantown, OH
Swartzel, Park (Parke B.)	01/03/1940	Forest Lawn Memorial Park, Glendale, CA. Cremated.
Sweasy, Charlie (Charles James)	03/30/1908	Evergreen Cemetery, Hillside, NJ
Sweeney, Bill (William J.)	08/02/1903	Cathedral Cemetery, Philadelphia, PA
Sweeney, Bill (William John)	05/26/1948	St. Joseph's Cemetery, West Roxbury, MA

Name	DOD	Cemetery, City, State
Sweeney, Buck (Charles Francis)	03/13/1955	St. Mary's Roman Catholic Cemetery (Troy Hill), Pittsburgh, PA
Sweeney, Charlie (Charles J.)	04/04/1902	Cypress Lawn Memorial Park, Colma, CA
Sweeney, Dan (Daniel J.)	07/13/1913	St. John's Cemetery, Louisville, KY
Sweeney, Hank (Henry Leon)	05/06/1980	Leiper's Fork Cemetery, Columbia, TN
Sweeney, Jeff (Edward Francis)	07/04/1947	Mount Carmel Cemetery, Hillside, IL
Sweeney, Jerry (Jeremiah H.)	08/25/1891	Mount Calvary Cemetery, Roslindale, MA
Sweeney, Pete (Peter Jay)	08/22/1901	Holy Cross Cemetery, Colma, CA
Swentor, Augie (August William)	11/10/1969	Waterside Cemetery, Marblehead, MA
Swetonic, Steve (Stephen Albert)	04/22/1974	Jefferson Memorial Park, Pleasant Hills, PA
Swett, Pop (William E.)	11/22/1934	Holy Cross Cemetery, Colma, CA
Swift, Bill (William Vincent)	02/23/1969	Oak Hill Burial Park, Lakeland, FL
Swift, Bob (Robert Virgil)	10/17/1966	Roselawn Cemetery, Salina, KS
Swigart, Oad (Oadis Vaughn)	08/08/1997	Mount Olivet Cemetery, St. Joseph, MO
Swigler, Ad (Adam William)	02/05/1975	Arlington Cemetery, Drexel Hill, PA
Swindell, Josh (Joshua Ernest)	03/19/1969	Memorial Gardens Cemetery, Grand Junction, CO
Swindells, Charlie (Charles Jay)	07/22/1940	Portland Memorial Cemetery, Portland, OR
Swormstedt, Len (Leonard Jordan)	07/19/1964	Harmony Grove Cemetery, Salem, MA
Sylvestor, Lou (Louis J.)	05/05/1936	Evergreen Cemetery, Brooklyn, NY
Taber, John Pardon	02/21/1940	Acushnet Cemetery, Acushnet, MA
Taber, Lefty (Edward Timothy)	11/05/1983	Wyuka Cemetery, Lincoln, NE
Tabor, Jim (James Reubin)	08/22/1953	Beason Cemetery, Gurley, AL
Taff, John Gallatin	05/15/1961	Oakwood Cemetery, Austin, TX
Taitt, Doug (Douglas John)	12/12/1970	Riverview Abbey Mausoleum, Portland, OR
Talcott, Roy (Leroy Everett)	12/06/1999	Miami Memorial Park, Miami, FL
Tamulis, Vito (Vitautris Casimirus)	05/05/1974	Nashville National Cemetery, Madison, TN
Tankersley, Leo (Lawrence William)	09/18/1980	College Mound Cemetery, Terrell, TX
Tannehill, Jesse Niles	09/22/1956	Evergreen Cemetery, Southgate, KY
Tannehill, Lee Ford	02/16/1938	Antioch Baptist Church Cemetery, Live Oak, FL
Tappan, Walter Van Dorn	12/19/1967	Cremated, Los Angeles, CA
Tappe, El (Elvin Walter)	10/10/1998	Quincy Memorial Park, Quincy, IL
Tappe, Ted (Theodore Nash)	02/13/2004	Cremated, Wenatchee, WA
Tarbert, Arlie (Wilbur Arlington)	11/27/1946	Lake View Cemetery, Cleveland, OH
Tate, Al (Walter Alvin)	05/08/1993	Lakeview Memorial Estates, Bountiful, UT
Tate, Bennie (Henry Bennett)	10/27/1973	Boner Cemetery, West Frankfort, IL
Tate, Hughie (Hugh Henry)	08/07/1956	St. Michael's Cemetery, Greenville, PA
Tate, Pop (Edward Christopher)	06/25/1932	Riverview Cemetery, Richmond, VA
Tatum, Tommy (V T)	11/07/1989	Resurrection Memorial Cemetery, Oklahoma City, OK
Tauby, Fred (Frederick Joseph)	11/23/1955	Golden Gate National Cemetery, San Bruno, CA
Tauscher, Walt (Walter Edward)	11/27/1992	Woodlawn Memorium, Orlando, FL
Tavener, Jackie (John Adam)	09/14/1969	Greenwood Memorial Park, Fort Worth, TX
Taylor, Arlas Walter	09/10/1958	Dade City Cemetery, Dade City, FL
Taylor, Ben (Benjamin Harrison)	11/03/1946	Green Hill Cemetery, Bedford, IN
Taylor, Billy (William Henry)	05/14/1900	Woodlawn Cemetery, Jacksonville, FL

Name	DOD	Cemetery, City, State
Taylor, Chink (C L)	07/07/1980	Burnet Cemetery, Burnet, TX
Taylor, Danny (Daniel Turney)	10/11/1972	West Newton Cemetery, West Newton, PA
Taylor, Dummy (Luther Haden)	08/22/1958	Baldwin City Cemetery, Baldwin City, KS
Taylor, Ed (Edward James)	01/30/1992	Mount Greenwood Cemetery, Chicago, IL
Taylor, Fred (Frederick Rankin)	01/06/2002	Union Cemetery, Columbus, OH
Taylor, George J. *manager*	10/28/1911	Calvary Cemetery, Woodside, Queens, NY
Taylor, Harry (James Harry)	11/05/2000	Shepherd's Cemetery, Sheperdsville, IN
Taylor, Harry Leonard	07/12/1955	Cremated, Forest Lawn Cemetery, Buffalo, NY
Taylor, Harry Warren	04/27/1969	Woodlawn Cemetery, Toledo, OH
Taylor, Jack (John Budd)	02/07/1900	Fairview Cemetery, Castleton Corners, Staten Island, NY
Taylor, Jack (John W.)	03/04/1938	Green Lawn Cemetery, Columbus, OH
Taylor, Joe Cephus	03/18/1993	Greenwood Cemetery, Pittsburgh, PA
Taylor, Leo Thomas	05/20/1982	Mount Pleasant Cemetery, Seattle, WA
Taylor, Live Oak (Edward S.)	02/19/1888	Cypress Lawn Cemetery (Laurel Hill Mound), Colma, CA. Originally intered at Laurel Hill Cemetery, San Francisco. Cemetery removed in 1940.
Taylor, Pete (Vernon Charles)	11/17/2003	Baldwin United Methodist Church Cemetery, Millersville, MD
Taylor, Rube (Edgar Ruben)	01/31/1912	Greenwood Cemetery, Dallas, TX
Taylor, Tommy (Thomas Livingstone Carlton)	04/05/1956	Greenville Cemetery, Greenville, MS
Taylor, Wiley (Philip Wiley)	07/08/1954	Louisville Cemetery, Louisville, KS
Taylor, Zach (James Wren)	09/19/1974	Woodlawn Memorial Park, Winter Garden, FL
Teachout, Bud (Arthur John)	05/11/1985	Cremated, Laguna Beach, CA
Tebbetts, Birdie (George Robert)	03/24/1999	St. Bernard Catholic Church Cemetery, Bradenton Beach, FL
Tebeau, George E.	02/04/1923	Crown Hill Cemetery, Wheat Ridge, CO
Tebeau, Patsy (Oliver Wendell)	05/15/1918	Calvary Cemetery, Cleveland, OH
Tebeau, Pussy (Charles Alston)	03/25/1950	St. Joseph's Cemetery, Pittsfield, MA
Tedrow, Allen Seymour	01/23/1958	Pioneer Cemetery, Westerville, OH
Temple, Johnny (John Ellis)	01/09/1994	Cremated, Anderson, SC. Ashes given to family
Tener, John Kinley	05/19/1946	Homewood Cemetery, Pittsburgh, PA
Tennant, Jim (James McDonnell)	04/16/1967	Lakeview Cemetery, Bridgeport, CT
Tennant, Tom (Thomas Francis)	02/15/1955	Holy Cross Cemetery, Colma, CA
Tenney, Fred (Frederick)	07/03/1952	Harmony Cemetery, Georgetown, MA
Terrell, Tom (John Thomas)	07/09/1893	St. John's Cemetery, Louisville, KY
Terry, Adonis (William H.)	02/24/1915	Forest Home Cemetery, Milwaukee, WI
Terry, Bill (William Harold)	01/09/1989	Evergreen Cemetery, Jacksonville, FL
Terry, John Buchard	04/27/1933	Forest Hill Cemetery, Kansas City, MO
Terry, Wallace W.	01/21/1916	Newtown Cemetery, Newtown, PA
Terry, Yank (Lancelot Yank)	11/04/1979	Cresthaven Memory Gardens, Bedford, IN
Terry, Zeb (Zebulon Alexander)	03/14/1988	Cremated, Los Angeles, CA
Terwilliger, Dick (Richard Martin)	01/21/1969	Rest Haven Memory Gardens, Belding, MI
Tesch, Al (Albert John)	08/03/1947	New York Bay Cemetery, Jersey City, NJ
Tesreau, Jeff (Charles Monroe)	09/24/1946	Pine Knoll Cemetery, Hanover, NH

Name	DOD	Cemetery, City, State
Tettelbach, Dick (Richard Morley)	01/26/1995	Cremated, East Harwich, MA
Textor, George Bernhardt	03/10/1954	West Lawn Cemetery, Canton, OH
Thacker, Moe (Morris Benton)	11/13/1997	Cremated, Louisville, KY
Thatcher, Grant (Ulysses Grant)	03/17/1936	Woodward Hill Cemetery, Lancaster, PA
Theis, Jack (John Louis)	07/06/1941	Confidence Cemetery, Georgetown, OH
Thevenow, Tommy (Thomas Joseph)	07/29/1957	Springdale Cemetery, Madison, IN
Thielman, Henry Joseph	09/02/1942	Calvary Cemetery, St. Cloud, MN
Thielman, Jake (John Peter)	01/28/1928	Calvary Cemetery, St. Cloud, MN
Thomas, Bill (William Miskey)	01/14/1950	Montgomery Cemetery, Norristown, PA
Thomas, Bud (Luther Baxter)	05/20/2001	Mt. Zion United Methodist Church Cemetery, Esmont, VA
Thomas, Claude Alfred	03/06/1946	El Reno Cemetery, El Reno, OK
Thomas, Fay Wesley	08/12/1990	Cremated, Chatsworth, CA
Thomas, Fred (Frederick Harvey)	01/15/1986	Cremated, Rice Lake, WI
Thomas, Frosty (Forrest)	03/18/1970	Memorial Park Cemetery, St. Joseph, MO
Thomas, Herb (Herbert Mark)	12/04/1991	Oak Hill Cemetery, Palatka, FL
Thomas, Ira Felix	10/11/1958	Holy Sepulchre Cemetery, Wyndmoor, PA
Thomas, Kite (Keith Marshall)	01/07/1995	Abilene Cemetery, Abilene, KS
Thomas, Lefty (Clarence Fletcher)	03/21/1952	Knollkreg Memorial Park, Abingdon, VA
Thomas, Myles Lewis	12/12/1963	Woodlawn Cemetery, Toledo, OH
Thomas, Ray (Raymond Joseph)	12/06/1993	Cremated, Wilson, NC
Thomas, Red (Robert William)	03/22/1962	Lindsey Cemetery, Lindsey, OH
Thomas, Roy Allen	11/20/1959	Riverside Cemetery, West Norristown, PA
Thomas, Tom (Thomas W.)	09/23/1942	Shawnee Cemetery, Shawnee, OH
Thomas, Tommy (Alphonse)	04/27/1988	Druid Ridge Cemetery, Pikesville, MD
Thomas, Walt (William Walter)	06/06/1950	Alto Reste Park Cemetery, Altoona, PA
Thomason, Art (Arthur Wilson)	05/02/1944	Fairview Cemetery, Liberty, MO
Thompson, Andrew M. *manager*	02/17/1895	Watson Cemetery, Pecatonica, IL
Thompson, Bill (Will McLain)	06/09/1962	Homewood Cemetery, Pittsburgh, PA
Thompson, Danny Leon	12/10/1976	Capron Cemetery, Capron, OK
Thompson, Dave (David Forrest)	02/26/1979	Iredell Memorial Gardens, Statesville, NC
Thompson, Frank E.	06/27/1940	Fairview Cemetery, Joplin, MO
Thompson, Fresco (Lafayette Fresco)	11/20/1968	Queen of Heaven Cemetery, Rowland Heights, CA
Thompson, Fuller Weidner	02/19/1972	Cremated, Los Angeles, CA
Thompson, Gus (John Gustav)	03/28/1958	Conrad Memorial Cemetery, Kalispell, MT
Thompson, Hank (Henry Curtis)	09/30/1969	Odd Fellows Cemetery, Fresno, CA
Thompson, Harry (Harold)	02/14/1951	Golden Gate National Cemetery, San Bruno, CA
Thompson, Homer Thomas	09/12/1957	Westview Cemetery, Atlanta, GA
Thompson, Jocko (John Samuel)	02/03/1988	Cremated, Gate of Heaven Cemetery, Silver Spring, MD
Thompson, John Parkinson	08/01/1938	Woodland Cemetery, London, Ontario, Canada
Thompson, Lee (John Dudley)	02/17/1963	Oak Hill Cemetery, Solvang, CA
Thompson, Sam (Samuel Luther)	11/07/1922	Elmwood Cemetery, Detroit, MI
Thompson, Shag (James Alfred)	01/07/1990	Linwood Cemetery, Graham, NC

Name	DOD	Cemetery, City, State
Thompson, Tommy (Rupert Lockhart)	05/24/1971	Cremated, Auburn, CA
Thompson, Tommy (Thomas Carl)	01/16/1963	Cremated, La Jolla, CA
Thoney, Jack (John)	10/24/1948	St. Stephen's Cemetery, Fort Thomas, KY
Thormahlen, Hank (Herbert Ehler)	02/06/1955	Fairview Cemetery, Fairview, NJ
Thorpe, Bob (Benjamin Robert)	10/30/1996	Gulf Pines Memorial Park, Englewood, FL
Thorpe, Bob (Robert Joseph)	03/17/1960	Greenwood Memorial Park, San Diego, CA
Thorpe, Jim (James Francis)	03/28/1953	Jim Thorpe Memorial Mausoleum, Jim Thorpe, PA
Thorton, Walter Miller	07/14/1960	Cremated, Los Angeles, CA
Throneberry, Faye (Maynard Faye)	04/26/1999	Fisherville Cemetery, Fisherville, TN
Throneberry, Marv (Marvin Eugene)	06/23/1994	Fisherville Cemetery, Fisherville, TN
Thuman, Lou (Louis Charles Frank)	12/19/2000	Holy Redeemer Cemetery, Baltimore, MD
Thurston, Sloppy (Hollis John)	09/14/1973	Holy Cross Cemetery, Culver City, CA
Tiefenauer, Bobby Gene	06/13/2000	St. Francois Memorial Park, Bonne Terre, MO
Tiemeyer, Eddie (Edward Carl)	09/27/1946	Vine Street Hill Cemetery, Cincinnati, OH
Tierney, Bill (William J.)	09/21/1898	Mount Calvary Cemetery, Roslindale, MA
Tierney, Cotton (James Arthur)	04/18/1953	Calvary Cemetery, Kansas City, MO
Tietje, Les (Leslie William)	10/02/1996	Maple Grove Cemetery, Kasson, MN
Tillman, Johnny (John Lawrence)	04/07/1964	Flat Brook Cemetery, Canaan, NY
Tincup, Ben (Austin Ben)	07/05/1980	Rose Hill Memorial Park, Tulsa, OK
Tinker, Joe (Joseph Bert)	07/27/1948	Greenwood Cemetery, Orlando, FL
Tinning, Bud (Lyle Forest)	01/17/1966	Pilger Cemetery, Pilger, NE
Tipple, Dan (Daniel E.)	03/26/1960	Hillcrest Cemetery, Omaha, NE
Tipton, Eric Gordon	08/29/2001	Williamsburg Memorial Park, Williamsburg, VA
Tipton, Joe Hicks	03/01/1994	Pleasant Grove Methodist Cemetery, Pleasant Grove, AL
Tising, Jack (Johnnie Joseph)	09/05/1967	Memorial Gardens Cemetery, Colorado Springs, CO
Titcomb, Cannonball (Ledell)	06/08/1950	Greenwood Cemetery, Kingston, NH
Titus, John Franklin	01/08/1943	I.O.O.F. Cemetery, Saint Clair (Schuylkill Co.), PA
Tobin, Bill (William F.)	10/10/1912	Mt. St. Benedict's Cemetery, Bloomfield, CT
Tobin, Jack (John Thomas)	12/10/1969	Calvary Cemetery, St. Louis, MO
Tobin, Jim (James Anthony)	05/19/1969	Holy Sepulchre Cemetery, Hayward, CA
Tobin, Johnny (John Patrick)	01/18/1982	Holy Sepulchre Cemetery, Hayward, CA
Tobin, Pat (Marion Brooks)	01/21/1975	Forest Park Cemetery, Shreveport, LA
Todd, Al (Alfred Chester)	03/08/1985	Maple Grove Cemetery, Horseheads, NY
Todd, Frank (George Franklin)	08/11/1919	Grove Cemetery, Aberdeen, MD
Todt, Phil (Philip Julius)	11/15/1973	SS. Peter & Paul Cemetery, St. Louis, MO
Tolson, Chick (Charles Julius)	04/16/1965	Harmony Cemetery, Landover, MD
Tomer, George Clarence	12/15/1984	Violet Hill Cemetery, Perry, IA
Tomney, Phil (Philip H.)	03/18/1892	Aulenbach Cemetery, Mt. Penn, PA
Tompkins, Chuck (Charles Herbert)	09/20/1975	DeAnn Cemetery, DeAnn, AR
Toney, Fred Alexandra	03/11/1953	Spring Hill Cemetery, Nashville, TN

Name	DOD	Cemetery, City, State
Tonneman, Tony (Charles Richard)	08/04/1951	Greenwood Memory Lawn Cemetery, Phoenix, AZ
Toole, Steve (Stephen John)	03/28/1919	Calvary Cemetery, Pittsburgh, PA
Tooley, Bert (Albert R.)	08/17/1976	Mount Ever-Rest Cemetery, Kalamazoo, MI
Toporcer, Specs (George)	05/17/1989	Melville Cemetery, Melville, NY
Torgeson, Earl (Clifford Earl)	11/08/1990	G.A.R. Cemetery, Snohomish, WA
Torkelson, Red (Chester Leroy)	09/22/1964	Mount Olivet Cemetery, Chicago,IL
Torphy, Red (Walter Anthony)	02/11/1980	St. Patrick's Cemetery, Fall River, MA
Tost, Lou (Louis Eugene)	02/21/1967	Golden Gate National Cemetery, San Bruno, CA
Toth, Paul Louis	03/20/1999	Riverside National Cemetery, Riverside, CA
Touchstone, Clay (Clayland Maffitt)	04/28/1949	Forest Lawn Memorial Park, Beaumont, TX
Towne, Babe (Jay King)	10/29/1938	Riverside Cemetery, Spencer, IA
Townsend, George Hodgson	03/15/1930	Alderbrook Cemetery, Guilford, CT
Townsend, Ira Dance	07/21/1965	Masonic Cemetery, Weimar, TX
Townsend, Jack (John)	12/21/1963	Townsend Cemetery, Townsend, DE
Townsend, Leo Alphonse	12/03/1976	Catholic Cemetery, Mobile, AL
Toy, Jim (James Madison)	03/13/1919	Beaver Cemetery, Beaver, PA
Tozer, Bill (William Louis)	02/23/1955	Cypress Lawn Memorial Park, Colma, CA. Cremated.
Traffley, Bill (William Franklin)	06/23/1908	Glendale Cemetery, Des Moines, IA
Traffley, John M.	05/15/1900	Mount Olivet Cemetery, Frederick, MD
Tragesser, Walt (Walter Joseph)	12/14/1970	St. Boniface Cemetery, Lafayette, IN
Trautman, Fred (Frederick Orlando)	02/15/1964	Oakwood Cemetery, Bucyrus, OH
Travers, Al (Aloysius Joseph)	04/19/1968	Jesuit Novitiate Cemetery, Wernersville, PA
Tray, Jim (James)	07/28/1905	St. John's Cemetery, Jackson, MI
Traynor, Pie (Harold Joseph)	03/16/1972	Homewood Cemetery, Pittsburgh, PA
Treadway, George	11/05/1928	Evergreen Memorial Park, Riverside, CA
Treadway, Red (Thadford Leon)	05/26/1994	Arlington Memorial Park, Sandy Springs, GA
Trechock, Frank Adam	01/16/1989	Fort Snelling National Cemetery, Minneapolis, MN
Trekell, Harry Roy	11/04/1965	Forest Cemetery, Coeur D'Alene, ID
Tremper, Overton (Carlton Overton)	01/09/1996	Cremated, Largo, FL.
Trenwith, George W.	02/01/1890	Holy Cross Cemetery, Yeadon, PA. Originally intered at St. Mary's Cemetery (Moore Street), Philadelphia. Cemetery removed in 1954.
Tresh, Mike (Michael)	10/04/1966	Michigan Memorial Park, Flat Rock, MI
Trice, Bob (Robert Lee)	09/16/1988	St. Paul's Catholic Cemetery, Weirton, WV
Trinkle, Ken (Kenneth Wayne)	05/10/1976	Stampers Creek Cemetery, Paoli, IN
Triplett, Coaker (Herman Coaker)	01/30/1992	Mount Lawn Memorial Park, Boone, NC
Trosky, Hal (Harold Arthur, Sr.)	06/18/1979	St. Michael's Cemetery, Norway, IA
Trott, Sam (Samuel W.)	06/05/1925	Loudon Park Cemetery, Baltimore, MD
Trotter, Bill (William Felix)	08/26/1984	Maple Hill Cemetery, Fairfield, IL
Trouppe, Quincy Thomas	08/10/1993	Calvary Cemetery, St. Louis, MO
Trout, Dizzy (Paul Howard)	02/28/1972	Homewood Memorial Gardens, Homewood, IL
Trowbridge, Bob (Robert)	04/03/1980	Cedar Park Cemetery, Hudson, NY

Name	DOD	Cemetery, City, State
Troy, Dasher (John Joseph)	03/30/1938	Calvary Cemetery, Woodside, Queens, NY
Truby, Harry Garvin	03/21/1953	Woodland Cemetery, Ironton, OH
Ttuesdale, Frank Day	08/27/1943	Sunset Memorail Park, Albuquerque, NM
Tucker, Ollie (Oliver Dinwiddie)	07/13/1940	Tucker Family Cemetery, Radiant, VA
Tucker, Thurman Lowell	05/07/1993	New Gordon Cemetery, Gordon, TX
Tucker, Tommy (Thomas Joseph)	10/22/1935	Calvary Cemetery, Holyoke, MA
Turbeville, George Elkins	10/05/1983	Greenlawn Memorial Park, Columbia, SC
Turbidy, Jerry (Jeremiah)	09/05/1920	Calvary Cemetery, Dudley, MA
Turgeon, Pete (Eugene Joseph)	01/24/1977	Crestview Memorial Park, Wichita Falls, TX
Turk, Lucas Newton	01/11/1994	Presbyterian Church Cemetery, Homer, GA
Turner, Earl Edwin	10/20/1999	St. Anne's Catholic Cemetery, Lenox, MA
Turner, Jim (James Riley)	11/29/1998	Woodlawn Memorial Park, Nashville, TN
Turner, Ted (Theodore Holhot)	02/04/1958	Lexington Cemetery, Lexington, KY
Turner, Terry (Terrance Lamont)	07/18/1960	Knollwood Cemetery, Mayfield Heights, OH
Turner, Tink (Thomas Lovatt)	02/25/1962	West Laurel Hill Cemetery, Bala Cynwyd, PA
Turner, Tom (Thomas Richard)	05/14/1986	Cremated, Kennewick, WA
Turner, Tuck (George A.)	07/16/1945	Ocean View Cemetery, Oakwood, Staten Island, NY
Tuttle, Bill (William Robert)	07/27/1998	Cremated, Anoka, MN
Tutwiler, Elmer Strange	05/03/1976	Barrancas National Cemetery, Pensacola, FL
Tutwiler, Guy Isbel	08/15/1930	Elmwood Cemetery, Birmingham, AL
Twining, Twink (Howard Earle)	06/14/1973	Forest Hills Cemetery, Huntingdon Valley, PA
Twitchell, Larry (Lawrence Grant)	04/23/1930	Lakewood Park Cemetery, Rocky River, OH
Twombly, Babe (Clarence Edward)	11/23/1974	Oakdale Memorial Park, Glendora, CA
Twombly, Cy (Edwin Parker)	12/03/1974	Stonewall Jackson Memorial Cemetery, Lexington, VA
Twombly, George Frederick	02/17/1975	Puritan Lawn Memorial Park, Peabody, MA
Tyack, Jim (James Frederick)	01/03/1995	Hillcrest Memorial Park, Bakersfield, CA
Tyler, Fred (Frederick Franklin)	10/14/1945	Forest Hill Cemetery, East Derry, NH
Tyler, Johnny (John Anthony)	07/11/1972	Transfiguration Cemetery, Russellton, PA
Tyler, Lefty (George Albert)	09/29/1953	St. Patrick's Cemetery, Lowell, MA
Tyng, Jim (James Alexander)	10/30/1931	Cremated, Fresh Pond Crematory, Middle Village, Queens, NY
Tyree, Earl Carlton	05/17/1954	Rushville Cemetery, Rushville, IL
Tyriver, Dave (David Burton)	10/28/1988	Peace Lutheran Church Cemetery, Oshkosh, WI
Tyson, Ty (Albert Thomas)	08/16/1953	Mt. Olivet Cemetery, Tonawanda, NY
Uchrinscko, Jimmy (James Emerson)	03/17/1995	West Newton Cemetery, West Newton, PA
Uhl, Bob (Robert Ellwood)	08/21/1990	Cypress Hill Memorial Park, Petaluma, CA
Uhle, George Ernest	02/26/1985	Lakewood Park Cemetery, Rocky River, OH
Uhler, Maury (Maurice William)	05/04/1918	Druid Ridge Cemetery, Pikesville, MD
Uhlir, Charlie (Charles Karel)	07/09/1984	Lake View Cemetery, Spirit Lake, IA
Ulrich, Dutch (Frank W.)	02/11/1929	Bohemian National Cemetery (formerly Oak Hill Cemetery), Baltimore, MD
Umbricht, Jim (James)	04/08/1964	Cremated, ashes scattered at Astrodome, Houston, TX

Name	DOD	Cemetery, City, State
Underhill, Willie Vern	10/26/1970	Roselawn Memorial Cemetery, Van Vleck, TX
Underwood, Fred (Frederick Theodore)	01/26/1906	Mount St. Mary's Cemetery, Kansas City, MO
Unglaub, Bob (Robert Alexander)	11/29/1916	Sunny Ridge Memorial Park, Crisfield, MD. Moved from Loudon Park Cemetery, Baltimore in 1969.
Unser, Al (Albert Bernard)	07/05/1995	Calvary Cemetery, Decatur, IL
Upchurch, Woody (Jefferson Woodrow)	10/23/1971	Buies Creek Cemetery, Buies Creek, NC
Upham, Bill (William Lawrence)	09/14/1959	Gate of Heaven Cemetery, East Hanover, NJ
Upp, Jerry (George Henry)	06/30/1937	Oakland Cemetery, Sandusky, OH
Upright, Dixie (Roy T.)	11/13/1986	Green Lawn Cemetery, China Grove, NC
Upshaw, Cecil Lee	02/07/1995	Eternal Hills Memory Gardens, Snellville, GA
Upton, Bill (William Ray)	01/02/1987	Cremated, San Diego., CA
Urban, Luke (Louis John)	12/07/1980	Notre Dame Cemetery, Fall River, MA
Urbanski, Billy (William Michael)	07/12/1973	Holy Trinity Church, Hopelawn, NJ
Ury, Lon (Louis Newton)	03/04/1918	Evergren Cemtery, Fort Scott, KS
Ussat, Dutch (William August)	05/29/1959	Dayton Memorial Park, Dayton, OH
Vache, Tex (Ernest Lewis)	06/11/1953	Overton Cemetery, Overton, TX
Vadeboncoeur, Gene (Onesime Eugene)	10/16/1935	St. Joseph's Cemetery, Haverhill, MA
Vahrenhorst, Harry Henry	10/10/1943	Bethlehem Cemetery, Bellefontaine, MO
Vail, Bob (Robert Garfield)	03/22/1942	Chelten Hills Cemetery, Philadelphia, PA
Valo, Elmer William	07/19/1998	Sacred Heart New Cemetery, Palmerton, PA
Van Alstyne, Clay (Clayton Emory)	01/05/1960	Firwood Cemetery, Stuyvesant, NY
Van Atta, Russ (Russell)	10/10/1986	Frankford Plains United Methodist Church Cemetery, Augusta, NJ
Van Buren, Deacon (Edward Eugene)	06/29/1957	Cremated, Portland, OR
Van Camp, Al (Albert Joseph)	02/02/1981	Mount Calvary Cemetery, Davenport, IA
Van Cuyk, Chris (Christian Gerald)	11/03/1992	Florida National Cemetery, Bushnell, FL
Van Dyke, Ben (Benjamin Harrison)	10/22/1973	Sarasota Memorial Park, Sarasota, FL
Van Dyke, Bill (William Jennings)	05/05/1933	Concordia Cemetery, El Paso, TX
Van Haltren, George Edward Martin	09/29/1945	St. Mary's Cemetery, Oakland, CA
Van Zandt, Ike (Charles Isaac)	09/14/1908	Woodlawn Cemetery, Nashua, NH
Van Zant, Dick (Richard)	08/06/1912	Earlham Cemetery, Richmond, IN
Vance, Dazzy (Clarence Arthur)	02/16/1961	Stage Stand Cemetery, Homosassa Springs, FL
Vance, Joe (Joseph Albert)	07/04/1978	St. Joseph Cemetery, Devine, TX
Vandagrift, Carl William	10/09/1920	Catholic Cemetery, Fort Wayne, IN
Vandenberg, Hy (Harold Harris)	07/31/1994	Lakewood Cemetery, Minneapolis, MN
Vander Meer, Johnny (John Samuel)	10/06/1997	Garden of Memories Cemetery, Tampa, FL
Vangilder, Elam Russell	04/30/1977	Fairmont Cemetery, Cape Girardeau, MO
Vann, John Silas	06/10/1958	Forest Park Cemetery, Shreveport, LA
Varga, Andy (Andrew William)	11/04/1992	Cremated, Orlando, FL

Name	DOD	Cemetery, City, State
Vargus, Bill (William Fay)	02/12/1979	Mount Wollaston Cemetery, Quincy, MA
Vasbinder, Moses Calhoun	12/22/1950	Cadiz Cemetery, Cadiz, OH
Vaughn, Arky (Joseph Floyd)	08/30/1952	Eagleville Community Cemetery, Eagleville, CA
Vaughn, Bobby (Robert)	04/11/1965	New Tacoma Memorial Park, Tacoma, WA
Vaughn, Farmer (Henry Francis)	02/21/1914	Cremated, Cincinnati, OH.
Vaughn, Fred (Frederick Thomas)	03/02/1964	Wildwood Cemetery, Bartow, FL
Vaughn, Hippo (James Leslie)	05/29/1966	Cremated, Chicago, IL.
Veach, Al (Alvis Lindel)	09/06/1990	Live Oak Cemetery, Selma, AL
Veach, Bobby (Robert Hayes)	08/07/1945	White Chapel Memorial Cemetery, Troy, MI
Veach, Peek-a-Boo (William Walter)	11/12/1937	Floral Park Cemetery, Indianapolis, IN
Vedder, Lou (Louis Edward)	03/09/1990	Cremated, Lake Forest Crematory, Avon Park, FL
Veil, Bucky (Frederick William)	04/16/1931	Wildwood Cemetery, Williamsport, PA
Veltman, Pat (Arthur Patrick)	10/01/1980	Sunset Memorial Park, San Antonio, TX
Verban, Emil Matthew	06/08/1989	St. Mary's Cemetery, Lincoln, IL
Verdel, Al (Albert Alfred)	04/16/1991	St. Mary's Cemetery, Trenton, NJ
Vereker, Tommy (John James)	04/02/1974	St. John's Cemetery, Baltimore, MD
Vergez, Johnny (John Louis)	07/15/1991	Cremated, Sacramento, CA
Vernon, Joe (Joseph Henry)	03/13/1955	Milltown Rural Cemetery, Brewster, NY
Versalles, Zoilo Casanova	06/09/1995	Cremated, Cremation Society of Minnesota, Minneapolis, MN.
Veselic, Bob (Robert Mitchell)	12/26/1995	Crestlawn Memorial Park, Riverside, CA
Viau, Lee (Leon A.)	12/17/1947	Laurel Grove Cemetery, Totowa, NJ
Vick, Ernie (Henry Arthur)	07/16/1980	Washtenong Memorial Park, Ann Arbor, MI
Vick, Sammy (Samuel Bruce)	08/17/1986	Forest Memorial Park, Batesville, MS
Vickers, Rube (Harry Porter)	12/09/1958	Leonardson Memorial Cemetery, Pittsford, MI
Vickery, Tom (Thomas Gill)	03/21/1921	I.O.O.F Cemetery, Burlington, NJ
Vico, George Steve	01/14/1994	Serbian United Benevolent Cemetery, Los Angeles, CA
Vinson, Rube (Ernest Augustus)	10/12/1951	Lawn Croft Cemetery, Linwood, PA
Viox, Jim (James Harry)	01/06/1969	Forest Lawn Memorial Park, Erlanger, KY
Virtue, Jake (Jacob Kitchline)	02/03/1943	Mt. Vernon Cemetery, Philadelphia, PA
Visner, Joe (Joseph Paul)	06/17/1945	Hansville Cemetery, Fosston, MN
Vitelli, Joe (Antonio Joseph)	02/07/1967	St. Mary's Cemetery, McKees Rocks, PA
Vitt, Ossie (Oscar Joseph)	01/31/1963	Mountain View Cemetery, Oakland, CA
Vogel, Otto Henry	07/19/1969	Memory Gardens Cemetery, Iowa City, IA
Voigt, Ollie (Olen Edward)	04/07/1970	Greenwood Memory Lawn Cemetery, Phoenix, AZ
Volz, Jake (Jacob Phillip)	08/11/1962	St. Joseph's Society Cemetery, San Antonio, TX
Von Fricken, Tony (Anthony)	03/22/1947	St. Peter's Cemetery, Troy, NY
Von Kolnitz, Fritz (Alfred Holmes)	03/18/1948	Magnolia Cemetery, Charleston, SC
Vorhees, Cy (Henry Bert)	02/08/1910	Woodlawn Cemetery, Wadsworth, OH
Vosmik, Joe (Joseph Franklin)	01/27/1962	Highland Park Cemetery, Cleveland, OH
Vowinkel, Rip (John Henry)	07/13/1966	St. Paul's Cemetery, Oswego, NY
Voyles, Phil (Philip Vance)	11/03/1972	Lakeview Cemetery, South Weymouth, MA

Name	DOD	Cemetery, City, State
Wachtel, Paul Horine	12/15/1964	Sunset Memorial Park, San Antonio, TX
Wacker, Charlie (Charles James)	08/07/1948	Oak Hill Cemetery, Evansville, IN
Waddell, Rube (George Edward)	04/01/1914	Mission Burial Park North, San Antonio, TX
Waddey, Frank Orum	10/21/1990	Memorial Park Cemetery, Memphis, TN
Wade, Ben (Benjamin Styron)	12/02/2002	Cremated, Los Angeles, CA. Ashes given to family
Wade, Ham (Abraham Lincoln)	07/21/1968	Lakeview Memorial Park, Cinnaminson, NJ
Wade, Rip (Richard Frank)	06/15/1957	Oneota Cemetery, Duluth, MN
Wadsworth, Jack (John L.)	07/08/1941	Greenwood Cemetery, Wellington, OH
Wagenhorst, Woody (Ellwood Otto)	02/12/1946	Glenwood Cemetery, Washington, DC
Wagner, Al (Albert)	11/26/1928	Chartiers Cemetery, Carnegie, PA
Wagner, Bill (William Joseph)	01/11/1951	Calvary Cemetery, Waterloo, IA
Wagner, Bull (William George)	10/02/1967	Oakwood Cemetery, Muskegon, MI
Wagner, Hal (Harold Edward)	08/04/1979	Lakeview Memorial Park, Cinnaminson, NJ
Wagner, Heinie (Charles F.)	03/20/1943	Gate of Heaven Cemetery, Hawthorne, NY
Wagner, Honus (John Peter)	12/06/1955	Jefferson Memorial Park, Pleasant Hills, PA
Wagner, Leon Lamar	01/03/2004	Riverside National Cemetery, Riverside, CA
Wahl, Kermit Emerson	09/16/1987	Lakeview Cemetery, Columbia, SD
Waitkus, Eddie (Edward Stephen)	09/15/1972	Cambridge Cemetery, Cambridge, MA
Waitt, Charlie (Charles C.)	10/21/1912	Sunset View Cemetery, Colma, CA. Cemetery closed in 1951. Site currently Cypress Hills Golf Course.
Wakefield, Dick (Richard Cummings)	08/26/1985	Resthaven Memory Garden, Avon, OH
Wakefield, Howard John	04/16/1941	Calvary Cemetery, Evanston, IL
Walberg, Rube (George Elvin)	10/27/1978	Cremated, Phoenix, AZ
Walczak, Ed (Edwin Joseph)	03/10/1998	St. Mary's & St. Joseph's Cemetery, Norwich, CT
Waldbauer, Doc (Albert Charles)	07/16/1969	Terrace Heights Memorial Park, Yakima, WA
Walden, Tom (Thomas Fred)	09/27/1955	Memorial Park Cemetery, St. Louis, MO
Waldron, Irv (Irving J.)	07/22/1944	Oak Ridge Cemetery, Southbridge, MA
Walker, Bill (William Henry)	06/14/1966	Valhalla Gardens of Memory, Belleville, IL
Walker, Buddy (Martin Van Buren)	04/24/1978	Northwood Cemetery, Philadelphia, PA
Walker, Curt (William Curtis)	12/09/1955	Glenwood Cemetery, Beeville, TX
Walker, Dixie (Ewart Gladstone)	11/14/1965	Elmwood Cemetery, Birmingham, AL
Walker, Dixie (Fred)	05/17/1982	Elmwood Cemetery, Birmingham, AL
Walker, Ed (Edward Harrison)	09/29/1947	Greenlawn Cemetery, Akron, OH
Walker, Ernie (Ernest Robert)	04/01/1965	Fraternal Cemetery, Birmingham, AL
Walker, Fleet (Moses Fleetwood)	05/11/1924	Union Cemetery, Steubenville, OH
Walker, Frank (Charles Franklin)	09/16/1974	Glenwood Cemetery, Bristol, TN
Walker, Harry William	08/08/1999	Cedar Grove Cemetery, Leeds, AL
Walker, Hub (Harvey Willos)	11/26/1982	Santa Clara Mission Cemetery, Santa Clara, CA
Walker, Johnny (John Miles)	08/19/1976	Cremated, Hollywood, FL
Walker, Oscar	05/20/1889	Evergreen Cemetery, Brooklyn, NY
Walker, Roy (James Roy)	02/10/1962	Garden of Memories, Metairie, LA
Walker, Rube (Albert Bluford)	12/12/1992	Blue Ridge Memorial Park, Lenoir, NC
Walker, Speed (Joseph Richard)	01/20/1959	Jefferson Memorial Park, Pleasant Hills, PA

Name	DOD	Cemetery, City, State
Walker, Tilly (Clarence William)	09/21/1959	Urbana Cemetery, Limestone, TN
Walker, Tom (Thomas William)	07/10/1944	Fernwood Cemetery, Bridgeton, NJ
Walker, Welday Wilberforce	11/23/1937	Union Cemetery, Steubenville, OH
Walkup, Jim (James Huey)	06/12/1990	Duncan City Cemetery, Duncan, OK
Wall, Howard C.	03/15/1909	Oak Hill Cemetery, Washington, DC
Wall, Joe (Joseph Francis)	07/17/1936	Green-Wood Cemetery, Brooklyn, NY
Wall, Murray Wesley	10/08/1971	Restland Memorial Park, Dallas, TX
Wallace, Bobby (Rhoderick John)	11/03/1960	Inglewood Park Cemetery, Inglewood, CA
Wallace, Doc (Frederick Renshaw)	12/31/1964	Church Hill Cemetery, Church Hill, MD
Wallace, Jack (Clarence Eugene)	10/15/1960	Winnfield City Cemetery, Winnfield, LA
Wallace, Jim (James L.)	05/16/1953	St. Mary's Cemetery, Lynn, MA
Wallace, Lefty (James Harold)	07/28/1982	Sunset Memorial Gardens, Evansville, IN
Wallaesa, Jack (John)	12/27/1986	St. Anthony's Cemetery, Easton, PA
Waller, Red (John Francis)	02/09/1915	Holy Name Cemetery, Jersey City, NJ
Walsh, Augie (August Sothley)	11/12/1985	Cremated, San Rafael, CA
Walsh, Austin Edward	01/26/1955	San Fernando Mission Cemetery, Mission Hills, CA
Walsh, Connie (Cornelius R.)	04/05/1953	Calvary Cemetery, St. Louis, MO
Walsh, Dee (Leo Thomas)	07/14/1971	Calvary Cemetery, St. Louis, MO
Walsh, Ed (Edward Arthur.)	10/31/1937	Sacred Heart Cemetery, Meriden, CT
Walsh, Ed (Edward Augustine)	05/26/1959	Forest Lawn Memorial Gardens, Pompano Beach, FL
Walsh, Jim (James Thomas)	05/13/1967	New Calvary Cemetery, Mattapan, MA
Walsh, Jimmy (James Charles)	07/03/1962	St. Agnes Cemetery, Syracuse, NY
Walsh, Jimmy (Michael Timothy)	01/21/1947	New Cathedral Cemetery, Baltimore, MD
Walsh, Joe (Joseph Francis)	01/06/1967	St. Bonaventure University Cemetery, St. Bonaventure, NY
Walsh, Joe (Joseph Patrick)	10/05/1996	Walnut Hills Cemetery, Brookline, MA
Walsh, Joe (Joseph R.)	08/08/1911	Holy Sepulchre Cemetery, Omaha, NE
Walsh, John Gabriel	04/25/1947	St. Mary's Cemetery, Wilkes-Barre, PA
Walsh, Junior (James Gerald)	11/12/1990	St. Joseph's Cemetery, Scranton, PA
Walsh, Mike *manager*	02/02/1929	St. Louis Cemetery, Louisville, KY
Walsh, Tom (Thomas Joseph)	03/16/1963	Mount Calvary Cemetery, Davenport, IA
Walsh, Walt (Walter William)	01/15/1966	St. Catherine's Cemetery, Sea Girt, NJ
Walter, Bernie (James Bernard)	10/30/1988	Hillcrest Cemetery, Dover, TN
Walters, Bucky (William Henry)	04/20/1991	Whitemarsh Memorial Park, Ambler, PA
Walters, Fred James	02/01/1980	Hickory Grove Cemetery, Laurel, MS
Walters, Roxy (Alfred John)	06/03/1956	Olivet Memorial Park, Colma, CA
Waltz, John William *manager*	04/27/1931	Greenmount Cemetery, Baltimore, MD
Wambsganss, Bill (William Adolph)	12/08/1985	Calvary Cemetery, Cleveland, OH
Waner, Lloyd James	07/22/1982	Rose Hill Cemetery, Oklahoma City, OK
Waner, Paul Glee	08/29/1965	Manasota Memorial Park, Bradenton, FL
Wanner, Jack (Clarence Curtis)	05/28/1919	Oakwood Cemetery, Geneseo, IL
Wanninger, Pee-Wee (Paul Louis)	03/07/1981	Forest Hill Cemetery, Birmingham, AL
Wantz, Dick (Richard Carter)	05/13/1965	Forest Lawn Memorial Park-Cypress, Cypress, CA
Ward, Aaron Lee	01/30/1961	St. Joseph Cemetery #3, New Orleans, LA
Ward, Chuck (Charles William)	04/04/1969	Cremated, St. Petersburg, FL

Name	DOD	Cemetery, City, State
Ward, Jim (James H. H.)	06/04/1886	Mount Benedict Cemetery, West Roxbury, MA
Ward, Joe (Joseph A.)	08/11/1934	Westminster Cemetery, Bala Cynwyd, PA
Ward, John Montgomery	03/04/1925	Greenfield Cemetery, Uniondale, NY
Ward, Piggy (Frank Gray)	10/24/1912	Cedar Grove Cemetery, Chambersburg, PA
Ward, Rube (John Andrew)	01/17/1945	Maplewood Cemetery, New Lexington, OH
Wares, Buzzy (Clyde Ellsworth)	05/26/1964	Riverview Cemetery, South Bend, IN
Warhop, Jack (John Milton)	10/04/1960	Lanark Cemetery, Lanark, IL
Warmoth, Cy (Wallace Walter)	06/20/1957	Highland Memorial Gardens, Mt. Carmel, IL
Warneke, Lon (Lonnie)	06/23/1976	Owley Cemetery, Mount Ida, AR
Warner, Ed (Edward Emory)	02/05/1954	Forest Hill Cemetery, Fitchburg, MA
Warner, Fred (Frederick John Rodney)	02/13/1886	Woodlands Cemetery, Philadelphia, PA
Warner, Jack (John Ralph)	03/13/1986	Mt. Vernon Memorial Gardens, Mt. Vernon, IL
Warner, John Joseph	12/21/1943	St. Mary Star of the Sea Cemetery, Lawrence, NY
Warren, Bennie Louis	05/11/1994	Ames Cemetery, Ames, OK
Warren, Bill (William Hackney)	01/28/1960	Melrose Cemetery, Whiteville, TN
Warren, Tommy (Thomas Gentry)	01/02/1968	Memorial Park Cemetery, Tulsa, OK
Warstler, Rabbit (Harold Burton)	05/31/1964	North Canton Cemetery, North Canton, OH
Wasdell, Jimmy (James Charles)	08/06/1983	Meadowland Memorial Gardens, New Port Richey, FL
Wasem, Link (Lincoln William)	03/06/1979	Cremated, Laguna Beach, CA
Washburn, George Edward	01/05/1979	Resthaven Gardens of Memory, Baton Rouge, LA
Washburn, Libe (Libeus)	03/22/1940	Morningside Cemetery, Malone, NY
Washington, George (Sloan Vernon)	02/17/1985	New Colony Cemetery, Linden, TX
Waters, Fred Warren	08/28/1989	Roseland Park Cemetery, Hattiesburg, MS
Watkins, Bill (William Henry)	06/09/1937	Lakeside Cemetery, Port Huron, MI
Watkins, George Archibald	06/01/1970	Broyles Chapel Cemetery, Palestine, TX
Watson, Art (Arthur Stanhope)	05/09/1950	St. Bernard's Cemetery, Lewiston, NY
Watson, Doc (Charles John)	12/30/1949	Cremated, San Diego, CA.
Watson, Johnny (John Thomas)	04/29/1965	Woodmere Memorial Park, Huntington, WV
Watson, Milt (Milton Wilson)	04/10/1962	Bellwood Cemetery, Pine Bluff, AR
Watson, Mother (Walter L.)	11/23/1898	Middleport Hill Cemetery, Middleport, OH
Watson, Mule (John Reeves)	08/25/1949	Arlington Cemetery, Homer, LA
Watt, Allie (Albert Bailey)	03/15/1968	Rosewood Memorial Park, Virginia Beach, VA
Watt, Frank Marion	08/31/1956	Fort Lincoln Cemetery, Brentwood, MD
Way, Boy (Robert Clinton)	06/20/1974	Grove Cemetery, Victory Twp, Venango County, PA
Wayenberg, Frank	04/16/1975	Mount Olive Cemetery, Zanesville, OH
Weatherly, Roy (Cyril Roy)	01/19/1991	Cremated, Woodville, TX
Weaver, Art (Arthur Coggshall)	03/23/1917	Fairmount Cemetery, Denver, CO
Weaver, Bill (William Frederick)	06/01/1994	Cheatham Hill Memorial Park, Marietta, GA
Weaver, Buck (George Daniel)	01/31/1956	Mount Hope Cemetery, Chicago, IL
Weaver, Farmer (William B.)	01/23/1943	Hillside Memorial Park, Akron, OH
Weaver, Harry Abraham	05/30/1983	Holy Sepulchre Cemetery, Rochester, NY

Name	DOD	Cemetery, City, State
Weaver, Jim (James Dement)	12/12/1983	Forest Lawn Memorial Park, Erlanger, KY
Weaver, Orlie (Orville Forest)	11/28/1970	Garden of Memories, Metairie, LA
Weaver, Sam (Samuel H.)	02/01/1914	Mount Peace Cemetery, Philadelphia, PA
Webb, Bill (William Joseph)	01/12/1943	Mount Olivet Cemetery, Chicago, IL
Webb, Earl (William Earl)	05/23/1965	Taylor Place Cemetery, Jamestown, TN
Webb, Lefty (Cleon Earl)	01/12/1958	Forest Cemetery, Circleville, OH
Webb, Red (Samuel Henry)	02/07/1996	Cheltenham Veterans Cemetery, Cheltenham, MD
Webb, Skeeter (James Laverne)	07/08/1986	Rose Hill-Magnolia Cemetery, Meridian, MS
Webber, Les (Lester Elmer)	11/13/1986	Dudley-Hoffman Columbarium, Santa Maria, CA
Weber, Charlie (Charles P.)	06/13/1914	Magnolia Cemetery, Beaumont, TX
Weber, Harry (Henry J.)	12/22/1926	Crown Hill Cemetery, Indianapolis, IN
Weckbecker, Pete (Peter)	05/16/1935	Hampton National Cemetery, Hampton, VA
Weekly, Johnny (John)	11/24/1974	Oak View Memorial Park Cemetery, Antioch, CA
Wehde, Biggs (Wilbur)	09/21/1970	Calvary Cemetery, Sioux City, IA
Wehmeier, Herm (Herman Ralph)	05/21/1973	St. John's Cemetery, Cincinnati, OH
Weigel, Ralph Richard	04/15/1992	West Tennessee Veteran's Cemetery, Memphis, TN
Weihe, Podge (John Garibaldi)	04/15/1914	Spring Grove Cemetery, Cincinnati, OH
Weiland, Bob (Robert George)	11/09/1988	Mount Emblem Cemetery, Elmhurst, IL
Weiland, Bud (Edwin Nicholas)	07/12/1971	Memorial Park Cemetery, Skokie, IL
Weilman, Carl Woolworth	05/25/1924	Greenwood Cemetery, Hamilton, OH
Weimer, Jake (Jacob)	06/19/1928	Mount Olivet Cemetery, Chicago, IL
Weinert, Phil (Philip Walter)	04/17/1973	Lakeview Memorial Park, Cinnaminson, NJ
Weintraub, Phil (Philip)	06/21/1987	Desert Memorial Park, Cathedral City, CA
Weir, Roy (William Franklin)	09/30/1989	Rose Hills Memorial Park, Whittier, CA
Weis, Butch (Arthur John)	05/04/1997	New St. Marcus Evangelical Cemetery, St. Louis, MO
Weiser, Bud (Harry Budson)	07/31/1961	Odd Fellow's Cemetery, Shamokin, PA
Weiss, Joe (Joseph Harold)	07/07/1967	Cremated, Cedar Rapids, IA
Welaj, Johnny (John Ludwig)	09/13/2003	Moore Memorial Gardens, Arlington, TX
Welch, Curt (Curtis Benton)	08/29/1896	St. Aloysius Catholic Cemetery, East Liverpool, OH
Welch, Frank Tiguer	07/25/1957	Elmwood Cemetery, Birmingham, AL
Welch, Herb (Herbert M.)	04/13/1967	Fairview Cemetery, Dyersburg, TN
Welch, Johnny (John Vernon)	09/02/1940	Calvary Cemetery, St. Louis, MO
Welch, Mickey (Michael Francis)	07/30/1941	Calvary Cemetery, Woodside, Queens, NY
Welch, Ted (Floyd John)	01/07/1943	Woodland Cemetery, Cleveland, OK
Welday, Mike (Lyndon Earl)	05/28/1942	Mount Muncie Cemetery, Lansing, KS
Welf, Ollie (Oliver Henry)	06/15/1967	Calvary Cemetery, Cleveland, OH
Wellman, Bob (Robert Joseph)	12/20/1994	Gate of Heaven Cemetery, Montgomery, OH
Wells, Ed (Edwin Lee)	05/01/1986	Greenwood Cemetery, Montgomery, AL
Wells, Jake (Jacob)	03/16/1927	St. Mary's Cemetery, Norfolk, VA
Wells, John Frederick	10/23/1993	Cremated, Olean, NY
Welsh, Jimmy (James Daniel)	10/30/1970	Holy Sepulchre Cemetery, Hayward, CA
Welzer, Tony (Anton Frank)	03/18/1971	Saint Adelbert Cemetery, Milwaukee, WI

Name	DOD	Cemetery, City, State
Wendell, Lew (Lewis Charles)	07/11/1953	Woodlawn Cemetery, Bronx, NY
Wentz, George (John George)	09/14/1907	St. Louis Cemetery, Louisville, KY
Wentzel, Stan (Stanley Aaron)	11/28/1991	Forest Hills Memorial Park, Reiffton, PA
Wera, Julie (Julian Valentine)	12/12/1975	St. Mary's Cemetery, Winona, MN
Werden, Perry (Percival Wheritt)	01/09/1934	Bellefontaine Cemetery, St. Louis, MO
Werrick, Joe (Joseph Abraham)	05/10/1943	State Hospital Cemetery, St. Peter, MN
Wertz, Del (Dwight Lyman Moody)	05/26/1958	Highland Cemetery, South Bend, IN
Wertz, Johnny (Henry Levi)	09/24/1990	St. Paul Lutheran Church Cemetery, Pomaria, SC
Wertz, Vic (Victor Woodrow)	07/07/1983	Holy Sepulchre Cemetery, Southfield, MI
West, Buck (Milton Douglas)	01/13/1929	Mansfield Cemetery, Mansfield, OH
West, Dick (Richard Thomas)	03/13/1996	Lindenwood Cemetery, Fort Wayne, IN
West, Frank (John Franklin)	09/06/1932	Grandview Cemetery, Johnstown, PA
West, Jim (James Hiram)	05/24/1963	Cremated, Los Angeles, CA
West, Lefty (Weldon Edison)	07/23/1979	Forest Lawn Memorial Park, Hendersonville, NC
West, Max (Walter Maxwell)	04/25/1971	Resthaven Memorial Gardens, Houston, TX
West, Max Edward	12/31/2003	Cremated, San Bernardino. Ashes scattered.
West, Sam (Samuel Filmore)	11/23/1985	Resthaven Memorial Park, Lubbock, TX
West, William O.	10/27/1928	Cypress Hills Cemetery, Brooklyn, NY
Westerberg, Oscar William	04/17/1909	Mountain View Cemetery, Oakland, CA
Westlake, Jim (James Patrick)	01/03/2003	St. Mary's Catholic Cemetery, Sacramento, CA
Weston, Al (Alfred John)	11/13/1997	Cremated, San Diego., CA
Westrum, Wes (Wesley Noreen)	05/28/2002	Silver Creek Cemetery, Clearbrook, MN
Wetzel, Buzz (Charles Edward)	03/07/1941	Pinal Cemetery, Central Heights, AZ
Wetzel, Dutch (Franklin Burton)	03/05/1942	Cremated, Hollywood, CA
Weyhing, Gus (August)	09/04/1955	Calvary Cemetery, Louisville, KY
Weyhing, John	06/20/1890	Eastern Cemetery, Louisville, KY
Whaley, Bill (William Carl)	03/03/1943	Crown Hill Cemetery, Indianapolis, IN
Whaling, Bert (Albert James)	01/21/1965	Los Angeles National Cemetery, Los Angeles, CA
Wheat, Mack (McKinley Davis)	08/14/1979	Los Banos Cemetery, Los Banos, CA
Wheat, Zach (Zachary Davis)	03/11/1972	Forest Hill Cemetery, Kansas City, MO
Wheatley, Charlie (Charles)	12/10/1982	Memorial Park Cemetery, Tulsa, OK
Wheaton, Woody (Elwood Pierce)	12/11/1995	Arlington Cemetery, Drexel Hill, PA
Wheeler, Dick (Richard)	02/12/1962	Westview Cemetery, Lexington, MA
Wheeler, Don (Donald Wesley)	12/10/2003	Fort Snelling National Cemetery, Minneapolis, MN
Wheeler, Ed (Edward L.)	08/15/1960	Greenwood Memorial Park, Fort Worth, TX
Wheeler, George Louis	03/21/1946	Cremated, Santa Ana, CA
Wheeler, Harry Eugene	10/09/1900	Spring Grove Cemetery, Cincinnati, OH
Wheeler, Rip (Floyd Clark)	09/18/1968	Mapleview Cemetery, Marion, KY
Wheelock, Bobby (Warren H.)	03/13/1928	Mount Auburn Cemetery, Cambridge, MA
Whelan, Jimmy (James Francis)	11/29/1929	Calvary Cemetery, Dayton, OH
Whelan, Tom (Thomas Joseph)	06/26/1957	St. Joseph's Cemetery, Lynn, MA
Whisnant, Pete (Thomas Peter)	03/22/1996	Cremated, Port Charlotte, FL
Whistler, Lew (Lewis W.)	12/30/1959	Bethany Cemetery, St. Louis, MO

Name	DOD	Cemetery, City, State
Whitcher, Bob (Robert Arthur)	05/08/1997	Crown Hill Memorial Park, Twinsburg, OH
White, Ade (Adel)	10/01/1978	Zion Baptist Church Cemetery, Braselton, GA
White, Barney (William Barney)	07/24/2002	Cathedral in the Pines Cemetery, Tyler, TX
White, Bill (William Dighton)	12/29/1924	Greenwood Cemetery, Bellaire, OH
White, Deacon (James Laurie)	07/07/1939	Restland Cemetery, Mendota, IL
White, Deke (George Frederick)	11/27/1957	St. Agnes Cemetery, Herkimer, NY
White, Doc (Guy Harris)	02/19/1969	Rock Creek Cemetery, Washington, DC
White, Ed (Edward Perry)	09/28/1982	Lakeland Memorial Gardens, Lakeland, FL
White, Ernie (Ernest Daniel)	05/22/1974	Floyd's Memorial Gardens, Jonesville, SC
White, Hal (Harold George)	04/21/2001	Florida National Cemetery, Bushnell, FL
White, Jack (John Peter)	06/19/1971	St. Raymond's Cemetery, Bronx, NY
White, Jack (John Wallace)	09/30/1963	Floral Park Cemetery, Indianapolis, IN
White, Jo-Jo (Joyner Clifford)	10/09/1986	Cremated, Tacoma, WA
White, Kirby (Oliver Kirby)	04/22/1943	Hillsboro Cemetery, Hillsboro, OH
White, Sam (Samuel Lambeth)	11/11/1929	East Cedar Hill Cemetery, Philadelphia, PA
White, Steve (Stephen Vincent)	01/29/1975	St. Mary's Cemetery, Randolph, MA
Whitehead, Burgess Urquhart	11/25/1993	St. Thomas Church Cemetery, Windsor, NC
Whitehead, John Henderson	10/20/1964	Carson Cemetery, Ector, TX
Whitehill, Earl Oliver	10/22/1954	Cedar Memorial Park Cemetery, Cedar Rapids, IA
Whitehouse, Charlie (Charles Evis)	07/19/1960	Crown Hill Cemetery, Indianapolis, IN
Whitehouse, Gil (Gilbert Arthur)	02/14/1926	Oak Hill Cemetery, Brewer, ME
Whiteley, Guerdon W.	11/23/1925	Oak Grove Cemetery, Hopkinton, RI
Whiteman, George	02/10/1947	Hollywood Cemetery, Houston, TX
Whiting, Jesse W.	10/28/1937	Greenmount Cemetery, Philadelphia, PA
Whitman, Frank (Walter Franklin)	02/06/1994	St. John's Evangelical Cemetery, Troy, IL
Whitney, Art (Arthur Wilson)	08/15/1943	Edson Cemetery, Lowell, MA
Whitney, Frank Thomas	10/30/1943	Greenmount Cemetery, Baltimore, MD
Whitney, Jim (James Evans)	05/21/1891	Spring Forest Cemetery, Binghamton, NY
Whitney, Pinky (Arthur Carter)	09/01/1987	Mission Burial Park South, San Antonio, TX
Whittaker, Walt (Walter Elton)	08/07/1965	Mount Pleasant Cemetery, Bryantville, MA
Whitted, Possum (George Bostic)	10/16/1962	Wilmington National Cemetery, Wilmington, NC
Wicker, Bob (Robert Kitridge)	01/22/1955	Forest Home Cemetery, Forest Park, IL
Wicker, Kemp Caswell	06/11/1973	Main Street United Methodist Church Cemetery, Kernersville, NC
Wickland, Al (Albert)	03/14/1980	Cremated, Port Washington, WI
Wiedemeyer, Charlie (Charles John)	10/27/1979	Keystone Heights Cemetery, Keystone Heights, FL
Wiedman, Stump (George Edward)	03/03/1905	Holy Sepulchre Cemetery, Rochester, NY
Wieneke, Jack (John)	03/16/1933	Roseland Park Cemetery, Berkley, MI
Wiggins, Alan Anthony	01/06/1991	Rose Hills Memorial Park, Whittier, CA
Wiggs, Jimmy (James Alvin)	01/20/1963	Cremated, Xenia, OH
Wigington, Fred Thomas	05/08/1980	Mountain View Memorial Gardens, Mesa, AZ
Wilborn, Claude Edward	11/13/1992	Bethel Hill Baptist Church Cemetery, Roxboro, NC
Wilhelm, Harry Lester	02/20/1944	Oak Grove Cemetery, Republic, PA
Wilhelm, Hoyt (James Hoyt)	08/23/2002	Palms Memorial Park, Sarasota, FL

Name	DOD	Cemetery, City, State
Wilhelm, Spider (Charles Ernest)	10/20/1992	Dulaney Valley Memorial Gardens, Timonium, MD
Wilhoit, Joe (Joseph William)	09/25/1930	Calvary Cemetery, Santa Barbara, CA
Wilie, Denney (Dennis Ernest)	06/20/1966	Cremated, Hayward, CA
Wilke, Harry (Henry Joseph)	06/21/1991	St. Stephen's Cemetery, Hamilton, OH
Wilkie, Lefty (Aldon Jay)	08/05/1992	Cremated, Tualatin, OR
Wilkinson, Ed (Edward Henry)	04/09/1918	Jacksonville Cemetery, Jacksonvile, OR
Wilks, Ted (Theodore)	08/21/1989	Forest Park (East) Cemetery, League City, TX
Willett, Ed (Robert Edgar)	05/10/1934	Caldwell Cemetery, Caldwell, KS
Williams, Al (Almon Edward)	07/19/1969	Shilo Cemetery, San Augustine, TX
Williams, Bob (Robert Elias)	08/06/1962	Greenlawn Cemetery, Nelsonville, OH
Williams, Cy (Fred)	04/23/1974	Three Lakes Cemetery, Three Lakes, WI
Williams, Dale (Elisha Alphonso)	10/22/1939	Highland Cemetery, Fort Mitchell, KY
Williams, Dave (David Owen)	04/25/1918	Dunmore Cemetery, Dunmore, PA
Williams, Denny (Evon Daniel)	03/23/1929	Mount Calvary Cemetery, Portland, OR
Williams, Dewey Edgar	03/19/2000	Riverview Cemetery, Williston, ND
Williams, Dib (Edwin Dibrell)	04/02/1992	Thorn Cemetery, Greenbrier, AR
Williams, Don (Donald Reid)	12/20/1991	Cremated, San Diego, CA. Ashes given to family.
Williams, Earl Baxter	03/10/1958	Highland Memorial Park, Knoxville, TN
Williams, Gus (August Joseph)	04/16/1964	Calvary Cemetery, Sterling, IL
Williams, Harry Peter	12/21/1963	Holy Sepulchre Cemetery. Omaha, NE
Williams, James Andrew *manager*	10/23/1918	Green Lawn Cemetery, Columbus, OH
Williams, Jimmy (James Thomas)	01/16/1965	Lakewood Cemetery, Minneapolis, MN
Williams, Johnny (John Brodie)	09/08/1963	San Fernando Mission Cemetery, Mission Hills, CA
Williams, Ken (Kenneth Roy)	01/22/1959	Hillrest Memorial Park, Grants Pass, OR. Cremated.
Williams, Lefty (Claude Preston)	11/04/1959	Melrose Abbey Memorial Park, Anaheim, CA. Cremated.
Williams, Leon Theo	11/20/1984	Arlington Memorial Park, Atlanta, GA
Williams, Mutt (David Carter)	03/30/1962	Fort Smith National Cemetery, Fort Smith, AR
Williams, Otto George	03/19/1937	Graceland Park Cemetery, Omaha, NE
Williams, Papa (Fred)	11/02/1993	Memorial Park, Meridian, MS
Williams, Pop (Walter Merrill)	08/04/1959	Riverview Cemetery, Topsham, ME
Williams, Rip (Alva Mitchell)	07/23/1933	Moss Ridge Cemetery, Carthage, IL
Williams, Steamboat (Rees Gephardt)	06/29/1979	Olivet Cemetery, Deer River, MN
Williams, Ted (Theodore Samuel)	07/05/2002	Frozen, Alcor Life Extension Foundation, Scottsdale, AZ
Williams, Tom (Thomas C.)	07/27/1940	New Straitsville Cemetery, New Straitsville, OH
Williams, Woody (Woodrow Wilson)	02/24/1995	Pamplin Community Cemetery, Pamplin, VA
Williamson, Al (Silas Albert)	11/29/1978	Memorial Gardens of Hot Springs, Hot Springs, AR
Williamson, Howie (Nathaniel Howard)	08/15/1969	Hillcrest Cemetery, Texarkana, AR
Williamson, Ned (Edward Nagle)	03/03/1894	Rosehill Cemetery, Chicago, IL

Name	DOD	Cemetery, City, State
Willigrod, Julius	11/27/1906	Riverside Cemetery, Marshalltown, IA
Willingham, Hugh (Thomas Hugh)	06/15/1988	El Reno Cemetery, El Reno, OK
Willis, Joe (Joseph Dank)	12/04/1966	Woodland Cemetery, Ironton, OH
Willis, Lefty (Charles William)	05/10/1962	Edge Hill Cemetery, Charles Town, WV
Willis, Les (Lester Evans)	01/22/1982	Memorial Park Cemetery, Jasper, TX
Willis, Ron (Ronald Earl)	11/21/1977	Zion Cemetery, Obion, TN
Willis, Vic (Victor Gazaway)	08/03/1947	St. John's Catholic Church Cemetery, Newark, DE
Willoughby, Claude William	08/14/1973	Buffalo Cemetery, Buffalo, KS
Wills, Dave (Davis Bowles)	10/12/1959	Arlington National Cemetery, Arlington, VA
Wilshere, Whitey (Vernon Sprague)	05/23/1985	Lakewood Cemetery, Cooperstown, NY
Wilson, Art (Arthur Earl)	06/12/1960	Graceland Cemetery, Chicago, IL
Wilson, Bill (William G.)	05/09/1924	Calvary Cemetery, St. Paul, MN
Wilson, Billy (William Harlan)	08/11/1993	Cremated, Broken Arrow, OK
Wilson, Bob (Robert)	04/23/1985	Lincoln Memorial Cemetery, Dallas, TX
Wilson, Chief (John Owen)	02/22/1954	Austin Memorial Park, Austin, TX
Wilson, Chink (William)	10/28/1925	Cremated, Seattle, WA
Wilson, Don (Donald Edward)	01/05/1975	Forest Lawn Memorial Park-Covina Hills, Covina, CA
Wilson, Eddie (Edward Francis)	04/11/1979	St. Lawrence Cemetery, West Haven, CT
Wilson, Fin (Finis Elbert)	03/09/1959	Auburn Cemetery, Auburn, KY
Wilson, Frank (Francis Edward)	11/25/1974	Pine Grove Cemetery, Leicester, MA
Wilson, Gary (James Garrett)	05/01/1969	New Cathedral Cemetery, Baltimore, MD
Wilson, George Washington	10/29/1974	Morningside Park Cemetery, Mount Holly, NC
Wilson, Grady Herbert	07/23/2003	Parkhill Cemetery, Cloumbus, GA
Wilson, Hack (Lewis Robert)	11/23/1948	Rosedale Cemetery, Martinsburg, WV
Wilson, Highball (Howard Paul)	10/16/1934	Cedar Hill Cemetery, Havre de Grace, MD
Wilson, Icehouse (George Peacock)	10/13/1973	St. Joseph Cemetery, San Pablo, CA
Wilson, Jack (John Francis)	04/19/1995	Holyrood Cemetery, Seattle, WA
Wilson, Jim (James Alger)	09/02/1986	Pacific View Memorial Park, Newport Beach, CA
Wilson, Jimmy (James)	05/31/1947	Manasota Memorial Park, Bradenton, FL
Wilson, John Nicodemus	09/23/1954	St. Anne's Cedar Bluff Cemetery, Annapolis, MD
Wilson, John Samuel	08/27/1980	Chattanooga National Cemetery, Chattanooga, TN
Wilson, Les (Lester Wilbur)	04/04/1969	Floral Hills Cemetery, Lynnwood, WA
Wilson, Maxie (Max)	01/02/1977	Pine Hill Cemetery, Burlington, NC
Wilson, Mike (Samuel Marshall)	05/16/1978	Boynton Memorial Park, Boynton Beach, FL
Wilson, Mutt (William Clarence)	08/31/1962	Lone Oak Cemetery, Leesburg, FL
Wilson, Parke Asel	12/20/1934	Inglewood Park Cemetery, Inglewood, CA
Wilson, Pete (Peter Alex)	06/05/1957	Memorial Park Cemetery, St. Petersburg, FL
Wilson, Roy Edward	12/03/1969	Clarion City Cemetery, Clarion, IA
Wilson, Squanto (George Francis)	03/26/1967	Glenside Cemetery, Winthrop, ME
Wilson, Tex (Gomer Russell)	09/15/1946	Burns Cemetery, Trenton, TX
Wilson, Tom (Thomas G.)	03/07/1953	Green Hills Memorial Park, Rancho Palos Verdes, CA

Name	DOD	Cemetery, City, State
Wilson, Tug (George Archer)	11/28/1914	Green-Wood Cemetery, Brooklyn, NY
Wilson, Walter Wood	04/17/1994	Glenn Cemetery, Glenn, GA
Wilson, Zeke (Frank Ealton)	04/26/1928	Oakwood Cemetery, Montgomery, AL
Wiltse, Hal (Harold James)	11/02/1983	Pythian Cemetery, Bunkie, LA
Wiltse, Snake (Lewis DeWitt)	08/25/1928	Paxtang Cemetery, Harrisburg, PA
Windle, Bill (Willis Brewer)	12/08/1981	Seaside Memorial Park, Corpus Christi, TX
Winegarner, Ralph Lee	04/14/1988	Benton Cemetery, Benton, KS
Winford, Jim (James Head)	12/16/1970	Meeker New Hope Cemetery, Meeker, OK
Wingard, Ernie (Ernest James)	01/17/1977	Oak Hill Cemetery, Prattville, AL
Wingfield, Ted (Frederick Davis)	07/18/1975	Happy Valley Memorial Park, Johnson City, TN
Wingo, Ivey Brown	03/01/1941	Norcross Cemetery, Norcross, GA
Winham, Lave (Lafayette Sharkey)	09/12/1951	Evergreen Cemetery, Brooklyn, NY
Winkelman, George Edward	05/19/1960	Mount Olivet Cemetery, Washington, DC
Winn, George Benjamin	11/01/1969	Orange Hill Cemetery, Hawkinsville, GA
Winsett, Tom (John Thomas)	07/20/1987	Memorial Park Cemetery, Memphis, TN
Winston, Hank (Henry Rudolph)	02/04/1974	Restlawn Memorial Park, Jacksonville, FL
Winters, Clarence John	06/29/1945	Woodmere Cemetery, Detroit, MI
Winters, Jesse Franklin	06/05/1986	Elmwood Memorial Park, Abilene, TX
Wirts, Kettle (Elwood Vernon)	07/12/1968	St. Mary's Catholic Cemetery, Sacramento, CA
Wise, Archie (Archibald Edwin)	02/02/1978	Hillcrest Burial Park, Waxahachie, TX
Wise, Bill (William E.)	05/05/1940	Glenwood Cemetery, Washington, DC
Wise, Hughie (Hugh Edward)	07/21/1987	Cremated, Fort Lauderdale, FL. Ashes scattered
Wise, Nick (Nicholas Joseph)	01/25/1923	Mount Calvary Cemetery, Roslindale, MA
Wise, Sam (Samuel Washington)	01/22/1910	Glendale Cemetery, Akron, OH
Wisner, John Henry	12/15/1981	Oakridge Cemetery, Marshall, MI
Wisterzil, Tex (George John)	06/27/1964	Odd Fellows Cemetery, San Antonio, TX
Witek, Mickey (Nicholas Joseph)	08/24/1990	St. John's Cemetery, Dallas, PA
Witherow, Charles Lafayette	07/03/1948	Glenwood Cemetery, Washington, DC
Witherup, Roy (Foster Leroy)	12/23/1941	Mt. Varnum Cemetery, North Washington, PA
Witt, Whitey (Lawton Walter)	07/14/1988	St. Joseph's Catholic Cemetery, Woodstown, NJ
Witte, Jerry (Jerome Charles)	04/27/2002	Forest Park (Lawndale) Cemetery, Houston, TX
Wittig, Johnny (John Carl)	02/24/1999	Lake View Memorial Park, Sykesville, MD
Wnter, George Lovington	05/26/1951	Riverview Cemetery, Wilmington, DE
Woehr, Andy (Andrew Emil)	07/24/1990	Greenlawn Memorial Park, Fort Wayne, IN
Woerlin, Joe (Joseph)	06/22/1919	Calvary Cemetery, St. Louis, MO
Wolf, Chicken (William Van Winkle)	05/16/1903	Cave Hill Cemetery, Louisville, KY
Wolf, Ernie (Ernest Adolph)	05/23/1964	Glendale Cemetery, Bloomfield, NJ
Wolf, Lefty (Walter Francis)	09/25/1971	Metairie Cemetery, Metairie, LA
Wolf, Ray (Raymond Bernard)	10/06/1979	Oak Grove Cemetery, Graham, TX
Wolfe, Bill (Wilbert Otto)	02/27/1953	Mount Auburn Cemetery, Fayette City, PA
Wolfe, Chuck (Charles Hunt)	11/27/1957	Schellsburg Cemetery, Schellsburg, PA
Wolfe, Polly (Roy Chamberlain)	11/21/1938	Mount Carmel Cemetery, Morris, IL
Wolff, Roger Francis	03/23/1994	St. Mary's Help of Christians Catholic Cemetery, Chester, IL

Name	DOD	Cemetery, City, State
Wolfgang, Mellie (Meldon John)	06/30/1947	St. Agnes Cemetery, Albany, NY
Wolstenholme, Abe (Abraham Lincoln)	03/04/1916	North Cedar Hill Cemetery, Philadelphia, PA
Wolter, Harry Meigs	07/06/1970	Hollister Cemetery, Hollister, CA
Wolters, Rynie (Reinder Albertus)	01/03/1917	Woodland Cemetery, Newark, NJ
Wolverton, Harry Sterling	02/04/1937	Cypress Lawn Memorial Park, Colma, CA
Wood, Bob (Robert Lynn)	05/22/1943	Churchill Cemetery, Churchill, OH
Wood, Doc (Charles Spencer)	11/03/1974	Metairie Cemetery, Metairie, LA
Wood, Harry (Harold Austin)	05/18/1955	Rock Creek Cemetery, Washington, DC
Wood, Joe (Joseph Perry)	03/25/1985	Forest Park (Lawndale) Cemetery, Houston, TX
Wood, Joe Frank	10/10/2002	Cremated, Old Saybrook, CT
Wood, Roy Winton	04/06/1974	Evergreen Cemetery, Fayetteville, AR
Wood, Smoky Joe (Joe)	07/27/1985	Wood Family Cemetery, Wood Estate, Shohola Twp., PA
Wood, Spades (Charles Asher)	05/18/1986	Twin Grove Cemetery, Severy, KS
Woodall, Larry (Charles Lawrence)	05/06/1963	Gate of Heaven Cemetery, Silver Spring, MD
Woodburn, Gene (Eugene Stewart)	01/18/1961	Oakland Cemetery, Sandusky, OH
Woodcock, Fred Wayland	08/11/1943	New Cemetery, Ashburnham, MA
Woodend, George Anthony	05/01/1980	Fairview Cemetery, West Hartford, CT
Woodhead, Red (James)	09/07/1881	Bennington Street Burying Ground, East Boston, MA
Woodling, Gene (Eugene Richard)	06/02/2001	Fairview Park Cemetery, Granger, OH
Woodman, Dan (Daniel Courtenay)	12/14/1962	Riverview Cemetery, Groveland, MA
Woodruff, Sam (Orville Francis)	07/22/1937	Spring Grove Cemetery, Cincinnati, OH
Woods, Clarence Cofield	07/02/1969	Rising Sun New Cemetery, Rising Sun, IN
Woods, John Fulton	10/04/1946	Forest Lawn Cemetery, Norfolk, VA
Woods, Pinky (George Rowland)	10/29/1982	Cremated, Los Angeles, CA. Ashes scattered in Pacific Ocean
Woods, Walt (Walter Sydney)	10/30/1951	Newington Cemetery, Newington, NH
Woodward, Frank Russell	06/11/1961	East Lawn Cemetery, East Haven, CT
Worden, Fred (Frederick Bamford)	11/09/1941	Calvary Cemetery, St. Louis, MO
Workman, Chuck (Charles Thomas)	01/03/1953	Sunset Hill Cemetery, Warrensburg, MO
Workman, Hoge (Harry Hall)	05/20/1972	Cremated, Fort Myers, FL
Works, Ralph Talmadge	08/08/1941	Mountain View Cemetery, Altadena, CA
Worth, Herb (Herbert)	04/27/1914	Green-Wood Cemetery, Brooklyn, NY
Worthington, Red (Robert Lee)	12/08/1963	San Gabriel Mission Cemetery, San Gabriel, CA
Wortman, Chuck (William Lewis)	08/19/1977	Bunker Brother's Memory Gardens Cemmetery, Las Vegas, NV
Woulfe, Jimmy (James Joseph)	12/20/1924	Metairie Cemetery, Metairie, LA
Wright, Ab (Albert Owen)	05/23/1995	Memorial Park Cemetery, Muskogee, OK
Wright, Al (Alfred Hector) *manager*	04/20/1905	Green-Wood Cemetery, Brooklyn, NY
Wright, Bob (Robert Cassius)	07/30/1993	South Park Cemetery, Greensburg, IN
Wright, Clarence Eugene	10/29/1930	Lakewood Cemetery, Akron, OH
Wright, Dave (David William)	01/18/1946	Union Cemetery, Uhrichsville, OH
Wright, Dick (Willard James)	01/24/1952	Holy Savior Cemetery, Bethlehem, PA
Wright, Ed (Henderson Edward)	11/19/1995	Fairview Cemetery, Dyersburg, TN

Name	DOD	Cemetery, City, State
Wright, George	08/21/1937	Holyhood Cemetery, Brookline, MA
Wright, Glenn (Forest Glenn)	04/06/1984	Cremated, Olathe, KS. Ashes given to family.
Wright, Harry (William Henry)	10/03/1895	West Laurel Hill Cemetery, Bala Cynwyd, PA
Wright, Jim (James)	04/11/1963	Golden Gate National Cemetery, San Bruno, CA
Wright, Lucky (William Simmons)	07/04/1941	Tontogany Cemetery, Tontogany, OH
Wright, Pat (Patrick W.)	05/29/1943	Calvary Cemetery, Springfield, IL
Wright, Rasty (Wayne Bromley)	06/12/1948	Union Cemetery, Columbus, OH
Wright, Rasty (William Smith)	10/14/1922	Calvary Cemetery, Duluth, MN
Wright, Sam (Samuel)	05/06/1928	St. Patrick's Catholic Cemetery, Stoneham, MA
Wright, Taffy (Taft Shedron)	10/22/1981	Meadowbrook Cemetery, Lumberton, NC
Wrightstone, Russ (Russell Guy)	02/25/1969	Woodland Memorial Gardens, Harrisburg, PA
Wrigley, Zeke (George Watson)	09/28/1952	Holy Cross Cemetery, Yeadon, PA
Wuestling, Yats (George)	04/26/1970	Oak Grove Cemetery, St. Louis, MO
Wurm, Frank James	09/19/1993	Glens Falls Cemetery, Glens Falls, NY
Wyatt, Joe (Loral John)	12/05/1970	Mount Calvary Cemetery, Vincennes, IN
Wyatt, John Thomas	04/06/1998	Cremated, Omaha, NE.
Wyatt, Whit (John Whitlow)	07/16/1999	Buchanan City Cemetery, Buchanan, GA
Wycoff, John Weldon	05/08/1961	Sheboygan Falls Cemetery, Sheboygan Falls, WI
Wylie, Ren (James Renwick)	08/17/1951	Homewood Cemetery, Pittsburgh, PA
Wynn, Early	04/04/1999	Cremated, Venice, FL. Ashes scattered
Wynne, Bill (William Andrew)	08/07/1951	Oakwood Cemetery, Raleigh, NC
Wyrostek, Johnny (John Barney)	12/12/1986	Lake View Memorial Gardens, Belleville, IL
Wyse, Hank (Henry Washington)	10/22/2000	Fairview Cemetery (aka Pryor Cemetery), Pryor, OK
Wysong, Biff (Harlan)	08/08/1951	Clarksville Cemetery, Clarksville, OH
Yaik, Henry	09/21/1935	Mount Elliott Cemetery, Detroit, MI
Yale, Ad (William M.)	04/27/1948	Park Cemetery, Bridgeport, CT
Yantz, George Webb	02/26/1967	St. Michael's Cemetery, Louisville, KY
Yarnall, Rusty (Waldo Ward)	10/09/1985	Fairview Cemetery, Westford, MA
Yarrison, Rube (Byron Wardsworth)	04/22/1977	St. John's Lutheran-Brick Church Cemetery, Montgomery, PA
Yaryan, Yam (Clarence Everett)	11/16/1964	Elmwood Cemetery, Birmingham, AL
Yde, Emil Ogden	12/04/1968	Cremated, Leesburg, FL
Yeabsley, Bert (Robert Watkins)	02/08/1961	St. Timothy's Episcopal Church Cemetery, Philadelphia, PA
Yeager, George J.	06/05/1940	Spring Grove Cemetery, Cincinnati, OH
Yeager, Joe (Joseph F.)	07/02/1937	Woodmere Cemetery, Detroit, MI
Yeargin, Jim (James Almond)	05/08/1937	Cross Roads Baptist Church Cemetery, Greer, SC
Yeatman, Bill (William Suter)	04/20/1901	Oak Hill Cemetery, Washington, DC
Yelle, Archie Joseph	05/02/1983	Monument Hill Memorial Park, Woodland, CA
Yellowhorse, Chief (Moses J.)	04/10/1964	North Indian Cemetery, Pawnee, OK
Yerkes, Carroll (Charles Carroll)	12/20/1950	St. Joseph Cemetery, San Pablo, CA
Yerkes, Stan (Stanley Lewis)	07/28/1940	Fairview Cemetery, Hyde Park, MA

Name	DOD	Cemetery, City, State
Yerkes, Steve (Stephen Douglas)	01/31/1971	Holy Sepulchre Cemetery, Wyndmoor, PA
Yewell, Ed (Edwin Leonard)	09/15/1940	Glenwood Cemetery, Washington, DC
Yingling, Earl Hershey	10/02/1962	Lebanon Cemetery, Lebanon, OH
Yingling, Joe (Joseph Granville)	10/24/1946	Manchester Cemetery, Manchester, MD. (aka Immanuel Evangelical Reformed Church Cemetery)
Yochim, Ray (Raymond Austin Aloysius)	01/26/2002	Metairie Cemetery, Metairie, LA
Yohe, Bill (William Clyde)	12/24/1938	Ivy Green Cemetery, Bremerton, WA
York, Lefty (James Edward)	04/09/1961	Mt. Rose Cemetery, York, PA
York, Rudy (Rudolph Preston)	02/05/1970	Sunset Memorial Gardens, Cartersville, GA
York, Tom (Thomas Jefferson)	02/17/1936	Holy Cross Cemetery, Brooklyn, NY
York, Tony Batton	04/18/1970	Fairview Cemetery, Hubbard, TX
Yoter, Elmer Ellsworth	07/26/1966	Jefferson Memorial Park, Pleasant Hills, PA
Young, Babe (Norman Robert)	12/25/1983	Veteran's Memorial Cemetery, South Windsor, CT
Young, Charlie (Charles)	05/12/1952	Lakeview Memorial Park, Cinnaminson, NJ
Young, Cliff (Clifford Raphael)	11/04/1993	Ebenezer Cemetery, Willis, TX
Young, Cy (Denton True)	11/04/1955	Peoli Methodist Church Cemetery, Peoli, OH
Young, Del (Delmer Edward)	12/08/1979	Olivet Memorial Park, Colma, CA
Young, Del (Delmer John)	12/17/1959	Calvary Cemetery, Cleveland, OH
Young, George Joseph	03/13/1950	Long Island National Cemetery, Farmingdale, NY
Young, Harley (Harlan Edward)	03/26/1975	Evergreen Cemetery, Jacksonville, FL
Young, Herman John	12/12/1966	Mount Hope Cemetery, Mattapan, MA
Young, Irv (Irving Melrose)	01/14/1935	Great Hill Cemetery, Columbia Falls, ME
Young, Nick (Nicholas Ephraim) manager	10/31/1916	Rock Creek Cemetery, Washington, DC
Young, Pep (Lemuel Floyd)	01/14/1962	Guilford Memorial Park, Greensboro, NC
Young, Russ (Russell Charles)	05/13/1984	Camellia Memorial Lawn, Sacramento, CA
Youngblood, Chief (Albert Clyde)	07/06/1968	Llano Cemetery, Amarillo, TX
Youngman, Henry	01/24/1936	Homestead Cemetery, Homestead, PA
Youngs, Ross (Royce Middlebrook)	10/22/1927	Mission Burial Park South, San Antonio, TX
Yount, Ducky (Henry Macon)	05/09/1970	Eastview Cemetery, Newton, NC
Yount, Eddie (Floyd Edwin)	10/26/1973	Eastview Cemetery, Newton, NC
Yowell, Carl Columbus	07/27/1985	Berryman Family Cemetery, Alto, TX
Yuhas, Eddie (John Edward)	07/06/1986	Forsyth Memorial Park Cemetery, Winston-Salem, NC
Zabala, Adrian	01/04/2002	Evergreen Cemetery, Jacksonville, FL
Zabel, Zip (George Washington)	05/31/1970	Tabor Cemetery, Beloit, WI
Zachary, Chris (William Christopher)	04/19/2003	Cremated, Knoxville, TN
Zachary, Tom (Jonathan Thompson Walton)	01/24/1969	Alamance Memorial Park, Burlington, NC
Zacher, Elmer Henry	12/20/1944	Elmlawn Cemetery, Tonawanda, NY
Zackert, George Carl	02/18/1977	Aspen Grove Cemetery, Burlington, IA
Zahner, Fred (Frederick Joseph)	07/24/1900	St. Louis Cemetery, Louisville, KY
Zahniser, Paul Vernon	09/26/1964	Oakland Cemetery, Sac City, IA

Name	DOD	Cemetery, City, State
Zak, Frankie (Frank Thomas)	02/06/1972	St. Michael's Cemetery, Lodi, NJ
Zalusky, Jack (John Francis)	08/11/1935	St. Mary's Cemetery, Minneapolis, MN
Zamloch, Carl Eugene	08/19/1963	Sunset View Cemetery, El Cerrito, CA
Zapustas, Joe (Joseph John)	01/14/2001	St. Mary's Cemetery, Randolph, MA
Zearfoss, Dave (David William Tilden)	09/12/1945	Northwood Cemetery, Philadelphia, PA
Zeider, Rollie Hubert	09/12/1967	Woodlawn Cemetery, Auburn, IN
Zettlein, George	05/23/1905	Evergreen Cemetery, Brooklyn, NY
Ziegler, George J.	07/22/1916	Jewish Waldheim Cemetery, Forest Park, IL
Zientara, Benny (Benedict Joseph)	04/16/1985	Riverside National Cemetery, Riverside, CA
Zies, Bill (William)	04/16/1907	Beardstown City Cemetery, Beardstown, IL
Zimmer, Chief (Charles Louis)	08/22/1949	Crown Hill Memorial Park, Twinsburg, OH
Zimmerman, Bill (William Frederick)	10/04/1952	Hollywood Memorial Park, Union, NJ
Zimmerman, Eddie (Edward Desmond)	05/06/1945	Northwood Cemetery, Emmaus, PA
Zimmerman, Heinie (Henry)	03/14/1969	Woodlawn Cemetery, Bronx, NY
Zimmerman, Jerry (Gerald Robert)	09/09/1998	Cremated, Neskowin, OR
Zimmerman, Roy Franklin	11/22/1991	Tremont Cemetery, Tremont, PA. Cremated Harrisburg, PA
Zink, Walt (Walter Noble)	06/12/1964	Blue Hill Cemetery, Braintree, MA
Zinn, Frank Patrick	05/12/1936	Westminster Cemetery, Bala Cynwyd, PA
Zinn, Guy	10/06/1949	Greenlawn Masonic Cemetery, Clarksburg, WV
Zinn, Jimmy (James Edward)	02/26/1991	Oakland Cemetery, Little Rock, AR
Zinser, Bill (William Francis)	02/16/1993	Cremated, Englewood
Zitzmann, Billy (William Arthur)	05/29/1985	East Ridgelawn Cemetery, Clifton, NJ
Zmich, Ed (Edward Albert)	08/20/1950	St. Mary's Cemetery, Cleveland, OH
Zoldak, Sam (Samuel Walter)	08/25/1966	Cemetery of Holy Rood, Westbury, NY
Zuber, Bill (William Henry)	11/02/1982	Middle Amana Cemetery, Middle Amana, IA
Zwilling, Dutch (Edward Harrison)	03/27/1978	Cremated, Los Angeles, CA

NEGRO LEAGUERS

Name	DOD	Cemetery, City, State
Allen, Tom (Toussaint L'Ouverture)	03/03/1960	Beverly National Cemetery, Beverly, NJ
Alston, Tom (Thomas Edison)	12/30/1993	New Goshen United Methodist Church Cemetery, Greensboro, NC
Anderson, Andy (Andrew)	07/24/1989	Woodlawn Cemetery, Syracuse, NY
Anderson, Bubbles (Theodore M.)	03/14/1943	Fairmount Cemetery, Denver, CO
Armenteros, Juan F.	10/08/2003	Dade Memorial Park, Miami, FL
Askew, Jesse	01/05/2000	St. Peter's Cemetery, St. Louis, MO
Awkard, Russell	04/01/2002	Gate of Heaven Cemetery, Silver Spring, MD
Bailey, Alonza	04/23/1984	Glenwood Memorial Cemetery, West Palm Beach, FL
Baker, Bake (Hudson Andrew)	05/21/1999	Cremated, Philadelphia, PA
Baker, Gene (Eugene Walter)	12/01/1999	Rock Island National Cemetery, Rock Island, IL
Baker, Scoop (Rufus)	06/22/1992	Oak Lawn Cemetery, Fairfield, CT
Baldwin, Tiny (Robert)	04/00/1979	Crown Hill Cemetery, Indianapolis, IN
Ball, George Walter	12/15/1946	Lincoln Cemetery, Blue Island, IL
Bankhead, Dan (Daniel Robert)	05/02/1976	Houston National Cemetery, Houston, TX
Bankhead, Fred	12/17/1972	New Park Cemetery, Memphis, TN
Bankhead, Joe (Joseph Calvin) 2\24	02/04/1988	Empire Cemetery, Empire, AL
Barnes, Joe	09/25/1995	Mt. Glenwood Cemetery, Glenwood, IL
Barnes, Sanford	03/06/2000	Terrace Heights Memorial Park, Yakima, WA
Barnes, Tobias	12/03/1979	Fair Lawn Memorial Cemetery, Fair Lawn, NJ
Barnhill, Dave	01/08/1983	Brownhill Cemetery, Greenville, NC
Baro, Bernardo	06/10/1930	Cemeterio de Cristobal Colon, Havana, Cuba
Baylis, Hank (Henry)	12/17/1980	Fort Leavenworth National Cemetery, Fort Leavenworth, KS
Bea, Bill (William Darius)	04/13/1987	Spring Grove Cemetery, Cincinnati, OH

Name	DOD	Cemetery, City, State
Belfield, Skinner	12/14/1995	Fairmount Cemetery, Newark, NJ
Bell, Cool Papa (James)	03/07/1991	St. Peter's Cemetery, St. Louis, MO
Bell, W (William)	03/16/1969	El Campo Cemmunity Cemetery, El Campo, TX
Benson, Gene (Eugene)	04/05/1999	Cremated, Philadelphia, PA
Benton, James E.	10/17/1999	Cremated, Renton, WA.
Bibbs, Junious Lloyd	09/11/1980	Crown Hill Cemetery, Indianapolis, IN
Binga, Jesse	06/14/1950	Oak Woods Cemetery, Chicago, IL
Biot, Charlie (Charles A.)	03/10/2000	Fairmount Cemetery, Newark, NJ
Bissant, Bob (Robert N.)	08/17/1999	Providence Memorial Park, Metairie, LA
Black, Joseph	05/17/2002	Cremated, Phoenix, AZ. Ashes given to family.
Blackwell, Charles	04/22/1935	Cap Anderson Cemetery, Brandenburg, KY
Blair, Chico (Lonnie J.)	01/27/1992	Montours Presbyterian Cemetery, Oakdale, PA
Blair, Garnett E.	01/12/1996	Forest Lawn Cemetery, Richmond, VA
Blanchard, Chester	11/13/1996	West Memory Gardens, Dayton, OH
Blueitt, Virgil	04/29/1952	Montrose Cemetery, Chicago, IL
Bolden, Ed (Edward) *owner*	09/17/1950	Eden Cemetery, Collingdale, PA
Bond, Walt (Walter Franklin)	09/14/1967	Houston National Cemetery, Houston, TX
Boston, Bob (Robert Lee	07/08/2002	Dayton National Cemetery, Dayton, OH
Bowser, Thomas	11/21/1943	Crown Hill Cemetery, Indianapolis, IN
Bracken, Doc (Herbert)	02/17/1994	Jefferson Barracks National Cemetery, St. Louis, MO
Bradley, Provine	12/31/1986	Greenlawn Memorial Park, Greenwood, MS
Bremmer, Gene (Eugene)	06/19/1971	Evergreen Cemetery, Bedford, OH
Brewer, Woody (Sherwood)	04/23/2003	Abraham Lincoln National Cemetery, Elwood, IL
Bridges, Marshall	09/03/1990	Garden Memorial Park, Jackson, MS
Briggs, Otto	10/28/1943	Philadelphia National Cemetery, Philadelphia, PA
Brisker, William Lee	01/12/1996	Florida National Cemetery, Bushnell, FL
Brown, Cap (William Harris)	12/30/1996	Elmwood Cemetery, Birmingham, AL
Brown, Ike (Isaac)	05/17/2001	New Park Cemetery, Memphis, TN
Brown, Jim (James)	01/21/1943	San Marcos Blanco Cemetery, San Marcos, TX
Brown, Larry	04/07/1972	New Park Cemetery, Memphis, TN
Brown, Lefty (Jesse J.)	05/25/1980	Mount Hope Cemetery, Mattapan, MA
Brown, Ray (Raymond L.)	02/08/1965	Greencastle Cemetery, Dayton, OH
Brown, Willard Jessie	08/08/1996	Houston National Cemetery, Houston, TX
Bruce, Clarence	01/23/1990	Homewood Cemetery, Pittsburgh, PA
Bryant, Lefty (Allen)	03/22/1992	Leavenworth National Cemetery, Leavenworth, KS
Bryany, Country (Elias)	12/25/1937	Frederick Douglass Memorial Park, Staten Island, NY
Burbage, Buddy (Knowlington O.)	08/30/1989	Mount Zion Cemetery, Collingdale, PA
Burke, Ernest Alexander	01/31/2004	Garrison Forest Veterans Cemetery, Owings Mills, MD

Name	DOD	Cemetery, City, State
Byrd, Bill (William)	01/04/1991	Ivy Hill Cemetery, Philadelphia, PA
Byrd, Prentice	06/14/1983	Hamline Chapel Cemetery, Monroe City, IN
Cabrera, Alfredo	01/00/1964	Cemeterio de Cristobal Colon, Havana
Campanella, Roy	06/26/1993	Cremated, Forest Lawn Memorial Park-Hollywood Hills, Los Angeles, CA. Ashes given to family
Cannady, Rev (Walter)	12/03/1981	Oak Ridge Cemetery, Ft. Myers, FL
Carney, Ted (Clement)	04/23/1966	Emmanuel United Methodist Cemetery, Cheswold, DE
Carr, Austin George	06/11/1994	Gate of Heaven Cemetery, Silver Spring, MD
Cash, Wayman Treadwell	09/19/1998	Hillside Memorial Park, Akron, OH
Castillo, Julian		Cemeterio de Cristobal Colon, Havana, Cuba
Catto, Octavius Valentine	10/08/1871	Eden Cemetery, Collingdale, PA. Originally intered at Lebanon Cemetery, Philadelphia. Moved in 1905.
Charleston, Bennie (Benjamin Franklin)	02/20/1988	Crown Hill Cemetery, Indianapolis, IN
Charleston, Oscar	10/05/1954	Floral Park Cemetery, Indianapolis, IN
Charleston, Porter R.	06/11/1986	Haven Memorial Park, Chester, PA
Clarkson, Buzz (James Buster)	01/18/1989	Brush Creek Cemetery, Irwin, PA
Claxton, Jimmy (James Edward)	03/03/1970	Oakwood Hill Cemetery, Tacoma, WA
Clayton, Zach (Zachary M.)	11/20/1997	Holy Sepulchre Cemetery, Wyndmoor, PA
Clifton, Sweetwater (Nathaniel)	08/31/1990	Restvale Cemetery, Alsip, IL
Cockrell, Phil (Phillip)	03/31/1951	Mt. Lawn Cemetery, Sharon Hill, PA
Cohen, Jim (James Clarence)	04/23/2002	Quantico National Cemetery, Triangle, VA
Coimbre, Pancho (Francisco)	11/04/1989	Alvarez Memorial Cemetery, Ponce, Puerto Rico
Connor, John W. *owner*	07/09/1926	Woodlawn Cemetery, Bronx, NY
Cook, Walter I. *owner*	06/26/1888	Mercer Cemetery, Trenton, NJ
Craig, Joe (Joseph)	02/22/1991	Mt. Lawn Cemetery, Sharon Hill, PA
Crutchfield, Jimmy (John)	03/31/1993	Burr Oak Cemetery, Alsip, IL
Cummings, Chance (Napoleon)	04/22/1974	Greenwood Cemetery, Pleasantville, NJ
Dabney, John M.	11/09/1967	Fairmount Cemetery, Newark, NJ
Dandridge, Ray	02/12/1994	Fountainhead Memorial Park, Palm Bay, FL
Davis, Cherokee (John Howard)	11/17/1982	Cremated, Fort Lauderdale, FL
Davis, Fritz (Otis)	08/14/1992	Houston National Cemetery, Houston, TX
Davis, Piper (Lorenzo)	05/21/1997	Elmwood Cemetery, Birmingham, AL
Davis, Riley Marcilous	02/04/1997	Sharp Street Memorial United Methodist Church Cemetery, Baltimore, MD
Day, Eddie (Edward E.)	03/23/1906	Charles Evans Cemetery, Reading, PA
Day, Leon	03/13/1995	Arbutus Memorial Park, Baltimore, MD
Deas, Yank (James Alvin)	05/00/1972	Long Island National Cemetery, Farmingdale, NY
Delgado, Felix	06/13/2001	Puerto Rico National Cemetery, Bayamon, Puerto Rico
DeMoss, Bingo (Elwood)	01/26/1965	Burr Oak Cemetery, Alsip, IL
Dennis, Doc (Wesley)	03/06/2001	Woodlawn Memorial Park, Nashville, TN
Dent, Carl J.	12/22/1995	Rosehill Cemetery, Linden, NJ

Name	DOD	Cemetery, City, State
Dibut, Pedro	12/04/1979	Vista Memorial Gardens, Hialeah, FL
Dihigo, Martin	05/20/1971	Cemeterio Municipal Cruces, Cruces, Cienfuegos, Cuba
Dimes, Edward	09/28/1999	St. James Methodist Church Cemetery, Cleveland, OH
Dixon, Rap (Herbert A.)	07/30/1944	Midland Cemetery, Steelton, PA
Doby, Larry (Lawrence Eugene)	06/18/2003	Cremated, Monclair, NJ
Drake, Plunk (William P.)	10/30/1977	Jefferson Barracks National Cemetery, St. Louis, MO
Drew, Johnny (John M.)	02/29/1976	Eden Cemetery, Collingdale, PA
Duany, Claro	03/28/1997	Calvary Cemetery, Evanston, IL
Duncan, Frank III.	10/02/1999	Woodmere Cemetery, Detroit, MI
Duncan, Frank, Jr.	12/04/1973	Highland Cemetery, Kansas City, MO
Dunn, Jake (Joseph)	07/24/1984	Lincoln Memorial Park Cemetery, Compton, CA
Easter, Luke (Luscious Luke)	03/29/1979	Highland Park Cemetery, Cleveland, OH
Easterling, Howard Willis	09/06/1993	Mount Pleasant C.M.E. Church Cemetery, Mount Olive, MS
Epps, Harvey	04/09/2002	Meadowbrook Memorial Gardens, Suffolk, VA
Evans, Charles		Arbutus Memorial Park, Baltimore, MD
Fauntleroy, Arthur	07/13/2000	Gibbs Memorial Gardens, Camden, DE
Favors, Thomas	12/11/2001	South-View Cemetery, Atlanta, GA
Fennar, Cleffie (Albertus A.)	06/15/2001	George Washington Memorial Park, Paramus, NJ
Fernandez, Jose Maria, Sr.	01/00/1971	Cemeterio de Cristobal Colon, Havana, Cuba
Fernandez, Rudy (Rodolfo, Jr.)	09/06/2000	Rosehill Cemetery, Linden, NJ
Ferrell, Toots (Howard Leroy)	10/11/2002	Delaware Veterans Memorial Cemetery, Bear, DE
Fiall, George	06/00/1978	Beverly Hills Cemetery, Mohegan Lake, NY
Finney, Mike (Edward)	03/17/1998	Mount Peace Cemetery, Akron, OH
Foster, Bill (William H.)	09/16/1978	Carbondale Cemetery, Lorman, MS
Foster, Rube (Andrew)	12/09/1930	Lincoln Cemetery, Blue Island, IL
Fowler, Bud	02/26/1913	Oak Hill Cemetery, Frankfort, NY
Frazier, Albert Edwin	08/08/1999	Restlawn Cemetery, Jacksonville, FL
Frazier, Joshua *owner*	02/22/1945	Glendale Cemetery, Bloomfield, NJ
Gaines, Lefty (Jonas George)	08/06/1998	Port Hudson National Cemetery, Zachary, LA
Gans, Jude (Robert Edward	02/13/1949	Beverly National Cemetery, Beverly, NJ
Garcia, Antonio		Cemeterio de Cristobal Colon, Havana, Cuba
Garcia, John Juan	10/01/1904	Evergreen Cemetery, Brooklyn, NY
Gardner, Chappy (James)	10/28/1943	Cremated, Fresh Pond Crematory, Middle Village, Queens, NY
Gardner, Gus (Glover C.)	07/18/1990	Cedar Hill Cemetery, Vicksburg, MS
Gerard, Alphonso	07/14/2002	Christainsted Cemetery, Christiansted, St. Croix, Virgin Islands
Gerard, Frenchy (Albert)	10/27/1967	Cremated, Tampa, FL
Gibson, Josh (Joshua)	01/20/1947	Allegheny Cemetery, Pittsburgh, PA

Name	DOD	Cemetery, City, State
Gibson, Josh (Joshua, Jr.)	09/10/2003	Homewood Cemetery, Pittsburgh, PA
Giles, George Franklin	03/03/1992	Sunrise Cemetery, Manhattan, KS
Gilliam, Jim (James William)	10/08/1978	Inglewood Park Cemetery, Inglewood, CA
Givens, Oscar C.	10/22/1967	Rosehill Cemetery, Linden, NJ
Gonzalez, Mike (Miguel Angel)	02/19/1977	Cemeterio de Cristobal Colon, Havana, Cuba
Gottlieb, Eddie (Edward) *owner*	12/07/1979	Har Nebo Cemetery, Philadelphia, PA
Govern, S.K. (Stanislaus Kostka)	11/03/1924	Eden Cemetery, Collingdale, PA
Grant, Charlie	07/09/1932	Spring Grove Cemetery, Cincinnati, OH
Grant, Frank	05/27/1937	East Ridgelawn Cemetery, Clifton, NJ
Graves, Whitt Allen	04/21/1997	Maury Cemetery, Richmond, VA
Gray, Chester (Chesley)	04/18/1996	United Memorial Gardens, Plymouth, MI
Gray, George	02/26/2001	Lincoln Cemetery, Atlanta, GA
Green, Chin (Leslie)	03/02/1985	Calvary Cemetery, St. Louis, MO
Greene, Joe (James Elbert)	07/19/1989	Stone Mountain Cemetery, Stone Mountain, GA
Greenlee, Gus (William Augustus) *owner*	07/07/1952	Allegheny Cemetery, Pittsburgh, PA
Griffin, C.B. (Clarence Bernard)	02/27/1991	Green Lawn Cemetery, Columbus, OH
Griffith, Bob (Robert)	11/07/1977	Salem Cemetery, Liberty, TN
Griggs, Wiley	08/23/1996	Elmwood Cemetery, Birmingham, AL
Grimes, Bounce (Lionel E.)	02/06/1993	Alliance City Cemetery, Alliance, OH
Gross, Theodore	10/12/1999	Lakeview Cemetery, Wichita Falls, TX
Guilbe, Juan	04/29/1994	Cementerio Civil, Ponce, Puerto Rico
Hairston, Sammy (Samuel Harding)	10/31/1997	Elmwood Cemetery, Birmingham, AL
Hall, Perry	04/03/1992	Mt. Glenwood West Cemetery, Glenwood, IL
Hamman, Ed P. *owner*	01/09/1989	Oak Ridge Cemetery, Inverness, FL
Hannibal, Leo H.	06/00/1968	Resurrection Cemetery, Mackenzie, MO
Harden, Lovell	11/22/1996	Lakeside Cemetery, Erie, PA
Hardy, Art (Arthur Wesley)	09/20/1980	Forest Lawn Cemetery, Buffalo, NY
Harness, O. (Robert Marseilles)	06/17/1991	Holy Sepulchre Cemetery, Worth, IL
Harris, Isaiah	09/18/2001	Memorial Park Cemetery, Memphis, TN
Harris, Teenie (Charles)	06/12/1998	Homewood Cemetery, Pittsburgh, PA
Harris, Vic (Elander Victor)	02/23/1978	Eternal Valley Memorial Park, Newhall, CA
Harrison, Abe (Abraham)	05/01/1932	Ewing Cemetery, Ewing, NJ
Harvey, Bill (Davis)	03/05/1989	Maryland National Memorial Park, Laurel, MD
Harvey, Bob (Robert A.)	06/27/1992	Rosedale Cemetery, Orange, NJ
Haynes, Sammy	11/11/1997	Inglewood Park Cemetery, Inglewood, CA
Haywood, Buster (Albert)	04/19/2000	Inglewood Park Cemetery, Inglewood, CA
Heard, Jay (Jehosie)	11/18/1999	New Grace Hill Cemetery, Birmingham, AL
Hendrix, Stokes Edward	02/05/2003	Middle Tennessee Veterans Cemetery, Nashville, TN
Henry, Preacher (Leo)	05/16/1992	Edgewood Cemetery, Jacksonville, FL
Henry, Roy M.	06/22/1999	Evergreen Cemetery, Louisville, KY
Hernandez, Ricardo		Cemeterio de Cristobal Colon, Havana, Cuba
Herrera, Ramon	02/03/1978	Cemeterio de Cristobal Colon, Havana, Cuba
Hill, Sam (Samuel Leslie)	04/23/1992	Grove Hill Memorial Park, Dallas, TX

Name	DOD	Cemetery, City, State
Holder, Bill (William J.)	11/30/1993	Resthaven Memory Gardens, Avon, OH
Holliday, Flit (Charles Durocher)	08/22/1992	Jefferson Barracks National Cemetery, St. Louis, MO
Holloway, Crush (Christopher)	06/24/1972	Mt. Calvary Cemetery, Baltimore, MD
Hooker, Elbow (Leniel C.)	12/18/1977	Glendale Cemetery, Bloomfield, NJ
Hopwood, Reginald	07/04/1984	Fort Snelling National Cemetery, Minneapolis, MN
Hoskins, Dave (David Taylor)	04/02/1970	River Rest Cemetery, Flint, MI
House, Red (Charles)	02/01/2001	Woodlawn Cemetery, Detroit, MI
Howard, Doc (Charles Allen)	08/14/1904	Spring Grove Cemetery, East Liverpool, OH
Howard, Elston Gene	12/14/1980	George Washington Memorial Park, Paramus, NJ
Hubbard, Jesse James	01/14/1982	Riverside National Cemetery, Riverside, CA
Hudson, Andrew	04/05/1995	Forest Hill Cemetery, Kansas City, MO
Hudspeth, Highpockets (Robert)	08/02/1935	Cypress Hills National Cemetery, Brooklyn, NY
Hueston, William C.	05/31/1979	Emmons Ridge Cemetery, Hilham, IN
Hughes, Luther	09/22/1998	Galilee Cemetery, Sarasota, FL
Hutchinson, Ace (Willie D.)	10/10/1992	Fort Logan National Cemetery, Denver, CO
Hyde, Bubba (Cowan Fontella)	11/20/2003	St. Peter's Cemetery, St. Louis, MO
Ingram, Alfred	05/20/1995	South-View Cemetery, Atlanta, GA
Isreal, Pint (Clarence Charles)	04/12/1987	Gate of Heaven Cemetery, Silver Spring, MD
Jackson, Sonnyman (Rufus) *owner*	03/06/1949	Homewood Cemetery, Pittsburgh, PA
Jackson, Thomas H. *owner*	05/21/1931	Atlantic City Cemetery, Pleasantville, NJ
Jackson, Thumper (Daniel M.)	08/15/1992	Black Hills National Cemetery, Sturgis, SD
Jacox, Cal (Calvin J.) *Norfolk sportswriter*	08/10/1989	Calvary Cemetery, Norfolk, VA
Jefferson, George L.	09/21/1985	Parier Springs Cemetery, Boley, OK
Jenkins, Fats (Clarence R.)	12/06/1968	East Cedar Hill Cemetery, Philadelphia, PA
Jethroe, Sam (Samuel)	06/16/2001	Erie Cemetery, Erie, PA
Jewell, Warner	12/24/1960	Crown Hill Cemetery, Indianapolis, IN
Jlimmenez, Hooks		Cemeterio de Cristobal Colon, Havana, Cuba
Johnson, Bill (William H.)	10/26/1988	Calverton National Cemetery, Calverton, NY
Johnson, Curtis T.	01/27/2004	Jefferson Memorial Gardens, Saint Rose, LA
Johnson, Josh (Joshua)	08/12/1999	Camp Butler National Cemetery, Springfield, IL
Johnson, Judy (William Julius)	06/15/1989	Silverbrook Cemetery, Wilmington, DE
Johnson, Tubby (Pearley)	12/19/1991	Mount Hope Cemetery, Mattapan, MA
Johnston, William Wade	03/08/1978	Union Cemetery, Steubenville, OH
Jones, Casey (Clinton)	11/17/1998	Memorial Park Woods South Cemetery, Memphis, TN
Jones, Sam (Samuel)	11/05/1971	Woodlawn Cemetery, Fairmont, WV
Jones, Slim (Stuart)	11/19/1938	Mt. Calvary Cemetery, Baltimore, MD
Kemp, Gabby (James Albert)	10/21/1993	Crest Lawn Memorial Park, Atlanta, GA
Kennedy, John Irvin	04/27/1998	Evergreen Cemetery, Jacksonville, FL
Kimbro, Henry	07/11/1999	Greenwood Cemetery, Nashville, TN
Kimbrough, Hilton	03/13/1923	Atlantic City Cemetery, Pleasantville, NJ

Name	DOD	Cemetery, City, State
Kimbrough, Schoolboy (Larry Nathaniel)	01/29/2001	Cremated, Philadelphia, PA
King, Pijo (Clarence)	09/11/1993	Highland Memorial Gardens, Bessemer, AL
Kitamura, Richard Shoji	01/15/1981	Cremated at Hosoi Gaerden Mortuary, Honolulu, HI
Klep, Eddie	11/21/1981	Wintergreen Gorge Cemetery, Erie, PA. Cremated Los Angeles, CA
Kountze, Mabray *writer*	09/27/1994	Oak Grove Cemetery, Medford, MA
Lacy, Sam (Samuel Harold) *writer*	05/08/2003	Lincoln Memorial Cemetery, Suitland, MD
LaMarque, Lefty (James)	01/15/2000	Forest Hill Cemetery, Kansas City, MO
Landers, Henny (Robert Henry)	01/07/1998	Lincoln Cemetery, Kansas City, MO
Lattimore, Al (Albert)	02/22/1986	Magnolia Cemetery, Norfolk, VA
Leland, Frank	11/14/1914	Lincoln Cemetery, Blue Island, IL
Leon, Isidoro (Becerra)	07/25/2002	Miami Memorial Park, Miami, FL
Leonard, Buck	11/27/1997	Gardens of Gesthemane, Rocky Mount, NC
Lewis, Rufus	12/25/1999	Gethsemane Cemetery, Detroit, MI
Lloyd, Pop (John Henry)	03/19/1965	Atlantic City Cemetery, Pleasantville, NJ
Lockhart, A.J. (Arthur)	02/10/1993	Forest Lawn Cemetery, Buffalo, NY
Long, The Kid (Ernest)	09/20/2000	East View Cemetery, Rome, GA
Louden, Tommy (Louis Oliver)	08/31/1989	Fairmount Cemetery, Newark, NJ
Mackey, Biz (Raleigh)	09/22/1965	Evergreen Cemetery, Los Angeles, CA
Magrinat, Kiki (Jose)		Cemeterio de Cristobal Colon, Havana, Cuba
Manley, Abe *owner*	12/09/1952	Fairmount Cemetery, Newark, NJ
Manley, Effa *owner*	04/16/1981	Holy Cross Cemetery, Culver City, CA
Manning, Max (Maxwell C.)	06/23/2003	Atlantic City Cemetery, Pleasantville, NJ
Marcelle, Ghost (Oliver)	06/12/1949	Riverside Cemetery, Denver, CO
Marquez, Luis (Angel)	03/00/1988	Municipal Cemetery, Aquadilla, Puerto Rico
Marsans, Armando	09/03/1960	Cemeterio de Cristobal Colon, Havana, Cuba
Marshall, Bobby (Robert Walls)	08/27/1958	Lakewood Cemetery, Minneapolis, MN
Martin, Ed (Edward)	02/25/2002	Middle Tennessee Veterans Cemetery, Nashville, TN
Martin, J.B. (John B.) *owner*	04/30/1973	Woodlawn Cemetery, Detroit, MI
Martinez, Francisco		Cemeterio de Cristobal Colon, Havana, Cuba
Marvray, Hawk (Charles Jefferson)	04/06/1998	Barrancas National Cemetery, Pensacola, FL
Mathis, Lefty (Verdell)	10/30/1998	Memphis Memorial Gardens, Memphis, TN
Matlock, Leroy	02/06/1968	Elmhurst Cemetery, St. Paul, MN
Mayo, Hot Stuff (George)	08/22/1987	Mount Zion Cemetery, Collingdale, PA
Mayweather, Eldridge	02/19/1966	Leavenworth National Cemetery, Leavenworth, KS
McClain, Jeep (Eugene Walter)	07/07/1997	Mt. Lawn Cemetery, Sharon Hill, PA
McDonald, Mac (Webster)	06/12/1982	Fairview Cemetery, Willow Grove, PA
McHenry, Henry L.	02/09/1981	Green-Wood Cemetery, Brooklyn, NY
McMahon, Jess (Jesse Roderick) *owner*	11/21/1954	St. Raymond's Cemetery, Bronx, NY
McMillen, Earl T.	01/28/1999	Mount Glenwood South Cemetery, Glenwood, IL
McNair, Hurley	12/02/1948	Highland Park Cemetery, Kansas City, KS

Name	DOD	Cemetery, City, State
McNeal, Junior (Clyde Cliffton)	04/14/1996	Fort Sam Houston National Cemetery, · San Antonio, TX
Meadows, Helburn L.	09/11/1989	Union Baptist Cemetery, Cincinnati, OH
Medley, Babe (Calvin R.)	10/13/1983	Lincoln Memorial Cemetery, Suitland, MD
Mellix, Lefty (Ralph B.)	03/23/1985	Homewood Cemetery, Pittsburgh, PA
Mendez, Jose	10/31/1928	Cemeterio de Cristobal Colon, Havana, Cuba
Merchant, Speed (Henry Lewis)	08/23/1982	Wesleyan Cemetery, Cincinnati, OH
Mesa, Andres	09/27/1994	Greenwood Memory Lawn Cemetery, Phoenix, AZ
Miro, Pedro	01/28/1996	Mount Olivet Cemetery, Tonawanda, NY
Mobley, Ira	12/16/1984	Eastern Cemetery, Louisville, KY
Molina, Tinti (Augustin)	01/10/1961	Cemeterio de Cristobal Colon, Havana, Cuba
Mongin, Sam	01/30/1936	Cypress Hills Cemetery, Brooklyn, NY
Moody, Lee	07/04/1998	Sunset Gardens of Memory, Millstadt, IL
Moore, Herbert Cato	06/07/2003	Woodlawn Cemetery, Detroit, MI
Moreland, Nate (Nathaniel Edmund)	11/27/1973	Los Angeles National Cemetery, Los Angeles, CA
Morgan, Connie (Contance Enola)	10/14/1996	Mount Lawn Cemetery, Sharon Hill, PA
Morrison, Felton	12/29/1981	Cremated, Chelton Hills Crematory, Philadelphia, PA
Morton, Ferdinand Quentin (League executive)	11/15/1949	Woodlawn Cemetery, Washington, DC
Moseley, Beauregard	12/01/1919	Lincoln Cemetery, Blue Island, IL
Munoz, Jose	12/25/1945	Cemeterio de Cristobal Colon, Havana, Cuba
Newberry, Richard A.	10/26/1982	Fort Snelling National Cemetery, Minneapolis, MN
Noble, Ray (Rafael Miguel)	05/09/1998	Cypress Hills Cemetery, Brooklyn, NY
O'Kelley, Stretch (Willie James)	06/09/1991	College Park Memorial Cemetery, College Park, GA
Oms, Alejandro	11/09/1946	Santa Clara Cemetery, Santa Clara, Cuba
Owens, Bill (William John)	05/05/1999	Holy Cross Cemetery, Indianapolis, IN
Page, Ted (Theodore Roosevelt)	12/00/1984	Allegheny Cemetery, Pittsburgh, PA
Paige, Satchel (Leroy Robert)	06/08/1982	Forest Hill Cemetery, Kansas City, MO
Palmer, Ralph Leon	10/10/1999	Limestone Cemetery, Limestone, WV
Parks, Charles	09/13/1987	Beatties Ford Memorial Gardens, Charlotte, NC
Parpeti, Agustin		Cemeterio de Cristobal Colon, Havana, Cuba
Parsons, Elwood (NgL promoter)	08/26/1995	Body donated to Wright State University Medical School, Dayton, OH
Partlow, Roy E.	04/19/1987	Mount Peace Cemetery, Philadelphia, PA
Patterson, Pat (Andrew Lawrence)	05/16/1984	Paradise Cemetery-South, Houston, TX
Payne, Jap (Andrew H.)	08/22/1942	Lincoln Cemetery, Blue Island, IL
Pearson, Frank	08/11/1997	Calvary Cemetery, Memphis, TN
Pearson, Len (Leonard)	12/07/1980	Rosedale Cemetery, Orange, NJ
Pendleton, Jim (James Edward)	03/20/1996	Houston National Cemetery, Houston, TX
Pettus, Zach (William Thomas)	08/22/1924	Mount Olivet Cemetery, Maspeth, Queens, NY
Petway, Bruce	06/28/1941	Lincoln Cemetery, Blue Island, IL

Name	DOD	Cemetery, City, State
Phiffer, Lester J.	08/10/1982	Fort Leavenworth National Cemetery, Fort Leavenworth, KS
Poles, Spotswood	09/12/1962	Arlington National Cemetery, Arlington, VA
Pollard, Nate (Nathaniel)	11/23/1996	Geo. Washington Carver Memorial Gardens, Birmingham, AL
Pompez, Alex (Alessandro) *owner*	03/14/1974	Woodlawn Cemetery, Bronx, NY
Pope, Dave (David)	08/28/1999	Lake View Cemetery, Cleveland, OH
Posey, Cum (Cumberland Willis) *owner*	03/28/1946	Homestead Cemetery, Homestead, PA
Powell, Dick (Richard D.) *owner*	02/03/2004	Garrison Forest Veterans Cemetery, Owings Mill, MD
Powell, Pee Wee (Willie Ernest)	05/16/1987	Parkville Cemetery, Parkville, MI
Prim, Randolph	11/26/1986	Gypsum Hill Cemetery, Salina, KS
Quinones, Tomas	03/00/1967	Cementerio Civil, Ponce, Puerto Rico
Ragland, Harlen Earl	08/12/1960	Fort Leavenworth National Cemetery, Fort Leavenworth, KS
Raines, Larry (Lawrence Glenn Hope)	01/28/1978	Evergreen-Mount Hope Cemetery, Lansing, MI
Ramos, Ezequiel		Cemeterio de Cristobal Colon, Havana, Cuba
Rasberry, Ted (Theodore R.) *owner*	04/17/2001	Chapel Hill Memorial Gardens, Grand Rapids, MI
Ray, Jaybird (Otto C.)	01/24/1976	Fort Leavenwoth National Cemetery, Fort Leavenworth, KS
Redd, Hickey (Ulysses)	11/18/2002	Southern Memorial Gardens, Baton Rouge, LA
Redding, Cannonball Dick (Richard)	10/30/1948	Long Island National Cemetery, Farmingdale, NY
Reed, Percy	06/18/2000	Spring Grove Cemetery, Cincinnati, OH
Renfroe, Chico (Othello Nelson)	09/03/1991	Lincoln Cemetery, Atlanta, GA
Riddick, Big Six (Vernon W.)	03/12/1979	Calvary Cemetery, Norfolk, VA
Riddle, Jif (Marshall Lewis)	09/02/1988	Jefferson Barracks National Cemetery, St. Louis, MO
Ritchey, John Franklin	01/14/2002	Greenwood Memorial Park, San Diego, CA
Roberts, Curt (Curtis Benjamin)	11/14/1969	Evergreen Cemetery, Oakland, CA
Roberts, Elihu	03/23/1975	Lincoln Memorial Park, Mays Landing, NJ
Robinson, Bobby (William)	05/17/2002	Restvale Cemetery, Alsip, IL
Robinson, Bojangles (Bill) *owner*	11/25/1949	Evergreen Cemetery, Brooklyn, NY
Robinson, Buck (Johnson K.)	11/28/1998	St. Jude's Cemetery, Monroe City, MO
Robinson, Jackie (Jack Roosevelt)	10/24/1972	Cypress Hills Cemetery, Brooklyn, NY
Robinson, Scoby (Edward J.)	12/23/1990	Riverview Cemetery, South Bend, IN
Robinson, Slow (Henry Frazier)	10/13/1997	Robinson Estate, King's Mountain, NC
Rogan, Bullet Joe (Wilbert)	03/04/1967	Blue Ridge Lawn Memorial Gardens, Kansas City, MO
Roth, Bobby (Herman)	04/08/1988	Mount Olivet Cemetery, New Orleans, LA
Ruffin, Lassas (Charles Leon)	08/14/1970	Lincoln Memorial Cemetery, Portsmouth, VA
Russell, Branch L.	05/01/1959	Jefferson Barracks National Cemetery, St. Louis, MO

Name	DOD	Cemetery, City, State
Sadler, Bill (William A.)	11/10/1987	Gracelawn Memorial Park, New Castle, DE
Sama, Pablo	07/21/1951	Cemeterio de Cristobal Colon, Havana, Cuba
Sanchez, Gonzalo		Cemeterio de Cristobal Colon, Havana, Cuba
Santop, Louis "Top" (buried under birth name: Loftin)	01/22/1942	Philadelphia National Cemetery, Philadelphia, PA
Saperstein, Abe *owner*	03/15/1966	Westlawn Cemetery, Chicago, IL
Scantlebury, Pat (Patricio Athelstan)	05/24/1991	Glendale Cemetery, Bloomfield, NJ
Schlicter, Walter (Henry Walter) *owner*	01/15/1944	West Laurel Hill Cemetery, Bala Cynwyd, PA
Schorling, John M. *owner*	03/23/1940	Mount Greenwood Cemetery, Chicago, IL
Scott, Cornelius Adolphus	05/07/2000	Lincoln Cemetery, Atlanta, GA
Seagraves, Sam (Samuel)	02/06/2000	Sunrise Memorial Gardens Cemetery, Douglasville, GA
Searcy, Kelly (Kelton)	11/29/1978	Nashville National Cemetery, Madison, TN
Semler, James Aloysius "Soldier Boy"	10/15/1955	Long Island National Cemetery, Farmingdale, NY
Shackleford, John Gerald	04/08/1979	Newark Memorial Gardens, Newark, OH
Shelby, Hiawatha	09/19/1996	New Crown Cemetery, Indianapolis, IN
Sheppard, Freddie (Frederick)	12/05/1999	Elmwood Cemetery, Birmingham, AL
Shively, Rabbit (George Anner)	06/07/1962	Rosehill Cemetery, Bloomington, IN
Sias, George	10/08/1985	Mount Olivet Cemetery, New Orleans, LA
Simpson, Harry Leon	04/03/1979	Dalton Cemetery, West Hill, Dalton, GA
Smallwood, Woody (Dewitt)	01/26/1995	Mount Moriah Cemetery, Kansas City, MO
Smith, Dode	09/26/1996	Ohio City Cemetery, Ohio City, OH
Smith, George Cornelius	06/15/1987	Lincoln Cemetery, Gulfport, FL
Smith, Hilton	11/18/1983	Mount Moriah Cemetery, Kansas City, MO
Smith, John Ford	02/26/1983	Greenwood Memory Lawn Cemetery, Phoenix, AZ
Smith, Milt (Milton)	04/11/1997	Greenwood Memorial Park, San Diego, CA
Smith, Wendell *writer*	11/26/1972	Burr Oak Cemetery, Alsip, IL
Snead, Bo Gator (Sylvester)	05/21/1995	Sunnyvale Cemetery, Quincy, FL
Snow, Skipper (Felton)	03/16/1974	Eastern Cemetery, Louisville, KY
Spedden, Charles P. *owner*	03/29/1960	Mount Olivet Cemetery, Baltimore, MD
Spencer, J.B. (Joseph B.)	05/17/2003	McDonoghville Cemetery, Gretna, LA
Starks, Lefty (Otis)	07/16/1965	Long Island National Cemetery, Farmingdale, NY
Stearnes, Turkey (Norman)	09/04/1979	Lincoln Memorial Park Cemetery, Mount Clemens, MI
Stephens, Jake (Paul Eugene)	02/05/1981	Mount Zion Cemetery, Delta, PA
Stewart, Riley	12/10/2000	Calvary Missionary Baptist Church Cemetery, Benton, LA
Stovey, George Washington	03/22/1936	Wildwood Cemetery, Williamsport, PA
Strong, Nat (Nathaniel C.) *owner*	01/10/1935	Green-Wood Cemetery, Brooklyn, NY
Strothers, Colonel W. *owner*	07/14/1933	Lincoln Cemetery, Harrisburg, PA
Sunkett, Pete (Golden L.)	05/09/1993	Sunset Memorial Park, Merchantville, NJ
Suttles, Mule (George)	07/09/1966	Glendale Cemetery, Bloomfield, NJ

Name	DOD	Cemetery, City, State
Sykes, Doc (Franklin Jehoy)	11/10/1986	Cremated. Ashes scattered at Morehouse College, Atlanta, GA
Taborn, Mickey (Earl)	12/21/1996	Fort Sam Houston National Cemetery, San Antonio, TX
Tate, Roosevelt	11/16/1978	Public Cemetery, Bigbee Valley, MS
Tatum, Goose (Reece)	01/18/1967	Fort Bliss National Cemetery, El Paso, TX
Taylor, Benjamin Harrison	01/24/1953	Arbutus Memorial Park, Baltimore, MD
Taylor, C.I. (Charles Isum)	02/23/1922	Crown Hill Cemetery, Indianapolis, IN
Taylor, Candy Jim (James)	04/03/1948	Burr Oak Cemetery, Alsip, IL
Taylor, Joe Cephus	03/18/1993	Greenwood Cemetery, Pittsburgh, PA
Taylor, School Boy (Johnny)	06/15/1987	Springdale Cemetery, Hartford, CT
Taylor, Steel Arm (Johnny)	03/25/1956	Springdale Cemetery, Peoria, IL
Thomas, Clint (Clinton)	12/03/1990	Cunningham Memorial Park, St. Albans, WV
Thompkins, Allie	07/06/2001	Restland Memorial Park, Monroeville, PA
Thompson, Frank Andrew	05/31/2002	Middle Tennessee Veterans Cemetery, Nashville, TN
Thompson, Hank (Henry Curtis)	09/30/1969	Odd Fellows Cemetery, Fresno, CA
Thompson, Orange	02/07/1989	Forest Hill Cemetery, Kansas City, MO
Tiant, Luis, Sr.	12/12/1977	Milton Cemetery, Milton, MA
Tinker, Harold	11/27/2000	Allegheny Cemetery, Pittsburgh, PA
Torriente, Cristobal	04/11/1938	Cemeterio de Cristobal Colon, Havana, Cuba. Originally intered at Calvary Cemetery, Queens, NY. Moved in the 1940s.
Trent, Theodore	01/10/1944	Burr Oak Cemetery, Alsip, IL
Trice, Bob (Robert Lee)	09/16/1988	St. Paul's Catholic Cemetery, Weirton, WV
Trouppe, Quincy Thomas	08/10/1993	Calvary Cemetery, St. Louis, MO
Tugerson, Schoolboy (Jim Clarence)	04/07/1983	Lakeside Memorial Park, Winter Haven, FL
Turner, Wyatt James	09/18/1986	Allegheny Cemetery, Pittsburgh, PA
Underwood, Eli	10/08/2000	Cremated, Olinger Chase Chapel, Aurora, CO.
Vann, Robert Lee *publisher*	10/24/1940	Homewood Cemetery, Pittsburgh, PA
Vargas, Tetelo (Juan)	12/30/1971	Guayama Cemetery, Guayama, Puerto Rico
Vierra, Big Chris (Justin Christopher)	02/09/2002	Fairview Cemetery, New Britain, CT
Villodas, Luis	08/22/1994	Cementerio Civil, Ponce, Puerto Rico
Walker, Edsall Elliott	02/19/1997	Memory's Gardens Cemetery, Albany, NY
Walker, Hoss (Jesse T.)	01/26/1984	Fort Sam Houston National Cemetery, San Antonio, TX
Wallace, Bo (James)	04/14/2000	Rosehill Cemetery, Linden, NJ
Warfield, Frank (Francis X.)	07/24/1932	Mt. Auburn Cemetery, Baltimore, MD
Waters, Theodore	03/29/1966	Rolling Green Memorial Park, West Goshen, PA
Watkins, Skeeter (Murray Clifton)	03/26/1987	Adams Chapel Cemetery, Baltimore, MD
Watrous, Sherman	06/13/1997	Houston Memorial Gardens, Houston, TX
Watts, Andy (Andrew)	01/31/1991	Mount Hope Memorial Gardens, Livonia, MI
Webster, Jim (Daniel)	06/05/1988	United Memorial Gardens, Plymouth, MI
Wells, Junior (Willie Brooks)	01/04/1994	Plummes Cemetery, Austin, TX

Name	DOD	Cemetery, City, State
Wells, Willie	01/22/1989	Evergreen Cemetery, Austin, TX
Welmaker, Snook (Roy Horace)	02/03/1998	Lincoln Cemetery, Atlanta, GA
Wheeler, Boom Boom (Samuel Wallace)	04/16/1989	Calvary Cemetery, St. Louis, MO
White, Chaney	02/00/1967	Mount Lawn Cemetery, Sharon Hill, PA
White, Jacob C.	11/11/1902	Merion Memorial Park, Bala Cynwyd, PA
White, Sol (Solomon)	08/26/1955	Frederick Douglass Memorial Park, Staten Island, NY
White, Stank (Eugene)	04/26/2002	Evergreen Cemetery, Jacksonville, FL
Whitney, Carl Eugene	07/00/1986	Calvary Cemetery, St. Louis, MO
Wiggins, Maurice Caldwell	03/23/2002	Abraham Lincoln National Cemetery, Elwood, IL
Wiggs, Fats (Leonard David)	06/29/2000	Memorial Park Cemetery, Tampa, FL
Wiley, Doc (Wabishaw Spencer)	11/03/1944	Fairmount Cemetery, Newark, NJ
Wiley, Joseph	03/13/1993	Carrollton Cemetery (aka Green Street Cem.), New Orleans, LA
Wilkins, Barron DeWare	05/24/1924	Mount Olivet Cemetery, Maspeth, Queens, NY
Wilkins, Wesley	02/22/1971	Media Cemetery, Media, PA
Wilkinson, J.L. (James L.) *owner*	08/21/1964	Mount Moriah Cemetery, Kansas City, MO
Williams, George L.	01/09/1918	Merion Memorial Park, Bala Cynwyd, PA
Williams, Jeff (Norldon Leroy)	07/23/1994	Florida National Cemetery, Bushnell, FL
Williams, Jesse Harold	02/27/1990	Mount Moriah Cemetery, Kansas City, MO
Williams, Lawrence	02/28/2003	Evergreen Cemetery, Detroit, MI
Williams, Nature Boy (James R.)	04/08/1980	Mount Moriah Cemetery, Albright, WV
Williams, Smokey Joe	03/12/1946	Lincoln Memorial Cemetery, Suitland, MD
Wilmore, Al (Alfred Gardner)	03/03/1996	Westminster Cemetery, Bala Cynwyd, PA
Wilson, Bob (Robert)	04/23/1985	Lincoln Memorial Cemetery, Dallas, TX
Wilson, Boojum (Ernest Judson)	06/26/1963	Arlington National Cemetery, Arlington, VA
Wilson, Emmett Dabney	02/26/1991	Jefferson Barracks National Cemetery, St. Louis, MO
Wilson, Rollo (Wesley Rollo) *writer*	11/11/1956	Beverly National Cemetery, Beverly, NJ
Winters, Nip (James A.)	12/12/1971	Union Hill Cemetery, Kennett Square, PA
Wright, Ernest L. *owner*	04/11/1985	Erie Cemetery, Erie, PA
Wyatt, John Thomas	04/06/1998	Cremated, Omaha, NE.
Wynn, Fourteen (Willie M.)	07/14/1992	New Camden Cemetery, Camden, NJ
Yokely, Norman (Laymon Samuel)	11/26/1975	Evergreen Cemetery, Winston-Salem, NC
Yokum, Lewis	02/14/1966	Berry Cemetery, Ash Grove, MO
Young, Faye (Franklin) *writer*	10/00/1957	Mt. Glenwood Cemetery, Glenwood, IL
Zomphier, Zomp (Charles)	01/31/1973	Jefferson Barracks National Cemetery, St. Louis, MO

OWNERS AND EXECUTIVES

Name	DOD	Cemetery, City, State
Adams, Ivers Whitney (Boston owner 1871)	10/10/1914	New Cemetery, Ashburnham, MA
Allyn, Arthur Cecil, Jr. (White Sox owner 1961–69)	03/22/1985	Memorial Park Cemetery, Evanston, IL
Allyn, Arthur Cecil, Sr. (White Sox owner)	10/07/1960	Memorial Park Cemetery, Evanston, IL
Allyn, John W., Jr. (White Sox owner 1970–75)	04/29/1979	Memorial Park Cemetery, Evanston, IL
Autry, Gene (Angels owner 1961–98)	10/02/1998	Forest Lawn Memorial Park, Hollywood Hills, Los Angeles, CA
Baker, William F. (Phillie owner 1913–30)	12/04/1930	Greenwood Cemetery, Philadelphia, PA
Ball, Philip DeCatsby (Browns owner 1916–33)	10/22/1933	Bellefontaine Cemetery, St. Louis, MO
Barnard, Ernest S. (AL president 1927–31)	03/27/1931	Knollwood Cemetery, Mayfield Heights, OH
Barnes, Donald L. (St. Louis Browns owner 1937–45)	07/20/1962	Auburn Cemetery, Auburn, IL
Barrow, Edward G. (Yankees executive 1921–45)	12/15/1953	Kensico Cemetery, Valhalla, NY
Benswanger, William Edward (Pirates owner 1932–46)	01/15/1972	West View Cemetery, Pittsburgh, PA
Bishop, Campbell Orrick (St. Louis owner 1875)	08/26/1929	Bellefontaine Cemetery, St. Louis, MO
Blong, Andrew F. (St. Louis owner 1875)	05/27/1909	Calvary Cemetery, St. Louis, MO
Bradley, Alva (Indians owner 1928–46)	03/29/1953	Lake View Cemetery, Cleveland, OH

Name	DOD	Cemetery, City, State
Briggs, Walter Owen, Jr. (Tigers owner 1936–52)	07/03/1970	Holy Sepulchre Cemetery, Southfield, MI
Briggs, Walter Owen, Sr. (Tigers owner 1952–56)	01/17/1952	Holy Sepulchre Cemetery, Southfield, MI
Britton, Helene (Cardinals owner 1916)	01/08/1950	Lake View Cemetery, Cleveland, OH
Brush, John J. (Giants owner 1903–1912)	11/26/1912	Crown Hill Cemetery, Indianapolis, IN
Bulkeley, Morgan (Hartford owner 1876–77; NL president 1876)	11/06/1922	Cedar Hill Cemetery, Hartford, CT
Burke, Joe (Royals executive)	05/12/1992	Resurrection Cemetery, Lenexa, KS
Busch, Gussie (August A. Jr.) (Cardinals owner 1953–89)	09/29/1989	Sunset Memorial Park, Affton, MO
Butler, Dick (Richard) (Major and minor league executive)	12/20/2003	Paris Cemetery, Paris, KY
Byrne, Charles H. (Brooklyn owner 1884–97)	01/04/1898	Calvary Cemetery, Woodside, Queens, NY
Cammeyer, William H. (NY Mutuals owner 1875)	09/04/1889	Green-Wood Cemetery, Brooklyn, NY
Campbell, James A. (Tigers executive)	10/31/1995	Scott Cemetery, Huron, OH
Carpenter, Robert P. (Phillies owner)	06/11/1998	DuPont Family Cemetery, Winterthur, DE
Carpenter, Robert R.M., Jr. (Phillies owner)	07/08/1990	DuPont Family Cemetery, Winterthur, DE
Chandler, Happy (Albert Benjamin) (Commissioner 1945–51)	06/15/1991	Pisgah Presbyterian Church Cemetery, Pisgah, KY
Chiles, Eddie (Texas owner 1980–87)	08/22/1993	Greenwood Memorial Park, Fort Worth, TX
Comiskey, Charles A. (White Sox owner 1901–31)	10/26/1931	Calvary Cemetery, Evanston, IL
Comiskey, Charles L. (White Sox owner)		Calvary Cemetery, Evanston, IL
Comiskey, Grace Lou (owner 1941–56)	12/10/1956	Calvary Cemetery, Evanston, IL
Comiskey, Lou (John Louis) (owner)	07/18/1939	Calvary Cemetery, Evanston, IL
Cox, George Barnesdale (Cincinnati owner)	05/22/1916	Spring Grove Cemetery, Cincinnati, OH
Crosby, Bing (Harry Lillis) (Pittsburgh owner)	10/14/1977	Holy Cross Cemetery, Culver City, CA
Crosley, Powell, Jr. (Cincinnati owner 1934–61)	03/28/1961	Spring Grove Cemetery, Cincinnati, OH
Dale, Francis L. (Cincinnati owner 1967–73)	11/28/1993	Spring Grove Cemetery, Cincinnati, OH

Name	DOD	Cemetery, City, State
Davidson, Mordecai (Louisville owner 1889)	09/06/1940	Cave Hill Cemetery, Louisville, KY
Day, John (Giants owner 1883–1892)	06/01/1941	Fairmount Cemetery, Newark, NJ
Devery, Bill (William) (Yankees owner 1903–1915)	06/20/1919	Calvary Cemetery, Woodside, Queens, NY
DeWitt, William (Browns owner 1949–51)	03/03/1982	Oak Grove Cemetery, St. Louis, MO
Doherty, Edward S. (executive)	07/08/1971	St. Joseph Cemetery, Pawtucket, RI
Dovey, George B. (Braves owner 1907–1909)	06/19/1909	Mt. Moriah Cemetery, Philadelphia, PA
Drexler, Fred (Louisville owner 1893–96)	01/19/1929	Cave Hill Cemetery, Louisville, KY
Dreyfuss, Barney (Louisville and Pittsburgh owner 1899–1932)	02/05/1932	West View Cemetery, Pittsburgh, PA
Dreyfuss, Samuel W. (Pittsburgh owner)	02/22/1931	West View Cemetery, Pittsburgh, PA
Dunn, James C. (Indians owner 1916–22)	06/09/1922	Riverside Cemetery, Marshalltown, IA
Durham, Israel W (Phillies owner 1909)	06/28/1909	Mt. Moriah Cemetery, Philadelphia, PA
Ebbets, Charles H. (Dodgers owner 1898–1925)	04/18/1925	Green-Wood Cemetery, Brooklyn, NY
Eckert, William (Commissioner 1965–68)	04/16/1971	Arlington National Cemetery, Arlington, VA
Ehlers, Arthur (Baltimore GM–1954)	02/07/1977	Gardens of Faith Memorial Gardens, Baltimore, MD
Farrell, Frank (Yankees owner 1903–1915)	02/10/1926	Calvary Cemetery, Woodside, Queens, NY
Feeney, Chub (Giants executive, NL president 1970–86)	10/01/1994	Skylawn Memorial Park, San Mateo, CA
Fetzer, John (Tigers owner 1961–89)	02/21/1991	Mountain Home Cemetery, Kalamazoo, MI
Finley, Charles O. (Athletics owner 1961–80)	02/20/1996	Calumet Park Cemetery & Mausoleum, Merrillville, IN
Fleischmann, Julius (Cincinnati owner 1902–25)	02/05/1925	Spring Grove Cemetery, Cincinnati, OH
Fleischmann, Max C. (Cincinnati owner 1902–27)	10/16/1951	Spring Grove Cemetery, Cincinnati, OH. Cremated
Fogel, Horace S. (Phillies president 1909–1912)	11/15/1928	Mount Peace Cemetery, Philadelphia, PA
Frazee, Harry (Red Sox owner 1917–23)	06/04/1929	Kensico Cemetery, Valhalla, NY
Freedman, Andrew (Giants owner 1895–1902)	12/04/1915	Salem Fields Cemetery, Brooklyn, NY
Frick, Ford (NL president 1934–1951, Commissioner 1951–1965)	04/08/1978	Christchurch Columbarium, Bronx, NY

Name	DOD	Cemetery, City, State
Fuchs, Judge (Emil Edwin) (Braves owner 1927–35)	12/05/1961	Sharon Memorial Park, Sharon, MA
Gaffney, James E. (Braves owner 1913–15)	08/17/1932	Calvary Cemetery, Woodside, Queens, NY
Galbreath, John (Pirates owner 1951–69)	07/20/1988	Sunset Cemetery, Galloway, OH
Gatto, Larry (Louisville owner)		St. Louis Cemetery, Louisville, KY
Giamatti, Bart (A. Bartlett) (Commissioner 1989; NL president 1986–89)	09/01/1989	Grove Street Cemetery, New Haven, CT
Giles, Warren (NL prsident 1951–69)	02/07/1979	Riverside Cemetery, Moline, IL
Grabiner, Harry Mitchell (White Sox executive)	10/24/1948	Rosehill Cemetery, Chicago, IL
Grant, George Washington (part owner of Boston Braves 1919–23)	04/05/1947	Forest Lawn Memorial Park, Glendale, CA
Grant, M. Donald (Mets executive)	11/28/1998	Cremated, Stuart, FL
Griffith, Calvin R. (Sentaors–Twins owner 1956–84)	10/20/1999	Fort Lincoln Cemetery, Brentwood, MD
Griffith, Clark Calvin (Senators owner 1920–55)	10/27/1955	Fort Lincoln Cemetery, Brentwood, MD
Gruner, Gustave A. (St. Louis owner 1899)	05/28/1909	Bellefontaine Cemetery, St. Louis, MO
Haas, Walter (Oakland owner 1990–95)	09/20/1995	Home of Peace Cemetery, Colma, CA
Haldeman, Walter (Louisville owner 1876–77)	05/13/1902	Cave Hill Cemetery, Louisville, KY
Hannegan, Robert E. (Cardinals owner 1947–49)	10/06/1949	Calvary Cemetery, St. Louis, MO
Harridge, Will (AL president 1931–59)	04/09/1971	Memorial Park Cemetery, Skokie, IL
Hart, James (Cubs owner 1892–1905)	07/18/1919	Girard Cemetery, Girard, PA. Cremated.
Hempstead, Harry Newton (Giants owner 1912–18)	03/26/1938	Crown Hill Cemetery, Indianapolis, IN
Hermann, Garry (August) (Cincinnati owner 1902–27)	04/25/1931	Vine Street Hill Cemetery, Cincinnati, OH
Heydler, John (NL president 1909, 1918–34)	04/18/1956	Cremated, San Diego, CA.
Hofheinz, Judge (Roy Mark) (Astros owner 1963–71)	11/21/1982	Glenwood Cemetery, Houston, TX
Hope, Bob (Indians owner)	07/28/2003	San Fernando Mission Cemetery, Mission Hills, CA
Hulbert, William (owner)	04/10/1882	Graceland Cemetery, Chicago, IL
Huston, Tillinghast L'H (Yankees owner)	03/29/1938	Frederica Christ Episcopal Church Cemetery, Brunswick, GA

Name	DOD	Cemetery, City, State
Hyneman, Edwin I. (Minority owner of Phillies, 1903)	08/03/1946	Mount Sinai Cemetery, Philadelphia, PA
Jackson, William (Louisville owner 1884)	12/29/1895	Cave Hill Cemetery, Louisville, KY
Jacobs, David H. (Indians owner 1987–92)	09/17/1992	Lakewood Park Cemetery, Rocky River, OH
Johnson, Arnold (Athletics owner 1955–59)	03/10/1960	Cremated, West Palm Beach, FL
Johnson, Ban (Byron Bancroft) (AL president 1901–27)	03/28/1931	Riverside Cemetery, Spencer, IN.
Johnston, James (Senators owner 1963–67)	12/28/1967	New Hope Church Cemetery, Chapel Hill, NC
Jones, Butch (Samuel) (owner)	08/12/1919	West Laurel Hill Cemetery, Bala Cynwyd, PA
Kauffman, Ewing M. (Royals owner 1969–93)	08/01/1993	Kauffman Foundation & Memorial Gardens, Kansas City, MO
Kauffman, Muriel M. (Royals owner)	03/17/1995	Kauffman Foundation & Memorial Gardens, Kansas City, MO
Kaye, Danny (Seattle owner 1969)	03/03/1987	Kensico Cemetery, Valhalla, NY
Kroc, Joan (Padres owner 1984–90)	10/12/2003	El Camino Memorial Park, La Jolla, CA
Kroc, Ray (Padres owner 1977–84)	01/14/1984	El Camino Memorial Park, La Jolla, CA. Cremated.
Landis, Kenesaw Mountain (Commissioner 1920–44)	11/25/1944	Oak Woods Cemetery, Chicago, IL. Cremated.
Lane, Frank (executive)	03/19/1981	Restland Memorial Park, Dallas, TX
Lannin, Joseph F. (Red Sox owner 1913–16)	05/15/1928	St. Brigid's Cemetery, Westbury, NY
Lucas, Henry V. (St. Louis owner 1884–86)	11/15/1910	Calvary Cemetery, St. Louis, MO
Lyons, William (Louisville owner 1888)	06/02/1911	Cave Hill Cemetery, Louisville, KY
Mack, Connie (Cornelius Alexander) (Athletics owner 1937–54)	02/08/1956	Holy Sepulchre Cemetery, Wyndmoor, PA
Mack, Roy (Athletics owner)	02/10/1960	Calvary Cemetery, West Conshohocken, PA
MacPhail, Larry (Dodgers owner 1939–42; Yankees owner 1945–47)	10/01/1975	Elkland Township Cemetery, Cass City, MI
McDirmid, Campbell J. (Cincinnati Pres, 1928–29)	05/13/1942	Spring Grove Cemetery, Cincinnati, OH
McKeever, Edward J. (Dodgers owner)	04/29/1925	Holy Cross Cemetery, Brooklyn, NY
McKeever, Stephen (Dodgers owner)	08/19/1938	Holy Cross Cemetery, Brooklyn, NY
McKnight, Denny (AA president 1882–85)	05/05/1900	Allegheny Cemetery, Pittsburgh, PA
Meyer, Stuart F. (St. Louis Card. president 1992–94)	05/21/2001	Bellerive Heritage Gardens, Creve Coeur, MO

Name	DOD	Cemetery, City, State
Morrissey, John C. (owner Troy Haymakers 1860s)	05/01/1878	St. Peter's Cemetery, Troy, NY
Muckerman, Richard C. (Browns owner 1946–48)	03/15/1959	Calvary Cemetery, St. Louis, MO
Murphy, Charles Webb (Chicago Cubs owner 1906–13)	10/16/1931	Sugar Grove Cemetery, Wilmington, OH
Navin, Frank (Tigers owner 1908–35)	11/13/1935	Holy Sepulchre Cemetery, Southfield, MI
Noyes, Thomas C. (Senators owner 1905–1912)	08/21/1912	Rock Creek Cemetery, Washington, DC
O'Connell, Dick (Richard Henry) (Red Sox executive)	08/18/2002	Mount Auburn Cemetery, Cambridge, MA
O'Malley, Walter (Dodgers owner 1950–1979)	08/09/1979	Holy Cross Cemetery, Culver City, CA
Owens, Paul (Phillies executive)	12/26/2003	Woddbury Memorial Park, West Deptford, NJ
Pank, John Henry (Louisville owner 1882–83)	03/14/1905	Graceland Cemetery, Chicago, IL
Payson, Joan (Mets owner 1962–1975)	10/04/1975	Pine Grove Cemetery, Falmouth, ME
Perini, Louis (Braves owner 1945–52)	04/16/1972	Woodlawn Cemetery, Wellesley, MA
Phelps, Zach (Louisville owner 1985–87, AA president 1890–91)	08/29/1901	Cave Hill Cemetery, Louisville, KY
Pulliam, Harry (NL president 1903–1909)	07/29/1909	Cave Hill Cemetery, Louisville, KY
Quesada, Pete (Elwood Richard) (Senators owner 1961–62)	02/09/1993	Arlington National Cemetery, Arlington, VA
Quinn, Robert (Boston owner and executive)	03/12/1954	St. Joseph's Cemetery, Lockbourne, OH
Rigney, Dorothy Comiskey (White Sox owner)	01/22/1971	Calvary Cemetery, Evanston, IL
Robison, Frank DeHass (Cleveland–St. Louis owner 1889–1906)	09/27/1909	Lake View Cemetery, Cleveland, OH
Robison, Martin Stanley (Cleveland–St. Louis owner 1889–1910)	03/27/1911	Lake View Cemetery, Cleveland, OH
Rowland, Pants (Clarence Henry) (executive)	05/17/1969	Holy Sepulchre Cemetery, Worth, IL
Ruckstuhl, George (Louisville owner 1893–1896)	12/28/1896	Cave Hill Cemetery, Louisville, KY
Ruppert, Jacob (Yankees owner 1915–1938)	01/13/1939	Kensico Cemetery, Valhalla, NY
Ryan, Ellis (Indians executive)	08/11/1966	Knollwood Cemetery, Mayfield Heights, OH
Saigh, Fred (St. Louis owner 1949–52)	12/29/1999	Oak Grove Cemetery, St. Louis, MO

Name	DOD	Cemetery, City, State
Schott, Marge (Cincinnati owner 1986–2004)	03/02/2004	Gate of Heaven Cemetery, Montgomery, OH
Shibe, Ben (Athletics owner 1901–21)	01/14/1922	West Laurel Hill Cemetery, Bala Cynwyd, PA
Shibe, Thomas S. (Athletics owner 1922–35)	02/16/1936	West Laurel Hill Cemetery, Bala Cynwyd, PA
Short, Robert (Senators– Rangers owner 1969–74)	11/20/1982	Resurrection Cemetery, Mendota Heights, MN
Sinclair, Harry F. (Newark owner 1915)	11/10/1956	Calvary Cemetery, Los Angeles, CA
Smith, C. Arnholt (Padres owner 1969–77)	06/08/1996	Greenwood Memorial Park, San Diego, CA
Somers, Charles (Indians owner 1910–15)	06/29/1934	Lake View Cemetery, Cleveland, OH
Stoneham, Charles A. (Giants owner 1919–35)	01/07/1936	Holy Name Cemetery, Jersey City, NJ
Stoneham, Horace (Giants owner 1936–75)	01/07/1990	Cremated, Phoenix, AZ Originally intered at St. Francis Cemetery, Phoenix. Ashes given to family.
Stucky, Thomas Hunt (Louisville owner 1892)	02/16/1917	Cave Hill Cemetery, Louisville, KY
Taft, Charles Phelps (Cubs owner)	12/31/1929	Spring Grove Cemetery, Cincinnati, OH
Taylor, Charles H. (Red Sox owner 1904–11)		Forest Hills Cemetery, Jamaica Plain, MA
Taylor, John I. (Red Sox owner 1904–11)		Forest Hills Cemetery, Jamaica Plain, MA
Thompson, George W. (Philadelphia owner)	07/20/1904	Princeton Cemetery, Princeton, NJ
Topping, Dan (Danile R.) (Yankees owner 1948–66)	05/18/1974	Woodlawn Cemetery, Bronx, NY
Trautman, George McNeal (executive)	06/24/1963	Cremated, Columbus, OH.
Tweed, William Marcy (NY Mutuals owner 1860s)	04/12/1878	Green-Wood Cemetery, Brooklyn, NY
Van Cott, Cornelius C. (New York owner 1890, 1893–94)	10/25/1904	Cypress Hills Cemetery, Brooklyn, NY
Veeck, Bill (Indians owner 1946–49, Browns 1951–53, White Sox 1959–61, 1976–80)	01/02/1986	Cremated. Oak Woods Cemetery, Chicago, IL. Ashes scattered over Lake Michigan
Veeck, William Louis, Sr. (Cubs executive)	10/05/1933	Bronswood Cemetery, Oak Brook, IL
Von der Ahe, Chris (St. Louis owner 1882–97)	06/05/1913	Bellefontaine Cemetery, St. Louis, MO
Von der Horst, Harry (Baltimore owner 1891–92)		Baltimore Cemetery, Baltimore, MD

Name	DOD	Cemetery, City, State
Von der Horst, John H. (Baltimore owner 1891–92)	07/04/1894	Baltimore Cemetery, Baltimore, MD
Webb, Del (Yankees owner 1948–66)	07/04/1974	Cremated, Phoenix, AZ. Ashes scattered
Weeghman, Charles Henry (Chicago owner 1914–18)	11/02/1938	Lutherania Cemetery, Richmond, IN
Weil, Sidney (Cincinnati president 1930–33)	07/05/1968	Spring Grove Cemetery, Cincinnati, OH
Weiss, George (New York executive)	08/13/1972	Evergreen Cemetery, New Haven, CT
Williams, Edward Bennett (Orioles owner 1983–88)	08/13/1988	St. Gabriel's Cemetery, Potomac, MD
Wilson, Myron H. (Indians executive)	08/19/1962	Lake View Cemetery, Cleveland, OH
Wiman, Erastus (Mets owner 1886–87)	02/09/1904	Silver Lake Cemetery, Richmond, Staten Island, NY
Wrigley, Phillip K. (Cubs owner 1934–77)	04/12/1977	Forest Lawn Memorial Park, Glendale, CA
Wrigley, William (Cubs owner)	01/26/1932	Forest Lawn Memorial Park, Glendale, CA
Yawkey, Tom (Red Sox owner 1933–76)	07/09/1976	Cremated, Cambridge, MA. Ashes scattered at Winyah Bay, SC
Young, Nick (Nicholas Ephraim) (NL president 1885–1902)	10/31/1916	Rock Creek Cemetery, Washington, DC

UMPIRES

Name	DOD	Cemetery, City, State
Ashford, Emmett Littleton	03/01/1980	Cremated, Los Angeles, CA
Barlick, Al	12/27/1995	Cremated, Springfield, IL. Ashes given to family
Boggess, Dusty	06/08/1968	Sparkman Hillcrest Memorial Park, Dallas, TX
Bremigan, Nick	03/29/1989	Irondequoit Cemetery, Irondequoit, NY
Chylak, Nestor	02/17/1982	SS. Cyril & Methodius Cemetery, Peckville, PA
Cockill, George W.	11/02/1937	Lewisburg Cemetery, Lewisburg, PA
Colliflower, Harry (James Harry)	08/12/1961	Mount Olivet Cemetery, Washington, DC
Conlan, Jocko (John Bertrand)	04/16/1989	Green Acres Memorial Gardens, Scottsdale, AZ
Connolly, Tom (Thomas Henry)	05/14/1966	St. Patrick's Cemetery, Natick, MA
Corcoran, Tommy (Thomas William)	06/25/1960	Pachaug Cemetery, Pachaug, CT
Cross, Monte (Montford Montgomery)	06/21/1934	Arlington Cemetery, Drexel Hill, PA
Dascoli, Frank	08/11/1990	Holy Cross Cemetery, Danielson, CT
Delmore, Victor	06/10/1960	Mount Carmel Cemetery, Dunmore, PA
Donatelli, Augie (August J.)	05/24/1990	Bay Pines National Cemetery, Bay Pines, FL
Donnelly, Charles H.	12/13/1968	Pinecrest Cemetery, Lake Worth, FL
Doyle, Walter James	03/02/1988	Bay Pines National Cemetery, Bay Pines, FL
Drummond, Cal (Calvin Troy)	05/02/1970	Greenwood Memorial Gardens, Greenwood, SC
Emslie, Bob (Robert Daniel)	04/26/1943	St. Thomas West Avenue Cemetery, St. Thomas, Ontario, Canada
Evans, Billy	01/23/1956	Knollwood Cemetery, Mayfield Heights, OH
Finneran, Bill (Wiliam F.)	07/30/1961	Trinity Cemetery, Erie, PA

Name	DOD	Cemetery, City, State
Flaherty, Red (John F.)	04/01/1999	Massachusetts National Cemetery, Bourne, MA
Friel, Bill (William Edward)	12/24/1959	Resurrection Cemetery, Mackenzie, MO
Froese, Grover A.	07/20/1982	Calverton National Cemetery, Calverton, NY
Geisel, Harry	02/20/1966	Crown Hill Cemetery, Indianapolis, IN
Goetz, Larry (Lawrence)	10/31/1962	Goshen Cemetery, Goshen, OH
Gorman, Tom (Thomas David)	08/11/1986	George Washington Memorial Park, Paramus, NJ
Groom, Bob (Robert)	02/19/1948	Walnut Hill Cemetery, Belleville, IL
Henline, Butch (Walter John)	10/09/1957	Manasota Memorial Park, Bradenton, FL
Holliday, Bug (James Wear)	02/15/1910	Spring Grove Cemetery, Cincinnati, OH
Holmes, Ducky (Howard Elbert)	09/18/1945	Woodland Cemetery, Dayton, OH
Honochick, Jim	03/10/1994	Resurrection Cemetery, Allentown, PA
Howell, Harry (Henry Harry)	05/22/1956	Greenwood Memorial Terrace, Spokane, WA
Hubbard, Cal	10/17/1977	Oakwood Cemetery, Milan, MO
Hurst, Tim	06/04/1915	Calvary Cemetery, Woodside, Queens, NY
Hyatt, Ham (Robert Hamilton)	09/11/1963	Holy Cross Cemetery, Spokane, WA
Klem, Bill	09/01/1951	Graceland Memorial Park, Miami, FL
Kolls, Louis Charles	02/23/1941	Rock Island National Cemetery, Rock Island, IL
Kunkel, Bill (William Gustave James)	05/04/1985	Cremated, Middletown, NJ. Ashes given to family
Landes, Stan (Stanley Albert)	01/23/1994	Sunland Memorial Park, Sun City, AZ
Luciano, Ron	01/18/1995	Calvary-St. Patrick Cemetery, Johnson City, NY
Magee, Sherwood Robert	03/13/1929	Arlington Cemetery, Drexel Hill, PA
Magerkurth, George	10/07/1966	Greenview Memorial Gardens, East Moline, IL
McCormick, Barry (William J.)	01/28/1956	St. Joseph's New Cemetery, Cincinnati, OH
McGowan, Bill	12/09/1954	Cathedral Cemetery, Wilmington, DE
McLaughlin, Edward J.	11/28/1965	Holy Cross Cemetery, Yeadon, PA
McLean, William	02/03/1927	Holy Cross Cemetery, Yeadon, PA
McSherry, John	04/01/1996	Gate of Heaven Cemetery, Hawthorne, NY
Merrill, Durwood	01/11/2003	Woodman Cemetery, DeKalb, TX
Moran, Charley (Charles Barthell)	06/14/1949	Horse Cave Cemetery, Horse Cave, KY
Moriarty, George Joseph	04/08/1964	St. Mary's Cemetery, Evergreen Park, IL
Mullaney, Dominic J.	08/21/1964	St. Mary's Cemetery, Jacksonville, FL
Nallin, Richard	09/07/1956	Mount Olivet Cemetery, Frederick, MD
O'Day Hank (Henry Francis)	07/02/1935	Calvary Cemetery, Evanston, IL
Ormsby, Red (Emmett T.)	10/11/1962	St. Mary's Cemetery, Evergreen Park, IL
Owens, Brick (Clarence B.)	11/11/1949	Fairmount Willow Hills Park, Worth, IL
Paparella, Joe (Joseph)	10/17/1994	St. Francis Church Cemetery, Eynon, PA
Pfirman, Cy (Charles H.)	05/16/1937	St. John's Cemetery (Hope Mausoleum), New Orleans, LA
Phelps, Ed (Edward Jaykill)	01/31/1942	East Greenbush Cemetery, East Greenbush, NY
Pinelli, Babe (Ralph Arthur)	10/22/1984	Holy Cross Cemetery, Colma, CA
Pryor, Paul	12/15/1995	Memorial Park Cemetery, St. Petersburg, FL

Name	DOD	Cemetery, City, State
Quinn, John Aloyisus	07/04/1968	Our Lady of Grace Cemetery, Langhorne, PA
Robb, Scotty (Douglas W.)	04/10/1969	Laurel Grove Cemetery, Totowa, NJ
Roberts, Harry R.	05/15/1999	Riverside Cemetery, Falmouth, KY
Rommel, Eddie (Edwin Americus)	08/26/1970	New Cathedral Cemetery, Baltimore, MD
Runge, Ed (Edward)	07/25/2002	Greenwood Memorial Park, San Diego, CA
Secory, Frank Edward	04/07/1995	Cremated, Port Huron, MI
Sentell, Paul (Leopold Theodore)	04/27/1923	St. Joseph Cemetery #3, New Orleans, LA
Soar, Hank (Albert Henry)	12/24/2001	Swan Point Cemetery, Providence, RI
Stevens, John William	09/09/1981	SS. Peter & Paul Cemetery, Springfield, PA
Stewart, Bill (William J.)	02/18/1964	St. Joseph's Cemetery, West Roxbury, MA
Summers, Bill (William)	09/22/1966	Lakeview Cemetery, Upton, MA
Tabbacchi, Frank T.	10/26/1983	Madonna Cemetery, Fort Lee, NJ
Umont, Frank William	06/20/1991	Cremated, Fort Lauderdale, FL
Van Graflan, Roy	09/04/1953	Mount Hope Cemetery, Rochester, NY
Walsh, Frank (Francis D.)	07/04/1985	Fort Sam Houston National Cemetery, San Antonio, TX
Walsh, Mike	02/02/1929	St. Louis Cemetery, Louisville, KY
Westervelt, Frederick E.	05/04/1955	Arlington Cemetery, Drexel Hill, PA
Williams, Art	02/08/1979	Union Cemetery, Bakersfield, CA
Wilson, Frank	06/22/1928	Canarsie Cemetery, Brooklyn, NY
Young, Nick (Nicholas Ephraim)	10/31/1916	Rock Creek Cemetery, Washington, DC

WRITERS AND BROADCASTERS

Name	DOD	Cemetery, City, State
Adams, Franklin P. (New York writer)	03/23/1960	Cremated, Ferncliff Cemetery, Hartsdale, NY. Ashes scattered
Addie, Bob (Robert R.) (Washington writer)	01/18/1982	St. Gabriel's Cemetery, Potomac, MD
Alcock, John J. (Chicgo sportswriter)	01/07/1944	Mount Carmel Cemetery, Hillside, IL
Allen, Lee (writer)	05/20/1969	Boca Raton Cemetery, Boca Raton, FL
Allen, Mel (New York broadcaster)	06/16/1996	Temple Beth El Cemetery, Stamford, CT
Aulick, Bill (William Wrothe) (New York sportswriter)	12/25/1913	Flushing Cemetery, Flushing, NY
Ballard, Duke (William Wood) (New York sportswriter)	11/05/1946	Cremated, Fresh Pond Crematory, Middle Village, Queens, NY
Barber, Red (Walter Lanier) (Reds, Dodgers, Yankees broadcaster)	10/22/1992	Cremated, Talahassee, FL. Ashes scattered on his property
Barry, Mike (Louisville sportswriter)	00/00/1992	St. Louis Cemetery, Louisville, KY
Bates, Elmer Ellsworth (Cleveland sportswriter)	02/18/1930	Middle Ridge Cemetery, Madison, OH
Brandebury, Carl Sherman (New York sportswriter)	09/15/1942	Rock Creek Cemetery, Washington, DC
Brickhouse, Jack (Chicago broadcaster)	08/06/1998	Rosehill Cemetery, Chicago, IL
Broun, Heywood Campbell (New York writer)	12/18/1939	Gate of Heaven Cemetery, Hawthorne, NY
Brown, Warren W. (Chicago sportswriter)	11/22/1978	Queen of Heaven Cemetery, Hillside, IL
Buck, Jack (John Francis) (Cardinals broadcaster)	06/18/2002	Jefferson Barracks National Cemetery, St. Louis, MO
Burick, Si (Dayton sportswriter)	12/10/1986	Beth Abraham Cemetery, Dayton, OH

Burnes, Bob/Derks, John C.   BASEBALL BURIAL SITES

Name	DOD	Cemetery, City, State
Burnes, Bob (St. Louis sportswriter)	07/11/1995	Resurrection Cemetery, Mackenzie, MO
Burns, Edward H. (Chicago sportswriter)	01/27/1955	Rosehill Cemetery, Chicago, IL
Burr, Harold C. (New York sportswriter)	07/07/1955	Green-Wood Cemetery, Brooklyn, NY
Cannon, Jimmy (New York sportswriter)	12/05/1973	Calvary Cemetery, Woodside, Queens, NY
Carey, Harry (St. Louis, Chicago broadcaster)	02/18/1998	All Saints Cemetery, Des Plaines, IL
Carmichael, John (Chicago sportswriter)	06/06/1986	All Saints Cemetery, Des Plaines, IL
Carolan, James S. (New York sportswriter)	11/16/1943	Whitemarsh Memorial Park, Ambler, PA
Cashman, Joseph S. (Boston sportswriter)	02/12/1993	Cambridge Cemetery, Cambridge, MA
Caylor, O.P. (Oliver Pery) (sportswriter)	01/31/1930	Woodland Cemetery, Dayton, OH
Chadwick, Henry (New York writer)	04/20/1908	Green-Wood Cemetery, Brooklyn, NY
Chapman, Lou (Louis) (Milwaukee sportswriter)	04/30/2004	Spring Hill Cemetery, Milwaukee, WI
Cobb, Irvin Shrewsbury (New York sportswriter)	03/10/1944	Oak Grove Cemetery, Paducah, KY
Cobbledick, Gordon (Cleveland sportswriter)	10/02/1969	East Lawn Palms Cemetery, Tucson, AZ
Collins, Dick (Richard J.) (St. Louis sportswriter)	02/12/1953	Calvary Cemetery, St. Louis, MO
Considine, Bob (Robert B.) (New York sportswriter)	09/25/1975	Gate of Heaven Cemetery, Hawthorne, NY
Conway, Jack (John E.) (Bos Sportswriter)	02/01/1950	St. Joseph's Cemetery, West Roxbury, MA
Corcoran, Jimmy (Chicago sportswriter)	02/03/1944	Mount Carmel Cemetery, Hillside, IL
Cosell, Howard (broadcaster)	04/23/1995	Cremated, Ferncliff Cemetery, Hartsdale, NY.
Curran, Bill (William C.) (author)	12/17/2002	Willamette National Cemetery, Portland, OR
Curtis, Bob (Robert W.) (New York sportswriter)	02/21/1939	Flushing Cemetery, Flushing, NY
Daley, Arthur (New York sportswriter)	01/03/1974	Gate of Heaven Cemetery, Hawthorne, NY
Daniel, Dan (New York sportswriter)	06/03/1905	Forest Lawn Memorial Gardens, Pompano Beach, FL
Danzig, Allison (New York sportswriter)	01/27/1987	Nassau Knolls Cemetery & Memorial Park, Port Washington, NY
Dawson, James P. (New York sportswriter)	03/06/1953	St. John's Cemetery, Middle Village, Queens, NY
Derks, John C. (Salt Lake City sportswriter)	04/08/1944	Logan City Cemetery, Logan, UT

Name	DOD	Cemetery, City, State
Desmond, Connie (Dodgers broadcaster)	03/10/1983	Calvary Cemetery, Toledo, OH
Dorgan, Tad (Thomas A.) (cartoonist)	05/02/1929	Cypress Hills Cemetery, Brooklyn, NY
Doyle, John Hadley (DC sportswriter)	09/12/1946	Oak Hill Cemetery, Washington, DC
Doyle, John T. (Pres-American Sports Publishing)	05/21/1942	Cremated, Fresh Pond Crematory, Middle Village, Queens, NY
Drebinger, John (New York sportswriter)	10/23/1979	Cremated, Greensboro, NC
Dryden, Charles (Chicago sportswriter)	02/11/1931	Monmouth Municipal Cemetery, Monmouth, IL
Dudley, Jimmy (James R.) (Cleveland broadcaster)	02/12/1999	East Lawn Palms Cemetery, Tucson, AZ
Eagle, Dean (Luther Dean) (Louisville sportswriter)	04/21/1973	Cave Hill Cemetery, Louisville, KY
Elson, Bob (Chicago broadcaster)	03/10/1981	Queen of Heaven Cemetery, Hillside, IL
Falzer, Gustav A. (1st WS broadcaster)	01/26/1953	Fairmount Cemetery, Newark, NJ
Farnsworth, Bill (Wilton Simpson) (New York sportswriter)	07/10/1945	Gate of Heaven Cemetery, Hawthorne, NY
Farrell, Henry L. (Dayton sportswriter)	04/09/1954	Woodland Cemetery, Xenia, OH
Farrell, James Thomas (writer–"My Baseball Diary")	08/22/1979	Calvary Cemetery, Evanston, IL
Farrell, John J. (New York sportswriter)	11/04/1979	Creat Haven Memorial Park, Clifton, NJ
Fischer, Leo H. (Chicago sportswriter)	08/27/1970	Memorial Park Cemetery, Skokie, IL
Fullerton, Hugh (Chicago sportswriter)	12/27/1945	Hillsboro Cemetery, Hillsboro, OH
Gallico, Paul (New York sportswriter)	07/15/1976	Cremated, Monte Carlo, Monaco
Geiger, Edward J. (Chiago sportswriter)	01/11/1949	St. Mary's Cemetery, Evergreen Park, IL
Gettelson, Leonard (editor Sporting News BB Record Book)	12/25/1977	Monmouth Fields Burial Grounds, West Long Branch, NJ
Gibbons, Frank A. (Cleveland sportswriter)	09/01/1964	Holy Cross Cemetery, Cleveland, OH
Gillespie, Raymond J. (St. Louis sportswriter)	02/08/1979	Resurrection Cemetery, McKenzie, MO
Gold, Eddie (Edward Alan) (Chicago writer)	12/28/2002	Shalom Memorial Park, Arlington Heights, IL
Gould, James M. (St. Louis sportswriter)	02/15/1943	Calvary Cemetery, St. Louis, MO
Graham, Frank (New York sportswriter)	03/09/1965	Holy Mount Cemetery, Tuckahoe, NY

Name	DOD	Cemetery, City, State
Granger, William James (New York sportswriter)	01/17/1945	Holy Cross Cemetery, Brooklyn, NY
Grey, Zane (writer – "The Red-Headed Outfield")	10/23/1939	Union Cemetery, Lackawaxen, PA
Gruber, John (Pittsburgh sportswriter)	12/18/1932	North Side Catholic Cemetery, Pittsburgh, PA
Haldeman, John Avery (Louisville sportswriter)	09/17/1899	Cave Hill Cemetery, Louisville, KY
Haley, Mike (Martin J.) (St. Louis sportswriter)	03/06/1977	Calvary Cemetery, St. Louis, MO
Hall, Halsey (Twins broadcaster)	12/30/1977	Fort Snelling National Cemetery, Minneapolis, MN
Harrison, James Renwick (New York sportswriter)	10/06/1931	Richland Cemetery, Dravosburg, PA
Helfer, Al (broadcaster)	05/16/1975	Cremated, Carmichael, CA
Hennigan, Willie (William S.) (New York sportswriter)	07/05/1942	St. John's Cemetery, Middle Village, Queens, NY
Hodges, Russ (Giants broadcaster)	04/19/1971	Mount Tamalpais Cemetery, San Rafael, CA
Holland, Jerry (Gerald M.) (St. Louis sportswriter)	06/18/1974	Calvary Cemetery, St. Louis, MO
Holmes, Tommy (Brooklyn sportswriter)	03/25/1975	Cremated, Brooklyn, NY
Hudson, Gunboat (Walter) (New York sportswriter)	11/23/1933	St. John's Cemetery, Middle Village, Queens, NY
Husing, Ted (broadcaster)	08/10/1962	Mountain View Cemetery, Altadena, CA
Hutchinson, Ira Kendall (Chicago sportswriter)	08/21/1973	Chapel Hill Gardens South, Oak Lawn, IL
Kaese, Harold (Boston sportswriter)	00/00/1975	Puritan Lawn Memorial Park, Peabody, MA
Kelly, Ray ∫ (Philadelphia sportswriter)	11/22/1988	Cremated, Philadelphia, PA
Keough, HEK (Hugh E.) (Chicago sportswriter)	06/09/1912	Oak Woods Cemetery, Chicago, IL
Kiernan, John (New York writer)	12/10/1981	Beech Grove Cemetery, Rockport, MA
King, Joe (Joseph P.) (New York sportswriter)	04/16/1979	Cremated, Cedar Lawn Crematory, Paterson, NJ
Kramer, Murray (Boston sportswriter)		Temple Emeth Memorial Cemetery, West Roxbury, MA
Lardner, Ring (Ringgold Wilmer, Sr.) (writer)	09/25/1933	Cremated, Fresh Pond Crematory, Middle Village, Queens, NY
Lawson, Earl (Cinccinnati sportswriter)	01/14/2003	Arlington National Cemetery, Arlington, VA. Cremated Sacramento, CA
Lieb, Fred (New York sportswriter)	06/02/1980	Cremated, Houston, TX
Linn, Ed (writer)	02/07/2000	Greenwood Memorial Park, San Diego, CA
Long, Paul (Pittsburgh broadcaster)	07/12/2002	Jefferson Memorial Park, Pleasant Hills, PA
Malamud, Bernard (writer)	06/08/1905	Mount Auburn Cemetery, Cambridge, MA
Mann, Howard (Cleveland and Chicago sportswriter)	06/08/1936	Cremated, Chicago, IL.

Name	DOD	Cemetery, City, State
Masterson, Bat (New York sportswriter)	10/25/1921	Woodlawn Cemetery, Bronx, NY
McCarthy, Clem (broadcaster)	06/04/1962	Mount Olivet Cemetery, Maspeth, Queens, NY
McConaughy, John W. (New York sportswriter)	10/12/1933	Flushing Cemetery, Flushing, Queens, NY
McGeehan, William O. (New York sportswriter)	11/29/1933	Frederica Christ Episcopal Church Cemetery, Brunswick, GA
McGoogan, William J. (St. Louis sportswriter)	05/09/1966	Calvary Cemetery, St. Louis, MO
McKay, Judge (William Kennedy) (Chicago sportswriter)	09/23/1944	Graceland Cemetery, Chicago, IL
McLinn, Stoney (George E.) (Philadelphia sportswriter)	03/08/1953	Westminster Cemetery, Bala Cynwyd, PA
McNamee, Graham (broadcaster)	05/09/1942	Mt. Calvary Cemetery, Columbus, OH
Meany, Tom (Thomas W.) (New York sportswriter)	09/11/1964	Holy Cross Cemetery, Brooklyn, NY
Mercer, Sid (James Sidney) (New York sportswriter)	06/19/1945	Cremated, Fresh Pond Crematory, Middle Village, Queens, NY
Merrill, Bill (William) (Rangers Broadcater)	03/29/2003	Moore Memorial Gardens, Arlington, TX
Messer, Frank (Wallace Frank) (Yankees broadcaster)	11/13/2001	Western Carolina State Veterans Cemetery, Black Mountain, NC
Miley, Jack (John Barrett) (New York sportswriter)	06/17/1945	Calvary Cemetery, Milwaukee, WI
Morrison, Robert (St. Louis sportswriter)	11/13/1969	Calvary Cemetery, St. Louis, MO
Morse, Jake (Boston sportswriter)	04/12/1937	Cremated, Boston, MA
Mulford, Ren J. (Cincinnati sportswriter)	12/30/1932	Spring Grove Cemetery, Cincinnati, OH
Mullen, Edward Bartholemew (New York sportswriter)	01/28/1944	Calvary Cemetery, Woodside, Queens, NY
Murnane, Tim (Timothy Hayes) (Boston sportswriter)	02/07/1917	Old Dorchester Burial Ground, Dorchester, MA
Murray, Jim (LA sportswriter)	08/16/1998	Holy Cross Cemetery, Culver City, CA
Nelson, Lindsay (Mets broadcaster)	06/10/1995	Polk Memorial Gardens, Columbia, TN
Norton, Joseph P. (Newark sportswriter)	06/03/1936	Cemetery of the Holy Sepulchre, East Orange, NJ
O'Boynick, Paul L. (Kansas City sportswriter)	06/22/1992	Mount Calvary Cemetery, Kansas City, KS
O'Donnell, Peter J. (Louisville sportswriter)	10/16/1973	Calvary Cemetery, Louisville, KY
Palma, Aloysius Charles (New York sportswriter)	05/25/1985	Long Island National Cemetery, Farmingdale, NY
Parker, Dan (New York sportswriter)	05/20/1967	New St. Joseph's Cemetery, Waterbury, CT
Parkere, Marion Frank (St. Louis sportswriter)	06/10/1950	Calvary Cemetery, St. Louis, MO

Name	DOD	Cemetery, City, State
Passe, Loel (Astros broadcaster)	07/15/1997	Forest Park (Westheimer) Cemetery, Houston, TX
Patrick, Van (Tigers broadcaster)	09/29/1974	Northview Cemetery, Dearborn, MI
Phelon, Bill (William Arlie) (Cincinntai sportswriter)	08/19/1925	Cremated, Cincinnati, OH
Porter, Wiliam Trotter (Porter's Spirit of the Times)	07/19/1858	Green-Wood Cemetery, Brooklyn, NY
Povich, Shirley (Washington sportswriter)	06/04/1998	Elesavetgrad Cemetery, Washington, DC
Powers, Francis J.(Cleveland and Dayton sportswriter)	09/03/1977	Calvary Cemetery, Dayton, OH
Prince, Bob (Pirates broadcaster)	06/10/1995	Westminster Presbyterian Church Cemetery, Upper Saint Clair, PA
Queen, Frank (owner NY Clipper)	10/19/1882	Ebenezer M.E. Church Cemetery, Philadelphia, PA
Quigley, Martin (writer)	01/07/2000	Calvary Cemetery, St. Louis, MO
Rankin, William M. (New York sportswriter)	03/29/1913	Green-Wood Cemetery, Brooklyn, NY
Reichler, Joe (New York sportswriter)	12/12/1988	Kensico Cemetery, Valhalla, NY
Rice, Grantland (New York sportswriter)	07/13/1954	Woodlawn Cemetery, Bronx, NY
Rice, Thomas Stevens (New York sportswriter)	02/14/1942	Cremated, Brooklyn, NY
Richman, Milton (New York sportswriter)	06/09/1986	Mount Ararat Cemetery, Farmingdale, NY
Richter, Francis (sportswriter)	02/12/1926	West Laurel Hill Cemetery, Bala Cynwyd, PA
Rickart, Paul Adlai (St. Louis sportswriter)	10/24/1965	Calvary Cemetery, St. Louis, MO
Romano, Robin A. (sportswriter)	01/03/2000	Waterside Cemetery, Marblehead, MA
Rowswell, Rosey (Pittsburgh broadcaster)	02/06/1955	Allegheny Cemetery, Pittsburgh, PA
Runyon, Damon (New York sportswriter)	12/10/1946	Ferncliff Cemetery, Hartsdale, NY. Cremated.
Saam, By (Philadelphia broadcaster)	01/16/2000	Calvary Cemetery, West Conshohocken, PA
Saidt, Bus (Harold) (Trenton sportswriter)	04/08/1989	Riverview Cemetery, Trenton, NJ
Salsinger, H. G. (Detroit Sportswriter)	11/27/1958	Woodlawn Cemetery, Detroit, MI
Schlicter, Walter (Henry Walter) (Philadelphia sportswriter)	01/15/1944	West Laurel Hill Cemetery, Bala Cynwyd, PA
Seymour, Harold (writer)	06/ /1992	Cremated, Ashes scattered at Doubleday Field, Cooperstown, NY
Sheridan, John Brinsley (St. Louis sportswriter)	04/14/1930	Calvary Cemetery, St. Louis, MO
Smith, Red (Walter) (New York sportswriter)	01/15/1982	Long Ridge Union Cemetery, Stamford, CT

Name	DOD	Cemetery, City, State
Spink, Alfred H. (Sporting News editor)	05/27/1928	Woodlawn Cemetery, Forest Park, IL
Spink, Charles Claude (Sporting News editor)	04/22/1914	Bellefontaine Cemetery, St. Louis, MO
Spink, J.G. Taylor (Sporting News editor)	12/07/1962	Bellefontaine Cemetery, St. Louis, MO
Stevens, Bob (Robert) (San Francisco sportswriter)	01/02/2002	Skylawn Memorial Park, San Mateo, CA
Stockton, J. Roy (St. Louis sportswriter)	08/24/1972	Cremated, St. Petersburg, FL. Ashes scattered.
Sullivan, Ed (Edward Vincent) (New York sportswriter)	10/13/1973	Ferncliff Cemetery, Hartsdale, NY
Swope, Tom (Edwin Thomas) (Cincinntai sportswriter)	02/11/1969	Rest Haven Memorial Park, Cincinnati, OH
Tarvin, A.H. (Albert Henry) (Louisville sportswriter)	03/24/1959	Vine Street Hill Cemetery, Cincinnati, OH
Thayer, Ernest Lawrence (poet "Casey At the Bat")	08/21/1940	Cremated, Santa Barbara, CA. Ashes scattered
Thurber, James (writer – "You Could Look It Up")	11/02/1961	Green Lawn Cemetery, Columbus, OH
Tidden, George Otto (New York Sportswriter)	06/30/1913	Green-Wood Cemetery, Brooklyn, NY
Turgeon, Arthur J. (Providence sportswriter)	06/ /1972	Notre Dame Cemetery, Fall River, MA
Vaughn, Mark Irving (Chicago sportswriter)	11/22/1963	Valhalla Cemeterey, Milwaukee, WI. Cremated Waukegan, IL
Vila, Joe (Joseph Spencer) (New York sportswriter)	04/27/1934	Green-Wood Cemetery, Brooklyn, NY
Ward, Arch (Chicago sportswriter)	07/09/1955	All Saints Cemetery, Des Plaines, IL
Wedge, William (New York sportswriter)	09/08/1951	Kensico Cemetery, Valhalla, NY
Woodruff, Harvey T. (Chicago sportswriter)	06/02/1937	Memorial Park Cemetery, Evanston, IL

OTHER BASEBALL NOTABLES

Not every person involved with creating baseball memories fits neatly into the game as a player, manager, or executive. All sorts of individuals participate and contribute to the sport in various ways.

You cannot play the game without some equipment. Perhaps the best-known name in the baseball business is the Louisville Slugger. The Hillerich & Bradsby Company has been producing bats for over a century and remain headquartered in Louisville, Kentucky. John A. "Bud" Hillerich along with family successors John A., Jr. and Ward Hillerich are buried in the family plot at Cave Hill Cemetery in Louisville. J. Frederick Hillerich, founder of the woodturning business that evolved into the current business, and who was reported to be somewhat cool to the idea of wasting time making baseball bats when there were butter churns and bed posts to be made, is buried in Louisville's St. Louis Cemetery. Hillerich's partner, Frank Bradsby is buried in Bellefontaine Cemetery, St. Louis. One other man associated with baseball equipment was Rolly Latina, known as "The Glove Doctor," for his ability to design and repair gloves, is also near St. Louis at Lake View Memorial Gardens in Belleville, Illinois.

Even before Bud Hillerich started turning bats on his lathe the game had produced a rich history of baseball that predated the organized leagues. Well known is Hall of Famer Alexander Joy Cartwright. Some of his compatriots on the New York Knickerbockers, who are given credit for developing many of the rules that still are observed in the game, include Duncan Fraser Curry and Daniel Lucius "Doc" Adams. Both men served as President of the Knickerbocker club. Curry is interred at Brooklyn's Green-Wood Cemetery while Adams subsequently moved to Connecticut and is buried at Evergreen Cemetery in New Haven. Another player and organizer of nineteenth century cubs was Arthur Pue Gorman who was involved with the Washington Nationals during the time they made one of the early national tours. Gorman subsequently served in the US Senate from Maryland. He is buried at Oak Hill Cemetery, Washington, DC. Jim

Creighton, an early baseball star with the Excelsior Club of Brooklyn is buried at Green-Wood Cemetery in Brooklyn with a large monument over his grave. Also connected to baseball, and incorrectly credited with inventing the game is Abner Doubleday. Doubleday never made such a claim and had a distinguished military career. He is buried at Arlington National Cemetery in Virginia. One last nineteenth century individual is Thomas Eakins. Eakins was a prominent painter from Philadelphia. His painting "Baseball Players Practicing" is a classic image in sports art. Eakins is buried at Woodlands Cemetery, Philadelphia.

The Twentieth Century brought the game to new heights in popularity but also saw the great scandal of the game. The 1919 Black Sox scandal has all the players and owners involved recorded in the lists earlier in this book. But a pair of characters who resided in the shadows of the event are Arnold Rothstein and Abe Atell. Rothstein is thought to be the gambler who drove much of the action. He was murdered in 1928 and was buried in Union Fields Cemetery in Flushing, Queens. Attell, who was also a successful boxer before becoming involved with Rothstein, is buried in Beaverkill Cemetery, Rockland, New York.

Fans usually are recognized collectively rather than as individuals. But occasionally someone breaks through into the public consciousness. In the 1910s the Boston Red Sox were blessed with a fervent collection of supporters dubbed "The Royal Rooters." They marched, and sang, and cheered for their Sox. One of their number was John F. Fitzgerald. Known to the Boston populace as "HoneyFitz", he served as Mayor of Boston and was the grandfather of President John F. Kennedy. He is buried at St. Joseph's Cemetery, West Roxbury, Massachusetts. In 1949 another fan became more that a face in the crowd. When the Cleveland Indians got off to a slow start following their championship season of 1948, Charley Lupica decided to inspire the Tribe by climbing a flagpole and declaring he would remain until Cleveland reclaimed the American League pennant. As we know that did not happen and Lupica returned to earth when the club was eliminated from the race. When he died in 2002 he was buried at Holy Cross Cemetery in Cleveland.

One of Roy Campanella's famous quotes involves the observation that you have to have a lot of little boy in you to play baseball. Little boys still play baseball and Little League is the most prominent organization in the field. One of Little League's founders, Carl Stotz was interred at Twin Hills Memorial Park in Muncy, Pennsylvania just outside Williamsport. When the first Little League World Series was played in 1939, it was Frank Sipe who threw the first pitch in the game. He is buried at Wildwood Cemetery in Williamsport.

Boys were not the only people playing baseball. During World War II the All American Girls Professional Baseball League was founded. In recent years there has been a rediscovery of the league and its players with numerous books and articles published and the movie "A League of Their Own" giving us a look at the organization. In my research of the major leagues I have also uncovered a few players from this league. Faye Dancer is buried at Woodlawn Cemetery in Santa Monica, California; Dorothy Ferguson Key is at Sunset Memorial Gardens in Machesney Park, Illinois; Mary Lawson is interred in West Virginia at Mount Loretto Cemetery in White Silver Springs; Marie "Blackie" Wegman is in St. Joseph's Old Cemetery, Cincinnati; and Helen Callaghan St. Aubin, mother of major leaguer Casey Candaele, is buried at Evergreen Cemetery, Lompoc, California. South Bend Blue Sox manager Karl Winsch is buried at St. Mark's Lutheran Cemetery, Pennsburg, Pennsylvania.

Part of baseballs appeal is the wealth is historical statistics that have been compiled since the game began. Two organizations that have continued that tradition are the Howe News Bureau and the Elias Sports Bureau. Howe owner John S. Phillips is buried at All Saints Cemetery, Des Plains, Illinois. Al Munro Elias is at Ferncliff Cemetery, Hartsdale, New York and Walter Bruce Elias is in Maimonides Cemetery, Elmont, New York.

Others who have contributed to the game but defy easy classification include Baseball Clown Prince Max Patkin who is buried at Mount Lebanon Cemetery in Collingdale, Pennsylvania outside Philadelphia and Concessionaire Harry M. Stevens who is at Niles Union Cemetery, Niles, Ohio. Walter Dilbeck attempted to found a third major league in the 1960s with his creation of the Global League. He is buried at Alexander Memorial Park, Evansville, Indiana. L. Robert "Bob "Davids founded my favorite organization, the Society for American Baseball Research. He is interred at Arlington National Cemetery in Virginia. Emil Praeger is buried in Holy Cross Cemetery, Brooklyn, New York. Praeger was the designer of Dodger, Shea, and Kauffman Stadiums.

Our last entry is a gentleman who lived a quiet live in Chicago producing food products. One day he was tinkering with a mix of peanuts, popcorn and caramel. Thus Louis Rueckheim invented Cracker Jacks. He reposes in Oak Woods Cemetery in Chicago. Rueckheim's invention was immortalized in the tune "Take Me Out to the Ball Game," written by Albert Von Tilzer and Jack Norworth. Von Tilzer was cremated and his ashes are at the Chapel of the Pines in Los Angeles. Norworth is buried at Melrose Abbey Memorial Park in Anaheim, California.

STATE BY STATE

ALABAMA

Autauga County, Montgomery Metro

Oak Hill Cemetery, Prattville
George Grant, Ernie Wingard

Baldwin County, Mobile Metro

Belforest Catholic Cemetery, Daphne
Harry Matuzak

Bibb County

Green Pond Cemetery, Green Pond
Dixie Parker

Pineland Memorial Park, Centreville
Frank Pratt

Calhoun County, Anniston Metro

Edgemont Cemetery, Anniston
Tommy, O'Brien, Tully Sparks

Oxford Cemetery, Oxford
Jim Stephens

Chambers County

Chapel Hill Cemetery, Lafayette
Hal Finney, Lou Finney

Chilton County

Clanton Cemetery, Clanton
Jackie Hayes

Clarke County

Gosport Cemetery, Gosport
Grant Gillis

Pine Crest Cemetery, Jackson
Lefty Bolen

Suggsville Cemetery, Suggsville
Red Barnes

Coffee County

Meadowland Memorial Park, Enterprise
Ed Sherling

Covington County

Fairmount Baptist Church Cemetery,
Red Level
Sam Barnes

Greenwood Cemetery, Florala
Ernie Manning

Holly Pond Cemetery, Holly Pond
Earl Reid

Dallas County

Live Oak Cemetery, Selma
Al Veach

Escambia County

Oak Grove Cemetery, Flomaton
Ed Morris

Houston County, Dothan Metro

Haywood Sullivan

Jefferson County, Birmingham Metro

Cedar Grove Cemetery, Leeds
  Harry Walker

Elmwood Cemetery, Birmingham
  Cap Brown, Ben Chapman, Joe Conzelman,
  Piper Davis, Spud Davis, Eddie Dent, Wiley
  Griggs, Sammy Hairston, Lum Harris, Red
  Holt, Bill Hughes, Dee Miles, Bill Morrell,
  Legrant Scott, Freddie Sheppard, Harry
  Swacina, Guy Tutwiler, Dixie Walker, Dixie
  Walker, Frank Welch, Yam Yaryan

Forest Hill Cemetery, Birmingham
  Lloyd Christenbury, Ernie Cox, J.C.
  Powers, Pee Wee Wanninger

Fraternal Cemetery, Birmingham
  Ernie Walker

George Washington Carver Memorial
Gardens, Birmingham
  Nate Pollard

Highland Memorial Gardens, Bessemer
  Pijo King, Paul Lehner

Marvin's Chapel Cemetery, Pinson
  Tom Drake

New Grace Hill Cemetery, Birmingham
  Jay Heard

Oak Hill Memorial Cemetery, Birmingham
  Lep Long

Pleasant Grove Methodist Cemetery,
Pleasant Grove
  Joe Tipton

Valhalla Cemetery, Birmingham
  Hugh East

Lamar County

Vernon Cemetery, Vernon
  Guy Morton, Sr.

Limestone County, Huntsville Metro

Athens City Cemetery, Athens
  Dick Coffman, Ray Pepper

Gatlin Cemetery, Ardmore
  Slick Coffman

Macon County

Tuskegee Cemetery, Tuskegee
  Dana Fillingim

Madison County, Huntsville Metro

Beason Cemetery, Gurley
  Jim Tabor

Gurley Cemetery, Gurley
  Lena Styles

Marshall County

Hebron Church of Christ Cemetery, Joppa
  Jack Lively

Mobile County, Mobile Metro

Catholic Cemetery, Mobile
  Tommie Aaron, Barnes Graham, Eddie
  Stanky, Milt Stock, Leo Townsend

Magnolia Cemetery, Mobile
  Orville Armbrust, Pickles Dillhoefer,
  Charlie Duffee, Charlie Fritz, George
  Jumonville

Mobile Memorial Gardens, Mobile
  Pete Milne, Walter Sessi

New Home Missionary Baptist Church
Cemetery, Citronelle
  Bama Rowell

Pine Crest Cemetery, Mobile
  Bill Adair, Tommie Agee, Herb Kelly,
  Rollings, Joe Schepner

**Montgomery County, Montgomery
Metro**

Greenwood Cemetery, Montgomery
  Gus Felix, Bill Higdon, Jimmy Hitchcock,
  Tom Oliver, Tommy Sewell, Ed Wells

Oakwood Cemetery, Montgomery
  Slim Foster, Zeke Wilson

Pickens County

Gordo Cemetery, Gordo
  Verdo Elmore

Shelby County, Birmingham Metro

Montevallo Cemetery, Montevallo
  Jack Nabors

Sumpter County

Belmont Community Cemetery, Belmont
  Doc Land

Talladega County

Evergreen Memorial Cemetery, Sylacauga
  Walton Cruise

Oak Grove Missionary Baptist Church
Cemetery, Oak Grove
Kyle Graham

Oak Hill Cemetery, Talladega
Art Decatur

Tuscaloosa County, Tuscaloosa Metro

Carroll's Creek Baptist Church Cemetery,
Northport
Al Lary

Memory Hill Gardens Cemetery, Tuscaloosa
Danny Boone

Tuscaloosa Memorial Park, Tuscaloosa
Ike Boone, Joe Sewell, Riggs Stephenson

Walker County

Empire Cemetery, Empire
Joe Bankhead

Shanghi Cemetery, Dora
Ivy Andrews

ALASKA

Southeast Fairbanks Borough

Eagle Cemetery (formerly Fort Egbert
Cemetery), Eagle
Charlie Fisher

ARKANSAS

Arkansas County

Lone Tree Cemetery, Stuttgart
Bill Kerksieck

Baxter County

Kirby's Tucker Memorial Cemetery,
Mountain Home
Red Evans

Benton County, Fayetteville Metro

Pea Ridge Cemetery, Pea Ridge
Pea Ridge Day

Columbia County

Magnolia Memorial Park, Magnolia
Bob Linton

New Hope Cemetery, Magnolia
George Harper

Waldo Cemetery, Waldo
Travis Jackson

Conway County

Atkins City Cemetery, Atkins
Fred Bennett, Leo Dickerman

Crittenden County, Memphis Metro

Crittenden Memorial Park, Marion
Benn Karr

Cross County

Cogbill Cemetery, Wynne
Billy Bowers, Wes Flowers,
Harry Kelley

Faulkner County, Little Rock Metro

Spring Hill Cemetery, Greenbrier
Otis Brannan

Thorn Cemetery, Greenbrier
Dib Williams

Franklin County

St. Mary's Catholic Church Cemetery, Altus
Boss Schmidt

Greene County

Linwood Cemetery, Paragould
Orlin Collier

Wood's Chapel Cemetery, Paragould
Marlin Stuart

Hot Spring County

Calvary Cemetery, Hot Springs
Mike Cvengros

Memorial Gardens of Hot Springs, Hot Springs
George Earnshaw, Al Williamson

Pleasant Hill Cemetery, Donaldson
Carey Selph

Jefferson County, Pine Bluff Metro

Bellwood Cemetery, Pine Bluff
Milt Watson

Johnson County

Oakland Cemetery, Clarksville
Paul Dean

Lafayette County

Walnut Hill Cemetery, Bradley
Ralph Hamner

Logan County

Carolan Cemetery, Booneville
  Floyd Speer

Oakwood Cemetery, Paris
  Bob Osborn, Art Parks

Madison County

Huntsville Cemetery, Huntsville
  Joe Berry

Miller County

Hillcrest Cemetery, Texarkana
  Howie Williamson

Montgomery County

Owley Cemetery, Mount Ida
  Lon Warneke

Nevada County

DeAnn Cemetery, DeAnn
  Chuck Tompkins

Phillips County

Sunset Memorial Park, West Helena
  Gene Bearden

Pike County

Oakdale Cemetery, Murfeesboro
  Red Bird

Pulaski County, Little Rock Metro

Calvary Cemetery, Little Rock
  Gene Paulette

Edgewood Memorial Park, North Little Rock
  Bill Luhrsen, Hank Robinson

Little Rock National Cemetery, Little Rock
  Witt Guise, Dutch McCall, John
  Perkovich, Earl Smith

Oakland Cemetery, Little Rock
  Jimmy Zinn

Pine Crest Memorial Park, Alexander
  Grady Adkins, Marv Blaylock, Earl
  Browne, Lindsay Deal, Joe Klinger, Carl
  Sawatski

Roselawn Memorial Gardens Cemetery,
Little Rock
  Bob Allen, Bill Dickey, George Dickey,
  Tom Gulley, Art, Jahn, Jim McLeod,
  Scrappy Moore, Lee Rogers

Saline County, Little Rock Metro

Bryant Cemetery, Benton
  Jack McAdams

Sebastian County, Fort Smith Metro

Calvary Catholic Cemetery, Fort Smith
  Emmett Rogers

Fort Smith National Cemetery, Fort Smith
  Bob Patrick, Mutt Williams

Roselawn Cemetery, Fort Smith
  Harry Feldman

Union County

Arlington Memorial Cemetery, El Dorado
  Dave Davenport, Odell Hale, Schoolboy
  Rowe

Van Buren County

Blackwell Cemetery, Bee Branch
  Jim McKnight

Washington County, Fayetteville Metro

Evergreen Cemetery, Fayetteville
  Sid Benton, Roy Wood

ARIZONA

Cochise County

Douglas Cemetery, Douglas
  Oscar Purner

Evergreen Cemetery, Bisbee
  John Henry, Clarence Maddern

Gila County

Pinal Cemetery, Central Heights
  Buzz Wetzel

Maricopa County, Phoenix-Mesa Metro

East Resthaven Park Cemetery, Phoenix
  Les Barnhart

Alcor Life Extension Foundation, Scottsdale
  Ted Williams

Green Acres Memorial Gardens, Scottsdale
  Jocko Conlan, Lee Daney

Greenwood Memory Lawn Cemetery,
Phoenix
  Earl Grace, Grover Land, Andres Mesa,
  Art Nehf, John Smith, Tony Tonneman,
  Ollie Voigt

Mesa Municipal Cemetery, Mesa
Jack Redmond

Mountain View Memorial Gardens, Mesa
Fred Wigington

National Memorial Cemetery of Arizona, Phoenix
Doyle Lade

Paradise Memorial Gardens, Scottsdale
Lefty Sullivan

Resthaven Park Cemetery, Glendale
Jack Roche

St. Francis Catholic Cemetery, Phoenix
Bill DeLancey, Red Hardy, Mike Mitchell, Bob Scheffing,

Sunland Memorial Park, Sun City
George Darrow, Harvey Kuenn, Stan Landes

Valley of the Sun Cemetery, Chandler
Ralph Erickson

Mohave County, Las Vegas Metro

Mountain View Cemetery, Kingman
George Grantham, Bill Malarkey

Pima County, Tucson Metro

East Lawn Palms Cemetery, Tucson
Gordon Cobbledick, Jimmy Dudley, Hank Leiber

Evergreen Cemetery, Tucson
Lou Criger, Rags Faircloth

Holy Hope Cemetery, Tucson
Ray Bates, Herb Herring

Santa Cruz County

Black Oak Cemetery, Elgin
Mal Eason

Nogales City Cemetery, Nogales
Alex Beam

Yavapai County

Valley View Cemetery, Clarksdale
Bert Graham

CALIFORNIA

Alameda County, Oakland Metro

Cedar Lawn Memorial Park, Fremont
Red Marion

Chapel of the Chimes, Oakland
Herb McQuaid

Evergreen Cemetery, Oakland
Curt Roberts

Holy Sepulchre Cemetery, Hayward
Stu Clarke, Len Dondero, Ed Fernandes, Ray French, Eddie Kearse, Eddie Lake, Willie Ludolph, Ed McCreery, Doc Moskiman, Ernie Sulik, Jim Tobin, Johnny Tobin, Jimmy Welsh

Mountain View Cemetery, Oakland
Linc Blakely, Babe Borton, Bill Brenzel, Glenn Burke, Bernie DeViveiros, Bill Kenworthy, Nub Kleinke, Ernie Lombardi, William Marriott, Limb McKenry, Biff Schaller, Ossie Vitt, Oscar Westerberg

St. Mary's Cemetery, Oakland
Bud Connolly, Tom Fitzsimmons, Dan Long, Hack Miller, George Van Haltren

Amador County

Jackson Catholic Cemetery, Jackson
Luke Glavenich

Butte County, Chico Metro

Glen Oaks Memorial Park, Chico
Jim Battle

Memorial Park Cemetery, Oroville
Bill James

Paradise Cemetery, Paradise
Fritz Coumbe

Calaveras County

Buena Vista Cemetery, Murphys
Len Rice

Coulsa County

Colusa Cemetery, Colusa
Charlie Beville

Contra Costa County, Oakland Metro

Holy Cross Cemetery, Antioch
Don Landrum, Harry Malmberg

Memory Garden of Contra Costa, Concord
Bill MacDonald

Oak View Memorial Park Cemetery, Antioch
Johnny Weekly

Oakmont Memorial Park, Lafayette
  Les Scarsella, Gale Staley

Rolling Hills Memorial Park, Richmond
  Vada Pinson

St. Joseph Cemetery, San Pablo
  Johnny Babich, Jim Cronin, Augie Galan,
  Bud Hafey, Icehouse Wilson, Carroll
  Yerkes

Sunset View Cemetery, El Cerrito
  Russ Christopher, Tom Hafey, Ray
  Kremer, Tony Lazzeri, Harl Maggert,
  Carl Zamloch

El Dorado County, Sacramento Metro

Georgetown Pioneer Cemetery, Georgetown
  Ferris Fain

Westwood Hills Memorial Park, Placerville
  Tracy Baker

Fresno County, Fresno Metro

Belmont Memorial Park, Fresno
  Herb Hall, Joe Jenkins, Earl Jones,
  Walt Kuhn

Fresno Memorial Gardens, Fresno
  Rocky Stone

Kingsburg Cemetery, Kingsburg
  Dutch Hinrichs

Mountain View Cemetery, Fresno
  Ned Garvin, Dutch Leonard, Alex
  Metzler

Odd Fellows Cemetery, Fresno
  Hank Thompson

Pleasant Valley Cemetery, Coalinga
  Frency Boragaray

Washington Colony Cemetery, Fresno
  Zeke Rosebraugh, Andy Rush

Humbolt County

St. Mary's Cemetery, Ferndale
  Joe Oeschger

Inyo County

Big Pine Cemetery, Big Pine
  Bert Griffith

Kern County, Bakersfield Metro

Greenlawn Memorial Park, Bakersfield
  Buckshot May, Jimmy O'Connell

Hillcrest Memorial Park, Bakersfield
  Jim Tyack

North Kern Cemetery, Delano
  Woody Main

Union Cemetery, Bakersfield
  Art Williams

Lake County

Lower Lake Cemetery, Lower Lake
  Ted Easterly

Lassen County

Susanville Cemetery, Susanville
  Hardin Barry

Los Angeles County, Los Angeles Metro

All Souls Cemetery, Long Beach
  Lou Berberet, Red Conkwright,
  Marty Griffin, John Kerr, Lyn Lary,
  Skipper Roberts

Angeles Abbey Memorial Park, Compton
  Shags Horan

Angelus-Rosedale Cemetery, Los Angeles
  Johnny Butler, Frank Chance, Byron
  Houck, Joe Marshall

Calvary Cemetery, Los Angeles
  Hi Bell, Jim Ball, Shad Berry, Charlie
  Chech, Tom Daley, Lefty Gervais,
  Specs Harkness, Johnny Lush,
  Ray Prim, Charlie Reilly, Ferdie Schupp,
  Harry F. Sinclair, Ecky Stearns

Chapel of the Pines, Los Angeles
  Albert Von Tilzer

Corona Cemetery, Corona
  Jesse Hill

Eden Memorial Park, Mission Hills
  Herb Karpel

Eternal Valley Memorial Park, Newhall
  Vic Harris

Evergreen Cemetery, Los Angeles
  Earl Bell Gilmore, Biz Mackey

Forest Lawn Memorial Park–Covina Hills,
Covina
  George Gerken, Don Wilson

Forest Lawn Memorial Park-Hollywood
Hills, Los Angeles
  Gene Autry, Ralph Capron, Leo
  Durocher, Al Mamaux, John Roseboro,
  Don Rudolph, Bill Salkeld

Forest Lawn Memorial Park-Long Beach, Long Beach
George Caster, Dad Lytle, Vern Stephens

Forest Lawn Memorial Park, Glendale
Clyde Barfoot, Joe Brown, Ray Brown, Cleo Carlyle, Hooks Cotter, Babe Dahlgren, Pop Dillon, Chuck Dressen, Mike Flynn, George W. Grant, Ed Halbriter, Babe Herman, Tom Hughes, Red Kress, Marty Krug, Erskine Mayer, Pat Ragan, Dave Rowe, Carl Sawyer, Jack Sharrott, Bud Sketchley, Carl Spongberg, Casey Stengel, Park Swartzel, Phillip K. Wrigley, William Wrigley

Glenwood Cemetery, Long Beach
Frank Demaree, Shorty Des Jardien

Grand View Memorial Park, Glendale
Walt Judnich, Jack Lelivelt, Wally Rehg, Homer Summa

Green Hills Memorial Park, Rancho Palos Verdes
Nanny Fernandez, Lefty Mills, Tom Morgan, Tom Wilson

Hillside Memorial Park, Los Angeles
Ike Danning, Moe Franklin, Hank Greenberg, Bud Swartz

Hollywood Forever Cemetery (formerly Hollywood Memorial Park), Hollywood
Bert Adams

Holy Cross Cemetery, Culver City
Fred Baczewski, John Berardino, Johnny Bero, Al Boucher, Frank Burke, Mike Gazella, Waly Golvin, Fred Haney, Bob Kahle, Art Kruger, Peanuts Lowrey, Effa Manley, Jim Murray, Rube Novotney, Walter O'Malley, Erv Palica, Bill Phyle, Les Powers, Jerry Priddy, Rip Russell, Tilly Shafer, Red Smyth, Jigger Statz, Sloppy Thurston

Inglewood Park Cemetery, Inglewood
Earl Battey, Beals Becker, Steve Behel, Wally Berger, Curt Bernard, Tony Boeckel, Lyman Bostock, Bobby Brooks, Walter Carlisle, Doc Crandall, Sam Crawford, Wheezer Dell, Bill Essick, Curt Flood, Jim Gilliam, Russ Hall, Charlie Hartman, Sammy Haynes, Buster Haywood, Art Herman, Oris Hockett, Bob Leadley, Al Lyons, Lou Mahaffey, Hank McDonald, John McGraw, Fred McMullin, Irish Meusel, Bert Niehoff, Elmer Rieger, Pete Schneider, Jim Scott, Fred Smith, Harry Spies, Bobby Wallace, Parke Wilson

Lincoln Memorial Park Cemetery, Compton
Jake Dunn

Live Oak Memorial Park, Monrovia
Dick Conger, Bill Schuster

Los Angeles National Cemetery, Los Angeles
Percy Coleman, Molly Craft, Mike Dejan, Heinie Elder, Scott hastings, Ed Hearne, Bill James, Bill Johnson, Pete Lapan, Dutch Lieber, Nate Moreland, Milo Netzel, Gordon Rhodes, Denny Sullivan, Bert Whaling

Mount Sinai Memorial Park, Los Angeles
Lefty Phillips

Mountain View Cemetery, Altadena
Dick Cox, Reddy Grey, Don Heffner, Ted Husing, Ralph Works

Oakdale Memorial Park, Glendora
Curt Davis, Roger Freed, Babe Twombly

Pacific Crest Cemetery, Redondo Beach
John Halla

Park Lawn Cemetery, City of Commerce
Al Benton

Pasadena Mausoleum, Altadena
Charlie Deal

Pomona Cemetery, Pomona
Jesse Baker, Roy Hitt

Queen of Heaven Cemetery, Rowland Heights
Jesse Flores, Greg Mulleavy, Fresco Thompson

Resurrection Cemetery, Montebello
Lou Koupal, Cliff Markle, Don Ross

Rose Hills Memorial Park, Whittier
Tod Davis, Rube Ellis, Art Fromme, Wally Hood, Hugh McMullen, Scat Metha, Bob Meusel, Walt Slagle, Roy Weir, Alan Wiggins

Russian Molokan Cemetery, City of Commerce
Lou Novikoff

San Fernando Mission Cemetery, Mission Hills
Gilly Campbell, Chuck Connors, Bob Hope, Ernie Orsatti, Hank Patterson, Austin Walsh, Johnny Williams

San Gabriel Mission Cemetery, San Gabriel
  Hank Aguirre, Jim McHale, Red
  Worthington

Serbian United Benevolent Cemetery,
Los Angeles
  George Vico

Valhalla Memorial Park, North Hollywood
  Fred Abbott, Harry Berte, George
  Hildebrand, Cy Malis, Wilbur Murdoch,
  Dwight Stone

Valley Oaks Memorial Park, Westlake Village
  Paul Edmondson

Woodland Memorial Park, Compton
  George Decker

Woodlawn Cemetery, Santa Monica
  Johnny Bassler, Guy Cooper, Faye
  Dancer, Wimpy Quinn

Marin County, San Francisco Metro

Mount Olivet Catholic Cemetery, San Rafael
  Duster Mails

Mount Tamalpais Cemetery, San Rafael
  Flame Delhi, Lefty Gomez, Russ Hodges,
  Joe Mellana

Valley Memorial Park, Novato
  Joe Gantenbein

Mendocino County

Rose Memorial Park, Fort Bragg
  Vince DiMaggio

Russian River Cemetery, Ukiah
  John Cullen

Merced County, Merced Metro

Los Banos Cemetery, Los Banos
  Mack Wheat

San Joaquin Valley National Cemetery,
Gustine
  Ben Guintini

Modoc County

Eagleville Community Cemetery, Eagleville
  Arky Vaughn

Monterey County, Salinas Metro

El Carmelo Cemetery, Pacific Grove
  Bob Loane

San Carlos Catholic Cemetery, Monterey
  Eddie Burns

Napa County, Vallejo-Fairfield-Napa Metro

Holy Cross Catholic Cemetery, St. Helena
  Cookie Lavagetto, Chick Hafey

St. Helena Cemetery, St. Helena
  Dick Egan, Chick Gandil

Tulocay Cemetery, Napa
  Pat Bohen, Pete Daglia, Lou Guisto,
  Elmer Leonard

Yountville Cemetery, Yountville
  Ernie Alten

Orange County, Orange County Metro

El Toro Memorial Park, Lake Forest
  Catfish Metkovich

Fairhaven Memorial Park, Santa Ana
  Chick Brandom, Harry DeMiller, Sam
  Dungan, Hank Edwards, Bill Hughes,
  Ernie Johnson, Bob Nieman

Forest Lawn Memorial Park–Cypress,
Cypress
  Kit Carson, Dick Wantz

Good Shepherd Cemetery, Huntington Beach
  Jess Buckles, Connie Creeden, Vern
  Freiburger, Frank Manush, Don
  McMahon, Pat McNulty

Harbor Rest-Mount Olive Cemetery,
Costa Mesa
  Al Demaree

Holy Sepulchre Cemetery, Orange
  Harry Gaspar, Ed Sadowski

Loma Vista Memorial Park, Fullerton
  Al Campanis, Jack Salveson, Mike Simon

Magnolia Memorial Park, Garden Grove
  Jim Baxes

Melrose Abbey Memorial Park, Anaheim
  Jimmy Austin, Earl Hamilton, Gavy
  Cravath, Jack Norworth, Lefty Williams

Pacific View Memorial Park, Newport Beach
  Dale Coogan, Bert Delmas, Bryan
  Stephens, Jim Wilson

Westminster Memorial Park, Westminster
  Jesse Barnes, George Blaeholder, Rex
  Cecil, Red Dorman, George Payne, Phil
  Slattery

Placer County, Sacramento Metro

Colfax Cemetery, Colfax
  Ed Hutchinson

Roseville Cemetery, Roseville
Pryor McBee

St. Patrick's Cemetery, Grass Valley
Mitch Chetkovich

Riverside County, Riverside-San Bernardino Metro

Banning-Cabazon Cemetery, Banning
Joe Hoover

Coachela Valley Cemetery, Coachella
Mays Copeland

Crestlawn Memorial Park, Riverside
Bob Veselic

Desert Memorial Park, Cathedral City
Pete Reiser, Phil Weintraub

Elsinore Valley Cemetery, Lake Elsinore
Homer Hillebrand

Evergreen Memorial Park, Riverside
George Cobb, Tom Dowse, Gene Packard, George Treadway

Olivewood Cemetery, Riverside
Eric Show

Pierce Brothers Crestlawn Memorial Park, Riverside
Mike Darr

Riverside National Cemetery, Riverside
Jack Brewer, Merl Combs, Marv Felderman, Cecil Garriott, Jesse Hubbard, Johnny Mackinson, Paul Toth, Leon Wagner, Benny Zientara

San Jacinto Valley Cemetery, San Jacinto
Red Ostergard

Welwood Murray Cemetery, Palm Springs
Carter Elliott

Sacramento County, Sacramento Metro

Calvary Catholic Cemetery, Citrus Heights
Orval Grove, Carmen Mauro, Harl Maggert

Camellia Memorial Lawn, Sacramento
Russ Young

East Lawn Memorial Park, Sacramento
Cliff Daringer, Joe Gedeon, Hal Rhyne, Charley Schanz, Earl Sheely, Sailor Stroud

East Lawn Sierra Hills Cemetery, Sacramento
Gordon Jones

Masonic Lawn Cemetery, Sacramento
Bill Clemensen, Bruce Edwards

Mount Vernon Memorial Park, Fair Oaks
Bill Conroy, Art Garibaldi, Earl McNeely

Sacramento City Cemetery, Sacramento
George Borchers

South East Lawn Memorial Park, Elk Grove
Nippy Jones

St. John's Catholic Cemetery, Folsom
Bob Keefe

St. Joseph's Cemetery, Sacramento
Charlie Enwright, Jim Hughes

St. Mary's Catholic Cemetery, Sacramento
Ernie Bonham, Vince Castino, Tony Freitas, Alex Kampouris, Ray Keating, Merlin Kopp, Earl Kunz, Bill Marshall, Joe Marty, Bob McHale, Herm Pillette, Buddy Ryan, Manny Salvo, Bobby Schang, Merv Shea, Hank Steinbacher, Jim Westlake, Kettle Wirts

Sylvan Cemetery, Citrus Heights
Steve Senteney

San Benito County

Hollister Cemetery, Hollister
Harry Wolter

San Bernardino County, Riverside-San Bernardino Metro

Montecito Memorial Park, Colton
Jay Dahl, Dee Fondy, Ken Hubbs, Freddie Fitzsimmons, Jack Rothrock

Bellevue Memorial Gardens, Ontario
Bill Collins, Lin Storti

Green Acres Memorial Park, Bloomington
Chief Meyers

Hermosa Cemetery, Colton
Camilo Carreon, Gordon Maltzberger

Mountain View Memorial Park, Barstow
Bob Rhodes

San Diego County, San Diego Metro

Alpine Cemetery, Alpine
Bob Christian

Cypress View Cemetery, San Diego
Al Carson, Roy Hutson, Bid McPhee, Bill Starr

Dearborn Memorial Park, Poway
Deron Johnson, Bob Miller

El Camino Memorial Park, La Jolla
  Cedric Durst, Bob Jones, Joan Kroc, Ray
  Kroc, Mike Reinbach, Chico Ruiz
Eternal Hills Memorial Park, Oceanside
  Buster Adams
Fort Rosecrans National Cemetery, La Jolla
  Jack Albright, Howard Craghead, Bud
  Hardin, Rolla Mapel, John Mohardt,
  Goldie Rapp, Red Smith
Glen Abbey Memorial Park, Bonita
  Dick Aylward, Dain Clay, Jess Pike
Greenwood Memorial Park, San Diego
  Earl Brucker, Bill Dalrymple, Bob Elliott,
  Ed Linn, Steve Mesner, John Ritchey,
  Ed Runge, C. Arnholt Smith, Milt Smith,
  Bob Thorpe
Holy Cross Cemetery, San Diego
  Sleepy Bill Burns
La Vista Memorial Park, National City
  Joe Orrell
Mission San Luis Rey Cemetery,
San Luis Rey
  Andy Karl
Mount Hope Cemetery, San Diego
  Hick Carpenter, Joe Quest
Oak Hill Memorial Park, Escondido
  Pete Coscarart, John Raleigh

San Francisco County, San Francisco Metro

Odd Fellows Columbarium, San Francisco
  Fred Carroll
San Francisco National Cemetery,
San Francisco
  Rowdy Elliott, Charlie Flanagan

San Joaquin County, Stockton-Lodi Metro

Casa Bonita Mausoleum, Stockton
  Hap Collard
Cherokee Memorial Park, Lodi
  Lloyd Johnson
Park View Cemetery, Manteca
  Milo Candini, Monte Pfyl
San Joaquin Catholic Cemetery, Stockton
  Leroy Hermann, Bob Joyce, Mel Mazzera
Stockton Rural Cemetery, Stockton
  Dusty Miller, George Harper, Harry
  Lochhead

San Luis Obispo County, San Luis Obispo Metro

Atascadero Cemetery, Atascadero
  Walt Leverenz
Odd Fellows Cemetery, San Luis Obispo
  Pug Cavet, Lafayette Henion

San Mateo County, San Francisco Metro

Alta Mesa Memorial Park, Palo Alto
  Johnny Couch, Muddy Ruel, Karl Schnell
Cypress Lawn Memorial Park, Colma
  Dolph Camilli, Bert Cole, George Crosby,
  Chicken Hawks, Willie Kamm, Eddie
  Kenna, Henry Krug, Bill Lawrence, Bill
  Leard, Lefty O'Doul, Bruce Ogrodowski,
  John Russell, Charlie Sweeney, Live Oak
  Taylor, Bill Tozer, Harry Wolverton
Eternal Home Cemetery, Colma
  Lou Rosenberg
Golden Gate National Cemetery, San Bruno
  Jim Begley, Grover Baichley, Eddie
  Brown, Kid Butler, Joe Connolly, Babe
  Ellison, John Grimes, Chris Hartje, Fred
  Hofman, Bill Knickerbocker, Hap Myers,
  Marv Peasley, Harlin Pool, Jackie Price,
  Pete Scott, Fred Tauby, Harry Thompson,
  Lou Tost, Jim Wright
Greenlawn Memorial Park, Colma
  Truck Eagan
Hills of Eternity Memorial Park, Colma
  Harry Rosenberg
Holy Cross Cemetery, Colma
  Bob Blakiston, Ping Bodie, Julio Bonetti,
  Jim Britt, Willard Brown, Jim Byrnes, Jake
  Caulfield, Ike Caveney, Joe Chamberlain,
  Italo Chelini, Joe Corbett, Roy Corhan,
  Marty Creegan, Frank Crosetti, Bill
  Cunningham, Bill DePangher, Joe
  DiMaggio, Cy Falkenberg, John J.
  Fogarty, Charlie Fox, Charlie Geggus, Joe
  Giannini, Charlie Graham, Ed Hallinan,
  Ham Iberg, Youngy Johnson, George
  Kelly, Harry Krause, Bill Lange, Jim
  McDonald, Pete Meegan, Ed Montague,
  Eddie Mulligan, Jim Nealon, Billy Orr,
  Marino Pieretti, Babe Pinelli, Tom Power,
  George Puccinelli, Josh Reilly, Jim
  Roxburgh, Hank Sauer, John Smith, Mule
  Sprinz, Pete Standridge, Pete Sweeney,
  Pop Swett, Tom Tennant

Home of Peace Cemetery, Colma
Walter Haas
Italian Cemetery, Colma
Joe Orengo
Olivet Memorial Park, Colma
Heinie Heitmuller, Elmer Pence, Gus
Suhr, Roxy Walters, Del Young
Skylawn Memorial Park, San Mateo
Bobby Bonds, Chub Feeney, Bob Stevens
St. John's Cemetery, San Mateo
Justin Fitzgerald
Sunset View Cemetery, Colma
Charlie Waitt
Woodlawn Memorial Park, Colma
Jim Asbell, Win Ballou, Charlie Dorman,
Sam Mertes, Andy Piercy, Tom Seats,
Tubby Spencer

Santa Barbara County, Santa Barbara Metro

Calvary Cemetery, Santa Barbara
Joe Wilhoit
Dudley-Hoffman Columbarium, Santa Maria
Les Webber
Evergreen Cemetery, Lompoc
Helen St. Aubin
Goleta Cemetery, Goleta
Gene Lillard
Oak Hill Cemetery, Solvang
Lee Thompson
Santa Barbara Cemetery, Santa Barbara
Eddie Mathews

Santa Clara County, San Jose Metro

Los Gatos Memorial Park, San Jose
Al Gould
Oak Hill Memorial Park, San Jose
Frank Arellanes, Hal Chase, Herb
Gorman, Willie Hogan, Frank Jelincich,
Ren Kelly, George Schmees, Happy Smith
Santa Clara Mission Cemetery, Santa Clara
Herb Hippauf, Marv Owen, Paddy
Siglin, Hub Walker

Santa Cruz County, Santa Cruz Metro

Aptos Cemetery, Aptos
Harry Hooper
Holy Cross Cemetery, Santa Cruz
Joe Brovia

Shasta County, Redding Metro

Ogburn Inwood Cemetery, Shingletown
Joe Hatten

Siskiyou County

Henly-Hornbrook Cemetery, Hornbrook
Ivan Howard
Mount Shasta Memorial Park, Mount Shasta
Swede Risberg

Solano County, Vallejo-Fairfield-Napa

Dixon Cemetery, Dixon
George Darby, Ray Rohwer
Rockville Cemetery, Fairfield
Darrell Johnson
St. Vincent's Cemetery, Vallejo
John Gillespie
Suisun-Fairfield Cemetery, Fairfield
Cliff Aberson

Sonoma County, Santa Rosa Metro

Chapel of the Chimes, Santa Rosa, CA.
Sam Agnew, Chick Autry
Cypress Hill Memorial Park, Petaluma
Billy Hulen, Bob Uhl
Santa Rosa Memorial Park, Santa Rosa
Carl Holling, Judge Nagle

Stanislaus County, Modesto Metro

Lakewood Memorial Park, Hughson
Buddy Gremp, Hal Leathers, Urbane
Pickering
St. Stanislaus Catholic Cemetery, Modesto
Jack Gilligan, Walter Schmidt

Sutter County, Yuba City Metro

Sutter Cemetery, Sutter
Dolly Gray

Tehama County

Sunset Hill Cemetery, Corning
Lee Grisson
Vina-Carter Cemetery, Vina
Roy Joiner

Tulare County, Visalia-Tulare Metro

Cemetery Tulare, Tulare
Vic Lombardi

Visalia Cemetery, Visalia
Larry French, Mike Garcia, Willard
Hershberger, Chris Mahoney

Ventura County, Ventura Metro

Conejo Mountain Memorial Park, Camarillo
Alex Ferguson

Ivy Lawn Memorial Park, Ventura
Josh Clarke, Charlie Hall, Lerton Pinto,
Tex Pruiett

Yolo County, Yolo Metro

Capay Cemetery, Esparto
Cliff Garrison, Erv Kantlehner

Monument Hill Memorial Park, Woodland
Archie Yelle

Yuba County, Yuba Metro

Sierra View Memorial Park, Marysville
Cotton Pippen

COLORADO

Alamosa County

Alamosa Cemetery, Alamosa
Jim Hyndman

Boulder County, Boulder–Logmont Metro

Mountain View Cemetery, Boulder
Lenny Metz

Sacred Heart of Mary Catholic Cemetery,
Boulder
Hilly Flitcraft

Delta County

Delta Municipal Cemetery, Delta
Ed Karger

Denver County, Denver Metro

Fairmount Cemetery, Denver
Bubbles Anderson, Henry Bostick, Les
Channell, Sam Childs, Jake Gettman,
Dud Lee, Bill McGilvray, Jim Moore,
Eddie Quick, Charlie Reynolds, Art
Weaver

Fort Logan National Cemetery, Denver
Ace Hutchinson

Riverside Cemetery, Denver
John Bass, Oliver Marcelle

El Paso County, Colorado Springs Metro

Memorial Gardens Cemetery, Colorado
Springs
Jack Tising

Jefferson County, Denver Metro

Crown Hill Cemetery, Wheat Ridge
Bill Everitt, Bill Hubbell, Marty Lang,
Cliff Lee, George Teabeau

Golden Cemetery, Golden
Roy Hartzell, Cowboy Jones

Mount Olivet Cemetery, Wheat Ridge
Gus Alberts, Gran Bowler, Joe Connor,
Bill Eagan, Cobe Jones, Buzz Murphy,
Tom O'Hara

**Larimer County, Fort Collins–Loveland
Metro**

Sunrise Ranch Cemetery, Loveland
George Shears

Mesa County, Grand Junction Metro

Orchard Mesa Municipal Cemetery,
Orchard Mesa
Ray Boggs, Bill Evans

Memorial Gardens Cemetery,
Grand Junction
Josh Swindell

Montezuma County

Fairview Cemetery, Yellow Jacket
Al Brazle

Pueblo County, Pueblo Metro

Imperial Memorial Gardens, Pueblo
Jim Bivin

Mountain View Cemetery, Pueblo
Frederick Fass

Roselawn Cemetery, Pueblo
Delos Brown, Bob McGraw, Joe Straub

CONNECTICUT

**Fairfield County; Bridgeport–Stamford–
Norwalk Metro**

Fairfield Memorial Park, Stamford
Ron Northey

Lakeview Cemetery, Bridgeport
  Ed Connolly, George Curry, Bob
  Emmerich, Jim Tennant

Lawncroft Cemetery, Fairfield
  Ed Buckingham

Long Ridge Union Cemetery, Stamford
  Red Smith

Mountain Grove Cemetery, Bridgeport
  Neal Ball, Roy Clark

Norwalk Cemetery, Norwalk
  Billy Lauder

Oak Lawn Cemetery, Fairfield
  Scoop Baker

Old Silvermine Community Cemetery,
New Canaan
  Frank Buttery

Park Cemetery, Bridgeport
  Kiddo Davis, Ad Yale

St. John's Cemetery, Darien
  Fred Demarais, John Scalzi, Bill Swarback

St. Mary's & St. Joseph's Cemetery, Norwalk
  Jack Dunleavy, Joe Rabbitt

St. Mary's Cemetery, Greenwich
  Eddie Lopat

St. Michael's Cemetery, Stratford
  Howard Baker, Tom Downey, Danny
  Hoffman, Ernie Lush, Joe Malay, Jack
  McMahon, Spike Merena, John Michaels,
  Tricky Nichols, Jim O'Rourke, John
  O'Rourke, Mike Pasquella, Jim Rogers,
  Dan Shannon

Temple Beth El Cemetery, Stamford
  Mel Allen

Union Cemetery, Rowayton
  Ole Olsen

Willowbrook Cemetery, Norwalk
  Hezekiah Allen

Hartford County, Hartford Metro

Cedar Hill Cemetery, Hartford
  Morgan Bulkeley

East Cemetery, Manchester
  Bob Brady

Emanuel Synagogue Cemetery, Wethersfield
  Reuben Ewing

Fairview Cemetery, New Britain
  Lefty Marr, Chris Vierira

Fairview Cemetery, West Hartford
  George Woodend

Mt. St. Benedict's Cemetery, Bloomfield
  Harry Beecher, Steve Brady, Ed Cotter,
  Ed Coughlin, Jack Farrell, Frank Gilmore,
  John Henry, Bill Murray, Bill Tobin

New St. Joseph's Cemetery, Bristol
  Swat McCabe

Rose Hill Memorial Park, Rocky Hill
  Monk Dubiel, Emil Planeta, Bunny Roser

Springdale Cemetery, Hartford
  School Boy Taylor

St. Patrick's Cemetery, Hartford
  James Lehan, Biff Sheehan

St. Thomas Cemetery, Southington
  Joe Regan, Jimmie Savage

Veteran's Memorial Cemetery, South
Windsor
  Babe Young

Litchfield County

Hillside Cemetery, Torrington
  Tad Quinn

Middlesex County, Hartford Metro portion

St. John's Cemetery, Middletown
  Ed Cassian, Jerry Dorgan

Middlesex County, New Haven Metro portion

Fountain Hill Cemetery, Deep River
  Paul Hopkins

New Haven County, New Haven Metro portion

Alderbrook Cemetery, Guilford
  George Townsend

All Saints Cemetery, North Haven
  Jim Sheehan

Beaverdale Memorial Park, New Haven
  Bob Barthelson

Congregation Sinai Memorial Park,
Allingtown
  Heinie Scheer

East Lawn Cemetery, East Haven
  Jumping Jack Jones, Frank Woodward

Evergreen Cemetery, New Haven
  Doc Adams, Steve Libby, Al Mahon,
  George Weiss

Grove Street Cemetery, New Haven
  Bart Giamatti

Mapledale Cemetery, New Haven
  Charlie Pabor

Oak Grove Cemetery, West Haven
  George Bone

Sacred Heart Cemetery, Meriden
  Jack Barry, Ed Walsh

St. Bernard's Cemetery, West Haven
  Pete Falsey, Henry Gruber

St. Lawrence Cemetery, West Haven
  Chick Bowen, Al Clauss, Tom Leahy,
  Beauty McGowan, Dan Phelan, Eddie
  Wilson

New Haven County, Waterbury Metro portion

Calvary Cemetery, Waterbury
  Candy LaChance

New North Cemetery, Woodbury
  Al Schacht

New St. Joseph's Cemetery, Waterbury
  Ed Begley, Red Donahue, Dan Parker

Old St. Joseph's Cemetery, Waterbury
  Joe Connor, Roger Connor

Pine Grove Cemetery, Waterbury
  Gene Derby, Fred Klobedanz

Riverside Cemetery, Waterbury
  George Fields

St. James Cemetery, Naugatuck
  Ray Foley, Spec Shea, Jack Hoey

New Haven County, Bridgeport-Stamford-Norwalk Metro portion

Mount St. Peter's Cemetery, Derby
  Dennis Fitzgerald

Oak Cliffe Cemetery, Derby
  Bob Pettit

Pine Grove Cemetery, Ansonia
  Lou North

St. Augustine's Cemetery, Seymour
  Alex Konikowski

New London County, Norwich–New London Metro

Comstock Cemetery, Montville
  Cyclone Miller

Jordan Cemetery, Waterford
  Jack Burns

St. Mary's & St. Joseph's Cemetery, Norwich
  Gus Dugas, Ed Walczak

Yantic Cemetery, Norwich
  Bill Hutchison

New London County

Pachaug Cemetery, Pachaug
  Tommy Corcoran

Tolland County; Springfield Metro portion

West Cemetery, Somers
  Herman Bronkie

Tolland County

St. Bernard's Cemetery, Rockville
  Frank Cox

Windham County

Holy Cross Cemetery, Danielson
  Frank Dascolli

St. Joseph Cemetery, Willimantic
  Art Nichols

DELAWARE

Kent County, Dover Metro

Emmanuel United Methodist Cemetery, Cheswold
  Ted Carney

Gibbs Memorial Gardens, Camden
  Arthur Fauntleroy

Hollywood Cemetery, Harrington
  Al Burris

New Castle County, Wilmington Metro

All Saints Cemetery, Newark
  Ed Cihocki

Cathedral Cemetery, Wilmington
  Pete Cassidy, Bill Day, Chick Hartley, Bill
  McGowan, Joe Myers, John Newell

Delaware Veterans Memorial Cemetery, Bear
  Toots Ferrell

DuPont Family Cemetery, Winterthur
  Robert P. Carpenter, Robert R. M.
  Carpenter, Jr.

Glenwood Cemetery, Smyrna
Barney Slaughter

Gracelawn Memorial Park, New Castle
Frank Bennett, Billy Bruton, Bill Sadler

Head of Christiana Presbyterian Church
Cemetery, Newark
Len Lovett

Riverview Cemetery, Wilmington
George Winter

Silverbrook Cemetery, Wilmington
Bill Higgins, Judy Johnson, Leo Meyer

St. John's Catholic Church Cemetery,
Newark
Vic Willis

St. Joseph's-on-the-Brandywine Church
Cemetery, Greenville
Sadie McMahon

Townsend Cemetery, Townsend
Harry Hoch, Jack Townsend

Wilimington & Brandywine Cemetery,
Wilmington
Harry Anderson, Bill Hawke, Flip Lafferty

Sussex County

Millsboro Cemetery, Millsboro
Huck Betts, Broadway Jones

Union Cemetery, Georgetown
Chris Short

DISTRICT OF COLUMBIA

Washington, Washington Metro

Congressional Cemetery, Washington
Art Devlin, John Graff, Tom Kinslow,
Bill McCauley

Elesavetgrad Cemetery, Washington
Shirley Povich

Glenwood Cemetery, Washington
Phil Baker, Gene DeMontreville, Walter
Hewitt, Holly Hollingshead, Sadie
Houck, Harry Mace, Pop Snyder, Woody
Wagenhorst, Bill Wise, Charles Witherow,
Ed Yewell

Mount Olivet Cemetery, Washington
Thomas Cantwell, Harry Colliflower,
Tom Crooke, Ed Daily, John Gilroy, Buck
Gladmon, Pop Joy, Mickey Keliher, Watty

Lee, Tony Madigan, Charles Moran,
Michael Scanlon, Joe Stanley, George
Winkelman

Oak Hill Cemetery, Washington
Bob Barr, John Doyle, Tom Evers, George
Joyce, Arthur Gorman, Charlie Kalbfus,
Howard Wall, Bill Yeatman

Prospect Hill Cemetery, Washington
Joe Gearhardt

Rock Creek Cemetery, Washington
Doug Allison, Carl Brandebury,
Thomas C. Noyes, Doc White, Harry
Wood, Nick Young

Woodlawn Cemetery, Washington
Ferdinand Morton

FLORIDA

Alachua County, Gainesville Metro

Evergreen Cemetery, Gainesville
Charlie Harris

Forest Meadows Memorial Park Central,
Gainesville
Bill Ferrazzi

High Springs Cemetery, High Springs
Myrill Hoag

Orange Hill Cemetery, Williston
Paul Florence

Bay County, Panama City Metro

Garden of Memories, Panama City
Jack Franklin

Kent-Forest Lawn Cemetery, Panama City
Jack Bolling

Bradford County

Crosby Lake Cemetery, Starke
Parson Perryman

**Brevard County, Melbourne–
Titusville Metro**

Brevard Memorial Park, Cocoa
Jake Early

Fountainhead Memorial Park, Palm Bay
Ray Dandridge, Gene Markland

Melbourne Cemetery, Melbourne
Andy Seminick

Broward County, Fort Lauderdale Metro

Evergreen Cemetery, Fort Lauderdale
  Orth Collins
Forest Lawn Central Cemetery,
Fort Lauderdale
  Jack Enright
Forest Lawn Memorial Gardens, Pompano
Beach
  Dan Daniel, Ed Walsh
Hollywood Memorial Gardens, Hollywood
  Allie Strobel, Karl Drews
Our Lady Queen of Heaven Cemetery,
North Lauderdale
  Cliff Happenny, Jimmy Shevlin
Star of David Memorial Gardens, North
Lauderdale
  Cal Abrams

Citrus County

Oak Ridge Cemetery, Inverness
  Ed P. Hamman, Bernie Neis
Stage Stand Cemetery, Homosassa Springs
  Dazzy Vance

Clay County, Jacksonville Metro

Keystone Heights Cemetery, Keystone
Heights
  Charlie Wiedemeyer

Columbia County

Oakland Cemetery, Lake City
  Stuffy Stewart

Dade County, Miami Metro

Dade Memorial Park-South, Miami
  Tony Ordenana
Dade Memorial Park, Miami
  Juan Armenteros
Flagler Memorial Park, Miami
  Jimmie Foxx, Mike Guerra, Roberto Ortiz
Graceland Memorial Park, Miami
  Bill Klem, Max Rosenfeld
Miami Memorial Park, Miami
  Ray Bare, Isidoro Leon, Roy Talcott
Mt. Nebo Memorial Gardens, Miami
  Mose Solomon
Southern Memorial Park, Miami
  Mike Schemer

Vista Memorial Gardens, Hialeah
  Chet Covington, Pedro Dibut, Bobby
  Estalella, Tony Martinez, Reggie Otero,
  Nap Reyes
Woodlawn Park Cemetery North, Miami
  Max Carey, Tiny Chaplin, Sandy Amoros,
  Jorge Comellas, George Ferguson, Tom
  Knowlson, Julio Moreno
Woodlawn Park Cemetery South, Miami
  Jose Lopez, Fred Frink, Charlie
  Gassaway
Woodlawn Park Cemetery West, Hialeah
  John Douglas

Duval County, Jacksonville Metro

Edgewood Cemetery, Jacksonville
  Preacher Henry
Evergreen Cemetery, Jacksonville
  Frank Butler, Dixie Carroll, Hi Church,
  Joe Dobson, Bob Fisher, Ben Geraghty,
  John Kennedy, Bill Terry, Stank White,
  Harley Young, Adrian Zabala
Greenlawn Cemetery, Jacksonville
  Les Peden
Oaklawn Cemetery, Jacksonville
  Don Bessent, John Chambers, Bob
  Gandy, Kenny Robinson
Restlawn Memorial Park, Jacksonville
  Albert Frazier, Hank Winston
Riverside Memorial Park, Jacksonville
  Jim Holmes, Paul Schreiber, Tige Stone
St. Mary's Cemetery, Jacksonville
  Dominic Mullaney
Woodlawn Cemetery, Jacksonville
  Billy Taylor

Escambia County, Pensacola Metro

Barrancas National Cemetery, Pensacola
  Hawk Marvray, Elmer Tutwiler
Bayview Memorial Park, Pensacola
  Wally Dashiell, Bill Henderson, Bill
  McGhee, Marshall Renfroe
Pfeiffer Cemetery, Pensacola
  Bill Holden
St. John's Cemetery, Pensacola
  Russ Scarritt
St. Michael's Cemetery, Pensacola
  Tom Gettinger

Gadsden County, Tallahassee Metro

Sunnyvale Cemetery, Quincy
   Bo Gator Snead

Gulf County

Magnolia Cemetery, Apalachicola
   Ned Porter

Hardee County

Wauchula Cemetery, Wauchula
   Hank Boney

Hernando County, Tampa–St. Petersburg Metro

Brooksville Cemetery, Brooksville
   Wilbur Good

Highlands County

Oak Hill Cemetery, Lake Placid
   Red Causey

Hillsborough County, Tampa–St. Petersburg Metro

Centro Austriano Memorial Park, Tampa
   Charlie Cuellar, Ralph Onis

Garden of Memories Cemetery, Tampa
   Jerry Akers, Johnny Burnett, Tony
   Cuccinello, Guy Curtright, Milt Gaston,
   Gene Schott, Johnny Vander Meer

Limona Cemetery, Brandon
   George Foss

Memorial Park Cemetery, Tampa
   Fats Wiggs

Oaklawn Cemetery, Plant City
   Rip Sewell

Indian River County

Crestlawn Cemetery, Vero Beach
   Karl Spooner

Lake County, Orlando Metro

Florida National Cemetery, Bushnell
   William Brisker, Chris Van Cuyk, Hal
   White, Jeff Williams

Hillcrest Memorial Gardens, Leesburg
   Frank Barrett

Lone Oak Cemetery, Leesburg
   Mutt Wilson

Lee County, Fort Myers Metro

Fort Myers Memorial Gardens, Fort Myers
   Joe Coleman, Jean Dubuc, Fred Heimach

Oak Ridge Cemetery, Ft. Myers
   Rev Cannady

Leon County, Tallahassee Metro

Meadowwood Memorial Park, Tallahassee
   Fred Hatfield

Tallahassee Memory Gardens, Tallahassee
   Dick Howser

Manatee County, Sarasota–Bradenton Metro

Fogartyville Cemetery, Bradenton
   Hank Johnson

Manasota Memorial Park, Bradenton
   Johnny Cooney, Butch Henline, Bill
   McKechnie, Johnny Moore, Hank
   Olmsted, Paul Waner, Jimmy Wilson

Mansion Memorial Park, Ellenton
   Billy Purtell

St. Bernard Catholic Church Cemetery,
Bradenton Beach
   Birdie Tebbetts

Martin County, Fort Pierce–Port St. Lucie Metro

All Saints Cemetery, Jensen Beach
   Emmett Seery

Riverside Memorial Park, Tequesta
   Billy Herman

Okaloosa County, Fort Walton Beach Metro

Beal Memorial Cemetery, Fort Walton Beach
   Jack Peerson

Live Oak Memorial Park, Crestview
   Lance Richbourg

Orange County, Orlando Metro

Glen Haven Memorial Park, Winter Park
   Harry Biemiller, Ray Kennedy, Red
   Miller, Len Schulte

Greenwood Cemetery, Orlando
   Mickey Doolan, Joe Tinker

Highland Memorial Park, Apopka
   Clarence Heise

Palm Cemetery, Winter Park
   Del Mason

Woodlawn Memoriaum Memorial Park, Gotha
  Tim Crews, Dick Hahn, Tommy
  McMillan, Heinie Mueller, Joe Stripp,
  Walt Tauscher, Zach Taylor

Palm Beach County, West Palm Beach–Boca Raton

Boca Raton Cemetery, Boca Raton
  Lee Allen

Boynton Memorial Park, Boynton Beach
  Mike Wilson

Eternal Light Memorial Gardens,
Boynton Beach
  Izzy Goldstein

Glenwood Memorial Cemetery,
West Palm Beach
  Alonza Bailey

Hillcrest Memorial Park, West Palm Beach
  Ned Harris, Whitey Platt

Our Lady Queen of Peace Cemetery,
West Palm Beach
  Jim Peterson

Palm Beach Memorial Park, Lantana
  George Fallon

Pinecrest Cemetery, Lake Worth
  Charles Donnelly, Jim Faulkner

Royal Palm Memorial Gardens,
West Palm Beach
  Hank Gornicki, Pep Rambert, Jack
  Sheehan

Woodlawn Cemetery, West Palm Beach
  Ed Andrews

Pasco County, Tampa–St. Petersburg Metro

Dade City Cemetery, Dade City
  Arlas Taylor

Meadowland Memorial Gardens, New Port
Richey
  Charlie Niebergall, Jimmy Wasdell

Oakside Cemetery, Zephyrhills
  Red Kelly

Pinellas County, Tampa–St. Petersburg Metro

Bay Pines National Cemetery, Bay Pines
  George Bamberger, Verne Clemons,
  Augie Donatelli, Walter Doyle

Curlew Hills Memory Gardens, Palm Harbor
  Joe Cicero, Bill DeKoning

Cycadia Cemetery, Tarpon Springs
  Elliot Bigelow

Dunedin Cemetery, Dunedin
  Watty Clark

Lincoln Cemetery, Gulfport
  George Smith

Memorial Park Cemetery, St. Petersburg
  Larry Bearnarth, Ford Garrison, Hooks
  Iott, Paul Pryor, Pete Wilson

Royal Palm Cemetery, St. Petersburg
  Frank Fletcher, Doc Shanley

Serenity Gardens Memorial Park, Largo
  Angel Aragon, Ted Kleinhans

Sylvan Abbey Memorial Park, Clearwater
  George Abrams, Gene Ford, Jack Russell,
  Eddie Silber

The Garden Sanctuary Cemetery, Seminole
  Nelson Burbrink

Woodlawn Memorial Gardens, St. Petersburg
  Spud Chandler, Red Nelson, Jim Scott

Polk County, Lakeland–Winter haven Metro

Forest Hill Cemetery, Haines City
  Tommy Leach

Lakeland Memorial Gardens, Lakeland
  Ed White

Lakeside Memorial Park, Winter Haven
  Schoolboy Tugerson

Oak Hill Burial Park, Lakeland
  Bill Swift

Rolling Hills Cemetery, Winter Haven
  Harry Chiti

Wildwood Cemetery, Bartow
  Bill Phebus, Fred Vaughn

Putnam County

Oak Hill Cemetery, Palatka
  Herb Thomas

West View Cemetery, Palatka
  Weldon Henley

Sarasota County, Sarasota–Bradenton Metro

Galilee Cemetery, Sarasota
  Luther Hughes

Gulf Pines Memorial Park, Englewood
  Bunny Hearn, Roy Spencer, Bob Thorpe

Palms Memorial Park, Sarasota
  Lew Krausse, Hoyt Wilhelm

Sarasota Memorial Park, Sarasota
　Heinie Manush, George Susce,
　Ben Van Dyke

Seminole County, Orlando Metro
All Souls Cemetery, Sanford
　Tom Delahanty
Evergreen Cemetery, Sanford
　Zinn Beck
Oaklawn Park Cemetery, Sanford
　Ed Chaplin

St. Johns County, Jacksonville Metro
San Lerenzo Cemetery, St. Augustine
　Lyle Judy, Bill Steinecke

St. Lucie County, Fort Pierce–Port St. Lucie Metro
Fort Pierce Cemetery/Riverview Memorial Park, Fort Pierce
　John Milligan, Ray Phelps

Suwanee County
Antioch Baptist Church Cemetery, Live Oak
　Lee Tannehill

Volusia County, Daytona Beach Metro
Bellevue Cedar Hill Memory Gardens, Daytona Beach
　Dick Brown, Bill Burwell, John Campbell, Napoleon Lajoie, Fred Merkle
Hillside Cemetery, Ormond Beach
　Vern Duncan
Oakdale Cemetery, Deland
　Horace Allen, Dave Fultz
Shady Rest Cemetery, Holly Hill
　Larry Cheney

GEORGIA

Banks County
Presbyterian Church Cemetery, Homer
　Lucas Turk

Bartow County
Sunset Memorial Gardens, Cartersville
　Rudy York
White Cemetery, White
　Paul Fittery

Bibb County, Macon Metro
Macon Memorial Park, Macon
　Mack Stewart
Mount Zion Baptist Church Cemetery, Macon
　Doc Bass
Riverside Cemetery, Macon
　King Bailey, Jack Robinson, George Stallings

Butts County
Jackson City Cemetery, Jackson
　Larry Bradford

Calhoun County
Morgan Cemetery, Morgan
　Tom Cheney

Carroll County
Mt. Pleasant Cemetery, Carrollton
　Carl East

Chatham County, Savannah Metro
Bonaventure Cemetery, Savannah
　Harry Hanson, Bobby LaMotte
Catholic Cemetery, Savannah
　Mike Handiboe
Greenwich Cemetery, Savannah
　Ivey Shiver

Clarke County, Athens Metro
Evergreen Memorial Park, Athens
　Bobo Holloman
Oconee Hill Cemetery, Athens
　Nolen Richardson

Clayton County, Atlanta Metro
College Park Memorial Cemetery, College Park
　A.J. Cochran, John Milner, Stretch O'Kelley
Forest Lawn Memorial Gardens, College Park
　Mark Mauldin

Cobb County, Atlanta Metro
Cheatham Hill Memorial Park, Marietta
　Bill Webb
Dawson Cemetery, Kennesaw
　Lew Carpenter
Georgia Memorial Park Cemetery, Marietta
　Tom Lanning

Marietta City Cemetery, Marietta
  Bob Hasty
Norcross Cemetery, Norcross
  Roy Carlyle, Ivey Wingo
Presbyterian Cemetery, Roswell
  Nap Rucker
Riverview Memorial Park, Smyrna
  Tiny Osborne

Columbia County, Augusta–Aiken Metro

Westover Memorial Park, Augusta
  Bill McCorry, Tripp Sigman, Harry
  Smythe

Coweta Conty, Atlanta Metro

Oak Hill Cemetery, Newnan
  Bill Ayers

Dade County

Lake Hills Memorial Gardens, Trenton
  Joe Bokina

Dekalb County, Atlanta Metro

Bethany Baptist Church Cemetery, Decatur
  Tim Bowden
Decatur City Cemetery, Decatur
  Sam Mayer
Resthaven Garden of Memories, Decatur
  Dave Harris, Jim Galvin, Lee Meadows
Stone Mountain Cemetery, Stone Mountain
  Joe Greene

Dougherty County, Albany Metro

Crown Hill Cemetery, Albany
  Alf Anderson, Bill McAfee
Oakview Cemetery, Albany
  Jack Slappey

Douglas County, Atlanta Metro

Douglasville City Cemetery, Douglasville
  Oliver Hill, Camp Skinner
Sunrise Memorial Gardens Cemetery,
Douglasville
  Sam Seagraves

Floyd County

East View Cemetery, Rome
  Kid Long, Willard Nixon
Oaknoll Memorial Gardens, Rome
  Leon Culberson

Forsyth County, Atlanta Metro

Sawnee View Memorial Gardens, Cumming
  Luke Appling

Franklin County

Stevens Family Cemetery, Sandy Cross
  Cy Moore

Fulton County, Atlanta Metro

Arlington Memorial Park, Atlanta
  Leon Williams
Arlington Memorial Park, Sandy Springs
  Red Treadway, Leon Williams
Crest Lawn Memorial Park, Atlanta
  Gabby Kemp, Doc Ozmer, Milt Reed
Greenwood Cemetery, Atlanta
  Johnny Echols, Ray Francis
Lincoln Cemetery, Atlanta
  George Gray, Chico Renfroe, Cornelius
  Scott, Snook Welmaker
Mt. Paran Cemetery, Atlanta
  Hugh Casey
Resthaven Cemetery, Alpharetta
  Phil McCullough
Rucker Family Cemetery, Crabapple
  Johnny Rucker
South-View Cemetery, Atlanta
  Thomas Favors, Alfred Ingram
Westview Cemetery, Atlanta
  Jim Bagby, Jr., Jim Bagby, Sr., Bob
  Barrett, Joe Bean, Ed Crowley, Hack
  Eibel, Paul Gillespie, Roy Massey, Roy
  Moran, Red Smith, Bob Smith, Homer
  Thompson

Glynn County

Christ Church Cemetery, Saint Simons
Island
  Charlie Butler, Tillinghast Huston,
  William O. McGeehan
Palmetto Cemetery, Brunswick
  Bob Gilks

Gwinnett County, Atlanta Metro

Eternal Hills Memory Gardens, Snellville
  Cecil Upshaw
White Rose Cemetery, Duluth
  Charlie Bishop

Habersham County

Clarksville City Cemetery, Clarksville
    Red Barron

Yonah View Memorial Gardens, Demorest
    Johnny Mize

Haralson County

Buchanan City Cemetery, Buchanan
    Whit Wyatt

Hollywood Cemetery, Tallapoosa
    Ralph Head

Hart County

Rosehill Cemetery, Royston
    Ty Cobb, Tinsley Ginn

Heard County

Glenn Cemetery, Glenn
    Walter Wilson

Henry County

Fairview Memorial Gardens, Stockbridge
    Jim Hayes

Houston County

King's Chapel Cemetery, Perry
    Eddie Solomon

Jackson County

Zion Baptist Church Cemetery, Braselton
    Ade White

Jenkins County

Millen Cemetery, Millen
    Jim Busby

Lamar County

Fredonia Congregational Christian Church
Cemetery, Barnesville
    Everett Bankston

Liberty County

Dorchester Cemetery, Dorchester
    Phil Lewis

Lowndes County

Lake Park Cemetery, Lake Park
    Paul Carter

McLane Riverview Memorial Gardens,
Valdosta
    Monroe Mitchell

Macon County

Felton Cemetery, Montezuma
    Jimmy Lavender

Marion County

Tazewell Cemetery, Tazewell
    Brad Hogg

Meriwether County

Woodbury Cemetery, Woodbury
    Dick Niehaus

Muscogee County, Columbus Metro

Parkhill Cemetery, Columbus
    Herb Bremer, Skeeter Newsome, Elmer
    Riddle; Grady Wilson

Polk County

Rose Hill Cemetery, Rockmart
    Bill Calhoun, Harry Dean

Pulaski County

Orange Hill Cemetery, Hawkinsville
    George Winn

Rabun County

Clayton Cemetery, Clayton
    Claud Derrick

Sumter County

Oak Grove Cemetery, Americus
    Jeff McCleskey

Tatnall County

Reidsville City Cemetery, Reidsville
    Paul Easterling

Thomas County

Laurel Hill Cemetery, Thomasville
    Ken Holloway, Charlie Letchas, Dummy
    Murphy

New Bethel Cemetery, Meigs
    Bill Hall

Toobs County

Pinecrest Cemetery, Vidalia
    Wally Moses

Troup County

Restlawn Memory Gardens, LaGrange
    Dernell Stenson

Union County
Union Memory Gardens, Blairsville
    Dale Matthewson

Ware County
Greenlawn Cemetery, Waycross
    Mickey McGowan

Washington County
Baptist Church Cemetery, Harrison
    Phil Bedgood

Wayne County
Odum Cemetery, Odum
    Woody Davis

Whitfield County
Dalton Cemetery-West Hill, Dalton
    Harry Simpson

HAWAII

Honolulu County, Honolulu Metro
Hawaiian Memorial Park, Kaneohe
    Joe DeSa
National Memorial Cemetery of the Pacific,
Honolulu
    Hal Elliott
Oahu Cemetery, Honolulu
    Alexander Joy Cartwright

IDAHO

Ada County, Boise Metro
Morris Hill Cemetery, Boise
    Paul Fitzke, Andy Harrington

Bannock County, Pocatello Metro
Mountain View Cemetery, Pocatello
    Bob Addy

Bingham County
Gibson Mission Cemetery, Blackfoot
    Charlie Roy

Bonner County
Pinecrest Memorial Park, Sandpoint
    Leon Cadore

Fremont County
Riverview Cemetery, St. Anthony
    John Kane

Jerome County
Jerome Cemetery, Jerome
    Chick Fraser

Kootenai County
Forest Cemetery, Coeur D'Alene
    Harry Trekell
St. Thomas Cemetery, Coeur D'Alene
    Bill Burdick

Twin Falls County
Hagerman Cemetery, Hagerman
    Freddy Leach

ILLINOIS

Adams County
Calvary Cemetery, Quincy
    Dutch Kemner, Fritz Ostermueller
Greenmount Cemetery, Quincy
    Luke Lutenberg
Quincy Memorial Park, Quincy
    El Tappe
St. Peter's Cemetery, Quincy
    Jim Finigan

Bureau County
Sheffield Cemetery, Sheffield
    Red Gunkel

Calhoun County
St. Norbett's Catholic Cemetery, Hardin
    Bill McGee

Carroll County
Lanark Cemetery, Lanark
    Jack Warhop

Cass County
Beardstown City Cemetery, Beardstown
    Bill Zies

**Champaign County, Champaign–
Urbana Metro**
Roselawn Cemetery (aka New Mount Hope
Cemetery), Champaign
    George Huff
St. Mary's Cemetery, Champaign
    Big Jeff Pfeffer

Christian County

Calvary Cemetery, Pana
John Dudra

Linwood Cemetery, Pana
Frank Kreeger

Mound Cemetery, Pana
Nin Alexander

Oak Hill Cemetery, Taylorville
Frank Lamanske

Clinton County

Carlyle Cemetery, Carlyle
Patsy McGaffigan, Ray Starr

Kendree Chapel Cemetery, Keyesport
Frank Harter

Coles County

Ashmore Cemetery, Ashmore
Bill Cox

Greasy Point Cemetery, Rardin
Al Shaw

Cook County, Chicago Metro

Acacia Park Cemetery, River Forest
Red Faber, John Hollison, Otto Jacobs,
Bob Meinke, Pat Pieper

All Saints Cemetery, Des Plaines
Harry Carey, John Carmichael, Cozy
Dolan, Paddy Driscoll, Lew Fonseca,
John Godar, Gabby Hartnett, Fred
Lindstrom, Phil Masi, Doug McWeeney,
Tony Murray, Pete O'Brien, Doc Parker,
Fred Pfeffer, John S. Phillips, Lew Post,
Hans Rasmussen, Arch Ward

Assumption Cemetery, Glenwood
Walt Moryn

Bohemian National Cemetery, Chicago
George Caithamer, Larry Hoffman, Pete
Kutina, John Skopec, Frank Smykal

Burr Oak Cemetery, Alsip
Jimmy Crutchfield, Bingo DeMoss,
Wendell Smith, Candy Jim Taylor,
Theodore Trent

Calvary Cemetery, Evanston
Mike Brannock, John Carbine, Charlie
Comiskey, Charles L. Comiskey, Grace
Comiskey, Lou Comiskey, Tom Connelly,
Harry Curtis, Claro Duany, James
Thomas Farrell, Lou Fiene, Pat Flaherty,
Jimmy Hallinan, Mortimer Hogan, Matty
Honan, Tim Manning, Frank Martin,
Gordon McNaughton, Mart McQuaid,
Tom Messitt, Hank O'Day, John Pickett,
Paddy Quinn, Dorothy Comiskey
Rigney, Jimmy Ryan, Edward Santry,
Mort Scanlan, Howard Wakefield

Cedar Park Cemetery, Calumet Park
Don Kolloway, Fred Kommers, Phil
Stremmel

Chapel Hill Gardens South, Oak Lawn
Ira Hutchinson, Ray Poat, Wally Millies,
Larry Strands

Concordia Cemetery, Forest Park
Charlie Getzien, Rudy Kemmler, Herman
Long, Skel Roach

Elmwood Cemetery, River Grove
Nick Polly, Harry Spence

Evergreen Cemetery, Evergreen Park
Paul Masterson, Ray Schalk

Fairmount Willow Hills Park, Worth
Don Hanski, Brick Owens

Forest Home Cemetery, Forest Park
Ed Gastfield, Moxie Hengle, John Otten,
Crazy Schmit, Jack Smith, Billy Sunday,
Bob Wicker

Glen Oak Cemetery, Hillside
Hank Erickson

Graceland Cemetery, Chicago
Bob Caruthers, Fred Cone, Edward
Flynn, Will Foley, Emil Gross, Bucky
Guth, William Hulbert, Walt Kinzie,
Judge McKay, Dutch Meier, John Henry
Pank, Bill Phillips, Hugh Reed, Art
Wilson

Holy Cross Cemetery, Calumet City
Phil Collins, Ted Pawelek

Holy Sepulchre Cemetery, Worth
Joe Benz, Bill Conroy, Leo Dixon, Newt
Fisher, Max Fiske, O. Harness, Jim
Hughes, Charlie Irwin, Tom McGuire,
George McNamara, Tommy Mee, Oscar
Melillo, Tony Mullane, Hal Reilly, Pants
Rowland

Homewood Memorial Gardens, Homewood
Dizzy Trout

Irving Park Cemetery, Chicago
Foster Blackburn, Earl Juul, Earl Pruess

Jewish Waldheim Cemetery, Forest Park
Hub Knolls, George Rooks, George Ziegler

Lincoln Cemetery, Blue Island
George Ball, Rube Foster, Frank Leland, Beauregard Moseley, Jap Payne, Bruce Petway

Memorial Park Cemetery, Evanston
Arthur Allyn, Jr., Arthur Allyn Sr., John Allyn, Harvey Woodruff

Memorial Park Cemetery, Skokie
Leo Fischer, Will Harridge, Art Jorgens, Bill Mueller, Bud Weiland

Memory Gardens Cemetery, Arlington Heights
George Meyer

Montrose Cemetery, Chicago
Virgil Blueitt, Frank Meinke, Chick Pedroes, Bugs Raymond

Mount Carmel Cemetery, Hillside
John Alcock, Lefty Atkinson, Jimmy Corcoran, Harry Croft, Cherokee Fisher, Jack Hendricks, Ed Hughes, Leo Kavanagh, Bill McCabe, Dan O'Leary, Jake Powell, Ken Silvestri, Eddie Stack, Jeff Sweeney

Mount Glenwood South Cemetery, Glenwood
Earl McMillan

Mount Greenwood Cemetery, Chicago
Norm Glockson, Laurie Reis, John Schorling, Ed Taylor

Mount Hope Cemetery, Chicago
Roy Henshaw, Dick Higham, Harry Salisbury, Buck Weaver

Mount Olive Cemetery, Chicago
Jack Farrell, Herb Juul

Mount Olivet Cemetery, Chicago
Dick Attreau, Art Ball, Tony Cusick, Bill Moriarty, Mike Moynahan, Charley O'Leary, Red Torkelson, Bill Webb, Jake Weimer

Mt. Glenwood Cemetery, Glenwood
Joe Barnes, Faye Young

Mt. Glenwood West Cemetery, Willow Springs
Perry Hall

Northshore Gardens of Memories, North Chicago
Bob O'Farrell

Oak Forest Cemetery, Oak Forest
Frank Hemphill

Oak Hill Cemetery, Chicago
Reggie Richter

Oak Woods Cemetery, Chicago
Henry Adkinson, Cap Anson, Jesse Binga, Frank Bishop, Pete Fries, Hek Keough, Ernie Krueger, Kenesaw Mountain Landis, Spike LaRoss, Ed Mars, Louis Rueckheim, Jake Stahl, Tony Suck

Oakridge Cemetery, Hillside
Grover Gilmore, Erv Lange, Ed Merrill, Jimmy Slagle, Tuffy Stewart

Parkholm Cemetery, LaGrange Park
Fred Beebe

Queen of Heaven Cemetery, Hillside
Warren Brown, Dick Drott, Bob Elson, Nick Etten, Johnny Rigney

Restvale Cemetery, Alsip
Sweetwater Clifton, Bobby Robinson

Resurrection Cemetery, Justice
Sig Gryska, Ray Jablonski, Frank Naleway, Johnny Ostrowski, Tony Piet

Ridgelawn Cemetery, Chicago
Milt Galatzer

Ridgewood Cemetery, Des Plaines
Tom Asmussen

Rosehill Cemetery, Chicago
Jack Brickhouse, Harry Buker, Edward Burns, Harry Grabiner, Ed Grimes, Snipe Hansen, Nat Hudson, Leonidas Lee, Bill McClellan, Ned Williamson

Rosemont Park Cemetery, Chicago
Ike Samuels

Shalom Memorial Park, Arlington Heights
Eddie Gold

St. Adalbert's Cemetery, Niles
George Halas, Jake Kafora, Dick Kokos, Bill Lelivelt, Al Piechota

St. Boniface Cemetery, Chicago
Adam DeBus, Emil Geiss, Bill Geiss, Spencer Heath, Mike Hechinger, Jack Kading, Germany Schaefer

St. Joseph Cemetery, River Grove
   Otto Denning, Martin Glendon, Newt
   Halliday, Vedie Himsl, Tom Hughes, Tom
   Kane, Emil Kush

St. Mary's Cemetery, Evergreen Park
   Hank Butcher, Clem Clemens, Eddie
   Gaedel, Edward Geiger, Jim Hackett, Frank
   McCue, George Moriarty, Red Ormsby,
   Jerry Standaert, Jim Stroner, John Sullivan

Westlawn Cemetery, Chicago
   Abe Saperstein

Woodlawn Cemetery, Forest Park
   Erv Dusak, Alfred H. Spink

De Witt County

Woodlawn Cemetery, Clinton
   Doc Marshall

DuPage County, Chicago Metro

Arlington Cemetery, Elmhurst
   Vern Olsen

Bronswood Cemetery, Oak Brook
   Bob Allen, William Veeck, Sr.

Chapel Hill Gardens West, Oakbrook Terrace
   Bill Donovan

Mount Emblem Cemetery, Elmhurst
   Tony Kaufmann, Frank Mack, Jumbo
   Schoeneck, Bob Weiland

SS. Peter & Paul Cemetery, Naperville
   Ken Polivka

Edgar County

St. Mary's Cemetery, Paris
   Tom Sunkel

Franklin County

Boner Cemetery, West Frankfort
   Bennie Tate

Greene County

White Hall Cemetery, White Hall
   Monte McFarland

Grundy County

Polly Wolfe

Hamilton County

IOOF Cemetery, McLeansboro
   Ray Blades

Hancock County

Moss Ridge Cemetery, Carthage
   Rip Williams

**Henry County–Davenport–Moline–
Rock Island**

Dayton Corners Cemetery, Colona
   Baby Doll Jacobson

Oakwood Cemetery, Geneseo
   Jack Wanner

Pleasant View Cemetery, Kewanee
   Tom Drohan

Iroquois County

Calvary Cemetery, Piper City
   Elmer Koestner

Jackson County

Ava Evergreen Cemetery, Ava
   Joe Grace, Andy High

Pleasant Grove Memorial Park, Murphysboro
   Gary Geiger

Jefferson County

Mt. Vernon Memorial Gardens, Mount Vernon
   Jack Warner

Oakwood Cemetery, Mount Vernon
   Jim McLaughlin

Jersey County

Oak Grove Cemetery, Jerseyville
   Ed Baecht, Larry Chappell

Jo Daviess County

Elmwood Cemetery, Warren
   Abner Dalrymple

Kane County, Chicago Metro

Bluff City Cemetery, Elgin
   Ed McDonough, Erwin Renfer

River Hills Memorial Park, Batavia
   Al Corwin

Knox County

Oak Lawn Memorial Gardens, Galesburg
   Evar Swanson

La Salle County

Elerding Cemetery, Sheridan
   Si Johnson

Ottawa Avenue Cemetery, Ottawa
    Charlie Jaeger
Peru City Cemetery, Peru
    Russ Meyer
Restland Cemetery, Mendota
    Deacon White
Riverview Cemetery, Streator
    Wally Roettger

Lake County, Chicago Metro
Ascencion Cemetery, Libertyville
    Johnny Dickshot, Johnny McCarthy

Lee County
Grand Detour Cemetery, Grand Detour
    Stan Hack
Oakwood Cemetery, Dixon
    Lou Bevil, Ward Miller

Livingston County
St. Paul's Cemetery, Odell
    Bud Clancy

Logan County
Atlanta Cemetery, Atlanta
    Lee Dunham
Mount Pulaski Cemetery, Mount Pulaski
    Ray Demmitt
St. Mary's Cemetery, Lincoln
    Emil Verban

Macon County–Decatur Metro
Calvary Cemetery, Decatur
    Bill Mizeur, Al Unser
Fairlawn Cemetery, Decatur
    Beany Jacobson, Walt Meinert, George
    Scharein
Lutheran Cemetery, Decatur
    Boom-Boom Beck
Mount Zion Cemetery, Mount Zion
    Paul Smith

Macoupin County
Ditson Cemetery (aka Stephenson
Cemetery), Girard
    Del Paddock
Union Miners Cemetery, Mount Olive
    Mike Kreevich

Madison County
Buck Road Cemetery, Glen Carbon
    Johnny Lucas
Frieden's Evangelical Church Cemetery,
Troy
    Roy Lee
Glenwood Cemetery, Collinsville
    Art Fletcher
Marine City Cemetery, Marine
    Russ Pence
St. John's Evangelical Cemetery, Troy
    Frank Whitman
Sunset Hill Memorial Estates, Edwardsville
    John Bischoff

Marion County
Peaceful Valley Cemetery, Odin
    Grover Lowdermilk
Summit Prarie Cemetery, Salem
    Lou Lowdermilk

Marshall County
Lacon Cemetery, Lacon
    Bob Barnes

Mason County
Laurel Hill Cemetery, Havana
    Fred Beck, Franklin Donnelly

McHenry County, Chicago Metro
Marengo City Cemetery, Marengo
    Carl Lundgren
St. Mary's Catholic Cemetery, Huntley
    Johnny Klippstein

**McLean County–Bloomington–
Normal Metro**
Evergreen Memorial Cemetery, Bloomington
    George Radbourne, Hoss Radbourne
St. Mary's Cemetery, Bloomington
    Ed Kinsella

Mercer County
Aledo Cemetery, Aledo
    James McDougal
St. John's Cemetery, Viola
    Luke Nelson

Monroe County

Waterloo City Cemetery, Waterloo
  Will Koenigsmark

Montgomery County

Calvary Cemetery, Witt
  Paul Chervinko

Fillmore Glendale Cemetery, Fillmore
  Ray Richmond

Nokomis Cemetery, Nokomis
  Andy Bednar

Ogle County, Rockford Metro

Byron Cemetery, Byron
  Gat Stires

Oakwood Cemetery, Mount Morris
  Nels Potter

River View Cemetery, Oregon
  Fred Roat

Stillman Valley Cemetery, Stillman Valley
  George Bird

Peoria County, Peoria–Pekin Metro

Chillicothe City Cemetery, Chillicothe
  Bill Kreig

Parkview Cemetery, Peoria
  Harry Bay, Hod Leverette, Hal Smith

Springdale Cemetery, Peoria
  Charlie Bartson, Ben Caffyn, Norwood
  Gibson, Bill Jackson, George Pinckney,
  Steel Arm Taylor

St. Joseph Cemetery, West Peoria
  Jim Bluejacket

St. Mary's Cemetery, Peoria
  John Roach

Perry County

Sunset Memorial Park, DuQuoin
  Ewald Pyle

Pike County

Crescent Heights Cemetery, Pleasant Hills
  Dave Alitzer

Randolph County

Caledonia Cemetery, Sparta
  Earle Gardner

Coulterville Cemetery, Coulterville
  Nick Kahl

Oakridge Cemetery, New Athens
  Warren Hacker, Mickey Haefner

St. Mary's Help of Christians Catholic
Cemetery, Chester
  Roger Wolff

**Rock Island County–Davenport–Moline–
Rock Island**

Calvary Cemetery, Rock Island
  Harry Sage, Tom Sexton

Greenview Memorial Gardens, East Moline
  George Magerkurth

Memorial Park Cemetery, Rock Island
  Joe Berger, Herb Crompton

Riverside Cemetery, Moline
  Warren Giles, Oscar Graham,
  Karl Swanson

Rock Island National Cemetery,
Rock Island
  Gene Baker, Louis Kolls, Jeff Pfeffer

Saline County

Wolf Creek Cemetery, Eldorado
  Joel Newkirk

Sangamon County, Springfield Metro

Auburn Cemetery, Auburn
  Donald L. Barnes, Dutch Leonard

Brittin Cemetery, Sherman
  Jack Brittin

Brush Creek Cemetery, Divernon
  Al Papai

Calvary Cemetery, Springfield
  Joe Bernard, Bob Kinsella, Pat Wright

Camp Butler National Cemetery,
Springfield
  Jim Hamby, Josh Johnson

Oak Ridge Cemetery, Springfield
  Fred Donovan

Schuyler County

Rushville Cemetery, Rushville
  Earl Tyree

Shelby County

Myers Cemetery, Herrick
  Joe Adams

St. Clair County, St. Louis Metro

Holy Cross Lutheran Cemetery, Collinsville
    Terry Moore

Lake View Memorial Gardens, Belleville
    Dutch Hoffman, Rolly Latina, Johnny
    Wyrostek

Mount Carmel Cemetery, Belleville
    Steve Biras, Jerry Kane

O'Fallon City Cemetery, O'Fallon
    Ed Busch

St. Joseph Cemetery, Dupo
    Ed Albrecht

Sunset Gardens of Memory, Millstadt
    Lee Moody

Valhalla Gardens of Memory, Belleville
    Al Glossop, Bill Walker

Walnut Hill Cemetery, Belleville
    Jess Doyle, Max Flack, Bob Groom, Otto
    Miller, Ham Patterson, George Starnagle

Stark County

Toulon Municipal Cemetery, Toulon
    Charlie Hall

Jefferson County, Birmingham Metro

Chapel Hill Memorial Park, Freeport
    Clyde Southwick

County Home Cemetery, Freeport
    Frank Harris

Wabash County

Highland Memorial Gardens, Mt. Carmel
    Don Liddle, Cy Warmoth

Warren County

Monmouth Municipal Cemetery,
Monmouth,IL
    Charles Dryden

Wayne County

Maple Hill Cemetery, Fairfield
    Bill Trotter

White County

Odd Fellows Cemetery, Norris City
    Lew Brockett

Whiteside County

Calvary Cemetery, Sterling
    Gus Williams

Will County, Chicago Metro

Abraham Lincoln National Cemetery, Elwood
    Woody Brewer, Maurice Wiggins

Elmhurst Cremetery, Joliet
    Sweetbreads Bailey

Mount Olivet Cemetery, Joliet
    Ed Lagger

Plainfield Cemetery, Plainfield
    George Pierce

Pleasant Hill Cemetery, Frankfort
    Lou Boudreau

South Lockport Cemetery, Lockport
    Jim Donahue

St. John the Baptist Cemetery, Joliet
    Jack Himes, Ed Murphy

St. Patrick's Cemetery, Joliet
    Bobby Burke, Bill Moran

Trinity Lutheran Cemetery, Crete
    Rube Ehrhardt

Williamson County

Herrin City Cemetery, Herrin
    Dallas Bradshaw

Lake View Cemetery, Johnston City
    Hank Keupper

Winnebago County, Rockford Metro

Arlington Memorial Park, Rockford
    Hal Carlson

Greenwood Cemetery, Rockford
    Ross Barnes, Charlie Sproull

St. Mary/St. James Cemetery, Rockford
    Mike Golden, Thomas Griffen, Harry
    Sullivan

Sunset Memorial Gardens, Machesney Park
    Dorothy Ferguson Key

Watson Cemetery, Pecatonica
    Andrew Thompson

Willwood Burial Park, Rockford
    Varney Anderson

INDIANA

Allen County–Fort Wayne Metro

Catholic Cemetery, Fort Wayne
    Fred Alberts, Tom McCarthy, Ralph
    Miller, Lou Nagelsen, Rabbit Nill, Tom

O'Meara, Carl Vandagrift

Concordia Cemetery, Fort Wayne
Bill Brandt

Covington Memorial Gardens, Fort Wayne
Bill Chambers

Greenlawn Memorial Park, Fort Wayne
Bill Cramer, Pinky Hargrave, Hub Hart,
Andy Woehr

Lindenwood Cemetery, Fort Wayne
Louis Heilbrunner, Sal Madrid, Chick
Stahl, Dick West

Cass County

Mt. Hope Cemetery, Logansport
Red Corriden, Al Scheer

Clark County, Louisville Metro

Pleasant Ridge Cemetery, Borden
Jim Porter

Walnut Ridge Cemetery, Jeffersonville
Red Fisher, Frank Friend

Clinton County, Lafayette Metro

Bunnell Cemetery, Frankfort
Elmer Johnson

DeKalb County, Fort Wayne Metro

Woodlawn Cemetery, Auburn
Rollie Zeider

Dearborn County, Cincinnati Metro

Greendale Cemetery, Lawrenceburg
Kirtley Baker, George Boehler, Walt Justis

Decatur County

Kingston Cemetery, Kingston
Cy Bowen

South Park Cemetery, Greensburg
Bob Wright

Delaware County

Beech Grove Cemetery, Muncie
Charlie Knepper

Elm Ridge Cemetery, Muncie
Buck Crouse

DuBois County

Fairmount Cemetery, Huntingburg
Ray Blemker

Shiloh Cemetery, Jasper
Bob Friedrich

Elkhart County, South Bend Metro

Rice Cemetery, Elkhart
Nig Cuppy, Pat Paige

Violette Cemetery, Goshen
Speed Kelly, Mike Knode

Floyd County, Louisville Metro

Fairview Cemetery, New Albany
Jouett Meekin

Kraft-Graceland Memorial Park, New
Albany
Wayne LeMaster

Franklin County

Maple Grove Cemetery, Brookville
Fred Miller

Fulton County

Lutheran Cemetery, Pershing
Glenn Chapman

Gibson County

Montgomery Cemetery, Oakland City
Edd Roush

Warnock Cemetery, Princeton
Al Mauck

Grant County

Grant Memorial Park, Marion
Art Herring

Riverside Cemetery, Gas City
Walt Miller

Greene County

Prairie Chapel Cemetery, Lyons
Stump Edington

Hamilton County, Indianapolis Metro

Oaklawn Memorial Gardens, Fishers
Johnny Riddle

Westfield Cemetery, Westfield
Ray Boyd

Harrison County, Louisville Metro

Cedar Hill Cemetery, Corydon
Pinky May, Roscoe Miller

Hendricks County, Indianapolis Metro

Maple Hill Cemetery, Plainfield
  Lyman Drake

Henry County

New Lisbon Cemetery, New Lisbon
  Jot Goar

Jefferson County

Springdale Cemetery, Madison
  Tommy Thevenow

St. Patrick's Cemetery, Madison
  Dutch Distel

Jennings County

Hayden Cemetery, Hayden
  Rolla Daringer

Hillcrest Cemetery, North Vernon
  Forrest More

Johnson County, Indianapolis Metro

Forest Lawn Memorial Gardens, Greenwood
  Oral Hildebrand

Greenwood Cemetery, Greenwood
  Elmer Brown

Knox County

Fairview Cemetery, Vincennes
  Ollie Pickering

Hamline Chapel Cemetery, Monroe City
  Prentice Byrd

Mount Calvary Cemetery, Vincennes
  Joe Wyatt

Lake County, Gary Metro

Calumet Park Cemetery & Mausoleum,
Merrillville
  Charles O. Finley

Maplewood Cemetery, Crown Point
  Pete Henning

Ridgelawn-Mount Mercy Cemetery, Gary
  Johnny Mostil

Lawrence County

Cresthaven Memory Gardens, Bedford
  Yank Terry

Green Hill Cemetery, Bedford
  Bill Rariden, Ben Taylor

Madison County, Indianapolis Metro

East Maplewood Cemetery, Anderson
  Eli Cates, Tom Fisher, Peaches O'Neill

Marion County, Indianapolis Metro

Crown Hill Cemetery, Indianapolis
  Thomas Bowser, Tiny Baldwin,
  Paddy Baumann, Junious Bibbs, John J.
  Brush, Charlie Carr, Bennie Charleston,
  Rex Dawson, Harry Deane, Hod Eller,
  Harry Geisel, Charlie Gray, John Grim,
  Harry Hempstead, Carmen Hill, Warner
  Jewell, Al McCauley, Willie McGill,
  Patrick Murphy, Doc Newton, Ducky
  Pearce, Toad Ramsey, Bill Sowders,
  John Sowders, Len Sowders, C.I. Taylor,
  Harry Weber, Bill Whaley, Charlie
  Whitehouse

Floral Park Cemetery, Indianapolis
  Oscar Charleston, George Orme, Peek-a-
  Boo Veach, Jack White

Holy Cross Cemetery, Indianapolis
  Donie Bush, Phil Coridan, Pete Daniels,
  Biddy Dolan, Jim Duggan, Mike Heydon,
  Johnny Hutchings, Mike Kelly, Chuck
  Klein, Bill Owens, Duke Reilley, Hank
  Schreiber

Memorial Park Cemetery, Indianapolis
  Bill Andrews, Fred Eichrodt

New Crown Cemetery, Indianapolis
  Hiawatha Shelby

Oaklawn Memorial Gardens, Indianapolis
  Bob Logan

St. Joseph's Cemetery, Indianapolis
  Dom Dellessandro, Reb Russell

Washington Park East Cemetery,
Indianapolis
  John Corriden, Charlie French

Marshall County

Argos Maple Grove Cemetery, Argos
  Jim Middleton

Martin County

Emmons Ridge Cemetery, Hilham
  William Hueston

New Trinity Cemetery, Trinity Springs
  Vic Aldridge

Miami County

St. Charles Catholic Cemetery, Peru
Al Bergman

Monroe County, Bloomington Metro

Rosehill Cemetery, Bloomington
Rabbit Shively

Montgomery County

Ladoga Cemetery, Ladoga
Ed Summers

Noble County

Oak Park Cemetery, Ligionier
Bert Inks

Ohio County, Cincinnati Metro

Rising Sun New Cemetery, Rising Sun
Clarence Woods

Orange County

Mount Lebanon Cemetery, French Lick
Charlie Biggs

Stampers Creek Cemetery, Paoli
Ken Trinkle

Owen County

Riverside Cemetery, Spencer
Ban Johnson

Porter County

Calvary Cemetery, Portage
Billy Holm

St. Paul Lutheran Church Cemetery, Kouts
Stew Hofferth

Putnam County

Forest Hill Cemetery, Greencastle
Ed Eiteljorge

Randolph County

Fountain Park Cemetery, Winchester
Troy Puckett

Ripley County

Greendale Cemetery, Osgood
Bill Richardson

St Joseph County, South Bend Metro

Cedar Grove Cemetery, South Bend
Harry Arndt

Highland Cemetery, South Bend
Ben Koehler, Del Wertz

Riverview Cemetery, South Bend
George Beck, Scoby Robinson, Ray
Shook, Buzzy Wares

St. Joseph Cemetery, South Bend
Stan Coveleski, Ed Hanyzewski,
Ollie Bejma

Steuben County

Hamilton Cemetery, Hamilton
Frank Oberlin

Metz Cemetery, Metz
Jock Somerlott

Sullivan County

Mt. Zion Cemetery, Sullivan
Hosea Siner

Tippecanoe County, Lafayette Metro

Grand View Cemetery, West Lafayette
Hugh Nicol

St. Boniface Cemetery, Lafayette
Walt Tragresser

St. Mary's Cemetery, Lafayette
Mike Kosman

**Vandenburgh County, Evansville–
Henderson Metro**

Alexander Memorial Park, Evansville
Walter Dilbeck

Locust Hill Cemetery, Evansville
Buster Bray, Punch Knoll, Syl Simon

Oak Hill Cemetery, Evansville
Al Schellhase, Charlie Wacker

St. Joseph Cemetery, Evansville
Bob Coleman

Sunset Memorial Gardens, Evansville
Lefty Wallace

Vigo County, Terre Haute Metro

Calvary Cemetery, Terre Haute
Johnny Mann

Highland Lawn Cemetery, Terre Haute
Bruce Connatser, Harry Glenn, Al Myers,
Ace Stewart

Roselawn Memorial Park, Terre Haute
Emil Bildilli, Three Finger Brown, Bill
Butland, Jumbo Elliott

Shepherd's Cemetery, Sheperdsville
  Harry Taylor
St. Joseph's Cemetery, Terre Haute
  Bill Nelson

Wabash County
Falls Cemetery, Wabash
  George Mullin

Washington County
Crown Hill Cemetery, Salem
  Ovid Nicholson

Wayne County
Earlham Cemetery, Richmond
  Claude Berry, Dick Van Zant
Lutherania Cemetery, Richmond
  Charles Weeghman

Wells County
Elm Grove Cemetery, Bluffton
  Everett Scott
Hoverstock Cemetery, Zanesville
  Bill Prough

IOWA

Benton County
St. Michael's Cemetery, Norway
  Hal Trosky

Black Hawk County, Waterloo Metro
Calvary Cemetery, Waterloo
  Bill Wagner

Boone County
Mount Hope Cemetery, Mardrid
  Jim Grant
Sacred Heart Cemetery, Boone
  Jimmy Archer

Buena Vista County
Barnes Township Cemetery, Linn Grove
  Wattie Holm
Buena Vista Cemetery, Storm Lake
  Joe Decker

Cass County
Brighton Cemetery, Marne
  Gil Paulsen

Cherokee County
Mount Calvary Cemetery, Cherokee
  Steve Melter

Chickasaw County
New Hampton City Cemetery,
New Hampton
  Duane Josephson

Clay County
Riverside Cemetery, Spencer
  Babe Towne

Dallas County, Des Moines Metro
Violet Hill Cemetery, Perry
  George Tomer

Des Moines County
Aspen Grove Cemetery, Burlington
  George Stovall, George Zackert

Dickinson County
Lake View Cemetery, Spirit Lake
  Charlie Uhlir
Lakeland Memory Gardens, Spirit Lake
  Vern Fear

Dubuque County, Dubuque Metro
Linwood Cemetery, Dubuque
  Charlie Buelow
Mount Olivet Cemetery, Dubuque
  Ed Keas, Tom Loftus, Tom Ryder

Floyd County
Calvary Cemetery, Charles City
  Vive Lindaman

Franklin County
Hampton Cemetery, Hampton
  Joe Jaeger

Hardin County
Alden Cemetery, Alden
  Charlie Frisbee
Oakwood Cemetery, Ackley
  Art Reinhart

Iowa County
Middle Amana Cemetery, Middle Amana
  Bill Zuber

Johnson County

Memory Gardens Cemetery, Iowa City
  Otto Vogel

Jones County

Mayflower Cemetery, Oxford Junction
  Joe Hovlik

Wyoming Cemetery, Wyoming
  Dutch Levsen

Kossuth County

Riverview Cemetery, Algona
  Jesse Duryea

Lee County

Greenglade Cemetery, Farmington
  Jack Saltzgaver

St. Peter's Catholic Church Cemetery,
Keokuk
  Ralph Bell

Linn County, Cedar Rapis Metro

Cedar Memorial Park Cemetery, Cedar
Rapids
  Orie Arntzen, Cy Slapnicka, Earl
  Whitehill

Linwood Cemetery, Cedar Rapids
  Bill Hoffer, Roy Radebaugh, Paul Speraw

Mt. Calvary Cemetery, Cedar Rapids
  Mike Chartak

Oak Hill Cemetery, Cedar Rapids
  Belden Hill

Madison County

Hartman Cemetery, Truro
  Ducky Holmes

Mahaska County

Forest Cemetery, Oskaloosa
  Cliff Knox

Marshall County

Riverside Cemetery, Marshalltown
  James C. Dunn, Julius Willigrod

Monona County

Graceland Cemetery, Onawa
  Tom Richardson

Onawa Cemetery, Onawa
  Buster Brown

Montgomery County

Villisca Cemetery, Villisca
  Lynn King

Plymouth County

St. Mary's Catholic Cemetery, Remsen
  Johnny Niggeling

Polk County, Des Moines Metro

Glendale Cemetery, Des Moines
  Charlie Dexter, Art Ewoldt, Jesse
  Hoffmeister, Adrian Lynch, Bill Traffley

Pine Hill Cemetery, Des Moines
  Ed Hahn

Woodland/St. Ambrose Cemetery,
Des Moines
  Pat Donahue

Pottawattamie County, Omaha Metro

Cedar Lawn Cemetery, Council Bluffs
  Hal McKain

Neola Township Cemetery, Neola
  Red Downs

Sac County

Oakland Cemetery, Sac City
  Paul Zahniser

**Scott County, Davenport-Moline-
Rock Island**

Fairmont Cemetery, Davenport
  Lefty Lorenzen

Mount Calvary Cemetery, Davenport
  Al Van Camp, Tom Walsh

Tama County

Woodlawn Cemetery, Toledo
  King Cole

Van Buren County

Dibble Cemetery, Stockport
  Al Lawson

Webster County

Corpus Christi Cemetery, Fort Dodge
  Gene Ford, Jimmie Long

Winneshiek County

Decorah Lutheran Cemetery, Decorah
  Ossie Orwoll

Woodbury County, Sioux City Metro

Calvary Cemetery, Sioux City
  Biggs Wehde

Graceland Cemetery, Sioux City
  Bob Black, George Clark

Memorial Park Cemetery, Sioux City
  Red Anderson

Wright County

Clarion City Cemetery, Clarion
  Roy Wilson

KANSAS

Allen County

Moran Cemetery, Moran
  Otis Lambeth

Barber County

Riverview Cemetery, Kiowa
  Willie Ramsdell

Bourbon County

Evergreen Cemetery, Fort Scott
  Frank Hansford, Lon Ury

Butler County

Douglass Cemetery, Douglass
  Jimmy Durham

Cherokee County

Columbus City Cemetery, Columbus
  Raleigh Aitchison

Clay County

Greenwood Cemetery, Clay Center
  Herb Bradley

Cloud County

Mount Hope Cemetery, Clyde
  George Dockins

Coffey County

Le Roy Cemetery, Le Roy
  Lore Bader

Cowley County

Cambridge Cemetery, Cambridge
  Clay Smith

Ninnescah Cemetery, Udall
  Nick Allen

Riverview Cemetery, Arkansas City
  Claire Patterson

St. Mary's Cemetery, Winfield
  Fred Clarke

Crawford County

St. Mary's Cemetery, Pittsburg
  Pete Kilduff

Dickinson County

Abilene Cemetery, Abilene
  Kite Thomas

Doniphan County

Highland Cemetery, Highland
  John Misse

Douglas County, Lawrence Metro

Baldwin City Cemetery, Baldwin City
  Dummy Taylor

Oak Hill Cemetery, Lawrence
  Bob Edmundson

Franklin County

St. Patrick's Cemetery, Williamsburg
  Lou McEvoy

Greenwood County

Twin Grove Cemetery, Severy
  Spades Wood

Jackson County

Holton Cemetery, Holton
  Virgil Barnes

Jefferson County

LeRoy Cemetery, Oskaloosa
  Deacon Jones

Johnson County, Kansas City Metro

Resurrection Cemetery, Lenexa
  Joe Bowman, Joe Burke

Spring Hill Cemetery, Spring Hill
  Charles Brown

Labette County

Memorial Lawn Cemetery, Parsons
  Gil Britton

Oakwood Cemetery, Parsons
    Harry Maupin

Leavenworth County, Kansas City Metro

Fort Leavenwoth National Cemetery,
Fort Leavenworth
    Hank Baylis, Lester Phiffer, Harlen
    Ragland, Jaybird Ray

Leavenworth National Cemetery,
Leavenworth
    Lefty Bryant, Eldridge Mayweather,
    Johnny O'Connor, Hal Quick

Mount Muncie Cemetery, Lansing
    Mike Welday

Sunset Memory Gardens, Leavenworth
    Murry Dickson

McPherson County

Elmwood Cemetery, Lindsborg
    Del Lundgren

McPherson Cemetery, McPherson
    Harry Chapman

Montgomery County

Caney Sunnyside Cemetery, Caney
    Charlie Rhodes

Ottawa County

Highland Cemetery, Minneapolis
    Archie McKain

Pottawatomie County

Louisville Cemetery, Louisville
    Wiley Taylor

Mount Calvary Cemetery, St. Mary's
    Frank Bushey

Rice County

Sterling Community Cemetery, Sterling
    Art Evans

Riley County

Sunrise Cemetery, Manhattan
    George Giles

Saline County

Assaria Cemetery, Assaria
    Rube Suter

Gypsum Hill Cemetery, Salina
    Randolph Prim

Roselawn Cemetery, Salina
    Bob Swift

Sedgwick County, Wichita Metro

Benton Cemetery, Benton
    Ralph Winegarner

Clearwater Cemetery, Clearwater
    Lloyd Bishop

Lake View Cemetery, Wichita
    Lu Clinton

Maple Grove Cemetery, Wichita
    Ike McAuley

Old Mission Cemetery, Wichita
    Fred Brickell, Frank Isball, Tex Jones,
    Red Phillips

Pleasant Valley Cemetery, Bentley
    Bull Durham

Resthaven Gardens of Memory, Wichita
    Rufus Meadows

White Chapel Cemetery, Wichita
    Pat Hardgrove

Wichita Park Cemetery, Wichita
    Tom Angley, Gus Hetling

Shawnee County, Topeka Metro

Memorial Park Cemetery, Topeka
    Charlie Bates, Steve Simpson

Mount Hope Cemetery, Topeka
    Dale Gear

Topeka Cemetery, Topeka
    Guy McFadden, Butch Nieman, Ray Pierce

Sumner County

Caldwell Cemetery, Caldwell
    Ed Willett

Wilson County

Altoona Cemetery, Altoona
    Ike Kahdot

Buffalo Cemetery, Buffalo
    Claude Willoughby

Wyandotte County, Kansas City Metro

Highland Park Cemetery, Kansas City
    Hurley McNair

Maple Hill Cemetery, Kansas City
    Bob Grim

Memorial Park Cemetery, Kansas City
    Pat Collins, Roy Meeker
Mount Calvary Cemetery, Kansas City
    Joe Ellick, Paul O'Boynick

KENTUCKY

Adair County
Columbia Cemetery, Columbia
    Cy Barger

Boone County, Cincinnati Metro
Burlington Cemetery, Burlington
    Jim McGlothlin

Bourbon County, Lexington Metro
North Middletown Cemetery, North
Middletown
    Vic Bradford
Paris Cemetery, Paris
    Dick Butler

Boyd County, Huntington–Ashland Metro
Catlettsburg Cemetery, Catlettsburg
    Fred Frank

Bracken County
Heck's Cemetery, Augusta
    Wiley Piatt

Campbell County, Cincinnati Metro
Evergreen Cemetery, Southgate
    Still Bill Hill, Alamazoo Jennings, Bill
    Kisinger, Pop Schwartz, Jesse Tannehill
St. Joseph Cemetery, Newport
    Hank Gastright, Ed Glenn, Reddy Mack
St. Stephen's Cemetery, Fort Thomas
    Ray Kolp, Red Lutz, Chick Smith, Jack
    Thoney

Carlisle County
Roselawn Cemetery, Bardwell
    Vern Curtis

**Christian County, Clarksville–
Hopkinsville Metro**
Powell Cemetery, LaFayette
    Erv Brame

Crittenden County
Mapleview Cemetery, Marion
    Rip Wheeler

Daviess County, Ownesboro Metro
Rose Hill Cemetery, Owensboro
    Johnny Morrison, Phil Morrison

Fayette County, Lexington Metro
Lexington Cemetery, Lexington
    Ted Conover, Jim Park, Ted Turner

Franklin County
Frankfort Cemetery, Frankfort
    Dick Crutcher
Peak's Mill Cemetery, Frankfort
    Eddie Bacon

Fulton County
Greenlea Cemetery, Fulton
    Mel Simons

Graves County
Maplewood Cemetery, Mayfield
    Buster Ross

**Greenup County, Huntington–
Ashland Metro**
Bellefonte Memorial Gardens, Flatwoods
    Dykes Potter, Squire Potter

Harrison County
Battle Grove Cemetery, Cynthiana
    Harvey McClellan, Stan Rees

Hart County
Horse Cave Cemetery, Horse Cave
    Charley Moran

Henry County
Eminence Cemetery, Eminence
    Johnny Marcum

Jefferson County, Louisville Metro
Calvary Cemetery, Louisville
    Jack Bellman, Rudy Hulswitt, Bill
    Ludwig, John McCloskey, Ed Monroe,
    Peter O'Donnell, Rudy Sommers,
    Gus Weyhing

Cave Hill Cemetery, Louisville
  George Boone, Pete Browning, Harry
  Camnitz, Howie Camnitz, Monk Cline,
  Billy Clingman, Hub Collins, Mordecai
  Davidson, John Dodge, Fred Drexler,
  Dean Eagle, Irv Hach, John Haldeman,
  Walter Haldeman, John A. Hillerick, Jr.,
  John A. Hillerich, Sr., Ward Hillerich,
  Dixie Howell, William Jackson, Jack
  Kerins, Fred Koster, Bob Langsford,
  William Lyons, Frank Pearce, Zach
  Phelps, Harry Pulliam, John Reccius,
  Phil Reccius, Nick Reeder, Charlie
  Reising, George Ruckstuhl, Rudy
  Schwenck, Lev Shreve, Thomas Stucky,
  Chicken Wolf

Eastern Cemetery, Louisville
  Hercules Burnett, Mike Jacobs, Ira
  Mobley, Skipper Snow, John Weyhing

Eastwood Cemetery, Eastwood
  Frank Pearce

Evergreen Cemetery, Louisville
  Arnold Carter, Roy Henry, Irv Jeffries,
  Mahlon Higbee

Louisville Memorial Gardens, Louisville
  Roy Sanders

Portland Cemetery, Louisville
  Burley Byers, George Stultz

Resthaven Memorial Park, Louisville
  Woody Abernathy, Roy Bruner, Milt
  Gray, Jim Long, Max Macon, Pee Wee
  Reese

St. John's Cemetery, Louisville
  Dan Sweeney, Tom Terrell

St. Louis Cemetery, Louisville
  Mike Barry, John Dyler, Larry Gatto, Jack
  Heinzman, Frederick Hillerich, Tom
  Long, Doc Powers, John Richter, Mike
  Walsh, George Wentz, Fred Zahner

St. Michael's Cemetery, Louisville
  Tom Mclaughlin, John Russ, George
  Yantz

Zachary Taylor National Cemetery, Louisville
  Dick Durning

Kenton County, Cincinnati Metro

Forest Lawn Memorial Park, Erlanger
  Jim Viox, Jim Weaver

Highland Cemetery, Fort Mitchell
  Ed Hohnhorst, Joe Sommer, Dale
  Williams

Linden Grove Cemetery, Covington
  Mox McQuery, John Shoupe

St. Mary's Cemetery, Fort Mitchell
  Neal Brady, Bob Clark, Joe Heving

Laurel County

A.R. Dyche Memorial Cemetery, London
  Jim Jones

Logan County

Auburn Cemetery, Auburn
  Fin Wilson

Greenwood Cemetery, Adairville
  Bert James

Madison County, Lexington Metro

Richmond Cemetery, Richmond
  Earle Combs

McCracken County

Maplelawn Park Cemetery, Paducah
  Pat McGehee

Mt. Carmel Cemetery, Paducah
  Ed Holley

Oak Grove Cemetery, Paducah
  Irvin Cobb

Meade County

Cap Anderson Cemetery, Brandenburg
  Charles Blackwell

Montgomery County

Machpelah Cemetery, Mount Sterling
  Tom Grubbs

Oldham County, Louisville Metro

Floydsburg Cemetery, Crestwood
  Alex McFarlan, Mike Powers

Pendleton County

Riverside Cemetery, Falmouth
  Roberts, Harry

Pulaski County

Somerset Cemetery, Somerset
  Doc Sechrist

Rowan County

Forest Lawn Memorial Gardens, Morehead
  Steve Hamilton

Shelby County

Flat Rock Cemetery, Shelby County
  Dan McFarlan
Grove Hill Cemetery, Shelbyville
  Dan McGann

Spencer County

Valley Cemetery, Taylorsville
  Scott Stratton

Todd County

Highland Cemetery, Guthrie
  Kent Greenfield, Hugh Poland

Union County

St. Ann Cemetery, Morganfield
  Ed Johnson

Warren County

Fairview Cemetery, Bowling Green
  Fred Blackwell

Woodford County, Lexington Metro

Pisgah Presbyterian Church Cemetery, Pisgah
  Happy Chandler

LOUISIANA

Avoyelles Parish

Pythian Cemetery, Bunkie
  Hal Wiltse

Bienville Parish

Arcadia Cemetery, Arcadia
  Pol Perritt

Bossier Parish, Shreveport–Bossier City Metro

Calvary Missionary Baptist Church Cemetery, Benton
  Riley Stewart

Caddo Parish, Shreveport–Bossier City Metro

Forest Park Cemetery, Shreveport
  Al Baird, Bill Massey, Walter Stephenson, Pat Tobin, John Vann

Greenwood Cemetery, Shreveport
  Bill Fincher, John Mercer

Calcasieu Parish, Lake Charles Metro

Big Woods Cemetery, Vinton
  Ted Lyons
Graceland Cemetery, Lake Charles
  Johnny Berger

Claiborne Parish

Arlington Cemetery, Homer
  Orie Kerlin, Mule Watson
Rocky Springs Cemetery, Lisbon
  Rebel Oakes

East Baton Rouge Parish, Baton Rouge Metro

Greenoaks Memorial Park, Baton Rouge
  Walker Cress, Buddy Myer, Larry Pezold
Port Hudson National Cemetery, Zachary
  Lefty Gaines
Resthaven Gardens of Memory, Baton Rouge
  George Washburn
Roselawn Memorial Park, Baton Rouge
  Roland Howell, Rudy Leopold
Southern Memorial Gardens, Baton Rouge
  Hickey Redd

Iberia Parish

McGowen Memorial Cemetery, Jeanerette
  Harvey Green

Iberville Parish

Grace Memorial Park, Plaquemine, LA.
Cremated, Baton Rouge, LA.
  Jim Holloway
Protestant Cemetery, Plaquemine
  Big Bill Lee

Jefferson Parish, New Orleans Metro

Garden of Memories, Metairie
  Rube Kroh, Mike Miley, Ed Morgan, George Stumpf, Roy Walker, Orlie Weaver
Providence Memorial Park, Metairie
  Bob Bissant

Lafayette Parish, Lafayette Metro

Presbyterian Cemetery, Lafayette
  Tony DeFate

Lincoln Parish

Greenwood Cemetery, Ruston
 Johnny Jones

Orleans Parish, New Orleans Metro

Carrollton Cemetery, New Orleans
 Tex Hoffman, Joseph Wiley

Greenwood Cemetery, New Orleans
 Hal Bevan, Jimmy Dygert, Oscar Georgy,
 Larry Gilbert, Al Jurisich, Jack Kramer,
 Oyster Joe Martina, Leo Moon

Lake Lawn Cemetery, New Orleans
 Larry Bettencourt, Fats Dantonio, Charlie
 Gilbert, Tookie Gilbert, Andy Pilney

Masonic Cemetery, New Orleans
 Lou Legett

McDonoghville Cemetery, Gretna
 J.B. Spencer

Metairie Cemetery, Metairie
 Zeke Bonura, Count Campau, Al Flair,
 John Humphries, Mel Ott, Johnny
 Oulliber, Connie Ryan, Lefty Wolf, Doc
 Wood, Jimmy Woulfe, Ray Yochim

Mount Olivet Cemetery, New Orleans
 Bobby Roth, George Sias

St. John's Cemetery, New Orleans
 Jake Atz, Ted Jourdan, Carl Lind, Bill
 Perrin, Cy Pfirman, Ab Powell

St. Joseph Cemetery #2, New Orleans
 Dick Robertson

St. Joseph Cemetery #3, New Orleans
 Lou Klein, Tom Reilly, Paul Sentell,
 Aaron Ward

St. Vincent de Paul Cemetery, New Orleans
 Joe Dowie

Valence Street Cemetery, New Orleans
 John Peltz, Frederick Smith

Ouachita Parish, Monroe Metro

Monroe City Cemetery, Monroe
 Lou Jackson

Riverview Burial Park, Monroe
 Bob Harmon

Sardis Cemetery, West Monroe
 Ed Head

Red River Parish

Mount Zion Cemetery, Hall Summit
 Clint Courtney

Holly Springs Cemetery, Martin
 Joe Adcock

St. Charles Parish, New Orleans Metro

Jefferson Memorial Gardens, Saint Rose
 Curtis Johnson

St. Helena Parish

Greensburg Cemetery, Greensburg
 Jim Lindsay

St. Landry Parish, Lafayette Metro

Myrtle Grove Cemetery, Opelousas
 Al Nixon

St. Mary Parish

Morgan City Cemetery, Morgan City
 Bill Burgo

St. Tammany Parish, New Orleans Metro

Dendinger Memorial Cemetery,
Madisonville
 Irv Stein

Terrebone Parish, Houma Metro

Garden of Memories Cemetery, Houma
 Sid Gautreaux

Union Parish

Shiloh Cemetery, Bernice
 Red Booles

**Webster Parish, Shreveport–Bossier City
Metro**

Sibley Cemetery, Sibley
 Bill Bagwell

West Carroll Parish

Epps Cemetery, Epps
 Jake Jones

Winn Parish

Winnfield City Cemetery, Winnfield
 Jack Wallace

MAINE

**Androscoggin County, Lewiston–Auburn
Metro**

Mount Hope Cemetery, Lewiston
 John O'Brien, Pat O'Connell

Riverside Cemetery, Lewiston
  Bill Carrigan

Aroostook County

Smyrna Cemetery, Smyrna
  Happy Iott

Cumberland County, Portland Metro

Calvary Cemetery, South Portland
  Tom Catterson, Kid Madden

Eastern Cemetery, Portland
  Cuke Barrows

Lower Gloucester Cemetery, New
Gloucester
  Charlie Small

New Gloucester Cemetery, New Gloucester,
ME.
  Ben Houser

Pine Grove Cemetery, Falmouth
  Desmond Beatty, Frank Dupee, Joan
  Payson

South High Street Cemetery, Bridgton
  Jim Mains, Willard Mains

Franklin County

Riverview Cemetery, Farmington
  Ralph Good

Kennebec County

Glenside Cemetery, Winthrop
  Del Bissonette, Squanto Wilson

Maine Veterans Memorial Cemetery,
Augusta
  Hy Gunning

St. Mary's Cemetery, Augusta
  Don Brennan

Knox County

Acorn Cemetery, Rockland
  Chummy Gray

Brookland Cemetery, Waldoboro
  Clyde Sukeforth

Lincoln County

Dunbar Cemetery, Nobleboro
  Val Picinich

Penobscot County, Bangor Metro

Indian Island Cemetery, Old Town
  Lou Sockalexis

Millinocket Cemetery, Millinocket
  Bill Jones, Chick Maynard

Oak Hill Cemetery, Brewer
  Gil Whitehouse

Sagadahoc County

Richmond Cemetery, Richmond
  Bobby Messenger

Riverview Cemetery, Topsham
  Pop Williams

Somerset County

Maplewood Cemetery, Fairfield
  Otis Lawry

Waldo County

Grove Cemetery, Belfast
  Roger Salmon

Washington County

Forest Hills Cemetery, Harrington
  Irv Ray

Great Hill Cemetery, Columbia Falls
  Irv Young

York County, Portland Metro

Hope Cemetery, Kennebunk
  Chester Emerson, Sid Graves

Riverside Cemetery, Cornish
  Eddie Files

Riverside Cemetery, Kezar Falls
  Harry Lord

Riverside Cemetery, Ogunquit
  Bobby Coombs

Riverside Cemetery, Springvale
  Harland Rowe

St. Ignatius Cemetery, Sanford
  Fred Parent

St. Mary's Cemetery, Biddeford
  Jim McCormick

MARYLAND

Allegany County, Cumberland Metro
Frostburg Memorial Park, Frostburg
  Lefty Grove

Rosehill Cemetery, Cumberland
  George Daisy

SS. Peter & Paul Cemetery, Cumberland
  Joe Buskey, Karl Kolseth

United Methodist Churchyard, Hancock
    Ike Powers

Ann Arundel County, Baltimore Metro

Baldwin United Methodist Church
Cemetery, Millersville
    Pete Taylor

Cedar Hill Cemetery, Brooklyn Park
    Bill Hohman

Dulaney Valley Memorial Gardens,
Timonium
    Elmer Burkart, Howie Moss, Lefty
    Russell, Frank Skaff

Glen Haven Memorial Gardens, Glen Burnie
    Barry Shetrone

Nichols Bethel United Methodist Church
Cemetery, Odenton
    Babe Phelps

St. Anne's Cedar Bluff Cemetery, Annapolis
    John Wilson

St. Paul's Cemetery, Arcadia
    Otis Stocksdale

Baltimore County, Baltimoe Metro

Druid Ridge Cemetery, Pikesville
    Boileryard Clarke, Brownie Foreman,
    Red Kellett, Ben Mallonee, Butch
    Schmidt, Jim Stevens, Tommy Thomas,
    Maury Uhler

Garrison Forest Veterans Cemetery, Owings
Mills
    Ernest Burke, Dick Powell

Moreland Memorial Park, Parkville
    Ray Flanigan, Charlie Lau

Baltimore city, Baltimore Metro

Adams Chapel Cemetery, Baltimore
    Skeeter Watkins

Arbutus Memorial Park, Baltimore
    Leon Day, Charles Evans, Benjamin Taylor

Baltimore Cemetery, Baltimore
    Jack Evans, Mike Hooper, John Kelly,
    Jimmy Macullar, Harry Von der Horst,
    John H. Von der Horst

Baltimore National Cemetery, Baltimore
    Bill Lamar, George Maisel

Bohemian National Cemetery, Baltimore
    Dutch Ulrich

Gardens of Faith Memorial Gardens, Baltimore
    Ed Carroll, Arthur Ehlers, Willie Miranda

Govans Presbyterian Cemetery, Baltimore
    Merwin Jacobson

Greenmount Cemetery, Baltimore
    Stub Brown, Vin Campbell, Jim Gilmore,
    Tommy Johns, George Popplein, Frank
    Sellman, John Waltz, Frank Whitney

Hebrew Cemetery, Baltimore
    Rube Marquard

Holy Cross Cemetery, Baltimore
    Icebox Chamberlain

Holy Redeemer Cemetery, Baltimore
    Bill Lyston, Cliff Melton, Lou Thuman

Immanuel Lutheran Cemetery, Baltimore
    Johnny Neun

Lorraine Park Cemetery, Baltimore
    Rex Barney, Rudy Kneisch, Charlie
    Maisel, Fritz Maisel, Jerry Scala

Loudon Park Cemetery, Baltimore
    Harry Aubrey, Ormond Butler, Bill Byers,
    Cupid Childs, Dave Danforth, Buttercup
    Dickerson, Dave Foutz, Sam Frock, Slats
    Jordan, Bill Keister, Harry Kohler,
    Dummy Leitner, Charlie Loudenslager,
    Allen Russell, Jimmy Say, Milt Scott, Bill
    Stumpf, Sam Trott

Mount Olivet Cemetery, Baltimore
    Charles P. Speeden

Mt. Auburn Cemetery, Baltimore
    Frank Warfield

Mt. Calvary Cemetery, Baltimore
    Cruch Holloway, Slim Jones

New Cathedral Cemetery, Baltimore
    Charlie Eakle, Ferd Eunick, Mike Gaule,
    Ned Hanlon, Joe Kelley, Bill Kellogg, Walt
    Lerian, John Lyston, Bobby Mathews,
    Jimmy Mathison, John McGraw, Ed
    McLane, Deacon Morrissey, Wilbert
    Robinson, Eddie Rommel, Nick Scharf,
    Walt Smallwood, Jimmy Walsh, Gary
    Wilson

Oak Lawn Cemetery, Baltimore
    Harry Baldwin, Ed Beatin, Charlie
    Fitzberger, Jake Miller, Queenie
    O'Rourke, Harry Smith

Parkwood Cemetery, Baltimore
    Al Rubeling

Sharp Street Memorial United Methodist
Church Cemetery, Baltimore
   Riley Davis

St. John's Cemetery, Baltimore
   Chick Fewster, Tommy Vereker

St. Mary's Cemetery, Baltimore
   Jack Dunn, Frank Foreman, Suter Sullivan

St. Patrick's Catholic Church Cemetery,
Baltimore
   Bill Smiley

Trinity Cemetery, Baltimore
   Charlie Gettig, Sandy Nava

Western Cemetery, Baltimore
   Fred Carl, Ed High

Woodlawn Cemetery, Baltimore
   Max Bishop, Steve Brodie, Harry
   Fanwell, Fred Ostendorf

Caroline County

Grace Methodist Church Cemetery, Denton
   Buck Herzog

Carroll County, Baltimore Metro

Lake View Memorial Park, Sykesville
   Johnny Wittig

Manchester Cemetery (aka Immanuel
Evangelical Reformed Church Cemetery),
Manchester
   Joe Yingling

Pleasant Grove Cemetery, Finksburg
   Jack Flater

Westminster Cemetery, Westminster
   Ben Spencer

Cecil County, Wilmington, Metro

Zion Cemetery (formerly Cecilton
Cemetery), Cecilton
   Ray Morgan

Charlestown Cemetery, Charlestown
   Ted Cather

Charles County, Washington Metro

St. Ignatius Cemetery, Port Tobacco
   Ed Edelen

Dorchester County

Cambridge Cemetery, Cambridge
   Jake Flowers

Dorchester Memorial Park, Cambridge
   Fred Lucas

Frederick County, Washington Metro

Christ Reformed Church Cemetery,
Middletown
   Charlie Keller

Mount Hope Cemetery, Woodsboro
   Archie Stimmel

Mount Olivet Cemetery, Frederick
   Clarence Berger, Clarence Blethen,
   Carlton Molesworth, Richard Nallin,
   Emory Nusz, Dorsey Riddlemoser, John
   Traffley

St. John's Cemetery, Frederick
   Ray Gardner

Garrett County

Philos Cemetery, Westernport
   Baldy Louden

Harford County, Baltimore Metro

Angel Hill Cemetery, Havre de Grace
   C.B. Burns, Alfred Gilbert

Baker Cemetery, Aberdeen
   Les German, Cal Ripken Sr.

Cedar Hill Cemetery, Havre de Grace
   Highball Wilson

Grove Cemetery, Aberdeen
   Frank Todd

Harford County Home Cemetery, Bel Air
   Lou Say

St. Louis Cemetery, Clarksville
   Buck Etchison

Kent County

Asbury Methodist Church Cemetery,
Millington
   Hanson Horsey

Old St. Paul's Episcopal Church Cemetery,
Chestertown
   Swish Nicholson

Montgomery County, Washington Metro

Friends Cemetery, Sandy Spring
   Jack Bentley

Gate of Heaven Cemetery, Silver Spring
   Russell Awkard, Austin Carr, Joe Giebel,
   Pint Isreal, Joe Judge, Larry Woodall

Parklawn Cemetery, Rockville
  John Smith

Rockville Union Cemetery, Rockville
  Bill Eagle, Walter Johnson

St. Gabriel's Cemetery, Potomac
  Bob Addie, Edward Bennett Williams

St. John's Cemetery, Forest Glen
  Jake Powell

St. Mark's Cemetery, Germantown
  Alan Clarke

Woodside Cemetery, Brinklow
  Sam Rice

Prince Georges County, Washington Metro

Cedar Hill Cemetery, Suitland
  Walter Beall, Earl Clark, Walt Herrell,
  George Keefe, Billy Martin, Earl
  Mattingly, Ray Moore

Cheltenham Veterans Cemetery, Cheltenham
  Dizzy Sutherland, Red Webb

Fort Lincoln Cemetery, Brentwood
  Tom Brown, Dan Casey, Ed Fuller,
  Charlie Gooch, Calvin Griffith, Clark
  Griffith, Joe Haynes, Charlie Luskey,
  Frank Watt

George Washington Cemetery, Adelphi
  Rollie Hemsley

Harmony Cemetery, Landover
  Chick Tolson

Lincoln Memorial Cemetery, Suitland
  Sam Lacy, Babe Medley, Smokey Joe
  Williams

Maryland National Memorial Park, Laurel
  Bill Harvey

Resurrection Cemetery, Clinton
  Bill Smith

St. John's Cemetery, Beltsville
  Johnny Beall

Queen Ann's County, Baltimore Metro

Church Hill Cemetery, Church Hill
  Doc Wallace

Sudlersville Cemetery, Sudlersville
  Frank Brower

Somerset County

Oriole Cemetery, Oriole
  Joe Muir

Sunny Ridge Memorial Park, Crisfield
  Bob Unglaub

Talbot County

Spring Hill Cemetery, Easton
  Frank Baker

Wye Mills Cemetery, Wye Mills
  Nick Carter

Washington County, Hagerstown Metro

Cedar Lawn Memorial Park, Hagerstown
  Clyde Barnhart

Rose Hill Cemetery, Hagerstown
  John Allen, Joe Matthews, Duke Shirley

Wicomico County

Asbury United Methodist Church Cemetery,
Allen
  Dick Porter

First Baptist Cemetery, Pembroke
  Vic Keen

Galestown Cemetery, Galestown
  Homer Smoot

Parsons Cemetery, Salisbury
  Alex McCarthy

MASSACHUSETTS

Barnstable County, Barnstable Metro

East Harwich Cemetery, East Harwich
  Cy Morgan

Massachusetts National Cemetery, Bourne
  Jocko Conlon, Red Flaherty, Walt Ripley,
  Jim Schelle

Mosswood Cemetery, Cotuit
  Ed Gallagher, Danny Silva

Old North Cemetery, North Truro
  Danny MacFayden

People's Cemetery, Chatham
  John Andre

St. Francis Xavier Cemetery, Centerville
  Joe Cronin

Berkshire County, Pittsfield Metro

Cheshire Cemetery, Cheshire
  Dale Long

Fairview Cemetery, Dalton
  Jim Garry

St. Anne's Catholic Cemetery, Lenox
Earl Turner

St. Joseph's Cemetery, Pittsfield
Mark Belanger, Ed Connolly, Cy Ferry,
Jack Ferry, Howie Storie, Pussy Tebeau

Berkshire County (non-Metro portion)

Hillside Cemetery, North Adams
Ervin Curtiss

Maple Street Cemetery, Adams
Pete McBride, Dave Murphy

South View Cemetery, North Adams
Art Madison

St. Joseph's Cemetery, Stockbridge
Doc Scanlan

St. Peter's Catholic Cemetery, Great
Barrington
Pete Noonan

Bristol County, New Bedford Metro

Acushnet Cemetery, Acushnet
John Taber

Oak Grove Cemetery, New Bedford
Daff Gammons, Harry Stovey

St. Mary's Cemetery, New Bedford
Benny Bowcock, Jim Canavan, Tom
Hernon, Connie Murphy

Bristol County, Providence–Fall River–Warwick Metro

North Burial Ground, Fall River
Tom Gunning, Jim Manning

Notre Dame Cemetery, Fall River
Art Butler, Arthur J. Turgeon, Luke
Urban

Oak Grove Cemetery, Fall River
Charlie Buffington, Chris McFarland,
Butch Sutcliffe

St. John's Cemetery, Attleboro
Hank Morrison

St. Mary's Cemetery, Fall River
Ed O'Neil

St. Patrick's Cemetery, Fall River
Frank Fennelly, Tommy Gastall, Joe
Harrington, Mike McDermott, John
O'Brien, Johnny Reder, Red Torphy

Thomas Cemetery, Swansea
Gus Salve

Bristol County, Taunton–Norton–Raynham Metro

Raynham Cemetery, Raynham
Ezra Lincoln

St. Joseph's Cemetery, Taunton
George Bignell, Tim Donahue

Bristol County, Boston Metro

St. Mary's Cemetery, Mansfield
John Quinn

Dukes County

Oak Grove Cemetery, Vineyard Haven
Dave Morey

Essex County, Boston Metro

Beech Grove Cemetery, Rockport
John Kiernan

Greenlawn Cemetery, Nahant
Frank Leja

Hamilton Cemetery, Hamilton
Joe Batchelder

Harmony Cemetery, Georgetown
Fred Tenney

Harmony Grove Cemetery, Salem
Len Swormstedt

Highland Cemetery, Ipswich
Joe Burns

Oak Grove Cemetery, Gloucester
Fred Doe, Cy Perkins

Oak Hill Cemetery, Newburyport
Chet Nourse

Rosedale Cemetery, Manchester-by-the-Sea
Stuffy McInnis

St. Mary Cemetery, Beverly
John Deering

Essex County, Lynn–Peabody–Salem Metro

Annunciation Cemetery, Danvers
Tom McNamara

Holten Cemetery, Danvers
Alex Gardner

King Cemetery, Peabody
Sam King

Pine Grove Cemetery, Lynn
Harry Agganis, Daisy Davis, Bernie
Friberg, Barney Gilligan, John Leighton,
Art McGovern

Puritan Lawn Memorial Park, Peabody
George Bullard, Harold Kaese, George
Twombly

St. Joseph's Cemetery, Lynn
Tom Bannon, Les Hennessy, Irv Porter,
Blondy Ryan, Tom Whelan

St. Mary's Cemetery, Danvers
Ed Caskin

St. Mary's Cemetery, Lynn
Tom Niland, Jim Wallace

St. Mary's Cemetery, Salem
Henry Mullin

Swampscott Cemetery, Swampscott
Les Burke, Bump Hadley, Jim Hegan

Waterside Cemetery, Marblehead
Joe Graves, Robin Romana, Augie
Swentor

**Essex County, Lawrence–Methuen–Salem
Metro**

Bellevue Cemetery, Lawrence
Klondike Smith, Andy Swan

St. Mary's Immaculate Conception
Cemetery, Lawrence
Johnny Broaca, Dick Conway, John
Crowley, Patsy Donovan, Jocko Flynn,
Mike Jordan, George Moolic, John
Murphy, John O'Connell

Essex County, Framingham Metro

Immaculate Conception Cemetery,
Marlborough
John Buckley, Duke Farrell, Frank
Quinlan

**Essex County, Haverhill–North
Andover–Amesbury Metro**

Mount Prospect Cemetery, Amesbury
Leon Chagnon

Ridgewood Cemetery, North Andover
Johnny Barrett

Riverview Cemetery, Groveland
Dick Blaisdell, Jim McGinley, Dan
Woodman

St. James Cemetery, Haverhill
Jack Ryan

St. Joseph's Cemetery, Haverhill
Gene Vadeboncoeur

Franklin County

Green River Cemetery, Greenfield
Steve Partenheimer

Highland Cemetery, Millers Falls
Doug Smith

Hampden County, Springfield Metro

Calvary Cemetery, Chicopee
Mike Hickey

Calvary Cemetery, Holyoke
Dick Burns, Tommy Dowd, Charles
Hackett, Joe Lucey, Ed Moriarty, Tommy
Tucker

Hillcrest Park Cemetery, Springfield
Phil Page

Oak Grove Cemetery, Springfield
George Hemming, Fred Mann, Bob
Reach

Pine Hill Cemetery, Westfield
Les Lanning

St. Anne's Cemetery, Palmer
Bill Karlon

St. Jerome Cemetery, Holyoke
Marty Barrett, Pat Conway, Kip Dowd,
Jack Doyle, Bill Gleason, Jack Hannifin,
Fran Healy, John Hummel, Denny
O'Neill, Bill Sullivan

St. Mary's Cemetery, Westfield
Ray Fitzgerald

St. Michael's Cemetery, Springfield
Tom Burns, Snooks Dowd, Pete Gilbert,
Pat Hannifan, Bob Keating, Dan
Mahoney, Rabbit Maranville, Paddy
O'Connor

St. Thomas the Apostle Cemetery, Palmer
Red Shea

St. Thomas Cemetery, West Springfield
Francis Rosso

Hampshire County, Springfield Metro

Aspen Grove Cemetery, Ware
Candy Cummings

Mount Hope Cemetery, Belchertown
Frank Loftus

Old Saint William's Cemetery, Ware
Pat McCauley

Our Lady of Mount Carmel Cemetery, Ware
Joe Giard

St. Mary's Cemetery, Ware
 Nap Shea

Middlesex County, Boston Metro

Belmont Cemetery, Belmont
 Jud McLaughlin

Brookside Cemetery, Stow
 Fred Mitchell

Calvary Cemetery, Waltham
 Lawrence Daniels, Tom Cotter, Chippy
 Gaw, John Leary, Tom Stankard

Calvary Cemetery, Woburn
 Doc McMahon

Cambridge Cemetery, Cambridge
 Bill Barrett, Joseph Cashman, Dad
 Clarkson, John Clarkson, Walter
 Clarkson, Gid Gardner, Mack Hillis, Tim
 Keefe, Eddie Waitkus

Forest Dale Cemetery, Malden
 Jim Chatterton, Frank Mahar

Glenwood Cemetery, Everett
 Al Pierotti, Dupee Shaw

Holy Cross Cemetery, Malden
 George Brickley, Tony Conigliaro,
 Sammy Curran, Leo Hafford, Jerry
 Hurley, Toby Lyons, Jim McKeever,
 Barney Olsen, Cyclone Ryan, John Shea,
 Jim Sullivan, Joe Sullivan

Lindenwood Cemetery, Stoneham
 Bill Annis

Linwood Cemetery, Weston
 Eddie Collins

Mount Auburn Cemetery, Cambridge
 Charlie Devens, Doc Gautreau, Bernard
 Malamud, Dick O'Connell, Bobby
 Wheelock

Mount Pleaseant Cemetery, Arlington
 Ty LaForest

Newton Cemetery, Newton
 Bill Cronin, Al Hubbard, Frank Shellenback

Oak Grove Cemetery, Medford
 Tom Daly, Howard Fahey, Shanty Hogan,
 Frank Kelliher, Mabray Kountze, Fred
 Lake

Sleepy Hollow Cemetery, Concord
 Dick Loftus

St. Bernard's Cemetery, Concord
 Bill McCarthy, Dinny McNamara

St. Patrick's Cemetery, Stoneham
 Joe Casey, Sam Wright

St. Patrick's Cemetery, Watertown
 Dee Cousineau, Bob Daughters

St. Paul's Cemetery, Arlington
 Bill Conway, Pete Cote, Cozy Dolan,
 Mert Hackett, Walter Hackett, Charlie
 Maloney, Dewey Metivier, Dave Shean,
 Neil Stynes

Westview Cemetery, Lexington
 Dick Wheeler

Wildwood Cemetery, Winchester
 Hod Ford

Woodbrook Cemetery, Woburn
 Harry Berthrong

Woodlawn Cemetery, Everett
 Al Blanche, Clarence Dow, Sam Gentile,
 Skinny Graham

Wyoming Cemetery, Melrose
 Joe Harris, Dominic Mulrenan, Frank Selee

Middlesex County, Framingham Metro

Dell Park Cemetery, Natick
 Frank Allen

Forestvale Cemetery, Hudson
 Fred Robinson

**Middlesex County–Lowell–Billerica–
Chelmsford Metro**

Edson Cemetery, Lowell
 Bill Hawes, Art Sladen, Art Whitney

Fairview Cemetery, Westford
 Rusty Yarnall

Lowell Cemetery, Lowell
 Lee McElwee, Alex McKinnon

Pine Hill Cemetery, Tewksbury
 Carl Sumner

St. Joseph's Cemetery, Chelmsford
 Skippy Roberge

St. Patrick's Cemetery, Lowell
 Roscoe Coughlin, Shorty Dee, Denny
 Driscoll, Ed Flanagan, William Gallagher,
 Bob Ganley, John Grady, Barney
 McLaughlin, Frank McLaughlin, Bill
 Merritt, Marty Sullivan, Lefty Tyler

St. Patrick's Cemetery, Natick
 Tom Connolly, Jack Coveney, Frank
 Leary, Pat Pettee

Tewksbury Hospital Cemetery, Tewksbury
Ted Firth

Nantucket County

St. Mary's Cemetery, Nantucket
Tom Earley

Norfolk County, Boston Metro

Blue Hill Cemetery, Braintree
Claude Davidson, Walt Zink

Brookdale Cemetery, Dedham
Buck Danner, Hal Deviney, Paul
Radford

Fairmount Cemetery, Weymouth
Buster Burrell

Highland Cemetery, Norwood
Marty Callaghan, John Kiley

Highland Cemetery, Weymouth
Ken Nash

Holyhood Cemetery, Brookline
John Bergh, Cannonball Crane, Bill
McCarthy, John Morrill, Miah Murray,
Dave Pickett, Art Rico, Mike Slattery,
George Wright

Lakeview Cemetery, South Weymouth
Phil Voyles

Milton Cemetery, Milton
Bill Chamberlain, Elbie Fletcher, Doc
Martin, Luis Tiant Sr.

Mount Wollaston Cemetery, Quincy
Bill Dam, Bob Dresser, Charlei Ganzel,
Bill Vargus

Pine Hill Cemetery, Quincy
Tom Jenkins

Sharon Memorial Park, Sharon
Judge Fuchs

St. Francis Xavier Cemetery, Weymouth
Dan Howley

St. Mary's Cemetery, Canton
Olaf Henriksen

St. Mary's Cemetery, Needham
Shano Collins

St. Mary's Cemetery, Randolph
Gene McAuliffe, John Rudderham, Steve
White, Joe Zapustas

Walnut Hills Cemetery, Brookline
Artie Clarke, John Kelleher, Fred
Newman, Joe Walsh

Woodlawn Cemetery, Wellesley
Hank Camelli, Louis Perini

Woodside Cemetery, Cohasset
Dick Donovan

**Plymouth County, Brockton–Bridgewater–
Easton Metro**

Calvary Cemetery, Brockton
Pat Creeden, Haddie Gill, Frank Kane,
Fred Moncewicz, Henry Porter

Immaculate Conception Cemetery, Easton
Mike Driscoll

St. Patrick's Cemetery, Brockton
Bill McGunnigle, Frank Sexton

Plymouth County, Boston Metro

Central Cemetery, Carver
Charlie Bold

Church of St. John the Evangelist Cemetery,
Hingham
Ted Olson

Long Neck Cemetery, Onset
Dicky Pearce

Mount Pleasant Cemetery, Bryantville
Walt Whittaker

St. Patrick's Cemetery, Rockland
Dan Burke, Jim Hickey

**Plymouth County, Taunton–Norton–
Raynham Metro**

Clark Cemetery, Lakeville
Jim Cudworth

Suffolk County, Boston Metro

Bennington Street Burying Ground, East
Boston
Red Woodhead

Beth El Cemetery, West Roxbury
Si Rosenthal

Cedar Grove Cemetery, Dorchester
Henry Lampe, Larry McLean

Dorchester North Cemetery, Dorchester
Tom Raftery

Evergreen Cemetery, Brighton
Jack Burns

Fairview Cemetery, Hyde Park
Stan Yerkes

Forest Hills Cemetery, Jamaica Plain
    Tommy Bond, Lew Brown, Pep
    Deininger, George Haddock, Bob Hall,
    Andy Spongnardi, Charles H. Taylor,
    John I. Taylor

Mount Benedict Cemetery, West Roxbury
    Ed Callahan, Dan Cotter, John Fox, Ed
    Gill, Lee King, Jim Ward

Mount Calvary Cemetery, Roslindale
    Kid Butler, John Butler, Dan Cronin,
    Steve Dignan, Hugh Duffy, Curry Foley,
    Jim Halpin, Andy Harrington, Ike Kamp,
    Walter Lonergan, Mike Mahoney,
    Tommy McCarthy, Marty Shay, Tom
    Smith, Mike Sullivan, Jerry Sweeney, Bill
    Tierney, Nick Wise

Mount Hope Cemetery, Mattapan
    Dave Birdsall, Lefty Brown, George
    Bryant, Charlie Daniels, John Irwin,
    Tubby Johnson, King Kelly, Frank
    Shannon, Tom Sullivan, Herman Young

New Calvary Cemetery, Mattapan
    Dennis Berran, Joe Callahan, Bill Cooney,
    John Fitzgerald, Gene Good, Andy
    Leonard, Jack Manning, Buck O'Brien,
    Denny Sullivan, Jim Walsh

Old Dorchester Burial Ground, Dorchester
    Tim Murnane

St. Joseph's Cemetery, West Roxbury
    Bob Brown, Frank Connaughton, Tom
    Connolly, Jack Conway, Art Corcoran,
    John Donahue, Jumping Joe Dugan,
    Honey Fitz Fitzgerald, John Freeman,
    Hank Garrity, Bunny Madden, Joe
    Mulligan, Andy O'Connor, Jack Slattery,
    Bill Stewart, Bill Sweeney

Temple Emeth Memorial Cemetery,
West Roxbury
    Murray Kramer

Winthrop Cemetery, Winthrop
    Curt Fullerton, Paul Howard

Worcester County, Worcester Metro

Calvary Cemetery, Dudley
    General Stafford, John Stafford, Jerry
    Turbidy

Eastwood Cemetery, South Lancaster
    Billy Hamilton

Holy Rosary-St. Mary's Cemetery, Spencer
    Frank Bird

Hope Cemetery, Worcester
    Freeman Brown, Bruno Haas, Art
    LaVigne

Oak Ridge Cemetery, Southbridge
    Irn Waldron

Pine Grove Cemetery, Leicester
    Frank Wilson

Riverside Cemetery, Grafton
    Asa Stratton

St. Denis Cemetery, East Douglas
    Henry Coppola

St. John's Cemetery, Lancaster
    Billy Burke, Yale Murphy

St. John's Cemetery, Worcester
    Bill Bergen, Hugh Bradley, Kitty
    Bransfield, Jesse Burkett, Hugh Canavan,
    pat Carney, Doc Carroll, Chick Gagnon,
    Henry Lynch, Freddie Maguire, Chippy
    McGarr, Jo-Jo Morrissey, Con Murphy,
    Pat Murphy. Tom O'Brien, Rosy Ryan

St. Joseph's Cemetery, North Brookfield
    Marty Bergen

St. Luke's Cemetery, Westborough
    Andrew Sullivan

St. Mary's Cemetery, Uxbridge
    Frank Fahey

St. Roch's Cemetery, Oxford
    Al Javery

Swedish Cemetery, Worcester
    John Anderson

Woodlawn Cemetery, Clinton
    Jack McGeachey

**Worcester County, Leominster–Fitchburg–
Gardner Metro**

Forest Hill Cemetery, Fitchburg
    Ed Warner

New Cemetery, Ashburnham
    Ivers Whitney Adams, Fred Woodcock
    St. Bernard's Church Cemetery, Fitchburg
    Nixey Callahan, Tom Hart, John Keefe,
    pat Moran, Martin Powell

Worcester County, Framingham Metro

Lakeview Cemetery, Upton
    Tom Fleming, Bill Summers

St. Mary of the Assumption Cemetery, Milford
    Doc Curley

Worcester County, Providence–Fall River–Warwick Metro

St. Charles Cemetery, Blackstone
    Joe Connolly, Tim McNamara

MICHIGAN

Alcona County

St. Ann's Cemetery, Harrisville
    Kiki Cuyler

Allegan County, Grand Rapids–Muskegon–Holland Metro

Hudson Corners Cemetery, Allegan
    Frank Kitson

Oakwood Cemetery, Allegan
    Dad Hale

Rowe Cemetery, Allegan
    Frank Miller

Barry County

Riverside Cemetery, Hastings
    Lady Baldwin

Bay County, Saginaw-Bay City Metro

Elm Lawn Park Cemetery, Bay City
    Ernie Gust

Berrien County, Benton Harbor Metro

Resurrection Catholic Cemetery, St. Joseph
    Bob Katz

Branch County

Lester Cemetery, California
    Jim Hughey

Calhoun County, Kalamazoo–Battle Creek Metro

Floral Lawn Memorial Gardens, Battle Creek
    Charlie Grover

Memorial Park Cemetery, Battle Creek
    Ray Knode

Oak Hill Cemetery, Battle Creek
    Allan Collamore, Harry Staley

Oakridge Cemetery, Marshall
    John Wisner

Riverside Cemetery, Albion
    Deacon McGuire

Charlevoix County

Greenwood Cemetery, Petoskey
    Chick Lathers

Clinton County, Lansing Metro

Eureka Cemetery, Eureka
    LaRue Kirby

Delta County

Lakeview Cemetery, Escanaba
    John Perrin

Dickinson County

Norway Township Cemetery, Norway
    Johnny Johnson

Eaton County

Riverside Cemetery, Bellevue
    John Eubank

Genesee County, Flint Metro

Crestwood Memorial Cemetery, Grand Blanc
    Alex Main

Flint Cemetery, Flint
    Bert Miller

New Calvary Catholic Cemetery, Flint
    Gene Desautels

River Rest Cemetery, Flint
    Dave Hoskins

Sunset Hills Cemetery, Flint
    Arnold Early, Red Bluhm

Gogebic County

Marenisco Cemetery, Marenisco
    John Michaelson

Grand Traverse County

Oakwood Cemetery, Traverse City
    Bunny Brief

Gratiot County

North Star Cemetery, North Star
    Jesse Altenburg

Riverside Cemetery, Alma
    Rex DeVogt

Hillsdale County

Leonardson Memorial Cemetery, Pittsford
  Rube Vickers

Houghton County

Lake View Cemetery, Calumet
  Bert Sincock

Ingham County, Lansing Metro

Evergreen-Mount Hope Cemetery, Lansing
  Bob Kuhn, Larry Raines

Maple Ridge Cemetery, Holt
  Bill Grahame

Mount Hope Cemetery, Lansing
  Jack Morrissey, Vic Saier

Oakwood Cemetery, Grand Ledge
  Jerry Byrne

Ionia County

Rest Haven Memory Gardens, Belding
  Dick Terwilliger

Iosco County

Tawas City Cemetery, Tawas City
  Roxy Roach

Jackson County, Jackson Metro

Maple Grove Cemetery, Concord
  Ernie Baker

Roseland Memorial Gardens, Jackson
  Ed Hendricks

St. John's Cemetery, Jackson
  Jim Tray

Woodland Cemetery, Jackson
  Benny Frey

**Kalamazoo County, Kalamazoo–
Battle Creek Metro**

Grand Prairie Cemetery, Kalamazoo
  Freddy Spurgeon

Mount Ever-Rest Cemetery, Kalamazoo
  Chris Burkam, Bert Tooley

Mount Olivet Cemetery, Kalamazoo
  Harvey Freeman

Mountain Home Cemetery, Kalamazoo
  John Fetzer, Rudy Miller

Riverside Cemetery, Kalamazoo
  Hod Fenner

Vicksburg Cemetery, Vicksburg
  Bill Snyder

**Kent County, Grand Rapids–Muskegon–
Holland Metro**

Chapel Hill Memorial Gardens, Grand Rapids
  Ted Rasberry

Fair Plains Cemetery, Grand Rapids
  Walter Anderson, Al DeVormer

Holy Trinity Cemetery, Grand Rapids
  Al Platte

Rest Lawn Memorial Park, Grand Rapids
  Luther Roy

Woodlawn Cemetery, Grand Rapids
  Wally Pipp

Lapeer County, Detroit Metro

Greenwood Cemetery, North Branch
  Glenn Crawford

Oregon Township Cemetery, Lapeer
  Ralph Judd

West Deerfield Cemetery, West Deerfield
  Danny Schell

Lenawee County, Ann Arbor Metro

Oakwood Cemetery, Adrian
  Bill Carrick, Emil Huhn, Rube Kisinger

Riverside Cemetery, Clinton
  Bunny Fabrique

Livingston County, Detroit Metro

Lakeview Cemetery, Howell
  Bill Crouch

Macomb County, Detroit Metro

Lincoln Memorial Park Cemetery, Mount
Clemens
  Turkey Stearnes

Memphis Cemetery, Memphis
  Clint Rogge

Resurrestion Cemetery, Clinton Township
  Ribs Raney, Wildfire Schulte

Romeo Cemetery, Romeo
  Frank Bowerman

St. Clement Cemetery, Center Line
  Chet Laabs

St. Mary's Cemetery, St. Clair
  Ted Goulait

Utica Cemetery, Utica
  Duke Maas

Manistee County

Oak Grove Cemetery, Manistee
  Henry Jones, Jack Lundbom

Mason County

Ludington Cemetery, Ludington
  Danny Claire

Mecotas County

Highland View Cemetery, Big Rapids
  Win Kellum

Montcalm County

Sheridan Cemetery, Sheridan
  Ed Hemingway

Muskegon County, Grand Rapids–Muskegon–Holland Metro

Mona View Jewish Cemetery, Muskegon
  John Dobb

Oakwood Cemetery, Muskegon
  Monte Beville, Bull Wagner

Newaygo County

Big Prairie-Everitt Cemetery, White Cloud
  Pete Fahrer

Oakland County, Detroit Metro

Birmingham Cemetery, Birmingham
  John Rainey

Christian Memorial Cultural Cemetery, Rochester
  Roy Cullenbine

Franklin Cemetery, Birmingham
  Fred Blanding

Holy Sepulchre Cemetery, Southfield
  Jack Bracken, Walter Owne Briggs Jr.,
  Walter Owen Briggs Sr., Al Cicotte,
  Charlie Gehringer, Steve Gromek,
  Mickey Harris, Harry Heilmann, Nemo
  Leibold, Clyde Manion, Barney
  McCosky, Mike Menosky, Frank Navin,
  Billy Rogell, Brad Springer, Vic Wertz

New Hudson Cemetery, New Hudson
  Vern Spencer

Oakland Hills Memorial Gardens, Novi
  Hal Newhouser

Oxford Cemetery, Oxford
  Elijah Kones

Pine Lake Cemetery, West Bloomfield
  Norm Cash

Roseland Park Cemetery, Berkley
  Fred Goldsmith, Davy Jones, Dutch
  Lerchen, Jack Wieneke

White Chapel Memorial Cemetery, Troy
  Clem Koshorek, Babe Sherman, Bobby
  Veach

Saginaw County, Saginaw–Bay City Metro

Forest Lawn Cemetery, Saginaw
  Red McKee

Mount Olivet Cemetery, Saginaw,
  Ed Albosta

Shiawassee County

Roselawn Cemetery, Perry
  Andy Messenger

St. Clair County, Detroit Metro

Lakeside Cemetery, Port Huron
  Billy Kelly, Bill Watkins

Mount Hope Catholic Cemetery, Port Huron
  Fred Lamlein

St. Joseph County

Oak Lawn Cemetery, Sturgis
  Harry Niles

Parkville Cemetery, Parkville
  Pee Wee Powell

Tuscola County

Elkland Township Cemetery, Cass City
  Larry MacPhail

Van Buren County, Kalamazoo–Battle Creek Metro

Maple Hill Cemetery, Hartford
  Jay Parker

Prospect Hill Cemetery, Paw Paw
  Bill Killefer

Washtenaw County, Ann Arbor Metro

Forest Hill Cemetery, Ann Arbor
  Clarence Lehr

Oakwood Cemetery, Saline
  George Burnham

Michigan

BASEBALL BURIAL SITES

St. Thomas Catholic Cemetery, Ann Arbor
  Lou Schiappacasse

United Memorial Gardens, Plymouth
  Chester Gray

Washtenong Memorial Park, Ann Arbor
  Ray Fisher, Ernie Vick

Wayne County, Detroit Metro

Cadillac Memorial Gardens West, Westland
  Tom Cafego, Ralph McConnaughey, Art Reinholz

Elmwood Cemetery, Detroit
  Jim Carleton, Mac MacArthur, Ed Stein, Sam Thompson

Evergreen Cemetery, Detroit
  Ed Kippert, Bobby Lowe, Lawrence Williams

Forest Lawn Cemetery, Detroit
  Augie Bergamo, Harry Daubert, Bert Hogg

Gethsemane Cemetery, Detroit
  Rufus Lewis

Glenwood Cemetery, Wayne
  Ed Fisher

Grand Lawn Cemetery, Detroit
  Irv Bartling, Gus Bono, Homer Davidson, Dick Littlefield, Frank Owen

Michigan Memorial Park, Flat Rock
  Frank Sacka, Mike Tresh

Mount Elliott Cemetery, Detroit
  Ben Guiney, Frank McIntyre, Frank Scheibeck, Henry Yaik

Mount Hope Memorial Gardens, Livonia
  Andy Watts

Mount Olivet Cemetery, Detroit
  Jimmy Barrett, Doc Casey, Frank Fuller, Ed Gagnier, Marty Kavanagh, Sam LaRocque, Sport McAllister, Cass Michaels, Johnny Mitchell, Frank Okrie

Northview Cemetery, Dearborn
  Van Patrick

Our Lady of Hope Cemetery, Wyandotte
  Leo Christante

Our Lady of Mount Carmel Cemetery, Wyandotte
  Larry LeJeune

Parkview Memorial Cemetery, Livonia
  Eddie Cicotte

St. Hedwig Cemetery, Dearborn Heights
  Bernie Boland, Joe Smaza

United Memorial Gardens, Plymouth
  Jim Webster

Woodlawn Cemetery, Detroit
  Burt Blue, Fritz Buelow, Red Downey, Pete Fox, Red House, Ed Killian, J.B. Martin, Herbert Moore, H.G. Salsinger, Ed Siever

Woodmere Cemetery, Detroit
  Charlie Bennett, Nig Clarke, Frank Duncan III, Wish Egan, Gene Krapp, Charlie Krause, Jimmy Peoples, Fred Schemanske, Bill Stellberger, Clarence Winters, Joe Yeager

MINNESOTA

Benton County

Trinity Lutheran Church Cemetery, Sauk Rapids
  Rip Repulski

Blue Earth County

Calvary Cemetery, St. Cloud
  Henry Thielmann

German Lutheran Cemetery, Mankato
  Lou Polchow

Carlton County

LaPrairie Cemetery, Cloquet
  Chief Chouneau

Clearwater County

Silver Creek Cemetery, Clearbrook
  Wes Westrum

Dakota County, Minneapolis–St. Paul Metro

Resurrection Cemetery, Mendota Heights
  Robert Short

Dodge County

Maple Grove Cemetery, Kasson
  Les Tietje

Hennepin County, Minneapolis–St. Paul Metro

Crystal Lake Cemetery, Minneapolis
  Bob Ingersoll

268

Fort Snelling National Cemetery,
Minneapolis
  Bill Antonello, Halsey Hall, Whitey
  Hilcher, Reginald Hopwood, Richard
  Newberry, Jesse Petty, Frank Trechock,
  Don Wheeler

Grand-View Park Cemetery, Hopkins
  Bill Carney

Hillside Cemetery, Minneapolis
  Ellis Johnson

Lakewood Cemetery, Minneapolis
  Buzz Arlett, Ossie Bluege, Bert Brenner,
  George Dumont, Elmer Foster, Paul Giel,
  Spencer Harris, Mike Kelley, Bobby
  Marshall, Sherry Robertson, Dick Siebert,
  Wib Smith, Hy Vandenberg, Jimmy
  Williams

St. Mary's Cemetery, Minneapolis
  Joe Crotty, Joe Fautsch, Bill Fox, Harry
  Ostdiek, Rube Schauer, Spike Shannon,
  Jack Zalusky

Sunset Memorial Park, Minneapolis
  Lew Drill, Ralph Miller, Hack Spencer

Itasca County

Olivet Cemetery, Deer River
  Steamboat Williams

Kanabec County

Oakwood Cemetery, Mora
  Rube Geyer

Le Seuer County

Mound Cemetery, Le Seuer
  Roger Denzer

Mower County

Calvary Cemetery, Austin
  Lou Ciola

Murray County

Restland Memory Gardens, Slayton
  Ed Pipgras

Nicollet County

State Hospital Cemetery, St. Peter
  Joe Werrick

Olmsted County, Rochester Metro

Calvary Cemetery, Rochester
  Moonlight Graham

St. Mary's Cemetery, Winona
  Julie Wera

Polk County

Oakdale Cemetery, Crookston
  Les Munns

**Ramsey County, Minnespolis–St. Paul
Metro**

Calvary Cemetery, St. Paul
  Jim Banning, Paul Castner, Tony Faeth,
  Leroy Matlock, Bill Wilson

Forest Lawn Memorial Park, St. Paul
  Henry Gehring, Hap Morse

Oakland Cemetery, St. Paul
  Lee Quillen

Resurrection Cemetery, St. Paul
  Larry Rosenthal

Roselawn Cemetery, Roseville
  Mickey Rocco

St. Mary's Cemetery, White Bear Lake
  Rip Conway

Union Cemetery, St. Paul
  Dwain Sloat

Red Lake County

Hansville Cemetery, Fosston
  Joe Visner

Renville County

St. Aloysius Catholic Cemetery, Olivia
  Blix Donnelly

Rice County

Maple Lawn Cemetery, Faribault
  Jimmy Pofahl

Scott County, Minneapolis–St. Paul Metro

Spirit Hill Cemetery, Jordan
  Ollie Fuhrman

St. Mark's Cemetery, Shakopee
  Ted Odenwald

**St. Louis County, Duluth–Superior
Metro**

Calvary Cemetery, Duluth
  Rasty Wright

Ely Cemetery, Ely
  Burt Keeley

Forest Hill Cemetery, Duluth
    Bill Otis
Oneota Cemetery, Duluth
    Rip Wade
Park Hill Cemetery, Duluth
    Newt Randall
Sunrise Memorial Park, Hermantown
    Wally Gilbert

Stearns County, St. Cloud Metro
Calvary Cemetery, St. Cloud
    Jake Thielman
St. Benedict's Catholic Cemetery, Avon
    Showboat Fisher

Washington County
Lakewview Cemetery, Mahtomedi
    Ray Rolling

MISSISSIPPI

Bolivar County
Cleveland Cemetery, Cleveland
    Clay Roe

Choctaw County
Concord Cemetery, Ackerman
    Aubrey Epps

Claiborne County
Carbondale Cemetery, Lorman
    Bill Foster

Copia County
Hazlehurst City Cemetery, Hazlehurst
    Willis Hudlin

Covington County
Mount Pleasant C.M.E. Church Cemetery,
Mount Olive
    Howard Easterling

DeSoto County, Memphis Metro
Boggan Cemetery, Lewisburg
    Culley Rikard

Forrest County, Hattiesburg Metro
Roseland Park Cemetery, Hattiesburg
    Wid Matthews, Fred Waters

Franklin County
Mount Zion Cemetery, Meadville
    Dick Jones

George County
Magnolia Cemetery, Lucedale
    Claude Passeau

**Harrison County, Biloxi–Gulfport–
Pascagoula Metro**
Evergreen Cemetery, Gulfport
    Jack Ryan

Hinds County, Jackson Metro
Garden Memorial Park, Jackson
    Marshall Bridges
Greenwood Cemetery, Jackson
    Pete Shields
Raymond Town Cemetery, Raymond
    George Gill
Terry Cemetery, Terry
    Phil Redding

**Jackson County, Biloxi–Gulfport–
Pascagoula Metro**
Griffin Cemetery, Moss Point
    Red Bullock
Jackson County Memorial Park, Pascagoula
    Hal Lee, Sam Leslie
Machpelah Cemetery, Pascagoula
    Jay Kirke

Jones County
Hickory Grove Cemetery, Laurel
    Fred Walters
Lake Park Cemetery, Laurel
    Gene Moore
Spring Hill Cemetery, Laurel
    John Davis

Lauderdale County
Memorial Park, Meridian
    Sammy Holbrook, Papa Williams
Rose Hill-Magnolia Cemetery, Meridian
    Danny Clark, Eric McNair, Charlie Moss,
    Skeeter Webb

Lee County
Glenwood Cemetery, Tupelo
    John Merritt, Randy Reese

Shannon Cemetery, Shannon
    Guy Bush
Sherman Cemetery, Sherman
    Dode Criss

Leflore County

Greenlawn Memorial Park, Greenwood
    Provine Bradley
I.O.O.F. Cemetery, Greenwood
    Hughie Critz, Homer Spragins

Lowndes County

Friendship Cemetery, Columbus
    Dixie McArthur, Jake Propst,
    Jim Roberts

Neshoba County

Cedar Lawn Cemetery, Philadelphia
    Bubba Phillips

Noxubee County

Brooksville Cemetery, Brooksville
    Dave Madison
Public Cemetery, Bigbee Valley
    Roosevelt Tate

Panola County

Forest Memorial Park, Batesville
    Sammy Vick
Rose Hill Cemetery, Sardis
    Willie Mitchell

Pontotoc County

Pontotoc Cemetery, Pontotoc
    Jim Joe Edwards

Quitman County

Lambert Cemetery, Lambert
    Ed Chapman

Rankin County, Jackson Metro

Union Baptist Church Cemetery, Puckett
    Anse Moore

Stone County

Bond Cemetery, Bond
    Dizzy Dean

Tunica County

Oakwood Cemetery, Tunica
    Paul Gregory

Warren County

Cedar Hill Cemetery, Vicksburg
    Gus Gardner

Washington County

Greenville Cemetery, Greenville
    Cecil Bolton, Tommy Taylor

Yalobusha

Oak Hill Cemetery, Water Valley
    Dolan Nichols

MISSOURI

Boone County, Columbia Metro

Memorial Park Cemetery, Columbia
    Ed Barnhart

Buchanan County, St. Joseph Metro

Memorial Park Cemetery, St. Joseph
    Bill Bishop, Frosty Thomas
Mount Olivet Cemetery, St. Joseph
    Joe Kelly, Barney Reilly, Oad Swigart

Cape Girardeau County

Fairmont Cemetery, Cape Girardeau
    Elam Vangilder

Carroll County

Mount Zion Cemetery, Bogard
    Ray Powell
Van Horn Cemetery, Tina
    John Jenkins

Cass County, Kansas City Metro

Freeman Cemetery, Freeman
    George Gillpatrick

Chariton County

Mendon Cemetery, Mendon
    Vern Kennedy

Clay County, Kansas City Metro

Fairview Cemetery, Liberty
    Art Thomason

Dent County

Cedar Grove Cemetery, Salem
    Elmer Jacobs

North Lawn Cemetery, Salem
    Ben Cantwell

Dunklin County

Kennett Cemetery, Kennett
    Moxie Manuel

Franklin County, St. Louis Metro

Anaconda City Cemetery, Anaconda
    Loy Hanning

I.O.O.F. Cemetery, Sullivan
    Jim Bottomley

Greene County, Springfield Metro

Berry Cemetery, Ash Grove
    Lewis Yokum

Evergreen Cemetery, Republic
    Skinny O'Neal

Greenlawn Memorial Gardens,
Springfield
    Herschel Bennett

Resurrection Cemetery, Springfield
    Mike Ryba

Rivermonte Memorial Gardens,
Springfield
    Sherm Lollar

Rose Hill Cemetery, Willard
    Ken Gables

Grundy County

Masonic Cemetery, Trenton
    Harry Patton

Harrison County

Mount Moriah Cemetery, Mount Moriah
    Babe Adams

Howell County

Howell County Memorial Park Cemetery,
West Plains
    Tedd Gullic

Iron County

Arcadia Valley Memorial Park, Ironton
    Tim McCabe

Jackson County, Kansas City Metro

Blue Ridge Lawn Memorial Gardens,
Kansas City
    Bullet Joe Rogan

Calvary Cemetery, Kansas City
    Jimmy Gleeson, Bill Kling, Bill Moore,
    Joe Riggert, Roy Sanders, Cotton Tierney

Floral Hills Memorial Gardens, Kansas City
    Louis Johnson, Don O'Riley

Forest Hill Cemetery, Kansas City
    Ad Brennan, Joe Crisp, John Farrell,
    Andrew Hudson, Joe Kuhel, Lefty
    LaMarque, Satchel Paige, John Terry,
    Orange Thompson, Zach Wheat

Highland Cemetery, Kansas City
    Frank Duncan Jr.

Kauffman Foundation & Memorial Gardens,
Kansas City
    Ewing M. Kauffman, Murial M.
    Kauffman

Lincoln Cemetery, Kansas City
    Henny Landers

Longview Memorial Gardens, Kansas City
    Darrell Porter

Memorial Park Cemetery, Kansas City
    John Perrine, John Peters

Mount Moriah Cemetery, Kansas City
    Johnny Kling, Art Loudell, Kid Nichols,
    Dan Quisenberry, Woody Smallwood,
    Hilton Smith, Don Songer, J.L. Wilkinson,
    Jesse Williams

Mount Olivet Cemetery, Kansas City
    Luther Harvel

Mount St. Mary's Cemetery, Kansas City
    Frank Bonner, Jim Lillie, Lynn Nelson,
    Billy O'Brien, Scott Perry, Danny Shay,
    Fred Underwood

Mount Washington Cemetery, Independence
    Mack Allison, Fred House,
    Herm Merritt

Salem Baptist Church Cemetery,
Independence
    Mort Cooper

Jasper County, Joplin Metro

Fairview Cemetery, Joplin
    Frank Thompson

Forest Park Cemetery, Joplin
    Dick Bayless

Friends Cemetery, Purcell
    Ken Boyer

Mount Hope Cemetery, Webb City
   Al Gerheauser
Ozark Memorial Park Cemetery, Joplin
   Ferrell Anderson, Gabby Street
Webb City Cemetery, Webb City
   Bill Peppers

Jefferson County, St. Louis Metro

Hematite Methodist Cemetery, Hematite
   Benny Meyer, Walter Holke

Johnson County

Sunset Hills Cemetery, Warrensburg
   Lou Fette, Charlie Miller, Chuck
   Workman

Linn County

Mount Olivet Cemetery, Marceline
   Ernie Herbert, Chuck Rose

Marion County

Holy Family Cemetery, Hannibal
   Bill Miller
Mount Olivet Cemetery, Hannibal
   Frank Hafner
Riverside Cemetery, Hannibal
   Jake Beckley, Bob Hart
St. Jude's Cemetery, Monroe City
   Buck Robinson

Miller County

Iberia Cemetery, Iberia
   Bill Humphrey

Mississippi County

Garden of Memories Cemetery, Sikeston
   Allyn Stout

Montgomery County

Montgomery City Cemetery, Montgomery
   Jim Bishop

Newton County, Joplin Metro

Diamond Cemetery, Diamond
   Marc Hall
Gibson Cemetery, Neosho
   Ed Hawk
Macedonia Cemetery, Stella
   Al Atkinson

Perry County

Mount Hope Cemetery, Perryville
   Bill Cissell, Bill Schindler

Pettis County

Memorial Park Cemetery, Sedalia
   Hal Schwenk

Phelps County

Masonic Cemetery, St. James
   Roy Parker
Rolla Cemetery, Rolla
   Marv Breuer

Pike County

Bowling Green Memorial Gardens,
Bowling Green
   Jack Graney

Platte County, Kansas City Metro

Line Creek Cemetery, Parkville
   Drummond Brown

Pulaski County

Dixon Cemetery, Dixon
   Wally Schang

Randolph County

Oakland Cemetery, Moberly
   Joe Klugmann

Saline County

Ridge Park Cemetery, Marshall
   Bob Clemens

St. Charles County, St. Louis Metro

St. Peter's Catholic Cemetery, St. Charles
   Ham Schulte

St. Francois County

Masonic Cemetery, Farmington
   Barney Pelty
St. Francois Memorial Park, Bonne Terre
   Bobby Tiefenauer

St. Louis city, St. Louis Metro

Bellefontaine Cemetery, St. Louis
   Philip DeCatsby Ball, Bill Bayne,
   Campbell O. Bishop, Frank Bradsby, Dug
   Crothers, Ned Cuthbert, Julie Freeman,
   Gustave A. Gruner, Bunny High, Bill

Joyce, Henry Overbeck, Hub Pruett, Jack Rowe, Charles C. Spink, J.G. Taylor Spink, Chris Von der Ahe, Perry Werden

Bethany Cemetery, St. Louis
Silver Flint, Willie Sudhoff, Lew Whistler

Calvary Cemetery, St. Louis
Hal Anderson, Tom Barry, William Beckmann, Herman Besse, Andrew F. Blong, Cliff Brady, Jimmy Burke, Bobby Byrne, Dick Collins, Gus Creely, Creepy Crespi, Art Croft, Jumbo Davis, Walt Devoy, Tom Dolan, Frank Figgemeier, Tim Flood, Joe Gannon, Bill Gleason, Jack Gleason, Bill Goodenough, Jack Gorman, James Gould, Chin Green, Mike Haley, Robert E. Hannegan, Ducky Hemp, Phil Hensiek, Charlie Hodnett, Art Hoelskoetter, Jerry Holland, Pat Hynes, Ted Kennedy, Ernie Koob, Charlie Levis, Henry V. Lucas, Felix Mackiewicz, George Mappes, Wally Mattick, Harry McCaffery, Mike McDermott, Jumbo McGinnis, William McGoogan, Marty McManus, Trick McSorley, Paul McSweeney, Daniel Morgan, Robert Morrison, Tom Morrison, Richard C. Muckerman, Joe Murphy, Bill Norman, Ray O'Brien, Jack O'Connor, Mickey O'Neil, Marion Parkere, Frank Pears, Joe Peitz, Bill Popp, Martin Quigley, Joe Quinn, Rip Reagan, Jim Reardon, Paul Rickart, Yank Robinson, Ray Schmandt, Johnny Schulte, Joe Schultz Jr., Joe Schultz Sr., John Schulze, Pat Seery, Gerry Shea, John Sheridan, Urban Shocker, Oscar Siemer, Ed Silch, Skyrocket Smith, Tom Stanton, Justin Stein, Sleeper Sullivan, Jack Tobin, Quincey Trouppe, Connie Walsh, Dee Walsh, Johnny Welch, Boom Boom Wheeler, Carl Whitney, Joe Woerlin, Fred Worden

Jefferson Barracks National Cemetery, St. Louis
Frank Biscan, Doc Bracken, Jack Buck, Plunk Drake, Harry Hanebrink, Flit Holliday, Hughie Miller, Billy Mullen, Floyd Newkirk, Jif Riddel, Branch Russell, Emmett Wilson, Zomp Zomphier

Lakewood Park Cemetery, St. Louis
John Brock

Memorial Park Cemetery, St. Louis
Maurice Archdeacon, Jewel Ens, Mutz Ens, Hi Jasper, John Kroner, Bill Steele, Tom Walden

Mount Hope Cemetery, St. Louis
Ray Sanders

Mount Olive Cemetery of Lemay, St. Louis
Joe Becker

New Bethlehem Cemetery, St. Louis
Bill Abstein, Solly Hofman

New St. Marcus Cemetery, St. Louis
Connie Blank, Silver King, Rudy Kling, Charlie Krehmeyer, Bob Larmore, John Peters, Butch Weis

Oak Grove Cemetery, St. Louis
William DeWitt, Frank Olin, Fred Saigh, Yats Wuestling

Park Lawn Cemetery, St. Louis
Heinie Mueller

Saint Lucas Cemetery, St. Louis
Joe Medwick

SS. Peter & Paul Cemetery, St. Louis
Mike Drissel, Charlie Hautz, Red Juelich, Joe Muich, Phil Todt

St. John's Cemetery, St. Louis
Harry Lunte

St. Matthews Cemetery, St. Louis
Jimmy Hudgens

St. Paul's Churchyard Cemetery, St. Louis
Phil Ketter

St. Peter's Cemetery, St. Louis
Jesse Askew, Cool Papa Bell, Ted Breitenstein, Ernie Hickman, Bubba Hyde, Ted Menze, Ed Pabst

St. Trinity Lutheran Cemetery, St. Louis
Heinie Meine

Valhalla Cemetery, St. Louis
Art Bader, Doug Baird, Toots Coyne, Jack Crooks, Frank Decker, Ray Jansen, Ronnie Miller

St. Louis County, St. Louis Metro

Allen Cemetery, Allenton
Bob Klinger

Bellerive Heritage Gardens, Creve Coeur
Cactus Keck, Stuart F. Meyer

Bethlehem Cemetery, Bellefontaine
Bobby Hofman, Oscar Roettger, Harry
Vahrenhorst

Laurel Hill Memorial Gardens, Pagedale
Allen Elliott

Mount Lebanon Cemetery, St. Ann
Walter Mueller

New Picker's Cemetery, Lemay
Dad Meek

Oak Hill Cemetery, Kirkwood
Charlie Hollocher, Tom Poholsky

Old Meeting House Presbyterian Church
Cemetery, Frontenac
George Sisler

Our Redeemer Cemetery, Affton
Milt Byrnes, Ken Miller

Resurrection Cemetery, Mackenzie
Dan Adams, Jake Boultes, Pat Burke, Bob
Burnes, Mark Christman, Bill Friel,
Raymond Gillespie, Gene Green, Leo
Hannibal, Joe Hoerner, Binky Jones, Hal
Kleine, Otto Krueger, Joe Mowry, Pat
Patterson, Jack Phillips, Joe Poetz, Dick
Reichle

St. John United Church of Christ Cemetery,
Manchester
Hank Arft

St. Paul Churchyard Cemetery, Affton
Scrap Iron Biecher

St. Peter's Catholic Cemetery, Kirkwood
Kid Durbin

Sunset Memorial Park, Affton
Gussie Busch, Hooks Dauss, John Kirby,
Kurt Krieger, Walt Schulz

Stone County

Blue Eye Cemetery, Blue Eye
Chuck Hostetler

Sullivan County

Oakwood Cemetery, Milan
Cal Hubbard

Taney County

Ozarks Memorial Park, Branson
Ernie Nevel

Vernon County

Newton Burial Park, Nevada
George Lyons

MONTANA

Big Horn County

Custer Battlefield National Cemetery,
Crow Agency
Jack Kibble

Rockvale Cemetery, Pryor
Doc Oberlander

Cascade County, Great Falls Metro

Old Highland Cemetery, Great Falls
Ed Colgan

Custer County

Miles City Cemetery, Miles City
Wiman Andrus

Fergus County

Lewistown City Cemetery, Lewistown
Jim Crabb

Flathead County

Conrad Memorial Cemetery, Kalispell
Gus Thompson

Silver Bow County

Holy Cross Cemetery, Butte
Mike Mattimore

Mount Moriah Cemetery, Butte
Jim Powell

Mountain View Cemetery, Butte
Jim St. Vrain

Yellowstone County, Billings Metro

Yellowstone Valley Memorial Park,
Billings
Dave McNally

NEBRASKA

Adams County

Parkview Cemetery, Hastings
Johnny Hopp

Cedar County

Alderson Family Cemetery, Belden
    Dale Alderson

Coleridge City Cemetery, Coleridge
    George Stone

Douglas County, Omaha Metro

Calvary Cemetery, Omaha
    Loren Babe, Mike Prendergast

Forest Lawn Memorial Park, Omaha
    Kid Camp, Lew Camp, Henry Clarke,
    Billy Earle, Roy Luebbe, Russ McKelvy,
    Carl Stimson

Graceland Park Cemetery, Omaha
    Otto Williams

Hillcrest Cemetery, Omaha
    Dan Tipple

Holy Sepulchre Cemetery, Omaha
    Joe Dolan, Jim Kane, Owen Shannon,
    Joe Walsh, Harry Williams

Westlawn Cemetery, Omaha
    Bill Shipke

Gage County

Evergreen Home Cemetery, Beatrice
    Pid Purdy

Liberty Cemetery, Liberty
    Harlan Pyle

Hall County

Grand Island City Cemetery,
Grand Island
    Fred Glade

Soldiers' & Sailors' Home Cemetery,
Grand Island
    Seem Studley

Hamilton County

Aurora Cemetery, Aurora
    Clarence Mitchell, Les Nunamaker

Howard County

Elwood Cemetery, St. Paul
    Grover Alexander

Jefferson County

Prairie Home Cemetery, Diller
    Lee Dressen

Lancaster County, Lincoln Metro

Calvary Cemetery, Lincoln
    Pug Griffin

Lincoln Memorial Park, Lincoln
    Jack Bruner, Bob Mahoney

Raymond Cemetery, Raymond
    Al Bool

Waverly Rose Hill Cemetery, Waverly
    Bill Davidson

Wyuka Cemetery, Lincoln
    Lefty Taber

Lincoln County

Fort McPherson National Cemetery, Maxwell
    Bob Harris

Otoe County

Wykula Cemetery, Nebraska City
    Harry Smith

Richardson County

Steele Cemetery, Falls City
    Charlie Abbey

Scotts Bluff County

Fairview Cemetery, Scottsbluff
    Charlie Jackson

Seward County

Blue Mound Cemetery, Milford
    William Rumler

Stanton County

Pilger Cemetery, Pilger
    Bud Tinning

Thurston County

Agency Cemetery, Winnebago
    Chief Johnson

Wayne County

Ridge Cemetery, Randolph
    Jim Buchanan

NEVADA

Clark County, Las Vegas Metro

Bunker Brother's Memory Gardens
Cemmetery, Las Vegas
    Bob Boken, Chuck Wortman

Palm Vally View Cemetery, Las Vegas
   Dick Strahs
Paradise Memorial Gardens, Las Vegas
   Wally Shaner

Washoe County, Reno Metro

Odd Fellows Cemetery, Reno
   Art Sunday
Sierra Memorial Gardens, Reno
   Archie Campbell

NEW HAMPSHIRE

Carroll County

Center Conway Cemetery, Conway
   Rip Jordan
Ossipee Cemetery, Ossipee
   Fred Brown

Grafton County

Dartmouth Cemetery, Hanover
   Fletcher Low
Pine Knoll Cemetery, Hanover
   Jeff Tesreau
St. Joseph's Cemetery, Bristol
   Walter Prince
Trinity Cemetery, Holderness
   Al Spohrer

Hillsborough County, Manchester Metro

Forest Vale Cemetery, Manchester
   Charlie Baker
Mount Calvary Cemetery, Manchester
   Ray Dobens
Pine Grove Cemetery, Manchester
   John Carney, Lew Cross
St. Joseph Cemetery, Bedford
   Tom Padden, Phenomenal Smith

Hillsborough County, Nashua Metro

Edgewood Cemetery, Nashua
   Bobby Murray
St. Patrick's Cemetery, Hudson
   John Connor
Woodlawn Cemetery, Nashua
   Ike Van Zandt

Merrimack County

Pine Grove Cemetery, Warner
   Allie Moulton
St. Paul School Cemetery, Concord
   Lester Dole
Woodlawn Cemetery, Penacook
   Red Rolfe

Rockingham County, Nashua Metro

Forest Hill Cemetery, East Derry
   Bill Anderson, Fred Tyler
Holy Cross Cemetery, Londonderry
   Duffy Lewis

Rockingham County, Haverhill–North Andover–Amesbury Metro portion

Exeter Cemetery, Exeter
   Hal Janvrin
Greenwood Cemetery, Kingston
   Cannonball Titcomb

Rockingham County, Rochester–Dover, Metro portion

Newington Cemetery, Newington
   Walt Woods

Strafford County, Rochester-Dover Metro

Cold Spring Cemetery, East Rochester
   George Magoon
Durham Community Cemetery, Durham
   Ted Lewis
Pine Grove Cemetery, Barrington
   Bob Barr
St. Mary's Cemetery, Rochester
   Jimmy Bannon

Sullivan County

Mountainview Cemetery, Claremont
   Pat Parker

NEW JERSEY

Atlantic County, Atlantic–Cape May Metro

Atlantic City Cemetery, Pleasantville
   Ed Haigh, Ty Helfrich, Thomas H.
   Jackson, Hilton Kinbrough, Pop Lloyd,
   Max Manning, Sandy Piez
Egg Harbor Cemetery, Egg Harbor
   Lou Bauer, Carl Husta

Greenwood Cemetery, Pleasantville
Chance Cummings

Holy Cross Cemetery, Mays Landing
Ed Schorr

Laurel Memorial Park Cemetery, Egg Harbor
Boardwalk Brown, Ferdie Moore

Lincoln Memorial Park, Mays Landing
Elihu Roberts

Bergen County, Bergen–Passaic Metro

Brookside Cemetery, Englewood
Davy Force

Fair Lawn Memorial Cemetery, Fair Lawn
Tobias Barnes

Fairview Cemetery, Fairview
Willie Garoni, Gil Hatfield, Willard
Marshall, Hank Thormahlen

Garden of Memories, Old Tappan
Buddy Hassett

George Washington Memorial Park,
Paramus
Walter Ancker, Harry Cheek, Jack Cusick,
Emerson Dickman, Cleffie Fennar,
Charlie Fuchs, Tom Gorman, Elston
Howard, Harry Otis

Hackensack Cemetery, Hackensack
Stan Pitula

Madonna Cemetery, Fort Lee
Frank Tabbacchi

Maple Grove Park Cemetery, Hackensack
Ed Goebel

Maryrest Cemetery, Mahwah
Dick Lajeskie

Mount Carmel Cemetery, Tenafly
Jack Doscher, Bill Foxen, William Kinsler

St. Michael's Cemetery, Lodi
Frankie Zak

St. Nicholas Cemetery, Lodi
Otto Huber

Valleau Cemetery, Ridgewood
Charlie Jamieson

Burlington County, Philadelphia Metro

Beverly National Cemetery, Beverly
Tom Allen, Robert Gans, Bill Nagel, Bill
Narleski, Frank Parkinson, Ed Roetz,
Socks Seibold, Rollo Wilson

Brigadier General William C. Doyle
Memorial Cemetery (formerly New Jersey
Veterans Memorial Cemetery), Wrightstown
Eddie Smith

Christ Churchyard, Bordentown
Doc Imlay

Evergreen Cemetery, Lumberton
Chick Holmes

I.O.O.F Cemetery, Burlington
William Coon, Tom Vickery

Lakeview Memorial Park, Cinnaminson
Jim Curry, Jack Meyer, Ham Wade, Hal
Wagner, Phil Weinert, Charlie Young

Morgan Cemetery, Riverton
Lena Blackburne

Mount Laurel Cemetery, Mount Laurel
Jim Spotts

Riverside Cemetery, Riverside
Charlie Stecher

St. Peter's Church Cemetery, Riverside
Chubby Dean, Redleg Snyder

Upper Springfield Cemetery, Jobstown
Joe Ohl

Camden County, Philadelphia Metro

Arlington Cemetery, Pennsauken
Frank Berkelbach, Farmer Steelman

Bethel Memorial Park, Pennsauken
Pop Corkhill

Evergreen Cemetery, Camden
Ed Lennox

Harleigh Cemetery, Camden
John Radcliffe

Locustwood Memorial Park, Cherry Hill
Harry Gleason

Mount Carmel Cemetery, Moorestown
Wid Conroy

New Camden Cemetery, Camden
Danny Green, John Riddle, Fourteen
Wynn

New St. Mary's Cemetery, Bellmawr
Mike Clark, Bill Crowley

Sunset Memorial Park, Merchantville
Pete Sunkett

Union Cemetery, Gloucester
Billy Shindle

Cape May County, Atlantic–Cape May Metro

Seaside Cemetery, Marmora
   George Lowe
South Dennis Cemetery, South Dennis
   Dummy Stephenson
St. Mary's Cemetery, Cape May
   Hal Kelleher

Cumberland County, Vineland–Millville–Bridgeton

Cohansey Bapist Church Cemetery, Roadstown
   Rube Oldring
Fernwood Cemetery, Bridgeton
   Tom Walker
Siloam Cemetery, Vineland
   Ray Steineder

Essex County, Newark Metro

Cemetery of the Holy Sepulchre, East Orange
   Hugh Campbell, Larry Corcoran, Jack Farrell, Jack Farrow, Joseph Norton, Hal O'Hagen
Fairmount Cemetery, Newark
   Skinner Belfield, Charlie Biot, Lew Carl, John Dabney, John Day, Gustav Falzer, Mike Goodfellow, Tommy Louden, Abe Manley, Bob Miller, Everett Mills, Dave Pierson, Dick Pierson, Doc Wiley
Gate of Heaven Cemetery, East Hanover
   Ownie Carroll, Double Joe Dwyer, Happy Finneran, Ed Stelecki, Bill Upham
Glendale Cemetery, Bloomfield
   Joshua Frazier, Elbow Hooker, Pat Scantlebury, Mule Suttles, Ernie Wolf
Immaculate Conception Cemetery, Montclair
   Bert Daniels, Mule Haas, Bob Hooper, Danny O'Connell, Ed Reulbach
Mount Pleasant Cemetery, Newark
   Henry Burroughs, Horatio Munn
Mt. Olivet Cemetery, Bloomfield
   Larry Hesterfer, Don Savage
Mt. Olivet Cemetery, Newark
   Charlie Berry, Micheal Campbell
Restland Memorial Park, East Hanover
   Kewpie Pennington

Rosedale Cemetery, Orange
   Cookie Cuccurullo, Bob Harvey, Len Pearson
St. Mary's Cemetery, East Orange
   George Kopshaw, Rupert Mills
Woodland Cemetery, Newark
   Rynie Wolters

Gloucester County, Philadelphia Metro

Eglington Cemetery, Clarksboro
   Pete Rambo
Cedar Grove Cemetery, Glassboro
   Bill Husted
M.E. Church Cemetery, Williamstown
   Bill Grevell
Wenonah Cemetery, Wenonah
   Norm Baker
Woodbury Memorial Park, West Deptford
   Paul Ownes

Hudson County, Jersey City Metro

Arlington Cemetery, Kearney
   Oliver Sax
Hoboken Cemetery, Hoboken
   Charlie Bierman
Holy Cross Cemetery, North Arlington
   Oyster Burns, Sam Dente, Leo Kiely, Fritz Knothe, Dots Miller, Cotton Minahan, Red Shannon
Holy Name Cemetery, Jersey City
   John Cuff, Bert Daly, Jocko Fields, Ed Forsyth, Mickey Hughes, John Kelty, Jim McCloskey, Mike McCormick, John Puhl, Charles A. Stoneham, Red Waller
Jersey City Cemetery, Jersey City
   John Corcoran
New York Bay Cemetery, Jersey City
   Jimmy Knowles, Rube Peters, Joe Simmons, Al Tesch
St. Peter's Cemetery, Jersey City
   Pete Donnelly
   St. Peter's Cemetery, Weehawken
   Nat Hicks

Hunterdon County, Middlesex–Somerset–Hunterdon Metro

Holcombe-Riverview Cemetery, Lambertville
   Andy Boswell, Charlie Hargreaves

Prospect Hill Cemetery, Flemington
Eric Rodin

Mercer County, Trenton Metro

Cemetery of the First Presbyterian Church,
Ewing
Ralph Caldwell, George Case

Ewing Cemetery, Ewing
Abe Harrison

Greenwood Cemetery, Trenton
Danny Napoleon, Rusty Saunders

Harbourton Cemetery, Harbourton Village
Freddie Green

Mercer Cemetery, Trenton
Walter I. Cook

Our Lady of Lourdes Cemetery, Trenton
George Hessessey

Princeton Cemetery, Princeton
Pop Foster, George W. Thompson

Princeton Memorial Park, Robbinsville
Ed Leip

Riverview Cemetery, Trenton
Fred Gaiser, Bus Saidt, Leo Smith

St. John's Cemetery, Trenton
Pat Powers

St. Mary's Cemetery, Trenton
Joe Burns, Charlie Hanford, Teddy
Kearns, Al Verdel

**Middlesex County, Middlesex–Somerset–
Hunterdon**

Fernwood Cemetery, Jamesburg
Frankie Hayes

Hillside Cemetery, Metuchen
Warren McLaughlin

Holy Cross Burial Park, Jamesburg
Ed Sanicki

Holy Trinity Church, Hopelawn
Billy Urbanski

Lake Nelson Cemetery, Piscataway
Alex Sabo

New Calvary Cemetery, Parlin
Eddie Popowski

Resurrection Cemetery, Piscataway
Dan Dugan, Bob Maier

St. Gertrude's Cemetery, Colonia
Pete Appleton, Frank Bruggy

St. Peter's Cemetery, New Brunswick
John Harkins

St. Peter's Episcopal Church Cemetery,
Spottswood
Pete Sivess

**Monmouth County, Monmouth–Ocean
Metro**

Glenwood Cemetery, Long Branch
Mike Donlin

Monmouth Fields Burial Grounds, West
Long Branch
Leonard Gettelson

Mt. Olivet Cemetery, Red Bank
Snuffy Sternweiss, Dutch Stryker

St. Catherine's Cemetery, Sea Girt
Walt Walsh

St. George Cemetery, Neptune
Joe Albanese

St. Joseph's Church Cemetery, Keyport
John Burke

Morris County, Newark Metro

Locust Hill Cemetery, Dover
Frank McCrea

Ocean County, Monmouth–Ocean Metro

Greenwood Cemetery, Tuckerton
Doc Cramer

Laurelton Cemetery, Laurelton
Jack Martin

Passaic County, Bergen–Passaic Metro

Calvary Cemetery, Paterson
Mike Meola

Cedar Park Cemetery, Paramus
Joe Bennett, Sid Schacht

Creat Haven Memorial Park, Clifton
John Farrell

East Ridgelawn Cemetery, Clifton
Frank Grant, Billy Zitzmann

Holy Sepulchre Cemetery, Totawa
Dick Cogan, John Kelly, Joe McGuckin,
The Only Nolan

King Solomon Cemetery, Clifton
Frank Scott

Laurel Grove Cemetery, Totowa
Ollie Hanson, Jim McCormick, Bill
Pounds, Scotty Robb, Lee Viau

Salem County, Philadelphia Metro

Baptist Cemetery, Salem
 Goose Goslin

Finn's Piont National Cemetery, Salem
 Charlie Gessner

Lawnside Cemetery, Woodstown
 Harry Smith

St. Joseph's Catholic Cemetery, Woodstown
 Whitey Witt

St. Joseph's Cemetery, Swedesboro
 Earl Rapp

**Somerset County, Middlesex–Somerset–
Hunterdon Metro**

Bound Brook Cemetery, Bound Brook
 George Pfister

Evergreen Cemetery, Basking Ridge
 Ben DeMott

Sussex County, Newark Metro

Frankford Plains United Methodist Church
Cemetery, Augusta
 Russ Van Atta

Hainesville Cemetery, Layton
 Harry Harper

Union County, Newark Metro

B'nai Abraham Memorial Park, Union
 Alta Cohen

Evergreen Cemetery, Hillside
 Swede Carlstrom, Charlie Hamburg,
 Charlie Sweasy

Fairview Cemetery, Westfield
 Joe Collins

Graceland Memorial Park, Kenilworth
 Blackie O'Rourke

Hollywood Memorial Park, Union
 Ed Fallenstein, Bill Zimmerman

Rosedale Cemetery, Linden
 Al Reiss

Rosehill Cemetery, Linden
 Rudy Fernandez, Carl Dent, Oscar
 Givens, Bo Wallace

Warren County, Newark Metro

Belvidere Cemetery, Belvidere
 Charlie Berry

Fairmount Cemetery, Phillipsburg
 Ed Fitzpatrick, Tommy Raub, Jack
 Stansbury

NEW MEXICO

Bernallilo County, Albuquerque Metro

Fairview Memorial Park, Albuquerque
 Elmer Ponder

Gate of Heaven Catholic Cemetery,
Albuquerque
 Joe Palmisano

Mount Calvary Cemetery, Albuquerque
 Emmett Bowles, Rip Hagerman

Sunset Memorail Park, Albuquerque
 Rudy Bell, Frank Truesdale

Eddy County

Carlsbad Cemetery, Carlsbad
 Bob Clark

Woodbine Cemetery, Artesia
 Fred Brainerd, Carl Manda

Santa Fe County, Santa Fe Metro

Fairview Cemetery, Santa Fe
 Al Clancy

NEW YORK

**Albany County, Albany–Schenectady–Troy
Metro**

Albany Rural Cemetery, Albany
 Billy Arnold, King Brady, Gene Lansing,
 John Pappalau, Cy Seymour

Memory's Gardens Cemetery, Albany
 Edsall Walker

Our Lady of Angels Cemetery, Albany
 Mickey Devine

St. Agnes Cemetery, Albany
 Mike Burke, Jimmy Esmond, Joe Evers,
 Bill Fagan, Matty Firzgerald, Tom Hess,
 Ed MacGamwell, Ed McDonald, Jack
 O'Brien, Mike Regan, Mellie Wolfgang

St. Agnes Cemetery, Cohoes
 Tom Lynch

St. Patrick's Cemetery, Watervliet
 Tom Donovan, Darby O'Brien, Pat
 Simmons

Allegany County

Hillside Cemetery, Andover
  Bill Lauterborn

St. Mary's Cemetery, Bolivar
  Patsy Dougherty

Woodlawn Cemetery, Wellsville
  Howard Armstrong

Bronx County, New York Metro

Christchurch Columbarium, Bronx
  Ford Frick

New York City Cemetery (Potters Field),
Bronx
  Bock Baker

St. Raymond's Cemetery, Bronx
  Tom Doran, Charlie Jones, Mike Ledwith,
  Jess McMahon, Phil Powers, Jack White

Woodlawn Cemetery, Bronx
  John W. Connor, Alex Farmer, Frankie
  Frisch, Jim Holdsworth, Bat Masterson,
  George McManus, Johnny Murphy, Dave
  Orr, Alex Pompez, Grantland Rice, Dick
  Rudolph, Aleck Smith, Dan Topping,
  Lew Wendell, Heinie Zimmerman

Broome County, Binghamton Metro

Calvary-St. Patrick Cemetery, Johnson City
  Dennis Casey, Doc Farrell, Bill Hallahan,
  Ron Luciano, John McGuinness, Mike
  Murphy

Floral Park Cemetery, Johnson City
  Otis Johnson, Harry Lumley

Glenwood Cemetery, Port Dickinson
  Bert Dorr

Riverhurst Cemetery, Endicott
  John Munyan

Riverside Cemetery, Endicott
  Jake Pitler

Spring Forest Cemetery, Binghamton
  Jim Whitney

Vestal Hills Memorial Park, Vestal
  Glenn Spencer

Cattaraugus County

Delevan Cemetery, Delevan
  Howie Krist

Randolph Cemetery, Randolph
  Ray Caldwell

St. Bonaventure University Cemetery,
St. Bonaventure
  Kid McLaughlin, Joe Walsh

Cayuga County, Syracuse metro

Fort Hill Cemetery, Auburn
  Alan Storke

Indian Mound Cemetery, Moravia
  Lew Carr

St. Joseph's Cemetery, Auburn
  Tug Arundel, Jerry Dorsey, John Mansell,
  Mike Mansell, Tom Mansell, Ed Murphy

Chautauqua County, Jamestown Metro

Bemus Point Cemetery, Bemus Point
  Walter Brown

Evergreen Cemetery, Portland
  Henry Matteson

Glenwood Cemetery, Silver Creek
  George Mohart

Holy Cross Cemetery, Jamestown
  Jack Harper

Levant Cemetery, Levant
  Hugh Bedient

Riverside Cemetery, Kennedy
  Harry Eccles

Sunset Hill Cemetery, Lakewood
  Leon Carlson, Eric Erickson

Chemung County, Elmira Metro

Maple Grove Cemetery, Horseheads
  Al Todd

SS. Peter & Paul Cemetery, Elmira
  Billy Ging, Abe Kruger, Bill Mack, Red
  Murray, Don Richmond

Woodlawn Cemetery, Elmira
  Joe Ogrodowski

Woodlawn National Cemetery, Elmira
  Packy Rogers

Columbia County

Cedar Park Cemetery, Hudson
  Bob Trowbridge

Firwood Cemetery, Stuyvesant
  Clay Van Alystine

Flat Brook Cemetery, Canaan
  Johnny Tillman

Cortland County

St. Mary's Cemetery, Cortland
 Jim Mahady, Pete O'Brien

Delaware County

Paige Cemetery, Downsville
 Fred Odwell

Dutchess County, Dutchess Metro

Fishkill Rural Cemetery, Beacon
 Bill Leith

Poughkeepsie Rural Cemetery,
Poughkeepsie
 Bill Daley, Elmer Steele

Rhinebeck Cemetery, Rhinebeck
 Myron Allen

St. James Churchyard Cemetery, Hyde Park
 Rube DeGroff

St. Mary's Cemetery, Wappinger Falls
 Dan Brouthers

St. Peter's Cemetery, Poughkeepsie
 George Browne

Stanford Cemetery, Stanfordville
 Austin Knickerbocker

Erie County, Buffalo–Niagara Falls Metro

Elmlawn Cemetery, Tonawanda
 Walt Chipple, Herm Doscher, Jim
 Gillespie, Heinie Smith, Elmer Zacher

Forest Avenue Cemetery, Angola
 Pi Schwert

Forest Lawn Cemetery, Buffalo
 Art Hardy, A.J. Lockhart, Sandy
 McDougal, Jim Neher, Monk Sherlock

Holy Cross Cemetery, Lackawanna
 Jimmy Collins, Mickey Corcoran, George
 Daly, Lefty Davis, Pat Dealy, Dave
 Eggler, Huck Geary, George Myers, Jim
 Riley, Chet Ross

Holy Spirit Church Cemetery, North Collins
 Marion Fricano

Lancaster Rural Cemetery, Lancaster
 George Davis

Mount Calvary Cemetery, Cheektowaga
 Dick McCabe, Eddie Phillips, Buddy
 Rosar, Hack Schumann

Mount Olivet Cemetery, Tonawanda
 Scrappy Carroll, Jocko Halligan, Joe

McCarthy, Pedro Miro, Jim Prendergast,
 Stan Rojek, Vince Sherlock, Ty Tyson

Oakwood Cemetery, East Aurora
 Walt Lynch

Ridge Lawn Cemetery, Cheektowaga
 Bill Hunter

St. Augustine Cemetery, Lancaster
 Johnny Mokan

St. Matthews Cemetery, Buffalo
 Billy Milligan

St. Stanislaus Cemetery, Cheektowaga
 Frank Drews, Stan Jok, Frankie Pytlak

Sweeney Cemetery, North Tonawanda
 Burt Lewis

United German & French Cemetery,
Cheektowaga
 Norm McNeil

White Chapel Memorial Park, Amherst
 Bill Duzen

Franklin County

Morningside Cemetery, Malone
 Libe Washburn

St. Bernard's Cemetery, Saranac Lake
 Larry Doyle

Fulton County

Fern Dale Cemetery, Johnstown
 Harry McNeal

Our Lady of Mount Carmel Cemetery,
Gloversville
 George Burns

Genesee County, Rochester metro

St. Joseph's Cemetery, Batavia
 S. Vinceny Maney

Greene County

Evergreen Cemetery, Tannersville
 Joe Doyle

Herkimer, Utica–Rome Metro

Oak Hill Cemetery, Frankfort
 Bud Fowler

St. Agnes Cemetery, Herkimer
 Deke White

St. Joseph's Cemetery, Dolgeville
 Hal Schumacher

St. Mary's Church Cemetery, Little Falls
  Ray Shepardson

Kings County, New York Metro

Canarsie Cemetery, Brooklyn
  Frank Wilson

Cypress Hills Cemetery, Brooklyn
  Jim Snyder, Tad Dorgan, Charlie Girard,
  Pete Lamer, Al Metcalfe, Charlie Mills,
  Sam Mongin, Candy Nelson, Ray Noble,
  Jackie Robinson, Bill Schenck, Josh
  Snyder, Cornelius C. Van Cott, William
  West

Cypress Hills National Cemetery, Brooklyn
  Sandy Burk, Henry Heitmann,
  Highpockets Hudspeth, Phonney Martin

Evergreen Cemetery, Brooklyn
  Emil Batch, Bill Dahlen, Artie Dede,
  Frank Diven, Bob Ferguson, John Juan
  Garcia, George Hall, Herman Pitz,
  Bojangles Robinson, Hack Simmons, Lou
  Slyvester, Oscar Walker, Lave Winham,
  George Zettlein

Flatbush Cemetery, Brooklyn
  John Cassidy

Green-Wood Cemetery, Brooklyn
  Bill Barnie, Asa Brainard, Oliver Brown,
  Josh Bunce, Harold Burr, William
  Cammeyer, Henry Chadwick, Jack
  Chapman, Larry Ciaffone, Fred Crane,
  Jim Creighton, Duncan Fraser Curry,
  Charles H. Ebbets, Dude Esterbrook,
  Wally Fessenden, George Fletcher, Count
  Gedney, Frank Hankinson, Dick Hunt,
  Fred Jacklitsch, Jim Korwan, Henry
  McHenry, Edward Mincher, Nealy
  Phelps, William Trotter Porter, William
  M. Rankin, Fred Siefke, Nat Strong,
  George Tilden, William Marcy Tweed, Joe
  Vila, Joe Wall, Tug Wilson, Herb Worth,
  Al Wright

Holy Cross Cemetery, Brooklyn
  Larry Battam, Ned Bligh, Jack Burdock,
  Doc Bushong, Dick Butler, Denny Clare,
  Dick Cotter, Tom Daly, Joe Farrell, John
  Galvin, William Granger, Gil Hodges, Joe
  Hornung, Charlie Malay, John McGlone,
  Edward J. McKeever, Stephen McKeever,
  Tom Meany, Danny Murphy, Emil H.
  Praeger, Phil Reardon, Tom York

Salem Fields Cemetery, Brooklyn
  Andrew Freedman, Lip Pike

Livingston County, Rochester Metro

Leicester Cemetery, Leicester
  Norm Lehr

St. Agnes Cemetery, Avon
  Ken O'Dea

Temple Hill Cemetery, Geneseo
  Jay Rogers

Monroe County, Rochester Metro

Holy Sepulchre Cemetery, Rochester
  Will Callahan, Tom Carey, Paul Cook,
  Red Dooin, Tex Erwin, Ray Gordinier,
  Wickey McAvoy, George Mogridge, Sam
  Moran, Lou Raymond, Joe Sargent,
  Harry Weaver, Stump Wiedman

Honeoye Falls Cemetery, Honeoye Falls
  Chet Carmichael

Irondequoit Cemetery, Irondequoit
  Nick Bremigan, Mike Kircher

Lake View Cemetery, Brockport
  Herbie Moran

Mount Hope Cemetery, Rochester
  Moose Eggert, Lew Groh, Gene Kimball,
  John McKelvey, Roy Van Graflan

Pine Hill Cemetery, West Rush
  Al Mattern

St. John the Evangelist Cemetery,
Spencerport
  Pat Murray

Webster Rural Cemetery, Webster
  Walter Bernhardt

**Montgomery County, Albany–
Schenectady–Troy Metro**

Fort Plain Cemetery, Fort Plain
  Myron Grimshaw

Hagamans Mills Cemetery, Amsterdam
  Roger Bowman

St. Mary's Cemetery, Fort Johnson
  Bugs Reisgl

Nassau County, Nassau–Suffolk Metro

Beth David Cemetery, Elmont
  Happy Foreman, Saul Rogovin

Cemetery of Holy Rood, Westbury
  Bob Chipman, Zip Collins, Tom Gorman,

Jerry McCarthy, Frank McCormick, Marty
McHale, Chuck Sheerin, Sam Zoldak

Greenfield Cemetery, Uniondale
Arlie Lathan, John Ward

Melville Cemetery, Melville
Specs Torporcer

Nassau Knolls Cemetery & Memorial Park,
Port Washington
Allison Danzig

Plain Lawn Cemetery, Hicksville
Al Moore

Rockville Cemetery, Rockville Center
Joe Kelly

St. Brigid's Cemetery, Westbury
Joseph F. Lannin

St. Mary Star of the Sea Cemetery, Lawrence
John Warner

Niagara County, Buffalo–Niagara Falls Metro

Holy Trinity Roman Catholic Cemetery,
Lewiston
Johnny Pasek

Mount Ridge Cemetery, Royalton Center
Carl Fischer

Oakwood Cemetery, Niagara Falls
Harry Stine

St. Bernard's Cemetery, Lewiston
Art Watson

St. Joseph's Italian Cemetery, Niagara Falls
Sal Maglie

Oneida County, Utica–Rome Metro

Calvary Cemetery, Utica
George Detore

Cedar Lake Cemetery, New Hartford
Steve Roser

Crown Hill Memorial Park, Kirkland
Steve Peek

Forest Hill Cemetery, Utica
Alonzo Breitenstein, Fred Lewis, Art
Mills, Hardy Richardson, Biff Schlitzer

Mount Olivet Cemetery, Whitesboro
Bill Clancy, Joe Kiefer

New Forest Cemetery, Utica
Sam Dodge, Jim Fairbank

St. Agnes Cemetery, Utica
Eddie Burke, Bill Dineen, Mike Griffin

St. Bernard's Cemetery, Waterville
Danny Mahoney

St. Helen's Church Cemetery, Sherrill
Ben Egan

St. Peter's Cemetery, Utica
Amby McConnell

Onondaga County, Syracuse Metro

Assumption Cemetery, Syracuse
Bob Becker, Pat Crisham, Dutch Dotterer

Oakwood Cemetery, Syracuse
Ensign Cottrell, Bob Shawkey

Sacred Heart Cemetery, Syracuse
Al Grabowski, Reggie Grabowski

St. Agnes Cemetery, Syracuse
Jim Devine, Mike Dorgan, Jim Doyle,
Will Kelly, Jimmy Walsh

St. Mary's Cemetery, Syracuse
Frank Corridon, Frank LaManna, Charlie
Osterhout, Bud Podbielan

St. Patrick's Cemetery, Jordan
Fred Burchell

Woodlawn Cemetery, Syracuse
Andy Anderson

Ontario County, Rochester Metro

Glenwood Cemetery, Geneva
Jogn Bogart

Gorham Cemetery, Gorham
Frank Hershey

St. Francis Cemetery, Phelps
Joe Gleason

Woodlawn Cemetery, Canadaigua
Jim McCauley, Frank Smith

Orange County, Newbergh Metro

St. Mary's Cemetery, Port Jervis
Larry McKeon

Oswego County, Syracuse Metro

Redfield Cemetery, Redfield
Bill Duggleby

St. Mary's Cemetery, Fulton
Honey Barnes

St. Paul's Cemetery, Oswego
She Donahue, Rip Vowinkle

Village Cemetery, Mexico
Ripper Collins, Fred Payne

Otsego County

Lake View Cemetery, Richfield Springs
Lou Bruce

Lakewood Cemetery, Cooperstown
Whitey Wilshere

Maple Grove Cemetery, Worcester
Jim Konstanty

Plains Cemetery, Oneonta
Ken Chase, Dick Fowler

Putnam County, New York Metro

Milltown Rural Cemetery, Brewster
Joe Vernon

Queens County, New York Metro

Acacia Cemetery, Jamaica, Queens
Monte Pfeiffer

Calvary Cemetery, Woodside, Queens
David Beadle, Frank Bowes, Charles H.
Byrne, Jimmy Cannon, Rody Carey,
Spider Clark, Jack Coffey, John Connally,
Pete Cregan, John Daily, Bill Devery,
Mike Donovan, Frank Farrell, Bill Finley,
Neal Finn, James E. Gaffney, Jerry
Hurley, Tim Hurst, Willie Keeler, Kick
Kelly, Ed Kennedy, Jim Kennedy, Walt
Kinlock, Al LeFevre, William Loughran,
Frank McCarton, Jack McDonald, Pat
McGee, Hugh McQuillan, Edward
Mullen, Tony Murphy, Tom O'Rourke,
James Shanley, Bill Swanson, George
Taylor, Dasher Troy, Mickey Welch

Flushing Cemetery, Flushing, Queens
Bill Aulick, Frank Brill, Bob Curtis, John
McConaughy

Linden Hill Cemetery, Flushing
Frank Fleet

Lutheran All Faiths Cemetery, Middle
Village, Queens
George Chalmers, Sam Crane, Con Daily,
Slats Davis, Charles Hodes, Bill Hogg,
Red Kleinow, Ernie Lindemann, Doggie
Miller, Bill Morgan, Charlie Reipshlager

Maimonides Cemetery, Elmont
Walter Elias

Mount Olivet Cemetery, Maspeth, Queens
Bill Collins, Jogn Hatfield, Clem
McCarthy, George Meakim, Zach Pettus,
Barron Wilkins

Mount St. Mary's Cemetery, Flushing, Queens
Louis Castro

New Montefiore Cemetery, Pinelawn
Sid Gordon

St. John's Cemetery, Middle Village Queens
Bill Boyd, Tommy Clarke, Al Burch,
James P. Dawson, Willie Hennigan,
Gunboat Hudson, Joe Lake, Gene
McCann, Jimmy Ring, Chief Roseman,
Frank Scanlan

Union Field Cemetery, Flushing, Queens
Arnold Rothstein

Rensselear County, Albany–Schenectady–Troy

East Greenbush Cemetery, East Greenbush
Ed Phelps

Oakwood Cemetery, Troy
Fatty Briody, Bill Craver, Marc Filley,
Mart King, Steve King

St. John's Cemetery, Troy
Jim Devlin, Bub McAtee, Jack Rafter

St. Joseph's Cemetery, Troy
Henry Cote, Dan Minnehan

St. Mary's Cemetery, Troy
Johnny Evers, Hughie Hearne, Mike
Lawlor

St. Peter's Cemetery, Troy
Ralph Ham, John C. Morrissey, Tony Von
Fricken

Richmond County, New York Metro

Fairview Cemetery, Castleton Corners,
Staten Island
Jack Taylor

Frederick Douglass Memorial Park, Staten
Island
Country Bryant, Sol White

Moravian Cemetery, New Dorp, Staten
Island
Jim Mutrie

Ocean View Cemetery (formerly Valhalla
Burial Grounds), Oakwood, Staten Island
Jack Cronin, Tuck Turner

Silver Lake Cemetery, Richmond,
Staten Island
Erastus Wiman

Silver Mount Cemetery, Staten Island
George Sharrott

St. Mary's Cemetery, Grassmere, Staten Island
    Fred Lear

St. Peter's Cemetery, Staten Island
    Harry Damrau, Walter Ockey

Rockland County, New York Metro

Germonds Presbyterian Church Cemetery,
New City
    Bill Kalfass

Nyack Rural Cemetery, West Nyack
    Mark Polhemus

Rockland Cemetery, Sparkill
    Doc Leitner

St. Peter's Cemetery, Haverstraw
    Bil Drescher

**Saratoga County, Albany–Schenectady–
Troy**

Greenridge Cemetery, Saratoga Springs
    Hiker Moran

St. Joseph's Cemetery, Waterford
    Chick Robitaille

St. Peter's Roman Catholic Church
Cemetery, Saratoga Springs
    Joe Gingras

**Schenectady County, Albany–Schenectady–
Troy**

Most Holy Redeemer Cemetery,
Schenectady
    Frank Mountain, Lee Riley

Park View Cemetery, Schenectady
    Johnny Grabowski

St. John's Cemetery, Schenectady
    Bill Cunningham

Vale Cemetery, Schenectady
    Chick Evans, Seth Sigsby

Seneca County

St. Patrick's Cemetery, Geneva
    Frank Dwyer

Steuben County

Grove Cemetery, Bath
    Edwin Curtis

Holy Sepulchre Cemetery, Bath
    Joe Genewich

Rural Cemetery, Hornell
    Vince Dailey

St. Mary's Cemetery, Corning
    Bill Moore

Woodlawn Cemetery, Canisteo
    Mort Flohr

Suffolk County, Nassau-Suffolk Metro

Babylon Cemetery, Babylon
    Leo Fishel

Calverton National Cemetery, Calverton
    Hank Behrman, Grover Froese, Bill
    Johnson, Jim Romano

Holy Trinity Cemetery, North Amityville
    George Ross

Long Island National Cemetery, Farmingdale
    Heinie Beckendorf, Yank Deas, Art
    Gardiner, Les Howe, Charlie Meara,
    Aloysius Palma, Cannonball Dick
    Redding, James Semler, Red Sheridan,
    Ernie Smith, Lefty Starks, George Young

Mount Ararat Cemetery, Farmingdale
    Milton Richman

Pinelawn Memorial Park & Cemetery,
Farmingdale
    Jumbo Brown, Duke Kelliher

Setauket Cemetery, Port Jefferson
    Frank Norton

Southold Presbyterian Cemetery, Southold
    Hal Goldsmith

St. Charles Cemetery, Farmingdale
    Joe Benes, Steve Lembo

St. Patrick's Cemetery, Southold
    Lew Malone

Sullivan County

Beaverkill Cemetery, Rockland
    Abe Attell

Tioga County, Binghamton Metro

Evergreen Cemetery, Owego
    Spence Pumpelly

Tompkins County

Lakeview Cemetery, Ithaca
    John Clapp

Ulster County

Mount Marion Cemetery, Mount Marion
    Dutch Schirick

St. Mary's Cemetery, Kingston
  Bud Culloton, Bill Dugan, Dick Johnston

Warren County, Glens Falls Metro

Glens Falls Cemetery, Glens Falls
  Frank Wurm

St. Mary's Cemetery, South Glens Falls
  Bob Cooney, Jack Gilbert, Ray Miner

Washington County, Glens Falls Metro

Our Lady of Angels Cemetery, Whitehall
  Ebba St. Claire

Union Cemetery, Fort Edward
  Arnie Stone

Wayne County, Rochester Metro

St. Thomas the Apostle Cemetery, Red Creek
  George Mangus

Westchester County, New York Metro

Beverly Hills Cemetery, Mohegan Lake
  George Fiall

Dale Historical Cemetery, Ossining
  Red Hoff

Ferncliff Cemetery, Hartsdale
  Clint Blume, Al Munro Elias, Sid Farrar,
  Red Morgan, Damon Runyon, Ed
  Sullivan

Gate of Heaven Cemetery, Hawthorne
  Angel Aragon, Bob Berman, Heywood
  Campbell Broun, Howie Carter, Bob
  Considine, Arthur Daley, Bill Farnsworth,
  Bill Froats, Billy Gilbert, Jack Lynch, Billy
  Martin, John McSherry, Babe Ruth, Walter
  Signer, Paddy Smith, Heinie Wagner

Greenwood Union Cemetery, Rye
  George Smith

Holy Mount Cemetery, Tuckahoe
  Frank Graham

Holy Sepuchre Cemetery, New Rochelle
  Bob Cremins

Kensico Cemetery, Valhalla
  Ed Barrow, Buck Becannon, Andy
  Coakley, Harry Frazee, Lou Gehrig, Nat
  Jewett, Danny Kaye, Paul Krichell, Louis
  Pelouze, Joe Reichler, Jacob Ruppert,
  William Wedge

Mount Hope Cemetery, Hastings-on-Hudson
  Tom Forster

Sleepy Hollow Cemetery, Tarrytown
  Frank Murphy

Westchester Hills Cemetery, Hastings-on-
Hudson
  Jonah Goldman

NORTH CAROLINA

**Alamance County, Greensboro–Winston–
Salem**

Alamance Memorial Park, Burlington
  Tom Zachary

Linwood Cemetery, Graham
  Shag Thompson

Pine Hill Cemetery, Burlington
  Bill Evans, Maxie Wilson

Rock Creek United Methodist Church
Cemetery, Snow Camp
  Lew Riggs

Spring Friends Cemetery, Snow Camp
  Boyd Perry

**Alexander County, Hickory–Morganton–
Lenior**

Friendship Lutheran Church Cemetery,
Taylorsville
  Charlie Frye

Linney's Grove Baptist Church Cemetery,
Hiddenite
  Jim Poole

Stony Point Cemetery, Stony Point
  Dave Jolly

Bertie County

St. Thomas Church Cemetery, Windsor
  Burgess Whitehead

Buncombe County, Ashesville Metro

Chambers Cemetery, Weaverville
  Rome Chambers
  Forest Lawn Memorial Park, Enka
  Noodles Hahn

Riverside Cemetery, Asheville
  Buck Redfern

Sunset Cemetery, Asheville
  Taylor Duncan

Tweed's Chapel Cemetery, Asheville
  Johnny Lanning

Western Carolina State Veterans Cemetery,
Black Mountain
  George Bradshaw, Frank Messer

Burke County, Hickory–Morganton–Lenior

Burke Memorial Park, Morganton
  Razor Ladbetter

Forest Hill Cemetery, Morganton
  Earle Mack

South Mountain Baptist Church Cemetery,
Morganton
  Woody Rich

**Cabarrus County, Charlotte–Gastonia–
Rock Hill Metro**

Carolina Memorial Park, Kannapolis
  Ron Blackburn, Fred Chapman, Herman
  Fink

Mount Olivet United Methodist Church
Cemetery, Concord
  Billy Goodman

Oakwood Cemetery, Concord
  Willy Fetzer, Herm Holshouser, Clem
  Llewellyn

**Caldwell County, Hickory–Morganton–
Lenior Metro**

Blue Ridge Memorial Park, Lenoir
  Rube Walker

**Catawba County, Hickory–Morganton–
Lenior**

Eastview Cemetery, Newton
  Wade Lefler, Buz Phillips, Eddie Yount,
  Ducky Yount

Cleveland County

Robinson Estate, King's Mountain
  Slow Robinson

Columbus County

Whiteville Memorial Cemetery, Whiteville
  Charlie Ripple, Dave Smith

Craven County

Cedar Grove Cemetery, New Bern
  Stuart Flyth

Cumberland County, Fayetteville Metro

Lafayette Memorial Park, Fayetteville
  Cap Clark, Cal Koonce

**Davidson County, Greensboro–Winston–
Salem Metro**

Barnes Family Cemetery, Churchland
  Junie Barnes

Holly Hill Memorial Park. Thomasville
  Cliff Bolton

**Edgecombe County, Rocky Mount
Metro**

Pinetops Baptist Church Cemetery,
Pinetops
  Herb Cobb

Gardens of Gesthemane, Rocky Mount
  Buck Leonard

**Forsyth County, Greensboro-Winston-
Salem Metro**

Evergreen Cemetery, Winston-Salem
  Norman Yokely

Faith Missionary Alliance Church Cemetery,
Winston-Salem
  Vinegar Bend Mizell

Forsyth Memorial Park Cemetery, Winston–
Salem
  General Crowder, Don Hankins, Glenn
  Liebhardt, Johnny Meador, Ernie Shore,
  Eddie Yuhas

Gardens of Memory, Walkertown
  Rufe Gentry

Main Street United Methodist Church
Cemetery, Kernersville
  Kemp Wicker

Parklawn Memorial Garden, Winston-Salem
  Bob Gillespie, Jack Krol

Salem Cemetery, Winston-Salem
  Fred Anderson, Wes Livengood

**Gaston County, Charlotte–Gastonia–Rock
Hill Metro**

Morningside Park Cemetery, Mount Holly
  George Wilson

Mount Holly Cemetery, Mount Holly
  Chink Outen

Oakwood Cemetery, Gastonia
  Skipper Friday

Stanley Cemetery, Stanley
  Doyt Morris

Guilford County, Greensboro–Winston–Salem Metro

Forest Lawn Cemetery, Greensboro
  Johnny Allen, Sam Gibson

Guilford College Cemetery, Greensboro
  Luke Stuart

Guilford Memorial Park, Greensboro
  Dave Barbee, Ray Hayworth, Mac McLean, Pep Young

Moriah United Methodist Church Cemetery, Gilmer
  Tom Glass

New Garden Friends Cemetery, Greensboro
  Bill Lindsay, Rick Ferrell, Wes Ferrell

New Goshen United Methodist Church Cemetery, Greensboro
  Tom Alston

Oak Ridge Cemetery, Greensboro
  Bob Stafford

Westminster Gardens, Greensboro
  Mace Brown

Harnett County

Buies Creek Cemetery, Buies Creek
  Woody Upchurch

Westview Memorial Gardens, Lillington
  Dusty Cooke

Henderson County

Forest Lawn Memorial Park, Hendersonville
  Lefty West

Shepherd Memorial Park, Hendersonville
  Ewell Blackwell

Hertford County

Catfish Hunter

Iredell County

Iredell Memorial Gardens, Statesville
  Dave Thompson

Johnston County, Raleigh–Durham Metro

Kenly Cemetery, Kenly
  Al Evans, Gary Fortune

Lenior County

Maplewood Cemetery, Kinston
  Stan Spence, George Suggs

Mecklenburg County, Charlotte–Gastonia–Rock Hill

Beatties Ford Memorial Gardens, Charlotte
  Charles Parks

Elmwood Cemetery, Charlotte
  Jule Mallonee

Evergreen Cemetery, Charlotte
  Mike Garbark, Jim Hopper

Forest Lawn Cemetery West, Charlotte
  Jack Cameron, Jimmy Jordan

Hopewell Presbyterian Church Cemetery, Huntersville
  Ben Shields

Sharon Memorial Park, Charlotte
  Pat Cooper, Bill Harris, Garland Lawing, Nig Lipscomb, Ben Paschal, Bob Porterfield

Williams Memorial Presbyterian Church Cemetery, Charlotte
  Paul Burris

Moore County

Mount Hope Cemetery, Southern Pines
  Joe DeBerry

New Hanover County, Wilmington Metro

Greenlawn Memorial Gardens, Wilmington
  Sam Bowens

Oakdale Cemetery, Wilmington
  Gus Brittain

Oleander Memorial Gardens, Wilmington
  Willie Stargell

Wilmington National Cemetery, Wilmington
  Possum Whitted

Northampton County

Davis Family Cemetery, Jackson
  Ron Davis

Orange County, Raleigh–Durham Metro

Chapel Hill Cemetery, Chapel Hill
  Bob Lawson

New Hope Church Cemetery, Chapel Hill
  James Johnston

Pasquotank County

New Hollywood Cemetery, Elizabeth City
  Dick Burrus

Person County

Allensville United Methdist Church
Cemetery, Roxboro
  Enos Slaughter

Bethel Hill Baptist Church Cemetery, Roxboro
  Claude Wilborn

Pitt County, Greenville Metro

Brownhill Cemetery, Greenville
  Dave Barnhill

Randolph County, Greensboro–Winston–Salem Metro

Fairview Cemetery, Liberty
  Tim Murchison

Floral Garden Park Cemetery, High Point
  Dick Culler

Mount Vernon United Methodist Church
Cemetery, Trinity
  Gil English

Springfield Friends Church Cemetery,
High Point
  Woody Crowson

Richmond County

Leak Family Cemetery, Rockingham
  Russ Ford

Robeson County

Meadowbrook Cemetery, Lumberton
  Taffy Wright

Oak Grove Cemetery, Maxton
  Dutch Holland

Rowland Cemetery, Rowland
  Nate Andrews

Rowan County, Charlotte–Gastonia–Rock Hill

Chestnut Hill Cemetery, Salisbury
  Buck Jordan

Green Lawn Cemetery, China Grove
  Dixie Upright

Rowan Memorial Park, Salisbury
  Johnnie Heving, Clyde Kluttz

West Lawn Memorial Park, Landis
  Fred Archer

Rutherford County

Concord Baptist Church Cemetery, Bostic
  Tim McKeithan

Sunset Memorial Park, Forest City
  Smoky Burgess

Sampson County

Baptist Church Cemetery, Salemburg
  Rube Benton

Crumpler Family Cemetery, Salemburg
  Roy Crumpler

Scotland County

Hillside Memorial Cemetery, Laurinburg
  Willie Jones

Stanly County

Fairview Memorial Park, Albemarle
  John Gaddy, Dick Mauney

Stokes County, Greensboro–Winston–Salem Metro

Wilson Primitive Baptist Church Cemetery,
Walnut Cove
  Steve Shemo

Union County, Charlotte–Gastonia–Rock Hill

Lakeland Memorial Park, Monroe
  Dave Coble

Vance County

Union Chapel Church Cemetery, Henderson
  Buster Maynard

Wake County, Raleigh–Durham Metro

Greenmount Cemetery, Raleigh
  Chuck Rowland

Montlawn Memorial Park, Raleigh
  Bill Clarkson, Snake Henry, Jackie May

Oakwood Cemetery, Raleigh
  Bill Wynne

Raleigh Memorial Park, Raleigh
  Vic Sorrell

Raleigh National Cemetery, Raleigh
  Buddy Crump

Wake Forest Cemetery, Wake Forest
  Lee Gooch

Warren County

Fairview Cemetery, Warrenton
  Jack Scott

Wautauga County

Mount Lawn Memorial Park, Boone
  Coaker Triplett

Wayne County, Goldsboro Metro

Fremont Cemetery, Fremont
  Johnny Peacock

Martin-Price Cemetery, Mount Olive
  Ray Scarborough

Willow Dale Cemetery, Goldsboro
  Bill Bell, Mule Shirley

Wilson County

Antioch Baptist Church Cemetery, Middlesex
  Sam Narron

Cedar Grove Cemetery, Elm City
  Vance Page

Evergreen Memorial Gardens, Wilson
  Red Barrett, Stan Partenheimer

Maplewood Cemetery, Wilson
  Bunny Hearn

Stantonsburg Cemetery, Stantonsburg
  Buck Stanton

NORTH DAKOTA

Cass County, Fargo-Moorhead Metro
Holy Cross Cemetery, Fargo
  Ken Hunt, Roger Maris

Ransom County

Enderlin Cemetery, Enderlin
  Cy Pieh

Williams County

Riverview Cemetery, Williston
  Dee Moore, Dewey Williams

OHIO

Adams County

Moore's Chapel Cemetery, Blue Creek
  Austin McHenry

Allen County, Lima Metro

Gethsemani Cemetery, Lima
  Larry Cox

Woodlawn Cemetery, Lima
  Frank Foutz

Ashland County

Ashland Cemetery, Ashland
  Marshall Locke

Ashtabula County, Cleveland–Lorain–Elyria

Chestnut Grove Cemetery, Ashtabula
  Al Humphrey

Mount Pleasant Cemetery, Geneva
  Alex McColl

Athens County

Green Lawn Cemetery, Nelsonville
  Estel Crabtree, John Lovett, Bob Williams

New Marshfield Cemetery, New Marshfield
  Josh Devore

West Union Street Cemetery, Athens
  George Kahler, Howard McGraner

Auglaize County, Lima Metro

German-Protestant Cemetery, New Bremen
  Mack Huenke

Mount Tabor Cemetery, Gutman
  Merle Settlemire

St. Joseph Cemetery, Wapakoneta
  Lefty Houtz

Walnut Hill Cemetery, New Hampshire
  Bob Ewing

Wheeler Cemetery, Wapakoneta
  Whitey Guese

Belmont County, Wheeling Metro

Greenwood Cemetery, Bellaire
  Brickyard Kennedy, Parson Nicholson, Bill White

Holly Memorial Gardens, Pleasant Grove
  Johnny Blatnik

Riverview Cemetery, Martins Ferry
  Cy Morgan

Southern Cemetery, Barnesville
  Gus McGinnis

St. Mary's Cemetery, Martins Ferry
  Dick Padden

Brown County, Cincinnati Metro

Confidence Cemetery, Georgetown
  Slim Sallee, Jack Theis

Butler County, Hamilton–Middletown Metro

Darrtown Cemetery, Darrtown
  Walt Alston
Greenwood Cemetery, Hamilton
  Carl Weilman
Hickory Flats Cemetery, Overpeck
  Dan Daub
Miltonville Cemetery, Miltonville
  Ollie Johns
  Shandon Cemetery, Shandon
  Charlie DeArmond
St. Stephen's Cemetery, Hamilton
  Bill Hobbs, Harry Wilke

Carroll County, Canton–Massillon Metro

Bethlehem Cemetery, Malvern
  Ed Poole

Champaign County

Oakdale Cemetery, Urbana
  Johnny Siegle

Clark County, Dayton–Springfield Metro

Asbury Cemetery, Springfield
  Harvey Haddix
Calvary Cemetery, Springfield
  John Dolan, Jiggs Donahue, Joe Dunn,
  Pat Lyons
Ferncliff Cemetery, Springfield
  Dick Harley, Bill Keen, Brooks Lawrence,
  Jack Mercer, Otto Neu, Bill Niles
Glen Haven Memorial Gardens, New
Carlisle
  Charlie Pickett
St. Bernard Cemetery, Springfield
  Joe Rickert

Clermont County, Cincinnati Metro

Calvary Cemetery, Moscow
  Bill Irwin
Goshen Cemetery, Goshen
  Larry Goetz, Sam Leever
Green Mound Cemetery, New Richmond
  Hank Schenz
Greenlawn Cemetery, Milford
  Ches Crist, Tacks Latimer, Eppa Rixey
Mount Moriah Cemetery, Withamsville
  Earl Mossor

Clinton County

Clarksville Cemetery, Clarksville
  Biff Wysong
Sugar Grove Cemetery, Wilmongton
  Charles Murphy

Columbiana County, Youngstown–Warren Metro

Columbiana County Memorial Park,
East Liverpool
  Bill Powell
Grove Hill Cemetery, Hanoverton
  Hi Myers
Spring Grove Cemetery, East Liverpool
  Scoops Carey, Doc Howard, Win Mercer
Spring Hill Cemetery, Wellsville
  John Godwin, Bill Mundy
St. Aloysius Catholic Cemetery, East Liverpool
  Curt Welch
Woodland Cemetery, Salineville
  Ed McNichol

Coshocton County

Fairfield Cemetery, West Lafayette
  Lem Hunter

Crawford County, Mansfield Metro

Oakwood Cemetery, Bucyrus
  Ray Mack, Fred Trautman
Union Cemetery, New Washington
  Bill Kuehne

Cuyahoga County, Cleveland–Lorain–Elyria

Acadia Memorial Park, Mayfield Heights
  Les Fusselman, Roger Peckinpaugh
All Saints Cemetery, Northfield
  Mike Goliat
Brooklyn Heights Cemetery, Brooklyn Heights
  Ed Kusel
Calvary Cemetery, Cleveland
  Bill Bradley, Buttons Briggs, Dick Carroll,
  Ed Delahanty, Frank Delahanty, Jim
  Delahanty, Joe Delahanty, Harley
  Dillinger, Frank Doljack, Steve Evans,
  Lee Fohl, James Green, Thomas Healy,
  Dutch Henry, Ed Hilley, Kenny Hogan,
  Glenn Lienhardt, Paddy Livingston, Ed
  McKean, George Rettger, Hank
  Ruszkowski, Fred Smith, Steve Sundra,

Patsy Tebeau, Bill Wambsganss, Ollie Welf, Del Young

Evergreen Cemetery, Bedford
Gene Bremmer

Fairview Park Cemetery, North Olmstead
Otto Hess

Highland Park Cemetery, Cleveland
Luke Easter, Joe Vosmik

Hillcrest Memorial Park, Bedford Heights
Eddie Morgan, Red Ruffing

Holy Cross Cemetery, Cleveland
Moxie Divis, Frank Gibbons, Charley Lupica, Harry Redmond

Knollwood Cemetery, Mayfield Heights
Ernest S. Barnard, Herb Conyers, Billy Evans, Pete Johns, Bill Miller, Ellis Ryan, Terry Turner

Lake View Cemetery, Cleveland
Heinie Berger, Alva Bradley, Helene Britton, Ray Chapman, Pete Hotaling, Ernie Kish, Milo Lockwood, Ed McFarland, Dave Pope, Frank DeHaas Robison, Martin Stanley Robison, Matthew Stanley Robison, Charles Somers, Arlie Tarbert, Myron H. Wilson

Lakewood Park Cemetery, Rocky River
Clint Brown, Jack Hardy, David H. Jacobs, Jim Rutherford, Bill Stemmeyer, Larry Twitchell, George Uhle

Lutheran Cemetery, Cleveland
Bill Schardt

Mount Olive Cemetery, Cleveland
Harry Eisenstat

Riverside Cemetery, Cleveland
Amos Cross, Frank Cross, Emil Leber, Jim McLaughlin

St. James Methodist Church Cemetery, Cleveland
Edward Dimes

St. John's Cemetery, Cleveland
Bill Reidy

St. Joseph's Cemetery, Cleveland
Jim Gilman, Bill Gleason, Charlie Smith

St. Mary's Cemetery, Cleveland
Ed Zmich, Dode Paskert

Sunset Memorial Park, North Olmstead
Oscar Grimes

West Park Cemetery, Cleveland
Reddy McMillan, Ed Seward

Whitehaven Park, Mayfield Village
Don Fisher, Ken Landenberger

Woodland Cemetery, Cleveland
Joe Ardner, Harry Arundel, Charlie Bohn, Sim Bullas, Ed Cermak, Charlie Dewald, Ed Spurney

Delaware County, Columbus Metro

Oak Grove Cemetery, Delaware
Cliff Curtis

Erie County

Calvary Cemetery, Sandusky
Al Halt

Oakland Cemetery, Sandusky
Jerry Upp, Gene Woodburn

Scott Cemetery, Huron
James A. Campbell

Fairfield County, Columbus Metro

Forest Rose Cemetery, Lancaster
Pete Sims

Franklin County, Columbus Metro

Forest Lawn Cemetery, Columbus
Ed Donalds

Glen Rest Memorial Estate, Reynoldsburg
Russ Miller, Earl Moore, Owen Scheetz

Green Lawn Cemetery, Columbus
Harry Fritz, Wally Gerber, James Gifford, C.B. Griffin, Fred Hunter, Bob Kline, Jack McCallister, Gus Schmeltz, Kip Selbach, Billy Southworth, Jack Taylor, James Thurber, James Williams

Mifflin Cemetery, Gahanna
Nick Cullop

Mount Calvary Cemetery, Columbus,OH
Ed Dundon, Graham McNamee

Pioneer Cemetery, Westerville
Allen Tedrow

Resurrection Cemetery, Worthington
Joe Sparma

St. Joseph's Cemetery, Lockbourne
John Fluhrer, Frank Gleich, Jim Handiboe, Bill Hinchman, Dick Hoover, Vic Janowicz, Lee Magee, Frank Magee, Robert Quinn, Arch Reilly

St. Michael's Cemetery, Columbus
  Chappie Geygan

Sunset Cemetery, Galloway
  John Galbreath

Union Cemetery, Columbus
  Hank Gowdy, Benny Kauff, Hal Kime,
  William Lackey, Fred Taylor, Rasty
  Wright

Fulton County, Toledo Metro

Greenlawn Cemetery, Delta
  Harvey Bailey

South Swanton Cemetery, Swanton
  Roy Beecher

Geauga County, Cleveland–Lorain–Elyria

All Souls Cemetery, Chardon
  George Anderson, Hank Riebe

Greene County, Dayton–Springfield

North Cemetery, Cedarville
  Bumpus Jones

Woodland Cemetery, Xenia
  Henry Farrell

Guernsey County

Northwood Cemetery, Cambridge,OH
  Welcome Gaston

Hamilton County, Cincinnati Metro

Arlington Memorial Gardens, Cincinnati
  Gordy Coleman, Claude Corbitt, Bob
  Geary

Baltimore Pike Cemetery, Cincinnati
  Charlie Bell, Red Ehret, Nellie Pott

Bridgetown Cemetery, Cincinnati
  Flea Clifton

Calvary Cemetery, Cincinnati
  Wally Kopf

Gate of Heaven Cemetery, Montgomery
  Jim Beckman, Gus Bell, Eddie Hunter,
  Ted Kluszewski, Marge Schott, Bob
  Wellman

Guardian Angel Cemetery, Cincinnati
  Roy Hughes

Longview Asylum Cemetery, Cincinnati
  Kid Baldwin

Mount Washington Cemetery, Cincinnati
  John Ewing, Buck Ewing

Mt. Moriah Cemetery, Cincinnati
  Rube Bressler, Larry Kopf

Oak Hill Cemetery, Cincinnati
  Ival Goodman, Johnny Hodapp, Bobby
  Mitchell, Jack Niemes, Tom Sullivan

Rest Haven Memorial Park, Cincinnati
  Bill Hart, Tom Swope

Spring Grove Cemetery, Cincinnati
  Les Backman, Frank Bancroft, Bill Bea, Jim
  Blackburn, Billy Campbell, Charlie Case,
  Boss Cox, Powell Crosley Jr., Francis L.
  Dale, Pat Deisel, Ernie Diehl, Julius
  Fleischmann, Max C. Fleischmann,
  Charlie Gould, Charlie Grant, Heinie
  Groh, Emil Haberer, Crese Heismann, Bug
  Holliday, Waite Hoyt, Miller Huggins,
  Larry Jacobus, Jim Keenan, Campbell J.
  McDiarmid, Lou Meyers, George Miller,
  Ralph Miller, Ren Mulford, Red Munson,
  Larry Pape, George Paynter, George
  Pechiney, George Proeser, Percy Reed,
  Icicle Reeder, John Reilly, Ralph Sharman,
  Ed Sperber, Clarence Stephens, Joe
  Strauss, Harry Steinfeldt, Charles Phelps
  Taft, Podge Weihe, Sidney Weil, Harry
  Wheeler, Harry Wheeler, Sam Woodruff,
  George Yeager

St. Aloysius Gonzaga Catholic Cemetery,
Cincinnati
  Ralph Brickner

St. John's Cemetery, Cincinnati
  Harry Armbruster, Herm Wehmeier

St. Joseph's New Cemetery, Cincinnati
  Bill Bartley, Buzz Boyle, Eddie Boyle, Jack
  Boyle, Jim Boyle, Carney Flynn, Denny
  Lyons, Barry McCormick, Billy Riley, Jack
  Sutthoff

St. Joseph's Old Cemetery, Cincinnati
  Larry Benton, Joe Burke, Moe Burtsch,
  Ed Hug, Al Kaiser, Al Niehaus, Ambrose
  Puttmann, Gus Shallix, Blackie Wegman

St. Mary's Cemetery, Cincinnati
  Ralph Birkofer, Tony Hellman, Marty
  Herrmann, Steve Larkin, Fred
  Mollenkamp, Heinie Peitz, Ed Sicking,
  Jake Stenzel

Union Baptist Cemetery, Cincinnati
  Helburn Meadows

Union Cemetery, Montgomery
  Bubbles Hargrave, Jack Pfiester

Vine Street Hill Cemetery, Cincinnati
  Nick Altrock, Al Bashang, Red Bittmann,
  Chink Heileman, Garry Hermann, Jack
  Reiss, John Singleton, A.H. Tarvin, Eddie
  Tiemeyer

Walnut Hills Cemetery, Cincinnati
  George Rohe

Wesleyan Cemetery, Cincinnati
  Frank Bell, Speed Merchant

Hancock County

Maple Grove Cemetery, Findlay
  Tot Pressnell

St. Michael's Church Cemetery, Findlay
  Delos Drake

Harrison County

Cadiz Cemetery, Cadiz
  Moses Vasbinder

Grandview Cemetery, Scio
  Eddie Onslow, Jack Onslow

Henry County

United Church of Christ Cemetery, Holgate
  Jack Hallett

Highland County

Greenfield Cemetery, Greenfield
  Al Strueve

Hillsboro Cemetery, Hillsboro
  Hugh Fullerton, Kirby White

Huron County

St. Paul's Catholic Cemetery, Norwalk
  Jerry Nops

York Chapel Cemetery, Bellevue
  Bob Rothel

Jackson County

Fairmount Cemetery, Jackson
  Pat Duncan

Ridgewood Cemetery, Wellston
  Lefty James

**Jefferson County, Steubenville–Weirton
Metro**

Mt. Calvary Cemetery, Steubenville
  JackLewis, Tom Needham

Richmond Cemetery, Richmond
  Doc Kerr

Tiltonsville-Indian Mound Cemetery,
Tiltonsville
  John Easton

Union Cemetery, Steubenville
  Johnny Bates, Harry Hardy, William
  Johnston, George Kaiserling, Fleet
  Walker, Welday Walker

Upland Cemetery, Yorkville
  Skeeter Scalzi

Knox County

Mound View Cemetery, Mt. Vernon
  Edgar McNabb

Lake County, Cleveland–Lorain–Elyria

Evergreen Cemetery, Painesvile
  Marv Hawley

Madison Memorial Cemetery, Madison
  Milt Shoffner

Middle Ridge Cemetery, Madison
  Elmer Bates

Lawrence County, Huntington–Ashland

Woodland Cemetery, Ironton
  Harry Truby, Joe Willis

Licking County, Columbus Metro

Cedar Hill Cemetery, Newark
  Al Schweitzer

Fredonia Cemetery, Fredonia
  Woody English

Newark Memorial Gardens, Newark
  John Shackleford

Wilson Cemetery, Newark
  Paul Carpenter

Lorain County, Cleveland–Lorain–Elyria

Butternut Ridge Cemetery, North Eaton
  Pit Gilman

Calvary Cemetery, Lorain
  Dad Clarke

Elmhurst Park Cemetery, Avon
  Harry Bemis, Bill Bonness

Greenwood Cemetery, Wellington
  Jack Wadsworth

Resthaven Memory Gardens, Avon
  Bill Holder, Dick Wakefield

Ridge Hill Memorial Park, Amherst
Irish McIlveen

Westwood Cemetery, Oberlein
Clay Fauver

Lucas County, Toledo Metro

Calvary Cemetery, Toledo
Roger Bresnahan, Connie Desmond,
Frank Gilhooley, Len Madden, Red Smith

Forest Cemetery, Toledo
George Kelb, Harry McCluskey, Lee
Richmond

Mt. Carmel Cemetery (formerly St. Mary's
Cemetery), Toledo
Erve Beck

Ottawa Hills Memorial Park, Toledo
Garland Buckeye, Dick Kimble, Emilio
Palmero

Swan Creek Cemetery, Monclova
Charles Brown

Toledo Memorial Park, Sylvania
Ralph Comstock, Cliff Fannin, Harry
Hinchman, Dick Marloew, Ollie
Marquardt, Pete McShannic, Roy
Parmelee, Al Schulz, Ed Scott

Woodlawn Cemetery, Toledo
Rollin Cook, Fred Cooke, Lave Cross,
Nig Fuller, Topsy Hartsel, Addie Joss,
Harry Taylor, Myles Thomas

Madison County, Columbus Metro

Kirkwood Cemetery, London
Bob Bescher, Neb Stewart

**Mahoning County, Youngstown–Warren
Metro**

Brunsteter Cemetery, Austintown
Bill Otey

Calvary Cemetery, Youngstown
Nick Goulish, Pat Griffin, Marty Hogan,
Billy Rhiel

Forest Lawn Memorial Park, Youngstown
Frank Mills, Lou Schettler

Lake Park Cemetery, Youngstown
Charlie Conway

Oak Hill Cemetery, Youngstown
Ed Cartwright, Jimmy McAleer, John
Scheible

St. John's Cemetery, Campbell
Johnny Kucab

Tod Homestead Cemetery, Youngstown
Mike Modak

Marion County

Marion Cemetery, Marion
George Hogan

St. Mary's Cemetery, Marion
John Malarkey

**Medina County, Cleveland–Lorain–Elyria
Metro**

Fairview Park Cemetery, Granger
Gene Woodling

Mound Hill Cemetery, Seville
C.V. Matteson

Myrtle Hill Cemetery, Valley City
Paul O'Dea

Woodlawn Cemetery, Wadsworth
Cy Vorhees

Meigs County

Middleport Hill Cemetery, Middleport
Mother Watson

Mercer County

North Grove Cemetery, Celina
Bruno Betzel

Saint Henry's Church Cemetery, Saint Henry
Wally Post

Miami County, Dayton–Springfield Metro

Harris Creek Cemetery, Bradford
Pete Bigler

Monroe County

Oak Lawn Cemetery, Woodsfield
Sad Sam Jones

**Montgomery County, Dayton–Springfield
Metro**

Beth Abraham Cemetery, Dayton
Si Burick

Bethel Cemetery, Phillipsburg
Jesse Haines

Calvary Cemetery, Dayton
Bernie Hungling, Francis Powers, Jimmy
Whelan

Dayton Memorial Park, Dayton
  Ollie Klee, Terry Lyons, Stubby Magner,
  Jack Rowan, Dutch Ussat

Dayton National Cemetery, Dayton
  Bob Boston, Stubby Magner

Germantown Cemetery, Germantown
  Dazzy Swartz

Greencastle Cemetery, Dayton
  Ray Brown

West Memory Gardens, Dayton
  Chester Blanchard

Woodland Cemetery, Dayton
  Dan Bickham, Amos Booth, O.P. Caylor,
  Clyde Engle, Howard Freigau, Ducky
  Holmes, Harry McIntire

Morrow County

Shauck Cemetery (formerly Johnsville
Cemetery), Shauck
  Palmer Hildebrand

Muskingum County

Greenwood Cemetery, Zanesville
  Howdy Caton

Mount Calvary Cemetery, Zanesville
  Sandy McDermott

Mount Olive Cemetery, Zanesville
  Frank Wayneberg

Ottawa County

Clay Cemetery, Genoa
  Babe Doty

Perry County

Maplewood Cemetery, New Lexington
  John Churry, Rube Ward

New Straitsville Cemetery, New Straitsville
  Tom Williams

Rose Hill Cemetery, Roseville
  Dizzy Nutter

Shawnee Cemetery, Shawnee
  Tom Thomas

Pickaway County, Columbus Metro

Forest Cemetery, Circleville
  Lefty Webb

Hitler-Ludwig Cemetery, Circleville
  Jack Compton

Pike County

Mound Cemetery, Piketon
  Wiley Dunham

Portage County, Akron Metro

Aurora Cemetery, Aurora
  Ben Shaw

Standing Rock Cemetery, Kent
  Will Sawyer

Preble County

Fairview Cemetery, West Alexandria
  Phil Saylor

Richland County, Mansfield Metro

Bellville Cemetery, Bellville
  Scott Hardesty

Mansfield Catholic Cemetery, Mansfield
  John Daley

Mansfield Cemetery, Mansfield
  Ernie Beam, Buck West

Ross County

Floral Hills Memory Gardens, Chillicothe
  Barnie Schreiber

Greenlawn Cemetery, Chillicothe
  Dany Friend

Sandusky County

Lindsey Cemetery, Lindsey
  Red Thomas

Oakwood Cemetery, Fremont
  Russ Kerns

Scioto County

Greenlawn Cemetery, Portsmouth
  Harry Blake, Al Bridwell, Algie McBride,
  Piggy Moore, Chet Spencer, Pinky
  Swander

Memorial Burial Park, Wheelersburg
  Earl Smith

Rushtown Cemetery, Rushtown
  Branch Rickey

St. Peter's Catholic Cemetery, Wheelersburg
  Ed Hock

Seneca County

St. Mary's Cemetery, Tiffin
  Paul Maloy

St. Wendelin Church Cemetery, Fostoria
Pat Hilly

Stark County, Canton–Massillon Metro

Alliance City Cemetery, Alliance
Bounce Grimes, Earl Moseley

Calvary Cemetery, Massillon
Kid O'Hara

Christ Evangelical Lutheran Cemetery
(formerly Mapleton Cemetery), Mapleton
Vince Shupe

East Lawn Cemetery, Minerva
Ray Grimes, Roy Grimes

Forest Hill Cemetery, Canton
Sig Broskie, Ed Gremminger, Joe Houser,
John O'Connell, Charley Stanceu

Glendale Cemetery, Akron
Charlie Morton

Greensburg Cemetery, North Canton
Ossie France

Magnolia Cemetery, Magnolia
John Dagenhart

Massillon Cemetery, Massillon
Bob Fothergill, Warren Shannabrook, Earl
Blackburn

North Canton Cemetery, North Canton
Rabbit Warstler

Rose Hill Memorial Park, Massillon
Fred Bratschi, Dick Gossett

St. John's Catholic Church Cemetery, Canton
Bill Delaney

St. Joseph's Cemetery, Massillon
Herm Malloy

Sunset Hills Burial Park, Canton
Thurman Munson

Warstler Cemetery, Middlebranch
Joe Agler

West Lawn Cemetery, Canton
Bill Batsch, George Textor

Summit County, Akron Metro

Chestnut Hill Memorial Park, Cuyahoga Falls
Tod Sloan

Crown Hill Memorial Park, Twinsburg
Bunk Congalton, Elmer Flick, Bob
Whitcher, Chief Zimmer

Glendale Cemetery, Akron
Joe Battin, Sam Wise

Greenlawn Cemetery, Akron
Ed Walker

Hillside Memorial Park, Akron
Wayman Cash, Farmer Weaver

Holy Cross Cemetery, Akron
Mike Kahoe

Lakewood Cemetery, Akron
Clarence Wright

Mount Peace Cemetery, Akron
Mike Finney, Joe Neale

Rose Hill Burial Park, Fairlawn
Frank Motz, Hank Ritter, Luke Sewell

Springfield Center Presbyterian Cemetery,
Akron
Bob Spade

St. Nicholas Russian Orthodox Cemetery,
Akron
Pete Susko

St. Vincent's Cemetery, Akron
Scotty Ingerton

**Trumbull County, Youngstown–Warren
Metro**

Churchill Cemetery, Churchill
Bob Wood

Niles Union Cemetery, Niles
Harry M. Stevens

Oakwood Cemetery, Warren
Red Ames

Tuscarawas County

Evergreen Burial Park, New Philadelphia
Rube Marshall

Grandview Cemetery, Strasburg
Larry Schlafly

Peoli Methodist Church Cemetery, Peoli
Cy Young

Union Cemetery, Uhrichsville
Frank LaPorte, Whitey Moore, Al Shaw,
Dave Wright

Van Wert County

Ohio City Cemetery, Ohio City
Dode Smith

Warren County, Cincinnati Metro

Lebanon Cemetery, Lebanon
Earl Yingling

Springboro Cemetery, Springboro
  Bert Hamric

Washington County, Parkersburg–Marietta Metro

East Lawn Memorial Park, Marietta
  Karl Meister

Valley Cemetery, Marietta
  Dick Hoblitzell, Frank Jones

Wayne County

Doylestown Cemetery (aka Chestnut Hill Cemetery), Doylestown
  Denny Galehouse

Wooster Cemetery, Wooster
  Harry Billiard, Guy Hecker

Wood County, Toledo Metro

New Belleville Ridge Cemetery, Dowling
  Jim Bilbrey

Tontogany Cemetery, Tontogany
  Lucky Wright

Union Hill Cemetery, Bowling Green
  Ernie Neitze

Weston Cemetery, Weston
  Dan Abbott

Wyandot County

Bethel Cemetery, Sycamore
  Luther Bonin

Oak Hill Cemetery, Upper Sandusky
  Fred Osborn

OKLAHOMA

Beckham County

Fairlawn Cemetery, Elk City
  Cal Dorsett

Caddo County

Carnegie Cemetery, Carnegie
  Bill Reynolds

Canadian County, Oklahoma City Metro

El Reno Cemetery, El Reno
  Claude Thomas, Hugh Willingham

Cleveland County, Oklahoma City Metro

Lexington Cemetery, Lexington
  Bill Shore

Creek County

South Heights Cemetery, Sapulpa
  Denver Grisby

Garfield County, Enid Metro

Memorial Park Cemetery, Enid
  Lil Stoner, Dud Branom, Rip Radcliff

Garvin County

Mount Olivet Cemetery, Pauls Valley
  Jennings Poindexter

Harmon County

Fairmount Cemetery, Hollis
  Wilcy Moore

Jackson County

Altus Cemetery, Altus
  Mike Balenti

Jefferson County

Ringling Memorial Cemetery, Ringling
  Howie McFarland

Johnston County

Atoka Cemetery, Atoka
  Ted Blankenship

Tishomingo Cemetery, Tishomingo
  Euel Moore

Kay County

IOOF Cemetery, Blackwell
  Harry Huston

Le Flore County

Milton Cemetery, Hot Springs
  Rube Foster

Lincoln County

Meeker New Hope Cemetery, Meeker
  Carl Hubbell, Jim Winford

Logan County, Oklahoma City Metro

Summit View Cemetery, Guthrie
  Ernie Burch

Major County

Ames Cemetery, Ames
  Bennie Warren

Mayes County

Fairview Cemetery (aka Pryor Cemetery), Pryor
  Chad Kimsey, Hank Wyse
Graham Memorial Cemetery, Pryor
  Cliff Mapes

Muscogee County

Citizens Cemetery, Fort Gibson
  Jim Gladd
Green Hills Cemetery, Muskogee
  Paul Hinson
Memorial Park Cemetery, Muskogee
  Ab Wright

Okfuskee County

Parier Springs Cemetery, Boley
  George Jefferson

Oklahoma County, Oklahoma City Metro

Chapel Hill Memorial Gardens, Oklahoma City
  Bruce Sloan
Fairlawn Cemetery, Oklahoma City
  Liz Funk
Memorial Park Cemetery, Oklahoma City
  Charlie Emig, Pepper Martin, Allie Reynolds, Red Shillings
Resurrection Memorial Cemetery, Oklahoma City
  Tommy Tatum
Rose Hill Cemetery, Oklahoma City
  Frank Kellert, Milt Steengrafe, Dick Stone, Lloyd Waner
Sunny Lane Cemetery, Oklahoma City
  Johnny Hall

Ottawa County

Lofland Cemetery, Wyandotte
  Roy Jarvis

Pawnee County

North Indian Cemetery, Pawnee
  Chief Yellowhorse
Woodland Cemetery, Cleveland
  Vallie Eaves, Ted Welch

Pittsburg County

Elmwood Cemetery, Hartshorne
  Warren Spahn
Oak Hill Cemetery, McAllister
  Joe McGinnity

Pontotoc County

Memorial Park Cemetery, Ada
  Uke Clanton
Rosedale Cemetery, Ada
  Harry Brecheen, Ross Reynolds

Pottawatomie County, Oklahoma City Metro

Techumseh Cemetery, Techumseh
  Cy Blanton

Seminole County

Maple Grove Cemetery, Seminole
  Hugh Alexander

Stephens County

Duncan City Cemetery, Duncan
  Peaches Davis, Joe Hassler, Ned Pettigrew, Jim Walkup
Marlow Cemetery, Marlow
  Eddie Palmer

Tulsa County, Tulsa Metro

Calvary Cemetery, Tulsa
  Jack Bradley, Tony Rego
Floral Haven Memorial Gardens, Broken Arrow
  Jim Brewer
Memorial Park Cemetery, Tulsa
  Bill Breckinridge, Cal Crum, Howie Gregory, Jack Killilay, Carl Morton, Jim Oglesby, Jim Shilling, Tommy Warren, Charlie Wheatley
Rest Haven Cemetery, Sperry
  Denny Burns
Rose Hill Memorial Park, Tulsa
  Ed Klepfer, Doc Reisling, Ben Tincup
Woodland Memorial Park, Sand Springs
  Jerry Adair

Wagoner County, Tulsa Metro

Elmwood Cemetery, Wagoner
  Chuck Corgan, Fred Olmstead

Washington County
White Rose Cemetery, Bartlesville
    Bugs Bennett

Washita County
Cloud Chief Cemetery, Cloud Chief
    Dale Mitchell

Woods County
Alva Municipal Cemetery, Alva
    Bill McGill
Capron Cemetery, Capron
    Danny Thompson

OREGON

Benton County, Corvallis Metro
Oaklawn Memorial Park, Corvallis
    Oscar Harstad

**Clackamas County, Portland–Vancouver
Metro**
Zion Memorial Park, Canby
    Ed Coleman, Harry Gardner

Coos County
Sunset Memorial Park Cemetery, Coos Bay
    Floyd Stromme

Deschutes County
Greenwood Cemetery, Bend
    Paul Gehrman

Douglas County
Odd Fellows Cemetery, Myrtle Creek
    Glenn Elliott

Jackson County, Medford–Ashland Metro
Jacksonville Cemetery, Jacksonvile
    Ed Wilkinson

Josephine County
Granite Hill Cemetery, Grants Pass
    Charlie Armbruster
Hillcrest Memorial Park, Grants Pass
    Mel Ingram, Hub Pernoll, Ken Williams

Lane County, Eugene–Springfield Metro
Laurel Hill Cemetery, Springfield
    Howie Fox

Rest-Haven Memorial Park, Eugene
    Hal Luby

Lincoln County, Eugene–Springfield Metro
St. Paul Cemetery, St. Paul
    Curt Coleman

Linn County
Liberty Cemetery, Sweet Home
    Lyle Bigbee

Marion County, Salem Metro
Belcrest Memorial Park, Salem
    Howard Maple, Max Marshall
Restlawn Memory Gardens, Salem
    Bill Bevens, Wally Flagler

**Multnomah County, Portland–Vancouver
Metro**
Lincoln Memorial Park (formerly Mount
Scott Park Cemetery), Portland
    Cliff Carroll, Carl Druhot, Jim Keesey,
    Al Kellogg, Ralph Kreitz
Lone Fir Cemetery, Portland
    Rudy Kalloi, Tom Parrott, Jiggs Parrott
Mount Calvary Cemetery, Portland
    Ad Liska, Denny Williams
Pioneer Cemetery, Portland
    Suds Sutherland
Portland Memorial Cemetery, Portland
    Charlie High, Syl Johnson, Fielder Jones,
    Charlie Swindells
River View Cemetery, Portland
    Carl Mays, Gus Fisher
Riverview Abbey Mausoleum, Portland
    Dixie Leverett, Harry Rice, Doug Taitt
Skyline Memorial Gardens, Portland
    Charley Moore
St. Mary's Cemetery, Portland
    Harry Kane
Willamette National Cemetery, Portland
    Carson Bigbee, Bill Curran, Joe Erautt,
    Howie Haworth, Bruce Hitt, John
    Leovich, Dink O'Brien,. Bill Pertica,
    George Scott

Polk County, Salem Metro
Buena Vista Cemetery, Independence
    Ed Mensor

Union County

Elgin Cemetery, Elgin
Byron Speece

Odd Fellows Cemetery, LaGrande
Pete Dowling

Wasco County

Odd Fellows Cemetery, The Dalles
Solly Salsbury

Washington County, Portland–Vancouver Metro

Valley Memorial Park, Hillsboro
Wes Schulmerich

Yamhill County, Portland–Vancouver Metro

St. James Catholic Cemetery, McMinnville
Billy Sullivan

PENNSYLVANIA

Adams County

Annunciation Church Cemetery,
McSherrystown
Bill Sherdel

Evergreen Cemetery, Gettysburg
Jake Boyd, Eddie Plank

Mt. Carmel Cemetery, Littlestown
Cliff Heathcote

Sunnyside Cemetery, York Springs
Elmer Myers

Allegheny County, Pittsburgh Metro

36th Ward Cemetery (Banksville), Pittsburgh
Ben Froelich

All Saints Church Cemetery, Pittsburgh
Ted Sadowski

Allegheny Cemetery, Pittsburgh
Mark Baldwin, Josh Gibson, Gus
Greenlee, Denny McKnight, Ted Page, Cy
Rheam, Rosey Rowswell, Harold Tinker,
Wyatt Turner

Allegheny County Memorial Park,
Allison Park
Deacon Phillippe

Braddock Catholic Cemetery, Braddock
Tom Quinn

Calvary Cemetery, Pittsburgh
Pud Galvin, Enos Kilpatrick, Bill Regan,
Jimmy Smith, Moose Solters, Steve Toole

Chartiers Cemetery, Carnegie
Al Wagner

Elizabeth Cemetery, Elizabeth
Andy Bruckmiller

Fairview Cemetery, Whitehall
Joe Connell

Grandview Cemetery, East McKeeysport
Jake Smith

Greenwood Cemetery, Pittsburgh
Joe Taylor

Homestead Cemetery, Homestead
Bill Armour, Alex Jones, Cum Posey,
Henry Youngman

Homewood Cemetery, Pittsburgh
Bill Bishop, Clarence Bruce, Earl Francis,
Jim Gardner, Josh Gibson Jr., Bob Gibson,
Reddy Gray, Ad Gumbert, Billy
Gumbert, Teenie Harris, Sonnyman
Jackson, Lefty Mellix, Lew Moren, Squiz
Pillion, John Tener, Bill Thompson, Pie
Traynor, Robert Lee Vann, Ren Wylie

Jefferson Memorial Park, Pleasant Hills
Luke Boone, Rip Collins, Dutch Jordan,
Paul Long, Rube Sellers, Jack Snyder,
Steve Swetonic, Honus Wagner, Speed
Walker, Elmer Yoter

Minersville Cemetery, Pittsburgh
Frank Smith

Montours Presbyterian Cemetery, Oakdale
Chico Blair

Mount Airy Cemetery, Natrona Heights
Dutch Rudolph

Mount Calvary Cemetery, McKees Rocks
Mike Hopkins

Mount Lebanon Cemetery, Mount Lebanon
Harry Kirsch

Mount Olivet Cemetery, Pittsburgh
Red Callahan

Mount Royal Cemetery, Glenshaw
Whitey Alperman, Harv Cushman

Mount Vernon Cemetery, Mckeesport
William Ford, Rube Parnham

North Side Catholic Cemetery, Pittsburgh
Grant Briggs, Dick Buckley, Jack
Cummings, Gus Dundon, John Gruber

Oakland Cemetery, Pittsburgh
  Tun Berger

Restland Memorial Park, Monroeville
  Allie Thompkins

Resurrection Cemetery, Coraopolis
  Frankie Gustine, Jeep Handley

Richland Cemetery, Dravosburg
  James Harrison

Smithfield East End Cemetery, Pittsburgh
  Ducky Swan

Southside Cemetery, Pittsburgh
  Jim Pastorius

St. Augustine's Cemetery, Pittsburgh
  Nick Maddox

St. George's Cemetery, Pittsburgh
  Frank Lobert

St. Joseph's Cemetery, East McKeesport
  Shine Cortazzo

St. Martin's Cemetery, Pittsburgh
  Marty Berghammer

St. Mary Church Cemetery (Sharpsburg),
Pittsburgh
  Ralph Michaels

St. Mary's Cemetery (Penn Ave.), Pittsburgh
  Bobby Cargo

St. Mary's Cemetery, McKees Rocks
  Joe Vitelli

St. Mary's Roman Catholic Cemetery (Troy
Hill), Pittsburgh
  Ray Miller, Tom O'Brien, Buck Sweeney

St. Paul's Cathedral Cemetery, Pittsburgh
  Regis Leheny

St. Wendelin Cemetery, Pittsburgh
  Elmer Knetzer

Union Dale Cemetery, Pittsburgh
  Dave Black, Eddie Miller, Ed Morris,
  Billy Otterson, Marr Phillips, Al Pratt,
  Elmer Smith, Gene Steinbrenner, Ed
  Swartwood

West View Cemetery, Pittsburgh
  William Benswanger, Barney Dreyfuss,
  Sameul W. Dreyfuss

Westminster Presbyterian Church Cemetery,
Upper Saint Clair
  Bob Prince

William Penn Memorial Cemetery, Churchill
  Walt Kimmick

Armstrong County

Ford City Cemetery, Ford City
  Bob Pepper

Freeport Cemetery, Freeport
  Charlie Kuhns

Kittanning Cemetery, Kittanning
  Ossee Schreckengost

Beaver County, Pittsburgh Metro

Beaver Cemetery, Beaver
  Jack Darragh, Tom McCreery, Hugh
  Mulcahy, Ted Reed, Jim Toy

Grove Cemetery, Beaver Falls
  Joe Hughes

Irvin Cemetery, Rochester
  Alex Pearson

Locust Grove Cemetery, Ellwood City
  Rube Dessau

Old Monaca Cemetery (aka Union
Cemetery), Monaca
  Chris Lindsay, Howie Shanks

Sylvania Hills Memorial Park, Rochester
  Vern Hughes

Bedford County

Everett Cemetery, Everett
  Earl Howard

Schellsburg Cemetery, Schellsburg
  Chuck Wolfe

Berks County, Reading Metro

Aulenbach Cemetery, Mt. Penn
  Sam Field, Jack Fox, Charlie Shoemaker,
  Phil Tomney

Charles Evans Cemetery, Reading
  Eddie Day, Bill Dunlap, Jake Goodman,
  Frank Heifer, Jesse Levan, Shadow Pyle

Forest Hills Memorial Park, Reiffton
  Carl Furillo, Epp Sell, Stan Wentzel

Gethsemane Cemetery, Reading
  Whitey Kurowski, Kohly Miller

Heidelberg Cemetery, Robesonia
  Stan Klopp

Jesuit Novitiate Cemetery, Wernersville
  Al Travers

St. Peter's Cemetery, Reading
  Henry Larkin, Larry Ressler

Blair County, Altoona Metro

Alto Reste Park Cemetery, Altoona
   Walt Thomas

Calvary Cemetery, Altoona
   Albert Bradley, Tommy Irwin,
   Joe Martin, Bob Ramazzotti,
   Germany Smith

Fairview Cemetery, Altoona
   John Gochnaur

Oakridge Cemetery, Altoona
   Charlie Manlove

Bradford County

Camptown Cemetery, Camptown
   Grover Powell

Monroeton Cemetery, Monroeton
   Jake Northrop

SS. Peter & Paul Cemetery, North Towanda
   Ed Larkin

St. Bernard's Cemetery, Bradford
   John Shearon

Tioga Point Cemetery, Athens
   Aaron Clapp

Bucks County, Philadelphia Metro

Bristol Cemetery, Bristol
   Dan Potts

Evergreen Memorial Park, Bensalem
   Tom Miller

Newtown Cemetery, Newtown
   Wallace Terry

Our Lady of Grace Cemetery, Langhorne
   John Quinn

Reform Cemetery, Perkasie
   Ed Ritterson

Resurrection Cemetery, Bensalem
   Tom Kirk

St. Mark's Cemetery, Bristol
   John Coleman

Sunset Memorial Park, Feasterville
   John Karst

Union Cemetery, Quakertown
   Lefty Smoll

Butler County, Pittsburgh Metro

Browndale Cemetery, Renfew
   Ron Kline

Mt. Varnum Cemetery, North Washington
   Roy Witherup

Cambria County, Johnstown Metro

Grandview Cemetery, Johnstown
   Elmer Cleveland, Frank West

St. John's Catholic Church Cemetery, Geistown
   Frank Gatins

Cameron County

Newton Cemetery, Emporium
   Carl Lindquist

Carbon County, Allentown–Bethlehem–Easton Metro

Evergreen Cemetery, Jim Thorpe
   Hob Hiller

GAR Cemetery, Summit Hill
   Joe Gormley

Jim Thorpe Memorial Mausoleum
   Jim Thorpe

Sacred Heart New Cemetery, Palmerton
   Elmer Valo

St. Mary's Slovak Church Cemetery, Mahanoy City
   Joe Boley

Centre County, State College Metro

Branch Cemetery, State College
   Bill Stuart

Fairview Cemetery, Millheim
   Paul Musser

Philipsburg Cemetery, Philipsburg
   Tom Phillips

Chester County, Philadelphia Metro

Birmingham-LaFayette Cemetery, West Chester
   Ted Baldwin

East Caln Friends Buring Grounds, Downingtown
   Walt Doane

Fairview Cemetery, Coatesville
   Doc Amole, John Jones

Greenmount Cemetery, West Chester
   Bud Sharpe

Haym Salomon Memorial Park, Frazer
   Harry Shuman

Oak Grove Cemetery, Parker Ford
 Roy Sherid

Oaklands Cemetery, West Chester
 Joe Borden, Levi Meyerle

Oxford Cemetery, Oxford
 Jack Ogden

Parker Ford Baptist Church Cemetery,
Parker Ford.
 Jing Johnson

Philadelphia Memorial Park, Frazer
 Hans Lobert, John Shetzline

Pughtown Baptist Cemetery, Spring City
 Dick Ricketts

Rolling Green Memorial Park, West Goshen
 Theodore Waters

St. Francis DeSales Cemetery, Chester
Heights
 Jim McTamany

St. Partick's Cemetery, Kennett Square
 Mike Grady

Union Hill Cemetery, Kennett Square
 Eddie Collins Jr., Herb Pennock, Nip
 Winters

Clarion County

Clarion Cemetery, Clarion
 Emmet Heidrick

New Bethlehem Cemetery, New Bethlehem
 Hutch Campbell

Clearfield County

Atlantic Cemetery, Atlantic
 Goat Anderson

Luthersburg Cemetery, Luthersburg
 Frank Shugart

Morningside Cemetery, DuBois
 Lee Gamble, Henry Smoyer

Clinton County

Highland Cemetery, Lock Haven
 Jim Brown, Davy Dunkle, Tom Poorman,
 Jake Shaffer

St. Mary's Cemetery, Lock Haven
 Jerry Donovan

Columbia County, Scranton–Wilkes-Barre–Hazleton

Elan Memorial Park Cemetery, Bloomsburg
 Bobby Rhawn

Hillside Cemetery, Catawissa
 Lew McCarty

New Rosemont Cemetery, Bloomsburg
 Jim Devlin

Pine Grove Cemetery, Berwick
 Ralph Savidge

Crawford County

Greendale Cemetery, Meadville
 George Grossart

Saegertown Cemetery, Saegertown
 Sal Campfield

St. Brigid's Cemetery, Geneva
 Bob Garbark

Cumberland County, Harrisburg–Lebanon–Carlisle Metro

Rolling Green Memorial Park, Camp Hill
 George Hunter, Lynn Myers, Billy Myers,
 Andy Oyler

Spring Hill Cemetery, Shippensburg
 George Noftsker

Dauphin County, Harrisburg–Lebanon–Carlisle Metro

Blue Ridge Memorial Gardens, Harrisburg
 Tom Buskey

Cathedral Cemetery, Harrisburg
 Henry Meyers

East Harrisburg Cemetery, Harrisburg
 Les Bell, Jimmie DeShong, Charlie Snell

Harrisburg Cemetery, Harrisburg
 John Brackenridge, Ray Mueller, Dutch
 Schesler, Harvey Smith

Hummelstown Cemetery, Hummelstown
 Phil Paine

Lincoln Cemetery, Harrisburg
 Colonel Strothers

Midland Cemetery, Steelton
 Rap Dixon

Mount Calvary Cemetery, Harrisburg
 Ed Sales

Oak Hill Cemetery, Millersburg
 Sumner Bowman

Paxtang Cemetery, Harrisburg
 Myrl Brown, Snake Wiltse

Prospect Hill Cemetery, Steelton
 Red Owens

Wiconisco Cemetery, Wiconisco
Ed Clough, Bill Hart

Woodland Memorial Gardens, Harrisburg
Bill Rodgers, Russ Wrightstone

Delaware County, Philadelphia Metro

Arlington Cemetery, Drexel Hill
George Bausewine, Jack Clements,
Monte Cross, Wes Curry, Joe Green,
Walter Huntzinger, Jim Jackson, Howard
Lohr, Sherry Magee, Jake Munch, Joe
Munson, Harry O'Neill, Morrie Rath, Ad
Swigler, Frederick Westervelt, Woody
Wheaton

Chester Rural Cemetery, Chester
Dave Anderson, Tom Berry, Will Serad

Eden Cemetery, Collingdale
Ed Bolden, Octavius Catto, Johnny Drew,
S.K. Govern

Fernwood Cemetery, Lansdowne
Ike Benners, Charlie Brynan, George
Craig, George Davis, Henry Easterday,
Chick Fulmer, Washington Fulmer, Bill
Harbridge, Hardie Henderson, Bill
Knowlton, Elias Peak, Harry Schafer

Glenwood Memorial Gardens, Broomall
Harvey MacDonald

Haven Memorial Park, Chester
Porter Charleston

Holy Cross Cemetery, Yeadon
John Barthold, Charlie Bastian, Henry
Boyle, Jim Brennan, Pat Carroll,
Ned Connor, Dan Coogan, Wild Bill
Donovan, Jim Field, John Kalahan, Dan
Kerwin, Ed Knouff, Bill Leinhauser, Ed
Lennon, Billy Lennon, Dan McGarvey,
Edward McLaughlin, William McLean,
John Munce, Simon Nicholls, Will
Pierson, Butch Rementer, Joe Rullo,
Bernie Snyder, George Trenwith, Zeke
Wrigley

Immaculate Heart of Mary Cemetery,
Linwood
Joe Cassidy

Lawn Croft Cemetery, Linwood
Bert Cunningham, Charlie Johnson, Bris
Lord, Curly Ogden, Rube Vinson

Leiper Church Cemetery, Swarthmore
John Leiper

Media Cemetery, Media
Wesley Wilkins

Middletown Cemetery, Media
Hinkey Haines

Montrose Cemetery, Upper Darby
Will Holland

Mount Lawn Cemetery, Sharon Hill
Phil Cockrell, Joe Craig, Jeep McClain,
Connie Morgan, Chaney White

Mount Lebanon Cemetery, Collingdale
Max Patkin

Mount Moriah Cemetery, Yeadon
John Deasley, Pat Deasley, George Dovey,
Israel Durham, George Ewell, Bill
Greenwood, Jocko Milligan, George
Snyder

Mount Zion Cemetery, Collingdale
Hot Stuff Mayo, Buddy Burbage

SS. Peter & Paul Cemetery, Springfield
Jim Baumer, Tom Ferrick, Harry Marnie,
Wedo Martini, John McGillen, Danny
Murtaugh, Si Pauxtis, John Stevens

St. Charles Cemetery, Drexel Hill
Pete Conway

St. Denis Cemetery, Havertown
John Abadie, Joe Burns, John Castle,
Jimmy Dykes, Jack Hayden

St. Francis DeSales Cemetery, Chester
Heights
Johnny Podgajny

Elk County

Sarah Thayer Memorial Cemetery, Ridgway
Billy Rhines

St. Mary's Catholic Cemetery, St. Mary's
Dan Costello

Erie County, Erie metro

Erie Cemetery, Erie
Lou Bierbauer, Ed Cushman, Sam
Jethroe, Charles Strick, Ernest L. Wright

Evergreen Cemetery, Union City
Fred Chapman

Girard Cemetery, Girard
James Hart

Lakeside Cemetery, Erie
Lovell Harden

Trinity Cemetery, Erie

Dell Darling. Bill Finneran, Gussie
Gannon, Mike Morrison

Wintergreen Gorge Cemetery, Erie
Eddie Klep

Fayette County, Pittsburgh Metro

Cochran Cemetery, Dawson
Jock Menefee

Indian Creek Baptist Church Cemetery,
Mill Run
Roger Miller

Lafayette Memorial Park, Brier Hill
Bill Forman, Pat Mullin

Mount Auburn Cemetery, Fayette City
Bill Phillips, Jim Russell, Bill Wolfe

Oak Grove Cemetery, Republic
Harry Wilhelm

Oak Lawn Cemetery, Uniontown
Dean Sturgis

Forest County

North Forest Cemetery, Marienville
Fritz Scheeren

Franklin County

Cedar Grove Cemetery, Chambersburg
Piggy Ward

Cedar Hill Cemetery, Greencastle
King Lear

Corpus Christi Cemetery, Chambersburg
Gus Dorner

Greencastle Cemetery, Greencastle
Togie Pittinger

Lincoln Cemetery, Chambersburg
Mike Mowrey

Norland Cemetery, Chambersburg
Charley Gelbert

Parklawns Memorial Gardens,
Chambersburg
Robert Moorhead

St. Thomas Cemetery, St. Thomas
Nellie Fox

Fulton County

Siloam United Methodist Church Cemetery,
Harrisonville
George Selkirk

Greene County

Greene County Memorial Park, Waynesburg
Chuck Coles

Hewitt Cemetery, Rices Landing
Pete Knisley

Jefferson Cemetery, Jefferson
Art Goodwin

Huntingdon County

Mount Union Cemetery, Huntingdon
Hank Eisenhart

Riverview Cemetery, Huntingdon
Gene Elliott

Indiana County

St. Bernard's Cemetery, Indiana
Doc Gessler

Juniata County

New Church Hill Cemetery, Port Royal
Fred Frankhouse

**Lackawanna County, Scranton–Wilkes-
Barre–Hazleton**

Abington Hills Cemetery, Clarks Summit
Chick Shorten

Cathedral Cemetery, Scranton
John Cananaugh, Bill Coughlin, Alex
Mustaikis, Joe Samuels

Dunmore Cemetery, Dunmore
Dave Williams

Forest Hill Cemetery, Scranton
Henry Fox

Mount Carmel Cemetery, Dunmore
Vic Delmore, John McDonald

SS. Cyril & Methodius Cemetery, Peckville
Nestor Chylak

St. Catherine's Cemetery, Moscow
Bill Howerton, Hughie Jennings, Jerry
Lynn, Jim Murray, Finners Quinlan, Joe
Shaute

St. Francis Church Cemetery, Eynon
Joe Paparella

St. John's Cemetery, Jessup
Ben Cardoni

St. Joseph's Cemetery, Minooka
Jack O'Neill, Jim O'Neill, Mike O'Neill,
Steve O'Neill, Mike McNally, Junior Walsh

St. Mary's Visitation Parish Cemetery,
Dickson City
  Joe Glenn

St. Rose of Lima Cemetery, Carbondale
  Jack Fee, Pete Gillespie

Lancaster County, Lancaster Metro

Fairview Cemetery, Denver
  Lou Knerr

Florin Cemetery, Mt. Joy
  Snake Deal

Lancaster Cemetery, Lancaster
  Whitey Gibson

Laurel Hill Memorial Gardens, Columbia
  Jimmy Sheckard

Masonic Cemetery, Elizabethtown
  Bob Rice

Millersville Mennonite Cemetery, Millersville
  Charlie Miller

Riverview Burial Park, Lancaster
  Tom Stouch

Woodward Hill Cemetery, Lancaster
  George Carman, Grant Thatcher

Lawrence County

Oak Park Cemetery, New Castle
  Paul McCullough

SS. Philip & James Cemetery, New Castle
  Chet Boak

**Lebanon County, Harrisburg–Lebanon–
Carlisle**

Hershey Cemetery, Hershey
  George Staller

Indiantown Gap National Cemetery, Annville
  Bill Miller

Mt. Annville Cemetery, Annville
  Ed Miller

Mt. Lebanon Cemetery, Lebanon
  Nelson Greene

Lehigh County, Allentown–Bethlehem–Easton

Arlington Memorial Park, Allentown
  Claude Hendrix

Cedar Hill Memorial Park, Allentown
  Johnny Bucha, Sam Fishburn

Northwood Cemetery, Emmaus
  Eddie Zimmerman

Resurrection Cemetery, Allentown
  Jim Honochick

Union Cemetery, Allentown
  John Meister

**Luzerne County, Scranton–Wilkes-Barre–
Hazleton**

Calvary Cemetery, Drums
  Billy Lee, Dan McGeehan

Evergreen Cemetery, Kingston
  Buck Freeman

Hazleton Cemetery, Hazleton
  Charlie Jordan

Laurel Cemetery, White Haven
  Brad Kocher

Oak Lawn Cemetery, Wilkes-Barre
  Dixie Howell

SS. Peter & Paul Ukrainian Catholic Church
Cemetery, Plymouth
  Pete Elko

St. Ann's Cemetery, Freeland
  Matt Broderick, Connie McGeehan, John
  Shovlin

St. Gabriel's Cemetery, Hazleton
  Gene Connell

St. Ignatius Cemetery, Pringle
  Adam Comorosky

St. John's Cemetery, Dallas
  Mickey Witek

St. Joseph's Church Cemetery, Nanticoke
  Steve Bilko

St. Joseph's Polish Catholic Cemetery,
West Wyoming
  Joe Ostrowski

St. Mary's Annunciation Church Cemetery,
Pringle
  Harry Dorish

St. Mary's Cemetery, Wilkes-Barre
  Frank Crossen, Steamer Flanagan, Pete
  Gray, Mickey Haslin, Mike Konnick, Abe
  Lizotte, John McCloskey, Tony Rensa,
  John Walsh

St. Nicholas Cemetery, Shavertown
  Billy Goeckel

St. Peter's Lutheran Church Cemetery,
Hughestown
  Bucky Harris

Lycoming County, Williamsport Metro
Jersey Shore Cemetery, Jersey Shore
  Frank Nicholson
Montoursville Cemetery, Mountoursville
  Adam Johnson
Mound Cemetery, Williamsport
  Ed Holly, Bob Lindemann
Twin Hills Memorial Park, Muncy
  Carl Stotz
Wildwood Cemetery, Williamsport
  Fred Applegate, Robert Asbjornson,
  Rube Manning, Don Manno, Thomas H.
  Richardson, Jimmy Sebring, Frank E.
  Sipe, George Stovey, Bucky Veil

McKean County
Oak Hill Cemetery, Bradford
  Elmer Bliss
St. Bernard's Cemetery, Bradford
  Petie Behan

Mercer County, Sharon Metro
Hadley Cemetery, Hadley
  Esty Chaney
Mercer Citizen's Cemetery, Mercer
  Harry Maskrey, Leech Maskrey
Oakwood Cemetery, Sharon
  Charles Gibson
St. Mary's Cemetery, Sharon
  Jack McAleese

Mifflin County
Church Hill Cemetery, Reedsville
  Dutch Sterrett

Montgomery County, Philadelphia Metro
Calvary Cemetery, West Conshohocken
  Roy Mack, Bing Miller, George O'Brien,
  By Saam
Edgewood Cemetery, Pottstown
  Harry Gilbert
Fairview Cemetery, Willow Grove
  Mac McDonald
Fernwood Cemetery, Royersford
  Ray Hartranft
Forest Hills Cemetery, Huntingdon Valley
  Foghorn Bradley, Charlie Eckert, Twink
  Twining

George Washington Memorial Park,
Plymouth Meeting
  Bill Patton
Gladwyn Methodist Church Cemetery,
Gladwyn
  Richie Ashburn
Hillside Cemetery, Roslyn
  Chief Bender, Sam Crane, Del Ennis,
  Charlie Mason, Bill Peterman, George
  Stutz
Holy Sepulchre Cemetery, Wyndmoor
  Stan Baumgartner, Zach Clayton, Terry
  Connell, Joe Daly, Bill Hallman, Fritz
  Henrich, Frank Hoerst, Chick Keating,
  Matt Kilroy, Connie Mack, Tommy
  Madden, Billy Maharg, Warren Miller,
  Joe O'Rourke, Patsy O'Rourke, Tony
  Parisse, Harry Pearce, Ira Thomas,
  Steve Yerkes
Lawnview Cemetery, Rockledge
  Bill Fouser, Andy Knox
Merion Memorial Park, Bala Cynwyd
  Jacob White, George Williams
Montgomery Cemetery, Norristown
  Bill Thomas
Pottstown Cemetery (West), Pottstown
  John Gilbert
Riverside Cemetery, West Norristown
  Roy Ellam, Roy Thomas
Rose Hill Cemetery, Ambler
  Lew Richie
St. John's Lutheran-Brick Church Cemetery,
Montgomery
  Rube Yarrison
St. Mark's Lutheran Cemetery, Pennsburg
  Karl Winsch
Valley Forge Gardens, King of Prussia
  Sam McConnell
West Laurel Hill Cemetery, Baba Cynwyd
  Joe Berry Jr., Pete Childs, Harry
  Diddlebock, Butch Jones, Harry Lyons,
  Walt Moser, Bob Peterson, Al Reach,
  Francis Richter, Walter Schlicter, Count
  Sensenderfer, Orator Shafer, Ben Shibe,
  Thomas S. Shibe, Cub Stricker, Tink
  Turner, Harry Wright
Westminster Cemetery, Bala Cynwyd
  Joe Berry Sr., Harry Davis, JohnJackson,

Sam Kimber, Stoney McLinn, Charlie
Nyce, Jack Ridgway, Al Sauter, Joe Ward,
Al Wilmore, Frank Zinn

Whitemarsh Memorial Park, Ambler
Hugo Bezdek, James Carolan, Cliff Ross,
Bucky Walters

Montour County

Odd Fellows Cemetery, Danville
Bill Banks, Art McCoy

**Northampton County, Allentown–
Bethlehem–Easton Metro**

Easton Cemetery, Easton
George Barclay, John Galligan, Frank
Grube, Bill Parks

Easton Heights Cemetery, Easton
Harry Keener, John McPherson

Holy Savior Cemetery, Bethlehem
Dick Wright

Schoenersville Cemetery, Schoenersville
Bert Kuczynski

St. Anthony's Cemetery, Easton
Jack Wallaesa

Northumberland County

Harmony Cemetery, Milton
John Sullivan

Odd Fellow's Cemetery, Shamokin
Bud Weiser

Pomfret Manor Cemetery, Sunbury
Birdee Cree

Shamokin Cemetery, Shamokin
George Gilham

St. Casimar's Church Cemetery, Kulpmont
Steve Filipowicz

St. Stanislaus Cemetery, Shamokin
Harry Coveleski .

**Perry County, Harrisburg–Lebanon–
Carlisle**

Liverpool Cemetery, Liverpool
Lew Ritter

Newport Cemetery, Newport
Billy Cox

Philadelphia County, Philadelphia Metro

Cathedral Cemetery, Philadelphia
Ben Conroy, Tom Gillen, Dick Harley,
Emmett McCann, Mark McGrillis, John
McMullen, Charles Snyder, Bill Sweeney

Cedar Hill Cemetery, Philadelphia
John Hanna

Chelten Hills Cemetery, Philadelphia
Bill Shettsline, Bob Vail

East Cedar Hill Cemetery, Philadelphia
Bill Black, Fats Jenkins, George Shoch,
Sam White

Ebenezer M.E. Church Cemetery, Philadelphia
Frank Queen

Greenmount Cemetery, Philadelphia
Jersey Bakely, Chris Rickley, Frank Siffell,
Amos Strunk, Jesse Whiting

Greenwood Cemetery, Philadelphia
William F. Baker, George Creamer, John
Hiland

Har Nebo Cemetery, Philadelphia
Eddie Gottlieb

Ivy Hill Cemetery, Philadelphia
Bill Byrd, William Gray, Ed Lafitte

Laurel Hill Cemetery, Philadelphia
Dicky Flowers, Lon Knight, Henry Luff,
Jack McFetridge, Tom Pratt

Leverington Cemetery, Philadelphia
George Heubel

Magnolia Cemetery, Philadelphia
Ben Culp, Joe Mulvey

Milestown Baptist Church Cemetery,
Philadelphia
Jud Birchall

Most Holy Redeemer Cemetery,
Philadelphia
Bart Cantz, Heinie Kappel, Joe Kappel,
Al Maul

Mount Peace Cemetery, Philadelphia
Nate Berkenstock, Fred Dunlap, Horace
Fogel, Bill Haeffner, Bill Hallman, Jack
Lapp, Pete Loos, Roy Partlow, Adam
Rocap, Sam Weaver

Mt. Vernon Cemetery, Philadelphia
Charlie Householder, Henry Myers, Bill
Sharsig, Jake Virtue

Mount Sinai Cemetery, Philadelphia
Edwin I. Hyneman

New Cathedral Cemetery, Philadelphia
Jim Devlin, Pete Hasney, Mike Kilroy,

Otto Knabe, Fergy Malone, Sparrow McCaffrey, Johnny Ryan

North Cedar Hill Cemetery, Philadelphia
Harry Brooks, Bill Clymer, John Greenig, Izzy Hoffman, Harry Jacoby, Ed Sixsmith, Joe Sugden, Abe Wolstenholme

Northwood Cemetery, Philadelphia
George Bradley, Duke Esper, Kid Gleason, Joe Gunson, George Hesselbacher, Ernie Padgett, Chick Spalding, Buddy Walker, Dave Zearfoss

Oakland Cemetery, Philadelphia
Bert Conn, Dave Oldfield, Jesse Purnell

Philadelphia National Cemetery, Philadelphia
Otto Briggs, Owen Conway, Louis Santop

St. Dominic's Cemetery, Philadelphia
Benny Bengough, Harry O'Donnell, Ty Pickup

St. Timothy's Episcopal Church Cemetery, Philadelphia
Bert Yeabsley

Woodlands Cemetery, Philadelphia
Thomas Eakins, Fred Warner

Pike County, Newburgh Metro

Union Cemetery, Lackawaxen
Zane Grey

Wood Family Cemetery, Wood Estate, Shohola Twp.
Smoky Joe Wood

Potter County

Fishing Creek Cemetery, Roulette
Don Hoak

Schuylkill County

Brock Cemetery, Ashland
Jack Stivetts

Calvary Cemetery, Mt. Carbon
Bill Matthews

Charles Baber Cemetery, Pottsville
Jake Daubert, Frank Eustace, Jack Quinn

I.O.O.F. Cemetery, Saint Clair
Eddie Delker, John Titus

New St. Jerome's Cemetery, Tamaqua
Chris Fulmer

Odd Fellows Cemetery, Tamaqua
Chick Fullis

Queen of the Universe Cemetery, Branchdale
Socks Holden

Reformed Cemetery, Tremont
Sparky Adams

Sky-View Memorial Park, Hometown
Bob Rinker

St. Andrews Church Cemetery, Valley View
Fred Stiely

St. Joseph's Cemetery, Fountain Springs
John Chapman

St. Michael's Lutheran Church Cemetery, Klingerstown
Dutch Romberger

Tremont Cemetery, Tremont
Roy Zimmerman

Snyder County

Fairview Cemetery, Freeburg
Ralph Mitterling

West Side Cemetery, Shamokin Dam
Tex Neuer

Somerset County, Johnstown Metro

St. Michael's Cemetery, Greenville
Hughie Tate

Susquehanna County

St. Anthony's Cemetery, Forest City
Tex Hoyle

Tioga County

Cherry Flats Cemetery, Cherry Flats
Charlie Parsons

Prospect Cemetery, Mansfield
Herb Goodall

Union County

Lewisburg Cemetery, Lewisburg
Walter Blair, George Cockill, Dick Kauffman, Christy Mathewson, Hal McClure, Moose McCormick

Venango County

Calvary Cemetery, Oil City
Leo Callahan

Emlenton Cemetery, Emlenton
Claude Ritchey

Grove Cemetery, Victory Township
  Boy Way

Grove Hill Cemetery, Oil City
  Jim Duncan

Jerusalem Corners Cemetery, Pleasantville
  Art Stokes

St. Joseph's Cemetery, Oil City
  Frank Boyd

Sunset Hill Memorial Gardens, Cranberry
  Joe Harris

Venango County Poor Farm Cemetery, Sugar Creek Township
  Henry Kessler

Washington County, Pittsburgh Metro

Beallsville Cemetery, Beallsville
  Bill Coulson

Charleroi Cemetery, Charleroi
  Claude Gouzzie, Katsy Keifer

Monongahela Cemetery, Monongahela
  Ody Abbott

Our Lady of Lourdes Cemetery, Burgettstown
  Eddie Lukon

Queen of Heaven Cemetery, Venetia
  Howie Gorman, Gene Layden

Wayne County

Pine Grove Cemetery, South Sterling
  Bill Herring

Queen of Peace Cemetery, Hawley
  Eddie Murphy

St. John's Cemetery, Honesdale
  Fred Sherry

Westmoreland County, Pittsburgh Metro

Brush Creek Cemetery, Irwin
  Buzz Clarkson, Socks Seybold

Eastview Cemetery, Delmont
  Jimmy Ripple

Greenwood Cemetery, New Kensington
  Joe Page

Irwin Union Cemetery, Irwin
  Howie Jones

Plum Creek Cemetery, New Kensington
  Bill Culp

Scottdale Cemetery, Scottdale
  Sam Brown

St. Clair Cemetery, Greensburg
  Stan Ferens

St. Mary's Cemetery, Latrobe
  Ed Abbaticchio

St. Vincent's Cemetery, Latrobe
  Andy Gilbert, Hal Haid

Transfiguration Cemetery, Russellton
  Johnny Tyler

Twin Valley Memorial Park, Delmont
  Bob Moose

Union Cemetery, Arnold
  Red Bowser

West Newton Cemetery, West Newton
  Danny Taylor, Jimmy Uchrinscko

Wyoming County, Scranton–Wilkes-Barre–Hazleton

Evergreeen-Woodlawn Cemetery (formerly Factoryville Cemetery), Factoryville
  Henry Mathewson

York County, York Metro

Church of the Annunciation Cemetery, Hanover
  Bob McKinney

Mount Rose Cemetery, York
  Ken Raffensberger, Lefty York

Mount Zion Cemetery, Delta
  Gene Snyder, Jake Stephens

New Freedom Cemetery, New Freedom
  Tom Lipp

Prospect Hill Cemetery, York
  Bill Clay, Lefty George, Jim Gill, Norman Plitt

Salem Union Cemetery, Jacobus
  Ray Shearer

RHODE ISLAND

Bristol County

North Burial Ground, Bristol
  John Hamill

Prince's Hill Burial Ground, Barrington
  Harry Pattee

Kent County

Knotty Oak Cemetery, Anthony
Hi Ladd

Providence County, Providence–Fall River–Warwick Metro

Acotes Cemetery, Chepachet
Bill Mellor

Moshassuck Cemetery, Central Falls
Charley Bassett

Mount Calvary Cemetery, Cumberland
Ed Conley

Mount St. Mary's Cemetery, Pawtucket
Jim Connor, Dennis Driscoll

North Burial Grounds Cemetery (Potter's
Field), Providence
Fred Corey

Notre Dame Cemetery, Pawtucket
Max Surkont

Oak Grove Cemetery, Pawtucket
John Cattanach

Oakland Cemetery, Providence
Charlie Babington

Precious Blood Cemetery, Woonsocket
Pete LePine, Henri Rondeau

Riverside Cemetery, Pawtucket
Joe Start

St. Ann's Cemetery, Cranston
Scoops Cooney, Jimmy Cooney, Pat Duff,
Rip Egan, Martin Flaherty, Art Hagan,
Tom Lovett

St. Francis Cemetery, Pawtucket
John Doyle, Joe Flynn, John Flynn, Pat
Friel, Dinty Gearin, Paddy Greene, Jim
Hanley, Mike Lynch, Morgan Murphy,
William Sullivan

St. Joseph Cemetery, Pawtucket
Edward S. Doherty

St. Joseph's Cemetery, Ashton
Pat Maloney

Swan Point Cemetery, Providence
Bruce Caldwell, Cap Crowell, Eddie Eayrs,
Edgar Smith, Wally Snell, Hank Soar

Union Cemetery, North Smithfield
Chet Nichols Jr., Chet Nichols Sr.

Washington County, Providence–Fall River–Warwick Metro

Oak Grove Cemetery, Hopkinton
Guerdon Whiteley

Washington County, Norwich–New London Metro

Riverbend Cemetery, Westerly
John Frill, Charlie Robinson, Joe Sherman

SOUTH CAROLINA

Abbeyville County

Forest Lawn Memorial Gardens, Abbeville
Russ Lyon

Aiken County, Augusta–Aiken Metro

St. Paul United Methodist Church Cemetery,
New Ellenton
Rufus Smith

Anderson County, Greenville–Spartanburg–Anderson

Forest Lawn Memorial Park, Anderson
Roy Mahaffey

Presbyterian Cemetery, Pendleton
Carl Sitton

Beaufort County

Beaufort National Cemetery, Beaufort
Mal Moss

Charleston County, Charleston Metro

Magnolia Cemetery, Charleston
Art Brouthers, Fritz Von Kolnitz

St. Lawrence Cemetery, Charleston
Tom Colcolough

Chesterfield County

First Baptist Church Cemetery, Pageland
Van Mungo

Hopewell Presbyterian Church Cemetery,
Blackstock
Ed Durham

Old St. David's Episcopal Churhyard, Cheraw
Doc McJames

Darlington County

Darlington Memory Gardens, Darlington
    Harry Byrd
Magnolia Cemetery, Hartsville
    Bobo Newsom

Dillon County

Magnolia Cemetery, Latta
    Norm McMillan

Florence County, Florence Metro

Lake City Memorial Park, Lake City
    Clise Dudley

Greenville County, Greenville–Spartanburg–Anderson

Cross Roads Baptist Church Cemetery,
Greer
    Jim Yeargin

Graceland Cemetery, Greenville
    Pel Ballenger, Walter Barbare

Greenville Memorial Gardens, Piedmont
    Virgil Stallcup

Rose Hill Cemetery, Piedmont
    Champ Osteen

Wood Memorial Park, Greer
    John McMakin, Flint Rhem

Woodlawn Memorial Park, Greenville
    Blackie Carter, Joe Jackson, Rube Melton

Greenwood County

Edgewood Cemetery, Greenwood
    Elbert Andrews

Greenwood Memorial Gardens, Greenwood
    Cal Drummond

Lancaster County

Bethlehem Baptist Church Cemetery,
Lancaster
    Mike Cunningham

Kershaw City Cemetery, Kershaw
    Art Jones

Zion Methodist Church Cemetery, Lancaster
    Aaron Robinson

Laurens County

Pinelawn Memorial Gardens, Clinton
    Cal Cooper

Rosemont Cemetery, Clinton

    Claude Crocker, Chick Galloway

Lee County

Bethlehem Methodist Cemetery, Bishopville
    Dan Griner

Lexington County, Columbia Metro

Old Lexington Baptist Church Cemetery,
Lexington
    George Jeffcoat

Pilgrim Lutheran Church Cemetery,
Lexington
    John Boozer

Marion County

Rose Hill Cemetery, Marion
    Roxy Snipe

Marlboro County

McColl Cemetery, McColl
    Ralph McLaurin

Sunset Hill Memorial Park, Bennettsville
    Norm Brown

Newberry County

Newberry Memorial Gardens, Newberry
    Mickey Livingston

St. Paul Lutheran Church Cemetery, Pomaria
    Johnny Wertz

Pickens County, Greenville–Spartanburg–Anderson

Travelers Rest Cemetery, Travelers Rest
    Red Howell

Westview Cemetery, Easley
    Jack Owens

Richland County, Columbia Metro

Crescent Hill Memorial Gardens, Columbia
    Bob Hazle

Elmwood Cemetery, Columbia
    Rufus Clarke, Logan Drake, Kirby Higby

Greenlawn Memorial Park, Columbia
    Barney Martin, Ted Petoskey, George
    Turbeville

Spartanburg County, Greenville–Spartanburg–Anderson

Bethel Cemetery, Woodruff
    Sam Lanford

First Presbyterian Church Cemetery,
Woodruff
    Sam Page

Floyd's Memorial Gardens, Jonesville
    Ernie White

Pacolet Memorial Gardens, Pacolet
    George Banks

Roselawn Memorial Gardens, Inman
    Al Lakeman

Zion Hill Baptist Church Cemetery,
Spartanburg
    Jesse Fowler

Sumter County

Haselden Family Cemetery, Sellars
    Frank Ellerbe

York County, Charlotte–Gastonia–Rock Hill

Grand View Memorial Park, Rock Hill
    Eddie Freed, Al Shealy

SOUTH DAKOTA

Brown County

Lakeview Cemetery, Columbia
    Kermit Wahl

Meade County

Black Hills National Cemetery, Sturgis
    Thumper Jackson

Minehaha County, Sioux Falls Metro

Zion Lutheran Church Cemetery,
Garrettsville
    Emmett Nelson

Pennington County, Rapid City Metro

Mountain View Cemetery, Rapid City
    George Disch

Yankton County

Gayville Cemetery, Gayville
    Marv Olson

TENNESSEE

Blount County, Knoxville Metro

Logan Chapel United Methodist Church
Cemetery, Maryville
    Art Ruble

Bradley County

Triplett Cemetery, Cleveland
    Guy Lacy

Campbell County

Jellico Cemetery, Jellico
    Larry Douglas

Coffee County

Maplewood Cemetery, Tullahoma
    Wilson Collins

Cumberland County

Crossville City Cemetery, Crossville
    Mel Bosser

Green Acres Memory Gardens, Crossville
    Lefty Stewart

Davidson County, Nashville Metro

Calvary Cemetery, Nashville
    Johnny Gill, Tiny Graham, Charlie
    Harding, Bill McTigue

Greenwood Cemetery, Nashville
    Henry Kimbro

Middle Tennessee Veterans Cemetery,
Nashville
    Hardin Cathey, Stokes Hendrix, Ed
    Martin, Frank Thompson

Mount Olivet Cemetery, Nashville
    George Archie, Johnny Beazley, Slim
    Embrey, Johnny Gooch, Ben Harris,
    Claude Jonnard

Nashville National Cemetery, Madison
    Ed Cole, Bob Schultz, Kelly Searcy,
    Vito Tamulis

Spring Hill Cemetery, Nashville
    Tony Jacobs, Mickey Kreitner, Red
    Lucas, Tom Rogers, Henry Schmidt,
    Fred Toney

Woodlawn Memorial Park, Nashville
    Harley Boss, Slick Castleman, Dory
    Dean, Doc Dennis, Kerby Farrell, John
    Mihalic, Jay Partridge, Bill Schwartz,
    Dick Sisler, Jim Turner

DeKalb County

Salem Cemetery, Liberty
    Bo Griffith

Dyer County

Fairview Cemetery, Dyersburg
Herb Welch, Ed Wright

Fentress County

Taylor Place Cemetery, Jamestown
Earl Webb

Gibson County

Oakwood Baptist Church Cemetery,
Milan
Turner Barber

Greene County

Shiloh Cumberland Presbyterian Church
Cemetery, Greeneville
Dale Alexander

Grundy County

Tracy City Cemetery, Tracy City
Phil Douglas

Hamilton County, Chattanooga Metro

Brainerd Methodist Church Cemetery,
Chattanooga
Doc Johnston

Chattanooga Memorial Park,
Chattanooga
George Cunningham, Kid Elberfield

Chattanooga National Cemetery,
Chattanooga
Bill Akers, Bill Andrus, Jery Lane, Lyle
Lutrell, Bobby Reeves, Sammy Strang,
John Wilson

Forest Hills Cemetery, Chattanooga
Pat Dillard, Johnny Dobbs, Joe Engel,
Tom Ford, Jimmy Johnston, Bill
McAllester, George McConnell, War
Sanders

Greenwood Cemetery, Chattanooga
Bob Higgins

Hamilton Memorial Gardens,
Chattanooga
Ray Moss

Mizpah Congregation Julia Cemetery,
Chattanooga
Fred Graf

Hardeman County

Melrose Cemetery, Whiteville
Bill Warren

Hardin County

Savannah Cemetery, Savannah
Hank DeBerry

Haywood County

Oakwood Cemetery, Brownsville
George Murray

Henry County

Maplewood Cemetery, Paris
Mark Stewart

Jefferson County

Hillcrest Cemetery, Dandridge
Bill Bolden

Johnson County

Sunset Memorial Park, Mountain City
Clyde Shoun

Knox County, Knoxville Metro

Calvary Cemetery, Knoxville
Dan Leahy

Forest Grove Freewill Baptist Church
Cemetery, Knoxville
Edward Hodges

Greenwood Cemetery, Knoxville
Bonnie Hollingsworth

Highland Memorial Park, Knoxville
Frank Callaway, Earl Williams

Lynnhurst Cemetery, Knoxville
Bob Baird, Carl Doyle, Bill Meyer

Lawrence County

Lawrence County Memorial Gardens,
Lawrenceburg
George Bradley, Doc Cook

Lewis County

Swiss Cemetery, Hohenwald
Walt Marbet

Madison County, Jackson Metro

Brown's Chapel Cemetery, Jackson
Bill Hopper

Highland Memorial Gardens, Jackson
Ellis Kinder

Marion County, Chattanooga Metro

City Cemetery, South Pittsburg
Harry Baumgartner

Maury County
Leiper's Fork Cemetery, Columbia
  Hank Sweeney
Polk Memorial Gardens, Columbia
  Lindsay Nelson

McMinn County
Cedar Grove Cemetery, Athens
  Jim Baskette

Montgomery County, Clarksville–Hopkinsville
Liberty Presbyterian Church Cemetery,
Clarksville
  Hod Lisenbee

Moore County
Odd Fellows–Masonic Cemetery, Lynchburg
  John Stone

Obion County
Zion Cemetery, Obion
  Ron Willis

Shelby County, Memphis Metro
Calvary Cemetery, Memphis
  John Antonelli, Dino Chiozza, Lou
  Chiozza, Slim Love, Ed McGhee, Frank
  Pearson
Elmwood Cemetery, Memphis
  Hunter Lane, Charlie Shields, Dolly Stark
Fisherville Cemetery, Fisherville
  Faye Throneberry, Marv Throneberry
Forest Hill Cemetery-Midtown Memphis
  Jim Henry, Fritz Clausen, Charlie Frank,
  Dusty Miller, Danny Moeller, Ginger
  Shinault, Glen Stewart
Memorial Park Cemetery, Memphis
  Bill Harper, Isaiah Harris, Gene Lambert,
  Buddy Lewis, George Merritt, Jimmy
  Moore, Leon Pettit, Doc Prothro, Frank
  Waddey, Tom Winsett
Memorial Park Woods South Cemetery,
Memphis
  Casey Jones
Memphis Memorial Gardens, Memphis
  Lefty Mathis
Memphis National Cemetery, Memphis
  Ike Pearson, Jack Powell

New Park Cemetery, Memphis
  Fred Bankhead, Ike Brown, Larry Brown
West Tennessee Veteran's Cemetery, Memphis
  Ralph Weigel
Woodhaven Cemetery, Millington
  Ross Grimsley

Smith County
Ridgewood Cemetery, Carthage
  Tommy Bridges

Stewart County
Hillcrest Cemetery, Dover
  Bernie Walter

Sullivan County, Johnson City–Kingsport–Bristol
Glenwood Cemetery, Bristol
  Frank Walker
Oak Hill Cemetery, Kingsport
  George Diehl, Lew Flick

Sumner County, Nashville Metro
Bethpage Cemetery, Bethpage
  Hub Perdue

Tipton County, Memphis Metro
Munford Cemetery, Covington
  Harvey Hendrick

Washington County, Johnson City–Kingsport–Bristol
Evergreen Cemetery, Erwin
  Jim Mooney
Happy Valley Memorial Park,
Johnson City
  Ted Wingfield
Monte Vista Burial Park, Johnson City
  Joe Price
Urbana Cemetery, Limestone
  Tilly Walker

TEXAS

Anderson County
Broyles Chapel Cemetery, Palestine
  George Watkins
St. Joseph's Cemetery, Palestine
  Jack Coombs

Austin County

Oak Knoll Cemetery, Bellville
  Red Lynn
Sealy Cemetery, Sealy
  Mel Preibisch

Bandera County

West Prong Cemetery, Medina
  Bob Darnell

Bee County

Glenwood Cemetery, Beeville
  Curt Walker

Bell County, Killeen–Temple Metro

North Belton Cemetery, Belton
  Roy Mitchell

Bexar County, San Antonio Metro

Fort Sam Houston National Cemetery,
San Antonio
  Buck Freeman, Tex Kraus, Johnny
  Lucadello, Junior McNeal, Pancho
  Snyder, Mickey Taborn, Hoss Walker,
  Frank Walsh
Holy Cross Cemetery, San Antonio
  Bernie James
Mission Burial Park North, San Antonio
  Frank Browning, Homer Ezzell, Paul
  Kardow, Rube Waddell
Mission Burial Park South, San Antonio
  Cotton Knaupp, Pinky Whitney, Ross
  Youngs
Odd Fellows Cemetery, San Antonio
  Tex Wisterzil
San Fernando Archdiocesan Cemetery, San
Antonio
  Tim Griesenbeck
San Jose Burial Park, San Antonio
  Harry Ables
St. Joseph's Society Cemetery, San Antonio
  Jake Volz
St. Mary's Cemetery, San Antonio
  Patrick Newnam, Dick Phelan
Sunset Memorial Park, San Antonio
  Del Baker, Gene Bedford, Charlie Engle,
  Ray Flaskamper, Cy Fried, Joe Hague,
  Sam Harshaney, Fred Johnson, Topper
  Rigney, Art Scharein, Hank Severeid,

  Charley Suche, Pat Veltman, Paul
  Wachtel

Bowie County, Texarkana Metro

Hillcrest Cemetery, Texarkana
  Footsie Blair, Durwood Merrill

Brazos County, Bryan–College Station Metro

Bryan City Cemetery, Bryan
  Johnny Hudson
College Station Cemetery, College Station
  Rip Collins, Marty Karow
Restever Memorial Park, Bryan
  Beau Bell

Brooks County

Falfurrias Burial Park, Falfurrias
  Ernie Maun

Brown County

Bangs Cemetery, Bangs
  Slim Harriss
Greenleaf Cemetery, Brownwood
  Jack Knott

Burleson County

Caldwell Masonic Cemetery, Caldwell
  Mel Deutsch

Burnet County

Burnet Cemetery, Burnet
  Chink Taylor

Caldwell County, Austin–San Marcos Metro

Luling City Cemetery, Luling
  Gene Cocreham

Cameron County, Brownsville–Harlingen Metro

Rose Lawn Memorial Gardens, Brownsville
  Frank Jude

Camp County

Leesburg Cemetery, Pittsburg
  Dixie Parsons

Cass County

New Colony Cemetery, Linden
  George Washington

Pine Crest Cemetery, Atlanta
  Hub Northen

St. Williams Cemetery, Douglassville
  Bernie Henderson

Cherokee County

Berryman Family Cemetery, Alto
  Carl Yowell

Cedar Hill Cemetery, Rusk
  Heinie Odom

Clay County

Byers Cemetery, Byers
  Ray Harrell

Collin County, Dallas Metro

Altoga Cemetery, McKinney
  Otho Nitcholas

I.O.O.F. Cemetery, Farmersville
  Tex McDonald

Ridgeview Memorial Park, Allen
  Jackie Sullivan

Collingsworth County

Dodson Cemetery, Dodson
  Von McDaniel

Colorado County

Masonic Cemetery, Eagle Lake
  Howard Fitzgerald

Masonic Cemetery, Weimar
  Ira Townsend

St. Michael's Catholic Cemetery, Weimar
  Ed Donnelly

Comanche County

Oakwood Cemetery, Comanche
  Tex Carleton

White Point Cemetery, Comanche
  Belv Bean

Dallas County, Dallas Metro

Calvary Hill Cemetery, Dallas
  David Howard

Crown Hill Cemetery, Dallas
  Wingo Anderson

Edgewood Cemetery, Lancaster
  Gene Moore

Frankford Cemetery, Dallas
  George Dickerson

Garland Memorial Park, Garland
  Bill McWilliams

Greenwood Cemetery, Dallas
  Otto McIvor, Rube Taylor

Grove Hill Memorial Park, Dallas
  Walt Alexander, Duff Cooley, Bobby
  Finley, Jim Haislip, Sam Hill, Percy Jones

Holy Redeemer Cemetery, DeSoto
  Pretzel Pezzullo

Hutchins Cemetery, Hutchins
  Buddy Napier

Laurel Land Memorial Park, Dallas
  Jim Avrea, Virgil Cheeves, Red Durrett,
  Uel Eubanks, Lefty Fuhr, John Goodell,
  Herbert Hill, Garth Mann

Lincoln Memorial Cemetery, Dallas
  Bob Wilson

Mesquite Cemetery, Mesquite
  Turkey Gross

Oakland Cemetery, Dallas
  Oscar Dugey, Walt Goldsby, Slim Kinzy

Restland Memorial Park, Dallas
  Heinz Becker, Boob Fowler, Sal Gliatto,
  Ziggy Hasbrook, Marty Hopkins, Frank
  Lane, Jim Levey, Danny Lynch, Reeve
  McKay, Norm McRae, Ray Morehart,
  Walter Morris, Murray Wall

Sparkman Hillcrest Memorial Park, Dallas
  Jimmy Adair, Dusty Boggess, Lum
  Davenport, Pinky Higgins, Bubber
  Jonnard, Mickey Mantle

Wheatland Cemetery, Dallas
  Snipe Conley

Denton County, Dallas Metro

IOOF Cemetery, Denton
  Rollie Naylor

DeWitt County

Meyersville Catholic Cemetery,
Meyersville
  Marv Gudat

El Paso County, El Paso Metro

B'nai Zion Cemetery, El Paso
  Andy Cohen, Syd Cohen

Concordia Cemetery, El Paso
  Bill Van Dyke

Evergreen Cemetery, El Paso
  Connie Doyle, Red Hill, Tom Seaton
Evergreen East Cemetery, El Paso
  Astyanax Douglass
Fort Bliss National Cemetery, El Paso
  Goose Tatum

Ellis County, Dallas Metro

Ferris Park Cemetery, Ferris
  Alex Malloy
Hillcrest Burial Park, Waxahachie
  Paul Richards, Archie Ward
Red Oak Cemetery, Red Oak
  Tex Shirley

Erath County

Hucksby Cemetery, Stephenville
  Don Flinn

Fannin County

Arledge Ridge Cemetery, Bonham
  Roy Leslie
Burns Cemetery, Trenton
  Tex Wilson
Carson Cemetery, Ector
  John Whitehead
Leonard Cemetery, Leonard
  Polly McLarry
Willow Wild Cemetery, Bonham
  Roy McMillan

Freestone County

Greenwood Cemetery, Teague
  Joel Hunt

Galveston County, Galveston–Texas City Metro

Calvary Cemetery, Galveston
  Sig Jakucki
Episcopal Cemetery, Galveston
  Jim Murray
  Galveston Memorial Park, Hitchcock
  Bob Cone, Tony Smith

Gillespie County

Der Stadt Friedhof, Fredericksburg
  Hugo Klaerner
  .

Goliad County

Berclair Cemetery, Berclair
  Bill Rodgers

Gonzales County

Gonzales Memorial Park, Gonzales
  Dick Midkiff

Grayson County, Sherman–Dennison

Cedarlawn Memorial Park, Sherman
  Tom McBride, Bob Muncrief
Fairview Cemetery, Denison
  Tex Covington
Oakwood Cemetery, Denison
  Sam Covington
Van Alstyne Cemetery, Van Alstyne
  Sam Gray

Gregg County, Longview–Marshall

Grace Hill Cemetery, Longview
  Charlie Neal
Lakeview Memorial Gardens, Longview
  Joe Dawson
Memory Park Cemetery, Longview
  Abe Bowman, Tex Jeanes
Spring Hill Cemetery, Longview
  Homer Blankenship

Guadalupe County, San Antonio Metro

Guadalupe Valley Memorial Park, New
Braunfels
  Ray Katt, Jim Riley

Hale County

Plainview Cemetery & Memorial Park,
Plainview
  Claude Cooper, Sam Langford

Harris County, Houston Metro

Brookside Memorial Park, Houston
  Maury Newlin
Cedarcrest Cemetery, Baytown
  Joe McDonald
Earthman Memory Gardens Cemetery,
Baytown
  Clem Hausmann
Forest Park (East) Cemetery, League City
  Frank Barnes, Pete Runnels, Ted Wilks

Forest Park (Lawndale) Cemetery, Houston
  Frank Croucher, Eddie Dyer, John
  Glaiser, Dickie Kerr, Gus Mancuso,
  Wayne McLeland, Chuck Miller,
  George Munger, Glenn Myatt, Glenn
  Myatt, Heinie Schuble, Jerry Witte,
  Joe Wood

Forest Park (Westheimer) Cemetery, Houston
  Dick Farrell, Salty Parker, Loel Passe,
  Johnny Rizzo

Glenwood Cemetery, Houston
  Judge Hofheinz, Chappie McFarland

Grand View Memorial Park, Pasadena
  Chet Morgan

Hollywood Cemetery, Houston
  Gene Bailey, Jack Berly, George
  Whiteman

Holy Cross Cemetery, Houston
  Jerry Denny, Con Lucid

Houston Memorial Gardens, Houston
  Sherman Watrous

Houston National Cemetery, Houston
  Dan Bankhead, Walt Bond, Willard
  Brown, Fritz Davis, Jim Pendleton

Memorial Oaks Cemetery, Houston
  Pat Anlenman, Jack Creel, Jeff Cross,
  Hoot Evers, Johnny Keane, Johnny
  Lipon, Walter Murphy, Howie Pollet

Paradise North Cemetery, Houston
  Jake Brown

Paradise South Cemetery, Houston
  Pat Patterson

Resthaven Memorial Gardens, Houston
  Pidge Browne, Pat McLaughlin, Tommy
  Neill, Max West

Rosewood Memorial Park, Humble
  Fred Link, Slim McGrew

Woodlawn Garden of Memories, Houston
  Neal Baker, Gordie Hinkle

Harrison County, Longview–Marshall Metro

Colonial Gardens Cemetery, Marshall
  Guy Sturdy

Hays County, Austin–San Marcos Metro

San Marcos-Blanco Cemetery, San Marcos
  Jim Brown

San Marcos Cemetery, San Marcos
  Tex Hughson

Wimberley Cemetery, Wimberley
  Al Hollingsworth

Hidalgo County, McAllen–Edinburg Metro

Laurel Hill Cemetery, Mission
  Paul Johnson

Palm Valley Memorial Gardens, Pharr
  Earl Caldwell

Hill County

Blum Cemetery, Blum
  George Jackson

Fairview Cemetery, Hubbard
  Tris Speaker, Tony York

Peaceful Gardens Memorial Park, Woodrow
  Donnie Moore

Hood County, Fort Worth–Arlington Metro

Acton Cemetery, Acton
  Les Mallon

Hopkins County

Restlawn Memorial Park, Sulphur Springs
  Buck Fausett

Hunt County, Dallas Metro

East Mound Cemetery, Greenville
  Walt Dickson

Memoryland Memorial Park, Greenville
  Gibby Brack, Monty Stratton

Jackson County

Layden Family Cemetery, Edna
  Pete Layden

Memory Gardens of Edna (formerly Edna
Cemetery), Edna
  Frank Gibson

Jasper County

Memorial Park Cemetery, Jasper
  Les Willis

Jefferson County, Beaumont–Port Arthur Metro

Forest Lawn Memorial Park, Beaumont
  Jim Clark, Dutch Dietz, Les Fleming,
  Thomas Houghes, Jesse Landrum,
  Clay Touchstone

Magnolia Cemetery, Beaumont
  Hugh Shelley, Charlie Weber

Johnson County, Fort Worth–Arlington Metro

Godley Cemetery, Godley
George Milstead

Grandview Cemetery, Grandview
Slim Harrell

Jones County

Highland Memorial Cemetery, Stamford
Bob Prichard

Karnes County

Butler Family Cemetery, Kenedy
Al Baker

Falls City Cemetery, Falls City
Fabian Kowalik

Kenedy City Cemetery, Kenedy
Evritt Booe

Kaufman County, Dallas Metro

College Mound Cemetery, Terrell
Leo Tankersley

Elmo Cemetery, Elmo
James Griffin

Lamar County

Chicota Presbyterian Church Cemetery, Chicota
Buck Frierson

Evergreen Cemetery, Paris
Bill Lattimore

Providence Cemetery, Paris
Rick Adams

Leon County

Concord Cemetery, Concord
Ray Benge

Liberty County, Houston Metro

Immaculate Conception Catholic Cemetery, Liberty
Tink Riviere

Limestone County

Mexia City Cemetery, Mexia
John Carden

Lubbock County, Lubbock Metro

Lubbock City Cemetery, Lubbock
Sled Allen, Bill Morley

Resthaven Memorial Park, Lubbock
Bill Brown, Sam West

Mason County

Gooch Cemetery, Mason
Lindsay Brown

Matagorda County

Roselawn Memorial Cemetery, Van Vleck
Willie Underhill

McCulloch County

Rest Haven Cemetery, Brady
Bert Maxwell

McLennan County, Waco Metro

Crawford Cemetery, Crawford
Strick Shofner

Harris Creek Cemetery, McGregor
Sarge Connally

Holy Cross Cemetery, Waco
Louis Drucke

Oakwood Cemetery, Waco
Buster Chatham, Jack Little, Buster Mills, Lloyd Russell

Restland Cemetery, Waco
George Edmondson

Rosemond Cemetery, Waco
Charlie Barnabe, Jack Conway

Medina County

Oakridge Cemetery, Hondo
Stan Hollmig

St. Joseph Cemetery, Devine
Bert Gallia, Joe Vance

Milam County

Gause Cemetery, Gause
Jo-Jo Moore

Montgomery County, Houston Metro

Ebenezer Cemetery, Willis
Cliff Young

Montgomery Cemetery, Montgomery
Norm Branch

Mount Bethel Cemetery, Gary
Vic Frasier

Morris County

Omaha Cemetery, Omaha
    Randy Moore

Nacogdoches County

Cushing Cemetery, Cushing
    Joe Gallagher

Navarro County

Birdston Valley Cemetery, Streetman
    Firpo Marberry

Oakwood Cemetery, Corsicana
    Harvey Grubb

Nueces County

Robstown Memorial Park, Robstown
    Claude Davenport, Howie Reed

Rose Hill Memorial Park, Corpus Christi
    Tim Hendryx

Seaside Memorial Park, Corpus Christi
    Bill Windle

Palo Pinto County

New Gordon Cemetery, Gordon
    Pat Caraway, Thurman Tucker

Palo Pinto Cemetery, Palo Pinto
    Charlie Robertson

Potter County, Amarillo Metro

Llano Cemetery, Amarillo
    John Middleton, Chief Youngblood

Red River County

Clarksville Cemetery, Clarksville
    Clyde Milan

Dodd Family Cemetery, Detroit
    Ona Dodd

Fairview Cemetery, Clarksville
    Horace Milan

Refugio County

La Rosa Cemetery, Woodsboro
    Chick Autry

Robertson County

Bremond Cemetery, Bremond
    Bill Stellbauer

Runnels County

Evergreen Cemetery, Ballinger
    Stan Gray

Rusk County

Overton Cemetery, Overton
    Tex Vache

San Augustine County

Shilo Cemetery, San Augustine
    Al Williams

San Jacinto County

Oakwood Cemetery, Coldspring
    Pete McClanahan

Scurry County

Hillside Memorial Gardens, Snyder
    Bill Atwood

Smith County, Tyler Metro

Cathedral in the Pines Cemetery, Tyler
    Barney White

Memorial Park Cemetery, Tyler
    Larry Drake
    Oakwood Cemetery, Tyler
    Fred Johnston

Springtown Cemetery, Springtown
    Joe Hutcheson

Somervell County

Squaw Creek Cemetery, Glen Rose
    Debs Garms

Stephens County

Billy Maloney

Tarrant County, Fort Worth–Arlington Metro

Arlington Cemetery, Arlington
    Ed Appleton

Garden of Memories Memorial Park, Fort Worth
    Oscar Jones

Greenwood Memorial Park, Fort Worth
    Tom Baker, Eddie Chiles, Pete Donohue,
    Bill Gannon, Ed Konetchy, Clarence
    Kraft, Bill McCahan, Jackie Tavener, Ed
    Wheeler

Moore Memorial Gardens, Arlington
    Joe Lovitto, Steve Macko, Bill Merrill,
    Johnny Welaj

Mount Olivet Cemetery, Fort Worth
    Joe Bratcher, Cecil Coombs, Jake Mooty,

Howard Murphy, Tommy Robello, Bill Sodd

Oakwood Cemetery, Fort Worth
Joe Pate

Shannon Rose Hill Memorial Park, Fort Worth
Scotty Barr, Hod Kibbie, Ray Murray, Doc Nance

Taylor County, Abilene Metro

Elmwood Memorial Park, Abilene
Bernie Duffy, Jesse Winters

Throckmorton County

Throckmorton Cemetery, Throckmorton
Jimmie Coker

Tom Green County, San Angelo Metro

Fairmount Cemetery, San Angelo
Jake Freeze

Lawnhaven Memorial Gardens, San Angelo
Joe Kracher

Tarvis County, Austin–San Marcos Metro

Assumption Cemetery, Austin
Eddie Kazak

Austin Memorial Park, Austin
Bibb Falk, Chet Falk, Hunter Hill, Chief Wilson

Capital Memorial Park, Austin
Tom Hamilton, Hank Helf

Evergreen Cemetery, Austin
Wilie Wells

Hornsby Cemetery,Hornsby Bend
Rogers Hornsby
Oakwood Cemetery, Austin
Forrest Crawford, Ox Eckhardt, John Taff, Prince Oana

Plummes Cemetery, Austin
Junior Wells

Trinity County

Glenwood Cemetery, Groveton
Lefty Scott

Van Zandt County

Oak Hill Cemetery, Edgewood
Alex Hooks

Victoria County, Victoria Metro

Resurrection Cemetery, Victoria
Dick Mulligan, Lou Rochelli

Webb County, Laredo Metro

Laredo Municipal Cemetery, Laredo
Clarence Huber

Wharton County

El Campo Cemmunity Cemetery, El Campo
W Bell

Wharton City Cemetery, Wharton
Carl Reynolds

Wheeler County

Shamrock Cemetery, Shamrock
Bob Seeds

Wichita County, Wichita Falls Metro

Crestview Memorial Park, Wichita Falls
George Blackerby, Pete Turgeon

Electra Cemetery, Electra
Dick Adkins

Lakeview Cemetery, Wichita Falls
Theodore Gross

New Electra Cemetery, Electra
Farmer Ray

Williamson County, Austin–San Marcos Metro

Odd Fellows Cemetery, Georgetown
Jim Galloway

Young County

Oak Grove Cemetery, Graham
Ray Wolk

Pioneer Cemetery, Graham
Roy Easterwood

UTAH

Cache County

Logan City Cemetery, Logan
John Derks

Davis County, Salt Lake City–Ogden Metro

Bountiful City Cemetery, Bountiful
Ed Heusser

Kaysville and Layton Memorial Park,
Kaysville
  Sparky Adams
Lakeview Memorial Estates, Bountiful
  Al Tate

**Salt Lake County, Salt Lake City–Ogden
Metro**
Holladay Cemetery, Holladay
  Ray Jacobs
Salt Lake City Cemetery, Salt Lake City
  Roy Castleton, Paul Strand

Utah County, Provo–Orem Metro
Orem City Cemetery, Orem
  Doug Hansen, Kent Peterson
Payson City Cemetery, Payson
  Red Peery

**Weber County, Salt Lake City–Ogden
Metro**
Aultorest Memorial Park, Ogden
  Clay Lambert
Ogden City Cemetery, Ogden
  Dad Clark
Plain City Cemetery, Plain City
  Elmer Singleton

VERMONT

Chittenden County, Burlington Metro
Colchester Village Cemetery, Colchester
  Ray Collins
Lakeview Cemetery, Burlington
  Doc Hazleton
Mountain View Cemetery, Essex Center
  Bert Abbey
Our Lady of the Holy Rosary Cemetery,
Richmond
  Dave Keefe
St. Stephen's Cemetery, Winooski
  Ralph LaPointe

Rutland County
Evergreen Cemetery, Rutland
  Harry Hulihan
St. Raphael Cemetery, Poultney
  Ed Donnelly

Washington County
Hope Cemetery, Barre
  Walt Lanfranconi, Lou Polli, Steve
  Slayton

Windham County
Catholic Cemetery, Brattleboro
  Frank O'Connor

VIRGINIA

Alexandria City, Washington Metro
Mount Comfort Memorial Park, Alexandria
  Harry Child, Bill Kennedy
St. Mary's Cemetery, Alexandria
  James Shaw

Amherst County, Lynchburg Metro
Amherst Cemetery, Amherst
  Jackie Jensen

Appomatox County
Pamplin Community Cemetery, Pamplin
  Woody Williams

Arlington City, Washington Metro
Arlington National Cemetery, Arlington
  Charlie Becker, Boze Berger, Oscar
  Bielaski, Lu Blue, Mike Cantwell, Dennis
  Coughlin, Bob Davids, Bill Deitrick,
  Abner Doubleday, William Eckert, Nemo
  Gaines, Gil Gallagher, Dale Jones, Doc
  Lavan, Earl Lawson, Doc Martel,
  Spotswood Poles, Pete Quesada, Bill
  Stearns, Dave Willis, Boojum Wilson
Columbia Gardens Cemetery, Arlington
  Eddie Foster

Augusta County
Lebanon Church of the Bretheran Cemetery,
Mount Sidney
  Jim Hulvey
Union Cemetery, Parnassus
  Jerry May

Buckingham County
Mount Zion Baptist Church Cemetery, New
Canton
  Vern Bickford

Charlottesville City, Charlottesville Metro

Maplewood Cemetery, Charlottesville
 Charlie Ferguson

Chesapeake City, Norfolk–Virginia–Newport News Metro

Chesterfield County, Richmond–Petersburg

Dale Memorial Park, Chesterfield
 Monte Kennedy

Sunset Memorial Park, Chester
 George Smith

Danville city, Danville Metro

Highland Burial Park, Danville
 Herb Brett, Wally Burnette

Dinwiddie County, Richmond-Petersburg Metro

Good Shepherd Church Cemetery, McKenney
 Don Black

Emporia City

Emporia Cemetery, Emporia
 Vern Morgan

Falls Church City, Washington Metro

National Memorial Park, Falls Church
 Al Cypert, Clay Kirby

Oakwood Cemetery, Falls Church
 Johnny Priest

Fauquier County, Washington Metro

Ivy Hill Cemetery, Upperville
 Harvey Russell

Halifax County

Christian Church Cemetery, Virgilina
 Dixie Davis

Hampton City, Norfolk–Virginia–Newport News

Hampton National Cemetery, Hampton
 Pete Weckbecker

Oakland Cemetery, Hampton
 Buck Hopkins

Hopewell City, Richmond–Petersburg Metro

Appomattox Cemetery, Hopewell
 Morrie Aderholt

Lexington City

Stonewall Jackson Memorial Cemetery, Lexington
 Cy Twombly

Lynchburg City, Lynchburg Metro

Fort Hill Memorial Park, Lynchburg
 Bernie Creger

Holy Cross Cemetery, Lynchburg
 Kit McKenna, Charlie Pick

Spring Hill Cemetery, Lynchburg
 Al Orth

Madison County

Tucker Family Cemetery, Radiant
 Ollie Tucker

Martinsville City

Roselawn Burial Park, Martinsville
 Cloy Mattox

Mathews County, Norfolk–Virginia–Newport News Metro

Gwynns Island Cemetery, Gwynn
 Reese Diggs

Mecklenburg County

Crestview Memorial Park, LaCrosse
 Bill Connelly

Montgomery County

Oak Grove Cemetery, Pilot
 Charlie Jackson

Sunset Cemetery, Christiansburg
 Buddy Dear

Newport News City, Norfolk–Virginia–Newport News

Peninsula Memorial Park, Newport News
 Buck Marrow

Norfolk City, Norfolk–Virginia–Newport News

Calvary Cemetery, Norfolk
 Cal Jacox, Big Six Riddick

Forest Lawn Cemetery, Norfolk
John Gallagher, Dave Robertson, Buck
Stanley, John Woods

Magnolia Cemetery, Norfolk
Al Lattimore

Riverside Memorial Park, Norfolk
Abie Hood, Mike Smith

St. Mary's Cemetery, Norfolk
Jake Wells

Woodlawn Memorial Gardens, Norfolk
Garland Braxton

Petersburg City, Richmond–Petersburg Metro

Blandford Cemetery, Petersburg
Bill Quarles

Pittsylvania County, Danville Metro

Gretna Burial Park, Gretna
Clarence Pickrel

Portsmouth City, Norfolk–Virginia–Newport News

Lincoln Memorial Cemetery, Portsmouth
Lassas Ruffin

Oak Grove Cemetery, Portsmouth
Sam Post

Prince William County, Washington Metro

Quantico National Cemetery, Triangle
Jim Cohen

Sudley United Methodist Cemetery, Catharpin
Ben Sanders

Pulaski County

Dublin Cemetery, Dublin
Jim Brillheart

Grantham Cemetery, Draper
Doc Ayers

Richmond City, Richmond–Petersburg Metro

Forest Lawn Cemetery, Richmond
Garnett Blair, Bucky Jacobs

Holy Cross Cemetery, Richmond
Joe Boehling

Maury Cemetery, Richmond
Whitt Graves, Owen Kahn

Oakwood Cemetery, Richmond
Reddy Foster

Riverview Cemetery, Richmond
Bob habenicht, Buck Hooker, Herm
McFarland, Pop Tate

Westhampton Memorial Park, Richmond
Harry Hedgpeth

Roanoke County, Roanoke Metro

Mountain View Cemetery, Vinton
Red Cox

Scott County, Johnson City–Kingsport–Bristol

Jack Bushelman

Shenandoah County

Cedarwood Cemetery, Edinburg
Vance Dinges

Suffolk City, Norfolk–Virginia–Newport News

Meadowbrook Memorial Gardens, Suffolk
Harvey Epps

Virginia Beach City, Norfolk–Virginia–Newport News

Colonial Grove Memorial Park, Viginia
Beach
Bud Metheny

Eastern Shore Chapel Cemetery, Virginia
Beach
Bill Dammann

Rosewood Memorial Park, Virginia Beach
Clyde McCullough, Bill Morrisette,
Allie Watt

Washington County, Johnson City–Kingsport–Bristol Metro

Knollkreg Memorial Park, Abingdon
Lefty Thomas

Williamsburg City, Norfolk–Virginia–Newport News

Cedar Grove Cemetery, Williamsburg
Red Proctor

Williamsburg Memorial Park, Williamsburg
Bud Davis, Eric Tipton

Winchester City

Mount Hebron Cemetery, Winchester
Mul Holland

WASHINGTON

Asotin County

Clarkston Vineland Cemetery, Clarkston
Dave Gregg

Chelan County

Cashmere City Cemetery, Cashmere
Wynn Noyes

Clallam County

Dungeness Cemetery, Dungeness
Joe Coscarart

Grays Harbor County

Fern Hill Cemetery, Aberdeen
Jack Fanning, Jack Fournier, Frank
Mulroney, Marty O'Toole

Jefferson County

Laurel Grove Cemetery, Port Townsend
Tom Baker, Art McLarney

King County, Seattle–Bellevue–Everett

Acacia Memorial Park, Seattle
Bill Bailey, Dick Gyselman, Irv
Higginbotham, Bill Lasley, Amos Rusie

Calvary Catholic Cemetery, Seattle
Tioga George Burns, Dan Dugdale, John
Hickey, Tim O'Rourke, Alan Strange,
Tom Sullivan

Evergreen-Washelli Cemetery, Seattle
Joe Abreu, Andy Anderson, Del Howard,
Bill Kennedy, Charlie Mullen

Hillcrest Burial Park, Kent
Red Badgro

Holyrood Cemetery, Seattle
Dick Barrett, Jack Wilson

Lake View Cemetery, Seattle
Emil Frisk, Jeff Heath

Mount Olivet Pioneer Cemetery, Renton
Fred Hutchinson

Mount Pleasant Cemetery, Seattle
Leo Taylor

Sunset Hills Memorial Park, Bellevue
Al Niemiec, Ray Oyler

Kitsap County, Bremerton Metro

Ivy Green Cemetery, Bremerton
Bill Yohe

Klickitat County

West Klickitat Cemetery, White Salmon
Floyd Ritter

Pierce County, Tacoma Metro

Calvary Cemetery, Tacoma
Eddie Hickey, Pip Koehler

Mountain View Memorial Park, Tacoma
Jesse Baker, Ron Herbel, Cy Neighbors,
Cap Peterson

New Tacoma Memorial Park, Tacoma
Con Starkel, Bobby Vaughn

Oakwood Hill Cemetery, Tacoma
Jimmy Claxton

Western Washington State Hospital
Memorial Cemetery, Tacoma
Victory Faust

Woodbine Cemetery, Puyallup
Jim Mosolf

**Snohomish County, Seattle–Bellevue–
Everett Metro**

Cypress Lawn Memorial Park, Everett
Karl Adams

Evergreen Cemetery, Everett
Bob Chesnes

Floral Hills Cemetery, Lynnwood
Les Wilson

G.A.R. Cemetery, Snohomish
Earl Avrill, Earl Torgeson

Spokane County, Spokane Metro

Fairmount Memorial Park, Spokane
Ed Brandt

Greenwood Memorial Terrace Cemetery,
Spokane
Moose Baxter, Harry Howell

Holy Cross Cemetery, Spokane
Ham Hyatt

St. Joseph's Cemetery, Spokane
Phil Geier

Stevens County

St. Mary of the Rosary Cemetery, Chewelah
Dave Skeels

Thurston County, Olympia Metro

Masonic Memorial Park, Olympia
Ray Callahan, Ira Flagstead, Bill Karns

Whitman County

Pine City Cemetery, Pine City
    Elmer Leifer

Yakima County, Yakima Metro

Terrace Heights Memorial Park, Yakima
    Sanford Barnes, Mike Lynch, Hunky
    Shaw, Doc Waldbauer

WEST VIRGINIA

Berkeley County, Washington Metro

Rosedale Cemetery, Martinsburg
    Hack Wilson

Brooke County, Steubenville–Weirton

Brooke Cemetery, Wellsburg
    Gene Curtis
Wellsburg Cemetery, Wellsburg
    Rabbit Robinson

Cabell County, Huntington–Ashland

Barboursville Cemetery, Barboursville
    George Baumgardner
Highland Cemetery, Huntington
    John Scheneberg
Ridgelawn Memorial Park, Huntington
    Admiral Schlei
Spring Hill Cemetery, Huntington
    Fred Bailey, Wayland Dean, Wilbur
    Fisher, Jay Fry, Skeeter Shelton
Woodmere Memorial Park, Huntington
    Larry McClure, Ezra Midkiff, Johnny
    Watson

Fayette County

Highlawn Memorial Park, Oak Hill
    Harry Moran

Greenbrier County

Mount Loretto Cemetery, White Sulphur
Springs
    Mary Lawson

Hancock County, Steubenville–Weirton

St. Paul's Catholic Cemetery, Weirton
    Frank Kalin, Bob Trice

Harrison County

Elk View Masonic Cemetery, Clarksburg
    Ken Ash
Greenlawn Masonic Cemetery, Clarksburg
    Guy Zinn
Shinnstown Masonic Cemetery, Shinnstown
    Lee King

Jefferson County, Washington Metro

Edge Hill Cemetery, Charles Town
    Lefty Willis

Kanawha County, Charleston Metro

Cunningham Memorial Park, St. Albans
    Clint Thomas
Grandview Memorial Park, Dunbar
    Bill Hall
Mountain View Memorial Park, Charleston
    Babe Barna, Johnny Stuart
Spring Hill Cemetery, Charleston
    Ed Kenna
Sunset Memorial Park, Charleston
    Guy Morrison

Logan County

Forest Lawn Cemetery, Pecks Mill
    Max Butcher

Marshall County, Wheeling Metro

Big Run Church Cemetery, Cameron
    Clarence Garrett
Highland Cemetery, Cameron
    Beryl Richmond
Limestone Cemetery, Limestone
    Ralph Palmer

Mason County

Kirkland Memorial Gardens, Point Pleasant
    Herman Layne
Suncrest Cemetery, Point Pleasant
    Clarence Fisher

Mercer County

Woodlawn Memorial Park, Bluefield
    Bob Bowman

Monongalia County

East Oak Grove Cemetery, Morgantown
    Charlie Hickman

Wadestown M.E. Cemetery, Wadestown
Harry Shriver

Woodlawn Cemetery, Fairmont
Sam Jones

Ohio County, Wheeling Metro

Greenwood Cemetery, Wheeling
Jack Glasscock, Sam Moffett

Mount Calvary Cemetery, Wheeling
Bill George, Joe Miller, Sam Nicholl

Peninsula Cemetery, Wheeling
Sam Barkley

Pleasants County

Odd Fellows Cemetery, St. Marys
Frank Barron

Preston County

Aurora Cemetery, Aurora
Al Braithwood

Mount Moriah Cemetery, Albright
Nature Boy Williams

Raleigh County

Blue Ridge Memorial Gardens, Prosperity
Walt Craddock

Sunset Memorial Park, Beckley
Sheriff Blake, Johnny Gorsica, Joe
McManus

Randolph County

Maplewood Cemetery, Elkins
Del Gainer

Wood County, Parkersburg–Marietta

Parkersburg Memorial Gardens (formerly
Odd Fellows Cemetery), Parkersburg
Charlie Hastings, Al Mays, Greasy Neale

WISCONSIN

Adams County

Mt. Repose Cemetery, Friendship
Len Koenecke

Barron County

Nora Cemetery, Rice Lake
Clay Perry

Columbia County

Hillside Cemetery, Columbus
Frank Lange, Bob Poser

Pardeeville Cemetery, Pardeeville
Claud Elliott

Dane County, Madison Metro

Resurrection Catholic Cemetery, Madison
Ed Barry, Art Bramhall

St. Barnabas Cemetery, Mazomanie
Gene Brabender

St. Francis Xavier Cemetery, Cross Plains
Connie Grob

Dodge County

Graceland Cemetery, Mayville
Bert Husting

Leipsic Cemetery, Beaver Dam
Lymie Linde

Oakwood Cemetery, Beaver Dam
Pink Hawley

Douglas County, Duluth–Superior

Calvary Cemetery, Superior
Russ Ennis

Greenwood Cemetery, Superior
Dave Bancroft, Jay Cashion

Hebrew Cemetery, Superior
Morrie Arnovich

Fond du Lac County

Shrine of Rest Mausoleum, Fond du Lac
Paul Erickson

Forest County

Laona Cemetery, Laona
Ernie Ovitz

Trinity Lutheran Cemetery, Wabeno
Russ Bauers

Iron County

Hurley City Cemetery, Hurley
Frank Rooney

Jackson County

Riverside Cemetery, Black River Falls
Phil Haugstad, Ernie Rudolph

Jefferson County

Village Cemetery, Waterloo
George Davies

Kenosha County, Kenosha Metro

All Saints Cemetery, Pleasant Prairie
Ollie O'Mara, Charlie Pechous

Green Ridge Cemetery, Kenosha
Ben Dyer

Sunset Ridge Memorial Park, Kenosha
Ed Corey, Press Cruthers

Manitowoc County

Evergreen Cemetery, Manitowoc
Stoney McGlynn

Milwaukee County, Milwaukee Metro

Arlington Park Cemetery, Milwaukee
Lou Manske

Calvary Cemetery, Milwaukee
Charlie Cushman, Jack Miley, Tom
Nagle, Ted Sullivan

Catholic Cemetery, Milwaukee
Tom Lee

Evergreen Cemetery, Milwaukee
Hi Ebright

Forest Home Cemetery, Milwaukee
Charlie Dougherty, Frank Luce, Jim
Magnuson, Adonis Terry

Good Hope Cemetery, Milwaukee
Al Eckert

Graceland Cemetery, Milwaukee
Otto Schomberg

Holy Cross Cemetery, Milwaukee
Jap Barbeau, Jack Kloza, George
McBride, Ralph Shinners

Mount Olivet Cemetery, Milwaukee
Ted Cieslak, Dan Lally, Dan Marion

Pinelawn Memorial Park, Milwaukee
Art Bues, Elmer Klumpp, Fred Luderus

Saint Adalbert Cemetery, Milwaukee
Bruno Block, Fabian Gaffke, Joe Just, Al
Simmons, Tony Welzer

Spring Hill Cemetery, Milwaukee
Lou Chapman

Union Cemetery, Milwaukee
Anton Falch

Valhalla Memorial Park, Milwaukee
Pep Clark, Rube Lutzke, Mark Vaughn

Wanderer's Rest Cemetery, Milwaukee
Frank Schneiberg

Oconto County

Community Bible Church Cemetery,
Lakewood
Milo Allison

Oneida County

Three Lakes Cemetery, Three Lakes
Cy Williams

Polk County

Clear Lake Cemetery, Clear Lake
Burleigh Grimes

St. Croix Falls Cemetery, St. Croix Falls
Roy Patterson

Price County

Hillside Cemetery, Ogema
Jack Boyle

Racine County, Racine Metro

Burlington Cemetery, Burlington
Bob Steele

Rochester Cemetery, Rochester
Ginger Beaumont

St. Charles Cemetery, Burlington
Frank Roth

St. Mary's Cemetery, Burlington
Braggo Roth

West Lawn Memorial Park, Racine
Jimmy Grant

Richland County

Viola Cemetery, Viola
Henry Benn

Rock County, Janesville–Beloit

Calvary Cemetery, Beloit
Patsy Gharrity

Eastlawn Cemetery, Beloit
Frank Gregory, Roy Hansen, Elmer
Miller, Nig Perring

Maple Hill Cemetery, Evansville
Cal Broughton, Stan Sperry

Milton Junction Cemetery, Milton
  Willis Cole

Mount Olivet Cemetery, Janesville
  Joe Cantillon, John Morrissey, Tom
  Morrissey

Oak Hill Cemetery, Janesville
  Frank Bliss, Bill Lathrop

Tabor Cemetery, Beloit
  Jimmy Breton, Zip Zabel

Sauk County

Calvary Cemetery, Reedsburg
  Charlie Kavanagh

Sawyer County

Greenwood Cemetery, Hayward
  Fritz Ackley

Shawano County

St. Francis Solanus Catholic Church
Cemetery, Gresham
  Louis LeRoy

Sheboygan County, Sheboygan Metro

Calvary Cemetery, Sheboygan
  Joe Hauser

Sheboygan Falls Cemetery, Sheboygan Falls
  John Wycoff

**St. Croix County, Minneaplois–St. Paul
Metro**

Willow River Cemetery, Hudson
  Otis Clymer, Phil Gallivan, Bobby Reis

Trempealeau County

Pine Cliff Cemetery, Galesville
  Sam Brenegan

Walworth County

Spring Grove Cemetery, Delavan
  Webb Schultz

Waukesha County, Milwaukee Metro

Wisconsin Memorial Park, Brookfield
  Tom Dougherty, Happy Felsch, Doc
  Hamann, Ken Jungels, Ken Keltner, Art
  Kores, Fritz Mollwitz

Winnebago County, Appleton–Oshkosh

Highland Memorial Cemetery, Appleton
  Clarence Currie

Peace Lutheran Church Cemetery, Oshkosh
  Dave Tyriver

Riverside Cemetery, Appleton
  George Hogriever

St. John's Catholic Church Cemetery,
Menasha
  Dave Koslo

WYOMING

Big Horn County

Greybull Cemetery, Greybull
  Ben Hunt

Converse County

Douglas Park Cemetery, Douglas
  Bill Meehan

Laramie County, Cheyenne Metro

Mount Olivet Cemetery, Cheyenne
  Ed Murray

AMERICAN SAMOA

Immediately outside his home in Village of
Nu'uuli
  Tony Solaita

PUERTO RICO

Alvarez Memorial Cemetery, Ponce
  Pancho Coimbre

Cementerio Civil, Ponce
  Juan Guilbe, Tomas Quinones, Luis
  Villodas

Guayama Cemetery, Guayama
  Tetelo Vargas

Municipal Cemetery, Aquadilla
  Luis Marquez

Puerto Rico National Cemetery, Bayamon
  Felix Delgado

VIRGIN ISLANDS

Christainsted Cemetery, Christiansted,
St. Croix
  Alphonso Gerard

Frederiksted Cemetery, Frederiksted
  Elmo Plaskett

INTERNATIONAL

CANADA

Alberta

Mountain View Memorial Gardens
Cemetery, Calgary
    Glen Gorbous

Ontario

Holy Sepulchre Cemetery, Burlington
    Joe Krakauskas

Marymount Cemetery, Guelph
    Dan O'Connor

Melville Cemetery, Stouffville
    Earl Cook

Memorial Park Cemetery, Scarborough
    Alex Hardy

Mount Pleasant Cemetery, London
    Billy Mountjoy, Bill O'Hara

Necropolis Cemetery, Toronto
    Ernie Ross

Park Lawn Cemetery, Toronto
    Andy Kyle

St. Augustine Cemetery, Dundas
    Chub Collins

St. James Cemetery, Toronto
    Kid Summers

St. Thomas West Avenue Cemetery, St. Thomas
    Bob Emslie

Woodland Cemetery, London
    Steve Dunn, John Thompson

CUBA

Cemeterio de Cristobal Colon, Havana
    Alfredo Cabrera, Adolfo Luque, Kiki
    Magrinat, Armando Marsans, Bernardo
    Baro, Julian Castillo, Jose Fernandez,
    Antonio Garcia, Mike Gonzalez, Ricardo
    Hernandez, Ramon Herrera, Hooks
    Jimenez, Francisco Martinez, Jose
    Mendez, Tinti Molina, Agustin Parpeti,
    Ezequiel Ramos, Pablo Sama, Gonzalo
    Sanchez, Cristobal Torriente

Cemeterio Municipal Cruces, Cruces,
Cienfuegos
    Martin Dihigo

Santa Clara Cemetery, Santa Clara
    Alejandro Oms

FRANCE

Meuse-Argonne American Cemetery, Romagne
    Eddie Grant